Luke

PHILIP GRAHAM RYKEN

VOLUME 1

LUKE 1-12

P&R
PUBLISHING
P.O. BOX 817 • PHILLIPSBURG • NEW JERSEY 08865-0817

Unless otherwise indicated, Scripture quotations are from The Holy Bible, English Standard Version, copyright © 2001 by Crossway Bibles, a division of Good News Publishers. Used by permission. All rights reserved.

Scripture quotations marked (NIV) are from the HOLY BIBLE, NEW INTERNATIONAL VERSION®. NIV®. Copyright © 1973, 1978, 1984 by International Bible Society. Used by permission of Zondervan Publishing House. All rights reserved.

Italics within Scripture quotations indicate emphasis added.

Page design by Lakeside Design Plus

Printed in the United States of America

Library of Congress Cataloging-in-Publication Data

Ryken, Philip Graham, 1966–
  Luke / Philip Graham Ryken.
      p. cm.
  Includes bibliographical references and index.
  ISBN 978-1-59638-070-7 (cloth vol. 1) — ISBN 978-1-59638-133-9 (cloth vol. 2)
  1. Bible. N.T. Luke—Commentaries. I. Title.
  BS2595.53.R95 2009
  226.4'077—dc22
                              2008051651

To

Kathryn Elaine Ryken

who was still little when I was working on this commentary

and

to everyone who still needs to know Jesus for sure

It seemed good to me also, having followed all things closely for some time past, to write an orderly account for you, . . . that you may have certainty concerning the things you have been taught.
Luke 1:3–4

CONTENTS

Series Introduction   xi

Preface   xv

1. Knowing for Sure (1:1–4)   3
2. Getting Ready for Jesus (1:5–25)   16
3. The Annunciation (1:26–38)   28
4. *Magnificat* (1:39–55)   41
5. *Benedictus* (1:56–80)   54
6. Away in a Manger (2:1–7)   65
7. *Gloria in Excelsis Deo* (2:8–20)   76
8. *Nunc Dimittis* (2:21–38)   88
9. The Boy Jesus (2:39–52)   101
10. Be Prepared (3:1–14)   114
11. The Baptism of the Son (3:15–22)   126
12. Son of God, Son of Man (3:23–38)   139
13. Paradise Regained (4:1–13)   151
14. The Gospel according to Jesus (4:14–21)   164
15. A Prophet without Honor (4:22–30)   178
16. All Authority and Power (4:31–44)   190
17. No Turning Back (5:1–11)   202
18. Faith Healer (5:12–26)   215
19. Feast or Famine? (5:27–39)   227

Contents

20. Lord of the Sabbath (6:1–11)   240

21. The Calling of the Twelve (6:12–26)   253

22. The Hardest Commandment (6:27–36)   267

23. Your Log, My Splinter (6:37–42)   279

24. Of Rocks and Trees (6:43–49)   291

25. Just Say the Word (7:1–10)   304

26. Dead Man Talking (7:11–17)   315

27. The Friend of Sinners (7:18–35)   327

28. The Debt of Love I Owe (7:36–50)   339

29. The Parable of Parables (8:1–15)   353

30. Just Do It (8:16–21)   368

31. Who *Is* This Guy? (8:22–25)   380

32. What Has He Done for You? (8:26–39)   393

33. Only Believe (8:40–56)   406

34. An Internship for the Apostles (9:1–9)   419

35. Five Loaves, Two Fish, Twelve Baskets (9:10–17)   432

36. Confessing Christ Crucified (9:18–22)   444

37. The Cross of Discipleship (9:23–27)   456

38. The Glory of God the Son (9:28–36)   469

39. Four Mistakes That Most Christians Make (9:37–50)   482

40. Don't Look Back (9:51–62)   496

41. The King's Messengers (10:1–16)   509

42. Joy, Joy, Joy! (10:17–24)   522

43. Whose Neighbor Am I? (10:25–37)   536

44. Having a Mary Heart in a Martha World (10:38–42)   552

45. When You Pray (11:1–4)   566

46. Boldly Persevering in Prayer (11:5–13)   581

47. Jesus or the Devil (11:14–26)   594

48. A Sign for All Times (11:27–36)   607

49. When Your Soul Is an Unmarked Grave (11:37–44)   618

50. The Blood of the Prophets (11:45–54)   631

51. Unafraid and Unashamed (12:1–12) 643

52. A Fool and His Money (12:13–21) 656

53. Anxious for Nothing (12:22–34) 668

54. Ready, or Not? (12:35–48) 681

55. Before the Fire Falls (12:49–59) 694

SERIES INTRODUCTION

In every generation there is a fresh need for the faithful exposition of God's Word in the church. At the same time, the church must constantly do the work of theology: reflecting on the teaching of Scripture, confessing its doctrines of the Christian faith, and applying them to contemporary culture. We believe that these two tasks—the expositional and the theological—are interdependent. Our doctrine must derive from the biblical text, and our understanding of any particular passage of Scripture must arise from the doctrine taught in Scripture as a whole.

We further believe that these interdependent tasks of biblical exposition and theological reflection are best undertaken in the church, and most specifically in the pulpits of the church. This is all the more true since the study of Scripture properly results in doxology and praxis—that is, in praise to God and practical application in the lives of believers. In pursuit of these ends, we are pleased to present the Reformed Expository Commentary as a fresh exposition of Scripture for our generation in the church. We hope and pray that pastors, teachers, Bible study leaders, and many others will find this series to be a faithful, inspiring, and useful resource for the study of God's infallible, inerrant Word.

The Reformed Expository Commentary has four fundamental commitments. First, these commentaries aim to be *biblical*, presenting a comprehensive exposition characterized by careful attention to the details of the text. They are not exegetical commentaries—commenting word by word or even verse by verse—but integrated expositions of whole passages of Scripture. Each commentary will thus present a sequential, systematic treatment of an entire book of the Bible, passage by passage. Second, these commentaries are unashamedly *doctrinal*. We are committed to the Westminster Confession of Faith and Catechisms as containing the system of doctrine taught in the Scriptures of the Old and New Testaments. Each volume will teach, promote, and defend the doctrines of the Reformed faith as they are found in the Bible. Third, these commentaries are *redemptive-historical* in their orientation. We believe in the unity of the Bible and its central message of salvation in Christ. We are thus committed to a Christ-centered view of the Old Testament, in which its characters, events, regulations, and institutions are properly understood as pointing us to Christ and his gospel, as well as giving us examples to follow in living by faith. Fourth, these commentaries are *practical*, applying the text of Scripture to contemporary challenges of life—both public and private—with appropriate illustrations.

The contributors to the Reformed Expository Commentary are all pastor-scholars. As pastor, each author will first present his expositions in the pulpit ministry of his church. This means that these commentaries are rooted in the teaching of Scripture to real people in the church. While aiming to be scholarly, these expositions are not academic. Our intent is to be faithful, clear, and helpful to Christians who possess various levels of biblical and theological training—as should be true in any effective pulpit ministry. Inevitably this means that some issues of academic interest will not be covered. Nevertheless, we aim to achieve a responsible level of scholarship, seeking to promote and model this for pastors and other teachers in the church. Significant exegetical and theological difficulties, along with such historical and cultural background as is relevant to the text, will be treated with care.

We strive for a high standard of enduring excellence. This begins with the selection of the authors, all of whom have proven to be outstanding communicators of God's Word. But this pursuit of excellence is also reflected in a disciplined editorial process. Each volume is edited by both a series editor and a testament editor. The testament editors, Iain Duguid for the Old Testament and Daniel Doriani for the New Testament, are accomplished pastors and respected scholars who have taught at the seminary level. Their job is to ensure that each volume is sufficiently conversant with up-to-date scholarship and is faithful and accurate in its exposition of the text. As series editors, we oversee each volume to ensure its overall quality—including excellence of writing, soundness of teaching, and usefulness in application. Working together as an editorial team, along with the publisher, we are devoted to ensuring that these are the best commentaries our gifted authors can provide, so that the church will be served with trustworthy and exemplary expositions of God's Word.

It is our goal and prayer that the Reformed Expository Commentary will serve the church by renewing confidence in the clarity and power of Scripture and by upholding the great doctrinal heritage of the Reformed faith. We hope that pastors who read these commentaries will be encouraged in their own expository preaching ministry, which we believe to be the best and most biblical pattern for teaching God's Word in the church. We hope that lay teachers will find these commentaries among the most useful resources they rely upon for understanding and presenting the text of the Bible. And we hope that the devotional quality of these studies of Scripture will instruct and inspire each Christian who reads them in joyful, obedient discipleship to Jesus Christ.

May the Lord bless all who read the Reformed Expository Commentary. We commit these volumes to the Lord Jesus Christ, praying that the Holy Spirit will use them for the instruction and edification of the church, with thanksgiving to God the Father for his unceasing faithfulness in building his church through the ministry of his Word.

Richard D. Phillips
Philip Graham Ryken
Series Editors

PREFACE

After nearly a decade of preaching at Tenth Presbyterian Church, I decided it was time for me to satisfy a growing hunger to preach all the way through one of the biblical Gospels. Although I take deep satisfaction in preaching Christ from all the Scriptures, I also agree with Robert Murray M'Cheyne, who once observed "how sweet and precious it is to preach directly about Christ, compared with all other subjects of preaching."

For me the choice of which Gospel to preach was obvious. My predecessor—the late Dr. James Montgomery Boice—had already preached masterful series through the Gospels of Matthew and John. Mark was still a possibility, of course, but I was drawn to the broader scope of Luke, which is the longest book in the New Testament. Luke also has the most urban feel of any of the Gospels, and thus it seemed especially appropriate to preach to a city congregation like the one I pastor in Philadelphia. Luke had a special concern for people on the margins—people broken by the troubles of life, including the many women we meet in the pages of his Gospel. So I decided to preach through Luke, which has proved to be one of the best experiences of my Christian life.

It is no exaggeration to say that a commentary this size is a monumental undertaking. These two volumes on Luke would never have been possible without the prayers and assistance of many people. Every week, the work I do in God's Word is helped immeasurably by the prayers of God's people at Tenth Church. As editorial work on these Bible expositions began, my friend Jonathan Rockey and my colleagues (who are also still my friends) Dan Doriani and Rick Phillips made the generous commitment to read and comment on the entire manuscript. Their suggestions led to countless improvements and corrections, which were helpfully and cheerfully entered into the manuscript by my assistants Anne Davies and Dora McFarland. As always, Lisa helped me know how to honor God as we integrated this project into the rest of family life.

In a 2007 interview for *Newsweek*, the well-known atheist and best-selling author Sam Harris said, "I don't want to pretend to be certain about anything I'm not certain about." I think Luke would agree with Mr. Harris, which is why he wrote his famous Gospel. We should never pretend, especially when it comes to what we believe about God. This does not mean that we can never be certain, however. On the contrary, Luke's Gospel was written to give greater certainty about the person and work of Jesus Christ (see Luke 1:1–4). My prayer is that this commentary will help you understand the gospel and come to full assurance of your salvation, as Luke intended.

Philip Graham Ryken
Philadelphia, Pennsylvania

Luke

KNOWING FOR SURE

1

KNOWING FOR SURE

Luke 1:1–4

*Inasmuch as many have undertaken to compile a narrative of
the things that have been accomplished among us, just as those
who from the beginning were eyewitnesses and ministers of the
word have delivered them to us, it seemed good to me also, having followed all things closely for some time past, to write an
orderly account for you, most excellent Theophilus, that you
may have certainty concerning the things you have been taught.*
(Luke 1:1–4)

*D*oubt. Little by little, it gnaws away at the soul. To be sure, there
are times when Christianity makes all the sense in the world.
The mysteries of the birth, death, and resurrection of God the
Son appear so certain that it would seem foolish even to call them into
question. Yet there are also times when, as the poet Roger White so aptly
put it, "A mosquito buzzes round my faith"—the mosquito of doubt.[1] In

---

1. Roger White, *One Bird—One Cage—One Flight: Homage to Emily Dickinson* (Happy Camp, CA:
Naturegraph, 1983).

solitary moments the nagging questions whine in our ears: Is the Bible really true? Does God actually hear my prayers? Can my sins truly be forgiven? Will I definitely go to heaven when I die?

Sometimes the doubting questions can lead to unbelief. In the opening chapter of his novel *In the Beauty of the Lilies*, John Updike describes the moment when a Presbyterian minister abandons the Christian faith. Doubt had been buzzing away at the man's soul, and then one day his faith vanished altogether. As Updike tells it,

> The Reverend Clarence Arthur Wilmot, down in the rectory of the Fourth Presbyterian Church at the corner of Straight Street and Broadway, felt the last particles of his faith leave him. The sensation was distinct—a visceral surrender, a set of dark sparkling bubbles escaping upward. . . . His thoughts had slipped with quicksilver momentum into the recognition, which he had long withstood, that . . . there is no . . . God, nor should there be.
>
> Clarence's mind was like a many-legged, wingless insect that had long and tediously been struggling to climb up the walls of a slick-walled porcelain basin; and now a sudden impatient wash of water swept it down into the drain. *There is no God.*[2]

Even if we ourselves have not abandoned the Christian faith, we can understand how this could happen. We too have had our doubts. There are times when our faith falters, when the whole story of salvation suddenly seems quite improbable, if not impossible. We still believe in Jesus, but sometimes it is hard to know for sure.

LUKE, THE HISTORIAN

So Luke decided to write a Gospel. Knowing that people sometimes have their doubts about Jesus Christ, and that even believers may struggle to gain greater assurance of their faith, he sat down to write "the Gospel of knowing for sure." He began with a formal dedication:

> Inasmuch as many have undertaken to compile a narrative of the things that have been accomplished among us, just as those who from the beginning were eyewitnesses and ministers of the word have delivered them to

2. John Updike, *In the Beauty of the Lilies* (New York: Knopf, 1996), 5–6.

us, it seemed good to me also, having followed all things closely for some time past, to write an orderly account for you, most excellent Theophilus, that you may have certainty concerning the things you have been taught. (Luke 1:1–4)

Although Luke does not mention himself by name, he has always been universally acknowledged as the writer of this book. In one long sentence, he tells us what kind of book he wanted to write: one that would help people to be more certain of their salvation in Christ. To accomplish this goal, he set out to write a historically accurate, carefully researched, and well-organized Gospel.

Luke is exactly such a Gospel. First, it is historically accurate. Luke was by no means the only person ever to write a biography of Jesus Christ. He was well aware that others had tried to record what Jesus had done. As he said, "Many have undertaken to compile a narrative of the things that have been accomplished among us" (Luke 1:1). Perhaps he was thinking of the Gospel of Mark, which has many similarities to Luke, and which Luke may well have used as one of his sources. But the word "many" indicates that there were other writings as well, including works that may no longer be in existence.

In mentioning what others had written, Luke was not trying to be critical. He gives no indication that he considered the other writings to be unreliable in any way. In fact, he says just the opposite. Others wrote down what they had received from "eyewitnesses and ministers of the word" (Luke 1:2), by which Luke meant the apostles. From the book of Acts, which is the sequel to this Gospel, we know that apostles like Peter and John were called to be witnesses for Christ (e.g., Acts 1:8; 4:33). What qualified them to preach the gospel was the fact that they were eyewitnesses of the risen Christ.

But eventually the apostolic gospel had to be written down. The apostles would not be around forever, and if their mission was to continue, their message needed to be handed down in a more permanent form. Others had begun to preserve the apostolic witness in writing, but Luke wanted to do it too. God had called him to write a Gospel that was similar to what others had written, but would also make a unique contribution. Partly drawing on the work of others, but also pursuing his own historical and evangelistic interests, Luke would write a more complete history, so that people would know for sure what Jesus had done.

Luke defined a Gospel as "a narrative of the things that have been accomplished among us" (Luke 1:1). A narrative is simply a story, so Luke wanted to tell a story. But this particular narrative was historical. It was about things that had been accomplished, things that had really happened, things that had been done in time and space. Therefore, Luke is careful to place the story of Jesus in its historical context. For example, when he tells the story of the Savior's birth, he says that it coincided with "the first registration when Quirinius was governor of Syria" (Luke 2:2). Luke was writing fact, not fiction, and he knew the difference, as did his original readers. Like Polybius, the Greek historian of Rome, he wanted to "simply record what really happened and what really was said."[3] In addition, as we shall see, he wanted to give a divinely inspired interpretation of the words and deeds of Jesus Christ.

During the nineteenth century, liberal Bible scholars tried to argue that Luke was a bad historian, that his books were riddled with factual errors. In the last one hundred years, however, their assessment of Luke's historiography has been almost completely reversed. The more we learn about the ancient world, the more we see how careful he was to get the facts straight. One historian concludes: "Wherever modern scholarship has been able to check up on the accuracy of Luke's work the judgment has been unanimous: he is one of the finest and ablest historians in the ancient world."[4] In the words of the famous archaeologist William Ramsay, "Luke is a historian of the first rank; not merely are his statements of fact trustworthy; he is possessed of the true historic sense; he seizes the important and critical events and shows their true nature at greater length, while he touches lightly or omits entirely much that was valueless for his purpose. In short, this author should be placed along with the very greatest of historians."[5]

Doubtless some scholars will continue to challenge Luke on historical grounds. But his concern for historical accuracy helps us to be more certain

3. Polybius, quoted in Clinton E. Arnold, ed., *Zondervan Illustrated Bible Backgrounds Commentary,* vol. 1, *Matthew, Mark, Luke* (Grand Rapids: Zondervan, 2002), 322.

4. Otto Piper, "The Purpose of Luke," *Union Seminary Review* 67.1 (Nov. 1945), 16.

5. William Ramsay, *The Bearing of Recent Discovery on the Trustworthiness of the New Testament* (London: Hodder & Stoughton, 1915), 222.

of our faith. If it could be shown that Luke's work contained basic errors of fact, then his whole Gospel would be discredited. A Christian is someone who believes that Jesus is who he said he is and did what the Bible says he did. But if Luke didn't have his facts straight on the governorship of Syria, how can we trust his testimony about miracles like the virgin birth or the bodily resurrection of Jesus Christ? Our entire salvation depends on the things that Jesus accomplished in human history, specifically through his sufferings and death.

Fortunately, Luke was a good historian. He did not write some fanciful account of things that people wanted to believe about Jesus, but an accurate historical record of what Jesus actually did. Through the testimony of Luke and others, the things that Jesus accomplished are as well established as any fact of ancient history, and this provides a rational basis for our faith. Of course, we still have to accept that what the Gospel says is true. We have to put our own personal trust in Jesus, believing that he died on the cross for our sins and that he was raised again to give us eternal life. But we believe these things with good reason, knowing that they are based on reliable history.

JUST THE FACTS

In order to write a book that was historically accurate, Luke had to do painstaking research. This is a second feature of his Gospel: it was carefully researched. This required someone with a scholarly temperament, and Luke was just the man for the job. We sense this from his literary style. Listen again to his dedication:

> Inasmuch as many have undertaken to compile a narrative of the things that have been accomplished among us, just as those who from the beginning were eyewitnesses and ministers of the word have delivered them to us, it seemed good to me also, having followed all things closely for some time past, to write an orderly account for you, most excellent Theophilus, that you may have certainty concerning the things you have been taught. (Luke 1:1–4)

Who would begin a book with a word like "inasmuch" or write in such an elevated style? Only a man of letters—a highly educated, cultured, and sophisticated writer. Luke's preface compares favorably to the formal introductions we find in works by Herodotus, Thucydides, Josephus, and other ancient historians. By way of comparison, consider this passage from the introduction Thucydides gave to his famous *History of the Peloponnesian War:* "But as to the facts of the occurrences of the war, I have thought it my duty to give them, not as ascertained from any chance informant, nor as seemed to me probable, but only after investigating with the greatest possible accuracy each detail, in the case of both the events in which I myself participated and of those regarding which I got my information from others. And the endeavor to discover these facts was a laborious task."[6] Like Thucydides, Luke was writing in the grand style, which was appropriate for a sophisticated audience across the Greek-speaking world.

For all his literary skill, Luke was not an eyewitness to the events he describes in his book. He admits this from the outset, honestly distinguishing his own work from those "who from the beginning were eyewitnesses and ministers of the word" (Luke 1:2). Luke was not an apostle. Nevertheless, he was a close companion of the apostles, and it seemed good for him to write a Gospel. He wrote on the basis of the testimony he received from the apostles, and he wrote as one who had "followed all things closely for some time past" (Luke 1:3).

What was Luke's background? His name is Greek, which means that he may have been a Gentile. This would explain why he wrote a book presenting Jesus as the Savior of the world—a Gospel for the Gentiles as well as the Jews. What we do know is that Luke was medically trained. At the end of Colossians, he is described as "the beloved physician" (Col. 4:14). We also know that he traveled with the apostle Paul. In addition to Colossians, he is mentioned in 2 Timothy 4:11 and Philemon 24, where Paul calls him a "fellow worker," and perhaps also in 2 Corinthians 8:18, where Paul mentions "the brother who is famous among all the churches for his preaching of the gospel." There are further hints of Luke's partnership with Paul in Acts. Starting with chapter 16, parts of that book are written in the first person plural. For example, the author writes: "we sailed away from Philippi after the days of Unleavened Bread, and in five days we came to them at Troas,

---

6. Thucydides, *History of the Peloponnesian War*, trans. Rex Warner (Baltimore: Penguin, 1954), 24.

where we stayed for seven days" (Acts 20:6). This seems to indicate that Luke was one of Paul's traveling companions.

What all of this means is that Doctor Luke, as we might call him, was in an excellent position to know the truth about Jesus Christ. He could describe Christ's work as something "accomplished among us" (Luke 1:1). He was an eyewitness of the apostolic ministry and a member of the early Christian community, and as such, he wanted to know everything there was to know about Jesus. By his own testimony, he had "followed all things closely for some time past" (Luke 1:3). Norval Geldenhuys explains how Luke must have done his work:

> Through long periods (during his travels along with Paul and also at other times) he made thorough researches concerning the Gospel stories so that he was able to set forth the actual course of events. He collected and studied all available written renderings of words and works of Jesus; wherever the opportunity was presented to him he discussed the Gospel stories with persons who possessed firsthand knowledge concerning Him; and during his stay in Jerusalem and in other parts of Palestine he collected as much information as possible concerning the buildings and places connected with the history of Christ. This is all clearly evidenced by the contents of the third Gospel.[7]

If Mark was a storyteller, and John was a philosopher, then Luke was an investigative reporter. The result of his research is a rich account of the person and work of Jesus Christ. With a doctor's gift for observation, Luke noticed things that other people overlooked. His is the most complete Gospel, which is why it is the longest book in the New Testament, including many precious details that the other Gospels omit. It is from Luke that we learn about the birth of John the Baptist and the infancy of Jesus the Christ—in all likelihood because he interviewed their mothers. It is from Luke that we learn the Christmas carols of Mary, Zechariah, Simeon, and the angel chorus of heaven. It is in Luke alone that we read parables like the good Samaritan, the prodigal son, and the Pharisee and the publican. Only Luke tells us what Jesus preached on the road to Emmaus. And only Luke

---

7. Norval Geldenhuys, *The Gospel of Luke*, New International Commentary on the New Testament (Grand Rapids: Eerdmans, 1951), 53.

gives us fuller portraits of the women who followed Jesus: Elizabeth, Mary, Anna, and Mary and Martha.

The result of Luke's careful research is that reading his Gospel helps us to know for sure. Luke did his work with all the rigor of a prize-winning journalist, asking the famous questions: Who? What? When? Where? How? And at the back of his mind were the questions that we sometimes ask: Who is Jesus? What did he do? Did he really do what people said he did? When Luke was satisfied that he had the story straight, he wrote it down. As a careful historian, he wrote a sober, straightforward, nonsensationalized account of what Jesus did to save the world. This strengthens the assurance of our faith. The Gospel of Luke bears all the marks of authentic history, and as such, it reassures us that we are reading the real story of Jesus.

In describing how Luke came to write his Gospel, we must never forget that he wrote under the inspiration of the Holy Spirit. As John MacArthur explains,

> Luke's acknowledgment that he compiled his account from various extant sources does not invalidate the claim of divine inspiration for his work. The process of inspiration never bypasses or overrides the personalities, vocabularies, and styles of the human authors of Scripture. The unique traits of the human authors are always indelibly stamped on the book of Scripture. Luke's research creates no exception to this rule. The research itself was orchestrated by divine Providence.[8]

Luke was the one who did the research and the writing, but God was the one who gave us this Gospel. The work that Luke did was under the sovereign control of God's Spirit, so that the Gospel he wrote is the very Word of God. Like everything else in the Bible, it is not merely a human book about God, but a divine book to humanity. As B. B. Warfield explained,

> The whole of Scripture is the product of divine activities which enter it, however, not by superseding the activities of the human authors, but confluently with them; so that the Scriptures are the joint product of divine and human activities, both of which penetrate them at every point, working harmoni-

8. John MacArthur, *The MacArthur Quick Reference Guide to the Bible* (Nashville: Thomas Nelson, 2001), 190.

ously together to the production of a writing which is not divine here and human there, but at once divine and human in every part, every word, every particular.[9]

GETTING ORGANIZED

One more feature of Luke's Gospel is worthy of mention. Not only is the book historically accurate and carefully researched, but also logically organized. Luke tells us that his goal was "to write an orderly account" (Luke 1:3). Therefore, we would expect his Gospel to be organized in some careful and coherent way, and this is precisely what we find.

For the most part, the third Gospel is organized chronologically. Luke tells about things in the order they happened. However, he did not and could not tell us everything. Rather obviously, he did not have the space to report everything that Jesus ever said or did. He had to be selective. And as he chose what to include in his Gospel, he also had to decide how to arrange it. How did one event relate to the next? What was the best way to present the person and work of Jesus Christ? How should each phase of his life and ministry be connected to the story line of the gospel?

We can analyze the structure of Luke in several different ways. One good place to start is with Luke 4:17–21, where Jesus announces his intention to preach the good news and to perform liberating miracles of healing power. Or we could start with a thematic verse that aptly summarizes the book's message. This verse comes at the end of the story of Zacchaeus, where Jesus describes his ministry: "The Son of Man came to seek and to save the lost" (Luke 19:10). Jesus often identified himself as "the Son of Man," especially in the Gospel of Luke. By using this ancient title, he was declaring his authority to judge the nations, for the Son of Man was prophesied as coming for judgment (see Dan. 7:13–14). Here he announces what the Son of Man has come to do, namely, "to seek and to save the lost." By this point Jesus had already told the parables of the lost sheep, the lost coin, and the lost son (Luke 15). Now he makes their meaning clear: he is the Savior who has come on a search-and-rescue mission.

9. Benjamin B. Warfield, "The Divine and Human in the Bible," in *Selected Shorter Writings of Benjamin B. Warfield*, ed. John E. Meeter, 2 vols. (Phillipsburg, NJ: Presbyterian and Reformed, 1973), 2:547.

This is the structure of Luke's Gospel, which is organized to show who Jesus is and what he has come to do. The opening chapters tell of Christ's coming—his birth and preparation for ministry. Then Jesus begins his public ministry, and as he goes through Israel, teaching and performing miracles, he seeks lost sinners. But Jesus came to do something more than seek; he also came to save. So Luke ends with the great saving events of the gospel: the death, resurrection, and ascension of the Son of Man. Jesus came to seek and to save the lost. Roughly speaking, in chapters 1 to 3 he comes; in chapters 4 to 21 he seeks; and in chapters 22 to 24 he saves.

This is a good start in understanding Luke's structure, but we can be more specific. Most scholars agree that the book has at least four major sections. The first section runs from the beginning through 4:13, at which point Jesus begins his public ministry. The opening chapters are about Christ's coming and about his preparation for ministry. A good title for them is "The *Coming* of the Son of Man."

The next section runs from Luke 4:14 to Luke 9:50. What separates this material from what comes before and after is a change of venue. In the opening chapters the Son of Man comes to the nation of Israel, but in chapter 4 he goes to Galilee in the north: "And Jesus returned in the power of the Spirit to Galilee" (Luke 4:14). There he remains for the next six chapters, doing some teaching, performing many miracles, and clarifying his divine identity. We may call this part of Luke "The *Ministry* of the Son of Man."

There is a significant turning point near the end of chapter 9, where Jesus moves on from Galilee. This is part of the orderliness of Luke's account. The order is not simply logical and chronological, but also geographical. Luke says of Jesus, "When the days drew near for him to be taken up, he set his face to go to Jerusalem" (Luke 9:51). From this point on, there could be no turning back. Jesus was on his way to Jerusalem—the most important journey in the history of the world. Jesus was going up to the city, up to the temple, up to the cross to die. His journey runs from Luke 9:51 to Luke 19:27, where he enters Jerusalem in temporary triumph. And as he makes his way to Jerusalem, we get hints of what will happen when he gets there. As he trains his disciples, the Son of Man begins to tell them what he must suffer for the salvation of sinners (Luke 9:21–22, 43–45; 18:31–34). He also starts to face opposition from people who reject his claim to be the Christ.

Hence these chapters are about "The *Disciples* of the Son of Man," or perhaps "The *Rejection* of the Son of Man."

Finally the book ends with "The *Salvation* of the Son of Man"—not his own salvation, but the salvation he brings to all who trust in him. The section of Luke that runs from 19:28 to the end tells what Jesus did to save us. These are the climactic events of the Gospel: the Savior's death on the cross, resurrection from the grave, and ascension into heaven.

THE ASSURANCE OF FAITH

Why did Luke organize his Gospel this way? As we study what Luke has written, we always want to keep his purpose in mind. Why was he so concerned about historical accuracy? Why did he do such painstaking research? Why did he arrange his Gospel so systematically? Luke tells us why at the end of his dedication: "that you may have certainty concerning the things you have been taught" (Luke 1:4).

When Luke says "you," he is speaking most directly to his friend Theophilus. There has been a good deal of scholarly discussion as to whether or not this man was a real person. He probably was. To be sure, a name that means "beloved of God" might well refer generally to the church of Jesus Christ. Yet the name Theophilus was common enough in those days. Furthermore, the fact that Luke refers to him as "most excellent" Theophilus suggests that he may have been a ranking official in the Roman Empire. In the book of Acts the same title is used for the Roman governor Felix (Acts 23:26). So in all likelihood, Theophilus was a real but to us otherwise unknown nobleman. Alternatively, it has been proposed that the man to whom Luke wrote may have been the high priest of Israel.[10]

When Luke says "you," however, he is also speaking to us. Because Theophilus means "lover of God," or "beloved of God," it is the kind of name that Luke might have used to describe anyone who wants to have a relationship with God. Who is Theophilus? *You* are Theophilus, if you love God and are loved by him; therefore, Luke's Gospel is for you.

The other main question about Theophilus concerns whether or not he was a Christian. At the very least, he knew something about Christianity.

10. Richard H. Anderson, "Theophilus: A Proposal," *Evangelical Quarterly* 69.3 (1997): 195–215.

13

In verse 4 Luke reminds Theophilus about what he had been taught. One way or another, the man had heard the basic gospel message. He had been instructed in the faith. Maybe he was a Christian, maybe not. Perhaps he was a new believer. What we know is that he did not yet have the full assurance of his faith, which is why Luke wrote him this Gospel.

Perhaps the most important word in Luke's dedication to Theophilus comes at the very end of verse 4. It is the Greek word *asphaleian*, meaning "certain," or even "infallible." The word indicates "the absolute certainty, the truthfulness of the report concerning the history of Jesus."[11] Luke puts this word at the end of his dedication for emphasis. This was his whole reason for writing! Theophilus knew about Jesus, but needed to know him for sure.

This is what we need as well: a sure and certain knowledge of Jesus Christ and the salvation that comes through faith in him. We need to know what Jesus accomplished. We need to know the perfection of his virgin birth, the obedience of his sinless life, the wisdom of his profound teaching, and the power of his divine miracles. We need to know these things because they prove that he is the Son of God. And we need to know what Jesus did to save us from the wrath of God. We need to know that he suffered and died on the cross for our sins. We need to know that he was raised from the dead to give eternal life to all who trust in him. And we need to know that he has ascended to heaven, where he rules over all things for the glory of God.

We need to know these things because sometimes we have our doubts. We are like the man who said to Jesus, "I believe; help my unbelief" (Mark 9:24), or like the disciples who said, "Increase our faith!" (Luke 17:5). This is part of our struggle as fallen creatures living in a fallen world. Assurance doesn't always come right away, any more than it came right away for the apostles. We believe the gospel, but sometimes we are tempted not to, and thus we long to have greater assurance of our faith. The Westminster Confession of Faith wisely admits that "faith is different in degrees, weak or strong," and that it "may be often and many ways assailed, and weakened" (14.3). If we are sometimes tempted to have our doubts, this does not mean that we are not Christians. It simply means that we are sinners who are struggling to live by faith. But God calls us to grow in our faith, seek-

11. Geldenhuys, *Luke*, 57.

14

ing what the Confession calls "the attainment of a full assurance, through Christ" (14.3). As the Scripture says, we need to make our "calling and election sure" (2 Peter 1:10).

So how do we know for sure? Luke gives us the answer at the beginning of his Gospel. We do not become certain by looking at our own outstanding spiritual performance. If the assurance of our faith rested on our own ability to follow God, we could never be sure. We would always have our doubts about our obedience, or even about our faith, wondering if we were trusting God as well as we should. Nor does assurance come by going back to the moment when we first trusted in Jesus, as if our conversion experience could save us. Assurance does not come by looking within or by having some special experience. The only way we become sure of our salvation is by looking to Jesus.

This is why Luke wrote "the Gospel of knowing for sure." He researched things carefully and wrote them down logically and accurately, giving us the real history of Jesus. He knew that like faith itself, the assurance of faith comes by hearing the gospel. So like a good doctor, he wrote a book that would heal the doubting soul.

Luke's Gospel is for anyone who needs to know Jesus. It is for people who have never met Jesus before, and for people who need to meet him again, as if for the very first time. It is for people who aren't quite sure about Jesus, for people who are just starting to trust in him, and for people who have known him a long time, but still need to become more secure in their faith. It is for anyone who wants to know for sure.

Do you know Jesus? Do you know him for sure? Are you so certain in your faith that you are able to live for Jesus, and even to die for him? If you want to be sure, study the Gospel of Luke and offer the prayer of the English Reformers: "Almighty God, who called Luke the Physician, whose praise is in the Gospel, to be an Evangelist, and Physician of the soul: May it please thee that, by the wholesome medicines of the doctrine delivered by him, all the diseases of our souls may be healed through the merits of thy Son Jesus Christ our Lord."[12]

---

12. *The Book of Common Prayer* (1662), quoted in Michael Wilcock, *The Message of Luke*, The Bible Speaks Today (Downers Grove, IL: InterVarsity, 1979), 16.

2

GETTING READY FOR JESUS

Luke 1:5–25

*But the angel said to him, "Do not be afraid, Zechariah, for
your prayer has been heard, and your wife Elizabeth will bear
you a son, and you shall call his name John. . . . And he will
turn many of the children of Israel to the Lord their God, and
he will go before him in the spirit and power of Elijah, to turn
the hearts of the fathers to the children, and the disobedient
to the wisdom of the just, to make ready for the Lord a people
prepared." (Luke 1:13, 16–17)*

One of the strange things about the New Testament Gospels is
the amount of attention they give to John the Baptist. The story
of Jesus does not begin with Jesus, but with John. This is especially true in Luke, which opens with a lengthy account of the background
to John's birth. What was so important about John the Baptist?

The Gospel writers had good reason to start with the story of John. After
all, the man had a memorable ministry. He was a strange prophet who
did strange things. More importantly, as the early Christians looked back
at what God had done through Jesus Christ, they realized that it had all

started with John the Baptist. He was the forerunner, the herald sent ahead to announce the coming of the Christ. In the ancient prophecies, God had promised that before the Messiah came, his messenger would prepare the way. John the Baptist was the man who got people ready for Jesus.

Something similar happens whenever any great person makes a public appearance; there is always someone to announce his arrival. When a star athlete takes the field, an announcer introduces him in the starting lineup. When the president makes a speech, someone says, "Ladies and gentlemen, the President of the United States." When a celebrity receives an award, another celebrity makes the presentation—the greater the honor, the more famous the presenter.

Jesus was introduced by none other than John the Baptist, whom Jesus himself regarded as the greatest man who had ever lived (Luke 7:28). Who better to introduce Jesus than the messenger of the Messiah? So Luke, who wanted to begin at the beginning, started with John the Baptist.

But They Had No Child

The announcement of John's birth comes in three dramatic scenes. In the first scene we meet a couple without a child: "In the days of Herod, king of Judea, there was a priest named Zechariah, of the division of Abijah. And he had a wife from the daughters of Aaron, and her name was Elizabeth. And they were both righteous before God, walking blamelessly in all the commandments and statutes of the Lord. But they had no child, because Elizabeth was barren, and both were advanced in years" (Luke 1:5–7).

As a good historian, Luke carefully sets his account in its political context. These events took place near the end of the reign of Herod the Great (37 to 4 b.c.)—a time of oppression for the people of God. During those troubled times, an elderly couple was living out in the hill country near Jerusalem. Their names were Zechariah and Elizabeth. Both of them came from the priestly line of Aaron—a double blessing. Both were active in ministry. We might think of them as an old country pastor and his wife, nearing the age of retirement. And both of them were distinguished by their godliness. Not that they were sinless, of course, but they had a right relationship with God. They lived in outward conformity with the law, and God regarded them as righteous.

17

There was only one cloud that cast a dark shadow on their happiness. Luke tersely describes their difficulty: "But they had no child, because Elizabeth was barren, and both were advanced in years" (Luke 1:7). We can well imagine the lifetime of heartache behind those words. This was the great disappointment of Elizabeth's life. She had always longed to hold a child in her arms—*her* child—but now that was impossible. She had been through menopause; her womb was old and barren.

Any woman who has ever wanted a child knows what Elizabeth must have endured: the prying questions, the insensitive remarks, the sharp pang of desire for someone else's baby, and the nagging doubts about the goodness of God. But for Elizabeth there was something even worse—the suggestion that somehow this was all her fault. Kent Hughes comments: "In any culture infertility is an aching disappointment, and for some an almost unbearable stress. But the burden cannot be compared to that borne by childless women in ancient Hebrew culture because barrenness was considered a disgrace, even a punishment."[1] Elizabeth's plight reminds us of similar stories from the Old Testament. Hagar had contempt for Sarai because she could not bear Abraham a son (Gen. 16:4). And when Leah could not conceive, she called it an "affliction" (Gen. 29:32). This is the way people thought in those days. In Luke 1:25 Elizabeth refers to the stigma that she had to endure from people who assumed that God was against her. It was hard enough not having a child, but people also looked on her with reproach, thinking that she was ungodly.

This was bad manners, but even worse theology. Elizabeth was not ungodly; she was righteous before God. Therefore, whatever heartache she suffered was not some kind of punishment for her sin. Our sins are not always the cause of our suffering. Sometimes they are, but not always. True, many sins have destructive consequences that make us rue the day we ever decided to disobey God. This is one of the ways that God trains us to pursue righteousness. But many of the things we suffer have nothing to do with our own sin. Sometimes Christians suffer for exactly the opposite reason—for the sake of righteousness. Sometimes we suffer from the sins of others. And sometimes God allows us to suffer because he wants to be glorified through our suffering. Most of the time we do not know what

---

1. R. Kent Hughes, *Luke: That You May Know the Truth*, 2 vols., Preaching the Word (Wheaton, IL: Crossway, 1998), 1:21.

his reasons are, and therefore we should be very careful not to reach the wrong conclusions about why something bad is happening to us, or to someone else.

In this case, Elizabeth was barren for the glory of God. God was not punishing her, but planning a miracle that would get his people ready for salvation (and also bring Elizabeth great joy). God had something special in mind, and the best way to show that John was a special child was to bring him from a barren womb. So Elizabeth was suffering because of the way that God wanted to be glorified through her life.

Part of the Christian perspective on suffering is that even in suffering, there is a way for us to glorify God. There are wonderful examples of this among the barren women of the Bible, such as Hannah (see 1 Sam. 1:1–2:11), or the wife of Manoah (see Judg. 13). Suffering heightened the spiritual sensitivity of these women and brought them into a closer relationship with God. This is not always what happens, however. Sometimes we get bitter when we don't get what we want, and this is as much a temptation for people who are childless as it is for anyone else. But by his grace the Holy Spirit can enable us to suffer in a trusting way that demonstrates our faith in God's sovereignty.

The question to ask about suffering is not "What have I done to deserve this?" but "How can I glorify God through this?" Elizabeth is the perfect example. She did not wait for a child before her life could begin. She was busy serving the Lord, walking blamelessly in his commandments. For her, what some people considered a tragedy was an opportunity. No matter what suffering we must endure—and everyone suffers—there is still a way for us to live for the glory of God.

THERE APPEARED TO HIM AN ANGEL

What happened next was totally unexpected and utterly amazing. The man without a child met an angel with a gospel: "Now while he was serving as priest before God when his division was on duty, according to the custom of the priesthood, he was chosen by lot to enter the temple of the Lord and burn incense. And the whole multitude of the people were praying outside at the hour of incense. And there appeared to him an angel of the Lord standing on the right side of the altar of incense" (Luke 1:8–9).

19

Even without the angel, Zechariah's ministry at the temple would have been a once-in-a-lifetime experience. In Zechariah's day, Israel's priests were divided into twenty-four divisions, with each division serving at the temple on a rotating basis for two weeks a year (plus the national festivals, such as Passover). So Zechariah was at the temple, serving with the other priests in his division. Then he received a further honor. Every day two priests were chosen to enter the Holy Place and offer incense on Israel's sweet altar of prayer—one in the morning and one in the afternoon. Since there were so many priests, the choice was made by lot. This time, in the providence of God, the lot was cast for Zechariah. It was the greatest moment of his priestly career—"the apex of his personal history"[2]—because once a priest was chosen, he was ineligible to serve again.

Perhaps we can picture the scene. With the anticipation of awe, Zechariah prepared to offer incense on God's altar. He put on the priestly robes symbolizing purity. He walked through the temple courts, passing through the crowds that had gathered to pray. Then he went up to the Holy Place where God was. As he entered, he saw the sacred furniture that the Israelites had made according to the instructions God gave to Moses on the mountain. On his left was the golden lampstand of life, flickering in the darkness. On his right was the table of bread. In front of him was the golden altar of incense, up against the curtain that guarded the entrance to the Holy of Holies.

Zechariah was standing in the presence of almighty God, burning the incense that wafted up to heaven with his prayers. His heart was pounding in his chest, and then suddenly it almost stopped! He was not alone, but in the presence of a heavenly being: "And there appeared to him an angel of the Lord standing on the right side of the altar of incense. And Zechariah was troubled when he saw him, and fear fell upon him" (Luke 1:11–12). The angel scared the priest half to death. This is what happens when people see angels—the glorious, supernatural creatures that God created to worship and work for him. Because angels live in the presence of God, they reflect his glory, which is more than fallen sinners can bear. So on those rare occasions when people see them, they are always terrified.

2. Hughes, *Luke*, 1:21.

This particular angel was Gabriel, the messenger of salvation that God also sent to Mary, and before her, to Daniel (see Dan. 8:15–16; 9:20–21). The first thing Gabriel did was to speak words of reassurance. Then he told the petrified priest that his prayers were answered: "But the angel said to him, 'Do not be afraid, Zechariah, for your prayer has been heard, and your wife Elizabeth will bear you a son, and you shall call his name John'" (Luke 1:13).

It is hard to be certain exactly what Zechariah had been praying. The implication is that he was praying for a son. Doubtless this was something that he and Elizabeth had prayed for many times during the course of their marriage, but by now they had probably given up. Zechariah and Elizabeth had prayed, but God had not answered, and now it was too late. They weren't just "getting up there," they were *old!* Yet perhaps Zechariah had decided to pray for a son one last time. After all, this was his golden opportunity, his once-in-a-lifetime shot to pray at the altar of incense.

We can imagine what might have passed between Zechariah and Elizabeth beforehand. "Don't forget to pray," she might have said, not daring to finish her request, for fear that it would sound too foolish. "Yes, dear," her husband would have answered, smiling sadly and kissing her on the forehead. "I'll remember." Maybe this is what happened, maybe not. But however it came about, Zechariah was standing in the Holy Place when the angel said to him: "your prayer has been heard, and your wife Elizabeth will bear you a son" (Luke 1:13). The fact that Elizabeth is mentioned by name suggests that Zechariah had been praying for her. Possibly the angel was referring to prayers that Zechariah had offered long ago. *When* God decides to answer our prayers is his business. But the important thing is that Zechariah's prayers were answered. Elizabeth would bear a son, and they would call his name John, which means—appropriately enough—"God has been gracious." By the grace of God, new life would come from a barren womb.

MANY WILL REJOICE AT HIS BIRTH

There is another way to interpret Zechariah's prayer, however. It was not wrong for him to make a personal request, interceding for his wife; however, this was not his primary purpose. He was in the Holy Place to pray for the people of God. They were outside in the courtyard, silently watching to

21

see the incense rise from the temple, and then falling down to worship God. Zechariah was inside the Holy Place, interceding for them as their priest.

Of all the things that Zechariah prayed, his main petition was for the salvation of Israel. His people, who in those days were under Roman oppression, were waiting for the ancient promises to be fulfilled and for God to come and save them. As their priest, Zechariah was called to present their request before God. He was praying for their salvation, and this prayer, too, would be answered, for as the angel went on to say:

> And you will have joy and gladness, and many will rejoice at his birth, for he will be great before the Lord. And he must not drink wine or strong drink, and he will be filled with the Holy Spirit, even from his mother's womb. And he will turn many of the children of Israel to the Lord their God, and he will go before him in the spirit and power of Elijah, to turn the hearts of the fathers to the children, and the disobedient to the wisdom of the just, to make ready for the Lord a people prepared. (Luke 1:14–17)

With these words, Gabriel began to explain the significance of John the Baptist. This was no ordinary child. The angel said that his birth would bring great joy, not only to his parents, but also to many others. Joy is a significant theme in Luke, and this is the first hint of the rejoicing that his Gospel brings. The angel also said that the child would be "great before the Lord" (Luke 1:15). And he *was* great. The fact that he was born of a barren woman testifies to his greatness, because in the Bible this is always a portent of some momentous event in the history of salvation.

Then the angel told Zechariah that his son would be set apart. As a sign of his holiness, he was not to have any strong drink. This was part of the Old Testament vow taken by the Nazirites (Num. 6:1–4). Under ordinary circumstances, moderate drinking was permissible, but John was set apart for the holy service of God. He was an unusual person, called to an unusual ministry. To make sure that people knew that what he said came from God, rather than under the influence of alcohol, he was not permitted to drink. Instead, he was "filled with the Holy Spirit" (Luke 1:15). Other prophets had been anointed by the Spirit, but John was the first to be filled with the Spirit from his mother's womb.

What Gabriel had said to this point went well beyond what any parent could hope. Under the circumstances, it was amazing enough for Zechariah and Elizabeth to have a son at all, let alone a son who was called to greatness. But then the angel said something even more astonishing: "And he will turn many of the children of Israel to the Lord their God, and he will go before him in the spirit and power of Elijah, to turn the hearts of the fathers to the children, and the disobedient to the wisdom of the just, to make ready for the Lord a people prepared" (Luke 1:16–17).

Zechariah's eyes were already wide with amazement, but when he heard this, his jaw may well have dropped all the way to the floor. To understand why, we have to go back to Malachi, which is the last book in the Old Testament, written some four hundred years earlier. The prophet Malachi looked forward to the coming of Christ. He prophesied that one day God would send the greatest prophet of all, whom he called "the messenger of the covenant" (Mal. 3:1). But first God would send a forerunner—a second Elijah to prepare the way. According to Malachi, God said, "Behold, I send my messenger and he will prepare the way before me. And the LORD whom you seek will suddenly come to his temple; and the messenger of the covenant in whom you delight, behold, he is coming" (Mal. 3:1). He also said, "Behold, I will send you Elijah the prophet before the great and awesome day of the LORD comes. And he will turn the hearts of fathers to their children and the hearts of children to their fathers" (Mal. 4:5–6).

These were the ancient promises, as Zechariah undoubtedly knew. So when Gabriel appeared and started talking about the spirit and power of Elijah, about turning the hearts of fathers to their children, and about getting people ready for God, he was announcing the ultimate salvation. These promises were for the ministry of Zechariah's son, but they went beyond John the Baptist to proclaim the coming of the Christ. Gabriel's prophecy clearly indicated that Zechariah would be the father of the forerunner. And if his son was the forerunner, the fulfillment was on its way.

This is confirmed by the word that Gabriel uses a few verses later, when he says, "I was sent to speak to you and to bring you this good news" (Luke 1:19). Here, for the first time, Luke uses the word that became the title for his book (cf. Luke 2:10 and 3:18). "Good news" is another word for "gospel," and what the angel proclaimed to Zechariah was nothing less. Because John would prepare the way for Jesus, the announcement of his birth *was* good news—not just for Zechariah and Elizabeth, but also for the nation of Israel and the entire world. Jesus was coming to save!

23

He Was Unable to Speak

The thing to do when Jesus is coming is to get ready. This is why the Gospel of Luke starts with John the Baptist. His calling was to get people ready for Jesus. He told them to repent and return to God. He restored relationships, turning the hearts of fathers back to their children. Getting ready for Jesus takes a change of heart, in which our lives are turned around for God. There is a vertical dimension to this: first we have to get right with God. But there is also a horizontal dimension as we learn to love one another. This was the message that John preached—a message of repentance that prepared people for Jesus.

Even John's birth announcement was part of the preparation, except that Zechariah wasn't ready. He knew that Gabriel was for real, but he still had his doubts: "And Zechariah said to the angel, 'How shall I know this? For I am an old man, and my wife is advanced in years'" (Luke 1:18). The man without a child did not believe the angel with the gospel, and because of his unbelief, he became a man without a voice: "And the angel answered him, 'I am Gabriel, who stands in the presence of God, and I was sent to speak to you and to bring you this good news. And behold, you will be silent and unable to speak until the day that these things take place, because you did not believe my words, which will be fulfilled in their time'" (Luke 1:19–20).

The objection Zechariah raised is the objection that people always raise: he did not believe in the supernatural power of God. He was looking at things from the merely human point of view. He had his biology right, but not his theology. According to John Chrysostom, the famous preacher from Constantinople, "Zechariah looked at his age, his gray hair, his body that had lost its strength. He looked at his wife's sterility, and he refused to accept on faith what the angel revealed would come to pass."[3] This is where people always struggle. They believe that the Bible was written by men, but they doubt that it was written by God. They believe that Jesus was a man, but they doubt that he was also God. They believe that Jesus died, but they doubt that he rose again. It takes faith to accept God's Word, to receive God's Son, and to enter God's salvation—faith in an all-powerful God.

3. John Chrysostom, "On the Incomprehensible Nature of God" (2.11), quoted in *Luke*, ed. Arthur A. Just Jr., Ancient Christian Commentary on Scripture, NT 3 (Downers Grove, IL: InterVarsity, 2003), 11.

Zechariah couldn't believe it. What is so ironic, of course, is that he had prayed for the very thing he ended up doubting that God could do! There he was, worshiping God in the Holy Place, praying for a son and a Savior. So when the angel told him that his prayers were answered, he had every reason to believe. The good news was delivered by Gabriel. It came from God's mouth to Zechariah's ear, by way of an angel. It fulfilled the ancient promise of salvation. But instead of believing, Zechariah asked for some kind of confirmation. Apparently, he didn't really expect God to answer his prayers. Sometimes even a good man has trouble believing in the power of prayer or the truth of God's Word.

Zechariah just wanted to be sure, which is exactly why his story is in the Bible. When Luke wrote his Gospel, he could have left this part out of the story. He could have ended at verse 17, with the words of the promise, and then skipped down to verses 24 and 25, where Elizabeth rejoices in God's grace. Instead, Luke tells us how God dealt with Zechariah for doubting his sovereign power. Why did Luke include this episode? Because he was writing the Gospel of knowing for sure, and this story strengthens our faith. As we read the Gospel, it is obvious to us that Zechariah should stop raising questions and start believing the angel's promise. The reason this is obvious is that as soon as *we* hear the promise, we know that it is true. We believe the good news, which is exactly why Luke wrote this Gospel. He tells us how Zechariah responded to the gospel so that unlike him, we will respond in faith.

Eventually God made a believer out of Zechariah, but not before chastising him for his unbelief: "And the people were waiting for Zechariah, and they were wondering at his delay in the temple. And when he came out, he was unable to speak to them, and they realized that he had seen a vision in the temple. And he kept making signs to them and remained mute" (Luke 1:21–22). This is one of the more humorous moments in the Bible. The people in the courtyard were starting to get worried. Usually the priest did not stay in the Holy Place for very long. He burned some incense, offered some prayers, and then came back out. But this time there was a problem, and by the time Zechariah left the temple, perhaps staggering, people really were starting to wonder. What was taking so long?

Unfortunately, Zechariah could not tell them what had happened. He couldn't say a word. He was speechless because God had struck him dumb. He couldn't even pronounce the priestly blessing that the people

25

were waiting to receive. Poor Zechariah! He had just heard the greatest news that anyone had heard in about four centuries, but he wasn't able to tell anyone about it. All he could do was make hand signals. But just imagine trying to play charades with Gabriel's prophecy!

God was teaching Zechariah to trust his word. The priest's temporary disability was a sign against his unbelief. God said, "You want a sign, Zechariah? I'll give you a sign. You ought to just take me at my word, but if you won't believe my gospel, I won't let you share it!" David Gooding comments:

> But a priest who cannot believe the authoritative word of an angel of God, because he cannot accept the possibility of divine intervention to reverse the decay of nature, has lost faith in the basic principle of redemption. Without redemption, he has no gospel. Without a gospel, any blessing he pronounced upon the people would be the emptiest of professional formalities. If Zechariah could not believe the angel's gospel, it were better that he did not pretend to bless the people. Fittingly the angel struck him dumb.[4]

When we get to the end of this chapter, we shall see what effect this disability had on Zechariah. Martin Luther described the gospel as "glad tidings, good news, welcome information, a shout, or something that makes one sing and talk and rejoice."[5] That is exactly what the gospel does, except that Zechariah couldn't do it! He couldn't even talk, let alone shout and sing. Imagine how desperate he was to tell people the good news about John and ultimately about Jesus. By the time God loosened his lips he could hardly contain himself.

Can you feel his frustration? Aren't you dying for Zechariah to tell somebody the good news? This is how the story works. Luke has written about Zechariah's unbelief so that we would be more certain of our faith, and more urgent to tell people about it. As we read about Zechariah, we believe the gospel that he was given and we want others to believe it, too. We want to share the good news that Zechariah was unable to announce. The telling of the gospel brings us to faith and sends us out to witness.

4. David Gooding, *According to Luke: A New Exposition of the Third Gospel* (Grand Rapids: Eerdmans, 1987), 36.

5. Martin Luther, "Preface to the New Testament," quoted in Mark R. Talbot, "God's Shout," *Modern Reformation* 12.5 (Sept./Oct. 2003): 2.

TAKING GOD AT HIS WORD

When God announces good news, it always comes true. The angel said that all the promises would be fulfilled at the right time, and they were. Zechariah finished his work, "and when his time of service was ended, he went to his home. After these days his wife Elizabeth conceived, and for five months she kept herself hidden, saying, 'Thus the Lord has done for me in the days when he looked on me, to take away my reproach among people'" (Luke 1:23–25).

It is typical for Luke to notice what the gospel meant for hurting people. Here he shows us what the good news meant for Elizabeth. The gospel was for the nations, but it was also for people like her—a woman upon whom God had looked with grace. And Elizabeth responded to God in faith. When she realized that she was pregnant, she stayed at home to rest, to worship, and to wait for God's promise to come true. Her prayers were answered. Her reproach had ended. And unlike her husband, she was able to lift her voice and praise God for what he had done. She believed what God said.

This is what God always wants from us: faith. He wants us to take him at his word. So whatever God says, believe it! He has said that Jesus died and rose again, so believe in the crucifixion and the resurrection. He has said that he will forgive anyone who comes to him trusting in Jesus; so if you are a sinner, believe in Jesus and know that your sins are forgiven. God has said that he will never leave you or forsake you; so whatever troubles you are facing, believe that God will help you to the very end. He has also said that Jesus is coming again to judge the world. If this is what God has said, then we need to get ready by turning away from sin and trusting in Jesus.

3

THE ANNUNCIATION

Luke 1:26–38

And the angel said to her, "Do not be afraid, Mary, for you have found favor with God. And behold, you will conceive in your womb and bear a son, and you shall call his name Jesus. He will be great and will be called the Son of the Most High. And the Lord God will give to him the throne of his father David, and he will reign over the house of Jacob forever, and of his kingdom there will be no end." (Luke 1:30–33)

John came first. He was the forerunner—the messenger sent ahead to announce the coming of the King. Then came Jesus—his Majesty, the King—to seek and to save the lost. In the opening chapters of Luke their stories are laid out side by side for comparison and contrast. John and Jesus: two cousins, two pregnancies, two hymns of praise, and two deliveries at the beginning of two great lives.

The similarities between the two stories are striking. Both John and Jesus were born to godly women who apart from divine intervention were unable to bear children. Writing in the fourth century, Maximus of Turin described how "Mary, conscious of her virginity, marvels at the fruit hidden in her belly, while Elizabeth, conscious of her old age, blushes that her womb is heavy with the one she has conceived."[1] The births of both cousins were announced by the same awesome angel, who told people not to be afraid, proclaimed the birth of a son, gave each child his name, and explained his mission in life. The people who heard these announcements—Zechariah the priest and Mary the virgin—questioned the angel and were given a confirming sign.

Yet for all their similarities, what Luke mainly wants us to see are the differences. Like a white paint chip next to an off-white paint chip, the comparison is made to show the contrast. So who is greater: John or Jesus? John's mother was barren; the mother of Jesus had never been with a man at all. John would be a prophet crying in the wilderness; Jesus would reign on David's everlasting throne. John would be "great before the Lord" (Luke 1:15). Jesus would be "great" without qualification (Luke 1:32), the Son of the Most High God. John would be filled with the Holy Spirit, but Jesus would be *conceived* by the Holy Spirit. John would prepare for God's coming, but when Jesus came, God was there, in the flesh. Who is greater: John or Jesus? Luke argues from the lesser to the greater to give more glory to Jesus. Jesus was like John, but superior in every respect—infinitely superior.

GABRIEL'S GREETING

The birth of Jesus, like the birth of John, was announced by the angel Gabriel, who began with a greeting: "In the sixth month the angel Gabriel was sent from God to a city of Galilee named Nazareth, to a virgin betrothed to a man whose name was Joseph, of the house of David. And the virgin's name was Mary. And he came to her and said, 'Greetings, O favored one, the Lord is with you!'" (Luke 1:26–28).

It is doubtful whether Gabriel could have found a more unlikely person to greet anywhere in Israel. Mary was among the lowly. She was young— possibly as young as twelve or thirteen years old, in that awkward stage between childhood and womanhood.[2] Like many people in Israel, she was a

---

1. Maximus of Turin, "Collectio sermonum antiqua" (5.3–4), quoted in *Luke*, ed. Arthur A. Just, Jr., Ancient Christian Commentary on Scripture, NT 3 (Downers Grove, IL: InterVarsity, 2003), 10.

2. Joachim Jeremias, *Jerusalem in the Time of Jesus* (Philadelphia: Fortress, 1978), 364–65, reports that in those days the usual age for betrothal was twelve or twelve and a half.

poor, uneducated peasant living in a small country town far from the center of power. As people said in those days, "Can anything good come out of Nazareth?" (John 1:46). Mary was also a female in a culture that discounted women. From a merely human perspective, she was insignificant. Kent Hughes calls her "a nobody in a nothing town in the middle of nowhere."[3]

Yet Mary was given the greatest honor that any woman has ever been given. She was chosen to be the mother of Jesus, and her lowly estate was part of God's plan. By choosing Mary, God was beginning to show what humiliation his Son would have to endure for the salvation of sinners. Martin Luther observed that God might well "have gone to Jerusalem and picked out Caiaphas's daughter, who was fair, rich, clad in gold embroidered raiment and attended by a retinue of maids in waiting. But God preferred a lowly maid from a mean town."[4] God preferred this because the plan of salvation required Jesus to humble himself, and only then to be exalted. To rescue us from our sins and lift us to glory, Jesus first had to enter into the misery of our lost and fallen condition. What better way to show what he had come to do than for him to be born to a woman like Mary from a town like Nazareth?

God's grace is for the lowly. God certainly showed grace to Mary. This is the meaning of the angel's salutation: "Greetings, O favored one, the Lord is with you!" (Luke 1:28). With these words, Gabriel pronounced God's benediction on Mary. God was with her to bless her, not because of her own merit, but because of his grace. The word the angel used for "favor" *(kecharitōmenē)* comes from the Greek word for "grace" *(charis)*. It means to be treated with undeserved kindness. Martin Luther paraphrased Gabriel's greeting like this: "O Mary, you are blessed. You have a gracious God. No woman has ever lived on earth to whom God has shown such grace."[5]

The angel's greeting has often been misunderstood. Gabriel was not worshiping Mary; nor did he say that she was "full of grace." These ideas come from a prayer commonly used by Roman Catholics: "Hail Mary, full

---

3. R. Kent Hughes, *Luke: That You May Know the Truth*, 2 vols., Preaching the Word (Wheaton, IL: Crossway, 1998), 1:30.

4. Martin Luther, quoted in Roland Bainton, *The Martin Luther Christmas Book* (Philadelphia: Fortress, 1948), 22.

5. Martin Luther, quoted in Bainton, *Christmas Book*, 21.

of grace; the Lord is with thee. Blessed art thou among women, and blessed is the fruit of thy womb, Jesus, Holy Mary, Mother of God, pray for us sinners now and at the hour of death." This is not a biblical prayer, although it has some biblical language in it. The problem is that it treats Mary as the *source* of grace rather than as an *object* of grace. People pray to Mary because they think she has grace to give. But the phrase "full of grace" is based on a Latin translation (the Vulgate) that is really a *mis*translation. Even Roman Catholic Bible scholars admit this, although most still think that Christians should pray to Mary.[6] What the Bible actually says is that Mary was the *recipient* of God's grace, not a *repository* of grace. The word that the English Standard Version rightly translates as "favored one" is a passive participle. In other words, it refers to the grace that Mary was given by God, and not to any grace that she can give to others.

It is important to know what to believe about Mary because so many people go wrong at this point. The Bible never says that Mary was without sin, that she remained a virgin, or that she is able to give grace to sinners. We can only imagine how much it would grieve her to know that some people worship her! What the Bible does say—beyond the fact that she was the mother of Jesus—is that she was saved by grace. The way Mary helps us is not by giving us grace, but by showing that God can give us the same kind of grace that he gave to her. Mary is the blessed virgin, who alone was called to give birth to the Son of God. Her experience is not our experience; nevertheless, her example *is* for us. Since she received grace from God, her example proves that God shows unmerited favor to lowly sinners. Even when we feel small and insignificant, overlooked by the world, we can know that God is for us. Gabriel's greeting shows God's grace for the lowly.

THE ANGEL'S ANNOUNCEMENT

What the angel said was meant to be reassuring, yet Mary was still troubled. She wasn't hysterical, as some teenagers might have been, but she was more than a little upset. As Luke tells it, "She was greatly troubled at the saying, and tried to discern what sort of greeting this might be" (Luke 1:29).

6. See Raymond E. Brown, *The Birth of the Messiah: A Commentary on the Infancy Narratives in the Gospels of Matthew and Luke*, rev. ed., Anchor Bible Reference Library (New York: Doubleday, 1993), 325–27.

Naturally Mary wanted to know what this meant. What was happening? Why was an angel talking to her? What had he come to say?

Gabriel did not leave Mary in suspense, but followed his greeting with an announcement. The announcement—which came in two parts because it was divided by Mary's question in verse 34—began as follows: "Do not be afraid, Mary, for you have found favor with God. And behold, you will conceive in your womb and bear a son, and you shall call his name Jesus. He will be great and will be called the Son of the Most High. And the Lord God will give to him the throne of his father David, and he will reign over the house of Jacob forever, and of his kingdom there will be no end" (Luke 1:30–33).

With these words, the angel announced the greatest event in human history: the coming of the Son of God. First Gabriel told Mary not to be afraid, because she had found favor with God. "Favor" is a different form of the same word that the angel used in verse 28: *charin*, which is the Greek word for grace. God was showing unmerited favor to Mary; by his grace she would give birth to a son.

Then Gabriel proceeded to explain the significance of this child, telling about his person and work. Who was he? What would he do? The angel told Mary to call his name Jesus, which means "God saves," or "the Lord is salvation." This was the first hint that Jesus would be the Savior. He would bring salvation to sinners by dying on the cross in shame and then rising again in glory. Even from the announcement of his birth, his name testified to his saving work. Jesus is the salvation of God.

Next the angel said that Jesus would be "great." When Gabriel appeared to Zechariah, he said that John the Baptist would be "great before the Lord" (Luke 1:15). But Jesus *is* the Lord, so when Gabriel said that he would "be great," he did not limit his greatness in any way. Jesus is great. In the Old Testament, whenever this word is used without qualification, it almost always refers to God himself. God's wisdom is great; his works are great; his power is great; his mercy is great (e.g., Ps. 92:5; 103:11). So great is God's greatness that he alone deserves to be called "great." By saying that Jesus would be great, therefore, Gabriel was testifying to the deity of Jesus Christ.[7] No one is greater than he is. Jesus is great in wisdom, great

---

7. R. Laurentin, quoted in Darrell L. Bock, *Luke 1:1–9:50*, Baker Exegetical Commentary on the New Testament 3A (Grand Rapids: Baker, 1994), 113.

in power, great in love, and great in the majesty of his divine being. His greatness is the greatness of God.

Already we see the strange juxtaposition of meekness and majesty that define the life and ministry of Jesus Christ. He was born in the humblest of circumstances. While on earth he suffered the humiliation of poverty, loneliness, homelessness, rejection, persecution, and torture. Jesus humbled himself to the very death. Yet he was still the divine Son of God, and God exalted him back to greatness by raising him from the dead. We usually get this backwards. We exalt ourselves, trying to make ourselves greater than we are, and then God has to humble us. Jesus did the exact opposite: he humbled himself and let God do the exalting. In fact, this was part of his greatness. Later, when the disciples wanted to know who was the greatest, Jesus said, "He who is least among you all is the one who is great" (Luke 9:48). God does not define greatness by status, but by service (see Luke 22:27). Jesus was the greatest because by his sacrifice on the cross he became the servant of all.

After testifying to his greatness, the angel said that Jesus would be called "the Son of the Most High" (Luke 1:32). Gabriel used similar terminology a few moments later, calling Jesus "the Son of God" (Luke 1:35). "The Most High" was a favorite expression of King David, who used this title to praise the Lord (e.g., Ps. 7:17). Here Gabriel identifies Jesus as the *Son* of the Most High God. This phrase could be used for any child of God. There is a sense in which every believer is a son or daughter of the Most High. But this title belongs to Jesus in a unique way. Divine sonship is his eternal identity as the Second Person of the Trinity—God the eternal Son. There is one God in three persons: Father, Son, and Holy Spirit. What Luke gradually reveals—in Jesus' conception (Luke 1:35), at his baptism (Luke 3:22), at his transfiguration (Luke 9:35), and in his resurrection (Acts 13:33)—is that Jesus of Nazareth is God the Son. What joy it must have given Gabriel to announce this mystery for the very first time, declaring that Jesus is the Second Person of the Trinity, the divine Son of God.

Gabriel also said that Jesus would rule in majesty, sitting on the ancient throne of David. As Luke has already indicated (Luke 1:27), his earthly father Joseph came from the house of David, which meant that Jesus was David's rightful heir. Long ago God had promised David that his son would have a kingdom that would never end: "I will establish the throne of his kingdom forever. I will be to him a father, and he shall be to me a son. . . . Your throne shall be established forever" (2 Sam. 7:13–14, 16). These ancient promises were fulfilled in Jesus Christ, who is the son of David and Israel's eternal King.

This was the angel's announcement: Mary would give birth to a son named Jesus, who would be the great Savior and the Son of God, the most powerful ruler in the history of the world. Do you trust the angel's promise? It was written so that you would know for sure—so that you would believe in Jesus as your Savior, worship him as your great God, and serve him as your everlasting King.

Mary's Question

Mary believed the angel's prophecy, but she still had a question: "How will this be, since I am a virgin?" (Luke 1:34).

Mary obviously understood the angel to say that her child would be conceived before she got married. As everyone knows, she was engaged to Joseph. In those days a betrothal was formalized in a public ceremony and generally lasted for a year, during which the bride was sometimes referred to as the man's wife.[8] But the couple did not live together, and they did not have sexual relations, for in those days "an engagement was regarded as a definite promise of mutual fidelity and its violation was looked upon as adultery."[9]

Since she was a godly woman, Mary was saving herself for marriage. She was preserving her sexual purity as a prize, the way every woman should. But this raised an obvious question. How could she conceive and bear a son if she had never been with a man? Mary knew enough about the reproductive process to know that this was impossible. So she had to ask: "How will this be, since I am a virgin?"

Mary did not ask this question in unbelief. Here Luke is drawing a clear contrast between Zechariah's doubt and Mary's faith. When old Zechariah received the promise of a son, he asked, "How shall I *know* this?" (Luke 1:18). He wasn't sure whether to believe the angel or not, so he wanted

8. Bock, *Luke 1:1–9:50*, 107.
9. Norval Geldenhuys, *The Gospel of Luke*, New International Commentary on the New Testament (Grand Rapids: Eerdmans, 1951), 75.

some kind of confirmation. Mary asked a completely different question: "How will this be?" (Luke 1:34). In other words, she wanted to know how it would happen. Unlike Zechariah, she believed that the angel's promise would come true. But she was still curious to know *how* it would happen, and perhaps to know whether there was anything she needed to do.

It was a good, honest question, and Gabriel gave her the answer, as well as a sign to confirm the promise: "The Holy Spirit will come upon you, and the power of the Most High will overshadow you; therefore the child to be born will be called holy—the Son of God. And behold, your relative Elizabeth in her old age has also conceived a son, and this is the sixth month with her who was called barren. For nothing will be impossible with God" (Luke 1:35–37).

As a good historian, Luke gives us the facts: Mary's son would be conceived by the power of the Holy Spirit. Like a good physician, he also puts these facts into their medical context, telling us that Elizabeth was getting close to the end of her second trimester. The story of Jesus and his birth is not some bizarre myth. It is not, as some Bible scholars say, "a collection of largely uncertain, mutually contradictory, strongly legendary" accounts.[10] This is factual history, and what the facts declare is one of the most stupendous miracles God has ever performed: the virgin birth of Jesus Christ.

Mary asked the same question that people still ask today: How can this be? How can a woman become pregnant without having sexual relations? The answer is very simple—if you believe in the power of God. The answer is that Jesus was conceived by the Holy Spirit. This is the miracle of the virgin birth that Christians have always confessed. We say it in the Apostles' Creed: "he was conceived by the Holy Ghost, and born of the Virgin Mary." We also say it in the Nicene Creed: God the Son "was incarnated by the Holy Spirit of the Virgin Mary and was made man." This is how Mary had a son. The child in her womb came from the Holy Spirit: "Her pregnancy is an act of divine grace, explicable not in terms of human insemination . . . but in terms of the creative power of the Holy Spirit."[11]

Gabriel told Mary that the Holy Spirit would "overshadow" her. This language echoes the Old Testament and reminds us that the Holy Spirit has

10. Hans Küng, *On Being a Christian* (London: Collins, 1977), 451.
11. Donald MacLeod, *The Person of Christ*, Contours of Christian Theology (Downers Grove, IL: InterVarsity, 1998), 27.

been actively involved in everything that God has ever done. The Spirit was present at creation, when he overshadowed the waters of the earth (Gen. 1:2). The Spirit was there at the exodus, when he overshadowed the tabernacle in a cloud of glory (Ex. 40:34–35). Later the Spirit would overshadow Jesus, anointing him for his earthly ministry. It was by the Spirit that Jesus made atonement for our sins (Heb. 9:14), and by the Spirit that he was raised from the dead (Rom. 1:4). Then Jesus sent the Spirit to overshadow the church (Acts 1:8); it is by the power of his presence that we serve Christ today. The Holy Spirit has been overshadowing God's people from the very beginning, working with the Father and the Son for our salvation.

But no work of the Spirit is more miraculous than the work he did in Mary's womb, enabling the virgin to give birth to the Son of God. The virgin birth of Jesus Christ is one of the essential facts and great mysteries of the Christian religion. If we deny this, we deny the faith. According to Luke, Mary had a child before she had intercourse. Do we believe this, or not? If we say that Jesus was *not* born of a virgin, then either we believe that Mary was sexually immoral, or that Luke was a writer of fiction, or both. In any case, we defame the character of these godly people and contradict the plain teaching of Scripture.

Even worse, we deny the deity of Jesus Christ, because it is his conception by the Holy Spirit that makes him the holy Son of God. Jesus had to be born of a woman to be a man. But if he had been the physical offspring of Joseph, then he would have been nothing more than a man. His virgin birth, his divine conception by the Spirit—these things were necessary for his incarnation. Only the virgin birth preserves the humanity *and* the deity of Jesus Christ. His conception by the Spirit points to his deity. His birth from a woman points to his humanity. One person, two natures—a divine nature and a human nature. And because he was conceived by a unique creative act of the Holy Spirit, Jesus was not corrupted by the guilt of Adam. Fallen humanity could not produce its own Savior; he had to come from somewhere outside, by way of divine initiative and intervention. Therefore, God sent Jesus into the world as the perfect Son of God, born without sin.

In case she had any trouble believing, God gave Mary a sign. Unlike Zechariah, she had not asked for a sign, but God gave her one just the same. It was a sign that proved his sovereignty over the womb. Mary's relative Elizabeth—barren old Elizabeth—was six months pregnant! The angel told

Mary this to prove the power of God, which he declared in a memorable phrase: "Nothing will be impossible with God" (Luke 1:37; cf. Gen. 18:14). God was able to bring a child from a barren womb. If he was able to do this, then by the power of his Holy Spirit he could just as well make a virgin conceive and bear a son. And if God could perform the miracle of the virgin birth, then he is quite capable of handling the difficulties of our daily lives. Nothing is impossible with God. This is a verse to live by. As J. C. Ryle has said, "A hearty reception of this great principle is of immense importance to our own inward peace."[12]

Is there anything in your life that seems impossible? Perhaps it seems impossible for your great sin to be forgiven, especially after all the times you have tried not to do it again, but failed. Perhaps it seems impossible for your family to be restored after all the heartbreak and for joy to come again. Maybe it seems impossible for your physical and financial needs to be met, or for your work, your studies, or your ministry to succeed. It may seem impossible to endure the suffering that has come into your life, or for someone you love to come to Christ. But the Bible says, "Nothing will be impossible with God." He is the God of the virgin birth! There is no sin he cannot forgive, no relationship he cannot reconcile, no problem he cannot resolve, no need he cannot meet, no ministry he cannot bless, no grief he cannot comfort, no life he cannot reclaim, no sinner he cannot save. The God of the virgin birth is the God who makes all things possible.

MARY'S RESPONSE

Do you believe this? Mary believed it, and what a difference it made in her life. Her encounter with the angel ends with her great confession of faith: "Mary said, 'Behold, I am the servant of the Lord; let it be to me according to your word.' And the angel departed from her" (Luke 1:38).

The Bible says that "faith is the assurance of things hoped for, the conviction of things not seen" (Heb. 11:1). Mary had that assurance. Unlike Zechariah, meeting an angel did not leave her speechless. On the contrary, she was able to confess her faith and accept God's call. In the words of Maximus of Turin, "[Zechariah] lost his voice because he doubted. But [Mary],

12. J. C. Ryle, *Expository Thoughts on the Gospels, Luke* (1858; reprint Cambridge: James Clarke, 1976), 1:28.

because she believed immediately, conceived the saving Word."[13] She was able to do this because she took God at his word. She said, "Let it be to me according to your word" (Luke 1:38). Mary did not raise any objections. She did not hold out for an easier calling. She did not ask God to explain what would happen later if she said yes. All she needed to know was what God wanted her to do. Once she knew, that was enough for her; she was ready to do it!

How rare it is to find someone who is willing to trust God for the impossible and then obey him without hesitation or qualification. Even some of the great heroes of the faith tried to wiggle out of doing what God said. Think of Moses, who asked God to send someone else to lead the exodus (Ex. 4:13). Or of Gideon, who said he couldn't deliver Israel because he was the weakest man from the weakest tribe (Judg. 6:15). Or of Jeremiah, who said he was too young for the job (Jer. 1:6). But Mary was a woman of great faith. She understood that once we know what God wants us to do, any delay is a sign of unbelief. In the words of the English bishop Joseph Hall, "All disputations with God after His will is known, arise from infidelity. There is not a more noble proof of faith than . . . without all questionings to go blindfold whither He will lead us."[14]

Mary trusted God, even when it seemed impossible. In her own words, she was "the servant of the Lord" (Luke 1:38). The word "servant" could also be translated "slave." Mary was identifying herself as God's bondservant, his handmaiden. She wanted to offer God humble, trusting, submissive obedience. She was committed to doing whatever she was told to do. Her calling was to serve.

This was a great honor—the greatest honor that any woman has ever been given. To this day, Mary is blessed as the mother of Jesus. But her service also led to great suffering. To accept the virgin birth, Mary had to be willing to give up almost everything she knew and loved. She had to be willing to give up Joseph, the man she was engaged to marry. How could he consent to take her as his wife if she was pregnant with a child that was not his own? She had to be willing to give up her reputation. Imagine the village gossip in a town like Nazareth, where everyone would wonder who the father was. To be frank, there would always be some people who would call

13. Maximus of Turin, "Collectio," 10.
14. Joseph Hall, quoted in Ryle, *Expository Thoughts*, 1:30.

her son a bastard. Some might even say that she deserved to die, because the law demanded the death penalty whenever a woman who was engaged was convicted of adultery (Deut. 22:23–24).

There were other trials as well. There were all the physical pains that went with pregnancy and childbirth. There were also many hardships that Mary could not have predicted: the journey to Bethlehem, the exile in Egypt, the hatred of Herod. But the greatest suffering came when Jesus grew to be a man and began to fulfill his ministry. There was so much controversy surrounding Jesus that at one point the family tried to get him to go to another part of the country, or even to leave the ministry altogether (Mark 3:21). It was obvious that he was on a collision course with death. And at the very end Mary had to endure his arrest, his trial, his crucifixion, and his bloody burial. This is what it meant for Mary to submit to God's will for her life. When she said, "Behold, I am the servant of the Lord; let it be to me according to your word" (Luke 1:38), she was consenting to a lifetime of suffering for the glory of God.

All of this leads David Gooding to wonder how Mary did it. He marvels that "an ordinary human girl of flesh and blood believed [that God could perform the impossible miracle of the virgin birth], and went on believing it, and bore the incalculable honour and the immeasurable burden without losing faith and nerve and proper humility and sanity itself."[15] How did she do it? How was she able to offer such costly service? The answer is that Mary did it by faith. She trusted God for all of it—her relationship with Joseph, her reputation in town, her physical suffering, and the anguish of her soul. Mary believed in God and followed him with trusting obedience.

This is what it means to be a Christian. Indeed, we might even say that Mary was the first Christian, for a Christian is simply a person who believes in Jesus and says, "Behold, I am the servant of the Lord; let it be to me according to your word." This means trusting God for our relationships—romantic and otherwise—not trying to make them go the way we want them to go, but letting God lead. It means trusting God in our daily work, allowing him to see to our success. It means trusting God for ministry, being content with whatever blessing he brings, or doesn't bring, as long as we are faithful. It means trusting God for our families, asking him

15. David Gooding, *According to Luke: A New Exposition of the Third Gospel* (Grand Rapids: Eerdmans, 1987), 41.

to carry our burden for the people we love. It means trusting God with our troubles—the impossible things we have to face. And it means trusting God when we suffer reproach, as Mary did. If we follow God, then people will be as opposed to us as they are to him, but by faith we will continue to follow him.

Are you willing to be God's servant? Then surrender to his will and submit to his word. Give up control, putting things into his hands rather than bending them to your own purpose. Live for God no matter what other people think. And do this even if it means suffering for the cause of Christ. By the grace of God, through faith in Christ and by the work of his Holy Spirit, we are able to say what Mary said: "Have it your way, Lord, not mine—I am ready to do your will."

4

MAGNIFICAT

Luke 1:39–55

*And Mary said, "My soul magnifies the Lord, and my spirit
rejoices in God my Savior, for he has looked on the humble
estate of his servant. For behold, from now on all generations
will call me blessed." (Luke 1:46–48)*

The old woman was at home, waiting. She was waiting for God, waiting for the promise, and expecting her firstborn son. Who could believe it? An old woman like her—always childless— but now she was "starting to show." The young woman was out on the road, heading up to the hill country. She too was pregnant, but no one else knew about it yet. Who would believe it? A young girl like her—still a virgin—but soon she would bear a son.

Two women touched by God: a senior citizen and a teenager. Old barren Elizabeth was six months pregnant, staying at home to rest while she waited for the birth of John. The young virgin Mary had only just conceived. Was it really true? Would she really give birth to the Son of God? To confirm the promise, the angel told her about Elizabeth. So Mary took the hint and went to see her old cousin—a dangerous journey through almost a hundred miles of rugged wasteland.

Theologians call their meeting "the visitation." How precious it must have been for Mary and Elizabeth to embrace, share their good news, and discuss what God had done. What they shared was unique. They alone were chosen to bear the children of promise, and they were the first to know that God had come to redeem his people.

The visitation was not for Mary and Elizabeth alone, however, but also for their sons. John was the greatest prophet of the old covenant—the one called to announce the coming of the Christ. Jesus *was* the Christ, the Lord of the new covenant. So when Mary met Elizabeth, the covenants connected. Both sons were joined under one roof, and like the electrical contact between two power stations, the results were explosive. There was a spontaneous outburst of exultant joy, as the old covenant greeted the new. Poet Luci Shaw describes the encounter:

> Framed in light,
> Mary sings through the doorway.
> Elizabeth's six month joy
> jumps, a palpable greeting,
> a hidden first encounter
> between son and Son.[1]

ELIZABETH'S SONG

Luke was more a historian than a poet, so his account is more prosaic:

In those days Mary arose and went with haste into the hill country, to a town in Judah, and she entered the house of Zechariah and greeted Elizabeth. And when Elizabeth heard the greeting of Mary, the baby leaped in her womb. And Elizabeth was filled with the Holy Spirit, and she exclaimed with a loud cry, "Blessed are you among women, and blessed is the fruit of your womb! And why is this granted to me that the mother of my Lord should come to me? For behold, when the sound of your greeting came to my ears, the baby in my womb leaped for joy. And blessed is she who believed that there would be a fulfillment of what was spoken to her from the Lord." (Luke 1:39–45)

1. Luci Shaw, quoted in R. Kent Hughes, *Luke: That You May Know the Truth*, 2 vols., Preaching the Word (Wheaton, IL: Crossway, 1998), 1:42.

These verses show the joy that comes whenever anyone recognizes that Jesus is the Christ. The first to recognize him was John, whose calling it was to announce Christ's coming. What is remarkable is that he began to fulfill this calling while he was still in utero. "Not yet born, already John prophesies," wrote Maximus of Turin, "and while still in the enclosure of his mother's womb, confesses the coming of Christ with movements of joy."[2] John the Baptist was the only child ever to use a womb for a pulpit. In the liquid darkness of his mother's womb, the unborn child kicked for joy, leaping at the sound of Mary's voice, and in this way preparing people for the coming of Christ.

Elizabeth had felt John move before. The child was active, and at six months it was only natural for her to feel him kicking, as babies do. But this was different. Elizabeth could sense that her child was leaping for joy. She knew that a fetus is a person with emotions. She may also have known the angel's promise that John would "be filled with the Holy Spirit, even from his mother's womb" (Luke 1:15). By the inward witness of the Spirit, the child recognized the presence of Christ. Jesus was not yet viable—invisible in his mother's womb. Yet John knew him to be the Son of God. Later, when Jesus began his public ministry, John would testify that his joy was complete (John 3:29). But his joy began while he was still in his mother's womb.

The coming of Christ is a thing that makes a person leap for joy. This was true for John, and also for anyone who comes to faith in Christ. By the inward witness of the Holy Spirit we recognize that Jesus is the Son of God and our Savior from sin. When we recognize him, we rejoice in him, leaping for the joy of our salvation.

Elizabeth joined in the rejoicing. When John jumped, she shouted. And what was it that made the old woman shout? The coming of Christ. Like her son, Elizabeth was filled with the Holy Spirit, and like him, she recognized that she was in the presence of the Messiah. She lifted her voice and said, "Why is this granted to me that the mother of my Lord should come to me?" (Luke 1:43).

Notice Elizabeth's humility. For six months the big excitement in her life had been her own pregnancy. But rather than thinking of her own good news, she immediately praised God for what he had done for Mary. She was not jealous, but honored Mary as the mother of her Lord—the most

2. Maximus of Turin, "Collectio sermonum antiqua" (5.4), quoted in *Luke*, ed. Arthur A. Just Jr., Ancient Christian Commentary on Scripture, NT 3 (Downers Grove, IL: InterVarsity, 2003), 21.

blessed woman in the world. Like the angel Gabriel, she said that Mary was favored by God's grace.

Elizabeth was not worshiping Mary, of course, but blessing her faith. Mary was a woman who took God at his word. So Elizabeth said, "Blessed is she who believed that there would be a fulfillment of what was spoken to her from the Lord" (Luke 1:45). We may wonder whether Zechariah overheard this. If so, it was a rebuke to his unbelief, for although Zechariah also had a word from the Lord, he did not quite believe that God would fulfill his promise. But when Mary heard it, she believed it, and thus Elizabeth commended her faith. What an encouragement this must have been for Mary—a confirmation that she was right to believe in God. And what an encouragement it is for us to join her in believing that everything God has said about Jesus is absolutely true.

The most important thing Elizabeth said was not about Mary, however, but about Jesus. She referred to the child in Mary's womb as her Lord. What a remarkable thing for Elizabeth to say! She called the unborn child "my Lord" (Luke 1:43). This is a title from the psalms, where David referred to the Messiah as "my Lord" (Ps. 110:1). This was something that could have been revealed to Elizabeth only by the Holy Spirit. She had been resting quietly at home. How did she know that Mary was the mother of the Messiah? How did she know that she was even pregnant? Yet as soon as she heard her cousin's voice, she identified Mary's child as her Lord and God. By looking beyond his humanity to see his deity, Elizabeth was the first to confess her faith in Jesus as Lord.

This is how everyone should respond to Jesus Christ: by trusting in him as Savior and rejoicing in him as Lord. We have even better reason to believe in Jesus than John and Elizabeth had. They rejoiced over his conception, but we also rejoice for his crucifixion and resurrection. This is why Luke wrote his Gospel: so we would know for sure that Jesus died on the cross for our sins and was raised again to give us eternal life. Now everyone who believes in Jesus leaps for joy and calls him Lord.

Mary's Song

Elizabeth and John were not the only ones who rejoiced in the coming of Christ. Mary also rejoiced by breaking into song. Her song is called

Magnificat, a title taken from its first word in Latin: *magnificat*, or "magnifies." Mary said, "My soul magnifies the Lord, and my spirit rejoices in God my Savior" (Luke 1:46–47).

Mary's song is the first of four nativity hymns in Luke's Gospel: Mary's *Magnificat*, Zechariah's *Benedictus*, the angels' *Gloria*, and Simeon's *Nunc Dimittis*. Graham Scroggie rightly identified these Christmas carols as "the last of the Hebrew Psalms, and the first of the Christian hymns."[3] They appear only in Luke, which makes the good doctor the church's first hymnologist. Luke included these lyrics because he understood that the gospel is and must be a musical. What God has done in Christ demands to be praised. It is not enough simply to say what God has done to save us—what he has done also needs to be celebrated in song. R. Tannehill has observed that the *Magnificat* "is like an aria in opera; the action almost stops so that the situation may be savored more deeply."[4] This is exactly what the *Magnificat* does. It is written in the form of a poem; since poetry is a heightened form of expression, it forces us to slow down. And when we slow down, we are able to savor and celebrate the salvation we have in Christ. Mary's poem is a psalm that leads us into praise.

Some scholars have objected that a teenager like Mary could not possibly have composed a poetical and theological masterpiece like the *Magnificat*. They say that someone more sophisticated—like Luke—must have put these words into her mouth.

This objection overlooks the doctrine of inspiration, which teaches that Mary's words came from God the Holy Spirit. It is also flatly contradicted by the words of the song itself. Mary said, "My soul magnifies the Lord, and my spirit rejoices in God my Savior" (Luke 1:46–47). When she spoke of her "soul" and her "spirit," Mary was referring to the very center of her being. This song came from her heart. Perhaps it was a spontaneous response to Elizabeth's greeting, or perhaps she composed it on the way from Nazareth. But either way, it was *her* song. Mary worshiped God with all she was and everything she had, praising him with mind, soul, heart, and strength.

If we wonder how she was able to write such a famous poem, the answer is simple: Mary knew her Bible! Her song is similar to many songs from the

---

3. W. Graham Scroggie, *A Guide to the Gospels* (London: Pickering & Inglis, 1948), 371.

4. R. Tannehill, quoted in Arthur A. Just, Jr., *Luke 1:1–9:50*, Concordia Commentary (St. Louis: Concordia, 1996), 80.

Old Testament. It sounds like something from King David, or like something Hannah would have written. Hannah was another woman who was unexpectedly expecting. She said:

> My heart exults in the LORD;
>> my strength is exalted in the LORD. . . .
> The LORD makes poor and makes rich;
>> he brings low and he exalts.
> He raises up the poor from the dust;
>> he lifts the needy from the ash heap
> to make them sit with princes
>> and inherit a seat of honor. (1 Sam. 2:1, 7–8)

There are echoes from Hannah in Mary's song, but not just from Hannah. The *Magnificat* either quotes from or alludes to verses from Genesis, Deuteronomy, 1 and 2 Samuel, Job, Psalms, Isaiah, Ezekiel, Micah, Habakkuk, and Zephaniah.[5] Mary tried to put virtually the whole Bible into her song!

Mary was able to do this because the psalms and poems of the Bible were written on her heart. She had been raised on the Scriptures. She sang them at home and heard them at the synagogue. So when the plan of salvation intersected with her life, she was able to offer God the right kind of praise. Mary used the exalted language she had learned at her mother's knee by reading and singing the Bible. According to one literary scholar, "The style and language are those which would be natural to the speaker, as drawn from the storehouse of faith and piety, the sacred writings of her people, familiar to all by constant recitation, and dear to pious souls by use in their own devotions. . . . So here the words as well as the thoughts are those of a high-souled Hebrew maiden of devout and meditative habit, whose mind has taken the tone of the Scriptures in which she has been nurtured."[6]

From this we learn that the best way to train our children to glorify God is by studying and singing God's Word. When we know the Bible, it becomes the song of our hearts, and we are able to join Mary in say-

---

5. See Raymond E. Brown, *The Birth of the Messiah: A Commentary on the Infancy Narratives in the Gospels of Matthew and Luke*, rev. ed., Anchor Bible Reference Library (New York: Doubleday, 1993), 358–60.

6. Thomas Dehany Bernard, *The Songs of the Holy Nativity* (London: Macmillan, 1895), 57ff.

ing, "My soul magnifies the Lord, and my spirit rejoices in God my Savior" (Luke 1:46–47).

God Lifts the Humble

Mary had good reason to magnify the Lord. She had been promised a son—not just any son, but the Son of God, conceived by the Spirit of the Most High God. Her *Magnificat* is a song of gospel joy. Yet in it Mary says nothing specific about her son. This is the reason for her praise, but she does not mention it explicitly. Why not?

The answer is that Mary had the godliness to look beyond her gift and praise the God who gave it. To magnify means to enlarge, and what Mary wanted to enlarge was her vision of God. Her goal was to show his greatness. She wanted to magnify *God*, not her own position as the mother of the Son of God. She knew that she was blessed because of who God was, not because of who she was. Therefore, she wanted God to be seen to be great, not herself. The way to show this was not by thinking only about what God was doing in her life, but by enlarging her vision to see the majesty of God.

In her song Mary praised God for many of his divine attributes. She worshiped his mighty power (Luke 1:49, 51)—the power that brought forth the virgin birth. She honored his pristine holiness (Luke 1:49)—the holiness of his sinless Son. She magnified his mercy for sinners (Luke 1:50). She praised his everlasting faithfulness in keeping his promises (Luke 1:54–55). This was real worship. Mary did not dwell on her own happy circumstances, but rejoiced in the being and character of God.

It is right for us to praise God for what he has done, as Mary did. But sometimes even our worship of God can be somewhat self-centered, as if the really important thing is what God has done *for us*. We need to look beyond this to see God as he is in himself, and to praise him for being God. Then, when we speak about what God has done for us—as we should—it will be more about him and less about us.

Mary did this, and as she magnified God, there were two great themes to her praise. Why did God deserve her worship? Because he lifts the humble and humbles the proud. The first half of Mary's song is about God lifting the humble:

47

My soul magnifies the Lord,
and my spirit rejoices in God my Savior,
for he has looked on the humble estate of his servant.
For behold, from now on all generations will call me blessed;
for he who is mighty has done great things for me,
and holy is his name.
And his mercy is for those who fear him
from generation to generation. (Luke 1:46–50)

The mighty God reaches down in mercy, lifting the humble to greatness. Mary herself was the perfect example. No one was lowlier than she was—a poor young peasant girl from Nazareth. She was nobody from nowhere, and she knew it. She was also a sinner, which is why she praised God as her Savior. This is one of Luke's favorite titles for Jesus. Mary used it because she needed to be saved as much as anyone else. And by his grace, God saved her. He saw her lowly condition. He did great things for her, like putting a child in her virgin womb, and sending his Son to be her Savior. God reached down and saved her. This is why all generations call Mary blessed: she was blessed by the undeserved favor of a merciful God.

The way God worked in Mary's life is the way he always works. Not that anyone else could have borne the Son of God, of course, but God always exalts the humble. He does great things for people who honor him. In every generation he shows mercy to those who fear him, which simply means to worship him with reverence and awe: "To 'fear' God means to cherish reverence and respect for Him—not to be afraid, but to honour Him lovingly by avoiding what is contrary to His will and by striving after what pleases Him."[7] God-fearing people like Mary will be lifted up, no matter how low their situation in life.

An American doctor traveled to mainland China to serve as a medical missionary. As he visited remote villages in mountainous regions, he was sometimes shocked by the appalling living conditions he saw. But he was also reminded of the elevation that comes through knowing Christ:

---

7. Norval Geldenhuys, *The Gospel of Luke*, New International Commentary on the New Testament (Grand Rapids: Eerdmans, 1951), 85.

As I felt disgusted by the dirt and poverty, or felt anger as I saw begging street children with injuries or wounds likely inflicted by their "owners" so that they could get more cash, I also recalled that it was into a poor and backward corner of the Roman Empire that our Savior came. His arrival announcement was given to the marginalized, and He was accused of spending His time with the "wrong people." The greatness of His heart's love is seen in all this—for our nicest dwellings are a dump compared to His heavenly dwelling. But He bypassed all that and visited the neediest.[8]

Perhaps you are young and poor like Mary. Perhaps you are struggling with sickness or some other physical limitation. Perhaps you are in a low condition spiritually or emotionally. If this is your situation, do not complain that you deserve something better. Do not grasp after a higher position. Do not rage against your misfortune. But humble yourself to the providence of God and recognize your lowly position before him as a sinner. The Bible gives this promise: "Humble yourselves before the Lord, and he will exalt you" (James 4:10).

GOD HUMBLES THE PROUD

The same God who lifts the humble also humbles the proud, and in the second half of her song Mary praises God for humbling the nations:

He has shown strength with his arm;
   he has scattered the proud in the thoughts of their hearts;
he has brought down the mighty from their thrones
   and exalted those of humble estate;
he has filled the hungry with good things,
   and the rich he has sent empty away.
He has helped his servant Israel,
   in remembrance of his mercy,
as he spoke to our fathers,
   to Abraham and to his offspring forever. (Luke 1:51–55)

Here the personal becomes national and international. Mary moves beyond what God has done for her to rejoice in what God will do for

8. Quoted from a 2004 newsletter by Dr. Harvey Shephard.

Israel and the world. What is strange about these verses is that they were spoken in the past tense. Why did Mary do this? She was praising God for the gift of her son, but at the time he was still only a child in the womb. No proud armies had been scattered; no thrones had been overturned; no tycoons had been sent away. When would these things happen?

It is possible that Mary was remembering the great acts of God in history. The lines of her song sound like echoes from the Old Testament: God showed the strength of his arm by drowning Pharaoh's army in the sea; he scattered the proud Philistines by striking down Goliath; he brought mighty Nebuchadnezzar down from his throne and sent Belshazzar away from his feast. God did these things to save his people. God humbled the proud to show mercy to Israel, as he promised Abraham in the everlasting covenant (see Gen. 12:2–3).

Yet Mary was also praising God for what he would do in Christ. She was speaking in the past tense, but she was making prophecies about the future. She could get away with this because when God says that he will do something, it is as good as already done. His promises come with the guarantee of fulfillment. Furthermore, with the conception of Christ, the great reversal had already begun. The choice of Mary proved it: God was lifting the humble, and soon he would humble the proud. So her song spanned the past, the present, and the future. It was about what God had done, what God was doing, and what God would do in days to come.

The Son of God had come to establish his rule with justice and his kingdom with might. This meant the overthrow of every proud nation and the humbling of every proud heart. God alone deserves the power and the glory. Therefore, he must subdue everything and everyone that opposes his will. To be specific, he must humble the pride of intellect (Luke 1:51), the pride of position (Luke 1:52), and the pride of wealth (Luke 1:53). "Can you not see," wrote Martyn Lloyd-Jones, "that everything that man boasts in, his intellect, his understanding, his power, his social status, his influence, his righteousness, his morality, his ethics, his code—every one of them is utterly demolished by this Son of God?"[9]

9. Martyn Lloyd-Jones, "Bringing Down the Mighty," reprinted in *Evangelicals Now*, (Dec. 1998), 13.

Mary understood that the coming of Christ would turn the world upside down. He would be the exact opposite of anything anyone ever expected. Here is how Norval Geldenhuys summarized the message of Mary's *Magnificat:*

> The proud, those who exalt themselves and take no account of God, He puts down—beaten by His mighty arm. The powers that be, oppressors who tyrannize the poor and lowly, are deprived of their power and high standing, while those who are truly humble are exalted to great things. The hungry, those who realize their own need and yearn for spiritual food, are blessed. But the rich, those who are self-satisfied and proud, are shamed in the imagination of their hearts.[10]

In Christ, God takes the conventional standards of greatness and significance and stands them on their heads. The person he exalts is the humble servant who does his will. The person he humbles is the powerful leader who refuses to acknowledge his need for God. We see this happen all the way through the Gospel of Luke. The rich man goes to hell, while the poor man is carried home to be with the people of God (Luke 16:19–31). The prayers of the self-righteous Pharisee are denied, but the sinful tax collector goes home justified (Luke 18:9–14). As Jesus said, "Everyone who exalts himself will be humbled, and he who humbles himself will be exalted" (Luke 14:11; 18:14). At the end of the Gospel comes the greatest reversal of all: God the Son—who had once humbled himself to become a man and then to endure the painful, shameful death of the cross—is raised from the dead in triumph. Having humbled himself, he is exalted.

Now Christ is busy turning things upside down in the world. He does not leave things as they are. He does not stand for the status quo; in that sense, he is not a conservative. He is radical, subversive, revolutionary. This is why it is so deadly for the church to follow the culture. Jesus opposes the pride that rules the world, and if we are on the side of injustice, he is opposed to us. The child who put the song into Mary's heart was the world's most dangerous baby!

Here is how Martyn Lloyd-Jones described the reversal that Jesus brings to human events, as Mary celebrated:

10. Geldenhuys, *Luke,* 86.

When the King of Kings and the Lord of Lords came into this world, he came into a stable. If you do not feel a sense of holy laughter within you, I do not see that you have a right to think that you are a Christian. Thank God, this is gospel, this is salvation. God turning upside down, reversing everything we have ever thought, everything we have taken pride in. The mighty? Why, he will pull them down from their seats. He has been doing so. He is still doing so. Let any man arise and say he is going to govern, to be the god of the whole world; you need not be afraid—he will be put down. Every dictator has gone down; they all do. Finally, the devil and all that belong to him will go down to the lake of fire and will be destroyed for ever. The Son of God has come into the world to do that.[11]

This is the way God operates: the humble are shown mercy, while the proud receive justice. The lowly are lifted and the lofty are brought low. This is true for nations. The proud rulers who try to conquer the world always get destroyed in the end. It will happen to our own nation, unless we humble ourselves before God. The kingdoms of this world are temporary and transitory. God will not rest until Christ alone is Lord, and then he will see to it that justice is done, putting all wrongs to right.

God does the same thing with churches. Nothing is more deadly to spiritual health than spiritual pride. Churches that boast about their ministry will be humbled until they learn to give all the glory to God, while churches that humbly go about the Lord's work will see lives changed by the gospel.

What is true for churches and nations is also true for individuals: "God opposes the proud, but gives grace to the humble" (James 4:6). This is what Mary meant when she said that God "has filled the hungry with good things, and the rich he has sent empty away" (Luke 1:53; cf. 6:21, 24). Of course this verse has implications for social justice. God does not leave the poor to look after themselves, but provides for them, and so should we. People who feed the hungry have God's priorities at heart, while those who ignore the poor are exactly the kind of proud people that God likes to humble.

But Mary was also speaking about our spiritual need for God. God only satisfies people who are hungry for him. When we get stuffed on the pleasures of this life, we do not feel our need for God, and then he has nothing more to give us. If we are too proud to admit that we need God the way a

11. Lloyd-Jones, "Bringing Down the Mighty," 13.

beggar needs bread, he will send us away empty. But if we have a heart that hungers after God—if we long for the forgiveness of our sins; if we thirst for the knowledge of God; if we crave eternal life in Christ—then God will satisfy us with his grace.

This was the God that Mary magnified: the God who satisfies. Martin Luther said that her song was about "the great works and deeds of God, for the strengthening of our faith, for the comforting of all those of low degree, and for the terrifying of all the mighty ones of earth. We are to let the hymn serve this threefold purpose; for she sang it not for herself alone but for us all, to sing it after her."[12] Luther was right. The words of Mary's song strengthen our faith in Jesus Christ. They comfort us with the promise that God will lift us when we are low. They also chasten our pride, destroying the proud thoughts of our hearts.

As Mary's words do this sanctifying work, they teach us to sing a *Magnificat* of our own. God has done great things for us. We magnify him for the mighty deeds of our salvation—the death and resurrection of Jesus Christ. And we magnify him for the gracious work of the Holy Spirit, who humbles our pride so that God can lift us up to glory.

12. Martin Luther, *Luther's Works*, 21:306, quoted in Just, *Luke 1:1–9:50*, 79.

5

BENEDICTUS

Luke 1:56—80

*"Blessed be the Lord God of Israel, for he has visited and
redeemed his people and has raised up a horn of salvation for us
in the house of his servant David, as he spoke by the mouth of his
holy prophets from of old."* (Luke 1:68–70)

The opening chapters of Luke are like a duet from an oratorio. One voice begins to sing, followed by another, and then the two voices harmonize. For a while the second voice is silent while the first voice sings alone. Then the first voice leaves off and the second carries the music until finally the song ends with a chorus of angels.

The first melody we hear belongs to John the Baptist. It is the promise of his birth, given to his father Zechariah by an angel, but fully believed only by his mother Elizabeth. Then we hear the song of the Savior: the virgin Mary will give birth to the Son of God. When the two mothers meet, their melodies harmonize into one song. But after three months Elizabeth is ready to give birth, and Mary goes back to Nazareth. It is time again to sing the song of John the Baptist.

ZECHARIAH NAMES THE BABY

As Luke tells the story of John's nativity, he starts with the facts: "Mary remained with her about three months and returned to her home. Now the time came for Elizabeth to give birth, and she bore a son. And her neighbors and relatives heard that the Lord had shown great mercy to her, and they rejoiced with her" (Luke 1:56–58).

Imagine the scene. After long months of pregnancy and hard hours of labor, old Elizabeth had her baby and the whole town came to celebrate. In a small village any birth is a public event, but especially under these circumstances. The people praised God for his mercy to Elizabeth in giving her a son. The angel's promise had come true: "You will have joy and gladness, and many will rejoice at his birth" (Luke 1:14).

On the eighth day it was time for John to be circumcised. According to the law (Gen. 17:12–13), he needed to be given the sign of the covenant that God made with Abraham. Zechariah and Elizabeth believed the promise of salvation, and by faith they presented their son to God. This was the baby's big day. Like baptism, circumcision was the sacrament that marked a person's entrance into the covenant community. Everyone in the village showed up at the family's house to welcome their child into fellowship with the people of God.

It was at this time that a child was formally given his name. Naturally people expected Elizabeth to name her son Zechariah. According to custom, a firstborn son was always named after his father. But Elizabeth surprised everyone by calling him John: "On the eighth day they came to circumcise the child. And they would have called him Zechariah after his father, but his mother answered, 'No; he shall be called John'" (Luke 1:59–60). Elizabeth was emphatic. The baby's name was John, not Zechariah. Whether by direct revelation or by written communication with her husband, Elizabeth knew that this was the name the angel had given to Zechariah.

Immediately her family and friends started to protest: "And they said to her, 'None of your relatives is called by this name'" (Luke 1:61). This happens sometimes: parents give their child an unusual name, and some people can't resist making snide remarks or offering alternative suggestions. In this case, the name John was common enough, but people really thought that Elizabeth should call him Junior. This was the only way to carry on Zechariah's good name. Calling the baby John didn't make any sense. It wasn't even a family name!

In their consternation, the people appealed to the child's father. Elizabeth wasn't playing by the rules, but maybe Zechariah would listen to reason. To this point the old priest had been watching in silence. Because he had balked at God's promise, his encounter with the angel had left him unable to speak, and apparently also unable to hear (note that people make signs for Zechariah in verse 62, rather than speaking to him). Zechariah had been deaf and dumb for nearly a year, and his disabilities kept him out of the conversation, as disabilities often do. Presumably he did not even know what Elizabeth had called their son. But now everyone wanted to hear what he had to say, so they played charades until he could figure out what they were asking: "And they made signs to his father, inquiring what he wanted him to be called. And he asked for a writing tablet and wrote, 'His name is John.' And they all wondered" (Luke 1:62–63). Zechariah was as stubborn about the child's name as Elizabeth was. Both parents were willing to go against the wishes of their family and friends to do the will of God. According to the Greek New Testament, the first word Zechariah scribbled down was "John." Rather than writing something tentative like "We're thinking about calling the baby John," Zechariah wrote "*John* is his name."

This was not a name that Zechariah had chosen, but a name that was given by God to express the child's true identity. As we listen to the names in this story, we begin to sense that God is up to something big. Zechariah means that God remembers. Elizabeth means that God is faithful. John means that God is merciful. Then there is the sweetest name of all: Jesus, which means "God saves." Luke is telling the story of salvation, and these people are part of the story. The faithful God who shows mercy to sinners has remembered his promise to save.

At the very moment Zechariah wrote down John's name he finally found his voice: "And immediately his mouth was opened and his tongue loosed, and he spoke, blessing God. And fear came on all their neighbors. And all these things were talked about through all the hill country of Judea, and all who heard them laid them up in their hearts, saying, 'What then will this child be?' For the hand of the Lord was with him" (Luke 1:64–66). God's blessing on the boy is confirmed at the end of the chapter: "And the child grew and became strong in spirit, and he was in the wilderness until the day of his public appearance to Israel" (Luke 1:80).

The timing of Zechariah's speech was significant. The angel had said to him, "Behold, you will be silent and unable to speak until the day that these things take place, because you did not believe my words, which will be fulfilled in their time" (Luke 1:20). Given this prophecy, we might have expected the man to get his voice back the day the baby was born. Yet strangely Zechariah was speechless for another week. He did not find his voice until he named his son John. Only then did the angel's promise fully come true. Or to put it another way, God waited until Zechariah acted on his faith. By calling him John, the priest showed that he truly believed what the angel had said. For nine months he had been alone with his thoughts, pondering the angel's message. He had come to believe that his son would prepare the way for the Savior. By naming the boy John—in obedience to God—Zechariah was proving his faith in God's promise.

The words on the tablet showed that God had done a gracious work in Zechariah's life, bringing the old man to sure and certain faith. At first Zechariah doubted, but God disciplined him in a way that taught him to trust. This is something God often does, and it is always a mercy when he does it. He uses the hard experience of suffering to teach us to trust in him.

God works in our lives to bring us to the point where we trust his promise of salvation. Some people believe right away, like Mary and Elizabeth. As soon as they hear God's word, they know that it is true. They believe that Jesus died on the cross to save them from the hell that sin deserves. Believing right away is always better, because as soon as we believe, we receive the joy of knowing Christ. But some people are more skeptical, like Zechariah. They want to believe, but they're still not quite sure. They haven't rejected Jesus Christ, but they haven't accepted him either. How do cynics and skeptics ever come to trust in Christ for their salvation? And what is God doing to bring you to the full assurance of faith?

If necessary, God can deal with us the way he dealt with Zechariah, striking us deaf and dumb. This is not the way he usually works, however. Instead, he brings people to faith in a simpler way: by the reading and preaching of the gospel. God uses our personal circumstances to show us our need of a Savior. But in the end it is the gospel itself that persuades us to believe. Paul Ricoeur has rightly observed that "what progressively happens in the Gospel is the *recognition* of Jesus as being the Christ. We can say in this regard that the Gospel is not a simple account of the life, teaching, work, death, and resurrection of Jesus, but the communicating of an act of confession, a communication by means of which the reader in turn is rendered capable of performing the same recognition that occurs inside the text."[1] In other words, as we read the Gospel of Luke we are drawn to reach the same conclusion that Luke reached when he wrote it: Jesus is the Christ. Whether we believe this sooner like Elizabeth or later like Zechariah, the important thing is to make sure that we believe it in the end, because everyone who trusts in Jesus Christ will be saved.

ZECHARIAH BREAKS HIS SILENCE

Zechariah was not able to speak for at least nine months, which is a long time to remain silent. So perhaps it is not surprising that when he finally broke his silence, he had something important to say. The first words out of his mouth were "Praise the Lord!" This showed the true condition of Zechariah's heart. His suffering had done him spiritual good. Before he did anything else, he wanted to give praise to God.

What came out next was an exuberant eruption of praise. All of the joy that had been pent up inside the priest during the long months of Elizabeth's pregnancy now came pouring out in a cascade of exultation. Luke tells us that as soon as he had named his son, Zechariah's "mouth was opened and his tongue loosed, and he spoke, blessing God" (Luke 1:64). Once he believed, he had to worship, because whenever we know what God has done for our salvation, we are compelled to praise him for it. Genuine faith always expresses itself in jubilant praise, and where there is no real worship, we may wonder if there is any true faith at all.

After telling how people responded to what Zechariah said (Luke 1:65–66), Luke goes back and provides the lyrics to his song (Luke 1:67–79). Zechariah's hymn of thanksgiving is usually called the *Benedictus*, meaning "blessed," because this is the song's first word in Latin. The priest blessed God for blessing him. Perhaps this priestly benediction was spontaneous,

---

1. Paul Ricoeur, quoted in Michael S. Horton, *Covenant and Eschatology: The Divine Drama* (Louisville: Westminster John Knox, 2002), 205.

or perhaps it was composed during Zechariah's long months of silence. Either way, it was the song of his heart. It is also the word of God, for the Bible says, "Zechariah was filled with the Holy Spirit and prophesied" (Luke 1:67).

The *Benedictus* has many similarities to Mary's *Magnificat*. Both Mary and Zechariah were among the principal soloists who sang the first oratorio praising God for the Messiah's birth. Both of them spoke in the past tense, although both of them were also looking to the future. As one scholar has explained it, "The retrospect of prophecy and the prospect of fulfillment are commingled in the speaker's mind."[2] The words for both songs came from the Old Testament. Like the *Magnificat*, the *Benedictus* is full of biblical references, especially from the prophets. Zechariah wove the tapestry of his song from the threads of ancient prophecy.

Zechariah's benediction comes in two parts: a blessing for God (Luke 1:68–75) and a blessing for his son (Luke 1:76–79). First Zechariah blesses God for coming to save his people:

> Blessed be the Lord God of Israel,
>   for he has visited and redeemed his people
> and has raised up a horn of salvation for us
>   in the house of his servant David,
> as he spoke by the mouth of his holy prophets from of old,
> that we should be saved from our enemies
>   and from the hand of all who hate us;
> to show the mercy promised to our fathers
>   and to remember his holy covenant,
> the oath that he swore to our father Abraham, to grant us
>   that we, being delivered from the hand of our enemies,
> might serve him without fear,
>   in holiness and righteousness before him all our days. (Luke 1:68–75)

This blessing tells us all about salvation. Apparently Zechariah understood the staggering implications of what the angel had promised, or else, under the inspiration of the Holy Spirit, he spoke better than he knew. His son would be the forerunner to prepare the way for the coming of Christ. And

---

2. Thomas Dehany Bernard, *The Songs of the Holy Nativity* (1895), quoted in Leland Ryken, ed., *The New Testament in Literary Criticism*, A Library of Literary Criticism (New York: Ungar, 1984), 207.

if his son was the forerunner, then salvation was on its way. At stake in the birth of these two babies was nothing less than the salvation of the world. God had raised what Zechariah called "a horn of salvation." This phrase comes from the Old Testament (e.g., Ps. 148:14), where horns are often used as the symbol of an animal's power and strength. Horns are an animal's "business end," so to speak, and in a similar way, the Messiah is the business end of God's saving plan. With the coming of Christ, he was tossing the mighty horn of his salvation.

What is salvation? According to Zechariah, it is something that comes from God, and not from us. The priest blessed God for visiting his people (Luke 1:68). This was something he had experienced personally when the angel appeared to him at the temple. But this visitation was not for him alone. By sending the angel, by giving Elizabeth a baby, and especially by putting his Son in the virgin's womb, God was visiting his people. He was entering our situation from the outside, because without his intervention, we could never be saved. Salvation is not a human invention, but a divine visitation. It is not something we achieve by going to God, but something God has done by coming to us in Christ. No one is ever saved except by the grace of God.

God's gracious salvation comes in fulfillment of his promise. Zechariah mentions King David and the ancient prophecies about him (Luke 1:69–70). This makes it clear that the priest was not speaking about his own son, who came from Levi, but about Jesus, who came from the house and line of David. After spending three months with Mary, Zechariah knew about her child. He also knew that God had promised to lift up a horn of salvation for David (Ps. 132:17), giving him a son to rule on this eternal throne (2 Sam. 7:12–13). Then Zechariah went back even farther, to the holy covenant God made with Abraham (Luke 1:72–73), that the nations would be saved through his son (Gen. 17:4–7). All the prophecies were coming true: Jesus was the Savior God had always promised to send.

This salvation—the salvation that comes from God, in fulfillment of his promise—means deliverance. In verse 68 Zechariah calls it redemption, which is a release from bondage through the payment of a price. In verse 71 he describes it as being saved "from our enemies and from the hand of all who hate us." God's people have always had enemies. Since people hate God, it is only natural for them to hate his followers. In the

Old Testament Israel's enemies included the Egyptians, the Canaanites, the Assyrians, and the Babylonians. For Zechariah the great enemy was the Roman Empire. People were longing for a new exodus, in which God would rescue them from Rome. So when Zechariah spoke of deliverance, he may partly have been thinking in political terms. But as we shall see, he was also looking for a more lasting liberation—one that would bring freedom from sin.

The last thing Zechariah did in the first part of his song was to explain God's purpose. God was raising up a horn of salvation so that "we, being delivered from the hand of our enemies, might serve him without fear, in holiness and righteousness before him all our days" (Luke 1:74–75). Again, Zechariah may have been thinking partly in political terms. In order to serve God without fear, his people needed freedom from the tyranny of Rome. Few things are more precious than the freedom of religion. However, as Norval Geldenhuys has pointed out, "Although there may be a reference here to political liberation as well, something far more glorious is meant: the whole-hearted service of the Lord in complete freedom from all bonds of sin, guilt, punishment, curse, Satan and destruction."[3] To serve God is to glorify him in our worship and in everything else we do, leading holy lives. And this is the goal of our salvation. God wants to do something more with us than simply get us to heaven. His goal is for us to live for his glory, but to do this we first have to be liberated from the selfishness of our sin. God's salvation is for our sanctification, and this always leads to service.

This was Zechariah's song—a song of salvation. Now everything he promised has been fulfilled for us in Jesus Christ. Jesus is the salvation that comes from God. God had to intervene. Unless he sent his Son to be our Savior, we never could have been saved. We needed someone to live a perfect life and die an atoning death in our place. This was the promised salvation, and it was a mighty deliverance, as salvation always is. The crucifixion and resurrection of Jesus Christ have delivered us from sin, death, and Satan. We are no longer enslaved by our selfishness, but are free to give our lives away in service to others. This is why God has saved us: he has given us his grace so that we can live for his glory.

3. Norval Geldenhuys, *The Gospel of Luke*, New International Commentary on the New Testament (Grand Rapids: Eerdmans, 1951), 94.

Zechariah Blesses His Son

There were two parts to Zechariah's blessing. First, he blessed God for the visitation of his salvation (Luke 1:68–75). Then he blessed his newborn son (Luke 1:76–79). The order is significant. In spite of his fatherly pride, Zechariah recognized the subordinate position of his son. John was the last and greatest prophet of the old covenant, but what made him great was his relationship to Jesus. He was first in the birth order, but second in significance. Zechariah understood this, so his benediction was mainly for Jesus. Nevertheless, John had an important part to play in the coming of salvation, so he too received a blessing.

The child had already been circumcised, which was his birthright. But as the firstborn son, John also had a right to his father's blessing. We can imagine the emotion in the old man's voice as he turned to his only son and said, with fatherly affection:

> And you, child, will be called the prophet of the Most High;
>> for you will go before the Lord to prepare his ways,
> to give knowledge of salvation to his people,
>> in the forgiveness of their sins,
> because of the tender mercy of our God,
>> whereby the sunrise shall visit us from on high
> to give light to those who sit in darkness and in the shadow of death,
>> to guide our feet into the way of peace. (Luke 1:76–79)

The blessing Zechariah gave his son was in keeping with the promises he received from God. John was the forerunner—the prophet who went ahead to prepare the way. He would do this preparatory work by preaching the message of salvation. But what does it mean to be saved? The salvation Zechariah promised was not deliverance from earthly enemies. It was not a new form of religious freedom. Rather, John was called "to give knowledge of salvation to his people in the forgiveness of their sins" (Luke 1:77). Fundamentally, salvation is the forgiveness of sins.

By and large, the people of John's day were looking for the wrong kind of salvation. They were thinking primarily in political terms. They wanted a better economy, with more personal freedom. But that was not the kind of salvation God had in mind. So before the Savior even came, someone else had to get people ready. According to Geldenhuys, "it was necessary that John, the forerunner of Christ, should summon the people to a realization of guilt and to a confession of sins, and should make as many of them as possible see that the real redemption needed by them was deliverance from the power of their spiritual enemies—sin and the forces of darkness, so that they might escape from the wrath of God."[4]

Like the people of Israel, we are usually wrong about what we really need. We tend to look first at our outward circumstances. We want God to save us from things like a bad work situation, a financial setback, or a troubled marriage. Of course God is able to handle these problems, and it is right for us to pray for his help. But the first thing he has to deal with is our sin. Eventually salvation changes society, but that is not where it starts. There can be no social transformation without spiritual regeneration. Salvation begins when the Holy Spirit changes a sinner's heart. Michael Wilcock writes: "We must believe, as clear-thinking Christians in every age have believed, that it is the will and plan of God for all wrong relationships, political as well as spiritual, eventually to be put right. We include therefore in our preaching of salvation the need for the righting of wrong social structures and physical conditions. But we keep at its centre the need for the cleansing of sinful human hearts. That is the primary concern of the people of God."[5]

What we need more than anything else is to have a right relationship with God, and this can only come through the forgiveness of our sins. To be specific (although we will not see this until we get to the end of Luke's Gospel), a right relationship with God can only come through the cross where Jesus died for sinners. As Luke was later to write, "Everyone who believes in him receives forgiveness of sins through his name" (Acts 10:43). When we trust in Christ, God forgives our sins—all of them, no matter what we have done. He does this because of his mercy, which the *Benedictus* describes as "the tender mercy of our God" (Luke 1:78; cf. 1:58; 1:72). Mercy is "God's loyal, faithful, gracious love as he acts for his people."[6] Zechariah took the biblical term for mercy (*eleos*) and intensified it by connecting it to a word

---

4. Geldenhuys, *Luke*, 95.

5. Michael Wilcock, *The Message of Luke*, The Bible Speaks Today (Downers Grove, IL: InterVarsity, 1979), 38.

6. Darrell L. Bock, *Luke 1:1–9:50*, Baker Exegetical Commentary on the New Testament 3a (Grand Rapids: Baker, 1994), 183.

for deep feeling (*splanchna*). Forgiveness is the supreme expression of God's compassionate mercy for sinners.

Nothing is more wonderful for a sinner than to receive mercy. As Zechariah thought about how wonderful it was, he made a comparison. He imagined a group of pilgrims on a long journey. As they traveled through the wilderness, they were overtaken by darkness. Far from the safety of home, they were exposed to the terrors of night: vicious animals and violent enemies. They sat "in darkness and in the shadow of death" (Luke 1:79). This was Israel's situation during the dark days before Christ was born. It is the situation we are all in until we are saved. We are sitting in the darkness of our sin, waiting for death to devour us.

All that long night the pilgrims wondered if they would ever make it to the morning. They prayed for deliverance, waiting for the dawn. Then they saw it on the horizon: the first glimmer of the morning light. It was the sunrise of their salvation. In earlier days people would have called it the "dayspring"—the dayspring of deliverance. Zechariah said, "the sunrise shall visit us from on high to give light to those who sit in darkness and in the shadow of death, to guide our feet into the way of peace" (Luke 1:78–79; cf. Isa. 9:2; 60:3; Mal. 4:2). With the coming of the light, the pilgrims were able to find their way.

After darkness, light—this is what it means to be saved. Salvation is like the first glimmer of dawn after the blackest night. Until we come to faith in Jesus Christ, we are still living in the darkness of unforgiven sin. But when we trust him, as Zechariah did, his light comes into our lives and we are able to see our way. Believe in Jesus! The dark night of your sin will be over, and the dayspring of his light will rise in your heart.

6

AWAY IN A MANGER

Luke 2:1—7

*And while they were there, the time came for her to give birth.
And she gave birth to her firstborn son and wrapped him in
swaddling cloths and laid him in a manger, because there was no
place for them in the inn.* (Luke 2:6–7)

Death and taxes. Nothing demonstrates the worldly power of nations more clearly than their ability to take people's money and send them off to war. And when it comes to taxation and militarization, few nations have ever wielded comparatively more power than the Romans. The Roman army ruled the Mediterranean world, and this enabled Roman officials to collect revenue from all parts of their empire. To this day, we call paying our taxes "rendering unto Caesar" (see Luke 20:25).

The imperial power of Rome was consolidated by Octavian, who was famous for defeating Antony and Cleopatra at Actium, and who was the first Caesar to receive the august title of emperor. Octavian was so powerful that he achieved godlike status in parts of the Roman Empire.

Indeed, an inscription at Halicarnassus hails him as the "savior of the whole world."[1]

This Octavian is the Caesar we meet at the beginning of Luke's Gospel. He was then at the height of his powers, and Luke describes him doing what the Romans did best: "In those days a decree went out from Caesar Augustus that all the world should be registered. This was the first registration when Quirinius was governor of Syria. And all went to be registered, each to his own town" (Luke 2:1–3). All it took was a word from the emperor, and people thousands of miles away were set in motion. Every man in every province had to be registered—almost certainly for the purpose of levying taxes. According to Tacitus, Octavian kept the grand totals by hand, and according to Justin, writing in the second century, the census of Quirinius could still be viewed in Rome.[2] No taxation without registration—this was a basic principle of Roman government.

ONCE, IN ROYAL DAVID'S CITY

In chapter 2 Luke shows the far reach of Caesar's power, and also its undoing. As Kent Hughes describes it, Octavian's "relentless arm stretched out to squeeze its tribute even in a tiny village at the far end of the Mediterranean. Thus it came about that a village carpenter and his expectant teenage bride were forced to travel to his hometown to be registered for taxation."[3]

Although Caesar would never know it, he had unleashed a chain of events that would turn the whole world upside down, for among the millions who had to register was a man named Joseph, with his fiancée Mary. This one little family, seemingly swept up in the tide of earthly power, gave birth to a son who would rule the world. Mary's song was starting to come true: "He has shown strength with his arm; he has scattered the proud in the thoughts of their hearts; he has brought down the mighty from their

1. Raymond E. Brown, *The Birth of the Messiah: A Commentary on the Infancy Narratives in the Gospels of Matthew and Luke*, rev. ed., Anchor Bible Reference Library (New York: Doubleday, 1993), 415.

2. Leon Morris, *The Gospel According to St. Luke: An Introduction and Commentary*, Tyndale New Testament Commentaries (Grand Rapids: Eerdmans, 1974), 82–83.

3. R. Kent Hughes, *Luke: That You May Know the Truth*, 2 vols., Preaching the Word (Wheaton, IL: Crossway, 1998), 1:82.

thrones and exalted those of humble estate" (Luke 1:51–52). God was taking Caesar's pawns and moving them to checkmate, so that the real Savior would stand alone as the King of kings.

The Roman registration required every man in Israel to return to his ancestral home: "And Joseph also went up from Galilee, from the town of Nazareth, to Judea, to the city of David, which is called Bethlehem, because he was of the house and lineage of David, to be registered with Mary, his betrothed, who was with child" (Luke 2:4–5). Here David receives double mention. Luke has already told us that Mary's child would be David's son. The angel said that God would "give to him the throne of his father David" (Luke 1:32). Zechariah said that God would raise up a savior in "the house of his servant David" (Luke 1:69). Now Luke tells us that Joseph, the earthly father of Jesus, came from the royal line of David.

The grand purpose of these statements is to establish the child's credentials. In order to fulfill the promise of salvation, Jesus had to be a direct descendant of King David (cf. Rom. 1:3; 2 Tim. 2:8). Joseph's lineage also explains why he took his family to Bethlehem. Bethlehem was "the city of David"—the hometown of the ancient king—and thus the place where Joseph was required to register. This was another part of the old promise: the Savior had to be born in Bethlehem. In the words of the prophet Micah, "But you, O Bethlehem Ephrathah, who are too little to be among the clans of Judah, from you shall come forth for me one who is to be ruler in Israel, whose origin is from of old, from ancient days" (Mic. 5:2). To qualify as the Savior, Jesus had to be born in Bethlehem.

What is so ironic is that God used Caesar to get him there! Proud Octavian became the unwitting servant of the divine plan. David Gooding writes: "For Augustus the taking of censuses was one of the ways he employed to get control over the various parts of his empire. But—and here is the irony of the thing—in the process, as he thought, of tightening his grip on his huge empire, he so organized things that Jesus, Son of Mary, Son of David, Son of God, destined to sit on the throne of Israel and of the world, was born in the city of David, his royal ancestor."[4] What at first appeared to be a great show of Caesar's power actually proved the supremacy of God's sovereignty. Even Caesar's decree was part of the divine plan. God rules all things for his own glory. This is true not

4. David Gooding, *According to Luke: A New Exposition of the Third Gospel* (Grand Rapids: Eerdmans, 1987), 52.

only for the great events of salvation history, but also for the ordinary events of daily life. God is working out his will, and he will see that he gets the glory in the end, even in spite of the things that we do.

Luke tells us where Jesus was born so that we can be sure of his credentials as the Savior. Yet some scholars deny that this part of the Gospel is historically reliable. L. T. Johnson says that Luke "has the facts wrong,"[5] and Raymond Brown claims that his "information is dubious on almost every score."[6]

One objection is that apart from the Bible, there is no record of a universal registration that spanned the entire Roman world. In response, it should always be remembered that the Bible is a record of historical events, and needs to be respected as such. Furthermore, when Luke speaks of the emperor's decree, he may be referring to a general policy rather than to a specific census, and it was indeed Caesar's law to count and tax his subjects. Another objection is that it would have been impractical to require everyone to return to his hometown. Yet we should not underestimate a tyrant's willingness to inconvenience people. Furthermore, a universal tax census would have been feasible in an age when most people spent their whole lives close to the place where they were born, and it would have been all the more necessary in Israel, where people's identity was so closely tied to their heredity.

A more serious objection is that Quirinius did not take a census until A.D. 6, which does not fit the chronology of Jesus' life. Luke was well aware of that census, and in fact mentions it in Acts 5:37. But he was also aware of another census—one taken perhaps a decade earlier. Undoubtedly this is why he specifies that Jesus was born during "the *first* registration when Quirinius was governor of Syria" (Luke 2:2). Some scholars reject this solution because they say that Quirinius did not even become governor until A.D. 6, so there was no time for an earlier census. Yet there is also evidence that he served an earlier term in office.[7] In any case, we may be sure that Luke knew more about all this than modern scholars do. There is no reason to deny or even to doubt that he has the facts straight.

5. L. T. Johnson, *The Gospel of Luke*, Sacra Pagina (Collegeville, MD: Liturgical, 1991), 49.

6. Brown, *Birth*, 413.

7. Norval Geldenhuys, *The Gospel of Luke*, New International Commentary on the New Testament (Grand Rapids: Eerdmans, 1951), 100.

No Vacancy

As Luke tells the true story of the nativity, he shows the contrast between the worldly power of Caesar and the apparent weakness of the baby Jesus. But there is another contrast we ought to notice—the one between the welcome Jesus deserved and the one he was actually given. Although he was the son of David and the true king of Israel, Jesus hardly received a royal welcome.

To understand what an indignity this was, we simply need to remember who Jesus was (and is!). Luke describes him as Mary's firstborn son (Luke 2:7), but he was more than that! By the power of the Holy Spirit, the child in the virgin's womb was the very Son of God. He was "the firstborn of all creation" (Col. 1:15), with a unique status as God the one and only Son. He was the Alpha and the Omega, the beginning and the end. He was the Creator of the universe, the Maker of heaven and earth. He was the King of kings and Lord of lords, the Supreme Ruler of all that lives. He was the Second Person of the Trinity, the only begotten Son, the radiance of the Father's glory. By his divine nature, he shared in the full perfection of God's triune being. This baby—born in Bethlehem—was the all-knowing, all-seeing, all-powerful, and all-glorious Son of God.

What kind of welcome did he deserve? Jesus deserved to have every person from every nation come and worship him. He deserved to have every creature in the entire universe—from the fiercest lion to the tiniest insect—come to his cradle and give him praise. He deserved to have the creation itself offer him worship, with the rocks crying glory and the galaxies dancing for joy. He is God the Son, and anything less than absolute acknowledgment of his royal person is an insult to his divine dignity.

But what kind of welcome did he receive? What accommodation was he given? Luke tells us, "And while they were there, the time came for her to give birth. And she gave birth to her firstborn son and wrapped him in swaddling cloths and laid him in a manger, because there was no place for them in the inn" (Luke 2:6–7). Here is another irony of the incarnation: when the Son of God came to earth—the Maker of the universe in all its vast immensity—he couldn't even get a room!

Most people have some notion where Jesus was born, but some of our ideas are incorrect. The Bible says that there was no room for him at the inn, but what does this mean? Some scholars think that the biblical term (*katalyma*) refers to a private dwelling, possibly one owned by Joseph's relatives. More likely it refers to a guesthouse where groups of travelers slept in a common room.[8] Such lodgings were fairly primitive in those days, so the Bethlehem inn was hardly a Motel 6, let alone a five-star hotel. In all likelihood it was squalid and dirty, especially by contemporary standards.

On this particular night, the inn was so crowded that there was no room left for Joseph, Mary, and Jesus. Without blaming the innkeeper or anyone else who was there that night, the fact is that there were no vacancies. So Mary and Joseph took the next best accommodation they could find, which was out with the animals. Perhaps they were stabled in another room, or another building, or even outside in the yard. One early Christian tradition, dating back at least to the second century, maintains that Jesus was born in a cave. According to Justin Martyr: "Since Joseph had nowhere to lodge in that village, he lodged in a certain cave near the village; and while they were there, Mary brought forth the Messiah and laid him in a manger."[9] This is not unlikely. In those days people often stabled their animals in caves like the ones in and around Bethlehem. But in any case, Mary and Joseph were sleeping with animals. We know this because the Bible mentions the manger, which was a feeding trough for livestock, probably not made of wood, but hollowed out of the ground.

This is where the Son of God was born. It was uncomfortable enough to sleep there, but imagine trying to give birth in such a place, and for the first time. This is part of what it meant for Mary to follow through on her promise: "Behold, I am the servant of the Lord; let it be to me according to your word" (Luke 1:38). It meant traveling nearly a hundred miles, either on foot or by donkey, during the later stages of pregnancy. It meant the anxiety of having labor pains in a strange city. It meant suffering her child's messy entrance into the world. It meant wiping him clean, tearing clothes to bundle him, and then praying that he would live. Kent Hughes vividly imagines the "sweat and pain and blood and cries as Mary reached up to the heavens for help. The earth was cold and hard. The smell of birth mixed with the stench of manure and acrid straw made a contemptible bouquet. Trembling carpenter's hands, clumsy with fear, grasped God's

8. Brown, *Birth*, 400.
9. Justin Martyr, *Dialogue with Trypho* (78.4), quoted in Morris, *Luke*, 84.

Son slippery with blood—the baby's limbs waving helplessly as if falling through space—his face grimacing as he gasped in the cold and his cry pierced the night."[10]

When people sing of the Savior's birth, they call it a "silent night." But as Andrew Peterson has written in his song "Labor of Love,"

> It was not a silent night
> There was blood on the ground
> You could hear a woman cry
> In the alleyways that night
> On the streets of David's town
>
> And the stable was not clean
> And the cobblestones were cold
> And little Mary full of grace
> With the tears upon her face
> Had no mother's hand to hold

In short, everything we know about the birth of Jesus points to obscurity, indignity, pain, and rejection. One of the great mysteries of our universe is that when God the Son became a man he spent his first night in a barn.

LET EVERY HEART PREPARE HIM ROOM

Why was Jesus born like this? What does the crude and unwelcome poverty of his birth tell us about the way of salvation?

First, the birth of Christ shows us *the depravity of our sin*. When God the Son was born in Bethlehem, he was unrecognized and unwelcome. Some Israelites were watching and waiting for the Messiah, as we shall see later in this chapter. But most were so preoccupied with their own concerns that they were unaware of what God was doing in the world. When the rightful King was born, they did not even know that he was the King! His birth went virtually unacknowledged. As God said through Isaiah the prophet, "The ox knows its owner, and the donkey its master's crib, but Israel does not know, my people do not understand" (Isa. 1:3). The welcome that Jesus

---

10. Hughes, *Luke*, 1:83.

failed to receive is the first hint of something that the Gospel of John said about his ministry as a whole: "He came to his own, and his own people did not receive him" (John 1:11).

Jesus was rejected all through his ministry, right up to the very end. He was driven out of his hometown. His family thought he was so crazy that they practically disowned him. Many people flocked to him when they heard that he could perform miracles, but when he started talking about suffering, most of them drifted away. The religious leaders scoffed at him, rejecting his claims and growing to hate him, until finally they tried to do away with him altogether. It wasn't just Bethlehem—there was *never* enough room for Jesus. As one commentator put it, "When Christ first came among us we pushed him into an outhouse; and we have done our best to keep him there ever since."[11]

This is an outrage! The way Jesus gets shoved aside ought to make us indignant. But honestly, what kind of welcome would you have given him? What kind of welcome are you giving him right now? Have you made room for Jesus in your heart, coming to him by faith? Are you keeping a place open for him in your morning routine? Is there room for him in your daily activities at work or at school? Are you making space for him in your home? Jesus does not deserve to be shoved aside. He wants to fill your life with his grace.

Sadly, many people today make the same mistake that people made when Caesar issued his famous decree: they do not make room for Jesus. As Norval Geldenhuys has observed, "What the inhabitants of Bethlehem did in their ignorance is done by many today in willful indifference— they refuse to make room for the Son of God. They give no place to Him in their feelings, their affections, their thoughts, their views of life, their wishes, their decisions, their actions, or their daily conduct."[12] Thus the story of the nativity shows us our sin. It shows how unwelcome Jesus is to us until God, by his grace, reveals him to us as our Savior and our God.

And of course this is why Jesus came. It was to save us from our sins. But in order to do this he first had to become one of us, and this is the second thing that his birth reveals: *the humanity of our Savior.*

---

11. J. R. H. Moorman, *The Path to Glory: Studies in the Gospel According to St. Luke* (London: SPCK, 1960), 19.

12. Geldenhuys, *Luke*, 102.

Does anything have more of the feel and smell of our humanity than childbirth? Not to dwell on the details, but anyone who has ever witnessed the birth of a child knows what an earthy experience it is. The birth of Jesus was earthier than most, and by giving us the details of his delivery, Luke shows that he entered the world just like any other person. When Mary bundled her baby close, she was caring for the body of a real human being, even though he was also the divine Son of God. Jesus didn't just *seem* to be a human being; he *was* a human being! He had red blood running through his veins and human DNA in all his cells. Martin Luther said that Jesus "did not flutter about like a spirit, but He dwelt among men. He had eyes, ears, mouth, nose, chest, stomach, hands, and feet, just as you and I do. He took the breast. His mother nursed Him as any other child is nursed."[13]

Do you believe this? Do you believe that the Second Person of the Trinity was once a babe in his mother's arms? This is what we mean by the incarnation. The God of the universe entered into our situation, taking on all the limitations of our physical existence. He did not save us from a distance, but came as close to us as he possibly could, sympathizing with us in our sufferings.

God did this because it was necessary for our salvation. It was only by becoming a man that the Son of God could offer his body as the sacrifice for our sins, or be raised bodily from the grave. Jesus had to become one of us to save us. Of course, we are saved by his death, not his birth; but without his birth, he could never die or live again. There could be no crucifixion and no resurrection without the incarnation. "Therefore," wrote Martin Luther, "whenever you are concerned to think and act about your salvation, . . . you must run directly to the manger and the mother's womb, embrace this Infant and Virgin's Child in your arms, and look at Him— born, being nursed, growing up, going about in human society, teaching, dying, rising again, ascending above all the heavens, and having authority over all things."[14] Salvation comes through faith in God incarnate—the Son of God who lived, and died, and lives again in true humanity.

13. Martin Luther, "Sermons on the Gospel of John," *Luther's Works*, trans. Martin Berman (St. Louis: Concordia, 1957), 22:113.
14. Martin Luther, "Lectures on Galatians" (1535), *Luther's Works*, trans. Jaroslav Pelikan (St. Louis: Concordia, 1963), 26:30.

THE HUMILIATION OF THE MANGER

Finally, the birth of Christ shows us *his humility in our salvation*. Understand that God is infinitely superior to us. He is not simply a bigger and better version of a human being, but something altogether different. He is God, and we are not. His attributes are infinitely superior to ours. He is the Creator; we are only his creatures. For God to take on our nature, therefore, was an act of infinite humility. Theologians say that for him to be born at all was a humiliation.

The circumstances of Christ's birth confirm this. If God the Son had received the universal welcome that he truly deserved, we might be tempted to think that it was some kind of honor for him to come to earth and become a man. It was not an honor—it was abject humility; it was infinite condescension. Although in becoming a man the Son did not cease to be God, he did lay aside the privileges and prerogatives of his deity. He abandoned the glories of heaven to accept the limitations of earth.

This is starkly demonstrated by the humble circumstances of his birth. When we see the Son of God lying in a manger, we know that this can only be a humiliation. In the words of J. C. Ryle, "We see here the grace and condescension of Christ. Had He come to save mankind with royal majesty, surrounded by His Father's angels, it would have been an act of undeserved mercy. Had He chosen to dwell in a palace, with power and great authority, we should have had reason enough to wonder. But to become poor as the very poorest of mankind, and lowly as the very lowliest—this is a love that passeth knowledge. It is unspeakable and unsearchable." Then Ryle goes on to say, "Never let us forget that through this humiliation Jesus has purchased for us a title to glory."[15]

There was a reason that Christ humbled himself. He knew that in the end he could save us only by suffering and dying for our sins, and he wanted to show this from the very beginning. The humility of his birth was the whole pattern of his life. Jesus humbled himself to the very death, and there are rumors of this already in his birth. The sufferings that commenced with his incarnation culminated with his crucifixion. The same body that was wrapped in swaddling cloths was also wrapped in a burial shroud. The

---

15. J. C. Ryle, *Expository Thoughts on the Gospels, Luke* (1858; reprint Cambridge: James Clarke, 1976), 1:52.

manger points us to the cross and to the grave. And this is how we are saved: by the humility of our Savior. We are saved by believing for sure that Jesus humbled himself in becoming a man and dying on the cross for our sins.

This is also how we are called to live: according to the pattern of his humble birth and saving death. The humility of Christ ought to humble us. We are inclined to insist on our own way—to think that we are more important than we really are. We get angry when people refuse to give us the credit we think we deserve or show us the honor we think we ought to be given. We want to be exalted, not humiliated. But there is divinity in humility. The same Jesus who humbled himself for our salvation also wants us to humble ourselves for the sake of others. He calls us to be like him in putting others first and taking the lowest place for ourselves. We must never forget that although he is the Son of God, the Savior we serve was wrapped in swaddling cloths and laid in a manger, because there was no room for him at the inn.

7

GLORIA IN EXCELSIS DEO

Luke 2:8–20

And suddenly there was with the angel a multitude of the
heavenly host praising God and saying, "Glory to God in
the highest, and on earth peace among those with whom he
is pleased!" (Luke 2:13–14)

esus Christ was born in poverty and obscurity. Although he was the Son of God and the Savior of the world, his birth was largely ignored. On the night he was born his mother had to lay him in a manger, because there was no room for them at the inn.

The welcome that Jesus received—or didn't receive—had spiritual significance. It showed that he was coming to live among sinners and demonstrated the humility that led him to the cross. But it was not right for his advent to go unrecognized. His birth was the most important event in the history of the universe! Somehow it had to be celebrated. It also had to be explained, so that people would understand that God the Son had become a man to save sinners. So God sent angels, of all creatures, to tell people the good news.

What is even more surprising than the appearance of angels is that the first people to hear this good news were shepherds: "And in the same region there were shepherds out in the field, keeping watch over their flock by night" (Luke 2:8). Why did God choose these men to be the first to learn the true meaning of Christmas?

Various explanations have been offered. Some say that the shepherds make a connection with King David, the royal ancestor of Jesus, who was also a shepherd. Then there is a prophecy in Jeremiah—often overlooked—that God would send the Messiah when shepherds were watching their flocks in Judea: "In the cities of the hill country . . . the places about Jerusalem, and in the cities of Judah, flocks shall again pass under the hands of the one who counts them. . . . In those days and at that time I will cause a righteous Branch to spring up for David, and . . . Judah will be saved" (Jer. 33:13, 15–16). By fulfilling this ancient prophecy, the shepherds proved that Jesus is the Christ.

There is another reason why the shepherds were chosen, however, and why Luke—alone among the Gospel writers—included them in his book. Shepherds were outcasts, and thus their presence at the manger shows that salvation is for everyone. We tend to romanticize the shepherds, especially since there are so many good shepherds in the Bible, but they did not enjoy a very good reputation in their day. Because they lived out in the fields, they were unable to keep the ceremonial law, and thus they were treated as unclean. They were also regarded as liars and thieves, which is why their testimony was inadmissible in a court of law. Shepherds were despised. With the exception of lepers, they were the lowest class of men in Israel.

Yet these were the men God wanted to hear the gospel: working-class sinners. Like everything else about the birth of Christ, this upsets our expectations. We tend to think that God is for the good people, when in fact he is for needy sinners who are desperate for grace. As Mary sang in her *Magnificat*, Jesus came to bring down the thrones of the mighty and exalt those of humble estate (Luke 1:52). Who better to exalt than lowly shepherds? We do not even know their names! If God had grace for them, he has grace for any poor sinner who will come to Jesus in faith.

Good News!

What the shepherds saw out in the fields that first Christmas night absolutely terrified them: "And an angel of the Lord appeared to them,

77

and the glory of the Lord shone around them, and they were filled with fear" (Luke 2:9). This is not the first time Luke has introduced us to an angel. His Gospel, writes one old commentator, "resounds with angel songs, and with the music of their wings."[1] Here it also blazes with the light of their glory. The shepherds saw a burning light that pierced the night-black sky. It was nothing less than the glory of God, reflected in the radiance of one of his holy messengers.

This was such a frightening experience that the first thing the angel had to tell the shepherds was not to be afraid: "And the angel said to them, 'Fear not.'" Then the angel told them why: "for behold, I bring you good news of a great joy that will be for all the people. For unto you is born this day in the city of David a Savior, who is Christ the Lord" (Luke 2:10–11). This was the gospel according to the angel.

Every word in the angel's announcement was important. The words "fear not" offered reassurance. The appearance of an angel is always a terrifying experience, and the shepherds needed to know that they were safe. The angel had come to give them good news, and the word he used for this eventually became the title for Luke's book. It is the Greek word for proclaiming the gospel *(euangelizō)*. The words of the ancient promise were starting to come true: good news was being preached to the poor (see Isa. 61:1; Luke 4:18). An angel was preaching to shepherds, of all people.

The good news brought "great joy." It was the real joy of Christmas, that God had become a man to save his people. This joyful good news was "for all the people" (Luke 2:10). At first it may seem that this promise refers to all people everywhere. After all, good news for all people is a biblical truth. Jesus is the Savior of the world, the only Savior there is, and this good news is for everyone. That is not the meaning of this phrase, however. The angel did not say "all people," but "all *the* people," and the definite article distinguishes these people from others. So what people did the angel have in mind? Elsewhere in Luke this phrase refers specifically to the people of Israel.[2] In those days "the people" was a common and general term for the Jews. Of course the good news is not just for the Jews. Later in the chapter we find that it is also for Gentiles. But the angel gave the good news to the

1. W. Graham Scroggie, *A Guide to the Gospels* (Grand Rapids: Kregel, 1995), 380.
2. Robert H. Stein, *Luke,* New American Commentary 24 (Nashville: Broadman, 1992), 108.

Jews first. As the Scripture says, the gospel is "to the Jew first and also to the Greek" (Rom. 1:16).

The joyful good news was about the birth of a baby: "For unto you is born this day" (Luke 2:11). By the time we get to the end of Luke, we will discover that the good news also includes a death and a resurrection. It is the gospel of the cross and the empty tomb. But here we are given the good news of the manger. A child is born! A Son is given! The angel was making a birth announcement about a boy of flesh and blood.

What is surprising is that this child was born *to* the shepherds. The angel said, "Unto you is born." These words are like the tag on a Christmas present that says "To" and "From." The angels were placing a tag on the manger that said "To: the shepherds / From: God." Here the good news takes on personal significance. The angel was doing something more than telling the shepherds what happened; the angel was also telling them why it mattered. Ordinarily, a baby is born to a family. They are the ones who receive the gift of the child's life. In this case, however, the child was for the shepherds and for their salvation. But he was not for them alone. Jesus is for everyone who receives him by faith. We too can have the gift of his life, because God says to us what the angel said to the shepherds: to you is born a Savior.

WHAT CHILD IS THIS?

To this point the angel had given the shepherds good news, but without actually identifying the child. To do this, the angel listed four titles and announced that they all came together in one person. Who was this child?

He was *the son of David*, to which the angel alluded by mentioning "the city of David," meaning Bethlehem. This is now the sixth time that Luke has mentioned David's name. The child born to the shepherds was David's royal son.

He was also *the Savior*. This is another special title in the book of Luke, which uses the language of salvation more than any other Gospel. A Savior is a deliverer—someone who rescues people from death and destruction. This implies that we need a Savior, which of course we do. The deliverance that God brings may come in the form of physical deliverance, but it is also spiritual. Jesus came to save us from sin, Satan, and the righteous wrath of God. He delivered us from these deadly enemies by dying on the cross for our sins and then rising again to give us everlasting life. This was more than the shepherds understood, of course, but by saying that Jesus was the Savior, the angel was telling them to look to Jesus for whatever salvation they needed.

Then Jesus is *the Christ*. Eventually this became part of the Savior's name, but it is really a title. "Christ" is the Greek term for Messiah, which signifies the Savior that God had always promised to send. Literally, the Christ is "the anointed one." This calls to mind the kings and priests of the Old Testament who were anointed with oil as a sign of their office and mission in life. God had always promised that one day he would send a Savior to end all saviors, and this Messiah—this anointed one—would save his people forever. The Jews had been waiting for this for centuries, but now the angel proclaimed that the Savior had come, making the great confession that Jesus is the Christ.

The last title the angel gave to Jesus was *Lord*. This term of honor points to his deity, and to his sovereign rule over our lives. Jesus is the Lord God. Luke has already used the term "Lord" more than a dozen times, and always with reference to the Lord God. But this was the first time that the words "Christ" and "Lord" had ever been brought together. It was an unprecedented combination: Jesus is the Lord Christ. This meant that the promised and anointed Savior was none other than God himself, appearing in the flesh.

Savior, Christ, and Lord—Jesus was given the highest titles that can be given: "*Savior* points to his role as deliverer; *Messiah* points to his office in terms of the promised Anointed One of God; and *Lord* indicates his sovereign authority."[3] The good news for the shepherds was that this child was born in Bethlehem to be their Savior and their God. They never would have known this unless God revealed it to them. If the angel had not appeared to them while they were out in the fields, keeping watch over their flocks by night, the shepherds never would have come to Christ. They acknowledged this when they referred to the good news as "this thing that has happened, which *the Lord* has made known to us" (Luke 2:15).

This shows how much we need the preaching of the gospel. To understand what God has done, we need to have someone explain it to us. By itself, what God had done could not save the shepherds, or anyone else.

3. Darrell L. Bock, *Luke 1:1–9:50*, Baker Exegetical Commentary on the New Testament 3A (Grand Rapids: Baker, 1994), 225.

They needed to know what it meant by faith, which could only happen by divine revelation. This is how God saves us: not simply by sending Jesus to be our Savior, but also by preaching us the gospel so that we can believe in his saving work. God doesn't just do things; he also says things, and we need to know what he says so that we can believe in what he has done.

To help the shepherds believe, God gave them a sign to confirm his promise, much like the signs he gave to Mary and Zechariah. The angel said, "And this will be a sign for you: you will find a baby wrapped in swaddling cloths and lying in a manger" (Luke 2:12). How would the shepherds know for sure that they had the right child? Which one was the Christ? All they had to do was find the baby who was lying in a manger. The point of this sign was not so much what Jesus was wearing, which was common enough, but where he was sleeping. The angel had to tell them this, because otherwise they never would have believed it. Who would ever expect to find a baby in a manger, especially one who was given to be our Savior, Lord, and Christ?

The shepherds would not find the child couched in royal splendor, as they might have expected, but lying in poverty. This was the humiliation of the incarnation, that the Son of God humbled himself to save us. The Venerable Bede, writing sometime in the seventh or eighth century, said: "It should be carefully noted that the sign given of the Saviour's birth is not a child enfolded in Tyrian purple, but one wrapped round with rough pieces of cloth; he is not to be found in an ornate golden bed, but in a manger. The meaning of this is that he did not merely take upon himself our lowly mortality, but for our sakes took upon himself the clothing of the poor."[4] We can recognize Jesus the same way that the shepherds recognized him: by his humility. When we see him wrapped in the swaddling cloths of his humanity—and even more, when we see him dying in the naked agony of the cross—we know that he is the Christ whom God has sent to save us.

THE GLORIA

After giving the shepherds the good news of the gospel, the angel punctuated his proclamation with praise. But he did not do this alone: "Suddenly there was with the angel a multitude of the heavenly host praising God and

4. The Venerable Bede, "In Lucam," quoted in Arthur A. Just Jr., *Luke 1:1–9:50*, Concordia Commentary (St. Louis: Concordia, 1996), 108.

saying, 'Glory to God in the highest, and on earth peace among those with whom he is pleased!'" (Luke 2:13–14). This is the third Christmas carol in the Gospel of Luke. Like the others, it was spoken rather than sung, yet it was written in a poetic form that has often been set to music. And like the other lyrics, it is commonly known by its first words in Latin: *Gloria in excelsis Deo*—"Glory to God in the highest."

What makes this song different from the others is that it was sung by a chorus of angels. It was not a hymn that rose up from the earth, but an anthem that came down from heaven. For this reason, the *Gloria* gives a fuller revelation of the true divine glory of Jesus Christ. God the Son had always enjoyed the adoration of angels. From eternity past, those sinless creatures had worshiped him with perpetual praise. But now God was sending his Son into the world, where he would be despised and rejected unto death for the salvation of a lost and fallen race. This was the most glorious demonstration that God had ever made of his grace. Therefore, it was only right for him to receive the highest praise. In the words of J. C. Ryle, "Now is come the highest degree of glory to God, by the appearing of His Son Jesus Christ in the world. He by His life and death on the cross will glorify God's attributes,—justice, holiness, mercy, and wisdom,—as they never were glorified before."[5]

Imagine what joy it must have been to sing in that angelic choir. The skies opened up and the countless chorus streamed from the courts of heaven—an army of angels revealed in all its glory. They were singing in a new venue, praising God on earth as they had always done in heaven. Imagine what joy they had in going out in the middle of the night and scaring people half to death with the glory of God. They were also singing in a new key, praising God for his grace to sinners. Imagine what joy they had in worshiping the newborn Christ and saying "Glory to God." God was highly glorified in sending his Son to be our Savior. The Christmas angels saw this glory and revealed it to the shepherds so that we could see it too.

Then the angels pronounced a benediction. The coming of Christ was not just for the glory of God, but also for the good of humanity. So after giving glory to God in the highest, they proclaimed peace on earth. What a contrast this was to the kind of peace that the Romans had to offer. This

5. J. C. Ryle, *Expository Thoughts on the Gospels, Luke* (1858; reprint Cambridge: James Clarke, 1976), 1:58.

story began with a decree from Caesar Augustus, which reminds us that this was the age of the *Pax Romana*, when the Romans often praised their emperor for bringing "peace on earth." But this peace came at a dreadful cost. Nations were subjugated and plundered; peoples enslaved; the poor oppressed. There were peace and prosperity for some, fear and poverty for others. For Caesar only "gave peace as long as it was consistent with the interests of the Empire and the myth of his own glory."[6]

Even those who had outward peace in Roman times did not have rest for their souls. The famous Stoic philosopher Epictetus—a contemporary of Luke—observed that "while the emperor may give peace from war on land and sea, he is unable to give peace from passion, grief, and envy. He cannot give peace of heart, for which man yearns more than even for outward peace."[7] Nor could the emperor offer peace with God, which is the most necessary peace of all.

But now a new King was born, and with his birth the angels pronounced peace on earth—peace like the Hebrew *shalom:* total peace for the whole person. This meant peace with God, first of all. Until we have peace with God, we cannot have any true peace at all. Our sins cry out against us and we are afraid to die, because deep down we know that we deserve judgment. But Jesus came to give us peace with God by paying the penalty that our sins deserve. The Bible says that in Christ, God was "making peace by the blood of his cross" (Col. 1:20). Once we have peace with God, we can have peace with one another by the power of his Holy Spirit. We no longer have to push to get our own way, but we can wait for God to work. "It is the work of Christ to bring peace into all human relations," wrote Norval Geldenhuys: "into man's relation to God, to himself (his own feelings, desires, and the like), to his life's circumstances (calamities and trials), and to his fellow-men. According as Christ is honoured and is given admission to human lives, to that extent the peace on earth, which He came to bring, becomes a glorious actuality. In so far as people live outside Him, the earth remains in a state of disorder and strife without real peace."[8]

---

6. Arnaldo Momigliano, quoted in N. T. Wright, "The Most Dangerous Baby," *Christianity Today* (Dec. 9, 1996).

7. Epictetus, quoted in Norval Geldenhuys, *The Gospel of Luke,* New International Commentary on the New Testament (Grand Rapids: Eerdmans, 1951), 112.

8. Geldenhuys, *Luke,* 113.

This peace is not for everyone, but only for the people whom God is pleased to bless. The *Gloria* is often taken as a promise of universal salvation: "Peace on earth, goodwill to men." But as surprising as it may seem, this song actually teaches the doctrine of election. Its wording is important: "Glory to God in the highest, and on earth peace among those with whom he is pleased!" (Luke 2:14). According to Darrell Bock, who has written the definitive commentary on Luke, the phrase "with whom he is pleased" is "almost a technical phrase in first-century Judaism for God's elect, those on whom God has poured out his favor."[9] The peace of God comes according to his sovereign pleasure. The shepherds are the perfect example. They did not choose God; God chose them. They had to respond in faith, of course, but it was by the sovereign grace of God that they heard the good news.

As one missionary studied this verse, he struggled to translate it into a native tongue. The term "peace" was especially difficult because there was no equivalent in the local language. But with the help of his assistant, he finally came up with a translation that captured the heart of this verse: "God in heaven is just so good! So the people who live in this world, if God's heart is happy with them, then their fear is all-gone now!"[10]

"Their fear is all-gone now." This is one of the happy results of the Savior's birth. When we come to God through faith in Jesus Christ, we have real peace. We do not always gain the full benefit of that peace because sometimes we forget to trust God for it. But as we trust in him, he gives us peace. We do not need to be anxious about the future. We do not need to be afraid what people will think. We do not need to try to solve our problems on our own. We do not need to worry how God will provide for us. We do not need to despair if we lose what we love. All we need to do is trust in God and he will give us peace.

Certain Shepherds

What the shepherds heard was not the kind of message that anyone could ignore: "When the angels went away from them into heaven, the shepherds said to one another, 'Let us go over to Bethlehem and see this thing that has

9. Bock, *Luke 1:1–9:50*, 220.
10. Quoted without attribution in a 2001 newsletter from Wycliffe Bible Translators in Orlando, Florida.

happened, which the Lord has made known to us'" (Luke 2:15). "Hurry up!" they said. "We've got to go see this!" Taking off at a run, they headed for Bethlehem, where they found everything just as the angel had promised: "And they went with haste and found Mary and Joseph, and the baby lying in a manger. And when they saw it, they made known the saying that had been told them concerning this child" (Luke 2:16–17).

The shepherds told everyone about the angels they had heard on high. What happened next is important because it shows how to respond to the gospel that the shepherds were given. Different people responded to the good news in different ways. Everyone agreed that it was amazing. Luke tells us, "And all who heard it wondered at what the shepherds told them" (Luke 2:18). But this is not to say that everyone believed them. People were surprised by the shepherds' story, and they probably talked about it for months afterwards, but this does not mean that they all came to faith in Christ. People wonder about all kinds of things that they never fully believe.

Many people have the same response today. They think that Christmas makes a great story, but they wonder if it's all true. They're just not sure. This baby that was born in Bethlehem—is he really the Savior and the Lord? Some people wonder, but they cannot keep wondering forever. Either the good news of great joy is true, in which case we should believe in Jesus Christ, or else the whole thing is a myth, in which case there is no one to save us from our sins.

Mary's response went deeper. Luke tells us—probably on the basis of Mary's own testimony—that she "treasured up all these things, pondering them in her heart" (Luke 2:19). The adoration of the shepherds must have been a great encouragement to Mary. What they said about the city of David, and about her child's identity as Lord and Christ, confirmed the promises that God had made to her some nine months before.

Mary believed the shepherds, but she did not fully understand what they were saying. The word "treasure" *(synetērei)* indicates that she was holding on to the words of the gospel by faith. But the word "ponder" *(symballousa)* shows that she still had some things to think about. This word refers to "a person who is puzzled by what they have heard but keeps it in mind in order to understand, often with divine help, its meaning."[11] It is "an indica-

11. Stein, *Luke*, 110.

tion of an extended period of sustained reflection" by someone "trying to make sense and plumb the depths of all that she had experienced."[12] Mary had a faith that was seeking understanding.

It took Mary a long time to come to a full grasp of the gospel. She did not always understand who Jesus was, or what he was doing. On several occasions she actually opposed his calling. But she kept mulling things over, believing that Jesus was the Son of God and trying to understand what this meant. In the end, Mary came to a full and certain faith in Jesus as her Savior and Lord. We know this because after he ascended into heaven, Mary gathered with the early believers to worship God (Acts 1:14). It takes some people longer than others to come to a full understanding of who Jesus is, what he has done, and what it means to trust in him. The thing to do is to believe as much as we can and to keep thinking about the gospel, asking God to make us more certain of our salvation in Christ.

The shepherds were simpler men, and they had a more immediate response to the gospel. They heard it, they believed it, they investigated it, and when they were satisfied that it was true, they shared it and celebrated it—all in a matter of hours.

First the shepherds had to hear the gospel. If God had not revealed it to them, they never would have believed at all. Faith comes by hearing the Word. But once they heard it, the shepherds still had to respond in faith, which they did without delay. They left their flocks to go and see Jesus. The verb used for seeing (*aneuriskō*; Luke 2:16) means to search with the result of finding. What a wonderful way to describe what it is like to come to Christ! People who go looking for him will reach the goal of their quest, because God has promised that those who seek will find. Anyone who looks for Jesus in faith will find him, as the shepherds did.

When the shepherds saw Jesus lying in the manger, they were certain that everything the angel said was true. They saw Jesus, and they knew for sure. Immediately they became the first evangelists, sharing the good news with anyone who would listen. They took the same gospel they had been given by the angel and started giving it to others. This is how God saves sinners. As soon as we come to Christ in faith, we start sharing the good news. By the love shown in our lives and by the words of our witness, we proclaim

12. Keith F. Nickle, *Preaching the Gospel of Luke: Proclaiming God's Royal Rule* (Louisville: Westminster John Knox, 2000), 26.

the gospel of Jesus Christ, as the shepherds did. And when we do this, other people hear God's word and get saved by the same good news that saved us. Salvation comes by hearing and believing the gospel of Jesus Christ, who was born in a manger to become a man, who died on the cross to pay for our sins, and who was raised from the dead to give us eternal life.

All this is for the glory of God. The story of the shepherds ends with a great and glorious joy, as the angel promised: "And the shepherds returned, glorifying and praising God for all they had heard and seen, as it had been told them" (Luke 2:20). Do you see what the shepherds were doing? They were imitating the angels by glorifying God in the highest and praising him for peace on earth. This is what the gospel does: it brings us to faith in Jesus Christ, and this, in turn, leads to witness and worship. First we come and see, and when we know for sure, we go and tell, glorifying and praising God along the way.

What is the gospel doing in your life? Are you sharing your faith? Are you spreading the good news about Jesus Christ? Are you praising God, glorifying him for the gift of salvation? If you have come to Christ, then you must be doing these things, because every Christian does. But perhaps you are still wondering about Jesus, pondering his gospel in your heart. If so, then God is calling you to believe the angels and follow the shepherds to Jesus; he will be born in your heart by faith.

8

NUNC DIMITTIS

Luke 2:21–38

"Lord, now you are letting your servant depart in peace,
according to your word; for my eyes have seen your salvation that
you have prepared in the presence of all peoples, a light for revela-
tion to the Gentiles, and for glory to your people Israel."
(Luke 2:29–32)

Most parents do everything they can for a new baby, especially their firstborn. Long before birth, they begin making arrangements for what the child will wear and where the child will sleep. Then, once the baby is born, they provide almost constant care—holding, feeding, burping, and changing. Good parents give their children everything they need, from booties and buggies to trundle-bundles.

But the most important things that parents do for their children are spiritual. Good parents pray for their children, asking God to bless them with good health and spiritual growth. They read and sing them the Scriptures. They take them to worship in God's house. And by faith they present their children to God, giving them the sacrament of the covenant, which is the sign of God's promise and the seal of his grace.

PURIFICATION AND PRESENTATION

Mary and Joseph did all of this for their firstborn son. They were godly parents who wanted to do what God required. Five times Luke tells us that they did something for their son in accordance with God's law (Luke 2:22, 23, 24, 27, 39).

The first thing they did was to have their child circumcised, which they did the week after he was born: "And at the end of eight days, when he was circumcised, he was called Jesus, the name given by the angel before he was conceived in the womb" (Luke 2:21). In those days it was customary for a son to receive his name at the time of his circumcision. The name that Mary and Joseph gave their firstborn was the name that God had revealed to each of them: Jesus (see Matt. 1:21; Luke 1:31). It is the name that saves, for this is what Jesus means: "The Lord saves." Sometimes the very name itself begins to bring salvation to sinners. People hear the name of Jesus, it strikes a responsive chord somewhere deep in their souls, and in an instant they sense that he will satisfy the longing of all their desires. Jesus is the Savior.

After he received his name, Jesus received the sign of the covenant. With one sharp cut of the blade, his foreskin was cut away from his body. This was the first shedding of his blood, in anticipation of the cross. "Alas," wrote John Milton, "how soon our sin / Sore doth bring / His Infancy to seize!"[1] Circumcision went back to the days of the patriarchs, when God promised to bless the children of Abraham to the ends of the earth. As a token of his promise, God told Abraham to circumcise his sons. This was the sign of God's covenant, sealed in blood. The fact that this sign was given to Jesus showed that as a true son of Abraham, he was one with his covenant people.

Five weeks later Mary and Joseph took Jesus to the temple: "And when the time came for their purification according to the Law of Moses, they brought him up to Jerusalem to present him to the Lord (as it is written in the Law of the Lord, 'Every male who first opens the womb shall be called holy to the Lord') and to offer a sacrifice according to what is said in the Law of the Lord, 'a pair of turtledoves, or two young pigeons'" (Luke 2:22–24).

1. John Milton, "Upon the Circumcision," in Robert Atwan and Laurance Wieder, *Chapters into Verse: Poetry in English Inspired by the Bible*, 2 vols. (Oxford: Oxford University Press, 1993), 2:36.

They went to the temple for two reasons. One was for purification.[2] According to the law of Moses, a woman who gave birth to a son was ceremonially unclean for forty days after his birth (Lev. 12:1–4). When her time was up, she was required to bring the priest a lamb for a burnt offering and a pigeon for a sin offering. In this case, Mary and Joseph didn't bring a lamb because they couldn't afford one. All they had to offer was two young pigeons. But this was still in keeping with the law, which said, "if she cannot afford a lamb, then she shall take two turtledoves or two pigeons, one for a burnt offering and the other for a sin offering. And the priest shall make atonement for her, and she shall be clean" (Lev. 12:8). This is a clear indication of the poverty into which Jesus was born, and thus a further reminder of the humility of his incarnation.

Ordinarily, the rite of purification presumed that the child was a sinner. Presumably what made the mother impure was the guilt of her child's sin, which he inherited from Adam. This is why sacrifices were made. As Norval Geldenhuys explains it, "The sacrifices symbolized that the sacrificer deserved death, but that the sacrificial animal is loaded with the guilt and death-penalty and for the sake of the sacrificer enters upon death to set him free from his guilt of sin."[3]

So why did Mary need to go through the process of purification? The child that came out of her womb was no sinner! Jesus was the sinless Son of God. He was completely without sin, either original or actual. He was conceived by the Holy Spirit, and thus he did not inherit the guilt of Adam's sin. Nor had he committed any willful sins of his own. So why did Mary have to be purified? Because God commanded it, and also because her son had come to take our sin upon himself. This association between Jesus and the need for cleansing was an early clue that one day he would be the bearer of our sin, as God made him "to be sin who knew no sin, so that in him we might become the righteousness of God" (2 Cor. 5:21).

There was a second reason why Mary and Joseph took Jesus to the temple: "to present him to the Lord" (Luke 2:22). The purification of the mother was tied to the presentation of her son. This too was part of God's

---

2. See I. Howard Marshall, *The Gospel of Luke*, New International Greek Testament Commentary (Grand Rapids: Eerdmans, 1978), 116.

3. Norval Geldenhuys, *The Gospel of Luke*, New International Commentary on the New Testament (Grand Rapids: Eerdmans, 1951), 118.

law, going all the way back to the exodus. God said to Moses, "Consecrate to me all the firstborn. Whatever is the first to open the womb among the people of Israel, both of man and of beast, is mine" (Ex. 13:2). With these words, God laid his rightful claim to the life of every firstborn son in Israel. Yet parents were still allowed to raise their own children. All they had to do was acknowledge God's sovereignty by redeeming their sons with a sacrifice (Ex. 13:13–15), which was offered not long after the children were born. When parents presented their children to God, they were setting them apart for his service.

From this we learn to set our own children apart for God, which we do through the covenant sign of baptism (see Col. 2:11–12). But even more, we see the complete obedience and total dedication of Jesus to the will of God. Jesus already belonged to God as the Son to the Father in the Trinity. When he came to earth, however, he also belonged to God in obedience. From the very beginning of his life, he fulfilled all righteousness by keeping God's law. The Bible says, "when the fullness of time had come, God sent forth his Son, born of woman, born under the law, to redeem those who were under the law" (Gal. 4:4–5).

In his circumcision, Jesus received the lawful sign of the covenant. In his presentation, Jesus was consecrated to God, as the law required. Then all through the rest of his life, he lived in perfect obedience to the whole will of God. He did this for our salvation. We are saved by Christ's death on the cross, but we are also saved by his life on earth, in which he fulfilled all the righteousness that we owe to God.

SIMEON'S SONG

When Jesus was presented at the temple, two godly old saints were waiting to receive him. One of the characteristics of Luke's literary style is to present people in pairs, like Mary and Elizabeth, or John the Baptist and Jesus. Here he introduces us to a man of faith and a woman of prayer. These were the people who first found the joy of salvation in Christ: an ordinary man and woman who walked with God.

The man of faith was Simeon: "Now there was a man in Jerusalem, whose name was Simeon, and this man was righteous and devout, waiting for the consolation of Israel, and the Holy Spirit was upon him. And it had been revealed to him by the Holy Spirit that he would not see death before he had seen the Lord's Christ" (Luke 2:25–26).

We do not know much about Simeon's personal circumstances. He may have been a priest, but the Bible does not say. The main thing we know about him is his character: he was a righteous and godly man who was waiting for the coming of Christ—the Lord's anointed. He believed that God would comfort his people, and by a special promise he knew that one day he would see the Messiah with his very own eyes.

Once he had this promise, Simeon patiently waited for its fulfillment. This is what it means to be a believer: it means waiting in faith for God to do what he has promised. How often Simeon must have walked the streets of the city, waiting for the salvation that God had promised to give. We can imagine him watching parents present their children at the temple—perhaps even pulling their baby clothes back, peering into their tiny faces, and wondering which child would be the Christ.

Then one day the Holy Spirit led Simeon into the outer courtyard, where he met the desire of his trusting heart. In the providence of God, he was in the right place at the right time to see the Christ. The Bible says: "He came in the Spirit into the temple, and when the parents brought in the child Jesus, to do for him according to the custom of the Law, he took him up in his arms and blessed God" (Luke 2:27–28). Simeon's heart soared, and by the revelation of the Holy Spirit, he uttered a prophetic word:

> Lord, now you are letting your servant depart in peace,
>   according to your word;
> for my eyes have seen your salvation
>   that you have prepared in the presence of all peoples,
> a light for revelation to the Gentiles,
>   and for glory to your people Israel. (Luke 2:29–32)

These verses seem to tell the story "of a slave who is instructed by his master to keep watch through the long, dark night on a high place to wait for the rising of a special star and then to announce it. After wearisome hours of waiting he at last sees the star rising in all its brightness. He announces it and is then discharged from keeping watch any longer."[4] In this case, God

---

4. Geldenhuys, *Luke*, 119.

had called Simeon to watch and wait for the star of salvation, the rising of God's Son. Now Simeon's eyes had finally seen the glory. He had seen Jesus, and in Jesus he had seen the salvation of his God.

Of course neither Simeon nor anyone else is saved simply by the birth of Jesus. Jesus still had to live a perfect life, die an atoning death, and rise to eternal glory. There is no salvation without the cross and the empty tomb. But already at this point Simeon could see that salvation had come in the person of Jesus Christ, and therefore that God would do everything else to save him. The child in his arms was not simply part of his salvation, but salvation itself. Jesus is all that anyone needs to be saved.

The coming of Christ had one very important implication for Simeon: It meant that he was ready to die. This is why he began his prophecy with words of dismissal—the words that give his song its Latin title *Nunc dimittis*, which means "now you are dismissing." The *Nunc dimittis* is Luke's fourth and final Christmas carol—a hymn of praise for the newborn Christ. Here is how the poet T. S. Eliot paraphrased it:

> My life is light, waiting for the death wind,
> Like a feather on the back of my hand.
> Dust in sunlight and memory in corners
> Wait for the wind that chills towards the dead land. . . .
> Now at this birth season of decease,
> Let the Infant, the still unspeaking and unspoken Word,
> Grant Israel's consolation
> To one who has eighty years and no to-morrow. . . .
> I am tired with my own life and the lives of those after me,
> I am dying in my own death and the deaths of those after me.
> Let thy servant depart,
> Having seen thy salvation.[5]

Simeon began his song by speaking of his final departure, his dismissal unto death. Some people (like T. S. Eliot) infer from this that he was an old man. That may be true; however, Luke never tells us how old he was. All he tells us is that once Simeon had seen Jesus, he was ready to die—to be released from his watch post. This was partly because of the special promise

---

5. T. S. Eliot, "A Song for Simeon," in Atwan and Wieder, *Chapters into Verse*, 2:37.

that he would not see death until he had seen the Christ. But the principle also has a wider application. *Anyone* who has seen Jesus with the eyes of faith is prepared to die. And anyone who has not seen him—whether young or old—is not ready to die at all. When we see Jesus and his salvation, we are ready to be dismissed from this life in peace and enter the life to come. Have you seen Jesus by faith? Have you seen him crucified for your sins? Have you seen him raised for your salvation? It is then and only then that you are prepared to die.

The baby in Simeon's arms was not only for Simeon to see, or just for the Jews, but for everyone. In the Gospel of Luke, every time someone prophesies about Jesus we learn a little bit more about who he is and what he came to do. Simeon is the one who takes the gospel and makes it global. Earlier, when the angel spoke to the shepherds, the good news about the coming of Christ was specifically for the people of Israel (Luke 2:10). But Simeon had good news for the whole world. The salvation that God provided in Jesus is for *everyone* to see. It is for "all peoples" (Luke 2:31). To make his meaning clear, Simeon went on to specify that Jesus came for the Gentiles as much as he came for the Jews.

This is the basis for our evangelistic outreach around the world. Simeon's prophecy was about global evangelism. Jesus is God's light to the nations. The whole world is covered with darkness through sin, but Jesus has come to dispel the darkness, to shine the light of salvation into every dark corner of every dim heart. It is because of him that we have a gospel we can take to all nations and offer to everyone. We can say to people, "Look, here is salvation. Jesus Christ is God's light for the world. See him and be saved." This was the sermon in Simeon's song.

THE SWORD OF SUFFERING

Mary and Joseph were amazed to hear the good news of the global gospel. Even if they did not fully understand it, they rejoiced in it. Luke says, with reference to the baby Jesus, "his father and his mother marveled at what was said about him" (Luke 2:33). What a remarkable promise to make about a poor child whose parents could barely scrape together enough pigeons to make an offering. Who in Israel would believe that their little boy would become the Savior of the world?

But then Simeon drew the blade that pierced Mary's soul. He uttered a further prophecy, and with it the dark shadow of the cross fell on the mother and child: "Simeon blessed them and said to Mary his mother, 'Behold, this child is appointed for the fall and rising of many in Israel, and for a sign that is opposed (and a sword will pierce through your own soul also), so that thoughts from many hearts may be revealed'" (Luke 2:34–36).

With these words, Simeon offered the first hint of the great suffering that Jesus would endure to bring salvation. From the former prophecies of Mary, Zechariah, and the angels, we have learned about the glory and greatness of Jesus Christ. We have heard of his royal kingship, his divine lordship, and the peace he brings to his people. But here we learn that he will also be the object of opposition. Jesus is the "sign that is opposed" (Luke 2:35). People will despise him, reject him, and take their stand against him. In the end, of course, they nailed him to a tree and left him to die.

This was the sword that pierced Mary's soul. Despite her intense joy over the birth of her firstborn son, the day would come when she would suffer a grief of such anguish that it would strike her to the heart. God used this prophecy to prepare Mary for the crucifixion, so that in the end she would believe and be saved. As she watched Jesus grow up, she always remembered what Simeon had said. And when she finally found herself at the foot of the cross, she knew that the prophecy had come true. The piercing sword was the death of her beloved son.

Simeon's prophecy shows that from the beginning, God had a mission for Jesus that required him to suffer and die for sinners. The crucifixion was not some surprising and unexpected development, but the fulfillment of a preordained plan.

God's plan was for the salvation of his people. It was not for the salvation of everyone, however, which is why Simeon spoke about people falling as well as rising. In his song Simeon identified Jesus as the Savior whom God had prepared "in the presence of all peoples" (Luke 2:31). This might lead us to think that all people everywhere will be saved. Indeed, this is what some people think today, like the well-known Christian writer who said, "All will be redeemed in God's fullness of time, all, not just the small portion of the population who have been given the grace to know and accept Christ. All the strayed and stolen sheep. All the little lost ones."[6]

However attractive this may sound to some people, it is not the biblical truth. Jesus came to judge as well as to save. Notice again what Simeon says: "Behold, this child is appointed for the fall and rising of many in Israel, and for a sign that is opposed . . . , so that thoughts from many hearts may be revealed" (Luke 2:34–35). Jesus exposes what is really in our hearts. If we are truly humbled by our sin, then we will see our need for grace and be drawn to Jesus, who will make us rise to glory. In fact, the word that Simeon uses for rising (*anastasin*) is used elsewhere in the New Testament for resurrection.[7] Everyone who believes in Jesus will rise to heaven, to the glory of God.

Yet some people refuse to be humbled by their sin. They stand proud, not recognizing their need to be forgiven. Thinking that they can make it on their own, they are offended by the idea that salvation comes only through Christ and his cross. Why would anyone else have to die for their sins? For them, Jesus only gets in the way. He is something they cannot get around, something they keep tripping over. This is what Simeon meant when he said that Jesus would cause the "fall of many in Israel." Jesus is a stumbling block (see Isa. 8:14; 1 Cor. 1:23). Although some receive him by faith, others reject him in unbelief. They "speak against this sign of God's love that has been offered to them, for it searches men's hearts and some will be scandalized by a salvation which can only be achieved by way of the cross."[8]

This is the way it has always been. When people truly understand the claims of Christ, most of them are scandalized. This explains why some of our family members scorn our commitment to Christ. It explains why there is so much resistance to Christian truth on the secular college campus. It explains why other world religions are all united in their opposition to Christianity. This is the very thing that Jesus came to do: to reveal the true inward condition of every heart, whether in faith or

---

6. Madeleine L'Engle, quoted in John Wilson, "A Distorted Predestination," *Christianity Today*, Sept. 2003, 73.

7. Leon Morris, *The Gospel According to St. Luke: An Introduction and Commentary*, Tyndale New Testament Commentaries (Grand Rapids: Eerdmans, 1974), 89.

8. Michael Wilcock, *The Message of Luke*, The Bible Speaks Today (Downers Grove, IL: InterVarsity, 1979), 48.

unbelief. When people are opposed to Christians, it is because they are opposed to Christ. Whatever opposition we face is a sign that he is truly present in us.

What is your response to Jesus? Are you for him or against him? Will you rise or will you fall? This is the great question of life and death, because what God will do with us for all eternity depends on what we do with Jesus right now. He is the Great Divide. God uses his cross to reveal our true character, working out his eternal decrees of election and reprobation. There is no neutrality. Either we are with Jesus or we are against him. And if we are against him, we will fall down to spiritual death, down to physical death, and down to hell itself.

Luke tells us this so that we will come to faith in Jesus Christ—not falling, but rising: "Those who imagine themselves to be strong and high, who rely on their own merit and power, will come to woeful ruin and undoing, because in their pride they do not realize their own need and doom and do not take refuge in Christ. But the humble ones, those who bend low at His feet with confession of sin and faith in Him, will be raised up by His mighty arm to eternal life."[9]

ANNA'S STORY

Anna was rising. She was the second person who was waiting for salvation at the temple—a woman of prayer. According to Luke,

> There was a prophetess, Anna, the daughter of Phanuel, of the tribe of Asher. She was advanced in years, having lived with her husband seven years from when she was a virgin, and then as a widow until she was eighty-four [more literally, for eighty-four years]. She did not depart from the temple, worshiping with fasting and prayer night and day. And coming up at that very hour she began to give thanks to God and to speak of him to all who were waiting for the redemption of Jerusalem. (Luke 2:36–38)

Anna was a great woman of God. It is typical of Luke to write about her because—and this was unusual for a man of his era—he seems to have taken special notice of the spiritual lives of women. But then this is typical

9. Geldenhuys, *Luke*, 120.

97

of the Bible generally, which everywhere affirms the full dignity of women and honors their service to God.

Luke tells us several important things about Anna. She was a prophetess—that is, a woman who spoke for God. This is a rare word in Scripture. Although many men served as prophets, traditionally the Jews counted only seven prophetesses in the Old Testament. There are several more in the New Testament, but it was still an uncommon calling. Anna had the rare privilege of knowing and proclaiming God's will for his people.

Anna was also a widow—an old widow. Sadly, her husband had died after only seven years of marriage. Since girls married so young in those days, she may have been no more than twenty when he died. This meant that Anna still had eighty more years to serve the Lord. Her life shows what it means to serve God through all the seasons of life. There was a time when Anna was a young virgin. In those days she served God by getting to know him and by preserving her purity. When she got married, she served God primarily by loving and helping her husband. But after only seven years of marriage, God called her to be a widow. He released her from the duty of caring for a family so that she could live in single-hearted devotion to him. What is your situation? Whatever God calls you to do—at whatever stage of life—serve him in the appropriate way, living for his glory.

Anna served God by offering him her praise. She participated in public worship, never missing a service. She also fasted. Fasting is an expression of our total dependence on God for both physical and spiritual life. It is a help to prayer because our physical hunger reminds us of our true spiritual need for God. From the example of Anna and others we learn that fasting is an ordinary part of a healthy spiritual life. Then Anna prayed. It seems appropriate that she was the daughter of Phanuel, because Phanuel means "face of God," and this is what Anna was seeking: the face of God. Like many godly old women, she had a special calling to pray.

The old widow—I say "old" because she was more than eighty at the time, and may have been more than a hundred—did all of these things without ceasing. Because of her deep spiritual hunger for God, she practically lived at the temple, staying there to worship God both night and day. She was not trying to earn any special favor with God; she was simply living out the joy of knowing him. Her works were the proof of her faith as she waited for her salvation.

Is it any wonder that Anna was the woman who knew that Jesus was the Christ? She saw Simeon hold the Christ-child in his arms, "and coming up at that very hour she began to give thanks to God and to speak of him to all who were waiting for the redemption of Jerusalem" (Luke 2:38). Anna recognized her redeemer—the Savior whom God sent to rescue his people by suffering and dying for their sins.

As soon as Anna saw Jesus, she did what everyone who comes to Christ should do. She thanked God for the gift of her salvation in Christ, the consolation of her widow's heart. Then she began to tell other people about Jesus and his redemption. The news was too good for Anna to keep to herself: she had to share it with everyone she knew. So like the shepherds, she became one of the first evangelists. Her life was all about worship and witness.

What is your life all about? Have you seen Jesus? Have you recognized him as your Savior from sin? If you have, praise God for the free gift of your salvation. Speak words about Jesus into the lives of your family and friends so that they can trust him too. And wait for Jesus, living in the hope that he will come again.

We can see Jesus even more clearly than Anna and Simeon did. We see him not only in his birth, but also in his death and resurrection, knowing for sure that in him we have the forgiveness of sins and the promise of eternal life. We also have the Holy Spirit to help us follow their example by looking in faith and waiting in prayer. J. C. Ryle wrote: "If they, with so few helps and so many discouragements, lived such a life of faith, how much more ought we with a finished Bible and a full Gospel. Let us strive, like them, to walk by faith and look forward."[10]

When I think of men of faith and women of prayer, I remember my grandparents—Frank and Eva Ryken. Like Simeon, my grandfather was a man who had seen salvation and was ready to depart in peace. I can remember as a young boy going to see him the day that he went in for heart bypass surgery. As he sat on the edge of his bed, with his feet dangling below his hospital gown, he told us how he had met with Jesus in the night, gaining full assurance of the gospel he had always believed. He told us that he was ready to die. And like Anna, my grandmother was a woman of prayer. As

10. J. C. Ryle, *Expository Thoughts on the Gospels, Luke* (1858; reprint Cambridge: James Clarke, 1976), 1:75.

her horizons narrowed in the last years of her life, she retreated more and more into the privacy of her own room, where she experienced an extraordinary intimacy with Christ that surpassed her earlier days. As she waited for Jesus, her life itself became a prayer.

I suppose I will spend the rest of my life wanting somehow to be like all those old saints—seeing Jesus and waiting for him. Don't you want to be like them, too?

9

THE BOY JESUS

Luke 2:39–52

And when they had performed everything according to the Law of the Lord, they returned into Galilee, to their own town of Nazareth. And the child grew and became strong, filled with wisdom. And the favor of God was upon him. (Luke 2:39–40)

One summer in the early 1970s the good people at the Topps chewing gum company printed baseball cards with "Boyhood Photos of the Stars." Each card featured an old black-and-white photograph of a baseball all-star when he was a young boy. There was also a small picture in the corner that showed what he looked like as a major leaguer, for comparison. It was fascinating to discover that these great baseball players had once been little boys, and fun to imagine what it was like to grow up being someone like Brooks Robinson or Johnny Bench.

Luke gives us a similar snapshot in his Gospel. After announcing the birth of Jesus Christ, and before presenting his public ministry, Luke shows us what Jesus was like as a young boy—the story of his visit to the temple in Jerusalem. It is a vivid portrait. In the words of one commentator, Luke gives us the only glimpse that we have of the boy Jesus, with a boy's hunger for knowledge and yearning for future service, this boy who already had the consciousness of a peculiar relationship to God his Father, and yet who went back to Nazareth in obedience to Joseph and Mary to toil at the carpenter's bench for eighteen more years. . . . No one who did not love and understand children could have so graphically pictured the boyhood of Jesus in this one short paragraph.[1]

Presumably, there were many things that Luke could have told us about the childhood of Jesus Christ. But of all the things that Jesus said and did during his first thirty years, this is the only incident recorded in the Bible. Therefore, it must have special significance. What does this story tell us about Jesus? What can we learn about the mysterious union of his deity with his humanity? What can we discover about his saving mission on earth? In this passage we see Jesus growing in stature, growing in wisdom, and learning obedience to his Father in heaven.

Jesus Grew in Stature

Luke sets the stage for his story by shifting the scene from Bethlehem and Jerusalem back to Nazareth. He does not mention the adoration of the magi or the flight to Egypt as recorded in the Gospel of Matthew. Perhaps he simply assumed that people were familiar with those episodes from the life of Christ. In any case, what Luke says is thoroughly consistent with Matthew: "And when they had performed everything according to the Law of the Lord, they returned into Galilee, to their own town of Nazareth" (Luke 2:39).

This little village, which was in the north near Galilee, became the Savior's hometown. Luke summarizes his childhood there by compressing the first twelve years of his life into a single verse: "And the child grew and became strong, filled with wisdom. And the favor of God was upon him" (Luke 2:40). There is a similar summary at the end of the chapter, where Luke describes his life from adolescence to adulthood: "And Jesus increased in wisdom and in stature and in favor with God and man" (Luke 2:52). These verses testify to the physical, intellectual, spiritual, and relational development of the Son of God.

His physical development is the easiest for us to understand. We know that when God the Son became a man he took on a human body. The baby

---

1. A. T. Robertson, *Luke the Historian in the Light of Research* (New York: Charles Scribner's Sons, 1930), 239.

in the manger was a real baby with all the physical needs that any baby has. As an infant Jesus woke up in the middle of the night hungry. He needed to be nursed, burped, and changed.

We also know that when Jesus was an adult he suffered all the limitations of our physical existence. He grew tired and hungry; he needed to eat and sleep. His temptation to turn stones into bread was a real temptation, faced when he was on the verge of starvation. And most importantly of all, it was a real body that Jesus offered on the cross for our sins. It was flesh like ours that was torn and bloodied by the nails. This was the only way that he could save us, for as the Bible declares, "He himself bore our sins in his body on the tree, that we might die to sin and live to righteousness. By his wounds you have been healed" (1 Peter 2:24).

But what happened to the body of Christ between the manger and the cross? Luke tells us that he "grew and became strong" (Luke 2:40). Jesus went through all the ordinary stages of physical development. He had to crawl like a baby before he could walk like a man. First he was a newborn. Six months later he could sit up. Then he learned to use his hands and his feet to move around. Somewhere around age one the Son of God became a toddler as he learned how to walk. Then he turned into a little boy, and almost before his parents knew it, Jesus was a teenager.

So Jesus grew from infancy through adolescence to adulthood. "What a big boy you are!" his parents would say when he was little. "You're getting bigger. Soon you'll be taller than I am!" When we read that Jesus "increased in stature" (Luke 2:52), we can almost imagine his parents keeping his growth chart on the wall of their family home in Nazareth. This is part of what we mean when we say that God the Son became a man. Jesus came to save us in the body, and to do this he took on all the difficulties and possibilities of our physical existence.

JESUS GREW IN WISDOM

But this is not all that we mean. We also mean that Jesus was growing intellectually:

The great historic doctrine of the church is that the Son of God became a real man—not just someone who only appeared to be a man. When he was born, God the Son placed the exercise of his all-powerfulness and all-presence and all-knowingness under the direction of God the Father. He did not give up those attributes, but he submitted their exercise in his life to the Father's discretion. Though he was sinless, he had a real human body, mind, and emotions—complete with their inherent weaknesses.[2]

This is the doctrine of the incarnation, that God the Son became a man, that the divine person of the Son assumed a human nature. Understand what this doctrine teaches: Jesus had a human mind as well as a human body. Many Christians think they believe in the incarnation, when what they actually believe is that Jesus had the mind of God in the body of a man. But this is the ancient heresy of Apollinarianism. What the Bible actually teaches is a full incarnation in which the divine nature and the human nature are joined in the one person of Jesus Christ. Because these two natures are united in one person, both divine and human attributes are properly connected to the person of Jesus Christ. His humanity was a full humanity, including reason, will, and emotions. How could we say that God became a man unless he had a human mind as well as a human body?

Like his body, the mind of Christ had to develop. If we doubt this, all we need to do is look again at the Scripture, which says that Jesus "increased in wisdom" (Luke 2:52). Here Luke "expressly tells us that the intellectual, moral and spiritual growth of Jesus as a Child was just as real as His physical growth. He was completely subject to the ordinary laws of physical and intellectual development."[3] As he submitted to the very laws that he had created, Jesus was taught things that he did not know. Donald MacLeod explains that he "had a human mind, subject to the same laws of perception, memory, logic and development as our own. . . . He observed and learned and remembered and applied. This would have been impossible if he had been born in possession of a complete body of wisdom and knowledge. Instead, he was born with the mental equipment

2. R. Kent Hughes, *Luke: That You May Know the Truth*, 2 vols., Preaching the Word (Wheaton, IL: Crossway, 1998), 1:85.

3. Norval Geldenhuys, *The Gospel of Luke*, New International Commentary on the New Testament (Grand Rapids: Eerdmans, 1951), 122.

of a normal child, experienced the usual stimuli and went through the ordinary processes of intellectual development."[4]

A critical difference is that Jesus did this without sin. His development was unhindered by depravity, and thus his intellect advanced to its full capacity. He was never lazy, but always tried to learn as much as he could. He exercised good stewardship of his intellectual abilities, achieving the maximum potential of the human mind. However, this does not mean that he was omniscient, as far as his human nature was concerned. With respect to his divine nature, yes, Jesus knew all things, but not with respect to his human nature. The human mind is not omniscient; there are boundaries to its knowledge. Here we stand at the threshold of one of the great mysteries of the incarnation. God the Son took on the intellectual as well as the physical limitations of our humanity. If we believe in the incarnation, then we must believe this. Jesus Christ was a real human person—body, mind, and soul.

Perhaps some examples will help put this into perspective. Consider some of the things that Jesus did not know. When Jesus was two, he was not able to perform the complex computations of differential calculus; he couldn't even "solve for x." When he was six, he did not know the percentage of hydrogen in Jupiter's atmosphere, or the distance from Earth to Alpha Centauri. When he was ten, he could not recite the capital cities of Africa or the presidents of the United States. With respect to his divine nature, these were things that he had always known, but with respect to his human nature, they were among the many things that he did not know during his time on earth. John Calvin went so far as to say that there would be "no impropriety in saying that Christ, who knew all things, was ignorant of something in respect of his perception as a man."[5] Apart from special revelation by the Spirit, Jesus did not know anything that was outside of his experience or beyond the capacity of a human mind at that age to know. These were the rules of engagement for his mission to save the world.

I say "apart from special revelation" because the Gospels give many examples of Jesus having supernatural knowledge. Sometimes he knew exactly

4. Donald MacLeod, *The Person of Christ*, Contours of Christian Theology (Downers Grove, IL: InterVarsity, 1998), 164.

5. John Calvin, *Commentary on a Harmony of the Evangelists, Matthew, Mark and Luke* (Edinburgh: Calvin Translation Society, 1845), 3:153.

what people were thinking, or what would happen in the future. Jesus had access to this information by virtue of his deity. Yet he did not know these things because as a man he was omniscient (any more than the prophets were omniscient, although they too received special revelation from God—there is a difference between infinite knowledge and supernatural knowledge, which may be limited in scope).[6] Jesus knew these things as much or more because God the Father revealed them by God the Holy Spirit. Jesus learned the will of God through both general and special revelation. For anything beyond ordinary human knowledge, Jesus could depend on the revelation of God. The Father revealed as much as the Son needed to know. But as a man he also knew things the old-fashioned way: he learned them. This is why the Bible says that Jesus "increased in wisdom" (Luke 2:52), that he "learned obedience through what he suffered" (Heb. 5:8), and even that there were things that he did not know (Mark 5:30; 13:32).

These statements stagger the mind. If we sometimes take the incarnation for granted, it can only be because we have not wrestled with its full implications. What infinite condescension it was for God the Son to become a man, with all the limitations of our humanity, except for sin. This too is part of what he suffered for our sake. What gratitude this gives us for the salvation we have in Christ, and what encouragement to know that he can sympathize with our weakness. There were things that Jesus had to learn, things he did not understand all at once, even things he had to take on faith. Our Savior understands what it is like to go through all the growing pains of life.

The Lost Boy

As the body of Jesus grew in stature, his mind grew in wisdom. Jesus also grew in his personal relationships with other people and with his Father God. Luke tells us that "the favor of God was upon him" (Luke 2:40), and that he "increased in favor with God and man" (Luke 2:52).

In between these two summary statements, Luke tells us the famous story of the boy Jesus in Jerusalem. Luke probably heard this story from Mary, who "treasured up all these things in her heart" (Luke 2:51). At first Mary

---

6. MacLeod, *Person of Christ*, 166.

and Joseph "did not understand the saying that he [Jesus] spoke to them" at the temple (Luke 2:50), but for years afterwards Mary tried to figure out what it meant. Of all the things that happened during his boyhood years, this was the one that most clearly declared his destiny.

Going to Jerusalem was an annual occurrence for Jesus and his family. Luke tells us, "his parents went to Jerusalem every year at the Feast of the Passover. And when he was twelve years old, they went up according to custom" (Luke 2:41–42). Only Joseph was required to go, but this was a godly family, so they all made the annual pilgrimage for Passover, which was one of the three major festivals in Israel's religious calendar. Mary and Joseph had made a covenant to raise their child right, and this included leading him in the public worship of God—a practice he maintained when he was an adult.

Going to Passover must have been a great experience for a twelve-year-old boy. The streets of Jerusalem were crammed with as many as two hundred thousand pilgrims and one hundred thousand sheep for sacrifices. At that age Jesus may well have had the run of the city, with all its sights and sounds. He would have feasted with friends. He would have gone up to the temple to pray and sing psalms. On the night of Passover he would have worshiped with his family. As his father prepared the sacrificial lamb, Jesus would have heard the story of salvation all over again. Joseph would have reminded his eldest son how God rescued his people from slavery and delivered them from death in Egypt.

All of this had special significance the year that Jesus turned twelve. In another year he would be thirteen, the age at which a young man became a full member of the synagogue. So Jesus was preparing to become "a son of the law," or as we say it today, *bar mitzvah*. The rabbis said that when a boy turned twelve, it was time for him to go up to Jerusalem with his father and learn the rituals for Passover, which is why Luke says that Jesus "went up according to custom" (Luke 2:42). This was the year for him to learn what it meant to be a man.

It was also the year of a famous mix-up: "And when the feast was ended, as they were returning, the boy Jesus stayed behind in Jerusalem. His parents did not know it, but supposing him to be in the group they went a day's journey, but then they began to search for him among their relatives and acquaintances, and when they did not find him, they returned to Jerusalem, searching for him" (Luke 2:43–45).

As far as Mary and Joseph were concerned, Jesus was lost. To understand how this happened, it helps to know that for reasons of safety and fellowship, pilgrims did not travel as individual families in those days, but in large caravans. We may infer that Jesus, Mary, and Joseph belonged to the kind of vibrant spiritual community that we pray to find in the church: a happy fellowship of family and friends who worship God and love to serve him together. They were probably traveling in two large groups, for

> it was the custom in those days that when a company of festival pilgrims went on their return-journey the women went on ahead with the younger children and the men followed them. The bigger boys then traveled either along with the fathers or with the mothers. Joseph, therefore, may have thought, when he did not notice Jesus, that He was with Mary, and Mary probably thought that He was with Joseph. In addition, it was a definite custom that in the evening, after the day's journey, the whole traveling company came together for the night at a place previously arranged.[7]

Mary and Joseph had so much confidence in their oldest son that they trusted him to be where they thought he was supposed to be. We can sympathize with their growing sense of panic when they discovered that Jesus was missing. Nothing is more frightening than to lose a child. We can well imagine the urgent questions they asked: "Where's Jesus?" "Has anyone seen Jesus?" "When was the last time you saw him?" We can also imagine the lump in Mary's throat as she searched for her son, and the ache in her mother's heart when she realized that he could be a whole day's journey away. Was this the sword that would pierce her soul? She may have wondered. Meanwhile, gentle Joseph would have tried to reassure her: "Don't worry, Mary," he might have said. "Jesus will be all right. You'll see. God will take care of him."

IN HIS FATHER'S HOUSE

For all the drama of parents looking for their firstborn son, what Mary and Joseph went through during those anxious days is not the main point of this passage. The primary verb does not relate to them, but to their boy

7. Geldenhuys, *Luke*, 126.

Jesus: "he stayed behind" (Luke 2:43). Jesus remained in Jerusalem, at the temple. This was the place that satisfied his soul. He wanted to learn as much as he could about the Scriptures and the promise of salvation. Thus he was irresistibly drawn to the house of God. He wanted to stay in his Father's presence, lingering at the place where his heart could echo the joy he had always experienced as the eternal and preexistent Son.

So it was that on the third day, when Mary and Joseph finally found Jesus, he was in the first place they ought to have looked—at home in the house of his Father: "After three days they found him in the temple, sitting among the teachers, listening to them and asking them questions. And all who heard him were amazed at his understanding and his answers" (Luke 2:46–47).

Jesus was sitting in the temple courts, having a seminar with learned theologians. It is sometimes thought that he was the one doing the teaching, testing the Bible scholars to see how much they knew. Yet Jesus was learning as well as teaching. The Bible says that he was "listening" to the teachers. It also says that he was "asking them questions." This was the style of theological instruction in those days: education by disputation. Students questioned their rabbis to learn what they had to teach. So it was natural enough for a boy to sit at the feet of his teachers—especially a boy who was about to become "a son of the law"—and talk theology.

What was unusual in this case was the boy's extraordinary precocity. As the dialogue went back and forth, it was obvious that the boy Jesus had an exceptional knowledge of theology. He was not omniscient with regard to his human nature, because he was still learning. But he had a passion for studying the Scriptures. He believed all the words and promises of the Bible. He had spiritual wisdom to apply them to daily life. And he knew God, which is the foundation for all true knowledge, because his sinless heart was in trusting communion with his Father in heaven.

The questions this twelve-year-old asked were so perceptive and the answers he gave so lucid that everyone was amazed, including the child's parents, who apparently had no idea that Jesus was becoming such an accomplished theologian: "And when his parents saw him, they were astonished" (Luke 2:48). But Mary, at least, did not remain astonished for long. Her indignation quickly returned as she interrupted the scholars to scold her son: "And his mother said to him, 'Son, why have you treated us so? Behold, your father and I have been searching for you in great distress'" (2:48).

Spoken like a true mother, right down to that reproachful phrase "your father and I." It is easy for us to sympathize with Mary. We appreciate her affection for her firstborn son, and her anxious concern for his safety. We understand her emotions, and how her relief at finding Jesus naturally turned into anger over all the worry she had been through. No doubt if we had been in Mary's place we would have given Jesus the same kind of reprimand. She was still trying to understand who Jesus was and what he had come to do. Thus there were times when she faced the temptation that all parents face to raise a child more out of fear over what could go wrong than by faith in what God would do. Mary's question came from her fears.

What is more important is the answer that Jesus gave: "And he said to them, 'Why were you looking for me? Did you not know that I must be in my Father's house?' " (Luke 2:49). These are the first recorded words of Jesus Christ. They form the climax of this episode, which Luke seems to have included in his Gospel specifically so that he could record this saying. What the boy Jesus said was monumental in what it revealed about his true identity as the Son of God and revolutionary in its implications for our own relationship to God as our Father.

Jesus referred to God as "my Father." This intimate expression was totally new. No one had ever said anything like it before. To be sure, the fatherhood of God is present in the Old Testament. There are at least a dozen places where the Scripture refers to God as Father. However, those who are speaking always refer to themselves in the plural. That is, people spoke of God as "our Father," but no one ever called him "*my* Father." God's paternity was more a general concept than a personal relationship. Even men like Moses and David, who enjoyed special intimacy with God, never dared to claim that he was their Father.[8] But Jesus said it as if it were the most natural thing in the world. If the temple was God's house, then it was his Father's house, because he knew that God was his Father.

Here we are drawn into mysteries of the triune being of God. We have already pondered the mystery of the incarnation, that the divine Son of God had a human nature in every sense of the word. Here we are reminded

---

8. See David Gooding, *According to Luke: A New Exposition of the Third Gospel* (Grand Rapids: Eerdmans, 1987), 61.

that the one true God exists in three persons—Father, Son, and Holy Spirit. As the incarnate Son, Jesus knew God as Father even when he was a boy. Liberal theologians claim that at age twelve he had only "vague stirrings of his own identity."[9] But the Scripture shows that the boy Jesus knew who he was. He had complete confidence that he was the Son of God. Already at this young age he was speaking to God the way he would always speak to him when he was a man, and the way he taught us to speak to God, calling him "Father."

This meant that when Jesus was at the temple, he was right where he was supposed to be. He was not sinning against his earthly parents. He was not disobeying any instructions they had given him about when to be where. He was exactly where they should have expected to find him. As his mother and father, Mary and Joseph had a right to expect him to be where he was supposed to be. But in this case they made the wrong assumption about where that was. By pointing this out, Jesus was not trying to be some sort of smart aleck. It was just so obvious that he was frankly amazed that his parents didn't know where to find him. They were only his earthly parents, but his real Father was God in heaven. So Jesus said, "I *must* be in my Father's house" (Luke 2:49). This was a matter of divine compulsion. Given his unique identity as the Father's Son, Jesus *had* to be at the temple. The temple was God's dwelling place on earth, and therefore it was the place for the Son to commune with the Father. In addition to all the other ways that he was growing, the boy Jesus (the incarnate Son of God, human as well as divine) was growing in his relationship to God.

PERFECT SUBMISSION

In this Father-Son relationship, the Son was called to do his Father's will. To see this, it helps to know that there is another way to interpret what Jesus said. Literally he said, "I must be in the things of my Father" (Luke 2:49). In context, this refers to the temple.[10] However, it also has a wider application. Jesus was called to be about his Father's business. This is why he was at the

---

9. Fred B. Craddock, *Luke*, Interpretation (Louisville: John Knox, 1990), 43.

10. Raymond E. Brown, *The Birth of the Messiah: A Commentary on the Infancy Narratives in the Gospels of Matthew and Luke*, rev. ed., Anchor Bible Reference Library (New York: Doubleday, 1993), 475–76.

temple: it was the place where his Father transacted his business, and Jesus had come to do his Father's work. Geldenhuys writes:

> It is remarkable that the first words of Jesus quoted in the Gospel narrative are these words in which He so clearly refers to His divine Sonship, and in which He points to His life's vocation to be about His Father's business—to serve and glorify Him in all things and at all times. The words indicate a divine inevitability: Jesus must be busy with the interests of His Father. With Him it is, however, not a case of external compulsion—His whole nature yearns to serve and obey His Father voluntarily.[11]

Jesus was always "in the things of his Father." Later he would say, "I have come down from heaven, not to do my own will but the will of him who sent me" (John 6:38), and "I always do the things that are pleasing to him" (John 8:29). Jesus was always minding his Father's business, doing his Father's work, and submitting to his Father's will. It was this obedience that finally led him to the cross. When the time came for Jesus to die for our sins, he said to his Father what he had been saying with his whole life: "Thy will be done."

There is a perfect example of his submission at the end of Luke 2. After Jesus explained to his parents why he had to be at the temple, "he went down with them and came to Nazareth and was submissive to them" (Luke 2:51). Jesus went back to Nazareth, back to the family business, and back to obeying his parents. If ever a child had the right to demand his own way, it was Jesus of Nazareth. He was God the Son! Yet it is the will of God for children to obey their parents. Therefore, as long as Jesus was a boy, he submitted to Mary and Joseph, his mother and father. With all humility, he cheerfully and willingly obeyed their God-given authority.

We often struggle with submission. As children we do not always want to obey our parents. As wives we do not always want to respect our husbands. As workers we do not always want to obey our bosses. As church members we do not always want to listen to our pastors and elders. As citizens we do not always want to follow our leaders. We are tempted to do exactly the opposite, to insist on our own way. But God calls us to serve him by submitting to the people he has placed in positions of authority. Rather than

11. Geldenhuys, *Luke*, 128.

struggling with this, Jesus embraced it. When we learn to embrace it the way that Jesus did, then we too will enjoy God's favor.

Jesus submitted to God's will for our salvation. God the Son became a human being, with a mind and a body like ours. He grew through the stages of life, facing all the struggles that we face. He endured the physical limitations of the body and did the hard intellectual work of learning the ways of God in the world. He submitted to God's will, even to the point of obeying his parents. Jesus did all this so that he could live a perfect life and then offer himself as the perfect sacrifice for our sins.

God calls us to believe in Jesus for our salvation. Then he calls us to follow his example in the way that we live. This means growing in stature, taking good care of the bodies that God has given us. It means growing in wisdom, expanding our minds by learning as much as we can, especially about the Bible and theology. It means growing in our love for God, learning to call him Father. It means serving God by submitting to the people he has placed in authority. And when we find it difficult to do these things— when we must endure the sufferings of the body, or wrestle with things it is hard for us to understand, or submit to imperfect authority—we can pray for Jesus to help us. Jesus understands. From the time that he was a boy, he experienced all of these difficulties himself, and now that he has reached his full and glorious maturity, he has grace to help us in all our need.

10

Be Prepared

Luke 3:1—14

As it is written in the book of the words of Isaiah the prophet,
"The voice of one crying in the wilderness: 'Prepare the way
of the Lord, make his paths straight. Every valley shall be
filled, and every mountain and hill shall be made low, and
the crooked shall become straight, and the rough places shall
become level ways, and all flesh shall see the salvation of God.'"
(Luke 3:4–6)

ou know what you people are? You're all a bunch of hypocrites! You go to church on Sunday, but then you forget about God the rest of the week. You're living a double life. You say that you belong to God, but then you secretly go indulge in all kinds of sinful pleasures. You live in your nice big houses and drive around in your fancy cars, but you never do anything to help the poor. You snakes! Do you really think that God is going to save you just because you've been baptized and belong to an evangelical church? Listen, unless you turn away from your sins, you're going straight to hell."

This was the kind of message that John the Baptist preached in the wilderness. His sermons may not have been very "seeker sensitive," but they can hardly be faulted for a lack of courage! John wasn't trying to win friends and influence people; he was trying to get them to repent. Therefore, he spoke with holy boldness, bluntly confronting their sin. I am reminded of the nineteenth-century Methodist preacher Peter Cartwright, who once preached to President Andrew Jackson. Before the service he was warned not to say anything out of line. So when Cartwright got up to preach, he said, "I understand Andrew Jackson is here. I have been requested to be guarded in my remarks. Andrew Jackson will go to hell if he doesn't repent." The congregation was shocked, but afterwards the president shook Cartwright's hand and said, "Sir, if I had a regiment of men like you, I could whip the world."[1]

Like Peter Cartwright—though perhaps unlike most preachers—John the Baptist was not afraid to offend. His outspoken ministry led the great Anglican preacher J. C. Ryle to comment that it would be well "for the Church of Christ, if it possessed more plain-speaking ministers, like John the Baptist, in these latter days. . . . There is no charity in flattering unconverted people, by abstaining from any mention of their vices, or in applying smooth epithets to damnable sins."[2] Surely no one ever accused John the Baptist of flattery. Here was a man who cared enough to confront!

THE VOICE CRYING IN THE WILDERNESS

Admittedly, John was a little odd. Matthew tells us that he lived in the wilderness, wearing wild clothes and eating wild food (Matt. 3:4). Even in those days he was considered strange, which is why people talked about him all over Israel. But the main thing John did was to preach. The Gospels present him as a man of action, striding across Israel and preaching reformation. Auguste Rodin expressed this beautifully in his sculpture of John the Baptist. Rodin's Baptist has long unruly hair and an animal skin around his waist. He is in mid-stride, with a finger raised, his head turned to the side, and his lips parted, as if in mid-sentence. The sculpture captures the essence of John's ministry. However odd people thought he was, the man was alive with passion for preaching the Word of God.

---

1. This story has circulated in many different versions.

2. J. C. Ryle, *Expository Thoughts on the Gospels, Luke* (1858; reprint Cambridge: James Clarke, 1976), 1:89.

Be Prepared

Luke begins his account of John's ministry by introducing it in the formal style: "In the fifteenth year of the reign of Tiberius Caesar, Pontius Pilate being governor of Judea, and Herod being tetrarch of Galilee, and his brother Philip tetrarch of the region of Ituraea and Trachonitis, and Lysanias tetrarch of Abilene, during the high priesthood of Annas and Caiaphas, the word of God came to John the son of Zechariah in the wilderness" (Luke 3:1–2). This elegant introduction is the beginning of the middle of Luke's Gospel. Its purpose is to locate the ministry of John the Baptist and the life of Jesus Christ in time and space. The events in this Gospel really happened. They are as real as anything on the evening news. In the words of one commentator, "Only a historian could have written like this, a man with an orderly mind, giving in a series of clauses duly subordinated to the main verb that is to follow, the names of all the officials of the country round in a particular year, and in order. . . . The number of officials, named with an accuracy only possible to one writing in the period that he describes, shows Luke's carefulness to prove that his narrative may be tested by reference to contemporary official records."[3]

By comparing what Luke says with other ancient sources, we are able to determine that John's ministry began sometime between A.D. 26 and A.D. 29, most likely in the year A.D. 27.[4] The mention of Lysanias is especially significant because liberal scholars used to say that this was a mistake. A king named Lysanias ruled Abilene more than sixty years earlier, around 36 B.C. So Luke had the right man, the argument went, but the wrong date. However, ancient inscriptions have since proven that there was a second Lysanias—probably a direct descendant of the first—and that he ruled as tetrarch over Abilene at the time of Christ. We can trust Luke to tell us the truth.

Lysanias and the other rulers that Luke mentions form the local and international context for his Gospel. Everything we know about this impressive list of leaders testifies to their pride, violence, and self-indulgence. The Romans ruled the world in rebellion against God; even the

3. P. C. Sands, *Literary Genius of the New Testament,* quoted in Leland Ryken, ed., *The New Testament in Literary Criticism,* A Library of Literary Criticism (New York: Frederick Ungar, 1984), 204.
4. See Norval Geldenhuys, *The Gospel of Luke,* New International Commentary on the New Testament (Grand Rapids: Eerdmans, 1951), 134–35.

116

high priests of Israel were under their pagan authority. And it was during this degenerate time that God once again spoke to his people. For centuries he had been silent. There had not been a true prophet in Israel for more than four centuries. But then "the word of God came to John" (Luke 3:2), and it spoke with greater power and authority than all the rulers in the world. This is the way the Word always comes. In dark and dangerous times, when people seem powerless against the godless forces of evil, God's Word comes to bring salvation.

As soon as he received God's Word, John began to speak it, "proclaiming a baptism of repentance for the forgiveness of sins" (Luke 3:3). The Baptist was getting people ready for salvation. This fulfilled the prophecies made at his birth. When the angel announced John's birth, he said, *Proph.* "he will be filled with the Holy Spirit, . . . and he will turn many of the *Prepared* children of Israel to the Lord their God, and he will . . . make ready for the Lord a people prepared" (Luke 1:15–17). Then there was the prophecy of Zechariah, his father: "And you, child, will be called the prophet of the Most High; for you will go before the Lord to prepare his ways, to give knowledge of salvation to his people in the forgiveness of their sins" (Luke 1:76–77). When John started preaching repentance and forgiveness, God's promise came true.

Luke knew that something deeper was at work. John's ministry fulfilled a more ancient prophecy, one "written in the book of the words of Isaiah the prophet": *High/Low*

Self-Reliance
Hiding Behind Religion
Secrets Sins

> The voice of one crying in the wilderness:
> Prepare the way of the Lord,
>   make his paths straight.
> Every valley shall be filled,
>   and every mountain and hill shall be made low,
> and the crooked shall become straight,
>   and the rough places shall become level ways, *Snakes chased out*
> and all flesh shall see the salvation of God. (Luke 3:4–6; cf. Isa. 40:3–5)

The end of Self-Illusion

In the ancient world it was customary for kings to receive a royal welcome. So "when an emperor or some other eminent personage was about to visit a city, the citizens could be required to prepare a well-constructed

Self Reliance —> Hiding —> Secrets — Snakes

approach-road along which he could advance with due pomp and dignity on his way into the city."[5] To make sure that people were ready to receive him, the king would send a messenger on ahead to herald the news of his coming.

Isaiah took this custom and turned it into a prophecy. One day a great king would come to God's people, and when he did, his approach would be announced by a herald in the wilderness. To prepare for the coming of the king, the prophet envisioned a massive public works project, in which whole mountains would be leveled and valleys would be raised up. There would be a superhighway through the wasteland. And the king who walked on it would be the Lord God himself, bringing salvation. This is the way the prophecy begins and ends: "Prepare the way of the Lord . . . and all flesh shall see the salvation of God" (Luke 3:4, 6).

Luke took Isaiah's prophecy and said that it applied to the coming of Christ. Isaiah had prophesied "a voice" crying in the wilderness (see Isa. 40:3); Luke called it "*the* voice" (Luke 3:4) and said that it belonged to John the Baptist. John was the forerunner. He was the publicist, the advance man for the gospel. Mary, Zechariah, and Simeon had all celebrated God's salvation (see Luke 1:47; 1:69; 2:30). John announced that it was about to arrive in the person of his cousin Jesus Christ.

Soon everyone would see salvation. It is characteristic of Luke to point out the global reach of the gospel. Matthew and Mark also quoted from Isaiah (see Matt. 3:3; Mark 1:2–3), but only Luke included the promise that "all flesh shall see the salvation of God" (Luke 3:6; cf. Isa. 40:5). This does not mean "that God will save every single individual of the human race, even those who willfully reject him; such a doctrine runs counter to the basic teaching of the New Testament. Rather, it means that there is no kind of person the gospel cannot reach, no boundary it cannot cross. Luke is saying not that everyone will be saved, but that anyone can be saved."[6] And the way that people are saved is by trusting in the Savior whom God has sent to the world.

5. David Gooding, *According to Luke: A New Exposition of the Third Gospel* (Grand Rapids: Eerdmans, 1987), 73.

6. Michael Wilcock, *The Message of Luke*, The Bible Speaks Today (Downers Grove, IL: InterVarsity, 1979), 17.

Repent!

John's calling was to get people ready, to help them be prepared for the coming of Christ. But how were they supposed to get ready? What does it mean to "prepare the way of the Lord" or to "make his paths straight" (Luke 3:4)? According to John the Baptist, it means turning away from sin. Our lives are rocky and crooked, like the wilderness of Israel. Mountains of pride need to be broken down and valleys of self-pity need to be raised so that God can come in. Christ the King finds easy entrance to any heart that is sorry for sin. To put it another way, repentance is the on-ramp to salvation. If we want God to save us, we need to turn away from our sin.

John needed to say this because most people were looking for the wrong kind of Savior. In those days many Israelites were praying for the Messiah, but they were thinking primarily in political terms. They wanted someone to deal with Caesar, Herod, Pilate, and the rest of their Roman rulers. But God wanted to address their spiritual condition. He wanted to deal with their sin. So he sent John to help them get ready. This is what we always need: the spiritual preparation of the heart. We may want God to do many things for us, but first things first—we need to repent! The way to get ready for what God wants to do in our lives is to turn away from sin.

So John preached repentance. To be specific, he proclaimed "a baptism of repentance for the forgiveness of sins" (Luke 3:3). The order of this phrase is difficult to understand. Baptism, repentance, and forgiveness—which comes first? How are they related? Do we need to be baptized before God will forgive us, or was Josephus right when he said that John's baptism was a consecration of the body implying that the soul was already thoroughly cleansed by right behavior?[7] Answering these questions is made even more complicated by the fact that John's baptism is not the same as Christian baptism, which was introduced only after the resurrection.

David Gooding sees John's baptism as an expression of repentance. People were baptized as a sign of their sincere desire to turn away from sin.[8] Similarly, Norval Geldenhuys says that John "called the people to repentance and then baptized those who confessed their sins and gave

---

7. Flavius Josephus, *The Antiquities of the Jews* (18.5.2), in *The Works of Josephus*, trans. William Whiston (Peabody, MA: Hendrickson, 1987), 484.

8. Gooding, *Luke*, 72.

indications that they desired to lead a different and better life, in the assurance that God grants pardon to those who sincerely repent. So the baptism is the outward sign and seal that God has forgiven their sins."[9] At the very least, we can say that there is no forgiveness without repentance. The act of repentance does not have the power to take away our sin. Forgiveness comes only through Christ and his cross. But unless we repent we will never be forgiven, because only people who are sorry for their sins will ever admit they need a Savior.

We can also say that John's baptism was a sign of the forgiveness that God grants to penitent sinners. Somehow his baptism represented the taking away of sin. However, there were some people who wanted to take baptism a little farther. They wanted God to forgive their sins, but they weren't all that interested in giving them up. So they went to John for baptism, hoping that the water itself would take away their sin. This seems to be the context for John's warning, which may seem rather harsh: "He said therefore to the crowds that came out to be baptized by him, 'You brood of vipers! Who warned you to flee from the wrath to come?'" (Luke 3:7).

John said this because some of his groupies were phonies. They were insincere. They wanted to get baptized, but they really had no intention of leading a godly life. So John compared them to snakes slithering away from a fire. They wanted to get out of danger, but they still wanted to be snakes! Their nature was unchanged. They wanted to escape God's judgment, but they also wanted to keep living the way they had always lived. They wanted the outward sign of God's forgiveness without the inner transformation that repentance requires. They were hoping to be saved by their baptism, but they were unwilling to turn away from their sin.

This is a warning for us not to think that we can be saved by some outward action without the inner transformation of the Holy Spirit. Sometimes people pray "The Sinner's Prayer" or go forward at an evangelistic rally because they are afraid of hell, yet they never really make a commitment to live the Christian life. Understand that simply praying or going forward will not save anyone: we need to turn our whole lives over to Christ. We should not even presume upon our baptism. Baptism is a sign of God's grace. It assures us that our sins are forgiven in Christ. But we are not saved

9. Geldenhuys, *Luke*, 136.

by the water of baptism; we are saved by the sacrifice that Jesus offered on the cross for our sins. The way we receive his salvation is by faith, with repentance, and not merely through baptism.

One of the best ways to tell if we really are trusting in Christ for our salvation is to examine our behavior. John said, "Bear fruits in keeping with repentance" (Luke 3:8). This is God's standard. If we are truly sorry for our sins, then we will show it by the way that we live. We will lead a baptized life—a life consecrated to God. If we are not living righteously, then it is clear that we have not really repented, even if we have been baptized. Repentance means turning away from sin.

Do Not Delay

Some people count on baptism to save them; they think they will be saved by receiving the sacrament. Others depend on their religious connections; they think they will be saved because of who they are. This was especially tempting for the Jews of John's day because they were direct descendants of Abraham, the man who had the promise of the everlasting covenant. But John said: "Do not begin to say to yourselves, 'We have Abraham as our father.' For I tell you, God is able from these stones to raise up children for Abraham" (Luke 3:8).

John was warning people not to presume upon their identity as Israelites. Some of them had a spiritual pride that was based on their ethnic identity. In effect, they were perverting the doctrine of election. They thought that belonging to the covenant community meant never having to say that they were sorry. But this was a false confidence. That they were children of Abraham did not mean that they would be saved automatically. They still needed to repent; otherwise, they would fall under the wrath of God, whether they were Jews or not. The only true children of Abraham are those who turn away from sin.

John's baptism demonstrated this in a powerful way. In those days baptism was only for Gentiles.[10] When Gentiles came to faith in the God of Israel, they went through a ritual cleansing. This baptism meant that they were no longer unclean; now they belonged to the covenant community.

10. Geldenhuys, *Luke*, 144.

But no one ever baptized any Jews. This was not considered necessary: they were already clean because they belonged to God's people. So when John invited his fellow Jews to go back out into the wilderness to be baptized, he was saying that it was not enough for them to be Jewish. Simply belonging to Israel did not make them right with God. They too were unclean; their sins needed to be washed away. They needed to come to God in penitent faith and receive a baptism of repentance for the forgiveness of sins.

The application is obvious: we cannot be saved by our religious connections. Coming from a Christian family will not save us. Belonging to a particular ecclesiastical denomination or to some evangelical institution will not save us. It is not enough to be in the right family or the right church; we need to be in a right relationship with God. We are not saved by who we are, but by who God is, and by what he has done for us in Jesus Christ.

Some people trust their baptism to save them; others count on their religious connections; and still others decide to delay the matter of salvation altogether. They want their sins to be forgiven, but they are not quite ready to give them up. They expect to come back to God eventually, but first they want to have some fun. They want a little more time to party, a little more time to make some money, a little more time to pursue their interests, a little more time to gratify their sinful desires. They say that they will get more religious after they graduate, or when they get married, or once they have kids, or as soon as they retire. It is never now; it is always later.

There were people like that in John's day too, but John warned them not to wait any longer. It was too risky! He said, "Even now the axe is laid to the root of the trees. Every tree therefore that does not bear good fruit is cut down and thrown into the fire" (Luke 3:9). Judgment was coming soon—so soon, in fact, that the axe of divine wrath was ready to strike. Who would be cut down? People who were not bearing fruit, who did not show repentance in the way that they lived. What would happen to them? They would be thrown straight into the fires of hell.

Of all the reasons to repent, this is the most serious. God has said that one day he will reveal his wrath against every sinner who does not turn away from sin. He has also said that the day of judgment is coming soon. So why wait any longer? Why take the chance? Anyone who has not yet turned to God had better do it as soon as possible. Do not delay! You will never have a better opportunity than you have right now to turn away from sin and trust in Jesus Christ.

MY KIND OF SINNER

John the Baptist preached repentance with such urgency that people were desperate to know how to escape the fire of God's judgment: "And the crowds asked him, 'What shall we do?'" (Luke 3:10). They knew that they were not living the way that God wanted them to live, and they were ready to do something about it, but they were not quite sure what they were supposed to do.

John answered by giving specific instructions for practical repentance. True repentance means much more than feeling sorry for what we have done. It means turning away from sin and living in obedience to God. What this requires of each person will be a little different. We all sin in different ways, so we all need to turn away from different sins. Luke gives three examples (his is the only Gospel to do this). No doubt John the Baptist gave people many other ways to repent (see Luke 3:18), but these are representative of his teaching. They show us how he applied God's Word to daily life, and thus they help us begin to see what repentance would look like in our own lives.

The first example was for everyone: "Whoever has two tunics is to share with him who has none, and whoever has food is to do likewise" (Luke 3:11). John knew that many of his listeners were stingy. They did not have the grace of generosity. They liked keeping things for themselves. The way for them to repent was to give away their possessions. It was fine for them to wear their own clothes, of course. Everyone needs clothing. But if they had more than enough—if they had an inner tunic as well as an outer tunic— then they needed to give it up for someone who had nothing to wear at all. They needed to do the same thing with their food, which is another basic necessity. If they had enough to eat, they needed to feed the hungry.

John was saying these things to people who did not have very much to begin with. Some of them had only one tunic to spare. Yet in their hearts they were guilty of greed. The way for them to repent was not simply to admit that they were selfish at heart, but to start giving as much as they could to the poor and needy.

123

Some of John's listeners were a little wealthier—a lot wealthier, in fact. These were the notorious taxmen who collected revenue from their fellow Jews and then passed it on to the Romans. Taxation was privatized in the Roman Empire, and by charging more than the Roman rate, tax collectors often lined their own pockets in the process. Their countrymen regarded them as traitors and thieves, and rightly so. Yet some of them "also came to be baptized and said to him, 'Teacher, what shall we do?' And he said to them, 'Collect no more than you are authorized to do.'" (Luke 3:12–13). John did not tell these crooked tax collectors to find a different line of work; he told them to do their jobs fairly and justly.

He gave similar counsel to a third group of men: "Soldiers also asked him, 'And we, what shall we do?' And he said to them, 'Do not extort money from anyone by threats or by false accusation, and be content with your wages'" (Luke 3:14). Like tax collectors, soldiers often took advantage of their position. Because of their superior authority and weaponry, they had ways of making people give them money. This was tempting in those days because soldiers were not very well paid. It was the perfect recipe for the abuse of power. But some of these military men were ready to repent. John did not tell them that they had to lay down their weapons and leave the army; the military is an honorable occupation. The issue was what kind of soldiers they ought to be. They needed to use their authority properly. They also needed to be content with their pay. Here was a deeper repentance that went to the inward attitudes of the heart. John told these soldiers to be satisfied with what God provided.

What is noteworthy about these three examples is that they all have to do with social justice. Fred Craddock summarizes by saying, "Food and clothing are to be shared with people who have none; taxes are not to be calculated according to the greed of the people who are in power; and the military must stop victimizing the poor people under their occupation by constant threats, intimidation, and blackmail."[11] Or to put it another way, all of these examples have to do with money. Money has great spiritual power, both for evil and for good. What we do with our wealth reveals our true priorities. Are we living for ourselves or for others? Our budgets and bank accounts are leading indicators of our spiritual health.

11. Fred B. Craddock, *Luke*, Interpretation (Louisville: John Knox, 1990), 48–49.

If you have more than you need, start giving it away. If you are in business and you are taking more than you have a right to take, start treating people fairly. If you are not getting what you think you deserve, stop complaining about it and stop scheming to get more. This is what it means to repent. It means being content with what God has given us. It means not taking advantage of people for personal gain. And it means sharing with people who are in greater need.

But don't stop there! These examples teach us that every situation in life has its own typical temptations, its own dominating forms of depravity. Office workers are tempted to grumble. Laborers are tempted to cut corners. Businessmen are tempted to be greedy. Scholars and musicians are tempted to be arrogant. Teachers are tempted to be impatient. Children are tempted to rebel against their parents. Men are tempted to use pornography and angrily abuse their authority. Women are tempted to gossip and use their words to manipulate people. People who have been wronged are tempted to become bitter. People who suffer are tempted to self-pity. And even these are only examples. The point is that God calls every one of us to repent of our own personal sins.

What kind of sinner are you? What is your spiritual struggle? Whatever kind of sinner you are, you need to repent. You need to turn away from your sins. And there is something else you must do: believe in Jesus Christ for salvation. When people asked John what to do about their sins, he told them to repent. But that was before Jesus died on the cross for sinners and was raised again with the power of eternal life. Now when we ask what we should do about our sins, we get the answer that Peter gave when he first preached the gospel. Peter did more than simply say "Repent!" the way that John did (although of course he did tell people to repent). And he did more than simply baptize people, too (although he did baptize them). Peter also called people to faith in Christ. He said, "Repent and be baptized every one of you *in the name of Jesus Christ* for the forgiveness of your sins" (Acts 2:38). Jesus is coming soon to judge the world. The way to prepare for his coming is to repent and believe his gospel.

11

THE BAPTISM OF THE SON

Luke 3:15–22

*Now when all the people were baptized, and when Jesus also
had been baptized and was praying, the heavens were opened,
and the Holy Spirit descended on him in bodily form, like a
dove; and a voice came from heaven, "You are my beloved Son;
with you I am well pleased." (Luke 3:21–22)*

According to Luke, the gospel of Jesus Christ begins with the
ministry of John the Baptist. If this seems surprising, it helps
to know that in those days John was a nationally recognized
figure. People all over Israel were talking about John's unusual lifestyle,
confrontational message, and cleansing baptism. Thus it made sense for
Luke to introduce Jesus by way of his cousin John.

John was so famous that some people wondered whether he might
even be the Messiah. They were all waiting for the Savior whom God had
promised to send. Who would be the Christ? When John arrived on the
scene, he was the best candidate anyone had ever seen. Speculation was
rampant. Could it be? Was it possible? Had God finally come to redeem
his people? If they had studied the Scriptures more carefully, they would
have realized that someone else had to come first—the Messiah's messen-

ger. But still, we can understand why "the people were in expectation, and all were questioning in their hearts concerning John, whether he might be the Christ" (Luke 3:15).

John's Rebuttal

John was not the Christ. So as soon as he heard people starting to say that he was, he "answered them all, saying, 'I baptize you with water, but he who is mightier than I is coming, the strap of whose sandals I am not worthy to untie. He will baptize you with the Holy Spirit and with fire. His winnowing fork is in his hand, to clear his threshing floor and to gather the wheat into his barn, but the chaff he will burn with unquenchable fire'" (Luke 3:16–17).

Whether he knew it yet or not (and he does not mention him by name), John was speaking about Jesus. We will see what John was saying about Jesus in a moment, but first consider the simple fact that he was speaking about Jesus, and not about himself. John was at the height of his popularity—the most successful preacher in Israel. People were flocking to him in the desert and asking him to be their Savior. But John would hear none of it. He cared nothing for the opinions of men. The only thing that mattered to him was pointing people to Christ.

This is the hallmark of authentic Christianity: to exalt the person and work of Jesus Christ. J. C. Ryle wrote that a faithful preacher "will never allow anything to be credited to him, or his office, which belongs to his divine Master. . . . To commend Christ dying, and rising again for the ungodly—to make known Christ's love and power to save sinners—this will be the main object of his ministry. . . . He will be content that his own name be forgotten, so long as Christ crucified is exalted."[1] Being Christ-centered is not just for ministers, however; it ought to be true of everyone who knows Jesus Christ as Savior and Lord. The whole direction of a truly Christian life is to make more of Jesus, and less of ourselves.

John the Baptist is the perfect example. His calling was to prepare people for the coming of Christ. Once he had done that, John all but disappeared from the scene. From this point forward, John will decrease so that Jesus

---

1. J. C. Ryle, *Expository Thoughts on the Gospels, Luke* (1858; reprint Cambridge: James Clarke, 1976), 1:95–96.

can increase (see John 3:30), to the glory of God. However, people still want to know what happened to John, so Luke briefly told the rest of his story: "So with many other exhortations he preached good news to the people. But Herod the tetrarch, who had been reproved by him for Herodias, his brother's wife, and for all the evil things that Herod had done, added this to them all, that he locked up John in prison" (Luke 3:18–20).

From this we learn that Luke knew more about John's ministry, but told us only enough to help us believe in Jesus. We also learn how costly it can be to live for Christ. John was a godly man who faithfully proclaimed God's Word. He even confronted Herod for his scandalous sin. Herod had divorced his wife in order to marry his sister-in-law, ruining two marriages and committing adultery in the process. Herod was a wicked man, and for preaching against him, John was thrown into prison and eventually murdered (see Luke 9:7–9). This hardly seems fair. Yet it was God's plan for John's life. Like the rest of the men who prophesied the coming of Christ, he was called to suffer persecution for the sake of God's name.

People who proclaim Christ are often called to suffer. Sometimes our only reward in this life is to be rejected, as John was. But we will have God's blessing in the end, for Jesus has promised to honor those who honor him.

A Worthier Man

The way John the Baptist honored Jesus was by telling people how great he was. The people wanted to talk about how great *John* was, but John responded by declaring the one true Christ to be much greater. He is greater in three ways: he is a worthier man; he performs a holier baptism; and he is a higher being—the only Son of God.

John makes his argument for the superiority of the Christ by way of comparison. He said to people, "Look, you think you're impressed with me, but wait until you see the Christ. Then you will know what true greatness really is." John said it like this: "he who is mightier than I is coming, the strap of whose sandals I am not worthy to untie" (Luke 3:16). We will see some of the mighty things that Christ does in a moment. But consider the worthiness of his person—his superiority. The Christ deserves such great honor that John is not even worthy to untie his shoes.

In those days it was customary for students to follow their teachers. They generally did not pay tuition, but they did show their devotion by performing menial acts of service. A great teacher hardly had to lift a finger. His students did everything for him—everything, that is, except unlace his sandals. According to one ancient rabbi, "Every service which a slave performs for his master shall a disciple do for his teacher except the loosing of his sandal-thong."[2] That would be going too far. Unlacing someone's sandals was so degrading that a student could not be compelled to do it.

But John the Baptist wasn't even worthy to do that! He was unworthy to unlace the sandals of the immensely and immeasurably worthy Christ. By comparison, he was not just the lowest of the low; he was even lower. The people wondered whether John might be the Christ, but John told them that he didn't even deserve to be his slave.

John said this to show the superiority of Jesus Christ, who is the worthiest of all men. He is so worthy of honor and worship that even the greatest man on earth is unworthy to serve as his slave. How amazing it is, therefore, that God has called us to be the servants of Christ. We are not worthy for his service, except by God's grace. Therefore, everything we do in the name of Christ—all our worship, teaching, witness, and service—should be done in humble gratitude. The opportunity to do anything at all for Jesus is a high privilege that we are given only by the grace of God.

Then consider something even more amazing: this worthy Christ has become *our* servant! Remember how Jesus unlaced his disciples' sandals to wash their feet (John 13:1–20). This was such a menial task that Peter told Jesus not to touch him. But Jesus insisted. It was a stunning reversal. Jesus is so worthy that he would have done his disciples an honor by asking them to wash his feet. Instead, he washed *their* feet. He did this to prepare for offering them the supreme service, the most degrading duty of all: dying for their sins on the cross. See how worthy Jesus is, see how unworthy you are, and see how gracious God is to save you into his service.

2. Herman L. Strack and Paul Billerbeck, *Kommentar zum neuen Testament aus Talmud und Midrasch*, 4 vols. (1:121), quoted in Leon Morris, *The Gospel According to St. Luke: An Introduction and Commentary*, Tyndale New Testament Commentaries (Grand Rapids: Eerdmans, 1974), 97.

A HOLIER BAPTISM

John identified Christ as a worthier person. Then he explained that Christ would do a mightier work through a holier baptism: "He will baptize you with the Holy Spirit and with fire" (Luke 3:16). Remember the context. John was giving people "a baptism of repentance for the forgiveness of sins" (Luke 3:3). This baptism was the hallmark of his ministry. People came to John to be baptized, which is why they called him "John the Baptist." But even in his most effective area of ministry—namely, baptism—John was inferior to Christ, who would come with a holier baptism.

We can see the difference by comparing the mode of these two baptisms. John baptized people with water at the Jordan River. His baptism was the outward sign of an inward cleansing. But when Christ came, he would baptize people with the Holy Spirit and with fire. This went far beyond anything that John could do. John could call people to repentance, and he could wash them with water, but he could not change them from the inside out. Only someone as mighty as God could do that. Here is how David Gooding explains the difference: "John could put repentant people in water; in a sense, anybody could. Only One who was God could put people in the Holy Spirit, or the Holy Spirit in people."[3]

What does it mean to baptize people with the Holy Spirit? Of course, Christians are still baptized with water. But this water baptism is an outward sign of an inward reality: the Spirit's work in a sinner's life. The Spirit regenerates, giving us new spiritual vitality. The Spirit adopts, claiming us as the children of God. The Spirit sanctifies, making us holy like Christ. The Spirit seals, preserving our faith to the end. The Spirit fills, equipping us for ministry. This is why the baptism of Jesus Christ is a holier baptism: it is baptism with the Holy Spirit.

Have you experienced this baptism? Every believer does, because it is the Holy Spirit who makes a Christian a Christian. Our baptism comes from Jesus Christ, who has the power and authority to send us the Spirit. And this shows the superiority of Christ. Whereas John baptized with water, Jesus baptizes with God the Holy Spirit. This reminds us that only God can do the inward work of salvation that leads to eternal life. We can share the

3. David Gooding, *According to Luke: A New Exposition of the Third Gospel* (Grand Rapids: Eerdmans, 1987), 76.

gospel, preach the Word, and reach out in practical deeds of mercy. We can even baptize people with water. We can do all the outward things, but only God can do the inward things, like change a sinner's heart. He does this by the Spirit of Christ, which shows how great Christ is.

John also said that Christ would baptize with fire. This may be another way of talking about the Holy Spirit. In the book of Acts, which is the sequel to this Gospel, Luke tells us that on the day of Pentecost "suddenly there came from heaven a sound like a mighty rushing wind, and it filled the entire house where they were sitting. And divided tongues as of fire appeared to them and rested on each one of them. And they were all filled with the Holy Spirit" (Acts 2:2–4). When Christ sent his Spirit on the church, he came with flaming fire. It was a visible manifestation of the invisible God.

But fire also refers to divine judgment, as John makes clear in the following verse: "His winnowing fork is in his hand, to clear his threshing floor and to gather the wheat into his barn, but the chaff he will burn with unquenchable fire" (Luke 3:17). This familiar image—which appears both in Psalm 1 and in the teaching of Jesus (e.g., Matt. 13:24–30)—comes from the farm. At harvesttime, a farmer has to separate the wheat from the chaff. In those days farmers did this by tossing their grain up in the air. The wheat would fall back to the ground, while the lighter chaff would get blown into a pile for burning.

John was saying that Christ would do the same thing with the human race. One day he would sift humanity to make a final separation between two kinds of people: the wheat and the chaff. The wheat would be gathered into the storehouse of heaven, while the chaff would be burned with fire. The reference to "unquenchable" fire makes it clear that John was talking about the wrath of God at the final judgment—everlasting punishment in the eternal fire of hell (see Matt. 25:41, 46). Here is how J. C. Ryle has described the great day of judgment:

> Believers and unbelievers, holy and unholy, converted and unconverted, are now mingled in every congregation, and often sit side by side. It passes the power of man to separate them. False profession is often so like true, and grace is often so weak and feeble, that, in many cases, the right discernment of character is an impossibility. The wheat and the chaff will continue together until the Lord returns. But there will be an awful separation at the last day. The unerring judgment of the King of kings shall at length divide

the wheat from the chaff, and divide them for evermore. The righteous shall be gathered into a place of happiness and safety. The wicked shall be cast down to shame and everlasting contempt. In the great sifting day, every one shall go to his own place.[4]

John described this separation as a fiery baptism. He also said that this baptism was coming soon. Christ already had the tools of harvest in hand. This is a stern reminder not to delay repentance. Christ is coming. The time to get right with God is now, while there is still time, and not later, when it might be too late.

John's purpose in saying this was to show how great Christ is—much greater than any mortal man. John could call people to repent, but Christ could actually hold them to account. He is the Judge as well as the Savior, and as such, he holds the power of judgment by fire—the holiest baptism of all. Norval Geldenhuys comments: "Just as fire consumes what is destructible and thus works in a purifying and cleansing manner, so the Messiah will through the Holy Ghost consume sin and the sinners in so far as they cling to sin. In this way those who persist in sin will be destroyed, but those who sincerely confess their sins and flee to Him for refuge will be purified from sin to their own salvation, and delivered from its penalty and power."[5]

This was John's witness, and also his warning: when Christ came, he would baptize people with fire. The word that Luke used to describe John's message may seem rather surprising. Luke calls John's preaching "good news" (Luke 3:18), which is another way of calling it the gospel. But how can judgment by fire be good news? It is good news because when we know the truth about God's wrath we will start looking for a way to escape. And this will lead us to believe in Jesus Christ and receive the baptism of his Spirit—the free gift of eternal life.

STRANGE BAPTISM

When people started asking John if he might be the Messiah, he responded by showing them the superior greatness of Christ. He built his

---

4. Ryle, *Luke*, 1:97–98.
5. Norval Geldenhuys, *The Gospel of Luke*, New International Commentary on the New Testament (Grand Rapids: Eerdmans, 1951), 140.

case by identifying the Christ as a worthier man, who would perform a holier baptism. But then something happened that exalted the true greatness of Christ infinitely higher, proving his supremacy as the very Son of God. Christ is not simply a worthier man; he is a higher being, for "when all the people were baptized, and when Jesus also had been baptized and was praying, the heavens were opened, and the Holy Spirit descended on him in bodily form, like a dove; and a voice came from heaven, 'You are my beloved Son; with you I am well pleased'" (Luke 3:21–22).

This was the second baptism of the Son. The first was the baptism he gives—a baptism with fire and the Spirit. But the second is the baptism he received—a baptism by the Spirit from the Father declaring him to be the absolute Son of God. But why did Jesus even need to be baptized? This is a real puzzle. It hardly seems appropriate. John was baptizing people into repentance for the forgiveness of sins. However, Jesus was no sinner, and therefore he needed neither to repent nor to be forgiven. So why was he baptized? We know from the Gospel of Matthew that John himself had the same question. When Jesus came for baptism, "John would have prevented him, saying, 'I need to be baptized by you, and do you come to me?'" (Matt. 3:14).

Obviously, Jesus did not need to be baptized for the forgiveness of his own sins. Nevertheless, he was baptized. He did not have to do this, but he chose to. He made a deliberate decision to join with sinners in baptism for the forgiveness of their sins. The baptism of Jesus was different from all the others. Luke hints at this in the way he describes it: "Now when all the people were baptized, and when Jesus also had been baptized" (Luke 3:21). Luke is drawing a distinction. All the people were baptized, but then Jesus was also baptized, and somehow his baptism fell into a different category. The difference was that Jesus did not have to be baptized for his own sins. Rather, he was identifying with sinners in *their* need of forgiveness.

This was an act of solidarity. Jesus was taking the place of sinners. So already at the beginning of his public ministry, we are reminded of the ancient prophecy that he would be "numbered with the transgressors" (Isa. 53:12). If we are amazed to see him baptized, we are all the more amazed to see him crucified. The choice that Jesus made at his baptism was the choice that ultimately led him to the cross. He was willing to be reckoned as a sinner so that sinners could be saved. And so he was baptized.

Luke was less interested in the baptism itself—he does not even describe it, in fact, or the person who performed it—than he was in what happened afterward. What attracted Luke's attention was the revelation of God in his triune being. All three persons of the Trinity were present at this baptism: Father, Son, and Holy Spirit.

Whenever God does anything important—which of course includes everything he has ever done—it is the work of the entire Trinity. Here we see trinitarian cooperation in action. God the Son, the Second Person of the Trinity, was praying. God the Holy Spirit, the Third Person of the Trinity, descended from heaven. And God the Father, the First Person of the Trinity, pronounced his benediction on the Son. The Son prayed, the Spirit descended, and the Father spoke.

THE DESCENT OF THE DOVE

It would be marvelous to know what the Son was praying. In Luke we often find Jesus at prayer, but we rarely know what he prayed. Maybe he was asking the Father to confirm his status as the Son. Maybe he was asking the Spirit to anoint him for ministry. Or maybe he was simply enjoying fellowship with the Father and the Spirit, reveling in the sweet communion that all three persons of the Trinity share within the Godhead.

All we know for certain is how his prayers were answered. As Jesus prayed, the Spirit of God and the Word of God came down from heaven. First, Luke says, "the heavens were opened" (Luke 3:21). This was true in a literal sense. The clouds were parted, the skies sundered by the hand of God. But this phrase also refers to divine revelation. Whenever the Bible says that the heavens were opened, it means that the God of heaven revealed himself to his people on earth. As we read this Scripture—or any Scripture—the heavens are also opened for us. Whatever we read in the Bible is a direct revelation from the living God.

As heaven opened, the Holy Spirit descended in the form of a dove. Again, Luke makes it clear that he was speaking literally. The Spirit came down in bodily form. This was a public event, not a private experience. It was not something that Jesus felt somewhere in his own consciousness; it was an objective reality. The other Gospels tell us that Jesus and John both saw the Holy Spirit come down like a dove (see Matt.

3:16 and John 1:32). Presumably other people saw this as well. It was a *theophany*—a visible appearance of God's invisible Spirit.

This was a new image for the Holy Spirit. It was the first time that the Spirit had manifested himself as a dove. Why did he come down this way? What was the meaning of this sign? Perhaps the dove symbolized purity and peace, or innocence and beauty—all things that are commonly attributed to the dove. The Puritan Thomas Goodwin pointed instead to the bird's faithfulness and gentleness. "For a dove," wrote Goodwin, "is the most meek and the most innocent of all birds; without gall, without talons, having no fierceness in it, expressing nothing but love and friendship to its mate in all its carriages, and mourning over its mate in all its distresses. And accordingly, a dove was a most fit emblem of the Spirit that was poured out upon our Saviour when He was just about to enter on the work of our salvation. For as sweetly as doves do converse with doves, so may every sinner and Christ converse together."[6] One way or another, the dove communicates something about the person and work of the Holy Spirit. But what may be more important is the simple fact that the Spirit descended on the Son.

This does not mean that Jesus did not yet have the Spirit. We know that he did. He was conceived by the Spirit's power (Luke 1:35) and filled with the Spirit's wisdom (Luke 2:40). But at his baptism the Spirit made a public declaration that he was with Jesus for ministry. We see the implications of this all the way through the Gospels. It was by the power of the Holy Spirit that Jesus resisted temptation (Luke 4:1), preached the kingdom of God (Luke 4:14, 18), worshiped his Father in heaven (Luke 10:21), and performed mighty miracles (Matt. 12:28). It was also by the Spirit that he offered his body on the cross for our sins (Heb. 9:14) and was raised to give us eternal life (Rom. 1:4). Even for all his dignity, Jesus did not do all these things alone and independently, by his own intrinsic power, but dependently, by the power of the Holy Spirit. This was publicly validated at his baptism in the descent of the dove, and it was subsequently demonstrated in his miraculous ministry. As Luke was later to write, "God anointed Jesus of Nazareth with the Holy Spirit and with power. He went about doing good and healing all who were oppressed by the devil, for God was with him" (Acts 10:38).

6. Thomas Goodwin, quoted in R. Kent Hughes, *Luke: That You May Know the Truth*, 2 vols., Preaching the Word (Wheaton, IL: Crossway, 1998), 1:125.

The same glorious Spirit has also descended on us. As we have seen, Christ gives the Spirit—a superior baptism to the one administered by John. The Spirit Jesus gives is the same mighty Spirit that was with him for ministry, working miracles and blessing his teaching. Now we serve Jesus in the power of the same Spirit, trusting him to make our words and deeds effective in bringing people to Christ and helping them grow in the knowledge of God.

OF THE FATHER'S LOVE BEGOTTEN

Then the Father spoke his word of blessing. This is the climax of the passage—the exaltation of the Christ as the only Son of God. Luke shows that this is the climax by making the speaking of God's voice in verse 22 the main verb. The most important thing in this passage is what the Father said about the Son. Everything else is subordinate to his declaration: "You are my beloved Son; with you I am well pleased" (Luke 3:22). God said this in an audible voice so that people could hear what he was saying. He wanted everyone to know that Jesus Christ is his eternal Son—the mightiest one of all.

The Father used two words to describe his relationship to the Son—a word of affection and a word of approval. The word of affection is "beloved." The Son is beloved by the Father, and this is their eternal relationship. The Greek word for "beloved" (*agapētos*) generally means what it says: "beloved." However, when it is applied to a son or a daughter, it also means "only."[7] So the Father was declaring Jesus to be his Son in a unique sense: he is God the eternal Son, the only begotten of the Father. This is what the Father loves to declare, that the Son is the Son—his Son, the Son that he loves.

This expression of the Father's love for the Son rings with echoes from the Old Testament. It sounds similar to the way God spoke about Isaac, Abraham's only son by God's promise (see Gen. 22:2, 12, 16). It also echoes God's declaration to Israel's king, and ultimately to Israel's Messiah: "You are my Son; today I have begotten you" (Ps. 2:7). Then there is Isaiah's prophecy: "Behold my servant, whom I uphold, my chosen, in whom my soul delights" (Isa. 42:1). These deep biblical connections are suggestive.

---

7. I. Howard Marshall, *The Gospel of Luke*, New International Greek Testament Commentary (Grand Rapids: Eerdmans, 1978), 156.

They speak to Christ's sovereignty and servanthood, identifying him as God's royal Son and the Suffering Servant who brings salvation.

There is something special about a father's affection for his son. I will always remember the way that I looked at my son when he was a small boy. Until I became a father, I had never realized how beautiful a boy could be. But once I became a father, I would look at the boy sitting on my lap and I would say in my heart, "You are my beloved son."

God the Father said to Jesus Christ: "You are my beloved Son" (Luke 3:22). This does not mean that Jesus was not the Son before this point. On the contrary, his sonship is eternal. The Father was not performing some new act of adoption, but simply declaring on earth what had always been true in heaven. John the Baptist knew something of the worthiness of Christ, and of the holiness of his baptism. But only the Father could declare Jesus to be the one and only eternal Son of his love.

This is the paternal affection at the heart of the Godhead. In his eternal sonship, the Son of God is loved by the Father. Here is a great mystery. What can it mean for God to be loved by God? Within the inward relations of the Trinity we see the most perfect of all affections. The one who loves—in this case, the Father—loves with a perfect love. His affection knows no imperfection. And the one who is loved—in this case, the Son—is perfectly worthy to be loved. Thus there can be no more perfect love than the Father's love for his beloved Son within the Trinity.

With the Father's expression of affection came a word of approval: "with you I am well pleased" (Luke 3:22). There is always something special about a father's approval. Is anything more important for a son than to have his father's blessing, to know that his father approves of what he has done? One of the most significant experiences of my adolescence came at the end of one of the best basketball games I ever played. As time expired, my father rushed out onto the court to embrace me. I can still feel the sensation of my bare, sweaty arms against the scratchy fabric of his tweed sport coat. Every son longs to hear his father say, "I'm proud of you, son."

This is what God the Father said to God the Son: "with you I am well pleased" (Luke 3:22). Notice the wording: "with *you* I am well pleased." It was the very person of the Son that pleased the Father. He was pleasing to the Father just because he was the Son. But the Father was also pleased with the Son's obedience. By submitting to baptism, Jesus was choosing to take the part of sinful humanity. He was agreeing to carry out the great task that the Father had given him: to suffer and to die for sinners. And so the Father blessed him.

The smile of fatherly approval rested on Jesus all the days of his life. As the Son did the work of our salvation, the Father was pleased with everything he did. He was pleased with his obedience to his parents. He was pleased with his resistance to temptation. He was pleased with his teaching and his miraculous deeds of mercy. He was pleased with his life of prayer. He was pleased most of all with the sinless sacrifice that he offered on the cross. We know this because he raised Jesus from the dead, which was the ultimate proof of his approval. The Father was pleased with all of it. He was pleased with what Jesus had done, what Jesus was doing, and what Jesus would do. He took pleasure in the person and work of his Son.

The good news of the gospel is that if you believe in Jesus Christ for your salvation, then God is just as pleased with you. The Father's words of affection and approval are for his Son *and* for everyone who has faith in his Son. Jesus came to bring us into the Father's love. The things that we do are not pleasing to God. If we had to stand before God the Father on our own merit, we would never gain his approval, and we would never deserve his affection. But we do not stand before him on our own merit. As soon as we trust in Jesus Christ for our salvation, we stand before the Father on the merit of his Son. Now God the Father looks on us with the same affection and approval that he has for Jesus Christ, his worthy Son.

This is our hope when we are lonely, or needy, or fearful, or anxious, or burdened by the great weight of our sin. It is our joy when we feel that no one has ever really loved us the way that we long to be loved. No matter who we are or what we have done, God is not unloving or disapproving, but says to every one of his children, "You are my beloved; with you I am well pleased."

12

SON OF GOD, SON OF MAN

Luke 3:23—38

Jesus, when he began his ministry, was about thirty years of age,
being the son (as was supposed) of Joseph, the son of Heli, . . .
the son of Enos, the son of Seth, the son of Adam, the son of God.
(Luke 3:23, 38)

n her novel *The Poisonwood Bible*, Barbara Kingsolver describes an angry encounter between a Baptist missionary named Nathan Price and a tribal chieftain in the African Congo. The missionary has been growing impatient with the tribe's unwillingness to adopt the customs of Western Christianity. Finally, in exasperation, he accuses their chief of being childish and ignorant. But rather than responding in anger, the chief calmly answers the missionary by appealing to the wisdom of his ancient tribe:

"Ah, Tata Price," he said, in his deep, sighing voice. "You believe we are *mwana*, your children, who knew nothing until you came here. Tata Price, I am an old man who learned from other old men. I could tell you the name of the great chief who instructed my father, and all the ones before him, but you would have to know how to sit down and listen. There are one hundred twenty-two. Since the time of our *mankulu* we have made our laws without help from white men."[1]

The chief did not respond in anger because he was rooted in his family tree. He knew who he was. He knew who he was because he knew who his father was, and his father's father, all the way back for more than a hundred generations. By preserving the memory of his ancestors, he was connected to the past and its wisdom.

WHO WE ARE

This was also how the Jews of Jesus' day maintained their identity. They remembered who their fathers were, all the way back to the twelve original tribes of Israel. At first the names of their ancestors were passed down by oral tradition. Later they were written down for posterity, as in the many genealogies of the Old Testament. There were other records as well. The Jewish historian Josephus tells us that he was able to trace his genealogy by consulting public records. Similarly, the famous Rabbi Hillel—who lived during the time of Christ—used official registers to document his descent back to King David.[2] In those days, knowing someone meant knowing his family tree.

Luke wanted people to know who Jesus was. To that end, he recorded the Savior's genealogy in the ancient style:

Jesus, when he began his ministry, was about thirty years of age, being the son (as was supposed) of Joseph, the son of Heli, the son of Matthat, the son of Levi, the son of Melchi, the son of Jannai, the son of Joseph, the son of Mattathias, the son of Amos, the son of Nahum, the son of Esli, the son of Naggai, the son of Maath, the son of Mattathias, the son of Semein, the son of Josech, the son of Joda, the son of Joanan, the son of Rhesa, the son of Zerubbabel, the son of Shealtiel, the son of Neri, the son of Melchi, the son of Addi, the son of Cosam, the son of Elmadam, the son of Er, the son of Joshua, the son of Eliezer, the son of Jorim, the son of Matthat, the son of Levi, the son of Simeon, the son of Judah, the son of Joseph, the son of Jonam, the

1. Barbara Kingsolver, *The Poisonwood Bible* (New York: Faber and Faber, 1998), 378–79.
2. Norval Geldenhuys, *The Gospel of Luke*, New International Commentary on the New Testament (Grand Rapids: Eerdmans, 1951), 151.

son of Eliakim, the son of Melea, the son of Menna, the son of Mattatha, the son of Nathan, the son of David, the son of Jesse, the son of Obed, the son of Boaz, the son of Sala, the son of Nahshon, the son of Amminadab, the son of Admin, the son of Arni, the son of Hezron, the son of Perez, the son of Judah, the son of Jacob, the son of Isaac, the son of Abraham, the son of Terah, the son of Nahor, the son of Serug, the son of Reu, the son of Peleg, the son of Eber, the son of Shelah, the son of Cainan, the son of Arphaxad, the son of Shem, the son of Noah, the son of Lamech, the son of Methuselah, the son of Enoch, the son of Jared, the son of Mahalaleel, the son of Cainan, the son of Enos, the son of Seth, the son of Adam, the son of God. (Luke 3:23–38)

This genealogy teaches us many things about what it means to be a human being. Here we see the basic pattern of human existence. It all starts with childbirth, with a man fathering children and a woman bearing them out of her womb. Each new child has a name, his own identity. But we are all born into a common humanity, which Luke traces all the way back to the first man, Adam. We are all in this together.

Most of the names in Luke's genealogy are unfamiliar. Nearly half of them do not appear anywhere in the Old Testament. But these men were people like us, with the same kinds of ambitions that we have, the same joys and sorrows. They suffered the things that we suffer and celebrated the things that we celebrate.

They were also guilty of the same kinds of sins. All of these men were sinners. It is nice to think that our ancestors were noble and good, that they did something heroic. This is one of the reasons why people like to study their family trees. But whether they were heroic or not, the people who came before us were as deeply flawed as we are. We could infer this from the mere fact that they were human beings, but we could also prove it from the pages of the Bible. Consider some of the skeletons in this family closet, as recorded in the Old Testament. Terah was an idolater. Abraham was a liar. Jacob was a cheater and a thief. Judah traded slaves and consorted with prostitutes. David was a murderer and adulterer. We usually remember these men as heroes, but they were also scoundrels—all the way back to Adam, at the taproot of the family tree. Like any genealogy, the one in Luke's Gospel records a long line of sinners.

Because they sinned, they also died (except perhaps for Enoch; see Gen. 5:24). These men are no longer alive. They lived only a short time on earth.

141

One day they were young and full of life, dreaming about the future; but almost before they knew it, they were old and tired, longing for the good old days. Eventually even that grand old man Methuselah—who lived to be 969 (Gen. 5:27)—had to be buried. The wages of sin is death. Thus there is something tragic about a genealogy like this one. Like the rose on a thorn bush, each new generation flowers in beauty, but in the end it withers and dies. In these verses we see

> *what a frail and dying creature is man.* We read . . . a long list of names, containing the genealogy of the family in which our Lord was born, traced up through David and Abraham to Adam. How little we know of many of the seventy-five persons, whose names are here recorded! They all had their joys and sorrows, their hopes and fears, their cares and troubles, their schemes and plans, like any of ourselves. But they have all passed away from the earth, and gone to their own place. And so will it be with us. We too are passing away, and shall soon be gone.[3]

This is what it means to be a human being, and we need to face it: we are born, we live, we sin, and because we sin, we die. But we do not have to die without hope, because Jesus is in the genealogy. From the very beginning, God had promised to send this long and fallen line of sinners a Savior.

For all their struggles and failures, these men had the guaranteed promises of God. God promised Adam that he would crush his old enemy the devil (Gen. 3:15); this was the first promise of the gospel. God promised Abraham that he would become the father of many nations, and that through him all the nations of the earth would be blessed (Gen. 12:2–3). God made the same promise to Jacob: "in you and your offspring shall all the families of the earth be blessed" (Gen. 28:14). To Judah God promised an eternal kingdom (Gen. 49:10). This promise was repeated to David, the son of Jesse and the king of Israel (see 2 Sam. 7:12–16; Isa. 11:1). One day his son would reign on God's everlasting throne.

All this was more than any of these men deserved. In spite of their sin, God would bring salvation to and through their family line. Their legacy would be the Savior of the world. What hope this gives to anyone who

---

3. J. C. Ryle, *Expository Thoughts on the Gospels, Luke* (1858; reprint Cambridge: James Clarke, 1976), 1:104.

comes from a fallen family—and indeed, to any son or daughter of Adam! As he works out his plan of salvation, God is gracious to sinners.

Whose Genealogy Is It Anyway?

The promises that God made to Adam's family were all fulfilled in Jesus Christ. Luke has been introducing us to Jesus since the beginning of his Gospel, and by now his introduction is almost complete. However, we have not yet read the Savior's genealogy, and as a careful historian, Luke wanted to provide his full family background. He chose to do this at the outset of Christ's public ministry. Matthew put his genealogy at the beginning of his Gospel, in the context of Jesus' birth. But Luke waited until Jesus reached the age of full maturity, saying, "Jesus, when he began his ministry, was about thirty years of age" (Luke 3:23). Thirty was the age at which a Jewish man was ready to enter public life. Thus it was a natural place to confirm Jesus' identity by establishing his heredity. Before we learn what he did, we need to know who he is, which includes knowing his family background.

Knowing the family background was especially necessary in this case because Luke has just told us what the Father said after Jesus was baptized: "You are my beloved Son; with you I am well pleased" (Luke 3:22). This was a strong affirmation of the deity of Jesus Christ. Jesus is fully divine; he is God the eternal Son. But right at this point we need to be reminded that he is also fully human. This is the mystery of the incarnation, that Jesus has a human nature as well as a divine nature. "We accept the marvel," wrote the great Philadelphia Presbyterian Henry Boardman, "because God hath affirmed it; not because we can explain it."[4] One of the ways that Luke affirmed this great truth was by giving the human genealogy of Jesus Christ, going all the way back to Adam. This proved his true humanity. Jesus Christ was born into our race as a man among men.

Knowing this is part of knowing who Jesus is. Luke was writing the Gospel of knowing for sure, and this includes believing in the humanity of Jesus Christ. What better way to show this than by giving his family tree? We are inclined to skim through the biblical genealogies, when in fact they

4. Henry A. Boardman, *Earthly Suffering and Heavenly Glory: With Other Sermons* (Philadelphia: Lippincott, 1878), 353.

143

are a significant confirmation of the truth of the gospel. They testify that this is the authentic history of the true man Jesus Christ.

A good illustration of the way that the genealogy of Jesus helps to confirm the gospel comes from the missionary work of Wycliffe Bible Translators:

> When a Bible translator in Papua New Guinea started to translate Matthew's Gospel, he thought, "The last thing I want to do is bog these people down with a genealogy." So he began with chapter 2.
>
> But the day came when all the other chapters were done. He called together the men who were helping him, and they decided on the best way to say "begat." Then they proceeded with Matthew chapter one: ". . . Abraham begat Isaac. Isaac begat Jacob. Jacob begat . . ."
>
> By the time they completed about six of these "begats," the translator could sense the men were becoming excited.
>
> "Do you mean that these were real men?" they asked.
>
> "Yes," he answered. "They were real men."
>
> "That's what we do!" they added, referring to their custom of keeping track of genealogies. "We had thought that these were just white man's stories. Do you really mean that Abraham was a real man?"
>
> "Yes," the translator said, "that's what I've been telling you."
>
> "We didn't know that," they said, "but now we believe."
>
> That night they gathered the village together and said, "Listen to this!" Then they read the first chapter of Matthew. This chapter was the key for belief in the tribe.[5]

In order for Luke's genealogy to help us know who Jesus is, it has to be accurate. Here we encounter a well-known difficulty: the genealogies in Matthew and Luke are not identical. We can see this quickly and simply by comparing the two men who are listed as the grandfathers of Jesus Christ. Matthew tells us that his grandfather was Jacob, whereas Luke tells us that it was Heli. Of course, everyone has two grandfathers. However, both of these men are connected to Jesus' father Joseph, and thus they both appear to come from the same side of the family. Matthew identifies Jacob as "the father of Joseph the husband of Mary, of whom Jesus was born, who is

---

5. This story is recounted without attribution in a newsletter from Wycliffe Bible Translators, Orlando, 2000.

called Christ" (Matt. 1:16); but Luke says that Jesus was "the son (as was supposed) of Joseph, the son of Heli" (Luke 3:23).

This is not the only discrepancy between Matthew and Luke. Matthew starts with Abraham and carries the line forward to Jesus. Luke starts with Jesus and works his way backwards to Adam, which makes his list much longer. And although there are many places where the two genealogies overlap, nearly forty names are different, especially in the generations between David and Jesus. As a result, some scholars say that there must be some mistake. Yet, whenever we encounter an apparent contradiction in the Gospels, we should heed the advice of Francis Quarles, who wrote:

> When two Evangelists shall seem to vary
> In one discourse, they're diverse, not contrary;
> One truth doth guide them both, one spirit doth
> Direct them; doubt not, to believe them both.[6]

MARY'S SON

How do we reconcile Matthew with Luke? There are two main options. One is to say that both Matthew and Luke record the family tree of Joseph—who was Jesus' father as far as the law was concerned—but they do it in two different ways. This was the view held by the great New Testament scholar J. Gresham Machen, who wrote: "Matthew gives the *legal* descendants of David—the men who would have been legally the heir to the Davidic throne if that throne had continued—while Luke gives the descendants of David in that particular line to which, finally, Joseph, the husband of Mary, belonged."[7] In other words, Luke gives us the biological bloodline—what we would ordinarily think of as the genealogy. However, Matthew lists the rightful heirs to Israel's throne, establishing Jesus as the true king of Israel. This genealogy is different from the one in Luke because (as anyone who has studied world history will know) kings do not always have sons of their own, in which case the royal line passes to another man's son.

---

6. Francis Quarles, quoted in Robert Atwan and Laurance Wieder, eds., *Chapters into Verse: Poetry in English Inspired by the Bible*, vol. 2: *Gospels to Revelation* (Oxford: Oxford University Press, 1992), 7.

7. J. Gresham Machen, *The Virgin Birth of Christ*, 2nd ed. (London: James Clarke, 1958), 204.

In effect, Matthew and Luke were asking two different questions. Matthew started at the beginning and asked, "Who was the next king of Israel?" Luke began at the end and asked, "Who was this person's father?" Thus they ended up with two different genealogies. This is a reasonable solution, although it cannot be proven.

The alternative is to say that Luke recorded Mary's family tree instead of Joseph's. This would make sense because Luke has so much material about Mary (and probably from Mary) in his Gospel. It would also explain why his genealogy is so different from Matthew's. Jesus was descended from David through two different lines, one on each side of the family. In other words, Mary and Joseph were distant cousins. Matthew's genealogy is paternal; it traces the family line from David's son Solomon down through Joseph. Luke's genealogy is maternal; it traces the family line from David's son Nathan down through Mary. Thus Jesus had a double claim to David's throne. He was the true king of Israel both by legal succession and by blood.[8]

Since Luke was tracing Jesus' biological birthright, he had to do it through Mary. It must be admitted that he does not mention her by name. He simply refers to Jesus "being the son (as was supposed) of Joseph, the son of Heli" (Luke 3:23). However, this may be a roundabout way of referring to Mary. People *thought* that Jesus was the son of Joseph, but Luke has already told us that he was really the son of Mary by the Holy Spirit. Thus Luke could count on his readers to recognize that this was Mary's genealogy. If so, then Heli was Mary's father. Strangely enough, the Jewish Talmud confirms this by identifying her as Heli's daughter.[9]

So why does Luke call Joseph "the son of Heli"? There are at least two possible explanations. One is that Joseph had become Heli's son by adoption. This is not as unlikely as it may sound. If Mary did not have

---

8. This would also solve the old problem as to how Jesus could have descended from Jeconiah, who was cursed by God and denied the right to have his sons rule over Israel (see Jer. 22:30). Although Jeconiah appears in Matthew's genealogy, he does not appear in Luke's because (on this interpretation) he was not related to Jesus by blood. Jesus was not under Jeconiah's curse and thus could rightfully ascend to Israel's throne. See Donald Grey Barnhouse, *Man's Ruin: Exposition of Bible Doctrines, Taking the Epistle to the Romans as a Point of Departure*, vol. 1: *Romans 1:1–32* (Grand Rapids: Eerdmans, 1952), 45–47.

9. F. Godet, *A Commentary on the Gospel of St. Luke* (New York: I. K. Funk, 1881), 130.

any brothers, then it would have been customary for her father to adopt one of his sons-in-law to be his heir. So perhaps he adopted Joseph when the couple got married. This would make Heli Jesus' grandfather on his mother's side of the family, and in a sense also Joseph's father (note that the word "son" in the phrase "the son of Heli" can also mean "son-in-law"). Joseph's natural father was Jacob, but his adoptive father by marriage was Heli, and both men were grandfathers to Jesus Christ.

The other possibility is that Joseph was not Heli's son at all. The phrase "son of Heli" does not refer to Joseph, but skips Joseph and refers back to Jesus. Luke may have given us a subtle clue about this by omitting the definite article before Joseph's name.[10] All of Jesus' other ancestors are referred to as "the Heli," "the Matthat," and so on. Joseph is simply called "Joseph," not "the Joseph," which seems to separate him from the other names in Luke's genealogy. Thus the reference to Joseph is a parenthesis reminding us of the virgin birth, but as far as his genealogy was concerned, Jesus was the son of Heli. Technically, he was Heli's grandson, but in those days people used the word "son" in a general way to refer to any offspring. So Luke called Jesus the son of Heli; since he did not have a biological father, Heli was his closest male ancestor. Machen disagreed with this interpretation, but did an excellent job of explaining it: "Jesus was *supposed* to be the son of Joseph, but was really the son of Heli, etc. Heli would then be the father of Mary, and the word 'son' would be taken in the wider sense of 'descendant,' the name of the mother of Jesus being omitted because it was not customary for women to be included in a genealogy."[11]

All things considered, this seems to be the best solution. Matthew and Luke give us two different genealogies, one on his father's side, and one on his mother's side: "While both lines trace Christ to David, each is through a different son of David. Matthew traces Jesus through Joseph (his *legal father*) to David's son, *Solomon* the king, by whom Christ rightfully inherited the throne of David. Luke's purpose, on the other hand, is to show Christ as an actual human. So he traces Christ to David's son, *Nathan*,

---

10. This exegesis comes from Godet, who still provides the best and fullest defense of the view that the genealogy in Luke belongs to Mary.

11. Machen, *Virgin Birth*, 203.

through his *actual mother*, Mary, through whom He can rightfully claim to be fully human, the redeemer of humanity."[12]

THE SAVIOR OF US ALL

This brings us back to Luke's purpose in providing a genealogy, which was to prove the common humanity of Jesus Christ. We know that Jesus is divine. We know this because the Father declared him to be the only beloved Son. We are also reminded of it at the beginning of Luke's genealogy, when he says that Jesus was "supposed" to be the son of Joseph (Luke 3:23). In other words, people thought that he was the son of Joseph, but we know better, because Luke has told us the full story. We know that Jesus Christ was conceived by the Holy Spirit in the womb of the virgin Mary. We know that he is fully God.

We also need to know that Jesus Christ is fully human. Luke has already revealed him as "the Son of the Most High" (Luke 1:32), "the Son of God" (Luke 1:35), the only beloved Son of the Father (Luke 3:22). Now he tells us that the Son of God is also a son of man. He is fully human as well as fully divine. What better way to show this than to trace his connection to the human race all the way back to Adam? Biologically speaking, the humanity of Jesus Christ came through his mother, not his father, so Luke has given us his genealogy through Mary.

The last words of Luke's genealogy are important. No other genealogy ends this way: "the son of Adam, the son of God" (Luke 3:38). This statement reminds us that Adam had a unique relationship to God. He was not born into this world, but made by a direct act of creation. Since he was created in God's image, Adam bore the family likeness of God. He was God's son. Yet tragically his relationship with his Father was broken by his sin, and this sin corrupted the whole family line.

There was only one way for Adam and his sons to be rescued. There had to be a new beginning, a new Adam, a new humanity. There had to be someone who could once again be called "the son of God" to redeem the broken sonship of Adam. While the words at the end of Luke's genealogy certainly apply to Adam, they also apply in a unique way to Jesus Christ,

---

12. Norman L. Geisler and Thomas A. Howe, *When Critics Ask: A Popular Handbook on Bible Difficulties* (1992; reprint Grand Rapids: Baker, 1997), 385–86.

who has come with a new and perfect divine sonship. He is both the son of man and the Son of God. According to Arthur A. Just, "Jesus now embraces in himself every generation from Adam, the beginning of humanity. As such he now proceeds in his work as Messiah to redeem the humanity he bears in his own flesh. He is both son of Adam and Son of God, both true God and true man, with these two natures in one person."[13]

In Jesus Christ all of the promises that God made to the sons of Adam have been fulfilled. Jesus is the King that God promised to David, the ruler that he promised to Judah, the international blessing that he promised to Abraham, and the Satan-crushing Savior that he promised to Adam. To quote again from Arthur Just, "Luke shows how Jesus, at the head of the list, is the true Son of God who now begins the restoration of what Adam lost. Jesus, the second Adam, does perfectly what the first Adam did not do. As the Son of God, Jesus will demonstrate complete obedience to the Father and faithfulness to the promises given to Abraham and David."[14]

The genealogy of Jesus Christ shows that he was born into the very humanity that he was promised to save. The Bible says, "For God so loved the world, that he gave his only Son, that whoever believes in him should not perish but have eternal life" (John 3:16). Jesus came to save Jews, so he was born among their people, in the royal line of their ancient kings. Jesus the Jew was the son of Abraham and Jacob, the father of all the children of Israel. But he also came to save Gentiles, so Luke traced his ancestry all the way back to Adam, who is the father of us all. Luke wanted to show "the universal, all-embracing significance of Jesus. For this reason, in the family tree, he draws attention very expressly to the fact that Christ (through Adam) is, in His manhood, related to the whole human race."[15]

This means that what Jesus has done pertains to anyone who belongs to the human race. The people that he came to save were people like us. They were sinners. They were idolaters, murderers, liars, cheaters, and adulterers. This is why we all need to be saved: our sins have separated us from God and doomed us to die. So God the Son became the son of the son of the sons of sinners. This did not make him a sinner in his own right. Jesus never sinned. By his virgin birth, by his perfect obedience, and by the protective

13. Arthur A. Just Jr., *Luke 1:1–9:50*, Concordia Commentary (St. Louis: Concordia, 1996), 169.
14. Ibid., 168.
15. Geldenhuys, *Luke*, 153.

power of the Holy Spirit, he lived a life that was holy unto God. But he was born into a fallen race of sinners so that he could rescue us from our sins.

The Bible says that Jesus "had to be made like his brothers in every respect, so that he might . . . make propitiation for the sins of the people" (Heb. 2:17). In other words, he had to become one of us to save us. His genealogy proves that he *did* become one of us. Therefore he was able to offer his body—the body of a true and perfect man—for all our sins when he died on the cross. This is the Savior that God has sent to save everyone who trusts in him. We can count on him for eternal life, believing for sure what the Bible says about who he is. He is Jesus, the son of Heli, the son of David, the son of Judah, the son of Abraham, the son of Adam, and the Son of God.

13

PARADISE REGAINED

Luke 4:1–13

*And Jesus answered him, "It is said, 'You shall not put the Lord
your God to the test.'" And when the devil had ended every
temptation, he departed from him until an opportune time.*
(Luke 4:12–13)

nd so it begins. The Savior whose birth was announced by
angels and celebrated by shepherds has come into the world.
He was born in Bethlehem, dedicated in Jerusalem, raised in
Nazareth, and baptized in the Jordan. Through these events and the witness
of John the Baptist, Jesus Christ was revealed as the Savior of the world.

But all this was only by way of introduction. Luke took three long chapters to introduce the person of Jesus Christ. His grand prologue ended with
a genealogy that triumphantly declares Jesus to be "the son of Adam, the
son of God" (Luke 3:38). Then finally it began—his great mission to seek
and to save the lost. And what a beginning! Jesus Christ had come to destroy
the devil, to liberate people who were enslaved to Satan by sin. Rather than
waging a secret war or launching a sneak attack, Jesus took the fight directly
to Satan. Back at the river, heaven had opened to reveal Jesus as God the
beloved Son. Now Jesus stepped right up to the gates of hell. He would not

defeat the dark lord by deception, but in close combat on an open field of battle. So the Bible says, "Jesus, full of the Holy Spirit, returned from the Jordan and was led by the Spirit in the wilderness for forty days, being tempted by the devil" (Luke 4:1–2).

Mortal Combat

Every detail in this story is important. Jesus was led into the wilderness by the Holy Spirit, which shows that his trials and temptations were part of God's plan. Jesus was full of the Spirit from his birth and by his baptism. Now, at the beginning of his ministry, the Spirit led him through the wilderness—not just into it, but also *in* it—guiding Jesus throughout his time of testing. Thus it was in the power of the Spirit that Jesus fought the devil.

Already here we see an important lesson for our own daily Christian experience. If Jesus followed the leading of the Spirit, so should we, trusting that even our trials and temptations are under the Spirit's sovereign control.

The leading of the Spirit brought Jesus directly into conflict with God's ancient adversary the devil, the mighty fallen angel whom the Bible also calls Satan. Luke does not tell us whether this conflict took place within the Savior's soul or whether the devil appeared to Jesus in a visible form, as he did in the Garden of Eden. At the very least, he spoke to Jesus in an audible voice, and thus he was present in all the wickedness of his cruel power. The devil could not yet discern what Jesus would do to bring salvation, but he knew that his evil empire was under attack. He knew that this man Jesus had come to do the work of God, so he made a savage preemptive strike.

The setting for this conflict is significant. Jesus and Satan squared off in the wilderness. This takes us back to the place where the Israelites wandered, not for forty days, but for forty years. Just as the children of Israel were tested, so also Jesus—the true Israel—would be tested in the wilderness. There he would do what God's people had failed to do: live in grateful obedience to God.

The wilderness also reminds us of the lost condition of fallen humanity. We are all in the wilderness, spiritually speaking. This is the unhappy result of our fall into sin. The first man faced the first temptation in a garden, and when he sinned, our entire race was cast out. To bring us back, therefore, Jesus had to go out into the wilderness and defeat the devil who first tempted us to sin. Michael Wilcock writes:

> He is in fact going right back to the beginning, back to square one: he is the new Adam. In Eden, the head of the human race was confronted by the tempter, disobeyed God's word, and set the whole of mankind off on the wrong track. Now comes the second Adam, and alone in the wilderness he in his turn confronts the tempter. The difference is that he will win. He will be the totally obedient Man, Man as he was meant to be, Man who is altogether righteous, Man who never loses his relationship with God through sin.[1]

By giving in to temptation, the first Adam banished us all to the wilderness. But by going out and resisting temptation, the last Adam brought us back to paradise. This is the premise of John Milton's famous poem *Paradise Regained*. First Milton wrote *Paradise Lost*, the epic story "Of Man's First disobedience, and the Fruit / Of that Forbidden Tree, whose mortal taste / Brought Death into the World, and all our woe."[2] But the loss of paradise was not the end of the story. Jesus Christ came to regain what Adam had lost. He did this by resisting the very devil who tempted Adam. So Milton wrote a second poem, based on the temptation of Christ, a poem about

> Recover'd Paradise to all mankind,
> By one man's firm obedience fully tri'd
> Through all temptation, and the Tempter foil'd
> In all his wiles, defeated and repuls't,
> And Eden rais'd in the waste Wilderness.[3]

It was in the wilderness that Christ began to regain paradise for his people. As he confronted the devil, the whole plan of salvation was in question. Satan had already snatched paradise away from us. If he could, he would

---

1. Michael Wilcock, *The Message of Luke*, The Bible Speaks Today (Downers Grove, IL: InterVarsity, 1979), 60.

2. John Milton, *Paradise Lost*, ed. Christopher Ricks (New York: New American Library, 1968), lines 1–3.

3. John Milton, *Paradise Regained*, ed. Christopher Ricks (New York: New American Library, 1968), lines 2–7.

also seize the kingdom of Christ. If Jesus failed at any point, then he too would be condemned as a sinner, and there would be no justifying righteousness for us—no atoning sacrifice, no bodily resurrection, and no hope of eternal life. Paradise would be lost forever.

But if Jesus could stand firm against Satan's assault, resisting all his temptations, then paradise would be regained. What the devil offered him in the wilderness was the essence of all the temptations he would later face—all the things that would try to distract him from being the Savior that God had called him to be. If Jesus could withstand these trials, he could withstand anything.

First Temptation: Stone into Bread

Satan tempted Jesus throughout his time in the wilderness, probing for a weakness. But his most savage attack came right at the end of the forty days, when he made three devilish temptations that related to provision, power, and protection.

The first temptation was to turn stone into bread. The Bible says that Jesus was tempted in the wilderness for forty days: "And he ate nothing during those days. And when they were ended, he was hungry. The devil said to him, 'If you are the Son of God, command this stone to become bread'" (Luke 4:2–3).

To understand how tantalizing this was, we would have to endure a forty-day fast. Imagine going without food for a week, drinking only water. Then imagine extending that fast for five more weeks. Imagine not having anything to eat from now until the month after next. Then imagine surviving such a fast out in the desert. Jesus must have been at the very limits of physical endurance. People who have fasted this long testify that after days of gnawing hunger, they experience a euphoric release from their appetite for food. But this is only temporary, and in the weeks that follow, the body again becomes desperate in its craving. What Jesus suffered in the wilderness would have killed a weaker man. His condition was critical. At the end of forty days he was closer to death than at any other point in his life, except the crucifixion.

It was just at this moment, right at the point when he was most vulnerable, that Satan tempted Jesus to fix himself a little food. He had the power

154

to do it, of course. It would only take an instant. One word from Jesus and the stone would become bread.

How tempting this must have been, simply from the standpoint of physical need. But this temptation also had a spiritual dimension. Satan was attacking Jesus as the Messiah.[4] His diabolical strategy was to get him to doubt his own sonship. Satan had heard that Jesus was the Son of God. Possibly he was present at his baptism, when the Father introduced him as his beloved Son (Luke 3:22). But was it true? What proof did Jesus have that he really was the Son of God? The devil was casting doubt on what God said, as he loves to do. And if Jesus was the Son of God, then why was he on the verge of starvation? How could this be God's will for his life?

So Satan tempted him with the first of his "so you say you're the Son of God" temptations: "If you are the Son of God, command this stone to become bread" (Luke 4:3). This was basically the same strategy that Satan used in the Garden of Eden, when he tried to get Adam and Eve to doubt that what God said about the tree of the knowledge of good and evil was really true. One way or another, all of Satan's attacks strike at God's Word. Whenever we are tempted to doubt the truth of the Bible, we may be sure that the devil is up to his old tricks.

In this case, Satan was trying to raise suspicion about the Father's declaration that Jesus was his only beloved Son. He was tempting Jesus to prove his sonship, not just to Satan, but also to himself. If he was the Son of God, then surely God did not want him to die out in the wilderness. He had a divine right to his daily bread. So why not verify his sonship by showing that he had the miraculous power to make bread?

This temptation went right to the heart of what it meant for Jesus to be the Son of God and the Savior of the world. Jesus had come to do the Father's will, not his own will. Among other things, this meant trusting God to provide for his needs. Soon the Father would send angels to care for him (see Matt. 4:11). But Jesus may not have known that, and for the moment, it was still the Father's will for him to go hungry. Satan was tempting him (as he often tempts us) to be impatient, to get ahead of God's timetable by meeting his own needs in his own way rather than waiting for God to provide. Kent Hughes writes: "Christ was tempted to provide for his material

4. See Norval Geldenhuys, *The Gospel of Luke*, New International Commentary on the New Testament (Grand Rapids: Eerdmans, 1951), 158.

needs apart from the will of the Father and, furthermore, to go outside the natural order to meet his needs, to momentarily suspend living like a real human."[5] Jesus was tempted, therefore, to use his power as God to alleviate his suffering as a man.

In the face of this severe temptation, Jesus answered Satan with a word from God. He said, "It is written, 'Man shall not live by bread alone'" (Luke 4:4). Notice the first word in his response. Satan was challenging him to prove that he was the Son of God, but Jesus did not need to prove his divine sonship to Satan or to anyone else, least of all himself. There was no "if" about it; he *knew* that he was the Son of God. He knew it because the Father had said it, and he believed what God said. So rather than defending his deity, Jesus highlighted his humanity. He said, "*Man* does not live by bread alone."

By saying this, Jesus was identifying himself as a human being. It was as a man that he stood against the devil. Jesus was not masquerading as a man—a divine mind trapped in a human body. He was fully human, body and soul. Thus it was in his humanity that he withstood the wiles of Satan. We need to see this because usually we think that it was easy for Jesus to resist temptation. He was God, after all! Yet the Bible also says that Jesus was made in our human nature, that he was fully man, and that therefore "in every respect [he] has been tempted as we are" (Heb. 4:15). Understand this: Jesus did not resist the temptations of Satan by the superior power of his deity, but in all the weakness of his humanity. This gives us hope. Sometimes we say that we sin because we cannot help it. But by the grace that we have in Jesus Christ, we too have the ability to resist the devil: "because he himself has suffered when tempted, he is able to help those who are being tempted" (Heb. 2:18).

If man does not live by bread alone, then how does he live? Jesus was quoting the book of Deuteronomy (God's word to his people Israel when they were wandering in the wilderness), and the rest of the verse gives us the answer: "Man does not live by bread alone, but man lives by every word that comes from the mouth of the Lord" (Deut. 8:3). This is how Jesus lived: not by bread alone, but by the Word of God.

It was God's Word that assured Jesus of his sonship, declaring that he was beloved of the Father. It was also God's Word that led him into the wilder-

---

5. R. Kent Hughes, *Luke: That You May Know the Truth*, 2 vols., Preaching the Word (Wheaton, IL: Crossway, 1998), 1:133.

ness. So if he was desperate for food, it was because his Father wanted him to be at the edge of starvation. However hard it was to understand, this was God's will for his life. Jesus trusted that God was working for good because he trusted his Father's Word. When it was time to leave the wilderness, the Holy Spirit would let him know. In the meantime, Jesus refused to take matters into his own hands. He wanted to do what God said. Therefore, he did not get his own food at his own time (especially not from the devil's menu!), but waited for God's provision.

Jesus was deeply dependent on God and his Word throughout his earthly ministry. No physical craving ever led him away from the path of obedience. He did not gratify his own desires, but subordinated his needs to the will of his Father. He performed many miracles for the benefit of others, but he never abused his divine power by using it in the service of his own human needs.

SECOND TEMPTATION: THE CROWN WITHOUT THE CROSS

Satan never gives in without a fight. He will continue to wage war against Jesus Christ until the last desperate moment when he is cast into the eternal fire of God's wrath (Rev. 20:10). So having failed at one temptation, he tried another. This time it was not a temptation to provision, but to power: "And the devil took him up and showed him all the kingdoms of the world in a moment of time, and said to him, 'To you I will give all this authority and their glory, for it has been delivered to me, and I give it to whom I will. If you, then, will worship me, it will all be yours'" (Luke 4:5–7).

It must have been a spectacular vision. We think of Satan as a dark, ugly, and rather desperate creature. But he has much greater power than any man. Though fallen, he is mighty in his splendor. In fact, the Bible says that he is able to disguise himself "as an angel of light" (2 Cor. 11:14). So when Jesus saw the devil in the wilderness, he was not looking at evil in all its squalor, but in all its sophistication.

Whether in body or spirit, the devil took Jesus to some lofty height. In an instant, he could see all the royal treasure, military power, and cultural achievements of the world's great civilizations—everything from the golden roof of the temple in Jerusalem to the mighty Roman Empire in all its proud splendor. Perhaps he could even see future kingdoms, from the Ottoman Empire to the global superpower of the United States. And Jesus could see the gates of all the great cities swing open to receive him as their king.

Satan told Jesus that these kingdoms were his to give. As Milton put it in *Paradise Regained*, "The kingdoms of the world to thee I give; / For given to me, I give to whom I please."[6] This may seem like a delusion of grandeur. Was Satan telling the truth? Did he really have the authority to offer Jesus the world? Perhaps he did. Once sin entered the world, Satan gained power over the kingdoms of men, which is why Jesus called him "the ruler of this world" (e.g., John 12:31). But if Satan did rule the world for a time, it was only by God's permission, never by his own possession. And even what was handed over to him in the power of sin was still under God's sovereign control. So Satan was telling Jesus a half-truth, at most. He was posing as the ultimate power broker, but he was offering more than he had the right to give.

It must have been a strong temptation nevertheless. As the Son of God, Jesus had the right to receive the kingdom, the power, and the glory. It was his calling to be the king, and one day what Satan showed him would all be his. But how would he receive it? That was the question. God's way was for Jesus to suffer and to die for sinners, and only then to receive the kingdom. But Satan offered it to Jesus on the spot. He could have the ecstasy without the agony. The kingdoms of this world could become the kingdom of Christ without the scorn, the scourging, the spitting, and the bloody crucifixion. Satan was tempting Jesus to seize the crown without suffering the cross.

All Jesus had to do was worship the devil. The kingdoms could all be his—just one quick bow of the knee and he would have the world at his feet. Satan was offering Jesus a shortcut. He could bypass Calvary and go straight on to glory.

If Jesus had done this, he would have had the greatest kingdom the world has ever seen. Just imagine what would have happened if Jesus had established an earthly kingdom that was allied to the power of Satan. Together they would have dominated the world. Jesus would have had his kingdom. But he never would have solved the problem of our sin. In order to do

---

6. Milton, *Paradise Regained*, 4.2, 163–64.

that, he had to suffer and die. Furthermore, his kingdom would not have endured. He would have ruled on earth as king, but never would have inherited the everlasting kingdom of his Father—the kingdom the Father had promised when he said, "You are my Son; today I have begotten you. Ask of me, and I will make the nations your heritage, and the end of the earth your possession" (Ps. 2:7–8).

Worst of all, if Jesus had given in to this temptation, Satan would have become his lord. This was the devil's ancient ambition, the one that first cast him out of heaven. He wanted to have all the glory for himself, and in this temptation he was grasping for some way to get it. But God's plan was for the kingdom to be taken away from Satan forever, and for the devil himself to be destroyed.

It did not take Jesus long to give his answer. As powerful as this temptation was, he did not weigh his options. He did not take time to consider the alternatives. He did not contemplate how much easier it would have been to seize the crown without suffering the cross. He simply refused to worship Satan, or to compromise with him in any way: "Jesus answered him, 'It is written, "You shall worship the Lord your God, and him only shall you serve"'" (Luke 4:8; Deut. 6:13).

Once again Jesus was quoting one of God's commandments, the law that man was given to live by. He knew that it was wrong to worship anyone except God, and this was all that mattered. By refusing to worship Satan, Jesus was repudiating the popular path of worldly power. He was refusing to become a lesser messiah who ruled over only an earthly kingdom. And he was rejecting Satan's desperate attempt to become his lord. Jesus was choosing instead to walk the way of the cross. His goal was not to gain a kingdom for himself, but to save his people. To do this he was willing to suffer and to die for our sins. As for the kingdom, he would wait to receive it from his Father's hand.

THIRD TEMPTATION: PUTTING GOD TO THE TEST

By this time Satan was getting rather desperate. Jesus had refused to use his divine power to satisfy his acute physical need. He had rejected the offer of the easy kingdom. Yet Satan thought he detected an area of weakness. He noticed that Jesus always went back to Scripture. If he could get

Jesus to sin, it would have to be on the basis of something God said in his Word. So with fiendish cunning, Satan took Jesus "to Jerusalem and set him on the pinnacle of the temple and said to him, 'If you are the Son of God, throw yourself down from here, for it is written, "He will command his angels concerning you, to guard you," and "On their hands they will bear you up, lest you strike your foot against a stone"'" (Luke 4:9–11).

This was the third temptation: putting God to the test. What Satan proposed was spectacular. He took Jesus to the apex of the temple, either on the roof over the sanctuary or the royal portico that soared five hundred feet above the Kidron Valley. From that dizzy height he challenged Jesus to throw himself on God's mercy. If Jesus jumped, then surely his Father would save him. After all, this was a promise from the Psalms: God would save his Messiah (Ps. 91:11–12).

If Jesus took this leap of faith, and landed safely, then everyone would know that he was the Son of God. Once again, the devil was trying to get Jesus to test his own identity. How could he be sure that he was the Son of God? All he had to go on was what God said, but what did that prove? If Jesus wanted to know for sure, he had to see if God would save him. Satan was tempting Jesus to demand a sign instead of taking God at his word, to live by sight rather than by faith.

Leaping from the temple would also prove his identity to others. The Jews of that day expected the Messiah to take his stand at the temple. The ancient writings known as Midrash record the traditional Jewish belief that when the Messiah came, he would appear at the temple: "Our teachers have taught," the writings say, that "when the King, the Messiah, reveals himself, he will come and stand on the roof of the Temple."[7] Satan was daring Jesus to go one step farther and jump off! It would be a public proof of his true identity as the Son of God, because when God saved him, the people and priests who were worshiping there would know that he was their Messiah.

But Jesus refused to presume upon his Father's protection or to demand any further proof that he was the Son of God. He had heard the Father say that he was, and this was enough for him. Nor did he need to prove it to anyone else. So he refused to jump. Instead, he rebuked Satan with a clear command from God, using Scripture to interpret Scripture: "You shall not

7. *Pesiqta rabbati* 36, quoted in Hughes, *Luke*, 1:137.

put the Lord your God to the test" (Luke 4:12; cf. Deut. 6:16). Satan was trying to get Jesus to put his Father to the test; but since Jesus is God incarnate, Satan was putting God to the test himself, which the Bible says no one should ever do.

If Jesus had jumped, presumably the Father would have been compelled to save him. But that would have inverted the proper order of things. The Son had come to do his Father's will, and not the other way around: "To jump off the temple would have been to take the initiative and force God into a situation where he would have no choice but to back up the action in order to avert disaster, or else to be accused of unfaithfulness if he did not. That would have been to reverse the role of man and God, and of Son and Father."[8]

The day came when Jesus *did* put his life in God's hands. It came on Good Friday, when he said, "Father, into your hands I commit my spirit!" (Luke 23:46). But then it was in obedience to God's will, not to pull some kind of daredevil stunt. The day also came when the Father proved to Jesus and to everyone else that Jesus was the Son of God. The proof came on Easter Sunday, when God raised Jesus from the dead. He did not save his Son from death, but brought him through death into everlasting life. And Jesus was willing to wait for all this. Rather than jumping ahead, he trusted the Father to prove his sonship at the right and proper time, waiting for the confirmation of his resurrection.

OUR SAVIOR IN THE FIGHT

Three diabolical temptations, met by three biblical responses—and when it was all over, Satan had to leave in disgrace. Here we see the truth of God's promise: "Resist the devil, and he will flee from you" (James 4:7). But Satan would not be gone for long, for "when the devil had ended every temptation, he departed from him until an opportune time" (Luke 4:13; cf. 22:3). Their struggle would not be over until they battled to the death. But for the time being, Jesus had triumphed, resisting and refusing every temptation. What Satan intended as a temptation actually turned out to be a test or trial that proved the saving innocence of Jesus.

8. David Gooding, *According to Luke: A New Exposition of the Third Gospel* (Grand Rapids: Eerdmans, 1987), 80.

From his example, we learn how to stand firm against the devil's schemes. For Satan tempts us in many of the same ways that he tempted Jesus. We are tempted to doubt the goodness of God's fatherly care and put our physical desires ahead of our obedience to God. Satan wants us to gratify ourselves with food, sex, and entertainment rather than to make costly sacrifices of our time, money, and strength for the kingdom of God. What comforts are you giving up to advance the gospel? What compromises with pleasure are sapping your holy strength to glorify God?

We are also tempted to seek earthly glory and gain rather than to suffer for the cause of Christ. We want to have what we think we deserve, any way we can get it. So Satan tempts us take the easy way out, even if it means bowing to his wicked will. What are you working to get without waiting for God to give it to you?

Then we face the temptation to put God to the test. Does the Father love us? Will he really care for us? Instead of simply taking God at his Word, we want him to prove it. So Satan tempts us to base our attitude towards God on our personal experience rather than on the promises of God's Word. We make our comfort and safety the measure of God's love. We live by sight, and not by faith. If life is good, we think God is good; but if we come to any harm, we immediately question his motives. What demands are you placing on God before you will trust in his plan, or even before you will accept Jesus as Savior and Lord?

If it is true that Satan tempts us in some of the same ways that he tempted Jesus, then Jesus also shows us how to resist. Remember that Jesus faced these temptations in the weakness of his humanity. Furthermore, he did not draw any weapons that we do not have at our disposal. He defeated the devil by wielding "the sword of the Spirit" (Eph. 6:17), resisting temptation by the power of God's Word. Jesus was able to do this because he knew his Bible word for word. This shows the importance of Bible memory work. We need to store God's Word in our hearts, as Jesus did, so that we might not sin against God (Ps. 119:11). It is the Bible that teaches us not to live for pleasure, but by every word that comes from God; it is the Bible that teaches us to worship God alone; and it is the Bible that teaches us not to put God to the test. If we want to stand firm against the devil, we need to know and to do what God says in his Word.

As true as all that is, and as useful as it is for the Christian life, it is not the main point of this passage. The main point is that Jesus stood alone against Satan as the Son of God and resisted the temptations that he alone could face and endure. It is only because Jesus stood firm in the wilderness that he was able to offer a perfect sacrifice on the cross and save us from our sins. And it is only because Jesus resisted first that we ever resist any temptation at all. In the words of Ambrose, the early church father, Jesus was "led into the desert for a purpose, in order to challenge the devil. If he had not fought, he would not have conquered him for me."[9]

Our victory comes through the victory of Jesus Christ. Jesus did what he did against the devil so that he could gain us victory in our struggle against sin. If we had to face the devil without the saving work of Jesus Christ and without the gracious help of his Spirit, we wouldn't last more than a millisecond. But we do not face temptation alone. Jesus is our great champion in the fight. By his obedience in the wilderness, by his sufferings on the cross, and by his resurrection from the dead, he has defeated the devil and opened the way for us to enter paradise.

9. Ambrose, "Exposition of the Gospel of Luke" (4.14), quoted in *Luke*, ed. Arthur A. Just Jr., Ancient Christian Commentary on Scripture, NT3 (Downers Grove, IL: InterVarsity, 2003), 73.

14

THE GOSPEL ACCORDING TO JESUS

Luke 4:14–21

> *"The Spirit of the Lord is upon me, because he has anointed
> me to proclaim good news to the poor. He has sent me to
> proclaim liberty to the captives and recovering of sight to the
> blind, to set at liberty those who are oppressed, to proclaim
> the year of the Lord's favor."* (Luke 4:18–19)

What is the best sermon that you ever heard? For some people it is the sermon that brought them to saving faith in Jesus Christ. For others it is a sermon that brought special comfort in a season of sorrow, or clear guidance at a time of indecision. Still others would say it was a sermon that brought them back to God after they had wandered far away, or that helped them see the glory of his sovereign grace.

But of all the great sermons that have been preached since the beginning of the world, no one has ever preached a better sermon than the first one that Jesus preached in his hometown of Nazareth. It brings people to saving faith, gives them hope in all their troubles, and helps them see the glory of the Son of God. What could be better than to hear our Savior preach, and preach about himself? This is what he did at the synagogue in Nazareth: he preached the gospel according to Jesus. Luke recorded this sermon because of all the things that he wanted us to know for sure, the most important is the good news of salvation in Christ. And what better way for us to hear it than from the Savior's own lips?

Jesus Begins to Preach

By the time he delivered his famous sermon, Jesus had earned something of a reputation as a preacher. The Bible says that after being tempted in the wilderness, "Jesus returned in the power of the Spirit to Galilee, and a report about him went out through all the surrounding country. And he taught in their synagogues, being glorified by all" (Luke 4:14–15).

Here we see the secret of our Savior's success; he preached in the power of the Spirit. This is the secret of any effective ministry. What empowers people who preach the gospel is the animating influence of God the Holy Spirit. The famous Welsh preacher Martyn Lloyd-Jones described this anointing as "God giving power, an enabling, through the Spirit, to the preacher in order that he may do this work in a manner that lifts it up beyond the efforts and endeavours of man to a position in which the preacher is being used by the Spirit and becomes the channel through whom the Spirit works."[1]

This power of the Spirit is accessible to anyone who comes to God in faith, but Jesus possessed it in a unique way, and to the fullest measure. As the divine Son of God, he was conceived by the Holy Spirit (Luke 1:35). He was also baptized by the Holy Spirit, who descended on him in the form of a dove (Luke 3:22). Then he went out to face the devil, and the Bible says he did it "full of the Holy Spirit" (Luke 4:1). The Spirit remained on him throughout his public ministry. Jesus did not operate independently, serving by his own strength, but dependently, relying on the Spirit's work. The same divine spiritual power that accomplished his incarnation and enabled him to defeat the devil, also empowered his ministry of word and deed. This is one of the great mysteries of the Godhead: in doing his saving work, the Son was vitally connected to the Father and the Spirit within the triune being of God. This mystery is also one of the main secrets to effective gospel

1. D. Martyn Lloyd-Jones, *Preaching & Preachers* (Grand Rapids: Zondervan, 1971), 305.

ministry: if Jesus depended on the Spirit, how much more should we rely on his gracious influence.

The opening verses of this passage also give us the location for Jesus' ministry. He was preaching in Galilee, which was the region where he was raised—the northern part of Israel that surrounded the Sea of Galilee. To be more specific, Jesus was preaching in the *synagogues* of Galilee. Each town had its own meeting place for worship. By going there, Jesus placed his divine seal of approval on the public worship of God.

If anyone had the right to think that he didn't need to go to worship, it was Jesus. Imagine how many times he had to sit through below average teaching. How easy it would have been for him to say that he didn't need to go to the synagogue, that he could commune with his Father better somewhere off by himself. Yet throughout his life, Jesus maintained a regular pattern of public worship. This was "his custom," as we learn in Luke 4:16. Jesus sang through the psalms. He listened to God's Word. He said his prayers. And if going to worship was good enough for him, then obviously it needs to be a priority for us as well. Weekly worship attendance is the foundation for any life that glorifies God. Therefore, "Let us not give up meeting together" (Heb. 10:25 NIV).

As Jesus traveled from synagogue to synagogue, he began to teach. He started having an itinerant ministry as a Bible teacher. And as Jesus preached, people began to respond, so that he became a sensation all over Galilee. The spiritual power of his teaching awakened people's minds and hearts. They began to praise his preaching—in a word, to *glorify* him. Even if they did not fully understand who he was, they were beginning to do the very thing for which they were made: to glorify God in the person of his Son, Jesus Christ. This is the way that everyone who hears his voice ought to respond. What Jesus says is thrilling to the soul, and whenever we hear it, we should give glory to God.

HOMETOWN SERMON

We do not know how many weeks or months Jesus spent teaching his way through Galilee, but eventually he went back home to Nazareth. There he preached the gospel of his very own grace. Luke records this remarkable incident in some detail:

And he came to Nazareth, where he had been brought up. And as was his custom, he went to the synagogue on the Sabbath day, and he stood up to read. And the scroll of the prophet Isaiah was given to him. He unrolled the scroll and found the place where it was written,

Spirit upon my

ANointed

Proclaim goodnew

"The Spirit of the Lord is upon me,
  because he has anointed me
    to proclaim good news to the poor.
He has sent me to proclaim liberty to the captives
  and recovering of sight to the blind,
    to set at liberty those who are oppressed,
to proclaim the year of the Lord's favor."

SeNT

And he rolled up the scroll and gave it back to the attendant and sat down. And the eyes of all in the synagogue were fixed on him. And he began to say to them, "Today this Scripture has been fulfilled in your hearing." (Luke 4:16–21; cf. Isa. 61:1–2; 58:6)

This account is fascinating for what it tells us about public worship in the time of Christ. Every Sabbath, people gathered to worship God at their local synagogue. We know from other sources that they began by singing the psalms. But the center of their worship was reading and preaching the Old Testament. It was always a dramatic moment: someone would take a sacred scroll of Holy Scripture out of its container. He would give it to the teacher, who would carefully unroll it to the passage he wanted to teach. Then he would read it, translating from Hebrew into Aramaic so that people could understand. While he was reading, he remained standing out of respect for God's Word. Often there were two readings, one from the Law and one from the Prophets. When this was finished, the scrolls were carefully put away and the teacher sat down in a chair on a raised platform that signified his spiritual authority and began to teach. Finally, the service ended with prayers known as the Eighteen Benedictions.

The service at Nazareth followed the usual pattern. During worship, someone took out the Isaiah scroll and handed it to Jesus. This was not surprising. In those days it was common for visiting rabbis to be invited to speak. In this case, Jesus had become a local celebrity, so it was natural for him to be asked to preach.

167

Jesus began by finding the part of Isaiah's prophecy that he wanted to read. This shows how familiar he was with the Scriptures of the Old Testament. The scroll that Jesus read was not divided into chapters and verses. In fact, it wasn't even divided into words! Ancient Hebrew texts simply placed one letter next to another, without any spaces or punctuation. So to find the right place, Jesus must have had an intimate knowledge of the Hebrew language in general and of Isaiah's prophecy in particular. He not only worshiped God, but he also knew his Word. This is a powerful example for us. If the very Son of God devoted himself to studying the Bible, then we must do the same. How can we possibly live without the Scriptures that satisfied our Savior's soul?

So far everything had gone according to custom. As usual, the people of Nazareth had sung their psalms and heard the reading of God's Word. What they heard this particular week came from the end of Isaiah, where the Suffering Servant spoke about the great day of salvation. If they had been listening carefully, they would have heard Isaiah promise liberation to four kinds of people: the poor, the prisoners, the blind, and the oppressed.

If they knew their Bibles well, they might even have caught the prophet's reference to the ancient custom of the jubilee. According to the law of God, every fiftieth year was a special year of celebration in Israel, called the year of jubilee. As we read in Leviticus, "You shall consecrate the fiftieth year, and proclaim liberty throughout the land to all its inhabitants. It shall be a jubilee for you, when each of you shall return to his property and each of you shall return to his clan" (Lev. 25:10). This is what Isaiah meant by "the year of the Lord's favor" (Luke 4:19). The jubilee was a year of amnesty, when slaves were set free from their servitude. It was a year of redemption, when debtors were released from their financial obligations. And it was a year of restoration, when lost property was returned to its rightful owners.

What Isaiah prophesied was a jubilee to end all jubilees, and when the people of Nazareth heard it, they should have known that he was speaking about the great day of salvation. They should have recognized it as a prophecy about the Messiah, for this is the meaning of "anointed" (Luke 4:18): the "anointed one" was the Messiah, or, to use the Greek word for it, the Christ. Therefore, when godly people heard Isaiah's prophecy, it gave them hope that one day God would come and save his people.

168

Some of us Need to Let go —
Some of us Need to Hold on —

When Jesus finished reading from Isaiah, he rolled up the scroll and gave it back to the attendant. Then he sat down in the seat of authority. A sense of expectancy hung in the air; everyone wanted to know what Jesus would say. Luke tells us, "the eyes of all in the synagogue were fixed on him" (Luke 4:20). This true, factual description of what happened that day contains a profound spiritual lesson. Like the people of Nazareth, we need to look to Jesus and listen to his gospel.

What the Savior said next was one of the most amazing statements in Luke's Gospel and one of the most radical claims that Jesus ever made: "Today this Scripture has been fulfilled in your hearing" (Luke 4:21). Jesus was announcing the fulfillment of Isaiah's prophecy. The anointed one, the Messiah, the Christ had come. The Suffering Servant had arrived, bringing salvation. And with him came all the things that Isaiah promised would only come on the great day of God: good news for the poor, freedom for the captives, sight for the blind, and liberty for people under oppression.

Jesus, the Preacher

The first word in Jesus' sermon was "today." Jesus used this word to give his sermon a sense of immediacy. He was announcing "the year of the Lord's favor" (Luke 4:19)—the prolonged period when salvation would come to God's people. The new epoch would begin that very day. For when Jesus said that the Scripture had been fulfilled, he meant, very simply, that everything Isaiah said was really about him. *He* was the fulfillment! Isaiah's prophecy identified his person and defined his work. It explained who Jesus was and what he had come to do.

Who was Jesus? He was the Christ. This was perhaps the first time Jesus had declared that he was Israel's Messiah. He did this implicitly by taking Isaiah's words and claiming them as his own: "The Spirit of the Lord is upon me, because he has anointed me" (Luke 4:18). This was a clear way of claiming to be the Christ. Jesus was saying that he was the anointed one, the Messiah. His anointing was his baptism, when the Holy Spirit descended on him like a dove. Jesus of Nazareth was God's chosen servant, the Spirit-anointed Christ. As he carried out his ministry, he did everything in obedience to the Father, by the power of the Spirit.

What had Jesus come to do? The very thing that Isaiah promised: "to proclaim good news to the poor," and in doing so, "to proclaim liberty to the captives and recovering of sight to the blind, to set at liberty those who are oppressed, to proclaim the year of the Lord's favor" (Luke 4:18–19).

These words were revolutionary, but not in the way that most people thought. When they heard what Jesus said, they assumed it was some kind of political manifesto. They expected an earthly salvation that would bring a physical deliverance. Some of them wanted him to give the poor a higher standard of living—a social revolution. Some of them wanted him to heal the sick—a medical revolution. Still others wanted him to overthrow the Romans—a political revolution. Jesus had the power to do all of that. In fact, that is what Satan tempted him to do, and it was a real temptation for him. But it was not what he was called to do.

People who were looking only for an earthly kingdom were frustrated when Jesus failed to bring it. Yes, he fed the hungry, gave sight to the blind, and released people from satanic oppression. Jesus cared for people's bodies as well as their souls. His miracles helped to prove that he was the Christ, showing that God's kingdom had come. Nevertheless, they were not his primary purpose.

First and foremost, Jesus came to bring spiritual deliverance from the power of sin. The key word in these verses is the word "proclaim," which occurs three times. Jesus was sent to proclaim good news, to proclaim liberty, to proclaim the Lord's favor. Although this good news has physical, social, medical, and political implications, it is first and foremost a proclamation. This is why Jesus told the people who were gathered at the synagogue in Nazareth that day that Isaiah's prophecy was fulfilled in their *hearing* (Luke 4:21). They did not see any prisoners gain their freedom or any blind people recover their sight. But they did hear Jesus preach the gospel, and when they heard it, Isaiah's prophecy came true. Salvation had come by the proclamation of God's Word.

In fulfilling Isaiah's prophecy, Jesus preached to four kinds of people. First, he preached to the poor. People often wonder whether this statement refers to people who are poor in financial terms, which of course it does, but it also goes deeper. When Jesus spoke about the poor, he was referring to the common people of the land, who lived in humble poverty. In biblical terms, the poor are "the downtrodden and disadvantaged, helpless in themselves and at the mercy of powerful people and adverse circumstances."[2] Most of the people in places like Nazareth were poor in this sense, as were many of the people that we meet in this Gospel. Luke had a special concern for the needs of the poor. So did Jesus, and what he came to bring them was good news, which is another way of saying that it was the gospel. Jesus did not come to raise their standard of living, although God often makes the righteous prosper. Jesus came to give the poor something richer: the good news that by trusting in him they would receive forgiveness for their sins and the guarantee of eternal life, with all the treasures of heaven.

Why did Jesus say that his gospel was for the poor? Wasn't it also for the rich? Yes, the gospel is for everyone who is willing to receive it. In fact, later in this very sermon, Jesus mentions two people who were saved by grace: one poor (the widow of Zarephath) and one rich (Naaman the Syrian).[3] Both of them recognized their true spiritual poverty and turned to God in faith. But Jesus said he had good news for the poor so they would know the grace of God. Usually the poor get overlooked, but Jesus said the gospel was for them as much as for anyone else. This was not a way of excluding anyone (not even the rich), but of including everyone (even the poor).

The gospel is also for captives. Jesus said, "He has sent me to proclaim liberty to the captives" (Luke 4:18). This echoes the great text from Leviticus that rings out from Philadelphia's famous Liberty Bell: "Proclaim liberty throughout all the land unto all the inhabitants thereof" (Lev. 25:10). The word Jesus used for captives (*aichmalōtois*) referred originally to prisoners captured in time of war. In the context of Leviticus and Isaiah, it also included people who sold themselves into slavery in order to pay their debts.

If Jesus meant to free captives only in this literal sense, then he would have had a rather narrow agenda, with little relevance for people in Nazareth. But this verse has a wider meaning. The key is the word "liberty," or "release," as some versions have it. The same word is used again at the end of the verse, where Jesus proclaims "liberty for those who are oppressed" (Luke 4:18). David Gooding writes, "The Greek word for 'release' on both occasions is *aphesis*. Its associated verb carries a wide range of meaning: 'to

---

2. J. Alec Motyer, *Isaiah: An Introduction and Commentary*, Tyndale Old Testament Commentaries (Downers Grove, IL: InterVarsity, 1999), 377.

3. David Gooding makes this point in *According to Luke: A New Exposition of the Third Gospel* (Grand Rapids: Eerdmans, 1987), 79–80.

send away, discharge, let go, release, allow' and then the specialized sense 'to forgive', since to forgive is to release someone from his debts, guilt, obligations and deserved penalties. The noun *aphesis* can mean 'release', 'discharge', 'setting free' in a general sense or else 'forgiveness.'"[4]

When we take the word this way—and Luke typically uses the various forms of *aphiēmi* and *aphesis* to mean forgiveness (e.g., Luke 1:77; 5:20–24; 7:47–49; 24:47)—we see that Jesus was referring to the most liberating, emancipating release of all: freedom from guilt through the forgiveness of sins. There is no greater captivity than bondage to sin. It imprisons the mind, enslaves the heart, and incarcerates the soul. If that is what sin does, then what Jesus did on the cross is the world's greatest deliverance. By dying for our sins, Jesus paid the debt that we owed to God and thereby freed us from our captivity to sin and guilt. As Charles Wesley put it in one of his famous hymns: "He breaks the pow'r of reigning sin, / he sets the pris'ner free; / his blood can make the foulest clean, / his blood availed for me."[5] This is the gospel according to Jesus.

THE BLIND AND THE CAPTIVES

Then Jesus preached to the blind. People ask whether this refers to physical or spiritual blindness, and again the answer is both. Later in his Gospel Luke will give an account of Jesus restoring sight to a blind man (Luke 18:35–43). This was a sign of the age to come, when every child of God will have perfect vision: God has promised that every believer will see Jesus Christ in all his glory (Matt. 5:8; 1 John 3:2).

If Jesus came to restore only physical sight, it would be a somewhat limited blessing. It would be great for blind people, but even for them, it would fail to address their deepest need. To be sure, the ability to see is a precious gift. I learned this in a powerful way as I watched my brother-in-law adjust to losing his sight. He would give almost anything to get his vision back. But even eyesight is nothing compared to the gift of being able to see the grace of God. Blind believers like my brother-in-law testify that it is infinitely more precious to them to see Jesus by faith than to see anything else in the world. This is what Jesus came to do: to give sight for the blind. He came to help us see our sin and our need

4. Gooding, *Luke*, 82.
5. Charles Wesley, "O for a Thousand Tongues to Sing" (1739).

of a Savior so that we would look to him for grace. Even when he gave people physical sight, as he sometimes did, it was so they would know that he had the power to help them see the day of salvation.

Like the healing of physical blindness, the recovery of spiritual sight is a prominent motif in Luke's Gospel (see Luke 2:30; 24:16, 31). This motif comes to a triumphant conclusion in the book of Acts, Luke's sequel, when the apostle Paul announces his divine mission to the Gentiles: "to open their eyes, so that they may turn from darkness to light and from the power of Satan to God, that they may receive forgiveness of sins and a place among those who are sanctified by faith in me" (Acts 26:18).

Fourth, and finally, Jesus preached to the oppressed, offering them the same thing that he offered the captives: liberty, freedom, release. The oppressed are people who are crushed in spirit and shattered by the hard experiences of life. When Jesus spoke about oppression, he was speaking to anyone dominated by the powerful forces of evil in the world, including people who have suffered the cruelty of verbal, emotional, or physical abuse. "Oppression" is the biblical category for what people today would call "abuse." It also describes anyone who is under spiritual oppression, such as the people whom Jesus freed from demons (e.g., Luke 4:31–36; 11:14).

Jesus cares for people who are oppressed, and he has come to set them free. One day all oppression will cease. But in the meantime, God has grace for people who have been wounded by wickedness. We have the comfort of knowing that Jesus himself endured oppression on his way to the cross, and by his Spirit he speaks hope to our wounded hearts. Norval Geldenhuys summarizes this all by saying that in his gospel, Jesus

> announced that He was the One anointed by God with the Spirit to proclaim the glad tidings to the poor. God had sent Him to heal those who were broken-hearted and found themselves in spiritual distress; to proclaim deliverance to those who were captives in the power of sin and in spiritual wretchedness; to give back to the spiritually blind the power of sight; to cause those who were downcast and inwardly bruised to go forward in triumph; and thus to *proclaim the acceptable year of the Lord*," i.e. to announce the Messianic age—*the period ushered in by His appearance,* in which God will grant His salvation to His people.[6]

6. Norval Geldenhuys, *The Gospel of Luke*, New International Commentary on the New Testament (Grand Rapids: Eerdmans, 1951), 168.

Free at Last!

The Puritans used to say that God had only one Son, and he made him a preacher. What Jesus preached at the synagogue in Nazareth was a simple sermon, based on a specific passage of Scripture, with a single point of application. It was the kind of sermon that every minister ought to preach: a Scripture-based, Christ-centered sermon—an expository sermon that explains what the Bible says and proclaims the good news of salvation in Jesus Christ.

The gospel according to Jesus has at least two great implications for us. First, it shows that Jesus can save us in all our need. In his prophecy, Isaiah listed some of the deepest forms of human distress: poverty, imprisonment, blindness, and oppression. Jesus came to save all those people, and if he can save them, he can save anyone.

His gospel is for us in our poverty. Darrell Bock comments, "it is the poor in general who sense their need in the greatest way and, as a result, respond most directly and honestly to Jesus. They characterize concretely the person in need. Their material deprivation often translates into spiritual sensitivity, humility, and responsiveness to God's message of hope. The message is offered to them and they tend to be the most responsive to it."[7] This is often true, but not always. Sometimes the poor are too proud to admit their spiritual poverty, in which case they never receive the gospel. This is especially true in a country like the United States where, compared to the rest of the world, even the poor have a high standard of living. But we are all poor, if only we will see it. We have nothing to offer God except the crushing debt of our sin. But Jesus offers us the riches of his grace: "For you know the grace of our Lord Jesus Christ, that though he was rich, yet for your sake he became poor, so that you by his poverty might become rich" (2 Cor. 8:9).

The gospel of Jesus is for us in our bondage. We are held captive by all kinds of evil passions, foolish pleasures, sinful lusts, and selfish ambitions. What sins are keeping us captive? What guilt is enslaving our souls? Jesus came to set us free. By his death on the cross, our sins are totally and completely forgiven; by his resurrection, we have power in the Spirit to resist

7. Darrell L. Bock, *Luke 1:1–9:50*, Baker Exegetical Commentary on the New Testament 3A (Grand Rapids: Baker, 1994), 408.

temptation and lead a holy life. In our struggle with sin, we are called to believe in the good news of Jesus Christ.

The gospel of Jesus is for us in our blindness. Did you know that sin is the world's leading cause of blindness? It blinds us to the Scriptures: we do not see the truth of God's Word. It blinds us to our sin itself: we do not see our need to be forgiven. It even blinds us to the Savior: we do not see the salvation that Jesus has to offer. We do not see any of these things until Jesus comes to cure our blindness. It is only by the illumination of his Spirit that we are able to believe the Bible, repent of our sin, and trust in him for our salvation. If you are still groping around in spiritual darkness, then pray for Jesus to show you the light.

Then the gospel of Jesus is for us in our oppression. He is our strong protector, and by his grace, we are safe with him. He is "the Friend of the poor in spirit, the Physician of the diseased heart, the Deliverer of the soul in bondage."[8] Jesus can save us in all our need. As his gospel is preached, he calls us to trust in him and be saved.

From this a second implication follows: the gospel that saved us is the same gospel that other people need. The same Holy Spirit that anointed Jesus has been poured out on us. Now we are called to proclaim his gospel to the people around us, who are just as needy as we are. Obviously, the gospel according to Jesus has implications for meeting people's physical needs. Like Jesus, we are called to care for people's bodies as well as their souls. This means meeting the material needs of the poor. It means visiting the captives in prison. It means helping the blind and people with other disabilities. It means comforting those who suffer abuse.

According to Jesus, the gospel calls us to this kind of concern. "What is in view," writes Darrell Bock, "is a spiritual and social transformation in a new community."[9] Earlier in the passage that Jesus read from Isaiah, God rebuked his people for not taking care of the poor. He asked them: "Is not this the fast that I choose: to loose the bonds of wickedness, to undo the straps of the yoke, to let the oppressed go free, and to break every yoke? Is it not to share your bread with the hungry and bring the homeless poor into your house; when you see the naked, to cover him, and not to

8. J. C. Ryle, *Expository Thoughts on the Gospels, Luke* (1858; reprint Cambridge: James Clarke, 1976), 1:117.

9. Bock, *Luke 1:1–9:50*, 407.

hide yourself from your own flesh?" (Isa. 58:6–7). In other words, God demands his people to have a heart for the poor.

Nevertheless, we need to make sure that the main thing always remains the main thing, and the main thing is to preach the gospel. What people call "the social gospel" often ends up being all social and no gospel. But this was not the kind of ministry that Jesus had, nor is it the kind of ministry that he calls us to have. His priority was to proclaim the good news. Thus the leading edge of Christ-centered ministry to a needy community is always the preaching of the gospel.

What people need most is the good news of salvation in Christ. What do poor people need? Maybe they need more money, and if they do, we need to provide for their basic needs. But the main thing poor people need is the gospel, which offers them all the treasures of heaven through faith in Jesus Christ. What do prisoners need? They may want to get out of prison, but what they need most is freedom from sin, which comes only through Christ and his cross. What do people with disabilities need? Often they need practical assistance, which we are called to help provide, but above all they need the hope that their sins are forgiven, and that one day Jesus will raise their bodies from the dead. What do people need when they are oppressed and abused? They need comfort and protection, which we should offer, but also the safety and security of eternal life.

This is what we *all* need: the gospel according to Jesus, in all its saving, liberating power. If we want to see people's lives transformed—including our own—we need to give people the gospel. The renewal of the church and the reformation of society come through preaching the cross and the empty tomb.

Some years ago Philadelphia's Tenth Presbyterian Church was part of a study on urban ministry. Sociologists examined the impact of the church's service to the city, and when their report was finished, staff members at the church were given an opportunity to read a draft before it went to print. The report contained many encouraging remarks about the church's compassion for the city, but it also reflected an unfortunate misunderstanding. It said that Tenth was committed to urban ministry almost in spite of its strong commitment to expository preaching. Somehow traditional Bible teaching was considered to be at odds with a real concern for the city.

Thankfully, the researchers were willing to revise their report, because there can be no contradiction between proclaiming the gospel and caring for people in need. We believe in the gospel according to Jesus. It is just *because of* our commitment to proclaiming God's Word that we are committed to the poor, the prisoners, the disabled, and the oppressed. We believe the gospel according to Jesus, which begins with the proclamation of good news.

Do you believe this gospel? If so, it has lifted you up from the poverty of your soul, released you from captivity to sin, and helped you see past your spiritual blindness. Now God is calling you to help others who have the same desperate needs. According to Jesus, what they need is the gospel. If we love Jesus, and listen to him, we will give it to them.

The Gospel for IPC

The Gospel for Memphis

mission of God in the world —

15

A PROPHET WITHOUT HONOR

Luke 4:22–30

When they heard these things, all in the synagogue were filled with wrath. And they rose up and drove him out of the town and brought him to the brow of the hill on which their town was built, so that they could throw him down the cliff. (Luke 4:28–29)

ho is Jesus, and what does he want with me?" This is the question that keeps coming up as we study the Gospel of Luke. From the opening lines of his book, Luke has been showing us Jesus. We have heard the news of his virgin birth, witnessed his baptism as the beloved Son, seen his struggle with Satan, and listened to his preaching of the gospel. As we look and listen, we are confronted with his claims. Luke wants us to know for sure that Jesus is the Christ. But do we believe that he is the God and Savior he claimed to be? And if he is, are we willing to follow him? These are questions we cannot avoid; we are compelled to ask them again and again: Who is Jesus, and what does he want with me?

Some people respond to Jesus in trusting faith. The more they listen to his teaching, the more they want to do what he says. The more they see his miracles, the more they want to worship him. The more they watch how he cares for people, the more they want to have a relationship with him.

Soon they are thinking about Jesus all the time, and in the words of one writer, "That is how falling in love happens. We cannot get a person out of our minds. We are captivated by his or her beauty, by what he or she is like as a person. And it happens that way when people encounter the real Jesus in Scripture. If you try to 'sell' him in a world that is constantly hawking products, it comes across as just one more sales pitch. But if you let people see Jesus, he sells himself."[1]

This was Luke's strategy in writing his Gospel: he showed people Jesus so that Jesus could "sell himself." However, Luke knew that not everyone would be ready to buy. Some people come to Jesus in faith, but others deny his claim to be the Christ. In fact, people even rejected him in his own hometown.

First Impressions

It happened the very first time that Jesus preached in Nazareth. He had been traveling from town to town, teaching the Bible. When he finally came back home, Jesus preached from the book of Isaiah. He said the poor would get the gospel: the captives would gain their freedom, the blind would see, and the abused would be released from their oppression. This was the gospel according to Jesus.

How did people respond to this gospel? This is something Luke always wanted to show. It is one of his basic literary strategies. First Jesus does something or says something. Then people respond, and their response tells us something about Jesus, and about the kind of relationship he wants to have with us.

In this case, people responded favorably, at least initially. At first Jesus was as popular in Nazareth as he was everywhere else. Luke tells us: "And all spoke well of him and marveled at the gracious words that were coming from his mouth" (Luke 4:22). People were very impressed. Most of them knew Jesus well. As they watched him grow up, they had always admired him, for the Scripture says that during his early years he "increased in favor with God and man" (Luke 2:52). Jesus was an attractive person; he had an excellent reputation. But the people of

---

1. From a promotional flyer for Paul Miller's book *Love Walked Among Us: Learning to Love Like Jesus* (Colorado Springs: NavPress, 2001).

Nazareth generally were unaware that he knew how to teach the Bible. They did not know how well he knew the Scriptures. So when Jesus started to preach, they felt the same way people feel when a familiar child unexpectedly turns out to be an all-star athlete or a musical virtuoso. They were surprised and pleased. Luke tells us they "marveled" at what he was saying.

It is easy to imagine the kinds of things that people said. Some probably commented that they were close friends of the family. Others would have said they were astonished to find out that Jesus was such a dynamic speaker. Still others undoubtedly said that they had known it all along, that there had always been something special about that young man. But all of them were proud of the local boy who made good.

Yet sadly this was as far as things ever went. Later Jesus would tell his disciples to watch out when people spoke well of them (Luke 6:26), and this was something he had learned from his own experience. People in Nazareth were amazed at his speaking ability, but they did not understand what he was actually saying. The proof comes in the question they asked: "Is not this Joseph's son?" (Luke 4:22). This was true as far as it went: Joseph was the earthly father of Jesus. The implication was that a carpenter like Joseph could not have a son who was a teacher; ordinarily, teachers came from the families of the rabbis. If people had really listened to the sermon, however, they would have realized that Jesus was much more than the son of Joseph. By announcing the fulfillment of Isaiah's prophecy, Jesus was claiming to be the Christ. The people were right to discuss his identity, but instead of wondering whether he was the son of Joseph, they should have wondered whether he was the Son of God.

Many people respond the same way today. They admire Jesus for his teaching. They are willing to recognize him as one of the best men who ever lived. But unfortunately they never think of him as anything *more* than merely a human being. This was part of the problem in Nazareth, where people identified Jesus as Joseph's son, but refused to worship him as the Son of God.

It is not enough to speak well of Jesus, or even to marvel at his gracious words. He demands a more definite response. He is not merely the best of men; he is also the glorious God. Therefore, we cannot put him in the same category with ordinary men, as people tried to do in Nazareth. If all we do is admire Jesus, then we dishonor him, because he deserves to be worshiped as God and served as Lord.

Dismissing Jesus in this way is a danger for people who have been in the church for a long time. We get familiar with Jesus—maybe too familiar. We are never in any danger of thinking too highly of Jesus, but we are often guilty of not thinking of him highly enough. We preach about Jesus. We sing about Jesus. We even speak well about Jesus. But this is not enough. Jesus Christ is God the Son. He is the sovereign Lord over all creation, the great and mighty God, with saving grace for sinners. His deity is supreme and his lordship is absolute. Therefore, Jesus deserves nothing less than all our obedience, all our worship, and all our service.

PROVE IT!

If the people of Nazareth had believed in Jesus and his gospel, they would have worshiped him as the Christ. But they were not ready to bow down and worship, so Jesus made a rather mysterious comment: "Doubtless you will quote to me this proverb, 'Physician, heal yourself.' What we have heard you did at Capernaum, do here in your hometown as well" (Luke 4:23).

In those days medicine was a rather haphazard science, if it could be called a science at all. People looked upon doctors with a fair amount of skepticism. When medical professionals proposed a remedy, their patients asked for some kind of reassurance that it would actually work. If this seemed doubtful (as it often did), they would say, "Physician, heal yourself." In other words, "Before you touch my body, or make me drink something nasty, let me see you try it first!"

As Jesus preached, he perceived that people in his own hometown were looking at him with the same kind of skepticism. They knew that he was Joseph's son, but they did not believe that he was the Christ, and they wanted some kind of proof. They had heard stories about the miracles he did in the nearby village of Capernaum. As far as they were concerned, if Jesus wanted them to believe, he had to show them what he could do. His preaching was not enough; they wanted him to perform. They were Jewish, after all, and "Jews demand signs" (1 Cor. 1:22). David Gooding writes:

> They did not believe him, that they admitted. But the fault was not theirs, but his, for not supplying adequate evidence. The cure was in his own hands. It was no good finding fault with them for not believing; they were prepared to believe if he provided them with sufficient evidence. It was up to him to provide it. They had heard that he had done many marvelous things in Capernaum. But that wasn't enough; if he wanted them to believe his claim, he would have to prove it true by doing many more works like that in his own home town.[2]

Furthermore, Jesus was every bit as poor and needy as they were. How could they trust him to do something for them unless he could do it for himself? So before they would believe that he had good news for the poor, liberty for the captives, or sight for the blind, Jesus had to prove that he had the power to work miracles. It was put up or shut up; they had to see it to believe it; they wanted a miracle on demand.

Many people have the same attitude today. Perhaps they have heard that Jesus Christ is the Son of God and Savior of the world, who died on the cross for sins and rose again with the power of eternal life. They are almost willing to believe it. Yet they feel they need something more than just the preaching of the gospel. They want some kind of *proof*. If only God would solve their financial problems, or give them the relationship they are hoping to have in life, or take away their pain. If only he would speak to them, *then* they would believe in him.

Such skeptics are like the philosopher Bertrand Russell, who once told the Voltaire Society what he would say if he met God face to face. Russell was an agnostic—a man who was not sure whether there was a God or not. So what would he say if he ended up meeting God at the final judgment? "Not enough evidence, Lord. Not enough evidence!"[3] Bertrand Russell was the kind of man who had to see it before he would believe it. He was not willing to take God at his word. Are you?

---

2. David Gooding, *According to Luke: A New Exposition of the Third Gospel* (Grand Rapids: Eerdmans, 1987), 84.

3. This story is recounted by John Searle in *Mind, Language, and Society* (Boulder: Perseus, 1998), 36–37.

The Gospel Is for Outsiders, Too

The problem for skeptics is that Jesus does not give in to our demands. Rather than allowing us to take him on our terms, he insists that we receive him on his terms, or not at all. This is why Jesus refused to give the kind of performance that all his old neighbors were looking for: they would not believe in his word. In fact, Mark tells us "he could do no mighty work there, except that he laid his hands on a few sick people and healed them" (Mark 6:5). Why couldn't Jesus do any mighty work there? "Because of their unbelief" (Mark 6:6). So instead of performing miracles in Nazareth, Jesus uttered one of his famous proverbs: "Truly, I say to you, no prophet is acceptable in his hometown" (Luke 4:24).

This is a general principle of human relationships. We often envy the success of those who come from the same circumstances that we do. Indeed, the people of Nazareth seemed to resent the fact that rather than staying at home, Jesus went off and became a success elsewhere. Then too, familiarity breeds contempt, and sometimes the people who are closest to us have the hardest time letting us grow into the people God is calling us to become. They knew us way back when, so they think they know us already, even if they know more about who we were than who we are. This is especially a problem for prophets, who get less respect than almost anyone else. People love their hometown heroes, but not their local prophets. Prophets have a way of confronting sin and unbelief, as Jesus did, and this is hardly the way to become popular.

Maybe this is one of the reasons why many Christians have trouble persuading their own family members to accept Jesus Christ. They speak to their families with a prophetic voice, exposing their sin and warning them about the coming judgment. Sometimes God calls us to this kind of ministry, but if so, we need to remember that prophets are without honor, especially at home. Often it is better simply to embrace our families with the love that we have found in Christ, taking the role of a caring servant rather than a confronting prophet.

To prove his point about prophets without honor, Jesus used two examples from the lives of two of the greatest Old Testament prophets: Elijah and Elisha (Luke 4:25–27). Like Jesus, these men often went without honor in their home country. Yet God used them to share his grace with two outsiders: the poor widow of Zarephath and Namaan the leper. Jesus emphasizes that these needy people were not from Israel: the widow lived in the land of Sidon; Naaman came from Syria. Since both of them were Gentiles, they came from somewhere outside the family of God.

Jesus was warning the people of Nazareth that the same thing could happen to them. The good news of his grace was not just for the Jews, but for anyone and everyone who would come to him in faith. If his neighbors rejected the Christ, then he would take his gospel and go elsewhere, because even if *they* would not receive him, others would. Here is how Michael Wilcock explains Jesus' message: "Now listen, I have come with the good news of salvation not for Nazareth only, but for all Galilee, and indeed for all Israel; and—although this will scandalize you—if Israel turns out to be as blinkered and narrow-minded as you are, then she will forfeit it, while the rest of the world receives it."[4] This was something Luke wanted to show in his Gospel: that Jesus came to save sinners from all nations and thus to fulfill God's ancient plan to show his grace to the world.

Two Who Believed

Jesus used the examples of Elijah and Elisha to show that the good news of his gospel is not just for Jews, but also for Gentiles. That much is obvious. Jesus was also saying something less obvious, however, and possibly more important, but to see it we need to look more carefully at these two stories from the Old Testament.

The first story came from the ministry of the prophet Elijah. Jesus said, "But in truth, I tell you, there were many widows in Israel in the days of Elijah, when the heavens were shut up three years and six months, and a great famine came over all the land, and Elijah was sent to none of them but only to Zarephath, in the land of Sidon, to a woman who was a widow" (Luke 4:25–26).

This woman was desperate: she was down to her last meal. But God sent Elijah to meet her, and to ask for a drink of water and a morsel of bread. At first the woman refused. She said to Elijah, "As the LORD your God lives, I have nothing baked, only a handful of flour in a jar and a

4. Michael Wilcock, *The Message of Luke*, The Bible Speaks Today (Downers Grove, IL: Inter-Varsity, 1979), 61–62.

little oil in a jug. And now I am gathering a couple of sticks that I may go in and prepare it for myself and my son, that we may eat it and die" (1 Kings 17:12). Elijah told her not to be afraid, but to go ahead and bake him a cake, then to feed herself and her son. He told her this on the basis of a promise from God: "The jar of flour shall not be spent, and the jug of oil shall not be empty, until the day that the LORD sends rain upon the earth" (1 Kings 17:14). Amazingly, the widow did what Elijah said. She went home to bake him some bread, and God provided for her in a miraculous way. Her supplies did not run out, just as God had promised.

Why did Jesus use this story for one of his examples? Partly because the widow lived in Zarephath, which was outside of Israel, and therefore confirmed what he said about prophets being without honor at home. But Jesus also used her story for another reason: the widow had to believe God's promise *before* she saw God's miracle. If she had waited for God to prove himself, she would have died of starvation long before she ever ate another mouthful of food. God would perform the miracle of the flour and oil only if she acted in faith by first making the bread. Only then would she see what God could do. In other words, she had to believe it before she could see it. And she did believe it! There were many widows in Israel, but this was the woman who had faith. She knew her need, recognizing "her extreme poverty and fatal lack of resources."[5] And she believed that God would do what he said.

Jesus was calling the people of Nazareth to do the same thing, to take God at his word. Did he have the power to perform miracles? Yes, he did. Could he have done the same things in Nazareth that he did in Capernaum? Of course. But first things first: the people had to believe the gospel according to Jesus. They had to recognize their spiritual poverty and captivity to sin, then trust in Christ to save them. They wanted Jesus to do his miracles first, but he wanted them to come to him through faith in his word. He said they had to believe it to see it.

The story of Naaman teaches the same lesson. Jesus said, "And there were many lepers in Israel in the time of the prophet Elisha, and none of them was cleansed, but only Naaman the Syrian" (Luke 4:27). Again, like

5. Gooding, *Luke*, 87.

the widow of Zarephath, Naaman was an outsider—a commander in the army of one of Israel's most hated enemies. Unlike the widow, Naaman was extremely wealthy; nevertheless, his leprosy made him just as needy. So he traveled all the way down from Syria to see if God's prophet Elisha could do anything to heal him.

Elisha had just the remedy that Naaman needed. All he had to do was bathe in the Jordan River seven times, and his skin would be restored. But in order to do this, Naaman had to trust God's word, and at first he was skeptical. Elisha's instructions made him angry because he was looking for a miracle that worked more like magic. He said, "Behold, I thought that he would surely come out to me and stand and call upon the name of the LORD his God, and wave his hand over the place and cure the leper" (2 Kings 5:11). But eventually Naaman's servants persuaded him to do what Elisha told him to do. After all, his need was desperate, and all he had to do was wash and be clean. "So he went down," the Scripture says, "and dipped himself seven times in the Jordan, according to the word of the man of God, and his flesh was restored like the flesh of a little child, and he was clean" (2 Kings 5:14). Naaman acted in faith on God's word, and when he did, he witnessed God's saving power in his life.

With these two stories, Jesus was calling the people of Nazareth—and us—to faith. If they refused to believe, he would give his grace to those who would believe, just as he did in the days of Elijah and Elisha. But if only they took him at his word, they would see the salvation of their God. This is one of the great paradoxes of the Christian faith. If we want to receive eternal life, we need to believe the promise of the gospel. God does not take us to heaven first, and then ask us if we want to go there. Instead, he invites us simply to believe in Christ, promising that when we do, we will be saved forever. We have to believe it to see it.

The same principle applies throughout the Christian life. When it comes to our education, our relationships, our calling, our ministry, our retirement, or our future, we do not know what God has in store for us. But we take it on faith, trusting that he will keep his promise to protect us and provide for us. God offers full salvation in Jesus, and anyone who believes in him will see everything that God has to offer. Can you believe it? If you can, you will see it.

AN ANGRY RESPONSE

The people of Nazareth still couldn't see it, and they were not ready to believe it. In fact, the longer Jesus preached, the angrier they became, until finally they were ready to put him to death: "When they heard these things, all in the synagogue were filled with wrath. And they rose up and drove him out of the town and brought him to the brow of the hill on which their town was built, so that they could throw him down the cliff" (Luke 4:28–29). Obviously, they liked the introduction to his sermon a lot better than the conclusion! Their admiration for Jesus quickly turned into exasperation. They did not even wait for the benediction; they just marched him right out of the synagogue and tried to kill him.

No prophet receives honor in his hometown, but even so, this was an extreme reaction, especially since the intended victim was the Son of God. What made these people so angry?

Maybe Jesus insulted their spiritual pride. People generally do not like to admit how needy they are, so when he attacked their self-sufficiency, they were greatly offended. They rejected Jesus—not because they did not have enough evidence, but because they would not admit their spiritual need. According to him, the gospel was for people who were poor, blind, and captive. But as far as the people of Nazareth were concerned, they were none of these things. They were good, law-keeping, Bible-believing, worship-attending Jews. Who did Jesus think they were? And who did he think *he* was? The answer is that Jesus is the all-sufficient Savior:

> If they were poor and resourceless, they had only to call on him and he would demonstrate to them in their own personal subjective experience that his claim was true. . . . But there, of course, lay the trouble; they were not poor, at least, in their own estimation they were not. They were respectable, spiritually resourceful people, kind parents, loyal citizens, honest traders, regular attenders of the synagogue. His claim to be the Messiah come to put the world right was fantastic enough for a young man whom they had known from infancy; but they were prepared to consider the objective evidence of further miracles if he could repeat what he was reported to have done in Capernaum. But they were not in any urgent personal need.[6]

6. Gooding, *Luke*, 87.

Jesus also wounded their ethnic pride. If there was one thing the people of Nazareth knew, it was that God was for the Jews, and not for the Gentiles. To understand their attitude towards outsiders, consider the inscription that was on the temple in those days: "Let no Gentile enter within the partition and barrier surrounding the Temple, and whosoever is caught shall be responsible for his subsequent death."[7] Yet here Jesus was telling them that even if *they* did not believe in him, the Gentiles would.

Whenever Jesus said that his gospel was for the world, it always touched a raw nerve of Jewish patriotism, not to say prejudice. Later the apostles faced the same kind of hostility (see Acts 13:46–50; 22:21–22). People in places like Nazareth wanted to believe that God was only for them, and not for others. They were offended by the idea that God would share his grace with people who did not even deserve it. So when Jesus started talking about lepers and foreigners, it made them angry. They resented the implication that Gentiles would receive something that they themselves did not have the faith to believe. David Gooding comments: "To be told that they were spiritually blind, resourceless and poverty-stricken was bad enough; now to be told that they were less wise than this Gentile leper was intolerable."[8] Fred Craddock makes the same point in a provocative way: "Jesus does not go elsewhere because he is rejected; he is rejected because he goes elsewhere."[9]

And so they tried to stone him, executing the ancient penalty for blasphemy. In those days there was more than one way to stone someone. Sometimes the guilty party was tied up so people could throw rocks at him. But sometimes it was easier simply to throw someone off a cliff, dashing him against the stones below. This is what the Nazarenes wanted to do with Jesus, so they dragged him up a steep slope and tried to push him over the edge. It was a clear case of mob violence.

This was not the first time that someone tried to kill Jesus, and it would not be the last. Herod tried to kill him when he was still a baby. When he was a man, many people plotted against Jesus, until finally they put him to death. What happened at Nazareth was a premonition of the

7. Joseph A. Fitzmyer, "Did Jesus Speak Greek?" *Biblical Archaeology Review* 18.5 (Sept./Oct. 1992): 58–63 (p. 61).

8. Gooding, *Luke*, 88.

9. Fred B. Craddock, *Luke*, Interpretation (Louisville: John Knox, 1990), 64.

cross. Already we can tell that something horrible will happen to this man. We see what kind of Savior he will become: someone "despised and rejected by men" (Isa. 53:3). No prophet was ever dishonored like Jesus, not only in his hometown, but also by the very world that he had made.

This time God delivered him. Luke tells us that "passing through their midst, he went away" (Luke 4:30). This mysterious verse does not explain quite how Jesus escaped. But however it happened—maybe by means of some miracle, or perhaps simply by the sheer force of his personality—Jesus emerged unscathed. Not that he was unwilling to suffer for the sake of the people that he had come to save. Indeed, this was the very reason he came: to suffer and die for sinners. But it was not yet time for him to die. When it came time, he would do it of his own accord (see John 10:18), but the hour of his greatest suffering had not yet come.

As far as we know from the Gospel of Luke, this was the last time that Jesus ever appeared in Nazareth. He went away and never returned. As John comments in his Gospel, "He came to his own, and his own people did not receive him" (John 1:11). For some of them it must have been the last opportunity they ever had to hear Jesus preach, to believe that he was the Christ, and to worship him as their Savior and their Lord. They missed their chance! Rather than receiving him by faith, they demanded more evidence, and when he refused to give in to their demands, they tried to kill him.

Luke tells us these things to confront us with the claims of Christ. The question comes back to us: Who is Jesus, and what does he want with me? As we see how people responded to Jesus, we start to realize that we need to make a response of our own. We do not wish to kill him, of course, but if Jesus is who he says he is, then even an indifferent response will condemn us. We have heard the same gospel that the people heard in Nazareth, preached by the same Christ. Jesus says that he can rescue us from our debt and bondage to sin and restore our spiritual sight. This is exactly what we need, if only we will admit it. If we trust in him, he will release us and rescue us.

16

ALL AUTHORITY AND POWER

Luke 4:31—44

And they were all amazed and said to one another, "What is this word? For with authority and power he commands the unclean spirits, and they come out!" (Luke 4:36)

ifferent people exercise authority in different ways. A general does it by giving out orders and enforcing strict military discipline. A teacher does it by passing out grades and sending her students to the principal's office. A traffic cop does it by blowing his whistle and handing out citations. A taxman does it by conducting an audit and assessing penalties. These are some of the many ways that people exercise their God-given authority.

But how did Jesus exercise *his* authority? In the simplest way we can imagine: just by saying the word.

ALL KINDS OF AUTHORITY

At the end of Luke 4 the scene shifts away from Nazareth—where Jesus was rejected—to Capernaum, a city by the sea. There we find Jesus doing what he always did: going to the synagogue and preaching the gospel. It was another city, another Sabbath, another sermon. "If this is Saturday," Jesus might have said while he was on this preaching tour, "it must be Capernaum."

The ruins of this particular synagogue are still standing, close by the Sea of Galilee. The foundation stones date back to the time of Christ,[1] when Capernaum was a prosperous fishing town. Over the course of a single day, the people who lived there witnessed an awesome display of the divine power of Jesus Christ. It was "all in a day's work," and as Luke describes what happened on that remarkable day, he shows Jesus exercising three different kinds of authority. He also shows how people responded. From these events we learn the priority of the Word of God in the ministry of Jesus Christ.

First, Jesus exercised *teaching* authority: "And he went down to Capernaum, a city of Galilee. And he was teaching them on the Sabbath, and they were astonished at his teaching, for his word possessed authority" (Luke 4:31–32).

People were completely amazed; they had never heard anything like it. All of their other teachers spoke with delegated authority. When they taught the Bible, they spent much of their time quoting from other teachers. Their theology came second-hand. In the words of one ancient rabbi, "I have never in my life said a thing which I did not hear from my teachers."[2] But Jesus spoke on his own authority. As Mark said in a parallel account of the same events: "They were astonished at his teaching, for he taught them as one who had authority, and not as the scribes" (Mark 1:22). Jesus did not just preach about God; he *was* God. So when he preached, what he said was the very Word of God, in all its almighty authority.

Jesus also had *exorcising* authority. In other words, he had the power to perform exorcisms—to cast out demons. After Jesus preached, he started to work miracles that showed his power over the dark spirits of supernatural evil. Luke reports that "in the synagogue there was a man who had the spirit of an unclean demon. . . . But Jesus rebuked him, saying, 'Be silent and come out of him!' And when the demon had thrown him down in their midst, he

---

1. See Stanislao Loffreda, "Capernaum," in *New Encyclopedia of Archaeological Excavations in the Holy Land* (New York: Simon & Schuster, 1993), 1:294–95.

2. R. Eliezer, *Sukkah* 28a, quoted in Leon Morris, *The Gospel According to St. Luke: An Introduction and Commentary*, Tyndale New Testament Commentaries (Grand Rapids: Eerdmans, 1974), 109.

came out of him, having done him no harm" (Luke 4:33, 35). Later in the passage we read that demons came out of many of the other people that Jesus healed (Luke 4:41).

What is "the spirit of an unclean demon"? Some people deny the existence of demons. They say that this man was really struggling with some psychological disorder. But Luke knew better. This poor man was not suffering from depression; he was under the personal domination of a fallen angel—a supernatural being who was trying to cause him spiritual and physical harm. Norval Geldenhuys rightly says that demon possession "was not merely an ordinary form of mental disease as some writers have alleged, but a special phenomenon which was particularly frequent during Jesus' earthly sojourn and thus was directly connected with His coming to destroy the power of darkness."[3]

This raises an obvious question: Are people still possessed by demons today? The answer is yes. We are in a spiritual battle, and the cosmic forces of darkness are still fighting against us (see Eph. 6:12). These powers seek to gain control any way they can. They are often at work promoting evil in the structures of sinful society, but in their wickedness, they sometimes seek to dominate particular individuals (perhaps especially in cultures that have not yet been penetrated by the power of the gospel). This goes well beyond the general way in which unbelievers are said to be "in the power of the evil one" (1 John 5:19). Demon possession also goes well beyond ordinary temptation. In some Christian circles it has become popular to attribute every sin to a particular demon. People who think too highly of themselves have a demon of pride; people who eat too much have a demon of gluttony; and so on. When people talk this way, they are really blaming Satan for their own sinful nature. Their sins are not the direct result of demonic control, but simply the expression of their own sinful desires.

Nor is demon possession merely a matter of mental illness. Not everyone who has a delusion is under satanic control, although demons may perhaps cause or exacerbate mental illness and often seem to attack people who are spiritually or psychologically weak, taking advantage of any opportunity to gain greater control. This means that demons can be hard to detect, or to separate from a person's other struggles. Someone who is demon-possessed

3. Norval Geldenhuys, *The Gospel of Luke*, New International Commentary on the New Testament (Grand Rapids: Eerdmans, 1951), 174.

may even have outward manifestations that are similar to other psychological disorders. But the origin of the oppression is different. People who are demon-possessed are dominated by an inward, personal evil.

Demon possession seems to happen relatively more rarely today than it did in the time of Christ. Perhaps this is because there are now so many more people in the world, but only so many demons to torment them. The number of demons is finite, and there are more people than they can ever hope to possess. Or maybe Satan threw the full weight of his power against Israel because he knew that the Savior would come there first. But whatever the reason, Jesus often came into direct contact with people who were oppressed by demons.

This was part of his ongoing war with the devil. In this war, Jesus had authority over the demons, which he exercised simply by speaking his word. As Martin Luther wrote in his famous hymn about God's victory over Satan, "One little word shall fell him." The same word that Jesus had used to defeat the devil in the wilderness—the word of God—he now used to cast out demons. In those days people who wanted to gain power over the darkness would resort to all kinds of magic spells, religious incantations, bizarre rituals, and other desperate forms of hocus-pocus. But Jesus had true spiritual authority. All he had to do was say the word, and out the demon came.

THE GREAT PHYSICIAN

Jesus had a third kind of authority: *healing* authority. The same Christ who taught people the Word and triumphed over their demons also had the power to touch their bodies. He demonstrated this power at the house of Simon Peter: "And he arose and left the synagogue and entered Simon's house. Now Simon's mother-in-law was ill with a high fever, and they appealed to him on her behalf. And he stood over her and rebuked the fever, and it left her, and immediately she rose and began to serve them" (Luke 4:38–39).

Luke does not explain who Simon was, possibly because he was such a famous disciple. We will certainly get to know him well enough by the end of the Gospel. What Luke does tell us is that Peter had a mother-in-law, which presumably means that he had married a local girl (cf. 1 Cor. 9:5).

The good doctor also describes the woman's medical condition: she was "ill with a high fever" (Luke 4:38). This was a medical term for a dangerous fever.[4] The woman must have been desperate for a cure.

After a brief consultation, Jesus stood over her bed and commanded the fever to come out. He had the same power over disease that he had over demons. Both the physical world and the spiritual world were under his divine authority. All he had to do was rebuke the fever, and it was gone. Peter's mother-in-law was totally and immediately better. Her cure was complete. Luke proves this by showing what she did next. One minute she was lying sick in bed; the next moment she was up on her feet making people feel at home. This shows what kind of woman she was: she had the gift of hospitality. It also shows what we should do when Jesus touches us with his healing power: we should get up and start to serve him by serving others. But mainly it shows that Jesus has complete control and total authority over the diseases and disabilities of the human body.

We know Jesus well enough to expect this kind of miracle, but to the people who were there that day, it was such an amazing occurrence that the word quickly spread: "Now when the sun was setting, all those who had any who were sick with various diseases brought them to him, and he laid his hands on every one of them and healed them" (Luke 4:40). Presumably the reason people waited until sunset was to avoid breaking the Sabbath. Remember, this all happened on God's day of rest, and when it had ended, people started streaming to Jesus. Peter's home became a house of healing as Jesus cured diseases, removed tumors, mended broken bones, and did whatever else people needed to be made sound in body. He cured them all by the power of his healing touch.

Again we ask the question: Does Jesus still have this healing power today? The answer is yes, of course he does. He is Creator and Lord of the human body, and he can work a miracle whenever he wants. However, this is not his usual way of working. Ordinarily he works to answer our prayers for healing through the normal means of medical care. This too is one of God's gracious gifts, but it is not miraculous. "Miracle" is a word that Christians use all too casually, and often unwisely. Most recoveries—however unexpected—are not miracles.

---

4. Darrell L. Bock, *Luke 1:1–9:50*, Baker Exegetical Commentary on the New Testament 3A (Grand Rapids: Baker, 1994), 436.

To understand this, it helps to know why Jesus performed so many miracles during his earthly ministry. He did not do it to teach us to "expect a miracle." Rather, he did it to confirm his identity as the Christ. The apostles did something similar when they preached the gospel. As the good news about Jesus spread to new communities, the wonder-working power of the apostles helped to authenticate their message. Their miracles proved that what they said was true. Sometimes Jesus still works in miraculous ways today, especially when his gospel first penetrates a godless culture. He certainly has the power and authority to overrule creation whenever he pleases. But this is something that he rarely does, which is exactly why it is called a miracle.

Since Jesus has healing authority, we should pray in his name whenever we are sick. But we need to recognize that God often chooses *not* to heal us. Some day "there will be no more death or mourning or crying or pain" (Rev. 21:4 NIV). But we are still living in a fallen world, where disability and disease are part of God's curse against sin. Eventually all our prayers for healing will be answered, but this will not happen until Jesus comes again. Furthermore, God often uses our physical difficulties to do his gracious work in our lives. The life of the Christian follows the pattern of the life of Christ, in which suffering is the road to glory.

Among other things, this means that we can never make our health the test of God's love. Often Jesus has a work of healing to do in us that goes much deeper than our bodies. In his commentary on these verses, Michael Wilcock imagines what Jesus might say to us when he chooses not to answer our prayers for healing. Perhaps he would say something like this: "I could of course give you immediate relief; but I would rather take the opportunity to do something more far-reaching, which will be to your greater benefit in the long run. You will find it more protracted and perhaps more painful, and you may not understand what I am doing, because I may be treating disorders of which you yourself are unaware."[5] And what would Jesus do then? Wilcock says he would "set to work to deal with the needs of the whole person, rather than with the obvious need only. He may aim at a calming of spirit, or a strengthening of courage, or a clarifying of vision, as more important objectives than what we would call healing. Indeed the

5. Michael Wilcock, *The Message of Luke*, The Bible Speaks Today (Downers Grove, IL: Inter-Varsity, 1979), 67.

latter may not be experienced at all in this life, but only at the final 'saving and raising' of the sick, when their mortal nature puts on immortality."[6]

In his healing work as our Great Physician, Jesus is concerned for the whole person—body and soul. Often he uses the hurts of the body to bring healing to the soul, much the way a doctor uses deadly chemotherapy to kill a cancer. Sometimes we wish that God would just hurry up and heal us. If he doesn't, it is not because he doesn't love us, but because he is working a better plan. In the meantime, we need to trust him to do his total work in our lives.

How People (and Demons) Responded

Jesus exercised three different kinds of authority, but he exercised them all the same way: he did it by his word. How did he exercise his teaching authority? By speaking an authoritative word. How did he exercise his authority over demons? Simply by rebuking them. How did he exercise his authority over disease? He did it the same way: by telling the fever to come out. Words may not seem very powerful, but when they come from God, they have the power to transform people's lives, to triumph over supernatural evil, and to overturn the effects of illness. The words of Jesus carry supreme divine authority over creation and all the powers of hell.

How did people respond to Jesus and the awesome authority of his word? As we have seen, his teaching astonished them, but they were equally amazed by his power over demons and disease. Some of them noticed how he exercised this power: "And they were all amazed and said to one another, 'What is this word? For with authority and power he commands the unclean spirits, and they come out!' And reports about him went out into every place in the surrounding region" (Luke 4:36–37).

This is how the gospel spreads: by word of mouth, from person to person. When we see what Jesus can do, we want others to know about it, so they can see for themselves. In this case, people not only saw his power, but they also saw how he exercised it: by speaking his word. Just as God once spoke the universe into being, so Jesus spoke, and it was so. Here was a

6. Wilcock, *Luke*, 67–68.

clear demonstration of his divine power. He spoke his words with the very authority of God.

Even if some people did not recognize the source of this authority, the demons certainly did. They knew exactly what they were up against, which is why they cried out against it. This happened at the synagogue, where the demon "cried out with a loud voice, 'Ha! What have you to do with us, Jesus of Nazareth? Have you come to destroy us? I know who you are—the Holy One of God'" (Luke 4:33–34). Jesus provoked a similar response at the end of the day, when he was healing the sick: "And demons also came out of many, crying, 'You are the Son of God!'" (Luke 4:41).

These demons knew who Jesus was, and it terrified them. The Bible says, "The reason the Son of God appeared was to destroy the works of the devil" (1 John 3:8). And as Jesus began to do this devil-destroying work, the demons recoiled in terror. "Unable to bear the presence of Christ," writes Kent Hughes, they "writhed in the presence of Jesus' holiness."[7] They were filled with unholy dread, shuddering at the power of his mighty word (see James 2:19). There is no good news for the demons. Jesus has no gospel to save them, but will only condemn them to hell.

This is why the demons asked if Jesus had come to destroy them. They knew that he was the Holy One of God, and they hated him for it. No doubt this explains why Jesus told them to be quiet. This happened at the synagogue, where he said to the demon, "Be silent and come out of him!" (Luke 4:35). It happened again at Peter's house, where Jesus rebuked the demons "and would not allow them to speak, because they knew that he was the Christ" (Luke 4:41).

Why did Jesus silence these demons? After all, they seemed to have a better idea who he was than did anyone else. This has led some to wonder whether Jesus was trying to keep his identity secret. Yet that does not seem to be the right explanation here. If Jesus did not want people to know who he was, then why was he preaching and performing all these miracles by the power of his word?

Perhaps a better explanation is that even if what the demons said happened to be true, Jesus did not want them to be the ones saying it. David Gooding comments that even if "Satan and his demons may for tactical

7. R. Kent Hughes, *Luke: That You May Know the Truth*, 2 vols., Preaching the Word (Wheaton, IL: Crossway, 1998), 1:150.

reasons sometimes say what is true—in the third temptation Satan even quoted Scripture—or they may be forced against their will to say what is true: they never say it out of loyalty to the truth or with any intention of leading people to believe the truth."[8] Jesus hardly needed the servants of hell to declare his true identity. When they said that he was "the Son of God," they were not saying it for his glory, but for a wicked purpose. What matters is not simply knowing that Jesus is the Son of God, but also worshiping him *as* the Son of God. Yet these demons were not worshiping Jesus at all. They were not treating him with reverence and respect. Instead, they were causing a commotion. And so, as Athanasius wrote back in the fourth century, "The Lord himself silenced them and forbade them to speak. He did this to keep them from sowing their own wickedness in the midst of the truth. He also wished us to get used to never listening to them even though they seem to speak the truth."[9]

This is the violent conflict that the word of Christ always brings. Some people believe it by faith and begin to share it, so that others can be saved. But the demons hate it—they absolutely hate it. There is nothing they hate more than God's word, whether it comes from Christ himself, or from one of his servants. They know its holy power, and for that very reason they cry out in fear against it.

Surely this explains why nothing in the world arouses so much spiritual opposition as does the proclamation of biblical truth. Anyone who shares the gospel of Jesus Christ can expect to face opposition and even hatred. And any church that takes a stand for God and his Word can expect to face the same. The devil hates the law of God and the gospel of Jesus Christ, and he will stop at nothing in his ferocious and ultimately futile attempt to destroy them. I say "futile" because the word we proclaim comes with Christ's own authority, and therefore our Savior defends it with his almighty power. As we preach the Word of God, proclaiming the forgiveness of sins through the death and resurrection of Jesus Christ, the Holy Spirit makes it the power of salvation to those who believe. And there is nothing the devil or any of his demons can say to stop it.

8. David Gooding, *According to Luke: A New Exposition of the Third Gospel* (Grand Rapids: Eerdmans, 1987), 91.

9. Athanasius, "Life of St. Anthony," in *Luke*, ed. Arthur A. Just Jr., Ancient Christian Commentary on Scripture, NT 3 (Downers Grove, IL: InterVarsity, 2003), 85.

The Priority of the Word

Certainly there was nothing Satan could do to stop Jesus that extraordinary day in Capernaum, on which the Savior exercised his authority by communicating God's Word, casting out demons, and curing diseases. Apparently he worked well into the night, for "when it was day, he departed and went into a desolate place" (Luke 4:42). In a parallel account, Mark tells us that Jesus went to the wilderness to pray (Mark 1:35). This is something that Jesus often did, as we will see throughout Luke's Gospel. He had a compelling desire to spend time alone with his Father—an example we are wise to follow. If finding opportunities to pray was important to Jesus, it must be all the more important for us.

In this case, he was not alone for long, because "the people sought him and came to him, and would have kept him from leaving them" (Luke 4:42). The response Jesus received in Capernaum was very different from the one he received in Nazareth. There they wanted him to go; here they wanted him to stay, and it is easy to see why. With his power at their disposal, they would never need anything ever again. He could be their teacher, their counselor, and their doctor all rolled into one.

But Jesus refused: "He said to them, 'I must preach the good news of the kingdom of God to the other towns as well; for I was sent for this purpose.' And he was preaching in the synagogues of Judea" (Luke 4:43–44). Part of his concern was that he had others to reach. Jesus did not come to be the Savior of Capernaum only, or even just Israel, but ultimately the world. People were trying to keep him under control, so that he would do what they wanted. But Jesus always refuses to be confined to our narrow agenda. In this case, his mission compelled him to move on from Capernaum.

And what was his mission? To preach the Word, which he called "the good news of the kingdom of God" (Luke 4:43). The kingdom of God is simply the rule of God—the extension of his divine authority and power. That power was now present in the person of Jesus Christ, whose calling was to expand God's dominion by spreading God's Word. The people wanted him to perform more signs and wonders. But Jesus did not come to be a miracle worker; he came to preach the gospel. His ministry was a ministry of the word. In fact, this was even true of the miracles he performed. How did he cast out demons and heal the sick? He did it by the word of God. And

199

for what purpose? So people would know that his word was true. People were always trying to get Jesus to be someone other than who he was and to do something other than what he was called to do. But Jesus said, "I must preach the good news of the kingdom, for I was sent for this purpose."

People do the same thing with Jesus today. They want to turn him into some kind of wonder worker, or entertainment act, or insurance policy. They want something other than what Jesus has to offer: physical healing, or happy feelings, or financial prosperity. These are all blessings that God can give. But his greatest blessing is salvation through his gospel word—the good news of eternal life through the death and resurrection of Jesus Christ.

This is why the church's first priority is to preach the gospel. Today many people do the same thing with the church that they do with Jesus: they turn it into something other than what God has called it to be. They turn it into a political agenda, or an entertainment venue, or a social project—anything and everything other than what it is intended to be: a community that is gathered to hear God's Word. Once we hear the Word, it has an impact on everything else because it changes the way we live. But our first priority is to preach the good news.

The pastor of one of Philadelphia's old downtown churches—a liberal congregation in sad decline—once asked me why so many people worship at Tenth Presbyterian Church. He wanted to know the secret of our apparent success. I told him, "We preach the Word of God." The man was not impressed. In fact, he may even have been offended. But what I told him was the truth. Whether people understand it or not, God does his work by the preaching of his Word. This is why J. C. Ryle warned people to "beware of despising preaching. In every age of the Church, it has been God's principal instrument for the awakening of sinners and the edifying of the saints. The days when there has been little or no preaching have been days when there has been little or no good done in the Church. Let us hear sermons in a prayerful and reverent frame of mind, and remember that they are the principal engines which Christ Himself employed, when He was upon earth."[10]

All authority has been given to Jesus. He exercises this authority simply by speaking his word. Do we believe in the power of that word? Does it have

---

10. J. C. Ryle, *Expository Thoughts on the Gospels, Luke* (1858; reprint Cambridge: James Clarke, 1976), 1:128–29.

the same priority for us that it had for Jesus? If it does, then we will read it, hear it, study it, memorize it, and do everything in our power to share it with others. The Word will be the center of our lives, exercising a controlling influence over what we think, say, and do. And it will be the main thing that we want to share with others. We will not be content simply to befriend people and to serve them with the love of Christ, although we must at least do that. But we will have a pressing, compelling desire for people to hear God's Word. We will encourage them to read it. We will invite them to study it. We will bring them to hear it preached. And as we have the opportunity, we will help to carry it around the world, so that it can do its authoritative and powerful work of extending the kingdom of Jesus Christ.

17

No Turning Back

Luke 5:1–11

*And Jesus said to Simon, "Do not be afraid; from now on you will
be catching men." And when they had brought their boats to land,
they left everything and followed him. (Luke 5:10–11)*

*T*here was a song that I used to sing when I was alone in my
bed, and that my father sometimes sang with me in the twilight. It was a simple old spiritual about following Christ in
the way of discipleship:

I have decided to follow Jesus,
I have decided to follow Jesus,
I have decided to follow Jesus—
No turning back, no turning back.

Then I would sing through the other stanzas: "Though none go with me,
I still will follow. . . . The world behind me, the cross before me—no turning back, no turning back." When I sang those words, I meant them with
all my heart. I had decided to follow Jesus, no matter what. I had to gulp a
little when I got to the second verse because I knew it would not be easy to

follow Jesus all by myself. But that is what I was singing, and I knew in my heart that I would do it. Once I decided to follow Jesus, it was forever and for always.

This is the kind of decision that Luke is pressing us to make in his Gospel. He wants us to know for sure that Jesus is the Christ. To that end, he gives us the facts of Jesus' life and ministry. He documents Jesus' birth as the son of David. He declares his gospel of the kingdom of God. He demonstrates his power and authority over men and demons. He does all this so that we will know Jesus as the Son of God and Savior of the world. But more than that, Luke does it so that we will follow him as our Lord and God. He wants to bring us to the point of making a decision for discipleship. As soon as we know for sure that Jesus is the Christ, we must follow him, which is what it means to be a disciple. A disciple follows Jesus and never turns back.

LISTENING TO JESUS

One of the ways that Luke encourages us to decide for Christ is by telling us the story of the first people who ever made that decision. Chapter 5 begins with Jesus calling his first disciples. From their call we learn at least four things about following Jesus.

First, a true disciple listens to Jesus. In those days Jesus had a growing reputation as a preacher, and people were coming from all over the place to hear him. Luke tells us: "On one occasion, while the crowd was pressing in on him to hear the word of God, he was standing by the lake of Gennesaret, and he saw two boats by the lake, but the fishermen had gone out of them and were washing their nets. Getting into one of the boats, which was Simon's, he asked him to put out a little from the land. And he sat down and taught the people from the boat" (Luke 5:1–3).

Gennesaret is another name for Galilee, the large lake in northern Israel that was the center of Jesus' early ministry. Jesus must have been teaching near Capernaum, because Simon Peter was there, and Capernaum was his hometown. A huge crowd of people had gathered, and they were coming to Jesus for the right reason. As Luke tells us, they were "pressing in on him to hear the word of God" (Luke 5:1). God sent his Son to preach the gospel, so these people were coming to receive the very thing that Jesus had come to give: the word of God.

203

The only problem was that it was hard for all of them to hear. So Jesus quickly looked around for some way to amplify his voice, and when he saw some boats on the shore, he had his solution. Commandeering one of the boats, he rode a little way from shore, and sat down to teach. Jesus was using Peter's boat for his pulpit and the Sea of Galilee for his sound system. His voice carried clearly across the water, so that everyone could hear what he was saying.

Some of the people standing on the shore were becoming disciples, because a disciple is someone who listens to Jesus. This is the context in which discipleship always begins, because in order to follow Jesus, we must hear what he says. For the people who lived in Galilee, this meant going to hear Jesus preach. For us it means reading what Jesus has said in God's Word. It means studying the Bible, both on our own and with other Christians. It also means listening to Spirit-filled, Bible-based, gospel-centered preaching. The Bible says, "Faith comes from hearing, and hearing through the word of Christ" (Rom. 10:17). So for anyone who wants to follow Jesus, the ear is the most important part of the body.

The person who heard Jesus most clearly was the pilot of his boat, Simon Peter. And Peter needed to hear Jesus. He had known Jesus for some time, even welcoming him into his home, but it seems that he had not yet made a full decision for discipleship. This is a good reminder that it is not enough to listen to Jesus without also doing what he says. The ear may be the most important part of a disciple, but it is not the only part. Jesus calls us to follow him, body and soul. Sadly, many people listen to sermons without all their listening ever doing them very much good. They more or less hear what Jesus says, and think, "Wasn't that interesting?" but that is as far as it ever goes. They do not follow through on following Jesus.

It is dangerous to listen to Jesus without deciding to become his disciple. Jesus warned about this later when he denounced the very people who listened to him by the lake but never turned away from their sins. He said, "Capernaum, will you be exalted to heaven? You will be brought down to Hades. . . . I tell you that it will be more tolerable on the day of judgment for the land of Sodom than for you" (Matt. 11:23–24). To put this more provocatively, if people are not willing to follow Jesus, then it would be better for them not to go to church at all. God will hold us accountable for what we hear, and if we do not follow Jesus, we will be judged for our sins.

Turning Away from Sin

This brings us to a second mark of discipleship: a true disciple is a penitent disciple. In order to follow Jesus, we have to turn away from our sins. The person who makes that turnaround in this story is Simon Peter, who was perhaps the first disciple to repent. Jesus led him to repentance by making a strange request: "And when he had finished speaking, he said to Simon, 'Put out into the deep and let down your nets for a catch'" (Luke 5:4). It must have seemed a little presumptuous for Jesus to say this to a salty old fisherman, and we can sympathize with Peter's skepticism. What did a carpenter like Jesus know about catching fish?

Peter had been up all night, because that was the time to fish, especially in deep water. The fish generally did not surface during the bright hours of sunshine, but stayed deeper down, so it was better fishing at night. Of course, fishermen do not always catch something, and on this particular occasion, Peter and his fishing buddies caught nothing at all. No doubt they were tired and discouraged: their livelihood depended on catching fish. Furthermore, they had just finished washing and mending their nets (Luke 5:2). This meant that they were done for the night, and it was time to let their tackle dry in the daylight sun. Just about the last thing they wanted to do was go back out and fish. Hence the annoyance we sense in Peter's voice: "Master, we toiled all night and took nothing!" (Luke 5:5).

Peter was trying to straighten Jesus out by suggesting that it was pointless to try again what he and his companions had been trying all night. No one likes to get on-the-job advice from someone in a different line of work. Peter was the professional here, not Jesus. If Jesus wanted to teach the Bible, that was one thing. He could even borrow Peter's boat, if he needed to. But when he started telling Peter how to fish, that was another matter entirely.[1] By climbing into his boat and giving orders, Jesus was invading Peter's personal space. He did this to teach his disciple that his life was not his own. It was more than Peter's worship that Jesus wanted; he also wanted his work. Jesus was saying, "Your whole life belongs to me, Peter, even your fishing!"

1. Michael Wilcock, *The Message of Luke*, The Bible Speaks Today (Downers Grove, IL: InterVarsity, 1979), 68: "As long as Simon's boat is being used for a pulpit, the owner has no objection to Jesus's saying in it what he likes. But when it reverts to being a fishing-boat, it is Simon's once more, and Jesus no longer has a say in how it is to be used. Fishing is Simon's job."

Peter may have thought that Jesus was meddling at this point, but he still did what Jesus told him to do. This is the important thing: even if he was a little bit reluctant, Peter still obeyed. Using a title that communicated respectful submission, he said, "Master, at your word I will let down the nets" (Luke 5:5). This shows that Peter was well on his way to becoming a disciple. He was willing to do what Jesus said, even before he was sure if it was the right thing to do. He was still something of a skeptic, but at some point he crossed over from not quite believing in Jesus to almost believing in him, even if he still wasn't certain. This encourages our faith, especially when we struggle with doubts of our own. The first disciples all had their doubts. They were born skeptics. But what happened to Peter is what Luke hoped would happen to us as we read his Gospel: he started knowing Jesus for sure, and trusting his word.

It took a miracle for Peter and his mates to know for sure. First they had to do what Jesus said, letting down their nets: "And when they had done this, they enclosed a large number of fish, and their nets were breaking. They signaled to their partners in the other boat to come and help them. And they came and filled both the boats, so that they began to sink" (Luke 5:6–7). It was a tense situation. From the shore, an experienced observer readily could see that there was trouble on the water. When the fishermen dragged their nets, they came up with a ton of fish—maybe literally. Immediately they sent a signal across the water, and a second boat was launched. These boats were more than twenty feet long, but as the fishermen began to pull in their catch, the weight of the fish was so great that they started to sink.

It was the catch of a lifetime—the kind of thing a fisherman could talk about for the rest of his days. It was also a miracle—something that went well beyond the ordinary laws of nature. Whether Jesus summoned the fish up from the sea, or whether in some miraculous way he knew exactly where they were, he was showing his power over creation. Jesus did far more abundantly than any fisherman could ask or imagine. David Gooding writes, "Here was the Lord of fish and fishermen, the Lord of nature, the Lord of men and of their daily work."[2]

2. David Gooding, *According to Luke: A New Exposition of the Third Gospel* (Grand Rapids: Eerdmans, 1987), 103.

Once again, Jesus performed this miracle by the power of his mighty word. It was at his word that Peter lowered his nets, and at his word that they were filled to breaking. This teaches us to take Jesus at his word. Even if at first we do not fully believe what he says, we should believe as much as we can and ask him to help us to believe it all.

Peter learned to take Jesus at his word, too, but the main thing he learned was the sinfulness of his sin. His reaction to this miracle was somewhat surprising: "But when Simon Peter saw it, he fell down at Jesus' knees, saying, 'Depart from me, for I am a sinful man, O Lord.' For he and all who were with him were astonished at the catch of fish that they had taken, and so also were James and John, sons of Zebedee, who were partners with Simon" (Luke 5:8–10). This was a spontaneous and impulsive act of humble repentance. Heedless of the danger that his boat was in, Peter fell down right then and there in the boat and confessed that he was a sinner. Suddenly he realized that he was so unworthy that he was not even fit to ride in the same boat with Jesus.

The Bible says it was the miraculous catch that led Peter to repent. But what was he repenting *for*? This is less obvious. Maybe Peter was sorry for doubting Jesus' word. Maybe he was deeply moved by a miracle in his own area of expertise. He had seen Jesus perform other miracles, but he had not yet seen his power over the sea. Norval Geldenhuys comments that this miracle spoke to Peter

> in a very special manner. For he was a fisherman by trade and knew how humanly impossible it was to catch fish successfully in the lake in the early morning hours. The Lord's revelation of power in the field of Peter's own particular calling—the trade of a fisherman—consequently made a very powerful impression on him. That is why it was precisely after this event that he fell down before the Saviour with an overwhelming sense of His superhuman, divine glory and with a deep realization of his own utter sinfulness.[3]

But Peter's repentance seems more comprehensive. By performing this miracle, Jesus had displayed his divine majesty, and in response, Peter called him "Lord" (Luke 5:8). Earlier he had called Jesus "Master"

---

3. Norval Geldenhuys, *The Gospel of Luke*, New International Commentary on the New Testament (Grand Rapids: Eerdmans, 1951), 182.

(Luke 5:5), recognizing his teaching authority. But here Peter reverently acknowledges Jesus' sovereign lordship, and in doing so, he also sees his own sin. In an old commentary on this text, Plummer writes: "It is the 'Master' whose orders must be obeyed, the 'Lord' whose holiness causes moral agony to the sinner."[4] Peter understood that he was in the presence of someone perfectly holy, and that by contrast, he himself was totally depraved. So he fell down and confessed the sin of his entire nature.

Sooner or later, every disciple must come to the point of full repentance. We have to see ourselves as we really are, in all our sin. The way we see ourselves as we really are is by seeing Jesus as he really is, in all his power and majesty. This is what happened to Job, who saw God's glory over all creation and repented in dust and ashes (Job 42:6). It is what happened to Isaiah, who said, "Woe is me! For I am lost; for I am a man of unclean lips, and I dwell in the midst of a people of unclean lips; for my eyes have seen the King, the LORD of hosts!" (Isa. 6:5). And it is what happened to Peter, who fell down in his boat to worship Jesus with reverence and repentance. This was the great turning point in his life, as it is for everyone who follows Jesus. The point is not so much that we need to repent of this sin or that sin, but that we need to repent of our whole sinful selves. Eventually every disciple says what Peter said: "I am a sinful man, O Lord"; "I am a sinful woman"; "I am a sinful boy or girl."

FISHING FOR MEN

When we see our sin, we do not need to run away from Jesus. This is what Peter tried to do, and it is easy to understand why. He said to Jesus, "Depart from me, for I am a sinful man, O Lord" (Luke 5:8). This was vintage Peter: as soon as he half understood who Jesus was and what he was doing, he immediately leaped to the wrong conclusion. When he saw what a sinner he was, he suddenly decided there was no way for him to have any kind of relationship with Jesus at all.

4. A. Plummer, *Gospel According to St. Luke*, International Critical Commentary (Edinburgh: T. & T. Clark, 1922), quoted in Leon Morris, *The Gospel According to St. Luke: An Introduction and Commentary*, Tyndale New Testament Commentaries (Grand Rapids: Eerdmans, 1974), 113.

Sometimes we feel the same way. When we finally see how sinful we really are, it is only natural for us to feel that we do not even deserve to come into God's presence. We are too guilty to be where God is. But this is exactly why Jesus came. He came to bring us close to God by dying on the cross for our sins. Our sinful, guilty hearts want to push Jesus away. But rather than pushing him away, we should hold on to him, asking for the forgiveness that only he can offer.

Jesus never leaves a sinner who truly repents, so he did not leave Peter, but said to him, "Do not be afraid" (Luke 5:10). Jesus was reassuring Peter, telling him that his sins did not disqualify him. Part of Peter's anxiety was that he was too sinful to be useful. But Jesus told him not to be afraid: God could still use him. There was something he could do to glorify his Lord; he could follow his repentance with service. To be specific, Peter could become a "fisher of men," for Jesus told him, "from now on you will be catching men" (Luke 5:10; cf. Matt. 4:19). This is a third mark of Christian discipleship: every true disciple tells people about Jesus.

The way Jesus described Peter's evangelistic work is significant. He told his new disciple that he would be catching men "from now on." This was a new calling, a decisive new direction for Peter's life. From this time forward he would be an evangelist. Furthermore, this would be his full-time job, because the word used here for catching *(zōgrōn)* is a participle that implies continuous action. There is something else important about this word. It is formed by joining the verb "to catch" *(agreuō)* with the word for life *(zōon)*. Thus it means "to catch alive," which conveys the idea of rescue from danger.[5] This is not what most fishermen have in mind. When a fisherman catches fish, he is usually hoping to eat them, not save them! But Jesus was calling Peter to be a new kind of fisherman—one who rescued people from the deep sea of their sin and brought them safely to the shore of salvation. People who fish for sport would probably call this "catch and release," because people who get "caught" by the gospel are released from their sins.

People often say, "Give a man a fish, and you feed him for a day; teach a man to fish, and you feed him for a lifetime." But Jesus shows us that if you teach a man to fish for men, the people he catches will live forever. Peter excelled at this kind of fishing. During the course of his apostolic ministry,

5. Darrell L. Bock, *Luke 1:1–9:50*, Baker Exegetical Commentary on the New Testament 3A (Grand Rapids: Baker, 1994), 461.

as he went around preaching repentance and faith, Peter hauled in boat-loads of believers. Luke wrote about this in the book of Acts. Not long after Jesus rose from the dead and ascended to heaven, Peter cast his gospel net by preaching the gospel in Jerusalem and brought three thousand people to faith in Jesus Christ (Acts 2:14–41).

This calling was not just for Peter, but also for everyone who follows Jesus. Sometimes we think of evangelism as something for Christians with a special gift. It is true that some people are more gifted at it than others. But the call to tell people about Jesus is for every Christian. Evangelism is an ordinary part of everyday discipleship. Everyone who follows Jesus is called to be a kind of fisherman.

Evangelism is a lot like fishing. We should be careful not to take this analogy too far, but the miraculous catch of fish was a kind of parable about evangelism. By performing this miracle and then calling Peter to fish for men, Jesus was drawing a comparison. A fisherman never knows what he is going to catch. The catch is up to the sovereignty of God, as any fisherman can tell you. But if a fisherman refuses to drag his net, he will never catch anything at all. The same is true in Christian evangelism. We are called to cast a wide net by inviting our neighbors to Bible study, bringing our friends to church, speaking to family members about spiritual things, testifying to God's goodness in our daily lives, supporting Christian broadcasting, sending out foreign missionaries, and sharing the gospel every way we can. This is our calling both as a church and as individual Christians.

As we do these things, we trust in the sovereignty of God. Will we catch anything? Not always, and never by our own abilities, but that is hardly a reason to stop fishing! We should never let what may seem like our ineffectiveness in evangelism prevent us from doing what God has called us to do. In the same way that a fisherman keeps casting his nets, we are called to keep sharing our faith. We may catch people in places where we least expect it. We may bring in more people than we could ever imagine. After all, that is what happened to Peter on the Sea of Galilee. But whatever the results, God has called us to keep casting our gospel net because this is how he saves sinners. And he *will* save them. When Jesus called Peter to fish for men, he also gave him a promise: "you will be catching men" (Luke 5:10). He has given the same promise to us. We may not preach like Peter, but God will use his word to bring people to faith in Christ.

The African evangelist Michael Cassidy applied these principles to evangelism by observing that Peter and his friends were better fishermen than Jesus and that they were using all the latest methods for catching fish. Yet without Jesus himself their nets remained empty; they had nothing to show for all their hard work. So too our own efforts to win the lost—whatever our methods—will fail without the saving power of Jesus Christ.[6]

The great Scottish theologian Thomas Boston testified to this principle in a little essay called "A Soliloquy on the Art of Man-Fishing." In his essay the young pastor lamented his lack of effectiveness in evangelism, yet he also trusted that by the grace of God, he would yet become a "fisher of men." Boston wrote:

> Seeing I am called out to preach this everlasting gospel, it is my duty to endeavour, and it is my desire to be (Lord, thou knowest) a fisher of men. But, alas! I may come in with my complaints to my Lord, that I have toiled in some measure, but caught nothing, for any thing I know, as to the conversion of any one soul. I fear I may say, I have almost spent my strength in vain, and my labour for nought, for Israel is not gathered. O my soul, what may be the cause of this, why does my preaching so little good? No doubt part of the blame lies on myself, and a great part of it too. But who can give help in this case but the Lord himself? And how can I expect it from him but by prayer, and faith in the promises, and by consulting his word, where I may, by his Spirit shining on my heart, (shine, O Sun of righteousness), learn how to carry, and what to do, to the end the gospel preached by me may not be unsuccessful? Therefore did my heart cry out after Christ this day, and my soul was moved, when I read that sweet promise of Christ, "Follow me, and I will make you fishers of men," directed to those that would follow him.[7]

What God does with our witness is his business, but our business is to fish for men. This means supporting the mission of the church locally and globally. It means inviting friends to church; it means praying for people in need; it means having a short gospel presentation ready to give at a moment's notice; it means praying for lost family members. It

---

6. Michael Cassidy, quoted in Anne Coomes, *African Harvest* (London: Monarch, 2002), 166.

7. Thomas Boston, "A Soliloquy on the Art of Man-Fishing," in *The Complete Works of the Late Rev. Thomas Boston of Ettrick*, ed. Samuel M'Millan, 12 vols. (London, 1853; reprint Wheaton, IL: Richard Owen Roberts, 1980), 5:6.

also means getting involved with ministries that share the gospel. And it means speaking up and not staying silent. So launch the gospel boat! Cast your net into the teeming shoals of humanity and see what God will catch by his sovereign grace.

LEAVING IT ALL BEHIND

Jesus was calling people to be his disciples, and each step seemed more difficult than the last. It is one thing to listen to Jesus, which many people do, but another thing to repent for sin, which happens only when we are humbled by God's holiness. It is one thing to turn away from sin, but another thing to go out and start witnessing for Jesus. Yet a true follower of Christ does all these things. In fact, this is an excellent way to test our own discipleship: Am I spending time with Jesus in the Word? Am I sorry for my sins? Am I sharing my faith?

But that is not all: a disciple leaves everything behind to follow Jesus—absolutely everything. This is what Peter and his friends did at the end of this episode: they left it all behind. Luke tells us, "And when they had brought their boats to land, they left everything and followed him" (Luke 5:11). This is one of the most dramatic moments in Luke's Gospel. Peter and his friends had been studying Jesus, thinking about Jesus, and talking about Jesus. They had listened to him teach and watched him perform miracles. In a way, they had even started to follow him, but they had not yet come to the point of making an all-or-nothing decision for discipleship.

Then came the day their lives were changed forever. There by the Sea of Galilee Jesus called them to be his disciples. When he called, they answered, leaving everything behind. With complete and willful abandon, they left their boats and their fishing tackle right on the shore. This was symbolic of all the other things they left behind. They left behind their career ambitions. They left behind their old sins. They left behind the safety and security of living the way they had always lived. And they left behind their right to call their lives their own.

This is what it means to be a disciple: it means leaving everything behind—*everything*—to follow Jesus. Many people say they want to follow Jesus, but instead of leaving everything behind, they try to take it all with them. They call themselves Christians, but they are not willing to give up their selfish ambitions, sinful pleasures, comfortable surroundings, bitter grudges, precious idols, or simply the right to live the way they want to live. Imagine if Peter and his fishing buddies had tried to follow Jesus without leaving everything else behind. Imagine them hauling their boats and nets around to all the towns and villages where Jesus preached. Imagine them dragging all their fishing equipment up to Jerusalem when Jesus went there to die. Obviously, if they had tried to do that, they never would have been able to follow Jesus at all.

How foolish it is for us to pretend that we are following Jesus when in fact we want to keep our lives intact the way they are. But it is not just one part of our lives that he tells us to give over to him; he demands all of us. True discipleship is always costly because it means giving up what we want for us so that we can have what Jesus wants for us. We do this in principle as soon as we begin to follow Christ. Then we do it in practice every time something threatens to stand between us and a total commitment to Christ.

When I think of leaving it all behind, I think of a hard experience that my friend and colleague Cora Hogue had during the summer of 2003, when her apartment building was destroyed by fire and water. When the alarms went off in the middle of the night, Cora had just a few moments to gather her things and get out in one piece. Since there were many personal treasures in her apartment, including artwork and family heirlooms, she had a mental list of what she would rescue if ever she faced such an emergency. She quickly began to bundle up a valuable silk rug. Then she stopped. She remembered that all she needed was Jesus. Instead of grabbing this, that, and the other thing, she left it all behind. And as she stood in the doorway, she prayed, "Lord, I'm giving all this stuff to you. I'm letting go of it, and if there is anything that I really need, please watch over it and preserve it."

In the end, although the building was condemned, my friend was able to salvage some of her possessions. This is the way God often works. We give up everything, completely resigning all that we are and have over to him, and then he graciously returns whatever he wants us to use for his glory. But first we need to experience the liberating release of leaving it all behind to follow Jesus.

What do you need to leave behind, and what are you still dragging around with you? Jesus is calling you to follow him. He is calling you to be a listening-to-his-Word, repenting-for-sin, fishing-for-men, leaving-it-all-behind disciple. Answer his call. Decide to follow Jesus. Then keep the cross before you, leave the world behind you, and never turn back.

18

FAITH HEALER

Luke 5:12–26

*"But that you may know that the Son of Man has authority on
earth to forgive sins"—he said to the man who was paralyzed—"I
say to you, rise, pick up your bed and go home." And immediately
he rose up before them and picked up what he had been lying on
and went home, glorifying God. And amazement seized them all,
and they glorified God and were filled with awe, saying, "We have
seen extraordinary things today." (Luke 5:24–26)*

People call them the Untouchables, and they are the ultimate
outcasts. Members of the lowest caste in the Hindu community, they spend their entire lives outside the socially
acceptable relationships of Indian society. They are so ostracized that generally they do not receive the ordinary protections of Indian law. They are
considered "too impure, too polluted, to rank as worthy beings." They are
"shunned, insulted, banned from temples and higher caste homes, made to
eat and drink from separate utensils in public places, and, in extreme but
not uncommon cases, are raped, burned, lynched, and gunned down."[1]

1. Tom O'Neill, "Untouchable," *National Geographic,* (June 2003): 9.

Because the Untouchables are considered physically and ceremonially unclean, they are compelled to do any "work that involves physical contact with blood, excrement, and other bodily 'defilements' as defined by Hindu law. Untouchables cremate the dead, clean latrines, cut umbilical cords, remove dead animals from the roads, tan hides, sweep gutters. These jobs, and the status of Untouchability, are passed down for generations."[2] Nobody wants to be an Untouchable; nobody even wants to touch one.

UNCLEAN! UNCLEAN!

Jesus once met a man who was equally untouchable. The man's story—together with the story that follows it in Luke's Gospel—shows what happens to people who have faith in the healing power of Jesus Christ.

These events took place some time after Jesus had called his first disciples. Luke writes, "While he was in one of the cities, there came a man full of leprosy" (Luke 5:12). The biblical term for leprosy refers to a wide variety of skin ailments, some of them fatal, especially in biblical times. In its most extreme form, leprosy is a neurological disorder that numbs all sensitivity to pain, and thus results in a disfigured body. One preacher describes this incurable and infectious disease as "a living death, which no medicine can check or stay."[3]

Even when it was not deadly, leprosy was a dreadful disease—the AIDS or the Ebola virus of its day. According to the ancient historian Josephus, lepers were treated "as if they were, in effect, dead men."[4] Lepers had to live in isolation. Since there was no cure, the only defense was quarantine, so lepers lived in separate communities. This was a matter of public health; it was also a matter of biblical principle. According to the Old Testament law, "The leprous person who has the disease shall wear torn clothes and let the hair of his head hang loose, and he shall cover his upper lip and cry out, 'Unclean, unclean.' He shall remain unclean as long as he has the disease. He is unclean. He shall live alone. His dwelling shall be outside the camp" (Lev. 13:45–46).

2. O'Neill, "Untouchable," 13.

3. J. C. Ryle, *Expository Thoughts on the Gospels, Luke* (1858; reprint Cambridge: James Clarke, 1976), 1:136.

4. Flavius Josephus, quoted in R. Kent Hughes, *Luke: That You May Know the Truth*, 2 vols., Preaching the Word (Wheaton, IL: Crossway, 1998), 1:167n.

This miserable and humiliating form of apartheid must have had a severe psychological effect. In addition to whatever physical discomfort they suffered, people in leper colonies were segregated from society. They were socially unacceptable and ceremonially unclean. They were not allowed to have any human contact. So if they survived at all, it was only by the charity of people who would leave them a little food, but would not come anywhere near them. "The leper was not just ill," writes Michael Wilcock; "he was outcast. He had not simply lost his health; he had lost his family, his friends, his home, his livelihood. No-one would, indeed no-one was allowed to, associate with him."[5] In a word, lepers were untouchable.

Leprosy is an ugly but accurate illustration of our spiritual condition before we are healed by the gospel. At the time of Christ, people generally assumed that leprosy was God's curse against sin. This was not necessarily true, but leprosy still serves as a symbol of our sin—what R. C. Trench has called an "outward and visible sign of innermost spiritual corruption."[6] Sin makes us unclean. Our depravity is a disfiguring disease that distorts the person God created us to be. Indeed, it is a kind of living death, because the Bible says that apart from Christ, we are "dead in our trespasses" (Eph. 2:5). This leads us to ask a question the apostle Paul once asked, and that the leper in Luke's Gospel knew how to answer: "Wretched man that I am! Who will deliver me from this body of death?" (Rom. 7:24).

The answer is Jesus, so the man went and "fell on his face and begged him, 'Lord, if you will, you can make me clean'" (Luke 5:12). This was a disturbing thing for a leper to do, and people must have been shocked by it. Lepers were strictly forbidden to come into town (Lev. 13:46), yet Luke tells us that this incident took place while Jesus "was in one of the cities" (Luke 5:12). We can only imagine how horrified people were as this man approached, violating every convention of polite society. Doctor Luke reports that he had an advanced case of the disease. He was "full" of leprosy, as anyone who looked at him could tell. People must have backed away in terror, with mothers clutching their children and bystanders gasping in disbelief.

But the man was desperate, and so he came to Jesus. He came out of his overwhelming sense of personal need, recognizing his situation for what

5. Michael Wilcock, *The Message of Luke*, The Bible Speaks Today (Downers Grove, IL: Inter-Varsity, 1979), 69.

6. R. C. Trench, quoted in Hughes, *Luke*, 1:167.

it was. This is the way everyone should come to Jesus: needy for grace. By asking Jesus to make him clean, the man was confessing the truth of what he always had to say whenever anyone came near, "Unclean! Unclean!" It is only the sick that come to Jesus for healing, and this man knew he needed a cure.

He also believed that Jesus could heal him. As desperate as he was, the leper came in faith. He said, "Lord, if you will, you can make me clean" (Luke 5:12). Apparently the man was not entirely sure whether Jesus would heal him or not. Maybe Jesus wouldn't even touch him. But the man knew that if he was willing to do it, Jesus could heal him. So he threw himself down at Jesus' feet. By doing this, he was humbling himself before God. He was submitting to God's sovereignty over the human body and abandoning himself to the mercy of Christ. The leper had a full and dependent faith in the power of the Son of God. This is how we all come to Jesus for salvation: recognizing our desperate need, begging for healing, and believing that he can make us clean.

TOUCHING THE UNTOUCHABLE

Then Jesus did something totally unexpected and completely amazing: he touched the man. Luke writes, "And Jesus stretched out his hand and touched him, saying, 'I will; be clean.' And immediately the leprosy left him" (Luke 5:13). Understand that this was something that nobody *ever* did. Touching a leper was forbidden—not by any specific command from the law of God, but by the very nature of the disease. It simply wasn't done. So when Jesus did it, the people who were there that day must have turned away in revulsion. For them, the thought of touching a leper was unspeakable because his physical and spiritual uncleanness was contagious.

But Jesus touched the man, firmly resting his hand on the dreadful disease. In that electric moment, as the high voltage of divine power coursed through the strong arm of Jesus, the leper was healed. Ordinarily, when something clean touches something unclean, it becomes unclean as well. But here, for the first time in history, things ran in the other direction, as the cleanliness of Jesus healed the unclean leper. It was a total cure. The man's cleansing was complete. He had brand new skin from head to toe.

Here we see Jesus in all the grace of his salvation. We see his mercy in hearing and responding to the man's cry for help. When the leper asked if he was willing, Jesus said that he *was* willing—as willing as can be. He was also able, because Jesus had the power to heal. With one touch and one word, he restored the man's body. He did this without getting contaminated, for he was immune to the defilement of this disease. His touch was like a positive infection that invaded the leper's scabrous skin and made him clean again. At the same time, this healing gesture was a prophetic symbol of Christ's atoning righteousness. Just as Jesus took away the man's disease and transferred healthy skin to his ailing body, so Jesus takes away the sin of every penitent sinner and imputes to us his saving righteousness.

We also see the compassion of Jesus. In one sense it was unnecessary to touch this man. Jesus easily could have performed this miracle simply by the power of his word. But first he touched the man. The Son of God incarnate reached out to make a connection with him, skin on skin. This displays the Savior's true humanity. At the same time, it shows the genuineness of his compassion. He was restoring a relationship, bringing the man back into fellowship with the people of God. It may have been the first time in many years that anyone other than another leper had dared to have any contact with him. But now he was back in touch. Here is how John Calvin summarized the healing effect of Jesus touching the leper:

> There is such purity in Christ he absorbs all uncleanness and pollution, He does not contaminate Himself by touching the leper, nor does He transgress the Law. . . . [He] stays whole, clears all our dirt away, and pours upon us His own holiness. Now, while He could heal the leper by His word alone, He adds the contact of His hand, to show His feeling of compassion: no wonder, since He willed to put on our flesh in order that He might cleanse us from all our sins. . . . Here is a thing which we pass over without much impression at an idle reading, but must certainly ponder, with much awe, when we take it properly—that the Son of God, so far from abhorring contact with the leper, actually stretched out His hand to touch his uncleanness.[7]

7. John Calvin, *A Harmony of the Gospels: Matthew, Mark and Luke*, 3 vols. (Grand Rapids: Eerdmans, 1972), 1:244.

In addition, the healing hand of Jesus "signalized a coming reunion with family and friends, a reintegration with the society from which the disease had cut him off."[8] The prospect of this reunion explains why Jesus sent the man off to find the nearest priest. As soon as he was clean, Jesus "charged him to tell no one, but 'go and show yourself to the priest, and make an offering for your cleansing, as Moses commanded, for a proof to them'" (Luke 5:14). According to the Old Testament regulations for cleansing—which Jesus clearly respected—the man had to go to his priest, who served as a kind of public health inspector. The priest would verify that the leper was clean, proving to everyone the mighty power of Christ. Once the priest said that the man was clean, he would then spend the next eight days making special sacrifices for atonement and cleansing (see Lev. 14:1–32). After that, he could rejoin the covenant community.

All of this shows what happens when someone gets in touch with Jesus. He alone has the power to make people whole and clean. His healing touch is not just for lepers; it is for anyone who is needy for grace. Jesus has the power to heal the body, although he will not bring full and final healing until the resurrection. He has the power to restore the soul. He has the power to reconcile relationships. Most of all, he has the power to cure the deadly disease of our sin. Whatever healing we need—whatever sin is troubling our conscience, whatever sorrow is grieving our hearts, whatever relationship is making us anxious— Jesus is able to touch the hurting places in our lives and make us whole. Then he sends us out into the world to touch the hurting places in the lives of others, including all the people with all the problems that most people don't even want to touch. Everyone who has been healed by the gospel is part of a healing community that the Holy Spirit uses to make people whole.

Jesus is also willing—willing to make us clean. The deep desire of his saving heart is to make dirty sinners clean. What Jesus said to the leper he says to everyone who comes to him by faith: "I will; be clean." Charles Spurgeon said: "The 'I will' of an emperor may have great power over his dominions; but the 'I will' of Christ drives death and hell before him, conquers disease,

---

8. Wilcock, *Luke*, 69.

removes despair, and floods the world with mercy. The Lord's 'I will' can put away your leprosy of sin, and make you perfectly whole."[9]

If we are not purified from our sin, therefore, it is not because Jesus is not willing; it is because we have not yet trusted him for forgiveness through his death on the cross. Jesus cleanses everyone who comes to him in faith, as the leper did. Therefore, whatever ails us, we may trust in Jesus and experience his healing touch.

THROUGH THE ROOF

The leper was not the only man who came to Jesus for healing. As we have seen, Jesus came to preach the gospel, and not simply to perform miracles. But as Luke tells us, "now even more the report about him went abroad, and great crowds gathered to hear him and to be healed of their infirmities" (Luke 5:15).

As his popularity grew, it became increasingly difficult for Jesus to make time for the things that were most important to him. So Luke tells us, "he would withdraw to desolate places and pray" (Luke 5:16). Once again we see the intimacy that Jesus loved to share with his Father—the strength of his prayer life. The more demands that were placed on him for ministry, the more important he thought it was to go somewhere quiet and pray. This is an example for our devotions and a challenge to our discipline. Do we have any less need to spend time with our Father than Jesus did? We have greater need for God's help, and thus an even greater need to "withdraw to desolate places and pray" (Luke 5:16). As it was for Christ, so it is for the Christian: private prayer is the root of fruitful service to God.

It was during this same time period that Jesus performed another memorable miracle:

> On one of those days, as he was teaching, Pharisees and teachers of the law were sitting there, who had come from every village of Galilee and Judea and from Jerusalem. And the power of the Lord was with him to heal. And behold, some men were bringing on a bed a man who was paralyzed, and they were seeking to bring him in and lay him before Jesus, but

9. Charles Haddon Spurgeon, *The Parables and Miracles of Our Lord*, 3 vols. (Grand Rapids: Baker, 1993), 2:59.

> finding no way to bring him in, because of the crowd, they went up on
> the roof and let him down with his bed through the tiles into the midst
> before Jesus. (Luke 5:17–19)

It must have been a dramatic moment. A large and impressive crowd had gathered to hear Jesus teach. Religious leaders from as far away as Jerusalem were there, possibly to investigate Jesus, which shows how famous he had become. There were so many people that it was impossible for anyone else to get inside the building.

This was frustrating to a small group of men standing outside. They had a friend who was paralyzed, and they were desperate for him to get the kind of healing that only Jesus could give. Yet there was no way to get inside, especially carrying a stretcher. So they were facing a significant obstacle, as people often do when they are trying to help bring their friends to Christ.

Suddenly one of them had an inspiration: if they could not get in from the side, maybe they could get in from the top. There is a time for waiting to see if God will open a door, but there is also a time to get inside, even if it means going through the roof to get there. So the men climbed the outside staircase common to buildings of that day and started tearing away at the roof. We can only imagine the commotion that this caused down below. First debris started to fall down. Then daylight appeared, and before they knew it, the people inside were looking up at the sweaty, determined faces of men who would stop at nothing to bring their friend to Jesus.

Their story is a powerful example of Christian compassion. These men loved their brother, and when they saw that something could be done about his disability, they did everything in their power to get him the help that he needed. This is strong encouragement for anyone who cares for people with disabilities or other physical problems. Caring for the needs of the body is a holy obligation for the people of God.

This story is also a powerful example of Christian evangelism. What people need more than anything else is for someone to bring them to Jesus, overcoming all the obstacles. Whatever trouble these men went through to bring their friend to Jesus was worth it. Yet so often we let little things get in the way of inviting a friend to church, or offering to pray for someone, or bringing a Christ-centered perspective into a conversation, or sharing the basic facts of the gospel. What people need is a direct, personal encounter with Jesus Christ. So we should do whatever we can to bring them to a place where they can experience his healing touch. Whom do you know that needs to know Jesus? To what lengths are you willing to go in order to introduce them?

These men set a worthy example in many ways, but what Jesus especially admired about them was their faith. He could see that they trusted in him. Why else would they go to so much trouble to bring their friend to see him? Obviously they had a trusting faith in his power to heal. They also had a persistent faith—one not easily discouraged. And it was by this faith that the paralytic was healed, for when Jesus "saw their faith, he said, 'Man, your sins are forgiven you'" (Luke 5:20). We may infer from this that the man with the disability had as much faith as his friends. When Luke referred to "*their* faith," this man was included. God does not forgive our sins on the basis of someone else's faith. To be forgiven, we must put our own personal trust in Jesus, as this man did.

What is surprising is that Jesus did not do anything to heal his body, at least not at first. Obviously the man was coming for physical healing. But rather than making him walk, Jesus forgave his sins. He almost seemed to be missing the point, as when a waitress brings a pair of size ten loafers, or when a mailman delivers a pizza. But Jesus knew what he was doing. He wanted to give this man a greater gift, for however terrible it is to be paralyzed, it is far worse to suffer the spiritual paralysis of sin. So when Jesus saw this man's faith, he forgave him all his sins. Donald Hagner comments: "The point of this narrative is that the problem of sin, though not as apparent to the eye as paralysis, is . . . the fundamental problem of humanity that Jesus has come to counteract. Compared to the healings, the forgiveness of sins is by far the greater gift Jesus has brought in his ministry."[10]

Here Luke draws us into the heart of the gospel. Jesus had preached the gospel, cast out demons, healed the sick, called disciples, and cleansed the leper. But now he was meeting an even deeper need. He was making a man right with God through the forgiveness of his sins—a gift that would last for all eternity. What Jesus said to the paralytic he says to everyone who trusts in him. He says it to anyone who comes to him in faith. On the basis

10. Donald Hagner, *Matthew 1–13* (Dallas: Word, 1993), 232.

of his death on the cross—the killing penalty that he suffered for sinners—Jesus says, "Your sins are forgiven" (Luke 5:20).

Reaction and Response

It is wonderful to hear Jesus say that our sins are forgiven, but the religious leaders who were there that day evidently disagreed. As Luke tells us, "the scribes and the Pharisees began to question, saying, 'Who is this who speaks blasphemies? Who can forgive sins but God alone?'" (Luke 5:21).

These powerful religious leaders had come to investigate. They had heard something about the gospel Jesus preached and the miracles he performed, but they wanted to see for themselves. They were watching him with suspicion, reserving the right to reach their own conclusions about his person and ministry. When Jesus claimed that he could forgive sins, they immediately and strenuously objected. "He can't do that!" they said. "Only God can forgive a sinner!"

When they said this, the scribes and Pharisees were speaking better than they knew. In a way they were right: sin is an offense against the holy righteousness of God, so only God *can* forgive a sinner. But this just shows that someone can have the right theological position and still not have a right relationship with God. The scribes and Pharisees failed to recognize that Jesus Christ *is* God the eternal Son. This is why they accused him of blasphemy. By forgiving people's sins, Jesus was effectively claiming to be God. But he *wasn't* God, at least as far as they could see. So when he claimed to be divine, he was guilty of a crime punishable by death (see Lev. 24:10–16).

There was only one problem with their reasoning: Jesus really *is* God! He is God incarnate, God almighty, the supremely and infinitely awesome God. Therefore, he has the authority to forgive sinners, as he proceeded to prove. By the witness of the Holy Spirit, Jesus knew what the religious leaders were saying. And when he "perceived their thoughts, he answered them, 'Why do you question in your hearts? Which is easier, to say, 'Your sins are forgiven you,' or to say, 'Rise and walk'?" (Luke 5:22–23).

Like everything else that Jesus said, these words were simple, but profound. Which is easier, to say, "Your sins are forgiven," or to say, "Get up and walk"? At one level, they are both easy to say. After all, words are just words. But there is a sense in which it is easier to say, "Your sins are forgiven," because no one can tell if the person who says it is bluffing. Forgiveness is something that comes from God's throne, so who knows whether it really has been granted? The claim cannot be falsified. But when someone says, "Rise and walk," everyone knows right away whether the person who says it has the power to heal. Either the paralytic will get up and walk or he won't, and if he doesn't, the person who told him to stand up will be exposed as a complete fraud. So it is harder to say, "Rise and walk." If someone says that, he has to prove it.

When we look at things from the perspective of the cross, forgiving sins is the hardest thing of all, of course, because it cost Jesus his very life. In order to offer forgiveness, he had to suffer and die in the bloody agony of the cross. But in the context of this encounter, the hardest thing for Jesus to say was, "Rise and walk," which is exactly what he went on to say: "'But that you may know that the Son of Man has authority on earth to forgive sins'— he said to the man who was paralyzed—'I say to you, rise, pick up your bed and go home.' And immediately he rose up before them and picked up what he had been lying on and went home, glorifying God. And amazement seized them all, and they glorified God and were filled with awe, saying, 'We have seen extraordinary things today'" (Luke 5:24–26).

By performing this miracle, Jesus proved for sure that he was the Son of God. At the beginning of this narrative, Luke stated that "the power of the Lord" was with Jesus for healing (Luke 5:17). This power included the power and authority to heal paralysis, and if Jesus had the power and authority to do that, he also had the power and authority to forgive sinners. There is no disability he cannot heal, no sinner he cannot forgive. He is God the Son, with power to save.

This is all for the glory of God. Luke ends this episode by showing what happens after people have a healing encounter with Jesus. They glorify God. This is what the man who was paralyzed did: he scrambled to his feet, rolled up his mat, and left the house, praising God. He may have come in through the roof, but he left by the front door, carrying the bed that once carried him. And as he walked through the crowd, he said, "Praise God! Praise God!" They too were praising God. This is the way to respond when Jesus saves a needy sinner, not with the frowning disapproval of a Pharisee, but with the smiling praise of a believer in Christ. The reason that Jesus saves sinners is for the glory of God.

Do you want to see that glory in your own life? Then come to Jesus in faith, trusting him for healing and forgiveness. He will touch your sin-sick soul and cleanse your unholy heart. His healing compassion is not just for you, but also for the people you love well enough to bring to him. Your hands are the hands God uses to reach out to people no one else is willing to touch. Your arms are the arms he uses to carry people to Christ. Your voice is the voice he uses to sing his glorious praise.

19

FEAST OR FAMINE?

Luke 5:27–39

*And they said to him, "The disciples of John fast often and offer
prayers, and so do the disciples of the Pharisees, but yours eat and
drink." And Jesus said to them, "Can you make wedding guests
fast while the bridegroom is with them?" (Luke 5:33–34)*

f you want the job done right, you have to find the right person to do it. If you need a chef, you have to find someone who
knows how to make a soufflé. If you are looking for a first base-
man, it has to be a player who hits for power. If you are having trouble with
your car, the only person who can help is someone who knows which part
is the carburetor. You need to have the right person for the job.

As logical as it is, this approach is one that Jesus seems studiously to have
avoided. When it came time to choose his disciples, he did not go out and
find twelve theologically trained, morally upright, spiritually disciplined
men. Instead, he gathered a motley crew of everyday sinners. They hardly
seemed like the kind of men who would set the world on fire. But when
they met Jesus, their lives were changed forever and they became courageous for Christ. There is no better example of this transformation than a
lowlife named Levi, who was later and better known as Matthew.

227

How a Sinner Gets Saved

As we read Levi's story, we see what happens when Jesus comes to save a sinner. The story starts with business as usual. Jesus was busy performing miracles, and even forgiving people's sins. "After this," Luke tells us, "he went out and saw a tax collector named Levi, sitting at the tax booth" (Luke 5:27).

Already from this we know almost everything we care to know about what kind of man Levi was. He was a tax collector; in other words, he was a thieving sinner. In those days the Romans subcontracted the collection of their imperial revenue. Anyone who wanted to collect taxes would place a bid for his region, with the Romans awarding the contract to the highest bidder. The winner paid off the government, then tried to levy as many taxes as he could. Anything he collected over and above the amount he bid was his to keep. Obviously, this system was open to corruption. With all the poll taxes, land taxes, income taxes, road taxes, and port taxes they gathered, most tax collectors were filthy rich.

Filthy is just the word for it, because taxmen were among the most despised men in Israel. Because they collaborated with the Romans, they were considered traitors. Because they collected more than they had any right to take, they were considered robbers. And because they had so much contact with Gentiles, they were considered unclean. In fact, some rabbis said that if a tax collector set foot in someone's house, everything and everyone inside became impure.[1] So Levi was among the lowest of the low. One commentator aptly describes him as "sinfully rich and socially ostracized."[2]

When people saw this man sitting in his tollbooth and counting his money, they hated him. Yet what we ought to see in Levi is our own sinful selves, because until we come to Christ, we are like him in many ways. We sit in the tollbooth of our sin, trying to get as much as we can for ourselves, and not caring too much what we have to do to other people to get it. We will keep sitting in our sin, going about our business, until Jesus interrupts

---

1. *Toharot* 7.6, quoted in Richard D. Phillips, *Encounters with Jesus: When Ordinary People Met the Savior* (Phillipsburg, NJ: P&R, 2002), 87.

2. David Gooding, *According to Luke: A New Exposition of the Third Gospel* (Grand Rapids: Eerdmans, 1987), 109.

us the way he interrupted Levi. Luke tells us that Jesus "said to him, 'Follow me.' And leaving everything, he rose and followed him. And Levi made him a great feast in his house, and there was a large company of tax collectors and others reclining at table with them" (Luke 5:27–29).

Levi's conversion teaches us never to despair of our own or anyone else's salvation. We should say, "If God can save someone like Levi, he can save anyone, even a sinner like me." When he does save us, Jesus generally does it the way that he did it here. Although the story of Levi's salvation is told in just a few short lines, it contains many important doctrines of salvation.

First there is the doctrine of *election*—the sovereign choice of God. Before Levi ever decided to follow God, Jesus decided to make him one of his followers. As Jesus later said to his disciples, "You did not choose me, but I chose you and appointed you that you should go and bear fruit" (John 15:16). When Jesus said this, Levi knew exactly what he was talking about, because Jesus came to him before he ever came to Jesus. He was chosen by grace. The same thing is true of everyone who comes to God through faith in Christ. God's grace is God's choice, for the Bible says we were chosen in Christ before the foundation of the world (Eph. 1:4).

Next comes what theologians describe as *effectual calling*. There is a general call that God sends out to everyone—the gospel call to turn away from sin and believe in Jesus Christ. Not everyone answers that call. But there is also an effective call, by which God actually draws his chosen people to himself. This is the call that the apostle Paul had in mind when he said that those whom God predestined, "he also called" (Rom. 8:30). According to the Westminster Shorter Catechism, "Effectual calling is the work of God's Spirit, whereby, convincing us of our sin and misery, enlightening our minds in the knowledge of Christ, and renewing our wills, he doth persuade and enable us to embrace Jesus Christ, freely offered to us in the gospel" (A. 31). This was the call that Levi received—the call that effectively drew him to Christ. Up until this point in his life, he was "a man greedy for dirty money, filled with an uncontrolled desire to possess, careless of justice in his eagerness to have what did not belong to him. . . . Yet he was snatched from the workshop of sin itself and saved when there was no hope for him, at the call of Christ the Savior of us all."[3] God issues the same call to every

---

3. Cyril of Alexandria, "Commentary on Luke," quoted in *Luke*, ed. Arthur A. Just Jr., Ancient Christian Commentary on Scripture, NT 3 (Downers Grove, IL: InterVarsity, 2003), 95.

Christian: Jesus says, "Come," and by the inward compulsion of the Holy Spirit, we choose to follow him.

Conversion comes only by the choice and calling of God. It is a gift of his grace, which may explain why people started to call this man Matthew, which means "gift of God." This is what happens in salvation: God turns Levis into Matthews. But of course Levi still needed to respond to God in repentance and faith, which he did, for Luke tells us that he left everything behind to follow Jesus. Levi had more to lose than most people, but like the other disciples, he left it all behind. He gave up the sinful structures that led to his financial advantage. Once he left, he could never go back. But this is what repentance requires: a definitive break with the old life of sin, no matter what the cost. We must let go of everything that stands in the way of going with Jesus. This is the doctrine of *repentance unto life*.

At the same time that God calls us away from sin, he also calls us to follow Jesus in the way of discipleship, as Levi also did. This is the doctrine of *saving faith*. Here we need to notice an important grammatical detail. When Luke tells us how Levi followed Christ, he uses an active participle—which typically indicates continuous, ongoing action. When Levi got up to follow Jesus, it was for the rest of his life. This is what it means to be a disciple. When God calls us to follow Christ, he calls us to a whole life of faith.

As soon as Levi started to follow Jesus, he began to *worship*. This is what happens when someone welcomes Jesus into his life and knows for sure that he has received the free gift of eternal life: he starts to have fellowship with Jesus, and to give him the honor that he deserves. Levi did this by throwing Jesus a party. Luke calls it "a great feast" (Luke 5:29), which shows how wealthy the man was. It also shows how happy he was. For years Levi had been starving for a meaningful relationship with God; now he was feasting with God the Son. As J. C. Ryle said,

> Nothing can happen to a man which ought to be such an occasion of joy, as his conversion. It is a far more important event than being married, or coming of age, or being made a nobleman, or receiving a great fortune. It is the birth of an immortal soul! It is the rescue of a sinner from hell! It is a passage from death to life! It is being made a king and priest forevermore! It is being

provided for, both in time and eternity! It is adoption into the noblest and richest of all families, the family of God![4]

As he entered into the joy of his salvation, worshiping Jesus, Levi also started to *witness*. He wanted his friends to know Christ. This too is part of what it means to become a Christian. As soon as a person comes to Christ, he or she becomes an evangelist. Levi did this by inviting everyone he knew—including his nefarious colleagues in the tax business—to have dinner with Jesus. He wanted them to share the joy that he had in knowing Christ. He said, "My friends have to hear this!" So he invited them to a place where they could meet Jesus and mingle with Christians.

The story of Levi's conversion is really the story of every believer in Christ. This is how God saves sinners. First he chooses us by grace *(election)* and calls us to follow Christ *(effectual calling)*. By the work of the Holy Spirit, he enables us to turn away from sin *(repentance unto life)* and follow Jesus *(saving faith)*. And as we follow Jesus, we glorify God *(worship)* and proclaim his gospel *(witness)*. Once we come to God through faith in Christ, we are called to invite our friends to a place where they can meet Jesus, so that he can do the same thing for them that he did for us.

THE PHARISEES' FIRST COMPLAINT

This would be a happy place to end, except it is not where the story ends. After all, what would a party be without the Pharisees—those party-poopers of the New Testament Gospels? The Pharisees were socially conservative teachers who refused to believe that Jesus could be the Christ. When they saw him going to Levi's party, they raised two objections, which—like most of their complaints—actually ended up clarifying Christ's person and work. Praise God for the Pharisees, because their very criticisms help us to know Christ!

First they accused Jesus of eating and drinking with the wrong crowd: "And the Pharisees and their scribes grumbled at his disciples, saying, 'Why do you eat and drink with tax collectors and sinners?'" (Luke 5:30). The Pharisees had a problem with Jesus and his guest list. To understand their

4. J. C. Ryle, *Expository Thoughts on the Gospels, Luke* (1858; reprint Cambridge: James Clarke, 1976), 1:148.

complaint, it helps to understand that for the Jews, sitting down to share a meal was an expression of spiritual fellowship. One scholar writes: "In the East, even today, to invite a man to a meal was an honor. It was an offer of peace, trust, brotherhood, and forgiveness; in short, sharing a table meant sharing life. In Judaism in particular, table-fellowship means fellowship before God."[5]

It also helps to understand that, according to the Pharisees, certain members of society were not eligible for this kind of fellowship. There were whole categories of people who did not qualify. These "sinners," as they were called, included "members of the despised trades such as tax collectors, herdsmen, peddlers, or tanners, the physically deformed, the *am ha-arez* or mass of the population, Samaritans, and, to a certain extent, women."[6] To eat with such people was considered unclean; it was to share in their sin, becoming spiritually impure. Thus it was something a teacher and his disciples *never* did.[7] It was beneath their dignity. One of the ways they showed their devotion to God was by not having any social contact with people who were not respectable.

In this context, it is easy to guess what the Pharisees were thinking when they saw Jesus go into Levi's house and sit down to feast with tax collectors and other sinners. They were scandalized! As far as they were concerned, the fact that he was eating with such people showed that he was guilty by association, or else that he was violating their rules for the way a rabbi ought to behave.

Before we see how Jesus responded, we need to examine our own hearts. The Pharisee is not someone we find outside a church, but inside. These men were committed to God. They knew their theology. But they did not share God's heart for ministry. They did not have the love of Jesus for lost and needy sinners.

There is more than a little of the spirit of the Pharisee in all of us. It is tempting for us to have a critical spirit about the way other people live, saying, "Well, that's just not what Christians are supposed to do." It is tempt-

---

5. J. Jeremias, *New Testament Theology: The Proclamation of Jesus* (New York: Scribner, 1971), 115.

6. G. Feeley-Harnik, *The Lord's Table: Eucharist and Passover in Early Christianity* (Philadelphia: University of Pennsylvania Press, 1981), 42.

7. *Berakoth* 43, cited in Norval Geldenhuys, *The Gospel of Luke*, New International Commentary on the New Testament (Grand Rapids: Eerdmans, 1951), 193.

ing to think that there are some people who do not belong in church and hardly deserve to hear the gospel. It is tempting to criticize the way that this denomination, that church, or some other Christian organization does ministry without ever getting personally involved in reaching out. It is tempting to become so attached to our own particular style of Christianity that we never introduce Jesus to the people outside who need him the most. But we are not called to stand somewhere off with the Pharisees; we are called to sit down with sinners so that we can share the gospel.

DOCTOR JESUS

How did Jesus respond to these men? For starters, he was willing to grant one of their major premises. They said that he was eating with sinners; true enough. But far from becoming contaminated by their sin, Jesus was restoring them to righteousness. So he said, "Those who are well have no need of a physician, but those who are sick. I have not come to call the righteous but sinners to repentance" (Luke 5:31–32).

This is the climactic moment to which the whole story has been building. Here Jesus makes one of his great mission statements. He announces who he is and what he has come to do. He explains the purpose for which he left the splendors of heaven and came down to earth. He did not come to save the righteous. He did not come to spend time with people who had it all together. Rather, he came to save the people who really needed him: messed-up, broken-down, law-breaking sinners.

To explain his mission, Jesus used a simple illustration from the field of medicine. He said he was a doctor. This would have had special significance for Luke, who was a medical man himself. His point was that if you are not sick, you do not need a doctor. The only people who need treatment are those who have something wrong with them. By way of illustration, when I turned thirty, I went in for a complete physical. When he was finished looking me over, my doctor said, "Well, you're in excellent health. I can only think of one reason why you're here: Your wife must have told you to get a physical." My doctor was telling me that I did not need a doctor.

In the same way, the only people who need a Savior are sinners. So Jesus said, "I have not come to call the righteous but sinners to repentance" (Luke 5:32). The Great Physician had come to bring the ultimate cure. He had come to heal people from sin, which is a sickness unto death. This explains why he was mixing with the wrong crowd. It is what a doctor does: he spends time with sick people. And rather than getting infected by their sin, Jesus had the power to make them well. In the words of one scholar, "Over against the Pharisaic idea of salvation by segregation Jesus sets up the new principle of salvation by association."[8] When Jesus comes into contact with sinners, far from getting contaminated, he makes them whole and clean by the power of his perfect holiness.

Jesus offers us the same treatment, but in order to receive it, we have to accept his diagnosis. As long as we keep insisting that we are righteous, we will never see our need for the gospel cure. This was the problem with the Pharisees. They divided the world into two kinds of people: the righteous and the sinners (and guess which group they belonged to!) By claiming to be righteous, they were saying that they did not need whatever medicine Doctor Jesus wanted to prescribe. They did not think that they were sinners, so if Jesus came to save sinners, they did not need his salvation.

The truth is that we all need Jesus because we are all sinners. The Bible says, "None is righteous, no, not one" (Rom. 3:10). So when Jesus talked about "the righteous," he was being ironic. He was talking about people who *thought* they were righteous. But they were only self-righteous, because no one is righteous—not even the Pharisees.

If no one is righteous, then we all need a Savior. When Jesus calls sinners to repentance, he is calling every one of us: "All we like sheep have gone astray; we have turned every one to his own way" (Isa. 53:6). But there is a cure for us. There is a cure for our pride, our lust, and our greed. We get this cure when we hear the gospel. It is just what the doctor ordered: forgiveness for sin through the death and resurrection of Jesus Christ. We can have this cure if only we will see the sickness of our sin. As long as we maintain our own righteousness, we will never see our need for Jesus. But when we recognize our spiritual condition for what it really is, we get down on our knees and confess that we are among the sinners that Jesus came to save.

Then we go out and get involved in the lives of other sinners, so that they too can come to know Christ. Kent Hughes tells the story of William Booth, the founder of the Salvation Army. At first Booth tried to bring street people

---

8. W. Manson, *The Gospel of Luke*, quoted in Geldenhuys, *Luke*, 194.

right into the church. His biographer describes the fateful Sunday when he entered the sanctuary with

> a shuffling shabby contingent of men and women, wilting nervously under the stony stares of mill-managers, shop-keepers and their well-dressed wives. . . . To his dismay the Rev. Dunn saw that young Booth was actually ushering his charges, none of whose clothes would have raised five shilling in his own pawnshop, into the very best seats. . . . This was unprecedented, for the poor, if they came to chapel, entered by another door, to be segregated on benches without backs or cushions, behind a partition which screened off the pulpit.[9]

The modern-day Pharisees in that congregation were scandalized, and they ran Booth right out of church. But William Booth knew that Jesus did not come to save the righteous; he came to save sinners. So he kept reaching out to poor and needy sinners, eventually through the Salvation Army. I praise God that he did, because it was through that ministry that my own great-grandfather was saved off the streets of Scotland.

What are you doing to reach sinners outside the church? There are plenty of ways to do it. Get involved in the life of the neighbor that everyone avoids. Spend time with the kid that no one likes. Serve in a ministry to people who are down and out. Invite people to church—even people who will probably say no. You never know what they will say, so at least give them the chance to turn you down. Do not avoid the difficult people, but seek them out for relationships that might lead to their salvation. Identify the sinners in your life that need to know Jesus, and reach out to them with gospel love.

Friends of the Groom

The Pharisees must not have been very impressed by the answer that Jesus gave them, because rather than confessing their sins, they came back with another objection. First they criticized Jesus for eating and drinking with sinners; then they criticized him for eating and drinking at all: "And they said to him, 'The disciples of John fast often and offer prayers, and so do the disciples of the Pharisees, but yours eat and drink'" (Luke 5:33).

9. See Richard Collier, *The General Next to God* (New York: E. P. Dutton, 1965), 31–32.

235

Their first criticism related to outreach and evangelism: Jesus was spending too much time with sinners. Their second criticism related to discipleship: his followers were doing too much celebrating.

Here the Pharisees appealed not only to their own example, but also to that of John the Baptist. All of these men were ascetics. In other words, they practiced severe self-discipline in their relationship to God, abstaining from certain pleasures for spiritual reasons. They fasted and they prayed. In the case of John the Baptist and his disciples, this was in preparation for the coming of Christ. In the case of the Pharisees, it was more because they wanted to show how religious they were. When they fasted, they tried to look gloomy, so people would know how much they were suffering for God (see Matt. 6:16–18). They thought that in order to be spiritual, they had to be unhappy and uncomfortable. They were rather like the woman that the humorist Erma Bombeck once overheard speaking to her daughter during a worship service: "Stop that grinning—," she said, "you're in church!"[10]

Jesus never said there was anything wrong with fasting. He fasted himself at times, and he accepted the discipline as an ordinary part of the spiritual life. Norval Geldenhuys says that Jesus rejected fasting "as a religious meritorious ceremony bearing a compulsory, ceremonial character; but He practiced it Himself at times and permits it as a voluntary form of spiritual discipline."[11] However, Jesus did not make his disciples fast. This was because it was not the time for it: "Jesus said to them, 'Can you make wedding guests fast while the bridegroom is with them? The days will come when the bridegroom is taken away from them, and then they will fast in those days'" (Luke 5:34–35).

Earlier Jesus said that he was a doctor; now he was comparing himself to a groom. This is a theme that runs all the way through the Bible. There is a match that God has made in heaven between his people and his Son. Jesus Christ is the faithful bridegroom. He is the lover of our souls, and our destiny is to be united to him forever.

Jesus makes the comparison here because weddings were made to celebrate. They call for special arrangements: fancy clothes, good food, and fine wine. In those days, the party went on for a full week, as family and

10. Erma Bombeck, quoted in R. Kent Hughes, *Luke: That You May Know the Truth*, 2 vols., Preaching the Word (Wheaton, IL: Crossway, 1998), 1:190.

11. Geldenhuys, *Luke*, 198.

friends ate and drank to the joy of the happy couple. But one thing no one ever did at a wedding was to fast. Not even the Pharisees, for all their fascination with fasting, would miss out on a good wedding reception. As it is said in one of the rabbinical writings, "All in attendance on the bridegroom are relieved of all religious observances which would lessen their joy."[12]

The same principle applied to the disciples of Jesus Christ. He was the bridegroom, and as long as they were with him, it was inappropriate for them to do anything that would lessen their joy. Salvation had come, and it was a time for feasting, not fasting. Somehow people have the idea that Christians are spoilsports. Maybe we are, but people never said that about Jesus. He was so full of laughter that, if anything, they had the opposite reaction. They said he was having too much fun. And when we are filled with his joy, they will say the same thing about us.

Of course, the bridegroom would not be with his disciples forever. He would be taken away. Then the disciples *would* fast, not as an exhibition of their piety, but as an expression of their grief. Jesus was referring specifically to his death. The word for "taken away" (*aparthē*) indicates an act of violence. This was the first hint Jesus gave that he would suffer "a violent removal by death."[13] It meant that his disciples would not feast forever. The time would come for them to fast.

What time is it for us: a time to feast or a time of famine? It is a time for both. Like the disciples, we are with Jesus—not by his physical presence, but by the ministry of his Spirit (see John 14:18). Therefore, we are called to feast with him at his holy table, sharing the fellowship of his body and blood. But this is also a time for fasting. The day is coming when we will sit down together at what the Bible calls "the marriage supper of the Lamb" (Rev. 19:9)—the eternal feast that God has planned for us to celebrate with Jesus. But that day has not yet come. We are still waiting for our bridegroom, and until he returns, we fast and pray for the coming of his kingdom. We have a hunger for joy that will not be fully satisfied until Jesus comes again.[14]

---

12. William Barclay cites this rabbinical ruling in *The Gospel of Mark* (Philadelphia: Westminster, 1956), 191.

13. Geldenhuys, *Luke*, 197.

14. For a thorough treatment of the subject of fasting, see John Piper, *A Hunger for God: Desiring God Through Fasting and Prayer* (Wheaton, IL: Crossway, 1997).

SOMETHING OLD AND SOMETHING NEW

In saying all this, Jesus was telling the Pharisees that they were in a new situation. Now that he had come to save sinners, it was a time for feasting. To drive this home, Jesus told them a kind of parable: "No one tears a piece from a new garment and puts it on an old garment. If he does, he will tear the new, and the piece from the new will not match the old. And no one puts new wine into old wineskins. If he does, the new wine will burst the skins and it will be spilled, and the skins will be destroyed. But new wine must be put into fresh wineskins. And no one after drinking old wine desires new, for he says, 'The old is good'" (Luke 5:36–39).

This "parable" was really three parables in one. They all seem to relate in some way to the wedding theme, because the friends of the groom always wear fancy clothes and drink fine wine. Furthermore, they all deal with something new: new garments, new wineskins, and new wine. Jesus was saying, "Out with the old and in with the new." Now that he had come, people could not simply live the same old way that they used to live or treat people the same old way that they used to treat them.

Jesus needed to say this because he knew that people like the Pharisees would fail to understand his mission. Some would try to take little pieces of Jesus and patch him on to their old way of doing things. But the gospel will not mix and match with man-made religion. This was the point of his parable about the garments. People do not cut pieces out of their brand new outfits and sew them into their old clothes. If they did, their old clothes would look strange and their new ones would be ruined. Yet this is exactly what the Pharisees were trying to do with Jesus. They saw him feasting with his disciples. Even worse, they saw him feasting with sinners. This did not fit their old ideas about what it meant to be holy. Jesus was telling them that it *wouldn't* fit. He was not there to patch up their tired old ways of being good enough for God. He was not there to stay separate from sinners, or to keep one of their grumpy old fasts; he was there to celebrate free forgiveness with the sinners he had come to save.

Some people would go a little bit farther. They would be willing to drink in what Jesus said, but they would try to keep it within the confines of their old way of life. This was the point of his parable about the wineskins. People do not put new wine into old wineskins, because as wine ferments, it expands. It is possible to put new wine into a *new* wineskin, because it still has room to stretch. But when new wine is put into an old wineskin, the wineskin bursts, and both the wine and the wineskin are wasted.

This parable is often misused. Any time that anyone wants to do anything new in the church, people say, "We have new wine, and we need to put it in new wineskins!" Taken out of context, the parable could be used to justify almost anything, including things that are not even biblical. But the parable is not so much a general principle for life in the church as it is a statement of the radically new thing that God has done in Christ. Jesus has come to bring explosive joy to people who desperately need to be saved. This is not something that can be contained within the religion of Pharisees who want to stay separate from sinners.

Some people try to patch Jesus on; some people try to bottle him up; and some people refuse to try him at all. This is the point of his third parable: "No one after drinking old wine desires new, for he says, 'The old is good'" (Luke 5:39). This statement is hard to understand because Jesus has been comparing his ministry to new wine, and usually we think that old wine is better. But this is not always true; it all depends on the vintage, and in the Bible, new wine is used to express exuberant joy (e.g., Ps. 4:7; John 2:9–10). This is the comparison that Jesus was making: his salvation is fresh, like new wine. Yet, sadly, some people are not even willing to try it. They are so convinced the old wine is better that they refuse to taste what Jesus has to offer. This was true of the Pharisees. They did not think that they were sinners, so they would not join the feast. They refused to taste the wine of his salvation.

Are you willing to try Jesus? You cannot simply patch a little bit of Jesus on to your old way of life. You cannot keep him bottled up inside your old religion. Jesus insists on giving sinners the new clothes of his righteousness, and the new wineskin of his grace, filled with the new wine of his Spirit. If you do not know Jesus for sure, you really ought to try him!

20

LORD OF THE SABBATH

Luke 6:1–11

But some of the Pharisees said, "Why are you doing what is not
lawful to do on the Sabbath?" . . . And he said to them, "The Son
of Man is lord of the Sabbath." (Luke 6:2, 5)

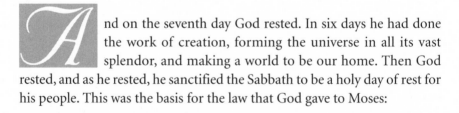nd on the seventh day God rested. In six days he had done
the work of creation, forming the universe in all its vast
splendor, and making a world to be our home. Then God
rested, and as he rested, he sanctified the Sabbath to be a holy day of rest for
his people. This was the basis for the law that God gave to Moses:

> Remember the Sabbath day, to keep it holy. Six days you shall labor, and
> do all your work, but the seventh day is a Sabbath to the LORD your God.
> On it you shall not do any work, you, or your son, or your daughter, your
> male servant, or your female servant, or your livestock, or the sojourner
> who is within your gates. For in six days the LORD made heaven and
> earth, the sea, and all that is in them, and rested the seventh day. There-
> fore the LORD blessed the Sabbath day and made it holy. (Ex. 20:8–11; cf.
> Gen. 2:2–3; Heb. 4:4)

This was the law of the Sabbath: one full day of rest in seven. The law was fundamental; it went back to the foundation of the world. It was also beneficial. God gave his people the Sabbath for their own good. By getting the rest they needed, they were able to flourish in all the activities of life. The law was relational. It helped to establish a bond of fellowship between God and his people. They were made in his image, and therefore their weekly rhythm was patterned after his work and rest in the creation of the world. To keep the Sabbath was to be like God, and therefore it was at the heart of what it meant to be godly.

For the children of Israel, the Sabbath was the best day of the week. It was a day for worship and for resting in the goodness of God. It was a day for ceasing from the labor and toil of the workday week. It was also a day for looking forward to the full and final salvation that God would provide in Christ: "when their vision was clearest the Jews understood that the weekly day of rest was a 'ritual anticipation of the advent of the messianic age'—a kind of picture, in the form of a religious observance, of what the whole of life would once again be like when God's Messiah came into the world to set things right—and therefore a thing of delight."[1]

PICKY, PICKY

It was on this delightful day that Jesus once again came into sharp conflict with the Pharisees. The whole thing started innocently enough: "On a Sabbath, while he was going through the grainfields, his disciples plucked and ate some heads of grain, rubbing them in their hands" (Luke 6:1).

Cutting through someone's field and picking a little grain was not against the law. In fact, it was one of the ways that God provided for his people. As it said in Deuteronomy, "If you go into your neighbor's standing grain, you may pluck the ears with your hand, but you shall not put a sickle to your neighbor's standing grain" (Deut. 23:25). As long as they did not try to do a full-scale harvest, it was acceptable for the disciples to help themselves. This was part of the legal code.

1. Michael Wilcock, *The Message of Luke*, The Bible Speaks Today (Downers Grove, IL: InterVarsity, 1979), 80.

241

The Pharisees did not see the situation that way, however. As the self-appointed Sabbath police, they thought they spotted a violation here. So they criticized the disciples for breaking God's law: "But some of the Pharisees said, 'Why are you doing what is not lawful to do on the Sabbath?'" (Luke 6:2). This was a serious accusation. Keeping the Sabbath was basic to biblical godliness, so to break it was to rebel against God. Such a sin would discredit the disciples, and by implication, it would also bring Jesus under reproach. The Pharisees thought they had caught the disciples red-handed.

Why did the Pharisees think that picking grain was against the law? The answer is that they had developed their own list of regulations for keeping the Sabbath. To make sure that they did not violate the fourth commandment, they specified all the different ways that someone could break the Sabbath, and then avoiding these activities became their law. According to the Mishnah, no fewer than thirty-nine different kinds of work were forbidden on the Sabbath, including reaping, threshing, winnowing, and preparing food.[2] When the disciples picked some heads of grain, the Pharisees thought they were reaping. When they rubbed them in their hands to separate the wheat from the chaff, they considered this threshing and winnowing. And when they started to eat the grain, they were guilty of preparing food on the Sabbath. So with every mouthful, the disciples were violating the law four different ways.[3] Thus said the Pharisees.

The problem was that this was their law, not God's law. The Pharisees were always telling people what to do and what not to do (especially what not to do), but they could not always tell the difference between their not-to-do list and God's command. They were legalists, and as a result, they ended up weighing people down with all kinds of extrabiblical regulations for the Sabbath. Instead of being a day of delight, under the repressive regime of the Pharisees it became a burden. This is a warning to us. We need to remember that most of the decisions we make about how to live out God's law in everything from our use of money to the education of our children are not binding for other Christians.

2. *Shabbath* 7.2, quoted in R. Kent Hughes, *Luke: That You May Know the Truth*, 2 vols., Preaching the Word (Wheaton, IL: Crossway, 1998), 1:200.
3. Leon Morris, *The Gospel According to St. Luke: An Introduction and Commentary*, Tyndale New Testament Commentaries (Grand Rapids: Eerdmans, 1974), 122.

WHAT DAVID DID

There were several ways that Jesus could have defended his disciples. He could have said that this was no big deal, that even if they *were* breaking the law, it was only a small violation. But Jesus did not say that. He could have said that what they did was not against the law at all, but only against the arbitrary opinions of the Pharisees. Jesus did not say that, either. He could even have said that it did not matter what people did on the Sabbath. He was the Messiah, and now that he had come, they were free from the old command. But Jesus wanted to go deeper. He wanted to free the law from the perversion of the Pharisees by explaining its underlying purpose. So he told a story from the Old Testament: "Have you not read what David did when he was hungry, he and those who were with him: how he entered the house of God and took and ate the bread of the Presence, which is not lawful for any but the priests to eat, and also gave it to those with him?" (Luke 6:3–4).

Jesus knew his Old Testament. Here he was referring to a story from the life of David. In those days God had rejected Saul and anointed David to serve as Israel's rightful king. But Saul was not dead yet, and because of his raging envy, David had to run for his life. This is where the story picks up in 1 Samuel 21, with David and his men fleeing from the wrath of Saul. They left in such haste that they did not have time to gather much in the way of provisions. So they went to the tabernacle, where Ahimelech was priest. And David said to him, "Now then, what do you have on hand? Give me five loaves of bread, or whatever is here" (1 Sam. 21:3). But Ahimelech said to David, "I have no common bread on hand, but there is holy bread—if the young men have kept themselves from women" (1 Sam. 21:4).

The priest was referring to the bread of the presence, which was kept in the tabernacle. This sacred bread of the covenant was baked fresh every week and then set out before the Lord on a golden table. It was only for the priests to eat, and no one else, for God had said to Moses:

> You shall take fine flour and bake twelve loaves from it; two tenths of an ephah shall be in each loaf. And you shall set them in two piles, six in a pile, on the table of pure gold before the LORD. . . . Every Sabbath day Aaron shall arrange it before the LORD regularly; it is from the people of Israel as a covenant forever. And it shall be for Aaron and his sons, and they shall eat it in

243

a holy place, since it is for him a most holy portion out of the LORD's food offerings, a perpetual due. (Lev. 24:5–6, 8–9)

Because the bread of the presence was consecrated to God, his holy priests were the only people who were allowed to eat it. But David and his men were famished. Technically, for them to eat the sacred bread was a violation of the ceremonial law that governed the worship of the tabernacle. But as Ahimelech considered the total righteousness of God, he recognized that he had a higher duty to meet a basic human need: "So the priest gave him the holy bread, for there was no bread there but the bread of the Presence" (1 Sam. 21:6).

This was the right thing to do in any case, but given who David was and what he was doing, it was especially necessary in this case. David was no ordinary citizen, and this was no ordinary situation. He was the Lord's anointed king, and thus his men were on a mission from God. David Gooding writes, "It was of paramount importance to the Lord that the Lord's anointed should be fed; and it was perfectly proper, therefore, that a symbol whose strict consecration was designed to teach Israel to revere the service of the Lord, should be used to serve the needs of the Lord's anointed. And if serving his needs meant serving the needs of his servants, there was nothing improper about it."[4]

By telling this story, Jesus was arguing from a harder case to an easier one. Follow his logic. If it was proper for David's men to eat the bread of the presence, as holy as it was, it was all the more appropriate for the disciples to pick a little grain on the Sabbath. In the words of Joseph Pipa, "if it was proper to violate a ceremonial law when the Lord's anointed was on the Lord's business on the Sabbath, then surely the Anointed and His followers may break a man-made law while they are doing the Lord's business on the Sabbath."[5] What David did violated the ceremonial law, but it was still the right thing to do because it was necessary to help people in need. God always desires mercy more than the observance of sacred rituals (cf. Matt. 12:6–7). What the disciples did on the Sabbath was not a violation of the law at all; it was per-

4. David Gooding, *According to Luke: A New Exposition of the Third Gospel* (Grand Rapids: Eerdmans, 1987), 114.
5. Joseph A. Pipa, *The Lord's Day* (Fearn, Ross-Shire: Christian Focus, 1997), 76.

fectly proper. Like the men of David, they were in the service of God's anointed king, they were on a holy mission, and they had a physical need. So if it was permissible for David to eat the bread of the presence, it was all the more appropriate for the disciples to eat enough grain to give them the strength they needed to follow Jesus. They were serving God's Son on God's Sabbath.

The problem with the Pharisees was not simply that they were too strict. Their problem was that they did not understand the true inward purpose of the law, which demands love for God and love for our neighbor. And because they did not understand this, they did not know how to apply the law properly, the way Jesus did. We are warned by their poor example not to use the Sabbath to avoid showing mercy, or to use our own ideas about how to live as an excuse for not doing what God requires.

THE SABBATH'S LORD

Jesus could have stopped there. The legal precedent he cited from the Old Testament cleared the disciples of any wrongdoing. But Jesus went on to make a dramatic declaration: "The Son of Man is lord of the Sabbath" (Luke 6:5).

Here Luke has done it again: he has told a story from the life of Jesus that builds up to a climactic statement about his person and work. This is in keeping with Luke's grand purpose of helping us know for certain that Jesus is the Christ. To that end, he has told us that Jesus is "the Son of the Most High" (Luke 1:32), "a Savior, who is Christ the Lord" (Luke 2:11), the beloved and well-pleasing Son of the Father (Luke 3:22). Luke has also shown the authority of Jesus to preach the gospel, heal the body, cast out demons, forgive sinners, and call disciples. Here at the beginning of chapter 6 he announces a new title, with new authority. Jesus is the Son of Man, and as the Son of Man, he is Lord of the Sabbath.

"Son of Man" is a messianic title that echoes the Old Testament, especially the prophecies of Daniel (see Dan. 7:9–14). By using this title, Jesus was testifying to his true humanity, and also hinting at his coming glory. He is the first man in the new humanity. But Jesus is also God, and this is the clear implication of his claim to lordship over the Sabbath. Who is the Lord of the Sabbath? Only God is.

245

As strange as it may seem, this statement is sometimes used to sweep aside the Sabbath. Some Christians have the impression that in this passage Jesus was saying that the Sabbath no longer mattered. As Lord of the Sabbath, he could do whatever he wanted with it, and what he wanted to do was eliminate the obligation to keep a day of rest. But the truth is almost exactly the opposite. By saying that he was Lord of the Sabbath, Jesus was making a strong claim to his deity, and also pointing to the abiding significance of the fourth commandment.

Remember that this Sabbath commandment came from God. The Sabbath was not a human invention, but a divine institution. God established it the week the world was made. He also reiterated it when he gave his law to Moses. The Sabbath came from God. He patterned it after his work in creation and revealed it in thunder from the mountain. Therefore, when Jesus claimed to be Lord of the Sabbath, he was claiming to be very God— the Creator and the Lawgiver.

Because he is God, Jesus Christ is supreme over the Sabbath. The Sabbath itself is an awesome institution. To this day, it orders the work and leisure of humanity by dividing our calendar into God-given weeks. By demanding us to set aside our regular work, it also gives special glory to God. Yet as great as the Sabbath is, Jesus is even greater, because he is the Sabbath's Lord. The law for this day was given at his command; the worship of this day returns to his honor; and the proper observance of this day is his sovereign prerogative.

Knowing that Jesus Christ is Lord of the Sabbath helps us to know that this day has abiding significance for the church. Far from being the only one of the Ten Commandments that Jesus abolished, as some Christians think, it is a commandment he taught as clearly as any other. J. C. Ryle comments: "We must not allow ourselves to be carried away by the common notion that the Sabbath is a mere Jewish ordinance, and that it was abolished and done away by Christ. There is not a single passage of the Gospels which proves this. In every case where we find our Lord speaking upon it, He speaks against the false views of it, which were taught by the Pharisees, but not against the day itself." Then Bishop Ryle offers an illustration to help us understand what Jesus does with the Sabbath. He writes, "The architect who repairs a building, and restores it to its proper use, is not the destroyer of it, but the preserver."[6]

Since the creation of the world, God has required his people to keep one holy day in seven for worship and rest. Jesus preserved this commandment, for when the Sabbath came, he worshiped at the synagogue (see Luke 4:16). We are called to follow his example: "Throughout the Gospels it is clear that the Lord taught that the Sabbath should be consecrated to God, and acted accordingly. It is therefore fitting that on the day of rest man should so disentangle himself from ordinary activities that he may be able to serve and glorify God to the best of his ability."[7]

Of course, the Sabbath is also a day for doing things that are truly necessary to meet our physical needs, which is what the disciples were doing when they picked grain. We need to be careful here, because not everything is quite as necessary as we think it is. We should resist the temptation to think that we need to be working, studying, or shopping on the Sabbath, when in fact we have not used our time wisely the rest of the week. But Jesus knows that we have real needs, and unlike the Pharisees, he liberates us from any man-made rules that would actually hinder us from observing the true purpose of the Sabbath, which is to put his glory at the center of our lives.

The primary change in the day is that now we celebrate it on the first day of the week, as the early Christians did (see Acts 20:7; 1 Cor. 16:2). This is because Sunday is the day that Jesus was raised from the dead (see John 20:19). By a mighty act of redemption—as mighty an act as creation itself—God has sanctified a new day, properly called "the Lord's day" (see Rev. 1:10). The Old Testament Sabbath was on the last day of the week, and on it godly people were looking forward to the rest that they would find in their Messiah. Now the Messiah has come in the person of Jesus Christ. Since he is the fulfillment of the Sabbath, we have already begun to enter his rest, and thus we begin our week by acknowledging his lordship over all of life. Nevertheless, we are still looking forward to our full and final rest with Christ in glory. "Our weekly Sabbath-rest," writes Richard Gaffin, "is a

---

6. J. C. Ryle, *Expository Thoughts on the Gospels, Luke* (1858; reprint Cambridge: James Clarke, 1976), 1:162.

7. Norval Geldenhuys, *The Gospel of Luke*, New International Commentary on the New Testament (Grand Rapids: Eerdmans, 1951), 200.

recurring pointer to that consummation. Weekly Sabbath keeping is a sign that points to the end of history and to the ultimate fulfillment of all God's purposes for his creation."[8]

The Lord's day is for resting from physical labor, so that our bodies can be restored and renewed. It is also for resting from spiritual labor. As the Scripture says, "So then, there remains a Sabbath rest for the people of God, for whoever has entered God's rest has also rested from his works as God did from his" (Heb. 4:9–10). Jesus Christ has finished the work of our salvation, so that we do not have to work our way to heaven. Then the Lord's day is for worship. It is for praising God with his people, for personal prayer and Bible study, and for fellowship with other Christians. It is for all of these things because it is for the Lord Jesus Christ. If we dishonor the day, we dishonor him; but as we honor the day, we honor him, because he is the Lord of this day.

A HAND TO HEAL

The Lord's day has one further purpose that becomes clear in the story that follows. Like many of the important events in Jesus' life, it happened on the Sabbath. And, as we might expect, given his commitment to keeping the fourth commandment, it happened while Jesus was at worship: "On another Sabbath, he entered the synagogue and was teaching, and a man was there whose right hand was withered. And the scribes and the Pharisees watched him, to see whether he would heal on the Sabbath, so that they might find a reason to accuse him" (Luke 6:6–7).

The Pharisees had heard that Jesus healed people on the Sabbath, and they wanted to see if he would do it again. Their sinister attitude shows that their confrontation with Jesus had continued to intensify. It did not take long for his ministry to arouse their opposition, and by this point they were actively seeking to attack him. Jesus was already on the collision course that would take him to the cross.

As far as the Pharisees were concerned, healing was a form of working, and thus it broke the fourth commandment. They might just be willing to accept a miracle if it were a matter of life and death. In fact, one of the old

---

8. Richard B. Gaffin, Jr., "A Sign of Hope," *New Horizons*, (March 2003), http.www.opc.org/nh.html?article_id=161.

rabbinic writings said, "Whenever there is doubt whether life is in danger this overrides the Sabbath."[9] But according to the Pharisees, the Sabbath was not a day for routine medical care. Unless the situation was truly life-threatening, mercy would have to wait for another day (cf. Luke 13:14). As one commentator puts it, "To heal on the Sabbath is permitted in the case of imminent danger of life; but where there is no danger in delay it is unconditionally forbidden."[10]

Admittedly, no one at the synagogue was dying. There was a man there who had a disability, however. He had an atrophied appendage, which Luke tells us with clinical accuracy happened to be his right hand. This was the hand that Jesus intended to heal, and that the Pharisees wanted to stay the way that it was.

Whether it was by his own divine omniscience or by the witness of the Holy Spirit, Jesus knew what the Pharisees were thinking, and his response was masterful: "But he knew their thoughts, and he said to the man with the withered hand, 'Come and stand here.' And he rose and stood there. And Jesus said to them, 'I ask you, is it lawful on the Sabbath to do good or to do harm, to save life or to destroy it?'" (Luke 6:8–9). What a question! We have already seen how good his answers were, but if anything, the questions that Jesus asked were even more devastating. This one searched the Pharisees right down to their very souls.

Obviously, the Sabbath was a day for doing good. But the do-nothing Pharisees were so concerned about keeping their man-made rules that they would not even lift a finger to help someone in need. "I'm sorry," they said. "You'll have to wait until tomorrow. This isn't a day for helping people; it's only for worshiping God." Because it did not leave any room for mercy, this interpretation had to be flawed in some fundamental way. Jesus wanted the Pharisees to see that by refusing to do good on the Sabbath, they were actually causing harm. Not only was it not wrong to help this man, but it was wrong *not* to. Jesus was not simply trying to show the Pharisees that their view of the Sabbath was inadequate; he was also saying that it was immoral![11] In this case, failing to act was morally equivalent to destroying someone's life. Therefore, far from keeping God's law, the Pharisees were actually breaking

---

9. *Yoma* 8.6, quoted in Morris, *Luke*, 123.
10. Strack-Billerbeck, quoted in Geldenhuys, *Luke*, 203.
11. Gooding, *Luke*, 113.

it. Their underlying attitude toward people in need was loveless, merciless, and cruel.

How easy it is to keep a list of things that make us good enough for God, while at the same time completely missing the things that are most important to him. The Pharisees had a long list of little things they did to be godly, but they overlooked the big things like loving mercy and doing justice. Their poor example is a warning that there is more to godliness than simply staying away from certain kinds of personal sin. God wants us to have a heart for people in need. Therefore, we need to ask ourselves the question that John asked the early church: "If anyone . . . sees his brother in need, yet closes his heart against him, how does God's love abide in him?" (1 John 3:17).

Jesus brought all of these issues right out into the open when he invited the man with the withered hand to stand in front of the Pharisees. First he asked if it was permissible for him to perform a miracle of mercy on the Sabbath. Jesus looked from one Pharisee to another, waiting for an answer. But none of them had anything to say, so "after looking around at them all he said to him, 'Stretch out your hand.' And he did so, and his hand was restored" (Luke 6:10).

This was a mighty work of salvation. One moment the man's arm dangled uselessly at his side, but the very next moment he was flexing his fingers. His hand was healed. At the command of Christ, he was able to do the very thing that he had always been unable to do: stretch out his hand. The man acted in faith, and when he did, he experienced the enabling power of God.

This is a picture of what happens in the salvation of a sinner. The gospel is preached by the power of the Holy Spirit, and the unbeliever hears the good news of salvation: "Believe in the Lord Jesus Christ, and by his death on the cross and resurrection from the grave, you will be saved." Up until that point, the unbeliever has been unable to believe the gospel. But God says, "Believe," and when he does, the unbeliever believes! By his amazing grace, God enables us to do what we cannot do for ourselves, which is to trust in Jesus Christ for our salvation.

Was it lawful for Jesus to heal a man's hand on the Sabbath? The answer is yes, because the Sabbath is for healing. By doing this miracle, the Lord of the Sabbath was not simply claiming his own personal right to do whatever he wanted on the day. Rather, he was revealing one of the true purposes of the day, which is to keep the law of mercy and love. Earlier Jesus told a story about David to show that there are certain things we *may* do on the Sabbath: works of necessity. By performing this miracle he was showing that there is also something we *must* do on the Sabbath, which is to show mercy.

A DAY FOR MERCY

Sadly, the Pharisees did not have the heart to show mercy, and thus their encounter with the Lord of the Sabbath ends on an ominous note: "But they were filled with fury and discussed with one another what they might do to Jesus" (Luke 6:11). The Greek word for fury *(anoias)* refers to an unthinking rage, almost a kind of madness. Ironically, in their fanatical hatred the Pharisees were really the ones who were breaking the Sabbath, because they were committing murder in their hearts. Rather than preserving life on the Sabbath, they were starting to look for a way to take it.

What made the Pharisees so angry? It was partly because Jesus broke one of their precious rules, but it was more because he exposed their lack of love for people in need. They were using the very law of God as an excuse for not showing mercy.

This forces us to examine our own response to Jesus and his miracle. More importantly, it challenges us to examine our commitment to people in serious need. Some Christians are like the Pharisees: always looking for some religiously justifiable way to avoid getting involved in other people's problems. They secretly think that people who have a drug addiction, get an abortion, end up in prison, join the gay lifestyle, or contract AIDS are getting what they deserve, and therefore that they themselves are off the hook as far as getting personally involved.

But Christ calls us to have a heart of compassion, and as the Lord of the Sabbath, he has given us a day to show mercy. Sunday is also a day of worship, of course, and a day of rest, but it is not just a day to take things easy. It is a day for helping people in need, especially if we can get some of our rest on Saturday, as most Americans can. Norval Geldenhuys is right when he says: "Jesus' words and actions teach us quite plainly that we should every Lord's Day place ourselves wholly at His disposal to perform works of love and mercy wherever and in whatever way it may be possible. We may not consecrate the day of rest in a merely passive manner, but must be active in His service and thus through Him be of use to those who suffer and need help, spiritually as well as physically."[12]

The Lord's day is for visiting the sick. It is for welcoming strangers, especially internationals. It is for helping people worship in the nursing home. It is for hosting the homeless to dinner. It is for giving fatherly care to orphans. It is for taking time to counsel friends who need encouragement. It is a day for giving all the service to God that we are unable to give the rest of the week. In addition to giving us a good day for rest and worship, the Lord has also given us a great day for the gospel—not just preaching it, but also practicing it through loving deeds of mercy.

There are great needs all around us. Thankfully, God has given us a day to help meet them. As John Calvin once said, referring to the urgent needs he saw around him in Geneva, "The city will be safe if God be truly and devoutly worshipped, and this is attested by the sanctification of the Sabbath."[13]

12. Geldenhuys, *Luke*, 203.
13. John Calvin, *Calvin's Commentaries*, 22 vols. (Grand Rapids: Baker, 1999), 9:387.

21

THE CALLING OF THE TWELVE

Luke 6:12–26

And when day came, he called his disciples and chose from
them twelve, whom he named apostles: Simon, whom he
named Peter, and Andrew his brother, and James and John,
and Philip, and Bartholomew, and Matthew, and Thomas,
and James the son of Alphaeus, and Simon who was called the
Zealot, and Judas the son of James, and Judas Iscariot, who
became a traitor. (Luke 6:13–16)

*T*he Bible does not give us many specifics about the architecture of heaven, but every splendid detail that it does give is full of spiritual significance. Consider what the book of Revelation says about the holy city of the New Jerusalem: "And the wall of the city had twelve foundations, and on them were the twelve names of the twelve apostles of the Lamb" (Rev. 21:14).

What a magnificent testimony this is to the ministry of the apostles! Their witness to the gospel—their message of salvation through the death and resurrection of Jesus Christ—is the foundation of the church, because it is only by believing the apostolic message that sinners can be saved. As a monument to their ministry, God has inscribed the names of the apostles in heaven, writing them on the bedrock of his holy city. This was the destiny God had in mind for these men from the beginning, but in order to reach it, they first had to endure poverty, hunger, sorrow, and persecution. Like Jesus himself, and like every one of his disciples, they had to pass through suffering on their way to glory.

Up All Night

Jesus told these twelve men what to expect the very day that he called them to be apostles. He had many followers in those days, but to fulfill his mission to the world, he appointed a smaller number of men to serve as his messengers. Luke tells us,

> In these days he went out to the mountain to pray, and all night he continued in prayer to God. And when day came, he called his disciples and chose from them twelve, whom he named apostles: Simon, whom he named Peter, and Andrew his brother, and James and John, and Philip, and Bartholomew, and Matthew, and Thomas, and James the son of Alphaeus, and Simon who was called the Zealot, and Judas the son of James, and Judas Iscariot, who became a traitor. (Luke 6:12–16)

The ministry of these twelve men was central to God's plan of salvation. First the apostles would spend several years with Jesus, learning to walk with him. At the end of their training they would witness his crucifixion and resurrection, which would show them for sure that Jesus was the Christ. Then they would go and preach the gospel to all nations, proclaiming the good news of salvation.

Since the apostles were the foundation for God's work in the world, it was absolutely essential for Jesus to choose the right men. So he prayed. He prayed privately, going up into the mountains to have time alone with God. He prayed fervently, spending the whole night in prayer. And he prayed dependently, asking his Father to help him. Later Jesus would tell the apostles that they were given to him by the Father (John 17:6). As he called men to ministry, he called the men who were his Father's choice.

This was even true of Judas, who ended up betraying Jesus. Luke's list of apostles ends on an ominous note, foreshadowing treachery. But this does not mean that God made a mistake. On the contrary, the betrayal of Judas Iscariot was part of God's plan for the death of his Son (see John 17:12), and thus for the salvation of the world.

The way that Jesus called the twelve proves the priority of prayer. This is the third time that Luke has mentioned Jesus going off somewhere to pray (cf. Luke 4:42; 5:16). As Hartley Coleridge wrote in one of his sonnets,

> He sought the mountain and the loneliest height,
> For He would meet his Father all alone,
> And there, with many a tear and many a groan,
> He strove in prayer throughout the long, long night.

The poet then asks why Jesus even needed to pray, and answers by reminding us of his incarnation:

> Why crave in prayer what was his own by might?
> Vain is the question,—Christ was man in deed,
> And being man, his duty was to pray.[1]

From this example we learn our own great need for prayer. Like Jesus, we need to meet with our Father in the mountain places of intercession. We need to pray for God's wisdom whenever we face a momentous decision, asking for his will to be done. We also need to pray for the work of the church, as Jesus did. His example shows us the priority of prayer in carrying forward the global work of the gospel. Prayer comes first. If Jesus began his mission with prayer, how can we expect to accomplish anything at all without it? We are never more like Jesus than when we get down on our knees to pray for people to go into the world and preach the gospel.

ORDINARY PEOPLE

As surprising as it may be to see Jesus pray, it is even more surprising to see how his prayers were answered. The twelve men that Jesus called were

1. Hartley Coleridge, quoted by Robert Atwan and Laurance Wieder, eds., in *Chapters into Verse: Poetry in English Inspired by the Bible*, vol. 2: *Gospels to Revelation* (Oxford: Oxford University Press, 1993), 72.

not the men that most people would have chosen. Yet the apostles were called by God, and thus they were the answer to Jesus' prayers.

An apostle is someone who is commissioned to carry a message or to perform an official duty on someone else's behalf. The word comes from the Greek verb that means "to send" *(apostellō)*. It is closely related to the Hebrew word *shaliach*, which at the time of Christ referred to an official representative in the Jewish community. By virtue of his commission, a *shaliach* had the authority to speak and to act for someone else. A modern example would be the power of attorney that authorizes a personal representative to sign legal documents, or the authority an ambassador has to sign a treaty for his country. Eventually the apostles would become Christ's ambassadors, his personal representatives. After his ascension, they would speak and act in Jesus' name—preaching the good news, performing miracles, and writing New Testament Gospels and Epistles. This was God's strategy for spreading the gospel.

What qualified these men to serve as apostles? All of them were disciples. They were among the men and women who followed Jesus. But what distinguished them from the other disciples? They were not religious leaders. In all likelihood, they were not well educated, well connected, or well funded. On the contrary, people regarded them as "unschooled, ordinary men" (Acts 4:13 NIV). All of them were poor—even Levi, who had left his lucrative tax business behind. It may seem rather surprising that these rather ordinary men became apostles. But they were called by God, and this was the secret of their success. What was important about them was not their credentials, but the calling they received by the sovereign election of God. "You did not choose me," Jesus later said to them, "but I chose you and appointed you that you should go and bear fruit and that your fruit should abide" (John 15:16).

The calling of the apostles was unique. They and they alone were called to represent Jesus Christ as his official messengers. In effect, by ordaining these twelve men, God was establishing a new Israel. Just as the twelve sons of Jacob founded the Old Testament people of God, so also the apostles established the foundation for God's new people in Christ. To this day, the church rests upon their ministry. We are "built on the foundation of the apostles and prophets" (Eph. 2:20). And since a building can have only one foundation, their ministry is nonrepeatable.

Nevertheless, the calling of the twelve teaches us important things about our own service to Christ. We too have been called by God. Like the apostles, we have been called to faith in Jesus Christ. We have also been called—by name—to serve our Lord in some particular ministry or ministries. We do not choose our calling in the church; God chooses it for us. This principle is basic to all Christian ministry.

When God calls us, he also provides the gifts that we need to carry out our calling. The mission of Jesus was not limited by the resources the apostles already had in their possession. He would give them whatever they needed, including his Spirit, who was the real power at work in their ministry. Therefore, as the apostles took the gospel to the world, they did not have to rely on their own abilities, but on the enabling and equipping work of God. Oswald Chambers was right when he said: "God can achieve his purpose either through the absence of human power and resources, or the abandonment of reliance on them. All through history God has chosen and used nobodies, because their unusual dependence on him made possible the unique display of his power and grace. He chose and used somebodies only when they renounced dependence on their natural abilities and resources."[2]

Whether we are nobodies like the apostles when Jesus called them, or somebodies such as they became, we need to put our confidence in Christ alone, and not in ourselves, so that his Spirit can do the real work of our ministry. It is only by the grace of the Lord Jesus Christ that we are able to care for people in need, see them come to faith, and help them grow in godliness.

The Ultimate Internship

As soon as Jesus called the apostles, he started showing them how to serve: "And he came down with them and stood on a level place, with a great crowd of his disciples and a great multitude of people from all Judea and Jerusalem and the seacoast of Tyre and Sidon, who came to hear him and to be healed of their diseases. And those who were troubled with unclean spirits were cured. And all the crowd sought to

2. Oswald Chambers, quoted in R. Kent Hughes, *Luke: That You May Know the Truth*, 2 vols., Preaching the Word (Wheaton, IL: Crossway, 1998), 1:209.

touch him, for power came out from him and healed them all" (Luke 6:17–19).

By now all of this is very familiar. Jesus kept gaining in popularity, so a great crowd gathered to hear him preach. Many identified themselves as his disciples, but others came from all parts of the country. They did not know what to think of Jesus yet, but they wanted to hear what he had to say. They also wanted to be healed. So Jesus cured their diseases and cast out their demons, healing everyone who could get close enough to touch him. By performing these miracles, he was demonstrating his power over evil and proving that he was the Christ.

Jesus was also showing his newly appointed apostles how to serve. They learned to carry out their calling by spending time with Jesus in ministry. Today we would call this an internship. Jesus started by letting the apostles observe his work firsthand. The next step was to give them simple opportunities to serve him in practical ways. Then he would encourage them to start exercising their gifts of preaching and healing. Eventually, he would send them all over the world as his gospel messengers. But it all began with personal discipleship in the context of mentored ministry. This is still the best pattern to follow in preparing for any form of service in the church. Watch and practice until God calls you into some more public form of ministry. And always spend time with Jesus, which today we do primarily through prayer and Bible study.

On the first day of their basic training, Jesus wanted to give the apostles a perspective on the Christian life that would help them know what to expect in ministry. Some of the things he says here are similar to things he said in his famous Sermon on the Mount (Matt. 5–7). In fact, some scholars say that Matthew and Luke both describe the same sermon. But then they have to reconcile all the differences between the two accounts. One obvious difficulty is that whereas Matthew says that Jesus "went up on the mountain" (Matt. 5:1), Luke tells us that he "came down with them and stood on a level place" (Luke 6:17). Some scholars resolve this apparent discrepancy by saying that Jesus delivered his sermon on a plateau halfway up the mountain. But the real problem is that there are so many differences in content. A simpler explanation is that Jesus preached the same but slightly different sermon on more than one occasion, as most preachers do sometimes. Matthew gives us the Sermon on the Mount; Luke gives us the same sermon, only different—what Kent Hughes cleverly calls "The Sermon on the Level."[3]

As Jesus began to preach this sermon, he gave his disciples four blessings, followed by a tale of woe. He was drawing a contrast between two ways of life. There are blessings that come with godliness, and woes that come from worldliness. But what brings blessing or woe is almost exactly the opposite of what most people think. How can you tell that God is blessing you? The answer Jesus gives is totally unexpected. He takes the things that no one wants—poverty, hunger, sorrow, persecution—and says that they have his blessing. Then he takes the things that everyone wants—money, food, entertainment, popularity—and says that they will never satisfy. Jesus thus teaches his disciples to "prize what the world calls pitiable, and suspect what the world thinks desirable."[4]

THE BEATITUDES

The first blessing is for the poor: "Blessed are you who are poor, for yours is the kingdom of God" (Luke 6:20). This was the gospel that Jesus had promised to preach: "good news to the poor" (Luke 4:18). Notice, however, that this benediction is not for everyone who is poor; it is specifically for poor Christians, because before he said these things, Jesus "lifted up his eyes on his disciples" (Luke 6:20). He was not pronouncing his blessing on humanity in general, but on his followers. He wanted them to know that in spite of their present poverty, they were in possession of an everlasting kingdom.

To understand the word "poor," we need to start by taking it fairly literally. In Matthew, Jesus says, "Blessed are the poor *in spirit*, for theirs is the kingdom of heaven" (Matt. 5:3). But in keeping with his special concern for the down and out, Luke's version is more literal: "Blessed are you who are poor" (Luke 6:20). Jesus wanted to encourage his people in financial hardship, perhaps especially if their hardships were related in some way to their service for him—as was the case for most of his disciples. J. C. Ryle comments:

3. Hughes, *Luke*, 1:213.
4. Michael Wilcock, *The Message of Luke*, The Bible Speaks Today (Downers Grove, IL: Inter-Varsity, 1979), 86.

> We must take good heed that we do not misunderstand our Lord's meaning, when we read these expressions. We must not for a moment suppose that the mere fact of being poor, and hungry, and sorrowful, and hated by man, will entitle any one to lay claim to an interest in Christ's blessing. The poverty here spoken of, is a poverty accompanied by grace. The want is a want entailed by faithful adherence to Jesus. The afflictions are the afflictions of the Gospel. The persecution is persecution for the Son of Man's sake.[5]

Unfortunately, there are always some people who think that the best way to measure God's blessing is by looking at someone's bank account. This is the error of the so-called prosperity gospel. In some African churches, a man is not considered ready for pastoral ministry until he becomes wealthy. Otherwise, the thinking goes, how will anyone know that he has God's blessing? Some Americans must have the same attitude, because we are endlessly afflicted with health and wealth preaching, especially on television.

How tempting it is to rely on money, both for ministry and for our own personal happiness. But this way of counting our blessings is spiritually impoverished. Among other things, it fails to recognize the grace that God gives to the poor. Although poverty itself is not a blessing, people who are poor in Christ *have* God's blessing. The whole kingdom of God belongs to them, with all of its spiritual riches in this life and unimaginable treasures in the life to come. But to receive these blessings, we have to admit our spiritual poverty and come to God for grace. According to Norval Geldenhuys, the blessing of God's kingdom is for people "who do not seek their wealth and life in earthly things, but who acknowledge their own poverty and come to Him to seek real life. Where outward poverty leads anyone to realize his utter dependence on God and to walk humbly with his Lord, such a person will be blessed—in measure even in this life, and more abundantly in the next, he may expect rich and glorious fullness of spiritual life and joy."[6]

Jesus also blessed the hungry—a second beatitude—saying, "Blessed are you who are hungry now, for you shall be satisfied" (Luke 6:21). In its most literal sense, this promise is closely connected to the first one. The same

---

5. J. C. Ryle, *Expository Thoughts on the Gospels, Luke* (1858; reprint Cambridge: James Clarke, 1976), 1:177.

6. Norval Geldenhuys, *The Gospel of Luke*, New International Commentary on the New Testament (Grand Rapids: Eerdmans, 1951), 210.

God who provides for the poor feeds the hungry. But we can also take the second beatitude in a more spiritual sense, as a hunger for God and his grace. This was the craving that the psalmist felt when he said, "O God, my soul thirsts for you; my flesh faints for you, as in a dry and weary land where there is no water" (Ps. 63:1; cf. 42:1–2).

We were made with a spiritual hunger for truth, an unfulfilled longing for eternity, and a desperate craving for the love that is at the heart of the universe. Only God can satisfy, and Jesus has promised that his disciples will be filled. We will drink deeply from the fountains of his grace. We will eat richly from the banquet of his Word. We will find our satisfaction in him.

We will also find our joy in Jesus, for he has promised us laughter. This is the third beatitude: "Blessed are you who weep now, for you shall laugh" (Luke 6:21). Here Jesus refers to all the sorrows that we suffer in a fallen world. We weep for our sins, repenting of all the wrong that we have done. We weep for the sins of others, lamenting the dishonor they do to God. We weep for the sins of our society, knowing that we ourselves are implicated in their iniquity. We weep for the lost, praying that God will rescue them. We weep for those who suffer, grieving over all the natural disasters, armed conflicts, and social injustices that happen every day. And we weep for the loved ones that we have lost, knowing that they are gone and will not return.

There are times when life is so full of sorrow that we wonder if we will ever laugh again. But as we weep, we hold on to this promise, that godly sorrow will turn to joy. One day God will take away our sinful nature, and we will never sin again. One day he will right every wrong and gather his people into his eternal city. One day all our sufferings and sorrows will come to an end. What laughter will ring through heaven then! As we stand in the golden city, reveling in the surprise of our redemption—the sudden realization that all our hopes have come true—we will burst into the everlasting laughter of joy.

The people who laugh loudest and longest will be the ones who suffered most for their faith. The fourth and final beatitude is for the persecuted church: "Blessed are you when people hate you and when they exclude you and revile you and spurn your name as evil, on account of the Son of Man! Rejoice in that day, and leap for joy, for behold, your reward is great in heaven; for so their fathers did to the prophets" (Luke 6:22–23).

Here Jesus is speaking about one particular kind of suffering: suffering for the sake of the gospel. He is speaking most specifically to his apostles, all of whom suffered violent persecution and most of whom died horrific deaths at the hands of their enemies. This was all for Jesus' sake. They were hated, excluded, reviled, and spurned, and in a way, this was the proof of their discipleship. To follow Jesus is to share in his sufferings. Dietrich Bonhoeffer went so far as to say:

> Suffering, then, is the badge of true discipleship. The disciple is not above his master . . . that is why Luther reckoned suffering among the marks of the true church, and one of the memoranda drawn up in preparation for the Augsburg Confession similarly defines the church as the community of those "who are persecuted and martyred for the Gospel's sake." . . . Discipleship means allegiance to the suffering Christ, and it is therefore not at all surprising that Christians should be called upon to suffer. In fact, it is a joy and a token of His grace.[7]

Bonhoeffer was right when he called this a joy, because Jesus told his apostles to rejoice in their sufferings. He did so for this reason: they would have great reward in heaven—a promise fulfilled in the foundations of the new Jerusalem, where their names are written in glory. The apostles must have taken this promise to heart, because in his later writing Luke tells us that when the apostles were beaten by the Sanhedrin, "they left the presence of the council, rejoicing that they were counted worthy to suffer dishonor for the name" (Acts 5:41).

This joy is not for the apostles only, but for everyone who is persecuted for Jesus' sake. At the beginning of 2004, thirty-six Chinese missionaries were commissioned to take the gospel westwards. Their goal was to make it all the way from China to Jerusalem, planting churches along the way and reaching some of the most unreached people in the world. All of these missionaries had already suffered at the hands of China's communist government. Most of them were likely to suffer again, as they traveled through Muslim lands. But they began their journey with rejoicing, hoping for an eternal reward.

What are you suffering for Jesus? As we live for Christ, we may well have struggles in our families, receive disparaging comments in our communities, and face difficulties in our work or ministry. But whatever we suffer, if

---

7. Dietrich Bonhoeffer, *The Cost of Discipleship* (New York: Macmillan, 1969), 101.

it is because of our faith in Jesus Christ, then we can rejoice in the hope of a great reward. God will bless us in the highest courts of heaven.

The Woes of the World

Most people say they want God to bless them, but how many people really want to live the kind of Christ-centered life that God has promised to bless? Most people do not want to be poor; they want to get rich. They do not want to go hungry; they want to get stuffed. They do not want to weep; they want to crack jokes. They do not want to get persecuted; they want to be popular. But Jesus said: "Woe to you who are rich, for you have received your consolation. Woe to you who are full now, for you shall be hungry. Woe to you who laugh now, for you shall mourn and weep. Woe to you, when all people speak well of you, for so their fathers did to the false prophets" (Luke 6:24–26).

When Jesus spoke about woe, he was not warning people about judgment, but expressing his sense of sadness over the way that they were living. The Greek word for woe *(ouai)* is more a word of lamentation than of condemnation. According to Leon Morris, it means something "like 'Alas' (NEB) or 'How terrible' (TEV). It is an expression of regret and compassion."[8] Jesus saw how tragic it was for people to live their own way rather than God's way, which is the only way of blessing.

Some people want to get rich. Jesus was not speaking about everyone who has money, because there are some godly rich people in the Bible. Rather, he is speaking about people "who seek their life and happiness only or primarily in material things, who do not realize their souls' need and do not acknowledge their dependence on God."[9] They are all about gaining more financial security and enjoying "the finer things in life." But if that is what they are living for, that is all the comfort they will ever get! As Jesus said, they have received their "consolation," and the verb he used for receiving *(apechō)* "is one often used in receipts with a meaning like 'Paid in full.'"[10] Jesus was warning people that money is a temporary blessing at best. It does

8. Leon Morris, *The Gospel According to St. Luke: An Introduction and Commentary*, Tyndale New Testament Commentaries (Grand Rapids: Eerdmans, 1974), 127.

9. Geldenhuys, *Luke*, 210.

10. Morris, *Luke*, 128.

not last forever, so rich people had better enjoy it while they can. To put it another way, earthly treasure always turns out to be a bad investment.

It is much better for us to recognize our true spiritual poverty and put all our stock in the kingdom of God. Consider the epitaph of Thomas Lowes, who is buried in Holyrood Abbey in Edinburgh:

> One instance among thousands of the uncertainty of human life and the instability of earthly possessions and enjoyments. Born to ample property, he for several years experienced a distressing reverse of fortune, and no sooner was he restored to his former affluence than it pleased Divine Providence to withdraw this together with his life. READER, be thou taught by this to seek those riches which never can fail and those pleasures which are at God's right hand for evermore: the gracious gift of God, and to be enjoyed through faith in JESUS CHRIST our Saviour.[11]

Jesus pronounced his second woe on people who are full, which is the opposite of being hungry. Someone who is full is already satisfied. Here Jesus seems to be speaking about people who are spiritually complacent. They do not have much of an appetite for God. They do not crave fellowship with Jesus Christ through prayer and Bible study. They feel satisfied, as if spiritually they have gone far enough already. They do not want to do anything too radical, or go outside their comfort zone.

This unhappy condition may be illustrated by telling the story of a duck who was flying across Europe in springtime. Along the way, the duck settled in a barnyard where tame ducks were fed corn every day. He intended to stay for only an hour, but there was so much good food that he decided to stay for the day, then a week, and finally the whole summer. Next autumn he heard a flock of wild ducks pass overhead. When he heard their wild call, he flapped his wings and rose to join them. But by this time he was so fat, that no matter how much he struggled, he failed to get any higher than the roof of the barn. So he dropped back to the ground and settled in for the winter. The next time the duck heard the call of the wild, he lifted his head excitedly, but he couldn't even get off the ground. Eventually he grew so satisfied with his life in the barnyard that he didn't notice the wild ducks at all.[12]

---

11. Quoted by Ligon Duncan in *First Epistle* 32.28 (July 26, 2001) n. p.

12. This story, which is sometimes attributed to Søren Kierkegaard, is recounted in Clarence McCartney, *Preaching without Notes* (Grand Rapids: Baker, 1976), 56–57.

The same thing can happen to anyone who starts gorging on what the world has to offer. You may fully intend to take off and fly again with the people of God. But you decide to stay a little longer and taste the sweet corn of ungodliness. For a while you are still willing to go to church and hear what God has to say, but eventually you decide that it is hardly worth the effort. The irony is that people who feel that they are full actually go hungry. People who do not have a craving for God do not feed on his Word. Soon they go starving for lack of fellowship with him.

Jesus knew that some people never do get serious about spiritual things. So he said, "Woe to you who laugh now, for you shall mourn and weep" (Luke 6:25). Not that God has anything against laughter. He invented it, after all, and Jesus said a lot of things that were quite funny, including some things right here in Luke 6. But his concern was people who live only for the laughs. They are silly, shallow, and superficial, even when it is time to get serious. Whenever anyone speaks to them about spiritual things, they laugh it off with a joke. They mock God, scorning his Word and ridiculing his followers. What a sad way this is to live, because people who never get serious about Jesus will never inherit eternal life. For them there will only be "weeping and gnashing of teeth" (e.g., Luke 13:28).

The last woe is for people who try to be popular: "Woe to you, when all people speak well of you, for so their fathers did to the false prophets" (Luke 6:26). Not that it is wrong for people to speak well of us. In fact, God wants us to have a good reputation with outsiders (e.g., 1 Tim. 3:7). But he does not want us to be people-pleasers. We cannot please everyone, after all, and the real danger comes when *all* people speak well of us. This is true for us both as individual Christians and as a church. Some churches try to please everyone, but as J. C. Ryle rightly observed, "To be universally popular is a most unsatisfactory symptom, and one of which a minister of Christ should always be afraid. It may well make him doubt whether he is faithfully doing his duty, and honestly declaring all the counsel of God."[13] If we are living like Jesus, then there are bound to be some people who will not speak well of us, any more than they speak well of him. We will be hated, and reviled, and all the rest of it. We should not be dismayed by this, but rejoice to suffer for Jesus' sake.

13. Ryle, *Luke*, 1:182.

By pronouncing these blessings and woes, Jesus was doing something that Puritan preachers used to call "dividing the audience." In other words, he was putting his listeners into two categories. In the process, he was forcing them to choose which kind of life they wanted to lead. We have to make the same choice. Do I want to have God's blessing, or do I want to follow the way of the world, with all of the woe it will bring me in the end? Which kind of life am I leading right now?

One way to answer these questions is to look at Luke 6 and see which list comes closer to describing the way that we live. Are we willing to be poor, sad, and persecuted for Jesus, or are we trying to be rich, happy, and popular? We say that we want the world to know Christ, but often we spend our time trying to be more like the world. Nobody wants to be poor. Nobody wants to be hungry. Nobody wants to be full of sorrow. Nobody wants to be rejected. But we have a Savior who was poor and hungry—a man of sorrows who was rejected unto death for our salvation. And when we learn to suffer for his sake, we will have his blessing.

22

THE HARDEST COMMANDMENT

Luke 6:27–36

"But I say to you who hear, Love your enemies, do good to those who hate you, bless those who curse you, pray for those who abuse you." (Luke 6:27–28)

Most of us find it hard enough to love our friends. Our desire for self-protection and self-advancement is so strong that often we fail to love the people we say we love as well as we should. We are willing to help our family and friends up to a point, but we have our limits. We want to give them loving service, but at the same time we are desperate to safeguard our time, our money, our emotional energy. We do not have the constant, compassionate, sacrificial love of Christ. But if we do not even love our friends very well, how could we ever love our enemies?

Ernest Gordon wrestled with this question during World War II while he was suffering in the infamous Japanese work camp on the River Kwai. Harsh conditions brought Gordon to the verge of death. Finally, he writes,

> I was headed for the Death House. I was so ill that I didn't much care. But I was hardly prepared for what I found there. The Death House had been

built at one of the lowest points of the camp. The monsoon was on, and, as a result, the floor of the hut was a sea of mud. And there were the smells: tropical ulcers eating into flesh and bone; latrines overflowed; unwashed men, untended men, sick men, humanity gone sour, humanity rotting. . . . The last shreds of my numbed sensibilities rebelled against my surroundings—against the bed-bugs, the lice, the stenches, the blood-mucous-excrement-stained sleeping platforms, the dying and the dead bed-mates, the victory of corruption. This was the lowest level of life.[1]

In the providence of God, and through the compassion of his army buddies, Gordon did not die, but survived. More than that, he and many of the other men in his camp came to faith in Jesus Christ. They learned to love each other. Yet they still found it impossible to love their enemies. As Gordon writes: "We had learned from the gospels that Jesus had his enemies just as we had ours. But there was this difference: he loved his enemies. He prayed for them. Even as the nails were being hammered through his hands and feet, he cried out, 'Father, forgive them, for they know not what they do.' We hated our enemies. We could see how wonderful it was that Jesus forgave in this way. Yet for us to do the same seemed beyond our attainment."[2]

LOVE YOUR ENEMIES

Whether it seems beyond our attainment or not, Jesus calls us to love our enemies. This is the hard commandment he gave his disciples—maybe the hardest one of all: "But I say to you who hear, Love your enemies" (Luke 6:27).

The context for this commandment is significant. Jesus had just called twelve men to be his apostles. These were the divinely appointed ambassadors who would preach his gospel to the world. But no sooner had he called them than he began to teach them what it would mean to follow him. Jesus pronounced four blessings on his apostles, and on everyone who would suffer for his sake. They would have to endure poverty, hunger, sorrow, and persecution, but in their suffering they would know

1. Ernest Gordon, *To End All Wars* (1963; reprint Grand Rapids: Eerdmans, 2002), 80–81.
2. Gordon, *To End All Wars*, 156.

his blessing. Jesus also pronounced four woes against self-satisfied people who were living for the pleasures of the moment and thought they could do without God. According to Jesus, therefore, there are two kinds of people: people who suffer for his sake and have his blessing, and people who live for themselves and will come to an unhappy end. But how should the first group relate to the second group? In other words, how should the true disciples of Jesus Christ respond to people who persecute them?

The natural response would be to hate them and to hurt them, or, at the very least, to stay away from them. This attitude was common among the pagan philosophers. Lysias wrote: "I consider it established that one should do harm to one's enemies and be of service to one's friends."[3] But this attitude was equally common among the people of God. According to Leviticus, "You shall not take vengeance or bear a grudge against the sons of your own people, but you shall love your neighbor as yourself" (Lev. 19:18). Yet at the time of Christ, many rabbis taught that this verse applied only to relationships within the community of faith ("your own people"). There were limits to brotherly love. The only people who counted as neighbors were fellow Jews. God's people had to love their friends, but not their enemies.

Like the rabbis, we are tempted to think of love as something we owe only to our friends. But Jesus says, "Love your enemies" (Luke 6:27). This is a harder commandment, based on a more powerful love. Leon Morris comments: "There are several words for love in Greek. Jesus was not asking for *storgē*, natural affection, nor for *erōs*, romantic love, nor for *philia*, the love of friendship. He was speaking of *agapē*, which means love even of the unworthy, love which is not drawn out by merit in the beloved but which proceeds from the fact that the lover chooses to be a loving person."[4]

Agapē is different from all other loves. Unlike *storgē*, it is *un*natural—it comes only by the supernatural work of God the Holy Spirit. Unlike *erōs*, *agapē* is not romantic. It is not the kind of love that anyone ever "falls into." Rather, it is the kind of love that disciples choose as part of their obedience to Christ. And unlike *philia*, *agapē* is not for friends only; it is also for

3. Lysias, *For the Soldier*, quoted in Darrell L. Bock, *Luke 1:1–9:50*, Baker Exegetical Commentary on the New Testament 3A (Grand Rapids: Baker, 1994), 590.

4. Leon Morris, *The Gospel According to St. Luke: An Introduction and Commentary*, Tyndale New Testament Commentaries (Grand Rapids: Eerdmans, 1974), 128–29.

enemies. Jesus called his disciples to show a deliberate affection that was not based on what people deserved, but on the grace of God.

We all have our enemies. Some of them are public: the greedy company that takes advantage of its employees; the unscrupulous politician who introduces ungodly legislation; the reckless driver who injures an innocent bystander; the dictator who persecutes the church; the terrorist who brings war and destruction. But others are more personal, like the demeaning boss, the scheming co-worker, the angry neighbor, the hostile spouse, or the former friend who has grown distant because of a disagreement. Who is *your* enemy? This is an important question to answer, because whoever your enemy is, he or she is the person Christ is calling you to love.

How Do I Love Thee?

Rather than speaking in general terms, Jesus gave his disciples specific instructions for loving their enemies. He took the same approach that Elizabeth Barrett Browning later took in her famous sonnet: "How do I love thee? Let me count the ways." Jesus knew that love is not simply a matter of what we think or feel, but also of the practical things we *do*. So he counted the ways that we can love our enemies: "Love your enemies, do good to those who hate you, bless those who curse you, pray for those who abuse you" (Luke 6:27–28).

There is a progression here. To "do good to those who hate" is to love with our actions, doing good to those who do us wrong. To "bless those who curse" is to love with our speech, using gentle words of grace when people speak to us in anger. To "pray for those who abuse" is to love with our hearts, asking God to rescue from sin the people who hurt us. Together our words, actions, and prayers form a powerful response to the hatred of our enemies. Rather than giving in to their evil by making an angry response, we triumph over evil with good.

I first learned this lesson when I was working at Burger King in high school. The working environment there was toxic (I refer to the workers, not the food). The shift leader made demeaning comments to her fellow workers. The manager was so abusive that one of the other managers ended up walking off the job. He was the kind of man who never told his employees what to do, or how, but then yelled at them for failing to do it. At first I hated working for these people; in a way, they were my enemies. But within several weeks God gave me the grace to pray that I would learn how to love them. I began to do good to them, finding extra ways to serve them. I began to bless them, speaking words of encouragement. I began to pray for them, asking God to show them his love. By the grace of God, the change was dramatic, not simply in my own attitude, and in my relationships with people I found it hard to love, but in the whole workplace.

One way to test whether we are keeping the hard commandment to love our enemies is to work through the list that Jesus gave his disciples. What good have I done for my enemy? What words of blessing have I spoken? What prayers of intercession have I offered? Ordinarily this is how the transformation starts: through prayer. We cannot long continue to hate someone we are constantly bringing before God's throne of grace. As we pray we begin to recognize that our enemies need the same things we need: forgiveness for sin and the power to lead a holy life. This gives us more sympathy for their situation, enabling us to love.

It seems significant that we are called to pray for our abusers rather than to do good to them. Some forms of abuse—especially physical violence—are too dangerous to endure. In such cases, we have a God-given responsibility to protect and preserve life, including our own. We need to be wise in our response to evil, and there are times when loving our enemies—including, in severe cases, within our own families—means praying for them at a safe distance. But we must continue to pray, because there is no form of hostility that excuses us from Christ's command to love our enemies.

LET ME COUNT THE WAYS

How else can we love our enemies? Jesus continued to count the ways: "To one who strikes you on the cheek, offer the other also" (Luke 6:29). At first this may seem to contradict what we have just said about self-protection. In fact, some people have understood this verse to mean that when we suffer physical abuse—such as a wife may suffer from her husband, or a child may suffer from a bully at school—we have to keep taking it.

This interpretation is wrong for many reasons. Obviously, Jesus is not teaching that we should allow evil to have its way. We have a God-given responsibility to make sure that physical violence is dealt with by the proper

271

authorities in the home, at work, or in the church. There is a striking example in the Gospel of John, where Jesus rebukes the priests for hitting him without cause (John 18:22–23). This too is love, as long as love is our real motivation. By caring enough to confront, we may help an abuser to recognize his sin and repent. In some situations, we may also have a responsibility to bring violence to the attention of the police. John MacArthur comments:

> The turn-the-other-cheek rule cannot be meant to keep civil government from punishing evildoers. To apply these principles in the civil arena would be to surrender society to chaos. Civil government is ordained by God precisely "for the punishment of evildoers and the praise of those who do right" (1 Pet. 2:13–14; cf. Rom. 13:4). Justice obligates us both to uphold the law and to insist that others do so as well. Reporting crime is both a civic responsibility and an act of compassion. To excuse or help cover up the wrongdoing of others is an act of wicked complicity with evil. To fail to protect the innocent is itself a serious evil.[5]

But if turning the other cheek does not mean accepting physical abuse, then what *does* it mean? As always, it helps to know the context. Jesus had just told his disciples that they would be persecuted for their faith (Luke 6:22–23). This is still the context for verses 27 to 29: the apostles would face suffering as followers of Christ, and they would have to endure it without fighting back. But there is also the cultural context to consider. In those days, striking someone's cheek was more an insult than an act of violence. As Darrell Bock explains, "The religious context makes it likely that a slap is intended and that an insult is in view. An ancient slap usually involved the back of the hand and may picture public rejection from the synagogue. . . . Such striking is really an abuse of power and a misuse of personal authority. Nevertheless, one is not to fight back in kind, but remain vulnerable to the insult again."[6]

The point is that we should be willing to suffer humiliation again and again for Christ. Rather than retaliating, or taking some form of revenge, we should endure insults with peace and patience, as Jesus did: "When

5. John F. MacArthur, *The Freedom and Power of Forgiveness* (Wheaton, IL: Crossway, 1998), 35.
6. Bock, *Luke 1:1—9:50*, 592.

he was reviled, he did not revile in return; when he suffered, he did not threaten, but continued entrusting himself to him who judges justly" (1 Peter 2:23). Sometimes the attacks that we face come from people at work. Sometimes neighbors make snide remarks about our involvement in the church. Sometimes friends pressure us to compromise our commitment to Christ. Sometimes family members try to discourage us from walking in the path of radical obedience. But no matter what forms of opposition we face, Christ calls us to keep reaching out to our enemies—even if it means that we might get hurt again.

Up to this point, Jesus has been talking about attacks against the dignity of our person, but in loving our enemies, we may also suffer the loss of our property. Jesus said, "from one who takes away your cloak do not withhold your tunic either. Give to everyone who begs from you, and from one who takes away your goods do not demand them back" (Luke 6:29–30).

Here Jesus calls us to have a giving spirit that is more concerned about the needs of other people than about the protection of our own property. A cloak was an outer garment, like an overcoat; a tunic was an inner garment, like a shirt. Jesus was saying that if someone is desperate enough to take your coat, let him have the shirt off your back, too. Obviously, this is just one example. The principle is that even if people mistreat us, we should give them above and beyond what they need, to the point of making a real sacrifice. This is the attitude we should take in helping our family members, in reaching out to people in our community, and in supporting the world-wide work of the church.

It is also the attitude we should take towards the poor. Jesus told his disciples to give to anyone who asks. The word at the beginning of verse 30 is not "beg," actually, but "ask" (aitounti). Jesus was not talking about giving money to panhandlers, or to people who will use it for an evil purpose, but about people with legitimate material needs. We should give them whatever they need, without demanding anything in return. At the end of verse 30 the context is not so much stealing as it is borrowing. Some people borrow things without ever giving them back. But rather than making them pay, we should be ready to forgive their debts. As disciples of Jesus Christ, the question for us is always "What can I give?" and never "What will I get in return?"

What is Jesus calling you to give? What has someone taken that he is calling you to let go? Some Christians are so concerned about somebody taking advantage of them that they never give anything to anyone. But Jesus calls us to err on the side of generosity. Of course there are limits to what we can give, and there are times when it is *not* loving to give, because giving will foster an unhealthy dependency. But *love* is what must decide—not love for ourselves and our possessions, but love for others and what they truly need. Even when it comes to our enemies, we should not look to hold on to what we have, but give it away as a demonstration of Christian love. Leon Morris summarizes by saying: "If Christians took this [command] absolutely literally there would soon be a class of saintly paupers, owning nothing, and another of prosperous idlers and thieves. It is not this that Jesus is seeking, but a readiness among his followers to give and give and give. The Christian should never refrain from giving out of a love for his possessions."[7]

The Reason behind the Golden Rule

Everything Jesus has been saying about loving our enemies is summarized in a famous statement that is usually called "The Golden Rule": "As you wish that others would do to you, do so to them" (Luke 6:31).

Some people think that this good old golden rule is hopelessly old-fashioned, but like everything else that Jesus said, it is as relevant today as it was the day that he said it. It is relevant for every situation in life. *Do unto others as you would have them do unto you.* This is a good rule to follow on the playground when kids are having trouble getting along. It is a good rule to follow at home when it comes to things like picking up clothes and putting away the toothpaste. It is a good rule to follow when merging in heavy traffic, or sharing an office, or resolving a dispute with a neighbor. Obviously, Jesus could not give specific instructions for any and every situation that anyone would ever face. But here is a rule to live by: one golden rule for all of life.

The Golden Rule is more than relevant, however; it is also radical. There were other teachers who gave similar counsel, but as far as we know, they always put it in the negative: "*Don't* do unto others what you *don't* want

7. Morris, *Luke*, 130.

them to do to you." This was not a law of love; it was merely a law of non-hatred. But Jesus said something more positive and, at the same time, more demanding: "As you wish that others would do to you, do so to them" (Luke 6:31). It is not simply *not* doing certain things that he is after, but doing everything we can to bless others. And not just our friends, either. The Golden Rule is for our enemies as well. We are called to treat people the way we want them to treat us, even if we are fairly sure they are still going to treat us the way that we *don't* want to be treated!

This is very different from the rule that most people follow. It is not what we typically see when businessmen are trying to close a deal, or when a husband and wife are having an argument, or when siblings are jockeying for position in the back seat of the minivan. The usual rule is more like, "Do whatever you can get away with," or "Do unto others what you have to do to get what you want out of them."

But Jesus said, "Do unto others what you would have them do to you, even if they are your enemies." Jesus said this for a reason: only this kind of love reveals the power of his grace. Most people are able to love the people who love them, at least to some extent. But who is able to love the people who *hate* them? Only someone whose life has been touched by the grace of a God who loved his enemies so much that he sent his Son to die for their sins. The very idea of loving our enemies takes us right to the heart of the gospel.

To show the difference between his love and our love, Jesus gave a series of three comparisons: "If you love those who love you, what benefit is that to you? For even sinners love those who love them. And if you do good to those who do good to you, what benefit is that to you? For even sinners do the same. And if you lend to those from whom you expect to receive, what credit is that to you? Even sinners lend to sinners, to get back the same amount" (Luke 6:32–34).

In each case, help is offered on the assumption of reciprocity. Almost anyone can offer this kind of love, because ultimately it is based on self-interest. Most people are willing to love people who love them in return. This is the kind of love that Philadelphia (the so-called City of Brotherly Love) advertises in its slogan, "The City That Loves You Back." Most people are also willing to do good to people who return the favor. As the saying goes, "I'll scratch your back if you scratch mine." They may even be willing to let people borrow their stuff, as long as they are sure they will get it back. It is always "tit for tat"—a quid pro quo. But what kind of love is that?

The love Christ calls us to show is more radical. It is not only for friends; it is also for enemies. It is not limited to people who love you, help you, and repay you, but extends to people who hate you, curse you, and abuse you. This is because it is not based on self-interest. Rather, it comes from the love that we ourselves have received from God, and now have the grace to give to others. It is a selfless, unselfish love, and the best way to prove this is by offering it to people who do not even deserve it. One of the main ways that people will come to know the infinite love of God is to see us showing it to people that nobody else would love.

LOVING THE WAY THAT GOD LOVES

Jesus taught his disciples to love this way because this is the way that God loves. So when we love our enemies, we show that we are God's true children. The family resemblance is unmistakable. Jesus said, "But love your enemies, and do good, and lend, expecting nothing in return, and your reward will be great, and you will be sons of the Most High, for he is kind to the ungrateful and the evil. Be merciful, even as your Father is merciful" (Luke 6:35–36).

God is love. It is his very character to show kindness and mercy, and more specifically, to show these virtues to his enemies. God shows kindness to evil, ungrateful people every day. He does it by giving us life and strength. He does it by sustaining the glorious universe where we live. He does it by sending rain from heaven, which he showers on the godly and the ungodly alike (Matt. 5:45). But God has shown his love supremely in sending his Son to die for the very people who hated him and rebelled against him. Salvation comes from the enemy-loving heart of God, who reconciles sinners—yes, sinners—to himself. The Bible says, "while we were *enemies* we were reconciled to God by the death of his Son" (Rom. 5:10).

This amazing love is not just the love of the Father, but also of the Son. When it comes to the love of God, it is "like Father, like Son." Jesus proved this in his sufferings and death, when he endured the very things that he told his disciples they would have to endure, yet still love their enemies (see Luke 6:27–30). As Luke will show us later in his Gospel, Jesus was hated.

He was hated by Judas, by the Pharisees, and by the people who demanded his crucifixion. Jesus was cursed—cursed by the false witnesses who testified against him, the soldiers who mocked him, and the governor who sentenced him to die a God-forsaken death. Jesus was abused. He was abused by the priests who whipped him, the soldiers who hung him up to die, and all the people who swore at him while he was dying on the cross. His enemies struck him on the cheek, and struck him again, insulting his true identity as the Son of God. They took away both his cloak and his tunic, leaving him to die naked. They stripped him of everything he had, down to his dignity.

What did Jesus demand from his enemies in return? Nothing except the opportunity to give his life for their sins. As he was dying on the cross, suffering at the hands of his enemies, Jesus was showing them his love—the very kind of love he called his disciples to show: "unselfish, disinterested, and uninfluenced by any hope of return."[8] Jesus was doing good to those who hated him, suffering the punishment they deserved for their sins. He was blessing those who cursed him, offering salvation to the thief on the cross. He was praying for those who abused him, saying, "Father, forgive them, for they know not what they do" (Luke 23:34).

This is where we learn to love our enemies: at the cross, where we were the enemies that Jesus died to forgive. Surely this is one of the reasons why Jesus gave us such a hard commandment. It is not a commandment that we could ever keep out of the strength of our own love. In order to keep it, we have to stay close to the cross, holding on to the love we know that Jesus showed us there. God has called us to love our enemies so that we can see the sin of our own loveless hearts and learn the true power of the love that comes from him. Jesus lived the love that he commanded, and now he gives the love that he lived. As Ambrose observed, writing in the fourth century, the gospel gives us "love for hostility, benevolence for hatred, prayer for curses, help for the persecuted, patience for the hungry and grace of reward."[9] It is only by the cross that we are able to be like Christ to our enemies—loving them without demanding anything in return.

8. J. C. Ryle, *Expository Thoughts on the Gospels, Luke* (1858; reprint Cambridge: James Clarke, 1976), 1:183.
9. Ambrose, "Exposition of the Gospel of Luke," 5.73, quoted in *Luke*, ed. Arthur A. Just Jr., Ancient Christian Commentary on Scripture, NT 3 (Downers Grove, IL: InterVarsity, 2003), 108.

Eventually, Ernest Gordon learned how to show this kind of love to his enemies, the Japanese. After the war ended, Gordon and the other POWs from the River Kwai made their long, slow way back to Britain, traveling through Asia by train. Along the way, they ended up in a rail yard next to a train full of wounded Japanese soldiers. Gordon describes their pitiable condition: "They were in a shocking state; I have never seen men filthier. Their uniforms were encrusted with mud, blood and excrement. Their wounds, sorely inflamed and full of pus, crawled with maggots. . . . The wounded men looked at us forlornly as they sat with their heads resting against the carriages waiting fatalistically for death. They were the refuse of war; there was nowhere to go and no one to care for them. These were the enemy."

Gordon tells how he and some other soldiers responded: "Without a word, most of the officers in my section unbuckled their packs, took out part of their ration and a rag or two, and, with water canteens in their hands went over to the Japanese train to help them. . . . We . . . knelt by the side of the enemy to give them food and water, to clean and bind up their wounds, to smile and say a kind word." But not everyone was pleased with this remarkable display of compassion. One Allied officer said, "What bloody fools you all are! Don't you realize that those are the enemy?"[10] Of course the officers realized it: that was exactly the point! The dying soldiers were the enemy, and for that very reason, Gordon and his friends were called to love them and do good to them.

They learned to give this kind of love from the same place where we can learn to give it: at the cross of Jesus Christ. The Savior who died for us there now calls us to give his love to others, including the people who hate us. Who are the enemies that God is calling you to love? Do good to them. Bless them and pray for them. Show them the love of God in Christ.

10. Gordon, *To End All Wars*, 196–97.

23

YOUR LOG, MY SPLINTER

Luke 6:37–42

"How can you say to your brother, 'Brother, let me take out the
speck that is in your eye,' when you yourself do not see the log that
is in your own eye? You hypocrite, first take the log out of your
own eye, and then you will see clearly to take out the speck that is
in your brother's eye." (Luke 6:42)

One of the many privileges of pastoral ministry is receiving correspondence that indicates—usually in no uncertain terms—one's failings as a pastor. This is a privilege because it promotes humility. When a pastor receives criticism, it is a reminder that whatever good he accomplishes in ministry is only by the grace of God. He is able to serve Jesus Christ in spite of himself, not because of himself.

As valuable as it can be, some criticism is easier to take than others. On one memorable occasion I received an unpleasant letter, written—as I recall—to complain about something I had said on the radio. Thankfully, I can recall neither the content of the letter nor the person who sent it. What I can remember is the tone, which was uncharitable and unkind. I can also remember the letter's conclusion. As my critic feverishly grasped for words adequate to characterize my offense, he finally said, "Why don't you take the log out of your own eye before taking the splinter out of someone else!"

At this point I had to laugh, because it seemed like my correspondent was doing the very thing that he was telling me not to do: he was trying to take the splinter out of my eye, but the log of his animosity kept getting in the way. But then this is how it always seems to us. The really obvious transgressions are the ones that other people commit, while our own sins seem small and insignificant by comparison. It is always "your log, but my splinter."

Judge Not

As disciples of the Lord Jesus Christ, we are called to see clearly and judge rightly, so that we can give people good spiritual care. To that end, Jesus has given us clear commands about how to respond to other people's sin, while always remembering that we ourselves are among the sinners.

Jesus gave these commands as part of his "sermon on the plain" in Luke 6. He had just finished telling his disciples how to love their enemies by offering mercy and grace to the very people who treated them with persecution and abuse. In verses 37 and following, Jesus continues talking about a godly response to sin: "Judge not, and you will not be judged; condemn not, and you will not be condemned; forgive, and you will be forgiven; give, and it will be given to you. Good measure, pressed down, shaken together, running over, will be put into your lap. For with the measure you use it will be measured back to you" (Luke 6:37–38).

Like many things that Jesus said, these verses are often misunderstood, especially the opening command, which is one of the few Bible verses that non-Christians still seem to know: "Judge not, lest ye be judged." No doubt this is because our culture considers judging people to be one of the ultimate sins. Nobody likes to be judged. People prefer to set their own standards, and to adjust them as they go, so that they never fail to meet them. The last thing they want is to have someone else telling them what to do. Sometimes they use this verse to tell other people to leave them alone—especially Christians. "Judge not," they say, "or you will be judged."

When Jesus said this, he did not mean that we are never called to render judgment. There are many life situations that demand a decision. Parents are called to make judgments when their children have a conflict. Teachers assess their students, managers evaluate their employees, elders decide cases of discipline in the church, and judges render verdicts in courts of law. The rest of the Bible makes it clear that "Judge not" is not a prohibition against any and every form of judgment. Whenever we are called to make moral or theological decisions, it is irresponsible for us not to judge.

There are also times when we are *not* called to make judgments, and this may be part of what Jesus means. Sometimes it is not our place to judge. The basketball team at Oxford University used to wear T-shirts that said, "Know your role." In other words, play your position. The point guard needs to pass, the center needs to rebound, and the shooters need to score. The same principle is a good one to apply when it comes to making judgments. We all have our opinions about what people ought to do, or how they ought to be treated. But before making any judgments, we need to consider whether it is really our place to judge. We need to ask ourselves what our role is. If it is not our place to judge—as it often isn't—then we should keep our opinions to ourselves. Otherwise, we run the risk of overstepping our bounds, or even putting ourselves in the place of God, who alone has the right to judge.

There are times when we have to judge (e.g., John 7:24), and times when we should not judge at all, but Jesus is mainly concerned about the attitude of our hearts. When he tells us not to judge, he is telling us not to treat people unfairly or unjustly in the court of our own opinion. In a word, we must not be *judgmental*. A judgmental person is someone who reaches unjust conclusions about someone else's motives. He or she is quick to criticize—usually putting things in the worst possible light—but slow to forgive. Someone who is judgmental also lacks any sense of proportion. Small offenses receive the same angry response that ought to be reserved for the most egregious sins. This is what Jesus is warning against: "a judgmental and censorious perspective toward others that holds them down in guilt and never seeks to encourage them toward God," or "evaluating others with such a harshness that the result is an unforgiving attitude and an approach that ceases to hold out hope as if someone is beyond God's reach."[1]

1. Darrell L. Bock, *Luke 1:1–9:50*, Baker Exegetical Commentary on the New Testament 3A (Grand Rapids: Baker, 1994), 607.

Instead, we are called to forgive others and offer them generous grace. Here Jesus draws a contrast between two attitudes of the heart. One is judging and condemning; the other is giving and forgiving. Most people are quick to criticize and slow to give other people room to grow, but Jesus calls us to have an attitude of open acceptance. This is the attitude that he himself took in laying down his life for our sins. Now, in the same way that he has forgiven us, he calls us to forgive others. Eric Wright says, "A forgiving person is one who, out of a profound sense of being personally forgiven a great debt by God, is quick to ask forgiveness from another, who repudiates anger, bitterness and a desire for revenge to initiate a loving approach to whoever may have hurt him or her, and who offers to freely forgive and forget the injury caused, with the hope that reconciliation may be achieved."[2]

Who is the person that you need to forgive? And what is the offense that needs to be forgiven? To offer forgiveness is to prove that we ourselves have been forgiven, because it shows the grace of God working in our hearts with power.

Jesus calls his disciples to do more than simply forgive, however; he also calls us to give. It is one thing to forgive people for what they have done to us, but it is another thing to go one step farther and do something to bless them. This is what Jesus has done for us. He has forgiven our sins through the cross, but more than that, he has granted us the free gift of everlasting life. Now he calls us to give the people who wrong us more grace than they deserve.

One woman who offered more grace was the victim of a horrible crime:

A Turkish officer raided and looted an Armenian home. He killed the aged parents and gave the daughters to the soldiers, keeping the eldest daughter for himself. Some time later she escaped and trained as a nurse. As time passed, she found herself nursing in a ward of Turkish officers. One night, by the light of a lantern, she saw the face of this officer. He was so gravely ill that without exceptional nursing he would die. The days passed, and he recovered. One day, the doctor stood by the bed with her and said to him, "But for her devotion to you, you would be dead." He looked at her and said, "We have met before, haven't we?" "Yes," she said, "we have met before." "Why

2. Eric E. Wright, *Revolutionary Forgiveness* (Auburn, MA: Evangelical Press, 2002), 147.

didn't you kill me?" he asked. She replied, "I am a follower of him who said 'Love your enemies.'"[3]

The Armenian woman did more for her enemy than simply forgive him. She offered him the gift of her love. She learned to do this from Jesus, who first loved her. This is another test of true discipleship. If you have forgiven your enemies, go the next step and give them more grace than they even deserve.

LEST YE BE JUDGED

To help his disciples have the right attitude towards fellow sinners—not condemning, but forgiving—Jesus said that we too will come under judgment. If we have a judgmental spirit, then we ourselves will be condemned. But if we give and forgive, we will receive God's blessing in return. It is measure for measure: God will apply the same standard to us that we apply to others. We should always remember, writes Friedrich Büchsel, "that God's judgment falls also on those who judge, so that superiority, hardness and blindness to one's own faults are excluded, and a readiness to forgive and to intercede is safeguarded."[4]

Büchsel goes on to say that this principle "has far-reaching consequences. It means that the Church cannot practice discipline with merciless severity. It means that the Church cannot take up a hard, contemptuous and supercilious attitude towards those whom it regards as sinners."[5] All too often, the people who render the harshest judgments and make the fewest allowances are people in the church—as if we ourselves were not in constant need of saving grace, or had never received any undeserved mercy from God. This was the problem with some forms of fundamentalism, which arose early in the twentieth century as a response to liberalism in theology. The fundamentalists faithfully defended core Christian doctrines like the inerrancy of Scripture and the deity of Jesus Christ, as well as his virgin birth, vicarious atonement, victorious resur-

---

3. L. Gregory Jones, *Embodying Forgiveness: A Theological Analysis* (Grand Rapids: Eerdmans, 1995), 265–66.

4. Friedrich Büchsel, "*krinō*," in *Theological Dictionary of the New Testament*, ed. Gerhard Kittel, trans. and ed. Geoffrey Bromiley (Grand Rapids: Eerdmans, 1965), 3:939.

5. Büchsel, "*krinō*," 3:939.

rection, and visible return. But some fundamentalists had a harsh and condemning spirit towards people who did not follow their man-made rules for Christian living. Such fundamentalists were rather like the Tin Woodsman in the Wizard of Oz, who had strong armor, but didn't have a heart. As a result of the heartlessness of fundamentalism, many people were hindered from hearing the gospel.

Sadly, the same thing still happens in the church today. It happens when we are overconfident in the conclusions we reach about other people's problems, without fully knowing their situation. It happens when we judge people's motives, wrongly assuming that we know why they did what they did. It happens when we withhold forgiveness from people who have done us wrong. It happens when we keep our distance from Christians struggling with difficult sins like self-pity or sexual immorality. It happens when we shun people with messy problems like poverty or drug addiction. It happens when we criticize the sins that other people commit more than we repent of our own unrighteousness. It happens when we use angry slogans to condemn hot-button issues like abortion or the gay lifestyle without befriending people and offering them grace. God forgive us. This is not the way that Jesus taught us to treat people, and when we do, it should not surprise us that they want nothing to do with his gospel.

The irony, of course, is that this is not the way Jesus judges us. He knows the whole truth about the full extent of our sin. Nevertheless, he reaches out to us in mercy, granting forgiveness through his death on the cross and offering eternal life through the power of his resurrection. Now the way that we treat others ought to demonstrate the mercy that we have received in Christ. The grace we give flows from the grace that we have received, and that we still need. But if we fail to treat people rightly, then we ourselves will come under judgment.

What Jesus says at the end of verse 38 can be taken either positively or negatively: "For with the measure you use it will be measured back to you." If we judge people with harsh condemnation, then we ourselves will be condemned. But the beginning of the verse makes it clear that Jesus expects something better from his disciples. The picture is entirely positive: a lapful of blessing. Here is how one scholar describes the ancient custom of "good measure, pressed down, shaken together, running over":

The seller crouches on the ground with the measure between his legs. First of all he fills the measure three-quarters full and gives it a good shake with a rotatory motion to make the grains settle down. Then he fills the measure to the top and gives it another shake. Next he presses the corn together strongly with both hands. Finally he heaps it into a cone, tapping it carefully to press the grains together; from time to time he bores a hole in the cone and pours a few more grains into it, until there is literally no more room for a single grain. In this way, the purchaser is guaranteed an absolutely full measure; it cannot hold more.[6]

This is the superabundant blessing that God gives his disciples when we show grace to sinners. He is gracious to the gracious, and generous with the generous, pouring a full measure of blessing right into our laps. Sometimes this happens in the present life, as God causes his people to prosper.

A legendary example of "measure for measure" comes from the life of a poor Scottish farmer named Fleming. One day the farmer heard a cry for help coming from a nearby bog. There, mired to his waist in black muck, was a terrified boy, screaming and struggling to free himself. Farmer Fleming saved the lad from what could have been a slow and terrifying death. The next day, a fancy carriage pulled up to the Scotsman's humble dwelling. An elegantly dressed nobleman stepped out and introduced himself as the father of the boy Farmer Fleming had saved. "I want to repay you," the nobleman said. "You saved my son's life." The Scottish farmer refused the offer, but at that moment, his own son came to the door. "Is that your son?" the nobleman asked. "Let me take him and give him a good education. If the lad is anything like his father, he'll grow to a man you can be proud of."

In time, the farmer's son graduated from St. Mary's Hospital Medical School in London. He later became better known throughout the world as Sir Alexander Fleming, the discoverer of penicillin. Many years later, when the nobleman's son was stricken with pneumonia, his life was saved by the very drug that Fleming had discovered. He too was a famous man. His name was Sir Winston Churchill.[7]

6. J. Jeremias, *The Parables of Jesus*, trans. S. H. Hooke, rev. ed., New Testament Library (Philadelphia: Westminster, 1963), 222.

7. Various versions of this story have circulated since the 1950's. I call it a "legendary example" here because there are reasons to doubt its accuracy. Even as a legend, though, the story can be used to illustrate a biblical point.

People say, "What goes around comes around." Jesus said it another way: "Give, and it will be given to you. Good measure, pressed down, shaken together, running over, will be put into your lap. For with the measure you use it will be measured back to you" (Luke 6:38).

Whether we receive a full measure now or not, we will receive it later, when we enter the measureless joy of heaven. We can never outgive God, who does "far more abundantly than all that we ask or think, according to the power at work within us" (Eph. 3:20)—the power of his grace in Jesus Christ.

Follow the Leader

Far from having a condemning spirit, Jesus was giving and forgiving. He showed mercy to sinners by offering them the gift of his life. So in his warnings not to be judgmental and in his command to be generous, Jesus was really telling his disciples to be like him. This seems to be the point of the verses that follow. After telling his disciples it would be "measure for measure," Jesus "also told them a parable: 'Can a blind man lead a blind man? Will they not both fall into a pit?'" (Luke 6:39).

The meaning of this parable, as Luke calls it, is fairly obvious: we need to be careful whom we choose to follow. If we follow the wrong leader, we will end up falling into a ditch. "Can a blind man lead a blind man?" No, because they have the same disability and thus they both need help to see where they are going. "Will they not both fall into a pit?" Yes, they will; sooner or later, they will have some kind of mishap. This happens from time to time in the city, where street workers sometimes leave potholes, ditches, and even manholes unguarded. Blind people face real danger.

The same thing can happen spiritually: church leaders who cannot see Jesus will lead their followers straight to the pit of hell. Some scholars think that when Jesus spoke of the blind leading the blind, he was referring specifically to the Pharisees. Certainly what he said applied to them. The Pharisees could not see the truth about grace, and therefore they led people down into the pit of legalism. Elsewhere Jesus called them "blind guides" (e.g., Matt. 23:16). But he says nothing about the Pharisees here, and the principle has a much wider application. Apart from the enlightening work of God's Spirit, we are spiritually blind. If we follow teachers who are equally blind, we will all end up in the ditch. This is the problem with following cult leaders who deny the deity of Jesus Christ, or radio person-alities who tell their listeners to leave the church, or theologians who add works to faith as the basis for our standing before God. They are all blind guides, and their way leads to destruction.

The parable of the blind leading the blind warns us to be careful whom we follow, and also to be careful how we lead. If we teach others, we are responsible for where we take them. In order to lead, we have to be able to see. We need to see the Bible as the perfect truth of God's holy Word. We need to see the majesty of God in his awesome power. We need to see the sinfulness of our sin and our desperate need for mercy. We need to see Jesus Christ crucified and raised from the dead. We need to see how the Spirit works to bring spiritual change. Only then can we lead our children or our church in the way that is right. Otherwise, we will only lead people astray.

Jesus also gave his disciples a related proverb: "A disciple is not above his teacher, but everyone when he is fully trained will be like his teacher" (Luke 6:40). The point of this general principle—which Jesus taught in a variety of contexts (cf. Matt. 10:24; John 13:16)—is "like teacher, like stu-dent." In those days—and it is not much different today—the way people learned religion was by spending time with a wise teacher. The more time they spent with him, the more their lives were patterned after his minis-try. This is basic to any form of discipleship: the teacher and the student have a close personal relationship in which the student becomes more like the teacher.

Obviously, it was (and is) very important to choose the right teacher. A beginning student could never hope to rise above the wisdom of his teacher in spiritual things—that would be the height of arrogance. The most that he could hope was to become *like* his teacher, and he would only reach that goal when he was fully trained. Therefore, it was crucial to select the right spiritual guide. When a disciple chose which master he wanted to follow, he was choosing what kind of person he would become.

Again, this has implications for how we teach as well as how we learn. For better and for worse, our students are bound to become like us. Often our virtues are only poorly imitated, while our flaws are highly exaggerated. So it is important for us to live and teach as well as we can. But why did Jesus say all this here? The general meaning of these two proverbs is fairly clear, but how do they relate to the verses that come before and after—verses that deal with exercising proper judgment?

Different scholars have given different answers. Maybe Luke has simply given us a list summarizing the things that Jesus said in his sermon, without making a strong logical connection between each item. Or maybe Jesus was speaking here about one specific kind of judgment: good judgment in choosing which teacher to follow. But whatever the precise connection may be, Jesus was calling his disciples to be like him. Remember the context: Jesus was speaking to his disciples as their teacher, so he was talking about their relationship with him. What is the best way for someone who is spiritually blind to avoid falling into the pit of destruction? The best way is to follow Jesus Christ, who has infinitely perfect vision and never leads anyone astray. Who is the best teacher for us to emulate? Jesus Christ, the holy Son of God, who is perfect in righteousness.

The obvious practical application is to follow Jesus Christ by faith. Let him lead you through life; he always knows the way. Listen to what he says about not being judgmental. Follow his example by showing forgiveness. To follow Jesus is to become like Jesus, as he transforms our lives through the powerful inward work of his Holy Spirit.

Log First, Then Splinter

Jesus finished what he had to say about judgment with a famous illustration. Back in verses 37 and 38, he had warned his disciples that they would be judged by the same standard they used to judge others. In verses 39 and 40 he warned them about the pitfalls of spiritual blindness. The danger in verses 41 and 42 is different, but it involves both bad judgment and bad eyesight. Jesus said: "Why do you see the speck that is in your brother's eye, but do not notice the log that is in your own eye? How can you say to your brother, 'Brother, let me take out the speck that is in your eye,' when you yourself do not see the log that is in your own eye? You hypocrite, first take the log out of your own eye, and then you will see clearly to take out the speck that is in your brother's eye" (Luke 6:41–42).

Here the problem is not that the person cannot see at all, but that he cannot see as well as he thinks he can. He thinks he can see so clearly that he can pick a speck out of someone's eye, yet somehow manages to overlook the big piece of wood sticking out of his own eye socket! Jesus was using this comic exaggeration to make a serious point. A "speck" is a little splinter of wood or straw. A "log" is the main beam of a building—not just a two-by-four, but a major pillar. The whole picture is so absurd that it would be laughable if it were not so common. How often we see this in daily life: the very person who criticizes other people is guilty of the most obvious sins of all. He has "some glaringly wrong habit or attitude in his life which everybody else can see; but strangely enough, not only can he apparently not see it himself, but he is the very one who is constantly pointing out other people's minor faults and failings."[8]

The word Jesus used for this common failing is *hypocrisy*. We are in danger of committing this great sin whenever we fail to see ourselves as we really are, pretending that we are not selfish, greedy, proud, or guilty of other log-sized sins. We are in danger of hypocrisy whenever we say that someone else has a problem, when in fact the problem is really our own. We are also hypocrites when we minimize our sin, pretending that it is smaller than it actually is. "Maybe it is pornography," we say, "but I'm only looking at it once a week." Or, "It's not really gossip; it's just something I feel you should know." Or, "Sure I yelled at her, but at least I didn't hit her." Whether we see it or not, our lust is adulterous, our words are treacherous, and our anger is murderous. When we examine our hearts, we always need to remember that our depravity is like something in the rearview mirror of a car: objects are larger than they may appear! Many of the sins we think are splinters are really more like two-by-fours, if not pillars.

We are also guilty of hypocrisy when we overestimate our ability to deal with other people's sin, or when we try to confront their sin before we confess our own. It is tempting to spend less time in private confession of sin than we spend thinking and talking (however charitably) about what is wrong with other people. A large part of our problem with logs and splinters is our sense of proportion: we are more concerned about someone else's minor issues than we are with our own major iniquities. But there is also a problem with our priorities: we have the nerve to try to straighten other people out before we have done business with God about our own personal sin. Like a lot of other things in life, we get things backwards.

8. David Gooding, *According to Luke: A New Exposition of the Third Gospel* (Grand Rapids: Eerdmans, 1987), 122.

Of course there is a place for confronting other people's sin, for giving constructive spiritual criticism, especially within the body of Christ. Jesus does not say that we can never help anyone else with a spiritual problem. In fact, he assumes that there are times when we are called to remove someone else's speck. But we should be slow to try to straighten other people out. First things first: we need to haul away the lumber in our own lives before we remove any splinters from anyone else. Nor does this mean that we have to be at a place of perfect sanctification before we can give people any spiritual help. But it does mean that we have to confess our own sins before we can ever hope to lead anyone else to repentance. "Whoever therefore is guided by good sense," wrote Cyril of Alexandria, "does not look at the sins of others, does not busy himself about the faults of his neighbor, but closely reviews his own misdoings."[9] It is only when our hearts have been broken by our own sin against God that we will have the humble grace to lead other sinners to repentance.

One way to see ourselves as we really are is simply to ask people who know us well to tell us what heavy timber they still see protruding from the eyeballs of our soul. But the most important thing is to follow Jesus, sticking close to his example, and living by his generous grace. Jesus sees us as we really are, down to the last speck. Because he is without sin, he is able to judge us with perfectly righteous clarity. But he does not condemn us—provided that we come to him in faith, trusting in the sacrifice he paid for our sins on the cross. With the help of his clear sight, we see both our sin and his forgiveness. Then perhaps we can begin to see other people the way that Jesus sees them: through the eyes of his grace.

9. Cyril of Alexandria, "Commentary on Luke," Homily 29, in *Luke*, ed. Arthur A. Just Jr., Ancient Christian Commentary on Scripture, NT 3 (Downers Grove, IL: InterVarsity, 2003), 110.

24

OF ROCKS AND TREES

Luke 6:43–49

*"For no good tree bears bad fruit, nor again does a bad tree
bear good fruit, for each tree is known by its own fruit. . . . Everyone who comes to me and hears my words and does them,
I will show you what he is like: he is like a man building a
house, who dug deep and laid the foundation on the rock. And
when a flood arose, the stream broke against that house and
could not shake it, because it had been well built."*
(Luke 6:43–48)

A young woman was walking alone in the city one Sunday evening when a couple of homeless people asked her for some
money. When they said they were hungry, she went to a store
and bought them a meal. Then they asked for $15 to pay for a room. Her
first reaction was, "I'm a young, single woman, walking through the city at
night. I didn't have to stop and go out of my way to do anything for them in
the first place! Now they're asking for more? Someone else can help them."
So she said no and walked on by.

But as soon as the woman stepped away, she remembered the words of Jesus from the sermon she had heard that day in church: "From one who takes away your cloak do not withhold your tunic either. Give to everyone who begs from you" (Luke 6:29–30). To obey this command would be a spiritual struggle, so the woman sat down to pray. What should she do? Did the homeless people really care? Were they even telling the truth?

Then she realized that for her, in this situation, it didn't matter. Jesus had told her to give, and all she needed to do was obey. So she pulled out her purse, remembering that she had only a few bills, and not knowing whether she had enough. As it turned out, she had exactly $15. When she caught up with the people that needed help, she explained why she was helping them and found out that they sometimes attended the same church. So in the providence of God, what at first seemed like a chance encounter turned out to be a wonderful opportunity for fellowship. And the woman learned an important lesson: the real proof of our discipleship is not whether we hear what Jesus has to say, but whether we actually do the things he tells us to do.

ROOT AND FRUIT

This was Jesus' concern as he pressed towards the practical conclusion of his "sermon on the plain." Many people had gathered to listen to him preach. They paid careful attention to what he said about patience in persecution, about loving enemies, and about not being judgmental. But listening was not enough. What mattered most was not simply hearing what Jesus had to say, but doing what Jesus said to do. This is the best test of Christian discipleship: Do we live the way that Jesus taught us to live? The truest profession of our faith is the *practice* of our faith.

In order to show the importance of being "doers of the word, and not hearers only" (James 1:22), Jesus gave his disciples two more little parables—one about fruit-bearing trees, and one about rock-solid houses. The first parable came from the orchard: "For no good tree bears bad fruit, nor again does a bad tree bear good fruit, for each tree is known by its own fruit. For figs are not gathered from thornbushes, nor are grapes picked from a bramble bush" (Luke 6:43–44).

It hardly takes a degree in horticulture to understand that a tree can only produce the kind of fruit that it was created to produce. Good trees do not produce bad fruit, and bad trees do not produce good fruit. On the contrary, fig trees produce figs and grape vines produce grapes, whereas thorn bushes and bramble bushes produce thorns and brambles. This is one of the basic laws of nature: every tree produces its own kind of fruit. A fruit-grower never gets the right kind of fruit from the wrong kind of tree, and the right kind of tree never produces the wrong kind of fruit.

This simple illustration has profound implications for the whole Christian life, for as Jesus went on to say, "The good person out of the good treasure of his heart produces good, and the evil person out of his evil treasure produces evil, for out of the abundance of the heart his mouth speaks" (Luke 6:45).

Every person is like a tree, and according to the divine laws of spiritual horticulture, we all produce the kind of fruit that is in our hearts to grow. The heart is the center of a person's being—the real you as you really are. Jesus said that a good life comes from a good heart, whereas an evil heart inevitably produces an evil life. There is a living, organic connection between the people we are on the inside and the lives that we lead out in the world. Whatever fruit we produce—whether good or evil—is rooted in the true condition of our souls. We can only produce the kind of spiritual fruit that it is our nature to produce. The reason we say the things we say and do the things we do is that we are the people we are.

Jesus says that some people have good hearts, and that out of the goodness of their hearts, they produce good fruit. Therefore, one of the truest ways for us to tell whether we have good hearts is by looking at the way that we live. Jesus said this mainly for the purpose of self-examination. He did not talk about good and bad fruit primarily so that we could examine what other people produce. Remember, he had just finished warning about judging others before judging ourselves. The principle of the log and the splinter applies to other people's fruit as much as it does to anything else. The main thing we need to check out is our own spiritual produce.

What is the fruit of a good heart? When God makes our hearts good by the powerful inward work of the Holy Spirit, what kind of life does he produce? The Bible says, "the fruit of the Spirit is love, joy, peace, patience, kindness, goodness, faithfulness, gentleness, self-control" (Gal. 5:22–23). Bearing good fruit, therefore, means loving others more than I love myself, making sacrifices so that someone else can advance. It means having joy even in the midst of sorrow, giving praise to the Lord at the same time I grieve. It means being at peace about the things that tempt me to worry, trusting the Lord with my anxieties about the future, the broken relationships in my life, and the safety of the people I love. Giving my fears over to God in faith is the fruit of a life of faith.

Bearing good fruit also means having patience in times of adversity, not pushing to make things go my way, but being content to wait and see what God will do. It means showing kindness and goodness, doing the little things to make life better for others. A fruitful life is characterized by consistent godliness, so that I am as good in private as I seem to be in public. Then come faithfulness, gentleness, and self-control. To be faithful means to work as hard now as I did at the beginning, rather than slacking off. To be gentle means giving a soft reply to a harsh criticism, rather than jumping to defend myself. To have self-control is to refuse to go off on reckless binges, and instead to resist the mounting pressures of temptation.

We are not yet perfect, so these are still areas of struggle for us. If we have received Jesus Christ by faith, however, then we should be starting to see some of the fruit of his work in our lives. When our hearts are good, his goodness always comes out. This goodness does not come from us, but from the Holy Spirit, who makes our hearts good by his grace. This is part of the proof of our salvation—one of the ways we know for sure that we know Jesus. We know it because we speak good words and do good deeds, for as Jesus said: "The good person out of the good treasure of his heart produces good" (Luke 6:45). Good fruit helps to assure us of our salvation because it shows that we have the good root of grace.

Out of the Heart

What, then, of the evil person with an evil heart? The same spiritual principle applies. If good is as good does, then evil is as evil does. Evil people can only speak and act in accordance with their nature, which means that they say and do what is evil, like all the evil deeds that the

Bible sets in contrast to the fruit of the Spirit: sexual sin, dissension, discord, fits of rage, envy, and drunkenness (see Gal. 5:19–21).

A bad heart produces bad fruit, and when we see bad fruit, we know that it can only come from a bad heart. We should not assume that people are any better on the inside than they seem to be on the outside. Usually people are much worse, as we ought to know from our own experience. J. C. Ryle said:

> Let it be a settled principle again in our religion, that when a man's general conversation is ungodly, his heart is graceless and unconverted. Let us not give way to the vulgar notion, that . . . although men are living wickedly, they have got *good hearts* at the bottom. Such notions are flatly contradictory to our Lord's teaching. Is the general tone of a man's communication carnal, worldly, irreligious, godless, or profane? Then let us understand that this is the state of his heart. When a man's tongue is generally wrong, it is absurd, no less than unscriptural, to say that his heart is right.[1]

Does this mean that Christians never say anything bad or do anything evil? No, of course sometimes we do, because we still struggle with our old sinful nature, and our sanctification is not yet complete. The difference is that whenever we see the fruit of our old evil nature, we recognize that it is evil and repent of our sin. As David Gooding comments, "The saintliest man may be appalled by the occasional overspill whose sudden eruption escapes the filter of his moral judgment and reveals what pollutants still remain in the depths. But if the general tenor of a man's conversation is evil, the source must be evil too. No excuse can break the connection between a tree's fruit and the nature of the tree."[2]

If it is true that the fruit of our outward actions grows from the root of our inward attitudes, then we never have any excuse for the wrong things that we say and do. This often happens when professional athletes or other public figures get caught doing something wrong. "That's not really what I'm like," they say. "It was out of character for me." Or they try to blame someone else, as if their reaction was some kind of automatic response

---

1. J. C. Ryle, *Expository Thoughts on the Gospels, Luke* (1858; reprint Cambridge: James Clarke, 1976), 1:192–93.

2. David Gooding, *According to Luke: A New Exposition of the Third Gospel* (Grand Rapids: Eerdmans, 1987), 122.

to the situation they were in. We are tempted to make the same kinds of excuses. We say, "That's not something I usually do; I've got that sin under control." We say, "You should have seen what he did first!" Or we say, "I only did what I did because she said what she said."

We need to be honest with ourselves, and with God. The truth is that what we do and say is *always* in character. As Paul Tripp writes in his excellent book *War of Words*, "It is very tempting to blame others or to blame the situation around us," but "word problems *reveal* heart problems. The people and situations around us do not *make* us say what we say; they are only the *occasion* for our hearts to reveal themselves in words."[3]

What *should* we say, then, when we get caught saying or doing something evil? What is the righteous response when we come out with a swear word, or when we say something rude, or when we have an angry outburst at home? What we ought to say is something like this: "You know, that really *is* what I'm like. I'm just embarrassed because usually I'm better at hiding it!" Or we should say: "It's not you; it's me. I know I said that you made me angry, but really it is because I am so angry that I treated you the way that I did."

To use a different analogy, the tongue is the sound system of the heart. Whatever is in our souls gets amplified whenever we put it into words. Our angry words come from a murderous heart; our salacious words come from an adulterous heart; our complaining words come from an envious heart. It is "out of the overflow of the heart" that the mouth speaks (Luke 6:45 NIV).

What Jesus said about the root and fruit of good and evil helps us make an accurate assessment of our true spiritual condition. This is important because—as we saw in the story of the log and the splinter—before we can be of any spiritual good to anyone else, we have to recognize and repent of our own personal sin. This calls for careful self-evaluation. The fruit that we produce—whether good or evil—grows from the root of who we are.

What Jesus said also helps us recognize the real problem at the root of all our sin: it comes from an evil heart—what I sometimes describe to my young children as "the bad naughty heart that you were born with." This means that real spiritual change can only happen when we first experience the total heart transformation that theologians call "regeneration." Far too

---

3. Paul David Tripp, *War of Words: Getting to the Heart of Your Communication Struggles* (Phillipsburg, NJ: P&R, 2000), 55.

often, people try to change their outward actions without asking God for a new heart. They can see that they are bearing bad fruit. They know that some of their actions and attitudes are sinful. They use bad language, for example, or they fall into sexual sin. They get absorbed in anxiety and self-pity. Or they get involved in some form of addiction, whether chemical or otherwise. Eventually they realize that their lives are a complete mess. They decide to stop doing whatever it is that they are doing; they start modifying their behavior. Sometimes they meet with some success, at least initially. They clean up their language. They try to have a more positive attitude. By sheer power of the will, they stay away from an old addiction.

Then, very unexpectedly, it happens again. They use a swear word, cursing God. They fall into anxious despair, without any hope that God will save them. They give in to the temptation to go back to an old beloved sin, just this once. Often they fall right back into the same old patterns of sin, or if not, they simply exchange one sin for another. But either way, mere behavior modification has failed. They are still bearing bad fruit, at which point it becomes painfully obvious that no real spiritual change has taken place in the heart.

The reason for this failure is very simple: no one can cultivate good fruit from a bad tree. A life that is rooted in sin can only produce sin. People generally assume that their hearts are basically good. In order to lead better lives, therefore, all we need to do is a little spiritual pruning, as if we could grow roses by cutting back the stinkweed. But in fact we need to dig all the way down and uproot the old tree of our sinful nature, asking God to plant a whole new life in our hearts.

Anyone who has not yet come to Christ in faith—personally trusting him for the forgiveness of sins and the free gift of eternal life through his death and resurrection—needs a whole new heart. This is a hopeful discovery, because the truth is that anyone can have a new heart. The problem we have is the very problem the gospel addresses. Therefore, all we have to do is ask, praying that God would give us a new life in Christ.

Yet even after we come to Christ, our sin issues are still heart issues. So as we struggle with sin, we need to ask God to do a heart-changing work of grace in us, which he does by the powerful inward work of the Holy Spirit. It is not enough simply to change our outward actions. The real change needs to take place inside. This means repenting of the evil desires in our sinful

297

hearts. It means putting to death our love for our selves and the things of this world. And it means asking God to replace those old sinful desires with new affections for him and for his holiness. Once our hearts are in the right place, then and only then will we begin to bear good spiritual fruit—the abundant harvest that only comes from having a new heart.

WALKING THE TALK

Jesus spoke with his disciples about root and fruit because he wanted them to do what he said. This is clear from the question he asked at the end of the parable: "Why do you call me 'Lord, Lord,' and do not do what I tell you?" (Luke 6:46). Apparently, there were already some hypocrites among the followers of Christ. They had been listening to Jesus teach, and they were identifying themselves as his disciples. They even called him "Lord," which was a term of respect for his teaching authority. They did not do what Jesus said, however, which was the main thing that really mattered. They were not living the good life that comes from a good heart.

We see the same thing in the church today. People call themselves Christians, and they talk about Christ, but they have many of the same sinful attitudes and are guilty of many of the same sinful actions as everyone else. It is not talking about Christ that makes a person a Christian, but living for Christ by faith. As Bishop Ryle wisely said, "obedience is the only sound evidence of saving faith, and the talk of the lips is worse than useless, if it is not accompanied by sanctification of the life."[4]

John Bunyan wrote about this in his famous allegory, *The Pilgrim's Progress*. On their journey to the Celestial City, Christian and Faithful met a man named Talkative, who was always conversing about spiritual things, but was not living the Christian life. He was talking the talk without walking the walk. Christian warned Faithful about this, saying,

> He talketh of prayer, of repentance, of faith, and of the new birth; but he knows but only to talk of them. . . . The soul of religion is the practice part. . . . This Talkative is not aware of; he thinks that hearing and saying will make a good Christian, and thus he deceiveth his own soul. Hearing is but as the sowing of the seed; talking is not sufficient to prove that fruit

4. Ryle, *Luke*, 1:196.

is indeed in the heart and life, and let us assure ourselves that at the day of doom, men shall be judged according to their fruits. . . . The end of the world is compared to our harvest, and you know men at harvest regard nothing but fruit, not that anything can be accepted that is not of faith.[5]

To help his disciples grow more good spiritual fruit, and not just talk about growing it, Jesus told them another little parable. This time it came from the world of architecture: "Everyone who comes to me and hears my words and does them, I will show you what he is like: he is like a man building a house, who dug deep and laid the foundation on the rock. And when a flood arose, the stream broke against that house and could not shake it, because it had been well built" (Luke 6:47–48).

The verbs in verse 47 outline a clear progression. The first is the verb for "coming" (erchomai), and it refers to the way people gathered around Jesus. They were coming to be near him, as we come near him today whenever we enter God's presence for worship. Next comes the verb for "hearing" (akouō). One of the main reasons people came to Jesus was to listen to him teach. Hearing involves paying careful attention to the things that Jesus says, meditatively concentrating on the meaning of his words and prayerfully considering their implications for our lives. Today we do this whenever we read and study the Bible, and whenever we listen to the preaching of the gospel. By the power of God's Word, by the witness of his Spirit, and by the action of our faith, we hear Jesus speaking to us in Scripture.

Coming and hearing are not enough, however. We must also respond, which is where the third verb comes in. The verb is poieō, the main Greek word for "doing," and the progression is not complete without it. It is not just the coming and hearing that Jesus is after, but the going and doing. Unless we reach the point of actually doing what Jesus says, we are not followers of Christ in the biblical sense. It is not enough to come to church and listen to the sermon; what God requires is a believing response. This means trusting in Jesus Christ alone for our salvation. It means giving our whole lives to worship his glory. It means offering sacrificial service to the people we are called to love. And it means living an obedient Christian life of outreach to people who are lost without Christ.

5. John Bunyan, The Pilgrim's Progress (New York: New American Library, 1964), 76–77.

How Firm a Foundation?

When we do what Jesus says—not just hearing it, but actually obeying it—we lay a solid foundation that can withstand all the trials of life. This is the main point of the parable. It is the doer, not the hearer, whose life is solid as a rock.

By telling his disciples that his words were the foundation for their lives, Jesus was making a strong claim to his deity. Who else has the right to tell people to build their whole lives on his word? Only the one true God. So when we do what Jesus says, we are building on the will of God, and our lives are like a house on the rock.

There is a house like this in Scotland, built into the rocky face of a cliff overlooking the Nidd Valley. In the year 1770 a humble weaver named Thomas Hill left his little cottage and climbed the cliff above the manor of his lord, Sir Charles Slingsby Bart. Armed only with a pick, a chisel, a hammer, and the desire to build a solid home for his family, Hill began his relentless assault on a sheer wall of limestone. It took him sixteen years to hollow out a cleft in the rock. Sixteen years—but what a house! As Hill chipped away at the cliff, he used the rocks and rubble to build the outer wall, until finally he completed a magnificent fortress with spectacular views of the surrounding countryside.[6]

Because it is built into the rock, Hill's house was all but impregnable, able to withstand any storm. This came at a great cost. It took years of blood, sweat, toil, and tears. Yet this is what it takes to build a house into the rock. A cottage on the ground can be completed in a matter of weeks, but a rock-solid fortress takes years of patience and perseverance.

The same thing is true in the spiritual life. The man Jesus described in his parable "dug deep and laid the foundation on the rock" (Luke 6:48). Building his house cost him something. Living the Christian life costs us something too. It takes discipline to work at understanding the Scriptures. It takes patience to persevere in prayer. It takes courage to put sinful desires to death. It takes dedication to grow in new areas of obedience. It takes sacrifice to serve others instead of ourselves. Above all, it takes faith to trust in Jesus Christ and not hold anything back.

6.. See www.knaresborough.co.uk/history/houseintherock.asp.

When we take the time to build the right spiritual foundation, though, we are ready for anything, including all the storms of life. Come what may, our foundation will hold:

> Such a man's religion may cost him much. Like the house built on a rock, it may entail on him pains, labour, and self-denial. To lay aside pride and self-righteousness, to crucify the rebellious flesh, to put on the mind of Christ, to take up the cross daily, to count all things but loss for Christ's sake,—all this may be hard work. But, like the house built on the rock, such religion will stand. The streams of affliction may beat violently upon it, and the floods of persecution dash fiercely against it, but it will not give way.[7]

To withstand the storms of life, lay a solid foundation. Anchor your life to the solid rock of Jesus Christ. Dig deep by obeying his word. Build a life that is strong enough to withstand every trial and tribulation.

Sadly, not everyone has a solid spiritual foundation. To warn people about this, Jesus finished his parable by making a contrast: "But the one who hears [my words] and does not do them is like a man who built a house on the ground without a foundation. When the stream broke against it, immediately it fell, and the ruin of that house was great" (Luke 6:49).

Rather than closing with a word of consolation, as some preachers always do, Jesus ended with a sharp warning. The situation he described was not uncommon in the arid climate of ancient Israel. Flash floods are always a danger in the desert, especially near the mountains. When the rains fall in the higher elevations, water cascades down the dry riverbeds and into the villages below without warning. When this happens, a house without a solid foundation—not with the wrong foundation, notice, but with no foundation at all—will collapse instantly.

Like some houses, some people do not have a solid foundation. Remember, Jesus was speaking to people who were coming to hear him, and who identified themselves as his disciples. But doing is what makes the difference, and these people were not doing what Jesus said. As a result, their lives were built on the shallow spirituality of man-made religion. Sad to say, the same thing is true of church-going people who call themselves Christians but are not living for Christ. They hear what

7. Ryle, *Luke*, 1:196.

Jesus says, but they do not *do* what Jesus says, and as a result, they do not have any real foundation for their lives.

Soon, Jesus said, they will be destroyed. Some stormy trouble will come—persecution perhaps, or one of life's many bitter disappointments—and their whole world will collapse, including any pretense of really trusting in God. If that does not happen in this life, it may happen at death, and it will certainly happen at the final judgment. Jesus called this tragedy a great ruin—the fatal torment of a lost soul.

Trouble is the test. When life is easy, it is difficult to determine what kind of foundation people have. The same is true with houses: it is hard to tell if they have a solid foundation simply by looking at the exterior. But wait until the storms come! Then everyone can see whether someone's house— or someone's life—is strong enough to stand. When trouble comes, a life without a solid foundation will fall apart, but a life anchored to the bedrock of obedience to Christ will keep on standing. Here it is worth noting that when Jesus told his disciples where to build their lives, he did not tell them to lay the foundation on "a" rock, but on "the" rock (Luke 6:48). "For no one," the Bible says, "can lay a foundation other than that which is laid, which is Jesus Christ" (1 Cor. 3:11).

What kind of life are you building? Are you digging down deep into the solid rock of Jesus Christ? And what kind of fruit are you yielding? Is it all talk, or are you walking in obedient faith? We can tell what kind of heart we have by the kind of fruit we are growing, and we can tell what kind of life we are building by seeing what happens when the storms come.

The great Scottish preacher Arthur John Gossip experienced this profound truth after the tragic and untimely death of his beloved wife. Gossip grieved deeply, but his faith did not fail, and upon his return to the pulpit, he said to his congregation:

> I don't think we need to be afraid of life. Our hearts are very frail, and there are places where the road is very steep and very lonely. But we have a wonderful God. And as Paul puts it, what can separate us from his love? Not death, he says immediately, pushing that aside at once as the most obvious of all impossibilities. No, not death. For I, standing here in the roaring of the Jordan, cold to the heart with its dreadful chill and very conscious of the terror of its rushing, I can call back to you who, one day

in your time, will have to cross it: Be of good cheer, my friend, for I feel the bottom and it is sound.[8]

The only person who can say something like this is someone who has solid footing, someone who has built his whole life on the rock-solid foundation of Jesus Christ. Build your life in obedience to the words of Christ, and you will be able to withstand anything—even the storms of the final judgment.

8. Arthur John Gossip, "But When Life Tumbles In, What Then?" *The Protestant Pulpit*, compiled by Andrew Blackwood (Nashville: Abingdon, 1947), 204.

25

JUST SAY THE WORD

Luke 7:1–10

*"Therefore I did not presume to come to you. But say the word,
and let my servant be healed. For I too am a man set under
authority, with soldiers under me: and I say to one, 'Go,' and he
goes; and to another, 'Come,' and he comes; and to my servant,
'Do this,' and he does it."* (Luke 7:7–8)

*Y*our wish is my command." This is the attitude of a servant who
understands what it means to be under authority. "Whatever
you need," the servant says, "I will get it. Just say the word, and
I will do it, because your wish is my command."

King David enjoyed this kind of authority when he was fighting
against the Philistines. David and his men were camped at the cave of
Adullam. The Philistines had made their stronghold nearby in Bethlehem—the city where David was born. As the military standoff continued, the king grew nostalgic for the sights and sounds of his hometown,
which was now in enemy-occupied territory: "And David said longingly,
'Oh, that someone would give me water to drink from the well of Bethlehem that is by the gate!'" (2 Sam. 23:15).

It was only an offhand remark, spoken in a moment of frustration. But David was the king, so the word quickly spread through the ranks: "The king wants a drink." "A drink?" "Yes, from the water of Bethlehem!" Since the city was then under enemy control, it sounded absurd. Yet there were three warriors in the camp—Joshebbasshebeth, Eleazar, and Shammah—for whom the king's wish was their command. So as soon as they heard what David wanted, "the three mighty men broke through the camp of the Philistines and drew water out of the well of Bethlehem that was by the gate and carried and brought it to David" (2 Sam. 23:16).

Of course David never intended for anyone to treat his idle wish like a royal command. In fact, he was so moved by what his men had done that he refused to drink the water, but poured it on the ground as a holy offering to God. Nevertheless, the story shows the supreme authority of a word spoken by God's anointed king.

A SICKNESS UNTO DEATH

Jesus Christ speaks with the same royal authority. We see this authority in the story of the Roman centurion at the beginning of Luke 7. The story shows the dying and desperate need of lost humanity. It shows the contrast between the apparent worthiness and the actual unworthiness of a person who seems to lead a good life. And it shows the only basis for salvation, which is faith in Jesus Christ.

The story begins with a man in desperate need. Jesus had just finished preaching his Sermon on the Plain. The Bible says, "After he had finished all his sayings in the hearing of the people, he entered Capernaum. Now a centurion had a servant who was sick and at the point of death, who was highly valued by him" (Luke 7:1–2).

As a physician, ordinarily we would expect Luke to tell us more about the man's condition, to offer some kind of diagnosis. But this time all he mentions is the man's prognosis. The situation was critical. The centurion's servant had a sickness unto death, and unless God intervened, he would surely die. He was "at the point of death," Luke tells us (Luke 7:2). Doubtless the people who cared for him could see the telltale signs of his imminent demise: listlessness, detachment, and a desperate struggle for every last breath. The deathwatch had begun.

The servant's plight is a reminder of our own mortality. Sooner or later, his situation is one all must face, because we are all under God's death sentence against our sin. This is the need behind all our other needs and the sum of all our fears. One day we are going to die, and unless there is some way for us to gain life after death, we will suffer without God for all eternity. It is something most people try to avoid thinking about, but can never escape entirely: the unavoidable reality that someday they will have to die.

One man who admitted that he was afraid to die was George Steinbrenner, the infamous owner of the New York Yankees. It was Steinbrenner who once said, "I will never have a heart attack. I give them." Yet a 2004 article poignantly described the rich man's growing fear of his own mortality. After collapsing at someone else's funeral, he said, "It makes you think. You're that close . . . you wonder if you're all right."[1]

Without the assurance of eternal life, George Steinbrenner wondered if he would be all right, but he did not know for sure. This is a doubt that many people share. As Bruce Milne writes in *Know the Truth*, "Death confronts us, as nothing else does, with our insignificance and weakness, and exposes the folly of our pretensions to greatness. Even when we attempt to face death with courage, we never succeed in finally overcoming it; it dominates us until at last we too go to receive the wages of sin."[2]

This is what the centurion's servant was up against: humanity's last and greatest enemy—death. But he was not dying alone and unloved. He had a master who cared for him. As the Bible says, the servant was "highly valued" (*entimos*). This may refer to his usefulness as a servant, but the word can also mean that he was "precious" in the sense that his master loved him. The centurion was a greathearted man with good affections. He loved his servant and wanted to do whatever he could to help him.

But what could he do? The centurion desperately wanted to help the servant he loved. Presumably he had tried everything he could think of, but there seemed to be nothing he could do to help. Again, this is a situation that we all encounter. We encounter it medically when the doctors say there is nothing else they can do for one of our family members. We encounter it relationally when we do not know how to bring people together. We encoun-

---

1. George Steinbrenner, quoted in Tom Verducci, "Mister Softie?" *Sports Illustrated*, (May 10, 2004), 66.
2. Bruce Milne, *Know the Truth: A Handbook of Christian Belief*, rev. ed. (Downers Grove, IL: InterVarsity, 1998), 136–37.

ter it financially when someone close to us is deep in debt. We encounter it spiritually when we share the gospel and people still do not want to know Jesus. What do you do when there is nothing else that you can do to help the people you love?

The thing to do is to ask Jesus for help, as the centurion did. He had heard about the power of Jesus to perform miracles. Luke tells us: "When the centurion heard about Jesus, he sent to him elders of the Jews, asking him to come and heal his servant" (Luke 7:3). The word used here for healing *(diasōzō)* comes from the group of words for salvation *(sōzō)*. Although "heal" is the proper translation here, the word's etymology aptly describes the situation. The word has the idea of carrying someone safely through a dangerous ordeal, which is what the centurion was praying that Jesus would do for his servant. He had nowhere else to turn. Jesus was his only hope. So he asked Jesus to work a saving cure that would rescue his friend from death.

The centurion's plea is a physical request that points to a deeper spiritual reality and reminds us that everyone needs the saving work of Jesus Christ. Who else can deliver us from death? Who else can carry us through our last ordeal and bring us safely to the other side? The only hope for meeting the dying and desperate need of lost humanity is the life that comes through Jesus Christ. As we suffer the sickness of sin—that sickness unto death—we should ask him to come with all the grace of his saving cure.

WORTHY OR NOT?

The centurion asked Jesus for help in true military fashion: he delegated the task to others, asking some of his Jewish friends to go and speak on his behalf. Their conversation with Jesus shows the contrast between the apparent worthiness and the actual unworthiness of a person who seems to lead a good life.

The elders asked Jesus to help the centurion on the basis of his good character: "And when they came to Jesus, they pleaded with him earnestly, saying, 'He is worthy to have you do this for him, for he loves our nation, and he is the one who built us our synagogue'" (Luke 7:4–5).

The elders were able to make a strong case that this man was worth helping. From the human point of view, there was every reason for Jesus to help the centurion. The centurion had a tender heart for people in need, as we have seen, and he cared for the people in his service. He was also powerful. As an officer in the Roman army he had roughly a hundred men serving under his command. He was strong. According to the historian Polybius, the Romans appointed to this rank only "men who can command, steady in action, and reliable; . . . when hard pressed they must be ready to hold their ground and die at their posts."[3] And he was wealthy. Centurions were well paid in those days, especially if they had been on a successful military campaign, and this man had enough money to finance public buildings.

Furthermore, he was active in his support for God's people. Despite the fact that he was an enemy officer, the centurion loved the Israelites, and he proved it by building them a synagogue (its foundations can still be seen in Capernaum today).[4] As a general rule, the Romans—especially in the army—looked down on the Jews. But this centurion was pro-Semitic; he was a friend of Israel. This does not necessarily mean that he worshiped with the Jews, but at least he was a God-fearing man, and he loved God's people so well that he built them a house for worship.

Now the Jews had a chance to return the favor. The elders of the community—prominent social and religious leaders—went to Jesus on the centurion's behalf. This was highly unusual: a group of Jews lobbying for a Roman soldier. Obviously they thought the man was worthy of their support, and they wanted Jesus to recognize this. In effect, they said, "Look, we really owe it to this guy to help him any way we can."

The elders were thinking in terms of merit.[5] They believed that someone who lived a good life was worthy to receive blessing. This is the way most people think; it is a basic presupposition of our fallen nature. We tend to think that people who do good things for others deserve to have good things done for them. Surely someone like the centurion—who supports the church and gives money to charity—can expect Jesus to answer his prayer for healing. Some people apply the same logic to

3. Polybius, quoted in Leon Morris, *The Gospel According to St. Luke: An Introduction and Commentary*, Tyndale New Testament Commentaries (Grand Rapids: Eerdmans, 1974), 136.

4. Arthur A. Just Jr., *Luke 1:1–9:50*, Concordia Commentary (St. Louis: Concordia, 1996), 304.

5. David Gooding, *According to Luke: A New Exposition of the Third Gospel* (Grand Rapids: Eerdmans, 1987), 129.

life after death. They believe that if they do enough good, they will be entitled to heaven. They hope that somehow the good they do will outweigh the bad, and that God will receive them on the basis of what they have done.

If good works could ever earn God's favor for anyone, surely the centurion deserved to have Jesus come and heal his servant. He had all the credentials anyone could ever hope to have. This is not the way God operates, however. In our pride we believe that we can be good enough for God. But who is ever good enough for God, especially when it comes to our eternal destiny? The Bible says that salvation "is not your own doing; it is the gift of God, not a result of works, so that no one may boast" (Eph. 2:8–9). Salvation has to be the gift of God, because otherwise we would take the credit for ourselves. Besides, God's standard is holy perfection. It is not enough to make friends with the people of God. It is not enough to go to church, give money to Christian causes, or get involved in ministry. What God requires is perfect righteousness. By that standard, no one is worthy—no one— except the Lord Jesus Christ. Therefore, if God is to help us, it will never be because of our merit, but only because of his mercy.

Not Worthy, Lord

Worthy or not, Jesus decided to help the centurion by healing his servant. With great compassion, he set off with the elders to find the centurion. As the Scripture says, "Jesus went with them" (Luke 7:6). This is what we see all the way through the Gospel: Jesus reaching out to help people in desperate need—people just like us. Jesus is able and willing to help us. The desire of his saving heart is to rescue people from sickness, sin, and death. Indeed, Luke tells us that this is why he came: to seek and to save the lost (Luke 19:10).

Except that in this case, Jesus never got there: "When he was not far from the house, the centurion sent friends, saying to him, 'Lord, do not trouble yourself, for I am not worthy to have you come under my roof'" (Luke 7:6). Apparently, the centurion had second thoughts. Earlier he sent a delegation to persuade Jesus to come and help. By now a messenger had returned to say that Jesus was on his way. Possibly the messenger had also reported what the elders had said to Jesus, that the centurion was worthy of his help. But the more he thought about it, the more the centurion realized that he was *un*worthy. In fact, he did not even deserve to have Jesus walk into his house.

Here we see the absolute contrast between the apparent worthiness and the actual unworthiness of a man who seems to lead a good life. Everyone else thought the centurion deserved whatever help he needed. He was a good man. He cared for his servants. He gave a lot of money to the local congregation. Surely such a man was entitled to some kind of special consideration! But by the grace of God, the centurion saw himself as he really was. He knew that he was not worthy at all—not compared to Jesus. He was not even worthy to be under the same roof!

Some commentators say that the centurion said this because he was concerned about ritual purity, that since he did not keep the food laws and other Jewish rituals, he assumed that a righteous Jew like Jesus would not want to enter his house. That is not what the man said, however. What he said was more personal.[6] He *himself* was unworthy, and what made him unworthy was the worthiness of Jesus. The basis for his comparison was the superior worthiness of this powerful healer. Somehow he could see that Jesus was more than a traveling teacher, that he had righteous authority (see Luke 7:8). When the centurion saw this, he set aside any thought that he had any merit of his own. It is not clear whether he was fully ready to confess his sins, but at the very least, he knew that he was not worthy of Jesus.

How do you see Jesus, and how do you see yourself? The two questions are connected, because when we see Jesus as he really is—in all his splendor—we also see our true spiritual need. The first and most important thing we need to see about ourselves is that we are sinners in desperate need of God's grace. And when we see ourselves as we really are—the way that God sees us, in all the unworthiness of our sin—we see the supreme worthiness of our Lord and Savior Jesus Christ. Jesus Christ is the worthy Son of God. He is the beginning and the end, the Creator of the universe, the one by whom and for whom all things were made. He is the mighty and supreme ruler of heaven and earth, the King of kings and Lord of lords. He is the holy Lamb of God, who was slain for our sins on the cross, who was

6. Robert H. Stein, *Luke*, New American Commentary 24 (Nashville: Broadman, 1992), 220.

raised from the dead for our justification, and who now deserves all honor, blessing, glory, and power.

If that is who Jesus is, then who are we? The answer is that we are needy sinners who do not even deserve the grace of God. We must never forget the unworthiness of our sinful nature or the unrighteousness of the sins that we commit against God. As the great preacher Alexander Whyte taught his congregation in Scotland, "The true Christian's nostril is to be continually attentive to the inner cesspool."[7]

This is not poisonous pessimism, but a healthy realism that helps us breathe the fresh air of the gospel. If we are proud of who we are and what we have accomplished, then we can never be saved, because "God opposes the proud" (1 Peter 5:5). But God also gives grace to the humble, and when we admit that we do not even deserve to be saved, we are ready to receive God's mercy in Christ. We are ready to say, "Lord Jesus, have mercy on me, a sinner. I am not even worthy to come into your presence. But I believe the promise of your word, that in the blood of your cross, there is enough grace for me."

MAKE IT SO

There is more to salvation than seeing our unworthiness before God. We also need true faith in Jesus Christ. The centurion had this as well. He believed that Jesus had the power to save. "I did not presume to come to you," he said to Jesus. "But say the word, and let my servant be healed. For I too am a man set under authority, with soldiers under me: and I say to one, 'Go,' and he goes; and to another, 'Come,' and he comes; and to my servant, 'Do this,' and he does it" (Luke 7:7–8). At the beginning of this incident, the centurion was trying to make things happen. But now he sees that this is unnecessary. If Jesus really has power over disease and death, then all he needs to do is speak, and the servant will be healed. The centurion had faith in Jesus Christ and the saving authority of his powerful word.

One of the reasons the centurion had this faith is that he knew how authority operates. As an officer in the Roman army, he was used to giving orders and then having them obeyed. All he had to do was say the word, and

---

7. C. S. Lewis, commenting on Alexander Whyte in R. Kent Hughes, *Luke: That You May Know the Truth*, 2 vols., Preaching the Word (Wheaton, IL: Crossway, 1998), 1:256.

his soldiers would carry out his commands. To give a contemporary illustration, it is like the story about the army captain who came to an impassible river. How could he possibly get to the other side? Easy; all he had to do was give a direct order: "Sergeant, get my jeep across this river!" The centurion gave similar orders all the time. When he said, "Go," people went; when he said, "Come," they came; and when he said, "Make it so," they made it so.

The centurion was able to give such orders because he was "a man set under authority" (Luke 7:8). Today we would say that he was "a man *in* authority," but as a Roman soldier, the centurion had a deeper understanding of how authority operates. Why did soldiers carry out his orders? Because he had military authority. But where did that authority come from? It came from the command structure of the Roman army. The centurion derived his authority from his superior officers, who derived their authority from their superior officers, going all the way up to Caesar himself. So when the centurion gave an order, it was backed by the entire Roman Empire. He was *in* authority because he was *under* authority.

Somehow the centurion knew that Jesus Christ had the same kind of authority. He may not have known that Jesus was God the Son. Presumably he could not define the doctrine of the Trinity, or explain how the words of the Son were backed by the full authority of the Father. But the centurion knew that Jesus had power over the physical needs of the human body. As far as he was concerned, the miracles of Jesus proved that he spoke with almighty authority. All Jesus had to do was say the word, and his wish was creation's command.

When Jesus heard what confidence the centurion had in the authority of his word, he was totally amazed. There are only two times in the Gospels when Jesus is said to experience this kind of astonishment. The first is when his family and friends rejected him at Nazareth. The Scripture says, "he marveled because of their unbelief" (Mark 6:6). This time it is not *un*belief that amazed him, but *belief:* "When Jesus heard these things, he marveled at him, and turning to the crowd that followed him, said, 'I tell you, not even in Israel have I found such faith'" (Luke 7:9).

Many things about the centurion's faith were amazing. It was amazing for such a mighty man to see that he needed help. It was amazing for such a good man to see his unworthiness. It was amazing to find someone who was willing to take Jesus at his word, with complete confidence in the power of his command. But it was totally amazing to find all this in a Gentile—someone outside the covenant community. It was hard enough to find an Israelite who trusted in Christ. But here was a Gentile—a Roman soldier, no less—with surpassing faith in the word of Christ.

It was because of the man's humble faith that Jesus healed his servant. Luke assures us that "when those who had been sent returned to the house, they found the servant well" (Luke 7:10). All Jesus had to do was say one single word, and the man's health was restored. It was one of the greatest miracles Jesus ever performed. He did not even go to the man; he just said the word at a distance. But by the time everyone went home, the servant was fully recovered. J. C. Ryle summarizes by saying: "A greater miracle of healing than this, is nowhere recorded in the Gospels. Without even seeing the sufferer, without touch of hand or look of eye, our Lord restores health to a dying man by a single word. He speaks, and the sick man is cured. He commands, and the disease departs."[8]

By the same word that once created the universe out of nothing, and that now brings sinners from darkness into light, Jesus delivered the centurion's servant from death. He did this because the centurion trusted in his power to heal. This serves as an example of a basic principle for our own salvation: we will not be healed by the worthiness of our works, but only by the trust of our faith. Believing the word of Christ brings salvation. David Gooding comments: "salvation is not granted on the basis of a man's good works, worth or merit. It is given on the grounds of faith. And faith according to this story, is not confidence that we have done the best we could, that God will assess our merits generously; faith is abandoning trust in our works and merit and any thought of deserving salvation, and relying totally and without reserve on the Person of Christ and the authority of his word."[9]

Luke tells us that at the end of his conversation with the centurion's final messenger, Jesus turned and spoke to the crowd. This simple gesture had profound significance for the people standing there that day, because it was an invitation for them to trust in Christ with their very own faith. When Jesus said, "Not even in Israel have I found such faith" (Luke 7:9), he was challenging people to put their trust in him. They too had heard about

---

8. J. C. Ryle, *Expository Thoughts on the Gospels, Luke* (1858; reprint Cambridge: James Clarke, 1976), 1:200.

9. Gooding, *Luke*, 132.

Jesus. They knew that he had the power to heal. Now they were invited to believe in his word.

Jesus turns to us with the same invitation. This story reminds us of our lost and desperate condition as dying sinners. We are not worthy of Christ either. But the story also shows us that Jesus has the power of God for salvation. He can give us whatever healing we need—whatever comfort in our grief, whatever forgiveness for our sin, whatever hope for our future—simply by saying the word. All we have to do is trust in Jesus, as the centurion trusted him, with a simple and confident faith.

26

DEAD MAN TALKING

Luke 7:11–17

*Then he came up and touched the bier, and the bearers stood
still. And he said, "Young man, I say to you, arise." And the
dead man sat up and began to speak, and Jesus gave him to his
mother. Fear seized them all, and they glorified God, saying,
"A great prophet has arisen among us!" and "God has visited
his people!" (Luke 7:14–16)*

*I*s anything as painful as the death of a child? Only parents who
have suffered such a loss can tell what agony they experienced
when they buried their son or daughter, or what anguish they
endure as they continue to lament everything they have lost, and everything that might have been.

The southern theologian Robert L. Dabney was away on church business
when he learned that his beloved son had come down with a serious illness.
The anxious father traveled all night to reach his son's bedside. Here is what
happened next, as Dabney relates in a letter to his brother:

> We used prompt measures, and sent early for the doctor, who did not think
> his case was dangerous; but he grew gradually worse until Sunday, when his

symptoms became alarming, and he passed away, after great sufferings, Monday. . . . A half hour before he died, he sank into a sleep, which became more and more quiet, until he gently sighed his soul away. This is the first death we have had in our family, and my first experience of any great sorrow. I have learned rapidly in the school of anguish this week, and am many years older than I was a few days ago. It was not so much that I could not give my darling up, but that I saw him suffer such pangs, and then fall under the grasp of the cruel destroyer, while I was impotent for his help. Ah! When the mighty wings of the angel of death nestle over your heart's treasures, and his black shadow broods over your home, it shakes the heart with a shuddering terror and a horror of great darkness. To see my dear little one ravaged, crushed and destroyed, turning his beautiful liquid eyes to me and his weeping mother for help, after his gentle voice could no longer be heard, and to feel myself as helpless to give any aid—this tears my heart with anguish.[1]

THE DEATH OF AN ONLY SON

As we mourn our losses—our own losses as well as the losses of the people we love—we wonder what comfort God has for grieving parents, and what hope we can have for life after death. Luke answers these questions in his Gospel by telling us what Jesus did for a mother who suffered the tragic loss of her only son. In this story we see the compassion of Christ, his power over death, and the worship and witness they inspire.

The woman's story begins in sorrow. Luke reports, "Soon afterward he [Jesus] went to a town called Nain, and his disciples and a great crowd went with him. As he drew near to the gate of the town, behold, a man who had died was being carried out, the only son of his mother, and she was a widow, and a considerable crowd from the town was with her" (Luke 7:11–12).

Jesus had been in Capernaum, healing the sick. As he approached the little town of Nain, some twenty-five miles to the south, he met a sad procession coming out of the city. It was a funeral. According to the custom of that time, the dead were buried outside the city, usually at twilight on the same day they died. Some of the people in the procession were musicians who played a mournful dirge on their flutes. Others were professional mourners—women who wept and wailed as a public expression of com-

---

1. Robert Lewis Dabney, quoted in James W. Bruce, III, *From Grief to Glory: Spiritual Journeys of Mourning Parents* (Wheaton, IL: Crossway, 2002), 37–38.

munal grief. Then there were all the people from town who had come to pay their last respects. Together they would lay their friend to rest in one of the rocky tombs in the cemetery by the side of the road.

As we picture this scene, we are reminded of the tragedy of the human condition. We ourselves have gone out to bury our dead—not walking out of the city, perhaps, but driving with a long line of cars behind a hearse. This is our common sorrow, and it is all because of sin. God gave us life, but we chose to sin, and in choosing sin, we have come under judgment. If there had never been any sin, there never would have been any death, any funerals, or any tears. But "sin came into the world through one man, and death through sin, and so death spread to all men because all sinned" (Rom. 5:12). This is the source of all our sorrow. As Martin Luther wisely said, "When you hear . . . of death, you must think not only of the grave and the coffin, and of the horrible manner in which life is separated from the body and how the body is destroyed and brought to naught, but you must think of the cause by which man is brought to death and without which death and that which accompanies it, would be impossible . . . namely, sin and the wrath of God on account of sin."[2]

So as Jesus watched this sad procession, he was witnessing the tragic and lost condition of dying humanity. It would have taken only a few moments to size up the situation. He could hear the sounds of lamentation. He could also see what was happening. Near the front of the procession was the dead man himself, wrapped in a burial shroud and lying on a bier—a flat, open stretcher carried on the shoulders of his friends. Walking in front of his lifeless body was the young man's mother. She was probably walking alone, because in those days it was customary for the family to precede the deceased, and in this case, very sadly, no one else was left.[3]

It was just about the saddest funeral that anyone could ever imagine. The woman was a widow, so she had been down this road before to bury her beloved husband. Now she was grieving again, for a loss that must have seemed too great to bear. The dead man was her only son, and now she had no one left to protect her and provide for her. Of course she knew that

2. Martin Luther, *Sermons of Martin Luther*, ed. John Nicholas Lenker, 8 vols. (Grand Rapids: Baker, 1983), 5:146–47.

3. Norval Geldenhuys, *The Gospel of Luke*, New International Commentary on the New Testament (Grand Rapids: Eerdmans, 1951), 223.

people were behind her—a large crowd of sympathizers—but in a very real sense, she was alone in the world. This was the death of a mother's only son, and when she buried him, she would bury a piece of her own heart.

Do Not Weep

This would have been just another forgotten tragedy, if it were not for one great fact: when the widow went out to bury her son, she met Jesus on the way. And when Jesus saw her situation, his heart went out to her. Luke loves to show Jesus caring for women in need, and here he tells us that "when the Lord saw her, he had compassion on her and said to her, 'Do not weep'" (Luke 7:13).

Jesus was sensitive to the woman's sorrow. He could see that she was alone in the world, with no husband and no children. She was losing what little was left of her family companionship and financial support. And when Jesus saw the helpless condition of the woman's great loss, he was drawn to her in love and sympathy. As "the protector of widows" (Ps. 68:5), he did not even wait to be asked, but graciously took the initiative to care for her needs. From this unsolicited sympathy, Martin Luther draws "the general rule that applies to all the merciful deeds of God, that they all overtake us without our merits, even before we seek them. . . . Thus you have here an example, not of faith, but of the pure grace and lovingkindness of God."[4]

Sadly, there are some people—including some Christians—who would rather not come anywhere close to people who are grieving, or hurt in other ways. Sometimes they are not sure what to say, or they are preoccupied with their own problems, or they are embarrassed by the untamed emotions of someone deep in pain. But Jesus cares. The word Luke uses to describe his response is a word of passionate feeling, an intense word for a gut response of loving sympathy for someone else's pain.

This is how Jesus always responded to people who were suffering. It is how he responded at the tomb of Lazarus, when he wept with Mary and Martha. It is how he responded to the people of Jerusalem in their harassed and helpless condition. It is how he responded to his own mother at the

4. Martin Luther, *Sermons of Martin Luther: The Church Postils*, ed. and trans. John Nicholas Lenker (1905; reprint Grand Rapids: Baker, 1995), 5:129, 135.

cross, when he committed her to the care of his beloved disciple. Joni Eareckson Tada marveled that every time she

> flipped through Matthew, Mark, Luke, and John, there He was, hanging out with someone else with a handicap—hob-knobbing with people with disabilities, reserving His most gentle touch for the blind and counseling the fathers of little boys with seizures. He seemed to go out of His way to strike up conversations with guys who were paralyzed on straw mats by the pool of Bethesda. Since Jesus was not caught up with his own concerns, he was able fully and selflessly to enter into someone else's sufferings.[5]

Jesus cares the same way for us. Luke has included this story in his Gospel so that we would know the compassion of Christ in all our sorrow. The same Jesus who reached out to the widow of Nain reaches out to us when we feel helpless in the face of death. The God of the universe—our Lord and Savior Jesus Christ—has deep compassion for people in pain. He remembers our losses. He knows our sufferings. He hears our cries of anguish. And when he does, his heart goes out to us. As the Scripture says, "Surely he has borne our griefs and carried our sorrows" (Isa. 53:4). This promise is for anyone grieving the death of a loved one, or mourning the loss of a friendship, or lamenting the days that are lost and gone forever. Jesus cares for every suffering soul. He says, "Blessed are those who mourn, for they shall be comforted" (Matt. 5:4; cf. Luke 6:21), and then he makes good on his promise by coming to us in all his comfort. So we go to him with our troubles, knowing that in his loving heart there is enough room for all our sorrows.

Then, as we experience the compassion of Christ for ourselves, we are called to share it with others. The Bible teaches that God "comforts us in all our affliction, so that we may be able to comfort those who are in any affliction, with the comfort with which we ourselves are comforted by God" (2 Cor. 1:4). The comfort we receive is the comfort we are called to give, and when we give it, we are following the example of Jesus. To be like Christ is to be drawn to people who suffer, to have an instinctive compassion for their sorrows. This means noticing people in pain—grieving parents, lonely widows, the chronically ill, and anyone else who is suffering. It means entering

5. Joni Eareckson Tada, "Sent to Serve," *Wheaton* (Autumn 2005): 58.

into their situation with sympathy. It means giving them the freedom to grieve without presuming to tell them how they ought to feel. It means showing them the Savior who died for them, who lives for them and loves them still. What a difference it makes when people who are suffering meet Jesus on the way! This is what happens when we reach out to them with the compassion of Christ.

ARISE!

Jesus had more to offer the widow of Nain than merely his sympathies. He told her not to go on weeping, but if that were all that he had done for her, it would have been extremely insensitive. Why shouldn't she weep? She had just lost her only son, and tears were the appropriate overflow of her grieving soul. People who have something to cry about should go ahead and cry. But Jesus had good reason to tell this woman to dry her tears, because he spoke in the expectation of a miracle. He went beyond caring for her grief to doing something about it, conquering the death that caused her sorrow.

As Jesus began to work his miracle, he made a dramatic gesture: "Then he came up and touched the bier, and the bearers stood still" (Luke 7:14). This must have shocked people, because according to the law, touching the place of the dead made a person ceremonially unclean (see Num. 19:16). But Jesus Christ is the Lord of life, and therefore he is not corrupted or contaminated by death.

On the contrary, Jesus has the divine authority to keep death in its place. A dramatic confrontation was taking place at the front of that funeral procession—a collision between life and death. An unstoppable force was meeting a seemingly immovable object. The grieving had come out to bury their dead; but when the funeral met Jesus, death had to stop in its tracks. Everyone else had to follow the procession, but Jesus had the authority to bring it to a halt. When he put out his hand, it was as if to say, "Death, you will come this far, but no farther."

Then, as the crowd watched and the pallbearers waited, Jesus spoke to the body that lay shrouded in death: "And he said, 'Young man, I say to you, arise.' And the dead man sat up and began to speak, and Jesus gave him to his mother" (Luke 7:14–15). How absurd it must have seemed when Jesus addressed these words to a cold and lifeless corpse. But he made good on his audacious command. Luke tells us that the young man "sat up" (Luke 7:15)—a phrase often used for a medical recovery.[6] Then, to show that his recovery was complete, he began to speak. This time the grave would not claim its victim, because by the power of his word, Jesus raised him from the dead. Reginald Quirk points out the seeming contradiction that is

> conveyed by the very absurdity of this verse of Scripture: "And the dead man sat up, and began to speak." What nonsense there is in that phrase: "the dead man sat up." If he were dead, he could not sit up. If he could sit up, he was not dead. What nonsense. Unless we are prepared to abandon an idea that is second nature to us—to say that with Christ death is neither an unstoppable force nor an immovable object. It is simply, as St. Paul had it, the last enemy to be overcome. Death is swallowed up in victory. This is, in fact, the death of death.[7]

The healing of the widow's son was a mighty demonstration of the divine power of Jesus Christ. He did not raise the dead by prayer, as prophets like Elijah had done, but simply by the power of his own command. When Jesus spoke, the dead obeyed. To perform this miracle, Jesus had to summon the young man's soul from the place of the dead. He had to reunite his body and soul. He had to reintegrate his person, so that he could get up and speak. All of this required supernatural power—power over the visible and the invisible, over the body and the soul, over life and death. Here we see the proof, wrote J. C. Ryle, "that the Prince of Peace is stronger than the king of terrors, and that though death, the last enemy, is mighty, he is not so mighty as the sinner's Friend."[8]

Rest assured that the widow's son was actually dead. There are always some people who want to cast doubt on Jesus and his miracles, especially the raising of the dead. Sigmund Freud spoke for many skeptics when he said that the miracles in the Gospels "contradicted everything that had been

---

6. Darrell L. Bock, *Luke 1:1–9:50*, Baker Exegetical Commentary on the New Testament 3A (Grand Rapids: Baker, 1994), 652.

7. Reginald Quirk, "Death vs. Life: An Unstoppable Force Meets an Immovable Object," *Modern Reformation* (Jan./Feb. 2002): 6.

8. J. C. Ryle, *Expository Thoughts on the Gospels, Luke* (1858; reprint Cambridge: James Clarke, 1976), 1:208.

taught by sober observation and betrayed too clearly the influence of the activity of the human imagination."[9] But Luke *was* a sober observer, and as a careful historian, he stuck to the facts. The young man was really and truly dead. It was between his death and his burial that Jesus raised him up.

There are three miracles like this in the Gospels: the son of the widow of Nain, the daughter of Jairus, and Lazarus of Bethany. In each case, there were plenty of witnesses, and the event was widely reported. As the Christian apologist Quadratus wrote to the Emperor Hadrian nearly a century later: "The persons who were healed and those who were raised from the dead by Jesus were not only seen when they were healed and raised, but were always present also afterwards; and not merely during the time that the Savior walked upon the earth—but after His departure also they were still there for a considerable time, so that some of them lived even until our times."[10]

Eventually all these people died, of course. This is the difference between the miracles that Jesus performed in the Gospels and his own resurrection from the dead. When Jesus rose from the dead, the Holy Spirit gave him a glorious and immortal body. But the people Jesus raised did not receive a resurrection body; they merely came back to life in their same old bodies. So what happened to them was more like a resuscitation than a resurrection. Their bodies were still mortal, and one day they would die again.

Nevertheless, the raising of the widow's son does point us to the death of death in the resurrection of Jesus Christ. It is one of the first hints in the Gospel that Jesus would rise from the dead. In compassion for our dead and dying race, Jesus had come to die for our sins, and after he died, to rise again. The miracle also shows that Jesus has the power to bring *us* back to life. He can do something more than show us sympathy. He can give spiritual life to our dead souls through faith in his cross. Now that he himself has indeed risen from the dead, Jesus has the power to grant us eternal life. His resurrection is the promise and proof of our own resurrection.

Earlier I quoted from Robert L. Dabney, who wrote to his brother about the loss of his young son. After giving full expression to his anguish, Dabney went on to affirm his confident hope in the resurrection:

9. Sigmund Freud, quoted in Armand M. Nicholi, Jr., *The Question of God* (New York: Free Press, 2002), 38.

10. Quadratus, according to Eusebius, *Historia Ecclesiastica*, as quoted in Geldenhuys, *Luke*, 224.

Our parting is not for long. This spoiled and ruined body will be raised, and all its ravished beauties more than repaired. . . . Our little boy, we hope and trust, is now a ransomed spirit. . . . This is a hope inexpressible and full of glory. As I stand by the little grave, and think of the poor ruined clay within, that was a few days ago so beautiful, my heart bleeds. But as I ask, "Where is the soul whose beams gave that clay all its beauty and preciousness?" I triumph. Has it not already begun, with an infant voice, the praises of my Savior? . . . He is in Christ's heavenly house and under His guardian love. Now I feel, as never before, the blessedness of the redeeming grace and divine blood, which have ransomed my poor babe from all the sin and death he inherited through me.[11]

This is the hope of every believer. Through the crucifixion of Jesus Christ we have forgiveness for our sins, and through the resurrection of Jesus Christ we have the hope of eternal life. We know for sure that when we die, God will receive our souls unto himself, and on the last day he will raise our bodies to glory.

On that great day we will be reunited with all the people we love in Christ. There is a clear indication of this in the Gospel. Luke tells us that after Jesus raised the young man from the dead, he "gave him to his mother" (Luke 7:15; cf. 1 Kings 17:23). The word "gave" is a reminder that life after death is a free gift of God's grace. Furthermore, without this detail the story would be incomplete. Remember that it was because of his compassion for the mother that Jesus got involved with this situation in the first place. He was sensitive to her suffering. So when Jesus brought the young man back to life, he restored him to his mother's arms.

This gives us a picture of the happy reunion we will have in heaven— the reunion of every believer in Christ. Jesus has promised that "an hour is coming when all who are in the tombs will hear his voice and come out" (John 5:28–29). He has promised that at the final resurrection every child of God will be raised to everlasting glory. He has promised that God "will wipe away every tear from their eyes, and death shall be no more" (Rev. 21:4). And on the great day when Jesus brings us to himself, he will also give us back to one another. Whom are you waiting to greet in glory? Norval Geldenhuys writes:

11. Dabney, quoted in Bruce, *From Grief to Glory*, 39.

In this story the Saviour's sympathy with the sorrowing and His absolute divine power over the invisible spirit-world are gloriously revealed. We see Him here as the loving Comforter, the Victor over death, and the Reuniter of separated dear ones. What He did here for the widowed mother and son He will one day do for all the faithful in a perfect and final form. He will bring full comfort, He will raise all His people in incorruptibility, and will reunite us, in the heavenly realm, with our loved ones who have died in Him.[12]

RESPONDING TO THE RESURRECTION

How should we respond to the glorious hope of the resurrection? The miracle stories in Luke always invite us to make some kind of response, and the story of the widow's son is no exception. Luke tells us: "Fear seized them all, and they glorified God, saying, 'A great prophet has arisen among us!' and 'God has visited his people!' And this report about him spread through the whole of Judea and all the surrounding country" (Luke 7:16–17). In keeping with this example, we are called to respond to the resurrection with worship and witness, so that everyone may know Jesus and his saving power.

When people saw the young man rise, they were filled with fear—not in the sense that they were scared, but in the sense that they were overawed by the miracle Jesus performed. Raising the dead put the fear of God into them (in a good way). They had a holy reverence for what Jesus had done, and this caused them to glorify God. They recognized that the dead could be raised only by the power of God. So they returned the praise back to God, glorifying him as the Lord and Giver of life after death.

The people also began to praise Jesus Christ. They did not yet know that he was God the Son, but they could not deny his power, and they knew that he was "a great prophet." Thus they testified that in Christ, God had "visited his people." This language echoed the promises that were made before Christ was born (see Luke 1:68, 78). It also harkened back to Elisha, who was the last prophet to raise the dead (see 2 Kings 4:18–37). It had been almost a thousand years since anyone in Israel had witnessed this kind of miracle. But now God had visited his people again, and they were full of praise.

12. Geldenhuys, *Luke*, 223.

We too should be full of praise. God has visited us in the person of his Son, Jesus Christ. Jesus died on the cross for our sins. He was raised from the dead to give us hope in the resurrection. Now every week we gather for worship on Sunday, the very day that Jesus was raised from the dead. We come before God in reverence and awe, worshiping the person of his Son, and glorifying him for the gift of resurrection life.

But this gift is far too wonderful to keep to ourselves; we have to share it with others. When the people of Nain saw someone come back to life, they couldn't possibly keep it a secret. They wanted to bear witness to what they had seen, and soon the whole country heard about it. So it is with the resurrection of Jesus Christ, or at least so it ought to be. When we know that on the third day after he died for our sins Jesus was raised from the dead, we want everyone else to know it too.

This is an important part of sharing the gospel. The gospel is not just the crucifixion, but also the resurrection. The good news about Jesus includes both his cross *and* his empty tomb. It is not simply the death of Jesus that saves us, but also his life. So when we tell people about Jesus, bearing witness to his saving grace, we have a duty to tell them about his victory over death. The Bible says that Jesus "must reign until he has put all his enemies under his feet. The last enemy to be destroyed is death" (1 Cor. 15:25–26).

There is a striking illustration of this death-defeating power on the frescoes in some of the Byzantine churches in Turkey, where the risen Christ is often portrayed standing over death in triumph. Underneath his feet are the keys of death, the gates of hell, and the body of Satan. Jesus has won the victory over death.

This is good news for people who are spiritually dead, because it means that Jesus can give us new spiritual life. He calls to us in his Word, and when we hear his voice, we come alive spiritually. It is good news for people who are afraid to die, because it gives them the hope of life after death. Death is not the end; through faith in Christ, we can receive the free gift of eternal life. The resurrection is also good news for people who are grieving, because it means that we may see our loved ones again. The Bible promises that Jesus "himself will descend from heaven with a cry of command. . . . And the dead in Christ will rise first. Then we who are alive, who are left, will be caught up together with them in the clouds to meet the Lord in the air, and so we will always be with the Lord" (1 Thess. 4:16–17).

When was the last time you told someone about Jesus and the resurrection? This news is so important that everyone needs to hear it. Everyone needs to know for sure that there is life after death, and that through faith in Jesus Christ, the dead will rise to everlasting glory.

To know the hope of the resurrection is to know the joy of salvation. This hope does not wipe away all our tears—not yet, at least—but it can give us joy in our sorrow. The great Southern Presbyterian preacher Benjamin Morgan Palmer and his wife experienced some of that joy when they went out to bury their teenaged daughter. The Palmers were heavy with grief that day. Nineteen years earlier they had lost an infant son. Now they were going to bury their daughter in the same spot, near the bank of a gentle stream. But as they began to dig, they made an unexpected discovery. Palmer writes:

> The pick-axe and the shovel threw aside the earth, which for many years had pressed upon the bosom of the infant. Only a few bones and a little skull. No, wait a second; and with trembling hand the father clipped one little curl from which the luster had faded, but twining still around the hollow temple. He placed it on the palm of his hand, without a word, before the eye of the mother. With a smothered cry she fell upon his neck. "It is our boy's; I see it as long ago, the soft lock that curled upon his temple." "Take it, Mother; it is to us the prophecy of the resurrection; the grave has not the power to destroy."[13]

The Palmers wept together by their children's grave—not tears of sorrow only, but also of joy, because they believed in the resurrection. They knew that the day is coming when Jesus will say to the dead, "Arise!" He will say to the living, "Weep no more," and all will be well.

13. Benjamin M. Palmer, *The Broken Home, or, Lessons in Sorrow*, quoted in Bruce, *From Grief to Glory*, 124.

27

THE FRIEND OF SINNERS

Luke 7:18–35

*And he answered them, "Go and tell John what you have seen
and heard: the blind receive their sight, the lame walk, lepers
are cleansed, and the deaf hear, the dead are raised up, the
poor have good news preached to them. And blessed is the one
who is not offended by me." (Luke 7:22–23)*

We all have our doubts—doubts about the future, about our abilities, about our relationships, about our health, about the meaning of life, and even about God. There are times when we wonder if God is really there, when our prayers seem to bounce back off the ceiling and we feel alone in the universe. Suddenly and often quite unexpectedly, everything we have ever believed about God and salvation seems extremely implausible. We are tempted to doubt whether the Bible really is the Word of God, whether Jesus really did rise from the dead, or whether we ourselves will ever experience the glories of eternal life.

Where do these doubts come from? Sometimes they come from Satan, who tempts us not to believe what God has said in his Word. Sometimes they come when we are bored, or tired, or suffering from physical weakness. Sometimes they come when we are grieving the death of someone we love. Sometimes they come when we are under spiritual attack, or have given in to destructive patterns of sin and are no longer able to think clearly and righteously about spiritual things. Often the doubts come when we are disappointed with God. We thought we knew what God would do for us; we had expectations of what salvation would be like. But when God fails to grant us the physical healing, the financial prosperity, or the family situation we prayed for, we are tempted to doubt whether he really is the God he claims to be.

Whatever the reason, we all have our doubts. Sometimes they almost seem to threaten the foundations of our faith.

DOUBTING JOHN

Even John the Baptist had his doubts—yes, even John the Baptist. This may seem surprising, because if ever a man seemed certain about God, it was John. From the time he was in his mother's womb, John the Baptist was set apart to bear witness to the coming of Christ. He had done this with great boldness, and without any apparent concern for what people thought of him. John went into the wilderness preaching repentance and declaring with complete conviction that God was coming in judgment. He did this without ever entertaining even the slightest doubt that what he said was the very word of God. John's whole life was based on the bedrock of his faith in God.

Yet even John the Baptist went through a dark night of the soul when suddenly and unexpectedly he had his doubts about Jesus. John was languishing in prison at the time, having been locked away by wicked King Herod. From time to time his disciples would come and tell him what was happening in Israel. Naturally they told him about Jesus—about the teaching he was doing and the miracles he was performing. But somehow this failed to meet John's expectations for the ministry of the Messiah. Luke writes: "The disciples of John reported all these things to him. And John, calling two of his disciples to him, sent them to the Lord, saying, 'Are you the one who is to come, or shall we look for another?'" (Luke 7:18–19).

John was having his doubts. He had always believed that Jesus was the Christ, but suddenly he was not so sure. He began to wonder whether perhaps he had baptized the wrong Messiah.

The Bible does not tell us why John was entertaining these doubts, or why he asked Jesus to confirm that he was the Christ. Maybe being in prison had something to do with it. With typical candor, John had criticized King Herod for marrying his brother's wife, and now he was locked in a high desert fortress near the Dead Sea (Luke 3:18–20; Matt. 11:2). That prison became John's Doubting Castle—the desolate place where he was tempted to spiritual despair. His personal difficulties started to dominate his perspective. He was in so much distress, it seems, that he could no longer see what God was doing, either in his own life or in the world at large.

There was another reason for John's sudden uncertainty. His imprisonment may have had something to do with it, but so did his expectations. John had prophesied that the Messiah would come "with the Holy Spirit and with fire" (Luke 3:16). This meant that the Messiah would bring spiritual salvation, but it also meant that he would come in judgment to destroy the enemies of God. As John preached about God's wrath, he said, "Even now the axe is laid to the root of the trees. . . . His winnowing fork is in his hand, to clear his threshing floor" (Luke 3:9, 17). John probably thought that God's judgment would come right away. So where was it?

According to the reports John was getting, Jesus was preaching sermons and performing miracles. But when would he get around to the really important stuff, like overthrowing the religious establishment, or inaugurating his kingdom? John was looking for a more militant Messiah, with a more aggressive timetable. David Gooding explains John's attitude like this: "It was all right his going about healing an odd slave here and raising a widow's son from the dead there—John had nothing against that. But what about the big issues? When was Jesus going to start putting oppressive governments right? Abolishing evil rulers like Herod? Putting down the Roman tyranny and giving Israel her political independence?"[1] To add just one more question to the list, when was Jesus going to get his prophet out of prison?

Jesus was not the Messiah that John expected. Although he was doing the miracles of the Spirit, he was not blazing with the fire of judgment. So John asked, somewhat impatiently: "Are you the one who is to come, or shall we look for another?" (Luke 7:19).

1. David Gooding, *According to Luke: A New Exposition of the Third Gospel* (Grand Rapids: Eerdmans, 1987), 134.

329

Jesus Is the One

It was a good question to ask, and a crucial question for anyone to answer. In fact, it is the very question that compelled Luke to write his Gospel, and that we read his Gospel to answer for ourselves: Is Jesus the Christ? Is he the Savior whom God promised to send? Is he the only true hope of salvation for the world? Jesus answers these questions in Luke 7 by showing us who he is and what he does (Luke 7:20–23), by declaring the high privilege of trusting in him (Luke 7:24–28), and by warning us to stop looking for someone or something else (Luke 7:29–35).

The way to know for sure whether Jesus is the Christ is to go back to his person and work. This is what we should always do when God fails to meet our expectations, when we are overwhelmed by our personal problems and plagued with doubt. We need to go back to Jesus and look again to see who he is and what he does. Here John the Baptist had the right instinct. Rather than simply brooding over his skeptical doubts, he sent his disciples to go and see Jesus: "And when the men had come to him, they said, 'John the Baptist has sent us to you, saying, "Are you the one who is to come, or shall we look for another?"'" (Luke 7:20).

How did Jesus answer? Not by trying to meet John's expectations, or giving in to the demand to change his ministry by suddenly performing mighty acts of judgment, but simply by continuing to do the work God had called him to do (which is also the work he has called us to do): showing mercy and preaching the gospel. Yes, Jesus will come to judge the world, but he came first to save it. Luke tells us: "In that hour he healed many people of diseases and plagues and evil spirits, and on many who were blind he bestowed sight" (Luke 7:20–21). Jesus gave John's disciples a dramatic demonstration of his miraculous power. Just in case they missed the point, he said to them, "Go and tell John what you have seen and heard: the blind receive their sight, the lame walk, lepers are cleansed, and the deaf hear, the dead are raised up, the poor have good news preached to them. And blessed is the one who is not offended by me" (Luke 7:22–23).

This is an excellent summary of the miracles that Jesus had performed. He healed the sick, like Peter's mother-in-law in Capernaum (Luke 4:38–40). He cast out evil spirits, rebuking them by the power of his word (Luke 4:31–37, 41). He cleansed lepers, like the man who came and said, "Lord, if you will, you can make me clean" (Luke 5:12). He made the lame to walk, like the man whose friends lowered him through the roof (Luke 5:17–26). Luke has reported one miracle after another, showing the authority Jesus had over demons and disease. With each new miracle, we get a clearer understanding of who Jesus is and what he has come to do, until finally—when he meets the funeral procession outside the town of Nain (Luke 7:11–17)—we see him bringing the very dead back to life.

On the basis of this evidence, what is the obvious conclusion we should reach about the true identity of Jesus Christ? Is he the one, or should we look for someone else? The facts speak for themselves, proving that Jesus is Savior, Christ, and Lord.

In case we have any lingering doubts, the clincher comes at the end of verse 22, where Jesus says, "the poor have good news preached to them." Jesus said the same thing when he preached his first public sermon in Nazareth: "The Spirit of the Lord is upon me, because he has anointed me to proclaim good news to the poor" (Luke 4:18). Now Jesus says it again, as the climax to his argument. His calling as the Messiah was not simply to perform miracles, but to proclaim the gospel of salvation to poor and needy sinners. Therefore, his preaching was part of the proof that he was the Savior whom God had always promised to send.

When John the Baptist heard what Jesus said, he would have recognized that his words came straight out of the Old Testament, from the promises of Isaiah. Isaiah was the prophet who said, "Your dead shall live; their bodies shall rise" (Isa. 26:19), and, "Then the eyes of the blind shall be opened, and the ears of the deaf unstopped; then shall the lame man leap like a deer, and the tongue of the mute sing for joy" (Isa. 35:5–6; cf. 29:18). Isaiah also prophesied, "the LORD has anointed me to bring good news to the poor" (Isa. 61:1). By echoing these words, Jesus was giving John a biblical and practical proof that he was the Christ. As he performed his miracles and preached his gospel, Jesus was doing the very things the Bible promised that the Savior would do.

Jesus was saying, therefore, that we should trust in him for salvation. This is the point of verse 23: "Blessed is the one who is not offended by me." These words also came from Isaiah. When Isaiah prophesied about the coming Savior, he said, "he will become a sanctuary and a stone of offense and a rock of stumbling to both houses of Israel, a trap and a snare to the inhabitants of Jerusalem. And many shall stumble on it. They shall fall and be broken; they shall be snared and taken" (Isa. 8:14–15). These are troubling verses. They mean that even when God comes to bring salvation, some people will reject him. They will stumble over the rock of salvation. They will be offended by the very idea that they need Jesus to be their Savior.

Jesus was warning John—and us—not to be offended by his saving work. Do not stumble over Jesus because he is not meeting your expectations, or because you are having spiritual doubts, or because you are disappointed with God. Do not get the wrong idea about Jesus, as John did. He *is* the one. If we try to find another savior, we will never be saved at all. But if we accept Jesus and what he has done for us in dying on the cross and rising from the dead, he will bless us with everlasting salvation. God has given us this promise: "Behold, I am laying in Zion a stone of stumbling, and a rock of offense; and whoever believes in him will not be put to shame" (Rom. 9:33). Trust in Jesus and you will never be ashamed, not even on the day of judgment.

The Messiah's Messenger

Jesus did and said these things because he loved John and wanted to help him become more sure of his faith. But he also wanted to make sure that people did not get the wrong idea about John. Yes, John was having his doubts, but he was still a great prophet, and God used his ministry to help people come to Christ. So Jesus made this comment on John's ministry: "When John's messengers had gone, Jesus began to speak to the crowds concerning John: 'What did you go out into the wilderness to see? A reed shaken by the wind? What then did you go out to see? A man dressed in soft clothing? Behold, those who are dressed in splendid clothing and live in luxury are in kings' courts'" (Luke 7:24–25).

Obviously, John was none of these things. He was hardly a reed, blown about by the latest winds of public opinion. No, John was more like a mighty oak tree, standing firm against the rough and stormy gales of opposition. Nor was he the kind of man who stood around the palace wearing fancy clothes and eating rich food. Everyone knew that John wore a camel skin around his waist and that his diet consisted almost entirely of locusts and wild honey. John the Baptist was one of the most popular teachers in Israel, but it was not because he told people what they wanted to hear or because he lived the lifestyle of the rich and famous.

So what was the meaning of John's ministry? Why did people go to hear him preach? Jesus said, "What then did you go out to see? A prophet? Yes, I tell you, and more than a prophet. This is he of whom it is written, 'Behold, I send my messenger before your face, who will prepare your way before you.' I tell you, among those born of women none is greater than John" (Luke 7:26–28).

Here Jesus gives high praise to John the Baptist, calling him a prophet and ranking him as the greatest of merely mortal men. What made John great was not his own personal identity, but his special calling to prepare the way for salvation. What made John important was who *Jesus* was. Since Jesus was the Messiah, John was more than just another prophet; he was the man promised to serve as the Messiah's messenger (Mal. 3:1). This made him the last and greatest prophet before Christ. The other prophets all looked for the Savior from a distance, but John saw him with his own two eyes. He alone had the privilege of pointing at Jesus and saying, "Behold, the Lamb of God, who takes away the sin of the world!" (John 1:29).

Then Jesus went on to make a surprising statement about our own personal privilege as believers in Christ. He said, "I tell you, among those born of women none is greater than John. Yet the one who is least in the kingdom of God is greater than he" (Luke 7:28). What a remarkable thing to say! Because of his witness to Christ, John the Baptist was the greatest man who ever lived. Yet even the newest, weakest Christian is greater than John. This is because we have experienced the finished work of Jesus Christ, and therefore, by the witness of the Holy Spirit, we know things that John could only dream of knowing. We know the mercy of Jesus in forgiving our sins through the cross. We know the power of Jesus in rising from the dead. We know the love of Jesus in the free gift of eternal life.

This is not to say that John was never saved. Of course he *was* saved, through his faith in the Messiah. Nevertheless, we have a more privileged place in the history of salvation. John saw only the beginning of what Jesus would do, but we have been given the whole gospel, and in our knowledge of the cross and the empty tomb, we have a fuller experience of Jesus Christ. We may have our doubts, but we should not miss out on the extraordinary opportunity we have to believe in Jesus Christ. John himself would be the first to tell us that there is nothing greater than belonging to the kingdom of God.

Two Responses to Jesus

The way to enter God's kingdom is by faith in Jesus Christ, but sadly, not everyone is willing to trust in him. At the end of this passage Jesus warns us to stop looking to someone or something else for our salvation.

When Jesus spoke about the kingdom, people responded in two radically different ways. This is what always happens when people listen to Jesus: they never stay where they are. Either they accept him by faith or they reject him to their own condemnation. So it was on this occasion: "(When all the people heard this, and the tax collectors too, they declared God just, having been baptized with the baptism of John, but the Pharisees and the lawyers rejected the purpose of God for themselves, not having been baptized by him)" (Luke 7:29–30).

The English Standard Version treats these verses as an aside, placing them in parentheses. However, it is not entirely clear what the people heard. Maybe they heard Jesus, which is the way the ESV has it: the word "this" refers back to what Jesus has just been saying. But in the original the Scripture simply says, "When all the people heard," not "heard this," so it is possible that Jesus is still talking. In that case, Jesus is commenting on something they heard previously, when John the Baptist was preaching and people either "declared God just" or "rejected the purpose of God."

Either way, the point is really the same. When some people heard the message of salvation—whether they had heard it earlier from John or now from Jesus—they accepted it by faith. They declared that God was just. In other words, they admitted that God was right about their sin and about everything else. The proof that they were willing to confess their sins was the baptism of repentance that they received from John (see Luke 3:3). As Norval Geldenhuys puts it, "they acknowledged that before God they were guilty and worthy of condemnation and that He was fully justified in demanding from them confession of sins and true repentance, not in word only, but outwardly and publicly by undergoing the baptism of John."[2]

But there were other people who did not accept God's verdict, did not confess their sins, and did not receive John's baptism of repentance for the forgiveness of sins. By and large, the people who rejected the message of salvation were the scribes and Pharisees, who in many ways were the religious fundamentalists of their day. These men prided themselves on their obedience to God and wanted to be accepted on their own merit. They did not think they had any reason to repent, which is why they never submitted to John's baptism. Frankly, they were offended by the idea that salvation came as a free gift for sinners. They thought people had to earn it, and for their own part, they were sure that they had done enough to deserve God's reward. So the Pharisees rejected Jesus, as they had rejected John, and thus, they were not saved. Luke puts it like this: the scribes and Pharisees "rejected the purpose of God for themselves" (Luke 7:30). This does not mean that they had the power to frustrate God's plans or overturn the decree of predestination. What it does mean is that they decided to reject the gift of salvation, which God freely and sincerely offers to everyone. God invited them to fulfill the true purpose of their existence by coming to him in repentance and faith, but instead they chose to live for themselves.

This is a serious warning for anyone involved in full-time Christian ministry. The Pharisees had the kind of spiritual pride that often goes with being a religious professional. It is a high privilege to study the sacred things of God, but as C. S. Lewis wisely said, "Sacred things may become profane by becoming matters of the job."[3] When that happens, we end up so far from God that we no longer see the seriousness of our sin.

This warning is not just for people in full-time ministry, however. It is for anyone who thinks that he or she is good enough for God. It is always tempting to think that we are better than the Bible says we really are. But Jesus tells us that we need to come to him confessing our sins. The only people who ever find salvation are the people who agree that God is right

2. Norval Geldenhuys, *The Gospel of Luke*, New International Commentary on the New Testament (Grand Rapids: Eerdmans, 1951), 228.

3. C. S. Lewis, quoted in R. Kent Hughes, *Luke: That You May Know the Truth*, 2 vols., Preaching the Word (Wheaton, IL: Crossway, 1998), 1:271.

to say that they are unrighteous. Once we agree with that, we are ready to come to Jesus with a sincere repentance and a certain faith.

PLAYING THE GAME RIGHT

To apply his teaching about faith and repentance, Jesus drew an analogy from daily life:

> To what then shall I compare the people of this generation, and what are they like? They are like children sitting in the marketplace and calling to one another, "We played the flute for you, and you did not dance; we sang a dirge, and you did not weep." For John the Baptist has come eating no bread and drinking no wine, and you say, "He has a demon." The Son of Man has come eating and drinking, and you say, "Look at him! A glutton and a drunkard, a friend of tax collectors and sinners!" Yet wisdom is justified by all her children. (Luke 7:31–35)

In those days, boys and girls loved to play weddings and funerals. These were common events, and it is not surprising that children imitated the rituals they saw in the streets of their city. Sometimes they played weddings, dancing around the boy and girl pretending to be the bride and groom. Sometimes they played funerals, singing sad songs and pretending to cry. But some children were bored with all that. They did not want to play weddings *or* funerals. In fact, they did not want to play anything at all. So the other children would singsong an old taunt from the Jewish playground: "We played the flute for you, and you did not dance; we sang a dirge, and you did not weep" (Luke 7:32).

This shows how much a man of the people Jesus was. He paid attention to children in the street and knew the nursery rhymes of his day. It also shows how much insight Jesus had into the true spiritual condition of the people who refused his grace, who were always looking for someone or something else. Jesus understood that it did not matter who preached to them: they simply refused to have anything to do with the salvation God had to offer.

First came John the Baptist—wearing wild clothes, eating strange foods, and preaching repentance. He would not play weddings; all he ever did was play funerals, crying about the judgment to come. John was much too primitive for the Pharisees, and far too condemning. When he had the audacity to tell them to repent of their sins, they decided that he had to be demon-possessed.

Then Jesus came, and the Pharisees did not want what he had to offer either. All of a sudden they changed their tune. The same people who demonized John for not playing weddings were scandalized by Jesus because he refused to play funerals! Strange as it may seem, Jesus had such a good time that he had a reputation for partying. All he ever did was spend time with notorious sinners, preaching about grace and offering mercy to people who did not even deserve it. His story was not a sad tragedy, but a joyful comedy, and Jesus spread this joy wherever he went. This violated people's spiritual sensibilities. As far as the Pharisees were concerned, the way to gain God's blessing was to be good and religious. Since they did not see any need to repent of their sin, they did not accept God's grace in the gospel. They thought salvation was theirs by right, and they were offended by the idea that it came as a gift for sinners.

Some people are never satisfied! These people did not like John, and they would not listen to Jesus: "They would neither have the holiness and wrath of God, nor the love and forgiveness of God. All they wanted was a God small enough to compromise and to pretend that their imperfect keeping of the law was adequate, a salvation small enough for their merits to earn it."[4] Here is how Michael Wilcock describes their attitude:

> When they "piped," and asked for a message that was undemanding and cheerful, John fasted and talked about sin; he was too gloomy, they wanted something brighter. But when they "wailed," and expected from the rabbi of Nazareth a solemn discussion on morals and religion, Jesus went to parties and talked about salvation; he was too exhilarating, they wanted something more proper. For the news of the kingdom . . . will not fit in with men's preconceived ideas, nor pander to their prejudices. It digs far deeper than their shallow understanding of the evils of Satan's kingdom, and soars far higher than their low view of the glories of God's kingdom.[5]

4. Gooding, Luke, 137.
5. Michael Wilcock, The Message of Luke, The Bible Speaks Today (Downers Grove, IL: InterVarsity, 1979), 92.

How easy it is to be critical about anything and everything without ever entering into a saving relationship with Jesus Christ. Some people are always finding fault. They object that the church is too judgmental, or that it is soft on sin. They say that this or that congregation is not friendly enough, or maybe a little too friendly. They criticize Christians for being too intellectual or too simple, for being too serious or too emotional. They say the same thing about Jesus: he is too strict for them, or too permissive; he is too hard to understand, or else too unsophisticated. Like the Pharisees, they are always looking for some other savior, and always finding some excuse for not believing in Jesus. But the problem is not with Jesus; the problem is with them.

How ironic, and how truly sad, that Jesus was the Savior the Pharisees needed all along. They were offended because Jesus was "a friend of sinners" (Luke 7:34). Since they did not think that they were sinners, Jesus was no friend of theirs! But instead of being offended by Jesus, the Pharisees should have believed in him. Then they would have become the kind of children Jesus talked about in verse 35: not foolish children who try to make God dance to their own tune, but wise children who accept the salvation that God has given.

The children of wisdom are people who are justified by faith, who are "wise for salvation through faith in Christ Jesus" (2 Tim. 3:15). The way for us to be so wise is to see our need of repentance and to trust in Jesus Christ for salvation. Anyone who still has any doubts should go back to Jesus. Learn from his teaching. Look at his miracles. Listen to what the Bible says about his death and resurrection. Stop looking for someone or something else. If you are a sinner who needs a friend, then Jesus is the Savior for you.

28

THE DEBT OF LOVE I OWE

Luke 7:36–50

"You did not anoint my head with oil, but she has anointed my
feet with ointment. Therefore I tell you, her sins, which are many,
are forgiven—for she loved much. But he who is forgiven little,
loves little." (Luke 7:46–47)

They will know we are Christians by our love. This was the attitude that Christians in Egypt embraced during the third century, when a terrible plague overwhelmed the famous city of Alexandria. According to Dionysius the Great, it was the followers of Christ who had compassion on the sick, even at the cost of their own lives. "Most of our brother Christians," he wrote, "showed unbounded love and loyalty, never sparing themselves and thinking only of one another. Heedless of danger, they took charge of the sick, attending to their every need and ministering to them in Christ, and with them departed this life serenely happy. . . . Many, in nursing and curing others, transferred their death to themselves and died in their stead."[1]

---

1. Dionysius of Alexandria, quoted in Rodney Stark, *The Rise of Christianity: How the Obscure Marginal Jesus Movement Became the Dominant Religious Force in the Western World in a Few Centuries* (San Francisco: HarperCollins, 1997), 82–83.

In those terrible days, the Christians showed a love that surpassed what anyone else was able to give. Dionysius went on to say this: "The heathen behaved in the very opposite way. At the first onset of the disease, they pushed the sufferers away and fled from their dearest, throwing them into the roads before they were dead, and treated unburied corpses as dirt, hoping thereby to avoid the spread and contagion of the fatal disease."[2] Even the famous physician Galen fled the city in fear.

What made the difference? What accounts for the extraordinary love that Christians showed to the dead and dying? Simply this: they had been forgiven. A life of love is the grateful response of a sinner who has found true forgiveness in Jesus Christ.

THE EXTRAVAGANCE OF HER LOVE

Nowhere do we see the connection between love and forgiveness more clearly than in the story Luke told about a woman who anointed Jesus' feet with her perfume. Here we see a clear contrast between the extravagant love of a forgiven sinner and the scornful contempt of a self-righteous man; Jesus also tells us what makes the difference.

Strangely enough, this incident occurred at a Pharisee's house. As Luke tells us, "One of the Pharisees asked him to eat with him, and he went into the Pharisee's house and took his place at the table" (Luke 7:36). Luke does not tell us why the Pharisee gave Jesus this invitation. Maybe he was curious. Maybe he wanted to test Jesus to see if he measured up to his spiritual standards. Maybe he wanted to earn the merit that was considered to come with hosting a rabbi for dinner.[3] But whatever his reason, the man invited Jesus to dinner, and Jesus accepted. He was willing to eat with anyone . . . even a Pharisee.

While they were eating, something surprising happened—something so surprising that Luke introduces it with an exclamation: "And behold, a woman of the city, who was a sinner, when she learned that he was reclining at table in the Pharisee's house, brought an alabaster flask of ointment, and standing behind him at his feet, weeping, she began to wet his feet with her tears and wiped them with the hair of her head and kissed his feet and anointed them with the ointment" (Luke 7:37–38).

---

2. Dionysius of Alexandria, quoted in Stark, *Rise of Christianity,* 84.

3. Joachim Jeremias, *The Parables of Jesus* (London: SCM, 1955), 101.

Here it helps to know something about dinner parties in biblical times. Homes had an open floor plan in those days, and a wealthy man like the Pharisee would host his guests in a courtyard. The meal would have been a semipublic occasion, more like a block party than a private dinner. It was not uncommon for people who were not invited to stop by for a chat, or even to sit around the edge of the courtyard.

What *was* uncommon was for a woman like this to show up at a house like this and do what she did for Jesus. We do not know her name. Some people have said that it was Mary Magdalene, but there is no reason to think that it was. Others say that it was a woman from Bethany, but that was something that happened much later in Jesus' ministry, at a different place, and with different results (see Matt. 26:6–13). The only thing we know about this woman is that she was a notorious sinner. This is mentioned three times: by Luke (Luke 7:37), by the Pharisee (Luke 7:39), and by Jesus himself (Luke 7:47). People usually assume that she was some kind of prostitute, and they may be right. Luke describes her as someone off the streets, which gives the connotation of sexual sin. But in a way it doesn't matter, because a sinner is a sinner. Whether she was a gossip or a call girl, she was still a sinner.

This is why she came to see Jesus. Sinful as she was, she knew that Jesus was the friend of sinners. His friendship has been apparent throughout this chapter as Jesus has shown compassion to the centurion, the widow, and other poor sinners who stand outside the people of God. Each episode

> describes a need which God alone can meet; and when we think of the people concerned, we realize that their "poverty" consists precisely in this—that in the eyes of Jesus's contemporaries such people have no resources to meet those needs, because they have no claim on God: the centurion is a mere Gentile, the widow a mere female, the woman at the party a mere sinner. They are outside the circle of privilege. For God to help them at all they have to receive his help gratis.[4]

The sinful woman was looking for free grace. So when she heard that Jesus was at the Pharisee's house, she ran to him with her perfume, hoping to

4. Michael Wilcock, *The Message of Luke*, The Bible Speaks Today (Downers Grove, IL: InterVarsity, 1979), 93.

worship at his feet. When she arrived, there he was, reclining in the ancient style, with his legs stretched behind him and his feet away from the table.

At first the woman simply stood there, looking at Jesus with adoring eyes, not daring to touch him. But as she stood there, she was overcome with emotion. She probably told herself not to cry, but somehow she couldn't help it. Here was the lover of her soul and the friend of her sinner's heart. She thought about all the wrong things that she had done, using her body and her soul in the service of Satan. But somehow she knew that Jesus had mercy on her, and then the tears started to flow—tears of relief, gratitude, and joy. I read this Bible story to my son when he was a small boy of perhaps two. He could not understand why the woman was crying. "Why tears, Daddy?" he asked. The answer is that she was overwhelmed by the grace that God had given her in Jesus Christ. She was weeping with the gratitude of sin forgiven.

As the woman looked down, she realized that her Savior's feet were wet with her tears. Without thinking, she began to wipe them with her hair. It was bad enough for a woman with her reputation to show up at a Pharisee's house uninvited. But in those days it was shameful for a woman to let down her hair in public. In fact, the Talmud went so far as to say that a man could divorce his wife if she showed her hair to another man.[5] But this woman no longer cared what other people thought. She was so in love with Jesus that she forgot herself entirely. Purely and passionately, but not erotically, she let her hair fall on his feet.

Nor did she stop there. The woman proceeded to pour her perfume on Jesus' feet, anointing them with oil. Perfume was highly prized in those dusty days, so the woman was giving Jesus an expensive gift. It may have been the most precious thing she owned, but now she was pouring it all out for the glory of Jesus.

This was a gesture of humility. Ordinarily, perfume would have been used to anoint someone's head. Only a slave would care for someone's feet. But this woman was willing to take the position of a servant, trusting Jesus not to use her and abuse her the way that other men would and some men had. With reverence and submission, she washed her Master's feet, giving him the highest honor.

5. Jeremias, *Parables*, 101–2.

This was also an expression of astonishing affection. When the woman poured out her perfume, she was pouring out her heart with the fragrance of her love. Then she kissed Jesus' feet, and according to the tense of the verb, she went on kissing them. Here we see the extravagant love of a forgiven sinner. As Luke has revealed the true identity of Jesus Christ, he has shown people responding to him in faith. Now he shows someone responding to him in love. Thus we see that a disciple is a lover; Jesus desires the affection of our hearts as well as the faith of our minds. So greet him with extravagant affection. Fall into the arms of his love, bow at his feet in worship, and weep for joy that all your sins are forgiven.

THE SCORN OF HIS CONTEMPT

The Pharisee who was with Jesus that day did none of these things. He was offended by what the woman was doing, embarrassed by her outward display of emotion. Luke tells us: "Now when the Pharisee who had invited him saw this, he said to himself, 'If this man were a prophet, he would have known who and what sort of woman this is who is touching him, for she is a sinner'" (Luke 7:39).

Spoken like a true Pharisee! The man's attitude was judgmental. He was quick to condemn other people for their sins, and when he did, he placed them in a different category from himself. *He* was righteous, but *they* were sinners. This was typical of the Pharisees we meet in the Gospels, with their holier-than-thou lifestyle. They were always looking down on people, snorting with indignation over their sins.

Notice the contempt in the Pharisee's words. Not only did he call the woman "a sinner," but he also alluded to "what sort of woman" she was. This was highly pejorative. Even the word "touching" may perhaps have sexual overtones, because elsewhere the same word is used with the connotation of sexual activity (see 1 Cor. 7:1). The Pharisee viewed the woman with disdain.

He had a similar attitude toward Jesus. Until now he had wondered whether Jesus might be a prophet. Now he was sure that he wasn't, because prophets do not associate with sinners. Or at least that is what the Pharisee thought. For him, religion was all about being good. God was for good people, not for people whose lives were a mess. A righteous man should not have contact with known sinners. So if Jesus were a real prophet, he would have known better than to associate with this kind of woman.

A prayer letter from a gospel partner serving in the Middle East helps to set Simon's attitude in its social context. She writes:

> The point that really struck me about Jesus' response to the woman was its complete departure from what was socially acceptable. I'm not sure if one can really begin to grasp how shocking it was unless one has spent enough time in the Middle East for its attitudes to start melding with his own. The worst sin a woman can commit here is to lose, or appear to have lost, her virginity outside of marriage. The most important asset she has as a woman is her reputation. The whole honor of the family hangs on the reputation of its women. If a woman has nothing but her reputation as a chaste woman, she always has a chance to succeed; if she has everything but her reputation she is lost before she begins. And in some parts of the Arab world, all it takes for a woman to lose her reputation is to be seen *speaking* to a man who is not a relative. If a man, particularly a religious man, is known to have even spoken with such a "lost" woman, his reputation will follow hers down the drain. It is a hard system and it crosses religious lines. Now consider that same system but take it back 2000 years to a less forgiving time. Then think about Jesus' encounter with the sinful woman. Shocking, isn't it?[6]

By thinking this way, the Pharisee thought that he was maintaining high moral standards, but in fact he was graceless, merciless, and loveless. As Kent Hughes puts it, he had "an arctic heart, a permafrost of the soul."[7] The only thing he could do with sinners was condemn them; he had no grace to give.

Here Luke is showing us two responses to Jesus, based on two totally different attitudes about sin and grace. There were many contrasts between these two people. One had a high social position, and the other was an outcast. One was a host, and the other was not even an invited guest. One was angry; one was overcome with joy. One was still evaluating Jesus, while the other had decided to trust him with her entire life. But the fundamental contrast was this: only one of them believed that God had grace for sinners.

---

6. Correspondence from Nancy Khalil, Dec. 1998.

7. R. Kent Hughes, *Luke: That You May Know the Truth*, 2 vols., Preaching the Word (Wheaton, IL: Crossway, 1998), 1:278.

Even without saying a word, the woman proved by her actions that she trusted Jesus for the forgiveness of her sins. But the Pharisee had no room for grace in his theology. He believed that grace was unavailable to sinners like that woman and unnecessary for a righteous man like himself.

From the spiritual standpoint, which of these two people is more attractive? Which of them has the right response to Jesus? And honestly, which of them is more like you? We do well to consider whether we are more like the woman who came to Jesus with the joy of a forgiven sinner, or more like the man who thought that some people were not even good enough to be forgiven.

One way to test our grasp of God's grace is to see how we respond to the people we think of as sinners. What we say about them, how we treat them, and what we do (or fail to do) to touch their lives with the love of Jesus Christ indicate our true understanding of God and his grace. Sadly, there are many Christians who refuse to get involved in the lives of people who are in spiritual trouble. They do not touch sinners, and they do not let sinners touch them.

Of course we need to stay away from unwise situations where we will be tempted to sin. But it is our calling as Christians to share the love of Christ with people who need his grace. In the same way that Jesus came to save lost sinners, and in the same way that he has touched our own lives, we are called to reach out with his love. The love of Christ is to govern our response to the girl at school who has a reputation for sleeping around, to the homeless man addicted to crack cocaine, to the openly gay couple in our apartment building, to the inmate with the violent record, to the family member who scorns the gospel, to the pastor who denies fundamental doctrines of the Christian faith. The love of Christ leads us to build relationships with the obvious sinners we know. Too often, we do not have relationships with them at all, or if we do, our contempt for their sin shows through. They can tell what we really think of them, and this hinders them from ever hearing the gospel we want to give them.

What would happen if we really believed that God has grace for sinners, loving them the way Jesus loved the woman at the Pharisee's house? We are called to an embracing love that shuns evil without shunning sinners. When we live with this kind of love, it has the power to change people's lives: not just the lives of others, but also our own.

WHAT MAKES THE DIFFERENCE

This true story from the life of Christ does something more than merely show the contrast between two people: it also tells us what makes the difference. As the Pharisee sat muttering to himself and thinking unkind thoughts, Jesus interrupted and "said to him, 'Simon, I have something to say to you.' And he answered, 'Say it, Teacher'" (Luke 7:40). The Pharisee was about to find out that Jesus really *was* a prophet. Not only did he know what kind of woman was washing his feet, but he also knew what kind of man was sitting across from him at the table! So Jesus told a little parable: "A certain moneylender had two debtors. One owed five hundred denarii, and the other fifty. When they could not pay, he cancelled the debt of both. Now which of them will love him more?" (Luke 7:41–42).

The answer was obvious, but Simon was wary, so he cautiously answered: "The one, I suppose, for whom he cancelled the larger debt." He was right, of course. Five hundred denarii was nearly two years' wages, and anyone forgiven a debt that large would be eternally grateful. So Jesus said, "You have judged rightly" (Luke 7:43).

Jesus was not really talking about economics, however; he was talking about the great debt of our sin, and about the grace of God that demands our gratitude. So he proceeded to apply his parable: "Then turning toward the woman he said to Simon, 'Do you see this woman?'" (Luke 7:44). In one sense Simon did see the woman; he had been looking at her with scorn ever since she started touching Jesus. But in another sense he did not see her at all—at least not the way God saw her. Simon was looking at her the way she used to be, not seeing the new woman she was becoming in Christ.

As Simon looked at her again, Jesus tried to help him see himself too. He said: "I entered your house; you gave me no water for my feet, but she has wet my feet with her tears and wiped them with her hair. You gave me no kiss, but from the time I came in she has not ceased to kiss my feet. You did not anoint my head with oil, but she has anointed my feet with ointment" (Luke 7:44–46). Simon had done almost nothing for Jesus. He did not even fulfill the basic duties of ordinary hospitality. He did not provide a basin of water for Jesus to wash his feet, or greet him with a kiss, or put oil on his forehead. He was barely hospitable. This rude response shows that Simon had almost as much contempt for Jesus as he had for the sinful woman. Rather than honoring Jesus with common courtesy, Simon treated him with arrogant indifference. Simon may have been religious, but he had no love for Jesus.

How often do we treat Jesus the same way? We have invited him into our hearts, perhaps, but there is more hospitality for us to give: the honor of our worship and the greeting of our prayer. If we have neglected these privileges, remaining indifferent to the presence of Jesus in our lives, then we have treated the Son of God with shocking contempt.

By contrast, the woman did everything she could for Jesus. She did everything the Pharisee failed to do, and more. She did not bring water; she wet Jesus' feet with her tears. She did not kiss him on the cheek; she kept on kissing and kissing his feet, like a servant. She did not anoint his head with oil; she anointed his feet, and wiped them with her long, beautiful hair. The woman surpassed the Pharisee in every respect. What made the difference? To Jesus, the answer was obvious: she had been forgiven. He said to Simon, "Therefore I tell you, her sins, which are many, are forgiven—for she loved much. But he who is forgiven little, loves little" (Luke 7:47).

At this point the meaning of the parable becomes clear. It is the forgiven who make the best lovers. The more people have been forgiven, the more they love, as even Simon had to admit. So what did the woman's passion for Jesus say about her? It proved that the great debt of her sin had been forgiven. Everyone knew that she was a sinner, including the woman herself, and also Jesus, who did not overlook her many sins. Jesus knew the full extent of her sin, as he always does. Nevertheless, this woman was fully forgiven, as the story tells us not once, but three times (verses 47, 48, and 49), and this meant that she was no longer defined by her depravity. She had discovered that with Jesus there is enough forgiveness for all our sin, even if we feel that we are the biggest sinners in the world. How do we know that she was forgiven? It was obvious from her love. Her gratitude was the proof that she had received God's grace.

But where did this leave Simon? What did his response reveal about the true condition of *his* heart? Well, the less people have been forgiven, the less they love, and since he loved so little, it is doubtful whether he had even been forgiven at all. Maybe his sins were less obvious, and maybe they were smaller than the kinds of sins that the woman committed, but he was a debtor too. The real difference between them was not the size of their debt, but the fact that only one of them had been forgiven. This was clear from the way that the Pharisee treated Jesus—not with warm gratitude, but with cold indifference. When Jesus said, "he who is forgiven little, loves little" (Luke 7:47), he was obviously talking about Simon the Pharisee.

Once again, this story searches our own hearts, compelling us to consider whether we have an obvious and extravagant affection for Jesus Christ, or else place all kinds of limits on how much of ourselves we are willing to give away in ministry. See the full extent of your sin, rather than always thinking that other people are bigger sinners than you are. Do not be like the wealthy duchess whom the Countess of Huntingdon invited to hear the great evangelist George Whitefield. That proud woman was offended to receive the invitation because she had heard about Whitefield's theology, and she did not want anyone telling her that she needed to repent. She wrote: "It is monstrous to be told, that you have a heart as sinful as the common wretches that crawl on the earth. This is highly offensive and insulting; and I cannot but wonder that your Ladyship should relish any sentiments so much at variance with high rank and good breeding."[8] Instead of insisting on our own righteousness, it is better for us to say, as Francis of Assisi said, "There is nowhere a more wretched and miserable sinner than I."[9]

The more we feel that we do not need to be forgiven, the more self-righteous we become, and the more self-righteous we become, the less love we give. We only do the minimum; we do not pour out our lives like fragrant perfume. If we love Jesus so little, it can only be because we have little idea how much we have been forgiven. The way to get a better idea about this is not to go out and become bigger sinners; all we need to do is see how big our sins already are. This means being honest about the sinfulness of our worry, our greed, our gossip, and our rage. And it means coming back to God again and again in repentance, even after we first come to Christ.

The power of gospel forgiveness can be illustrated from the dramatic difference it is making in the lives of Kurdish Muslim women. James Peterson of the Lutheran Orient Mission Society believes that "Jesus is great news for Muslim

8. This story is recounted by Arnold Dallimore in *George Whitefield*, 2 vols. (Edinburgh: Banner of Truth, 1975), 1:132.
9. Francis of Assisi, quoted in William Barclay, *The Gospel of Luke*, The New Daily Study Bible (Louisville: Westminster John Knox, 2001), 114.

women." Peterson recounts the conversation he had with a woman who had telephoned long distance from Kurdistan. When she claimed that she was meeting with thirty other women "in the name of Jesus," Peterson asked whether they had left Muhammad. "Of course, brother," she replied, "we need the gospel." One candidate for the Kurdish parliament agreed. "We have to do something for the women," he said. "The refugee women are being driven to prostitution to feed their children. It is our shame. It is the fruit of Muhammad; Islam shows no mercy to a woman once she is soiled. There is no salvation for her."[10]

But there is salvation for everyone in Jesus. When we have a deep sense of our own personal sin against God—seeing how sinful we really are—we may fully grasp the wonder of his grace for us in Christ. Only then do we know how large our debt was—the debt of sin that could be canceled only at Calvary. Only then do we know how many of our sins Jesus had to pay for when he died on the cross. And only then do we know the great debt of love that we now owe to God.

FAITH COMES FIRST

It is absolutely crucial to get these things in the right order. First comes the forgiveness of our sins through Christ's death on the cross; then comes our grateful response of love for Jesus.

Throughout this passage Jesus has been reasoning from love (or lack thereof) back to forgiveness (or its absence). But the forgiveness must come first. Sometimes the wording of verse 47 gives people the impression that it was the other way around, that it was the woman's love that led Jesus to forgive her: "her sins are forgiven—for she loved much" (Luke 7:47). The word "for" almost seems to suggest that her love was the cause of her forgiveness. Sometimes people get the same impression from the verse that follows, in which Jesus "said to her, 'Your sins are forgiven'" (Luke 7:48). Indeed, Roman Catholic theologians use this passage to argue that justification is not by faith alone, but by love combined with faith.[11] However, this interpretation goes against the sense of the entire passage. The woman did not earn forgiveness by her love. No, the point of the parable and of

10. James Peterson, "InterView," *Pulse* (Feb. 19, 1999), 5.
11. See Robert A. Sungenis, *Not By Faith Alone: The Biblical Evidence for the Catholic Doctrine of Justification* (Santa Barbara: Queenship, 1996), 203–6.

everything else Jesus said to Simon was that her love was the proof of her prior forgiveness.

This is confirmed by the grammar of verse 47. Here the word "for" has the sense of "seeing that," as the Greek allows. And when Jesus says that the woman's sins "are forgiven," he uses the perfect tense. He is talking about something that has already happened. He does not say when or how. Presumably the woman had been in contact with him and come under the influence of his teaching. But however it happened, her actions proved that she was forgiven. The Jerusalem Bible offers a helpful translation: "For this reason I tell you that her sins, her many sins, must have been forgiven, or she would not have shown such great love." Her love was not the cause of her forgiveness, but its confirmation.

Why, then, did Jesus tell the woman in verse 48 that her sins were forgiven? If she was already forgiven—and her actions proved that she was—then why did Jesus say it again? He may have done this to reassure the woman that she truly was forgiven. Sometimes sinners have trouble believing that God really does have grace for them, so Jesus said it again. The Bible does the same thing for us whenever we doubt that we can be forgiven. To help us know for sure that we are forgiven in Christ, it reminds us that "if we confess our sins, he is faithful and just to forgive us our sins and to cleanse us from all unrighteousness" (1 John 1:9).

Yet there is another reason why Jesus may have announced that the woman was forgiven: to show the other people who were there that he had the authority to forgive sins. J. C. Ryle calls verse 48 "a public and authoritative declaration" of forgiveness.[12] Whether this is what Jesus had in mind or not, what he said certainly attracted people's attention: "Then those who were at table with him began to say among themselves, 'Who is this, who even forgives sins?'" (Luke 7:49; cf. 5:21). When Jesus said that the woman's sins were forgiven, there was a buzz of astonishment around the table. People were surprised, not so much because they did not think the woman needed or deserved to be forgiven, but because they could not believe that Jesus had the authority to forgive her sins. As Hannah Arendt has said, "It is his insistence on the 'power to forgive,' even more than his performance

12. J. C. Ryle, *Expository Thoughts on the Gospels, Luke* (1858; reprint Cambridge: James Clarke, 1976), 1:242.

of miracles, that shocks the people."[13] Who did Jesus think he was? The question they asked is one of those gospel questions that invite us to make a response: who is this Jesus? He is God the Son, and therefore he has the divine right to forgive sinners. Once again, Luke is helping us know for sure that Jesus is the Christ.

Any lingering doubts we may have about the relationship between faith, love, and forgiveness are resolved in the final verse of the passage, where Jesus says, "Your faith has saved you; go in peace" (Luke 7:50; cf. Rom. 5:1). Having justified the woman by faith, Jesus sent her away in peace to serve God. This is a key verse, because Luke wrote his Gospel to show how Jesus came "to seek and to save the lost" (Luke 19:10). Here is a perfect example. To "save" is to do everything necessary to rescue us from our fallen situation. So how was this woman saved? Why were her sins forgiven? On what basis did she receive eternal life? Not by the merit of her love, but by the trust of her faith. The love came later, as a response to her forgiveness. But she was saved by faith.

This clarifies the true biblical way of salvation. God does not ask us to prove our love for him before he will save us. No, he offers forgiveness as a free gift of his love. Then, once our sins are forgiven, the right and natural response is for us to love him in return. It is not the love we show for Jesus that causes him to forgive us; it is his forgiveness that causes us to love.

Have your sins been forgiven through faith in Jesus Christ? If so, then what extravagant love are you showing Jesus in return? John Newton is famous for writing "Amazing Grace," which is a hymn of gratitude for sins forgiven. But Newton did not find it easy to love Jesus, any more than most of us do. "So much forgiven, so little, little love," he wrote just a few weeks before composing his famous hymn. "So many mercies, so few returns. Such great privileges, and a life so sadly below them."[14]

Most Christians feel like John Newton sometimes: loveless towards our loving and forgiving Savior. But there are ways for us to show more love to Jesus. Not by kissing him, or anointing him with perfume, or wiping his feet with our hair, perhaps, but there are other ways. We can do it by

13. Hannah Arendt, *The Human Condition* (Chicago: University of Chicago Press, 1958), 239.

14. John Newton, quoted in Steve Turner, *Amazing Grace: The Story of America's Most Beloved Song* (New York: HarperCollins, 2002), 110.

singing his praise with passion. We can do it by speaking words of affection to Jesus in prayer. We can do it by telling him that we are sorry for our many, many sins. And we can do it by reaching out to other sinners who need his grace—people no one else would touch. This is the debt we owe for all the sins that God has forgiven: not just tears and perfume, but lives poured out in love for Jesus.

29

THE PARABLE OF PARABLES

Luke 8:1–15

> *"A sower went out to sow his seed. . . . And some fell into good soil*
> *and grew and yielded a hundredfold." As he said these things, he*
> *called out, "He who has ears to hear, let him hear." (Luke 8:5, 8)*

Everyone loved Jesus (with the exception of a few Pharisees, scribes, and Sadducees). In the early days of his public ministry, large crowds followed him everywhere he went. But he was especially popular among women. Indeed, there has never been a man whose personality and teaching were more attractive to women than Jesus Christ.

From the beginning of his Gospel, Luke has paid special attention to the women whose lives were transformed by the coming of Christ. He introduced us to barren old Elizabeth, who trusted God for the gift of a son. He gave us a window into the soul of Mary, who sang Jesus his lullabies. He showed us salvation through the eyes of Anna, who waited for Christ at the temple. He documented the miracles that Jesus performed for Peter's mother-in-law and the widow of Nain. He poured perfume on the pages of his Gospel by introducing the sinful woman at the Pharisee's house.

Is it any wonder that these women loved Jesus? He satisfied their heart's desires with the gift of salvation. He had compassion on them in sickness and sorrow. He forgave their sins. In response, they became some of his first and most devoted disciples. Indeed, Burgon notes that "no woman is mentioned as speaking against our Lord in His life, or having a share in His death. On the contrary, He was anointed by a woman for His burial;—women were the last at His grave and the first at his resurrection;—to a woman He first appeared when He rose again;—women ministered to His wants;—women bewailed and lamented Him; a heathen woman interceded for His life with her husband, Pilate;—and, above all, of a woman He was born."[1]

THE WOMEN WHO SUPPORTED JESUS

Women are mentioned again at the beginning of chapter 8, where Luke tells us that Jesus "went on through cities and villages, proclaiming and bringing the good news of the kingdom of God. And the twelve were with him, and also some women" (Luke 8:1–2).

Jesus was on a preaching tour, fulfilling his mission to preach the gospel to the lost sinners of Israel. Town by town, he preached the good news of the kingdom of God. As usual, he had his entourage with him—loyal followers who helped him in his ministry and tried to learn as much as they could along the way. The twelve disciples were there, of course. These were the men Jesus had chosen to mentor in ministry. But there were also some women in the group. Luke thought it important for us to know that there were women near the inner circle of Jesus' disciples. He describes them as "some women who had been healed of evil spirits and infirmities," and he mentions three of them by name: "Mary, called Magdalene, from whom seven demons had gone out, and Joanna, the wife of Chuza, Herod's household manager, and Susanna, and many others, who provided for them out of their means" (Luke 8:2–3).

All of these women had experienced the saving power of Jesus Christ. Mary Magdalene had been possessed by seven demons—fallen angels who preyed upon her spiritual weakness and bent her will to their evil purpose. Many people have speculated about Mary's past, and she has often been accused of sexual immorality, but there is nothing about this in the Bible. All we know is that Jesus delivered her from demons. He

---

1. John William Burgon, in J. C. Ryle, *Expository Thoughts on the Gospels, Luke* (1858; reprint Cambridge: James Clarke, 1976), 2:465.

also delivered Joanna, who had connections at the royal palace, and a woman named Susanna. The Bible does not tell us anything more about how these women came to Christ. It simply tells us that they were healed from their infirmities. This is enough for us to know, because it assures us that Jesus has the power to heal both women and men from the ravages of sin.

The miracles that Jesus performed for these women were only the beginning of his work in their lives. He also invited them to learn from his teaching ministry. This was remarkable, because in those days rabbis generally did not teach women; theology was only for men. But Jesus wanted to do more for these women than forgive their sins: he wanted to disciple their minds. To that end, he instructed them in his Word.

These women, in turn, supported Jesus in his public ministry. This was necessary, because Jesus and his disciples owned almost nothing. They had nowhere to live, and as they traveled around Israel, they had no way to provide for their daily needs. But in the providence of God, these women supplied what Jesus needed. They may well have had a fair amount of money, but whether they were wealthy or not, they put what they had at Jesus' disposal. They wanted everyone to hear the good news of God's grace.

This shows that there is more than one way for a woman to show her love for Jesus Christ. Some women are called to anoint Jesus' feet, like the sinful woman at the Pharisee's house. There is a place for their love in the church—a place for adoring Jesus with the sweet perfume of extravagant worship, in which mind, heart, soul, and strength are totally absorbed in praising God. But there is also a place for serving Jesus in more practical ways, like paying the bills. This too is loving service for Christ. Whatever God has given us—whether it is the treasure of a loving heart or the gold of earthly gain—we are called to use it for his glory.

The women who followed Jesus served him to the very end. Unlike most of his other disciples, they followed their Savior to the cross and to the grave, before meeting him on the far side of the resurrection. None of them ever denied Jesus, which led Norval Geldenhuys to comment: "What a challenge and inspiration it must be for every woman to consider that, while nowhere in the four Gospels is mention made of any women who were hostile to Jesus, there are numerous references to ministration and marks of honor which they accorded Him."[2] The faithfulness of these worthy women is an example for every disciple. As we have the opportunity, and according to our gifts, we are called to share God's Word, pray for the ministry of those who preach the gospel, and give money to support Christian workers. As you follow Jesus, support the work of his Word in the world.

THE PARABLE OF THE SOILS

The women who provided for Jesus were devoted to his teaching—the kind of teaching we find in Luke 8. Jesus had been "bringing the good news of the kingdom of God" (Luke 8:1; cf. 4:43), and as he preached, he used an illustration from the world of agriculture:

> And when a great crowd was gathered and people from town after town came to him, he said in a parable: "A sower went out to sow his seed. And as he sowed, some fell along the path and was trampled underfoot, and the birds of the air devoured it. And some fell on the rock, and as it grew up, it withered away, because it had no moisture. And some fell among thorns, and the thorns grew up with it and choked it. And some fell into good soil and grew and yielded a hundredfold." As he said these things, he called out, "He who has ears to hear, let him hear." (Luke 8:4–8)

This is the first major parable in Luke's Gospel. We have already encountered one or two shorter parables, like the house on the sand (Luke 6:46–49) and the story of the two debtors (Luke 7:41–43), but this is the longest parable so far. In a way, it is the mother of all parables because Jesus used it to explain why he spoke in parables, and what they were supposed to accomplish in the lives of the people who heard them.

This particular parable is often called "The Parable of the Sower," because the sower seems to be the main character. It was a familiar scene in ancient Israel: a farmer with a bag of grain slung over his shoulder, rhythmically moving his arm back and forth, casting seed on the ground. In fact, the crowd may have been watching someone sow right then and there, while

---

2. Norval Geldenhuys, *The Gospel of Luke*, New International Commentary on the New Testament (Grand Rapids: Eerdmans, 1951), 239.

they were listening to Jesus. But as we shall see, the parable is about the seed and the soil as much as it is about the sower.

There are two steps in understanding any parable: first interpretation, then application. First we need to understand what the parable means, then we need to put it into practice. But interpretation always comes first. Since the disciples were new to all this, they came right out and asked Jesus for an explanation: "And when his disciples asked him what this parable meant, he said, 'To you it has been given to know the secrets of the kingdom of God, but for others they are in parables, so that "seeing they may not see, and hearing they may not understand"'" (Luke 8:9–10).

This explanation challenges the conventional wisdom about parables. People usually think of them as stories Jesus told to make it easier to understand the kingdom of God, and sometimes that is exactly what the parables do. That is not their usual purpose, however. Sometimes they actually *prevent* people from understanding the kingdom of God. The stories are easy enough to follow, but their meaning is much harder to discern. If we define a parable as "an earthly story with a heavenly meaning," it is the heavenly part that is hard to understand.

Jesus went so far as to describe his parables as "secrets of the kingdom of God" (Luke 8:10). The word "secret" suggests that parables conceal as well as reveal. In the Bible, a secret (or a "mystery," as it is sometimes translated) is not something only God knows, but something he has also revealed to his people. It is something about salvation that no one would know anything about unless God revealed it. But now that God *has* revealed it, it is more like an open secret.

In this case, Jesus told his disciples that they had been "given" the secrets of the kingdom, and then he explained the parable. He gave his disciples the gift of saving knowledge. But Jesus did not give this gift to everyone. Not everyone was in on the secret. Indeed, the very same parable that gave the disciples knowledge of the kingdom also kept some people from knowing Christ. The reason Jesus taught in parables was so that some people would not understand. By way of explanation, Jesus quoted the prophet Isaiah, who said: "Keep on hearing, but do not understand; keep on seeing, but do not perceive" (Isa. 6:9). In the context of Isaiah's ministry, people had rebelled against God's word, and as part of his judgment against their sin, God would harden them in their unbelief. According to the mysterious and sovereign will of God, some people are given to understand, and some are not. Understanding the parables requires spiritual discernment, which only comes from the Holy Spirit working in a person's life. Thus the parables have a twofold purpose: they teach spiritual truth to people who believe in Jesus, and at the same time they deliberately harden unbelievers in their unbelief. The same parable has different effects on different people, and what makes the difference is the grace of God and faith in Jesus Christ through the Holy Spirit.

Another way to say this is that the parables discriminate. God uses them to differentiate between those who are inside and those who are outside his kingdom. At the time Jesus began to teach in parables, huge crowds were following him. But how many people were there to listen—really listen—to what Jesus had to say? People were following him for all kinds of reasons. Because the parables were so enigmatic, they would reveal the difference between people who were there only to be entertained, and people (like the disciples) who were willing to make the effort to understand spiritual truth. As Leon Morris explains it, Jesus was looking "for more than a superficial adherence, so He intensified His use of parables, stories which yielded their meaning only to those who were prepared to search for them. The parables demand thought and spiritual earnestness. They separate the sincere seeker from the casual hearer."[3] We should not be surprised, therefore, when some people fail to grasp the clear meaning of a parable that can only be understood by faith. From the beginning, it was Jesus' intention that the parables would harden some people in their unbelief, while at the same time they would help other people understand his kingdom.

BAD SOIL

Having explained the general purpose of his parables, Jesus began to interpret the parable of the soils. He said, "Now the parable is this: The seed is the word of God" (Luke 8:11). Immediately we know that this parable (unlike some of the parables) is a kind of allegory. There is a direct connection between the down-to-earth details of the parable and deep spiritual

3. Leon Morris, *The Gospel According to St. Luke: An Introduction and Commentary*, Tyndale New Testament Commentaries (Grand Rapids: Eerdmans, 1974), 150.

truths. The seed represents the word of God, which implies that the sower is God himself, or perhaps one of the men who preaches his gospel.

Like a seed, the good news about Jesus Christ has the power of life in it, and under the right conditions of the heart, it will spring up to salvation. But the conditions have to be right, and whether the seed will grow or not depends on where it falls. Not everyone is equally receptive to the word of God. In order to show this, Jesus compared four kinds of people to four kinds of soil (or else two kinds of soil—good and bad—with the bad soil described three different ways). Each soil represents a different condition of the heart, a different response to the gospel, and a different destiny. Sadly, only one of the four ever bears any good spiritual fruit.

The first kind of heart is *hard and indifferent.* Jesus said, "The ones along the path are those who have heard. Then the devil comes and takes away the word from their hearts, so that they may not believe and be saved" (Luke 8:12). Here Jesus draws on a common experience for farmers in those days, when footpaths often cut right through their fields. Inevitably, some of their seed fell on hard pathways, where it never had a chance to germinate. Before long, it was trampled by passersby or became easy prey for hungry birds.

The same thing happens when the word of God falls on the heart of a hardened sinner: it never penetrates the mind, or touches the conscience, or enters the heart. It just seems to go in one ear and out the other. Such a heart is not prepared to receive the gospel. Before God's word has a chance to do any spiritual good, the devil swoops down like an angry old crow to snatch it away (which is easy to do when someone's heart is so hard).

This explains why some people can hear the gospel many times without ever having it make any impression on them. The problem does not lie in the word itself, or in the way it is presented, but in the hearts of the people who hear it. They may be hardened by bitter experiences in life, or by an unjustified prejudice against God, or by an unwillingness to turn away from their sin, or by cold indifference to spiritual truth. Whatever the reason, God's word never gets into their lives.

They also have someone working against them—a diabolical enemy who will do everything in his power to keep them from thinking about God's word. Notice why the devil does this: "so that they may not believe and be saved" (Luke 8:12). If he could, Satan would prevent everyone from ever hearing the gospel. He knows that hearing the gospel brings salvation, which is the last thing he wants to see. Also notice when the devil does this. He does it as soon as the word is preached, for Jesus said: "*Then* the devil comes and takes away the word" (Luke 8:12). Whenever the seed is sown, the devil is at work to steal it right from the hearers' hearts. He knows that if he waits, the person who hears God's word might think about it long enough to believe it and come to Christ. In order to prevent this from happening, he snatches the seed before it has a chance to grow. Nowhere is Satan more active in doing this than in a church that preaches the gospel. J. C. Ryle wrote:

> Nowhere does he labor so hard to stop the progress of that which is good, and to prevent men and women being saved. From him come wandering thoughts and roving imaginations,—listless minds and dull memories,— sleepy eyes and fidgety nerves,—weary ears and distracted attention. In all these things Satan has a great hand. People wonder where they come from, and marvel how it is that they find sermons so dull, and remember them so badly! They forget the parable of the sower. They forget the devil.[4]

Be sure not to forget the devil! Ask God to soften the hard ground of your heart so that you can take in the word, believe it before the devil stops you, and be saved.

More Bad Soil

A second kind of heart is *shallow and superficial.* Jesus said, "And the ones on the rock are those who, when they hear the word, receive it with joy. But these have no root; they believe for a while, and in time of testing fall away" (Luke 8:13). This, too, was a common difficulty for Palestinian farmers. In many places they had only a few inches of soil to work with before they reached the bedrock. A plant may grow in such conditions, sometimes quite rapidly, but it will not survive. The soil simply is not deep enough to sustain life. The plant cannot get enough moisture, so when the hot desert sun comes out, it will shrivel and die.

The same thing happens when some people hear the gospel. They are happy to hear it, and at first the word seems to give them life. They have a kind of faith. In some sense they believe in Christ, at least for a little

4. J. C. Ryle, *Luke*, 1:250–51.

while, and they seem to be full of joy. But it cannot last because they are not rooted. Soon trouble comes and they fall away from the Christian faith, or, to use the proper term for it, they "apostatize." What seemed to be a commitment to Christ turns out not to have been faith at all, because true saving faith perseveres. When it is tested in the burning heat, it does not wither, but as Peter said, it comes out shining like pure gold (1 Peter 1:7).

This helps us see how important it is to be honest about the hardships of the Christian life. When we first come to Christ, we may have so much joy that it is easy to imagine all our troubles are over. We need to know, therefore, that in following Christ we are walking in the footsteps of a suffering Savior. Times of testing are bound to come, and if we are not rooted in the gospel of the cross, our shallow and superficial faith will fail.

This also helps us see how important it is to become a disciple in the true biblical sense. Making a so-called decision for Christ can be the first step in a life of faith, but if that is all that ever happens, it quickly becomes apparent that we are not really Christians. According to Jesus, there is a kind of believing that springs up very quickly and enthusiastically, but does not endure because it never takes root in the gospel. The problem is not the enthusiasm, of course. There is real excitement in coming to Christ because it changes our whole perspective on everything. Furthermore, the gospel demands an emotional response, bringing feelings of deep, true joy. But these feelings alone are not sufficient. What we need is a firm grasp on the realities of Christ's saving work: his death on the cross and his resurrection from the grave. The only faith that endures is one that is based on who Jesus is and what he has done, not one that is based on how we happen to feel.

It is often surprising to see how far some people seem to go in the Christian life before falling away. Yet it has always been this way. Back in the third century Cyril of Alexandria lamented the way some people "joyfully receive instruction," yet "when they go out of the churches, at once they forget the sacred doctrines and go about in their customary course, not having stored up within themselves any thing for their future benefit. . . . When persecution troubles them and the enemies of the truth attack the churches of the Savior, their heart does not love the battle, and their mind throws away the shield and flees."[5]

5. Cyril of Alexandria, "Commentary on Luke" (Homily 41), in *Luke*, ed. Arthur A. Just Jr., Ancient Christian Commentary on Scripture, NT 3 (Downers Grove, IL: InterVarsity, 2003), 134.

J. C. Ryle observed the same thing when he was preaching in Liverpool back in the nineteenth century:

> It is quite possible to feel great pleasure, or deep alarm, under the preaching of the Gospel, and yet to be utterly destitute of the grace of God. The tears of some hearers of sermons, and the extravagant delight of others, are no certain marks of conversion. We may be warm admirers of favourite preachers, and yet remain nothing better than stony-ground hearers. Nothing should content us but a deep, humbling, self-mortifying work of the Holy Ghost, and a heart-union with Christ.[6]

It happens all the time: people who once seemed very excited about Christianity fall away from the faith. A high school student who was enthusiastic about going to youth group falls in with a bad crowd. A girl who grew up in Sunday school goes off to college and starts sleeping with her boyfriend. A couple that went to church when they were dating drifts away after they get married. A man who said he wanted to get serious about spiritual growth gets back into online pornography. A skeptic who seemed to be convinced about the truth of Jesus Christ moves on to another religion, or no religion at all. We pray that people like this will come back to Christ, and some of them probably will. But the sad reality is that some people who seem to believe never get rooted in the gospel. As Helmut Thielicke once wrote, "there is nothing more disintegrating than people who have been merely 'brushed' by Christianity, people who have been sown with a thousand seeds but in whose lives there is no depth and no rootage. Therefore, they fall when the first whirlwind comes along. It is half-Christians who always flop in the face of the first catastrophe that happens, because their dry intellectuality and their superficial emotionalism do not stand the test."[7]

Do you have a faith that can stand the test? Only if you are holding on to a gospel that goes down more than two inches deep. Otherwise, what you think is faith will fail and you will fall away the first time you face any real difficulty in the Christian life. Trouble is the test of true Christian faith. When troubles come, the rootless will fall away, but faithful Christians will grow stronger through their pain.

6. Ryle, *Luke,* 1:252.
7. Helmut Thielicke, quoted in R. Kent Hughes, *Luke: That You May Know the Truth,* 2 vols., Preaching the Word (Wheaton, IL: Crossway, 1998), 1:290.

THREE BAD WEEDS

There is a third kind of heart that seems to grow even faster than the others, but still never bears any good spiritual fruit. This kind of heart is *preoccupied and distracted*. Jesus said, "And as for what fell among the thorns, they are those who hear, but as they go on their way they are choked by the cares and riches and pleasures of life, and their fruit does not mature" (Luke 8:14). Every gardener has seen this happen. Good plants never seem to grow as fast as weeds, and sometimes weeds take over the whole garden. Vegetable plants have trouble getting the sunlight that they need to grow, and as a result, they never produce any good fruit. Whatever fruit they do produce is immature, and therefore useless.

The same thing can happen spiritually. Jesus mentioned three weeds that choke off spiritual growth. One is the weed of trouble. Sometimes the cares of life are so distracting that we forget to nurture the life of the soul. We spend so much time worrying about our health, or a family conflict, or a work situation that we fail to give God the service he requires. Our miseries get in the way of ministry.

But Jesus did not stop there. He went on to say that the *good* things in life can be just as distracting as the bad things. It is not just our toils and cares that stunt our growth, but also our riches and pleasures. Taking a vacation, buying a car, remodeling our home—these things are all good in themselves, but they easily distract us from the kind of sacrificial obedience that helps us to grow in Christ. J. C. Ryle wisely said:

> The things of this life form one of the greatest dangers which beset a Christian's path. The money, the pleasures, the daily business of the world, are so many traps to catch souls. Thousands of things, which in themselves are innocent, become, when followed to excess, little better than soul-poisons, and helps to hell. Open sin is not the only thing that ruins souls. In the midst of our families, and in the pursuit of our lawful callings, we have need to be on our guard. Except we watch and pray, these temporal things may rob us of heaven, and smother every sermon we hear. We may live and die thorny-ground hearers.[8]

There are many examples of this in the Bible. Consider Esau, who sold his birthright for a bowl of stew (see Gen. 25:29–34), or Demas, whose

8. Ryle, *Luke*, 1:252–53.

love for this world caused him to leave the mission field (see 2 Tim. 4:10). The same thing can happen to us. Like the people in the parable, we hear the word of God, but we are preoccupied with the cares of life. Or we are distracted by the endless opportunities we have for immediate gratification and the incessant buzz of entertainment media. We turn on the TV instead of opening our Bibles. We get on the Internet instead of having a meaningful conversation with a friend. We go out and have fun with people we enjoy rather than reaching out to someone in pain. The things we do may not be wrong in themselves, but they do not have to be wrong to get in the way of our spiritual growth. We make time for everything else except developing a deeper relationship with Jesus Christ. As a result, we never become the men and women that God is calling us to become. If we bear any fruit at all, it "does not mature," as Jesus said, and is of little use to the kingdom of God.

GOOD HEART, GOOD FRUIT

There are so many things that can get in the way of growing good spiritual fruit. William Cowper wrote about this in a poem called "The Sower":

The seed that finds a stony soil,
   Shoots forth a hasty blade;
But ill repays the sower's toil,
   Soon withered, scorched, and dead.

The thorny ground is sure to balk
   All hopes of harvest there;
We find a tall and sickly stalk,
   But not the fruitful ear.

The beaten path and high-way side
   Receive the trust in vain;
The watchful birds the spoil divide,
   And pick up all the grain.[9]

9. William Cowper, "The Sower," in *Chapters into Verse: Poetry in English Inspired by the Bible*, vol. 2: *Gospels to Revelation*, ed. Robert Atwan and Laurance Wieder (Oxford: Oxford University Press, 1993), 94.

Given all the bad things that can happen to good seed, it seems almost amazing that anything ever grows at all. But good fruit does grow. As Cowper also wrote:

But where the Lord of grace and power
    Has blessed the happy field;
How plenteous is the golden store
    The deep-wrought furrows yield!

Jesus ended his parable with a golden harvest from the last and best kind of soil—a heart that is *good and fruitful.* He said, "As for that in the good soil, they are those who, hearing the word, hold it fast in an honest and good heart, and bear fruit with patience" (Luke 8:15). When good seed is sown in good soil, it yields an abundant harvest—what Jesus described back in verse 8 as "a hundredfold."

A good heart is not so hardened by sin that Satan can snatch away the good seed of God's word. It is not so shallow that it withers in the heat of persecution. It is not so distracted that it gets choked off by life's troubles and pleasures. Instead, it stays rooted in the word of God, and as a result, it bears a bountiful harvest.

Notice how Jesus described this kind of heart. It is a heart that holds on to God's word: reading it regularly, believing what it says about sin and salvation, and living in obedience to its commands. This heart is also an honest heart—one that is sincere in its desire to grow in the knowledge of God. It is a good heart—one that has been made good by the grace of God. It is a patient heart—one that perseveres through life's trials without giving up on God. Such a heart will *always* bear good fruit, because when it is planted in a good heart, the good seed of God's word grows a harvest of love, patience, righteousness, and all the other fruits of godliness.

Knowing this encourages us to keep sharing God's word. Will everyone listen to it? Will everyone believe it and grow by it? No, depending on where the word falls, it may or may not grow. Some people would not even listen to Jesus himself, so it should not surprise us if they do not listen to us either. But we are called to keep sharing the gospel. In one of his sermons on this passage, Charles Spurgeon made this point in the strongest possible terms:

What the minister has to do, is to go forth in his Master's name and scatter precious truth. If he knew where the best soil was to be found, perhaps he might limit himself to that which had been prepared by the plough of conviction. But not knowing men's hearts, it is his business to preach the gospel to every creature—to throw a handful on that hard heart yonder, and another handful on that overgrown heart, which is full of cares and riches and pleasures of this world. He has to leave the fate of the seed in the care of the Master who gave it to him, for well he understands that he is not responsible for the harvest, he is only responsible for the care, the fidelity, and the integrity with which he scatters the seed, right and left with both his hands. . . . We are bound to preach the gospel, whether men will hear, or whether they will forbear. Let men's hearts be what they may, I am not loosed from my obligation to sow the seed on the rock as well as in the furrow, on the highway as well as in the ploughed field.[10]

Yet the parable ends with the good news that as we sow the gospel, some people will believe it and bear good fruit. God is faithful to his word, and in the end he will have his harvest. Simon Kistemaker comments:

The emphasis of the parable is the farmer's ups and downs in growing a crop. He may lose his crop, in this case three times, but in the end reap an abundant harvest. In the same way, missionaries, evangelists, and pastors are keenly aware of hardened hearts, hostile responses, and dismal failures among their hearers. But convinced of the innate power of God's Word, they continue to preach and, consequently, expect an astonishing harvest. The parable assures gospel preachers and teachers of growing success in spite of the fact that some of their hearers reject the message of salvation.[11]

Like the other parables, the parable of the soils searches our hearts. As Jesus talks about the different kinds of soil, and the different spiritual conditions they represent, we recognize that we are all in this parable somewhere. This should cause us to ask some serious questions: "How am I responding to God's word? Is my heart like shallow ground, or am I deeply rooted in the grace of God? Are pain and pleasure distracting me from the work that

10. Charles H. Spurgeon, "The Parable of the Sower," *The New Park Street Pulpit* (1861; reprint Pasadena, TX: Pilgrim, 1975), 6:173–74.
11. Simon Kistemaker, *The Parables: Understanding the Stories Jesus Told* (Grand Rapids: Baker, 1980), 37.

God wants to do in my life? Am I doing anything to help people hear the gospel, like the worthy women who supported Jesus in his public ministry? What is the real condition of my heart?"

Usually when people listen to a sermon they make some kind of evaluation. "I thought that was a really good sermon," they say, or perhaps they say that it wasn't very good at all. Either way, the sermon is what they want to assess. But according to the parable of the soils, it is really God's word that evaluates *us*, because the way we respond shows what is in our hearts. Good hearing is just as important as good preaching. If the gospel is truly preached, then what we say about the sermon says more about us than it does about the sermon. He who has ears to hear, let him hear.

30

JUST DO IT

Luke 8:16–21

"Take care then how you hear, for to the one who has, more will be given, and from the one who has not, even what he thinks that he has will be taken away." (Luke 8:18)

he opening ceremonies of the 2002 Winter Olympics in Salt Lake City were an amazing spectacle of sound and light. A worldwide television audience watched as thousands of singers, skaters, and other performers presented a pageant of the American West from its native inhabitants to the pioneers, the transcontinental railroad, and beyond.

One of the most captivating aspects of the celebration was the participation of young performers called "the children of light." First a boy in pioneer costume skated into the darkened stadium with a single lantern. He was followed by hundreds of other children, who carried bright lights and danced on the ice like stars in the moonlight. In keeping with the Olympiad's theme of "Light the Fire Within," these children of light represented the joy of life and the world's bright hope for the future.

The children also awakened echoes of eternity. In their glory, they were a reflection of God's promise in the gospel that people who believe in Jesus

Christ will become "children of light" (John 12:36 KJV). It was only a pale reflection, of course, because the Olympics make a poor substitute for the gospel. But as they grasped for transcendence, the opening ceremonies awakened a desire that only Jesus can satisfy—our desire to become the bright and glorious children of God.

The twin themes of light and children are brought together in two small episodes that appear side by side in the Gospel of Luke: a proverb about a lamp under a jar and a statement Jesus made about membership in his family. Together these incidents show that the true children of light are people who do what Jesus says.

THIS LITTLE LIGHT OF MINE

Jesus had just been speaking about the importance of good listening. He had many followers in those days, but not all of them were receiving his word by faith. So he told a parable that discriminated between good listeners and bad listeners. According to the parable of the soils, although some have good hearts, others are too hard, or too shallow, or too distracted to grow in the gospel. "He who has ears to hear," Jesus said, "let him hear" (Luke 8:8).

This is one of the first and most basic lessons of Christian discipleship. The disciples were still in spiritual kindergarten, and the main thing children learn in kindergarten is how to listen to their teacher. If the disciples never learned to listen, then everything else that Jesus had to teach them would be useless. How can we do what Jesus wants us to do unless first we hear what he has to tell us?

To make sure that his disciples learned this lesson well, Jesus added further application to the parable of the soils. He said to them: "No one after lighting a lamp covers it with a jar or puts it under a bed, but puts it on a stand, so that those who enter may see the light. For nothing is hidden that will not be made manifest, nor is anything secret that will not be known and come to light. Take care then how you hear, for to the one who has, more will be given, and from the one who has not, even what he thinks that he has will be taken away" (Luke 8:16–18).

These verses are puzzling, which reminds us that spiritual truth is spiritually discerned, and that this requires the help of the Holy Spirit. What did Jesus mean by this proverb or miniparable about the lamp under the jar?

369

The general point is that if you have something useful—like a lamp, for example—you use it! You do not cover it with a jar or hide it under a bed. If you did, it would not give off any light, which would be pointless. It would be like fixing dinner and then scraping it into the garbage disposal, or buying a car and then locking it away in the garage, or getting an exercise bike and never riding it. It wouldn't make any sense! If you get something to use, you use it, and use it properly. The way to use a lamp, of course, is to put it up on a stand where it can illuminate the entire house.

There is still some question as to what Jesus meant by the lamp. Was he referring to the light of his own teaching? This would fit in with what Luke has already said about Jesus coming as a "light to those who sit in darkness" (Luke 1:79) and "light for revelation to the Gentiles" (Luke 2:32). Or was he talking about the calling his disciples had to shine the gospel around the world? That is certainly the point of the proverb in Matthew, where Jesus says, "In the same way, let your light shine before others, so that they may see your good works and give glory to your Father who is in heaven" (Matt. 5:16).

This image occurs frequently in the Bible. The people of God are bright lights in a dark world, showing the way to God. The missionary focus seems to be somewhat less prominent in Luke, however, where the context is hearing and doing God's word. Jesus had just told his disciples that if they had good hearts, they would hold on to his word and bear good fruit. But they needed to put his word into practice. Like the lamp in a house, the truth of the gospel was meant to be put to use; it was never intended to be hidden away. The main point of this image is utility. Now that the disciples had heard the truth, what were they going to do with it?

Sadly, many people hear God's word without ever having it make any difference in their lives. As we learned from the parable of the soils, people can hear the good news about Jesus Christ and yet fail to bear any good spiritual fruit. By telling the proverb of the hidden lamp, Jesus was making a further application. Some people hear the gospel again and again, but when it comes to glorifying God, they are as useless as a lamp under a jar. They may even claim to be Christians, but they keep their so-called Christianity to themselves, and what good is that?

It is not enough to say or think that we are Christians. The question is: Are we really living the Christian life? J. C. Ryle said, "The Gospel which we possess was not given us only to be admired, talked of, and professed,—but to be practiced. It was not meant merely to reside in our intellect, and memories, and tongues,—but to be seen in our lives."[1] It's like the old children's song based on this passage: "This little light of mine, I'm gonna let it shine. This little light of mine, I'm gonna let it shine." And then the verse that follows: "Hide it under a bushel? No! I'm gonna let it shine!" Even on the lips of a preschooler, the song is a defiant manifesto. It expresses a bold commitment to living for Jesus in an open and obvious way.

To do this, we need to make good use of the truths that we know from Scripture. We make use of the law by confessing our sins, and we make use of the gospel by trusting in Jesus Christ. We make use of the doctrine of election by living with humility, remembering that there is nothing in us to deserve God's grace. We make use of the doctrine of justification by living free from any attempt to improve our standing with God, resting instead in the finished work of Jesus Christ. We make use of the doctrine of sanctification by growing in practical holiness—learning to live with the charity, purity, and generosity that Jesus showed us by his example. We make use of the doctrine of perseverance by remaining steadfast under trial. We make use of the doctrine of glorification by waiting in hope for Christ's return.

These are only examples, of course. The point is that if we know the truth, we are called to live by it. Every time we learn something from the Word of God, we should consider specific ways to put it to work in our daily lives. If Jesus has illuminated us with the gospel, it is time for us to shine.

USE IT OR LOSE IT

What happens if we *don't* make good use of what God has revealed to us in Jesus Christ? The lamp under the jar shows how absurd this would be, but we still need to ask the question, because some people hear about Jesus without ever responding in faith and obedience. What will happen to them in the end? According to Jesus, they will not get away with ignoring the Word of God forever, but will be held strictly accountable: "For nothing is hidden that will not be made manifest, nor is anything secret that will not be known and come to light" (Luke 8:17).

1. J. C. Ryle, *Expository Thoughts on the Gospels, Luke* (1858; reprint Cambridge: James Clarke, 1976), 1:256–57.

Everyone admits that this is a difficult verse, but not everyone agrees how it should be interpreted. Jesus is still using the idea of a hidden light, but he has changed the metaphor to make a different but related point. Some interpreters say that verse 17 is about the message of his gospel, which was hidden during the earthly ministry of Jesus Christ, but came to light after his death and resurrection. The secrets of salvation in Christ—secrets that Jesus shared only with his closest friends—were concealed for a time, but later revealed through the ministry of the apostles.[2]

That interpretation may be possible. However, it seems more likely that rather than making a historical-theological point about the manifestation of the gospel, Jesus is still making a practical point about hearing and obeying his word. People can fool themselves into thinking that they are standing in the faith, at least for a little while. But are they shining with the light of the gospel?

Eventually the real truth will come out. In a universe that is governed by an all-seeing and all-knowing God, nothing can be hidden forever. Michael Wilcock says, "It is impossible anyway permanently to hide where one stands in relation to the gospel. What is hidden will come out sooner or later—that is, it will if it is really there. The danger is . . . that the man who thinks he has received the gospel, and keeps it hidden and never lets the fact be known, may find one of these days, when he comes to look for the reality of the gospel within him, that it is not in fact there—and never was."[3]

When Jesus spoke about secrets coming to light, he may have been referring to the final judgment. The Bible says, "God will bring every deed into judgment, with every secret thing, whether good or evil" (Eccl. 12:14). It also describes the final judgment as the day when "God judges the secrets of men by Christ Jesus" (Rom. 2:16). On that awesome day, God will hold us accountable for every word that we have ever heard. Then it will all come out: all the things that we have done and all the things that we have left undone will be exposed. And if we fail to do what God has said in his word—to believe the gospel, for example, or to keep the commandments,

---

2. I. Howard Marshall is representative of this view; see *The Gospel of Luke*, New International Greek Testament Commentary (Grand Rapids: Eerdmans, 1978), 330.

3. Michael Wilcock, *The Message of Luke*, The Bible Speaks Today (Downers Grove, IL: Inter-Varsity, 1979), 141–42.

or to fulfill our calling in the world—then eventually this will come to light. If we hide what we have been given, our sins will find us out.

The practical application of this warning is obvious: we need to be very careful how we respond to God's word. As Jesus went on to say in the next verse, "Take care then how you hear, for to the one who has, more will be given, and from the one who has not, even what he thinks that he has will be taken away" (Luke 8:18). Through his parables and proverbs, Jesus had been telling people to make good use of the truth. Now he was saying that if they failed to make good use of it, they would lose the privilege altogether. When it comes to God's word, we either use it or lose it.

To make this point, Jesus drew a contrast between the "haves" and the "have nots." When he spoke about "the one who has," he was not speaking about material prosperity, or even about people who had special gifts and talents. He was speaking about people who listened to him, and were beginning to grasp the secrets of the kingdom of God. He was talking about the kind of people he had described at the end of verse 15—people who hold fast to God's word "in an honest and good heart, and bear fruit with patience" (Luke 8:15). People who make good use of what Jesus says will be given to understand even more of God's truth.

What about the "have nots"? They *think* they know the truth. They claim to be Christians. They go to church. They sit through sermons and receive the sacraments. But they are not living the gospel. Their religion does not do them any good because they are not making good daily use of what they have been given. They are just as angry and selfish and bitter as ever. To use the illustration that Jesus gave, they have taken the light of salvation and hidden it away. Eventually they will be found out, and when that happens, they will lose everything. Norval Geldenhuys says, "While those who listen to Him with a believing, surrendered and obedient heart, will be given a deeper and more intensive insight into the spiritual life and into His Word, the indifferent and disobedient ones will lose even the little measure of spiritual knowledge and joy of life which they possess."[4]

Jesus ended his comparison between the "haves" and the "have nots" with stern words of warning: "from the one who has not, even what he thinks that he has will be taken away" (Luke 8:18). When it comes to spiritual

---

4. Norval Geldenhuys, *The Gospel of Luke*, New International Commentary on the New Testament (Grand Rapids: Eerdmans, 1951), 248.

knowledge, the rich get richer and the poor get poorer. To some extent, Jesus was talking about what happens already in this life. People who do not believe and obey God's word move farther and farther away from the truth. But he was also referring to the final judgment, when people who reject his gospel will lose every last opportunity to hear the word of God.

Does this seem fair? The "haves" keep getting more and more, while the "have nots" lose everything, including everything they thought they had. Whether it seems fair or not, this is the way spiritual knowledge works. As it says in Proverbs, "Give instruction to a wise man, and he will be still wiser; teach a righteous man, and he will increase in learning" (Prov. 9:9). People who put God's word into action grow in Christ, and as a result, they are able to learn more and more of his truth. For example, they begin to share their faith, and as they share their faith, they come to a clearer understanding of the gospel. Or they begin to give their money to Christian work. The more they give, the more they want to give, and eventually they learn that everything they have belongs to the Lord, and is to be used for his glory. Knowledge builds on knowledge, especially when spiritual knowledge is put into practice. Knowing is by doing, and the more we do, the more we are able to know.

On the other hand, if we never do anything with what we know, then we never grow in spiritual knowledge, because we really know only what we use. In this respect, growing in Christ (or *not* growing in Christ, as the case may be) is something like learning a foreign language. People generally do not learn to speak Spanish or Turkish by listening to recordings. The way they really learn the language is by using it in personal conversation. And if they do not keep using it, they quickly forget what they thought they had learned. Spiritual knowledge works the same way: use it or lose it. If we do not put what Jesus says into practice, then even what we have heard will not be of any use, either to us or to anyone else.

This brings us back to the same point of practical application that Jesus has been pressing on us again and again: whenever we hear his word, we are called to believe it and do it. We start by putting our faith in the gospel of Jesus Christ, trusting in his death and resurrection for the forgiveness of our sins and the hope of eternal life. We also accept the Bible—the whole Bible—as the Word of God (see 1 Thess. 2:13). Then we live the kind of life that God has for us in Jesus, obeying the clear commands of Christ. What is the result of all your Scripture reading, Bible study, and attendance at public worship? What spiritual changes is God bringing into your life? In what specific ways are you living out the gospel you say that you believe?

THE CHILDREN OF GOD

At this point Luke introduces an incident that at first might seem to interrupt the flow of the narrative, but actually serves to reinforce the importance of hearing and doing what Jesus says. Luke is up to his usual literary strategy of putting things in pairs, placing them side-by-side to make the same point in two different ways. Here the point is that if we do what Jesus says, we show that we are the true children of God.

Jesus made this point in connection with his own closest relatives, who were trying to contact him: "Then his mother and his brothers came to him, but they could not reach him because of the crowd. And he was told, 'Your mother and your brothers are standing outside, desiring to see you'" (Luke 8:19–20). This gives us a fascinating glimpse into the relationship that Jesus had with his earthly family. Jesus Christ was a real man, with a real mother and brothers and sisters. As we read in the Gospel of Mark, he was "the son of Mary and brother of James and Joses and Judas and Simon," as well as of his sisters, whose names are not recorded (Mark 6:3).

Roman Catholic theologians deny that Jesus had any siblings, claiming instead that the brothers and sisters mentioned in the Gospels were either cousins or stepsiblings. This is because they believe that Mary was a perpetual virgin. If Jesus had any brothers at all, they say, they were the sons of Joseph by a previous marriage. Admittedly, the word that Luke uses for brothers *(adelphoi)* could possibly refer to other relatives, such as cousins or stepbrothers. However, there is no evidence for this anywhere in the Bible. The idea was introduced only later in church history, when people began to give greater prominence to Mary. The most natural meaning of Luke 8:19 and other verses referring to Jesus' earthly family is that he had full brothers and sisters who, like him, were the children of Mary and Joseph.[5]

Jesus loved his family, but his relationship with them was sometimes strained by his identity as God the Son and his calling as the Savior of

---

5. For a fuller discussion of this issue, see Darrell L. Bock, *Luke 1:1–9:50*, Baker Exegetical Commentary on the New Testament 3A (Grand Rapids: Baker, 1994), 752–53.

the world. We saw this when Jesus was twelve, and he stayed behind at the temple after Passover (Luke 2:41–51). His mother was worried sick. She did not realize that Jesus was *supposed* to be in his Father's house, but according to Jesus, she should have realized it. We sense the same family tension at Cana, where Jesus rebuked his mother for pushing him to engage in public ministry before it was time (see John 2:4).

Here we see it again. Jesus' mother and brothers wanted to see Jesus. They wanted to pull him aside. They wanted to talk with him. So they pressed their claim on him as members of his own family. Perhaps they needed his help with a family crisis. Perhaps they were concerned about the hectic pace of his ministry—you know how mothers can worry about a child's health. Perhaps they wanted to get Jesus away from teaching altogether. This is not unlikely. Mark tells us that his family "went out to seize him, for they were saying, 'He is out of his mind'" (Mark 3:21). Mary and the other members of the family were not perfect; they did not always understand Jesus and the mission he was called to fulfill. But whatever their motive, they came to interrupt his ministry.

Jesus took advantage of this opportunity to explain what it meant to belong to the most important family of all: the family of God. When someone came and told him that his mother and brothers were waiting outside, he said, "My mother and my brothers are those who hear the word of God and do it" (Luke 8:21).

This encounter teaches us both a minor lesson and a major lesson. The minor lesson is that our calling in the family of God sometimes has to take precedence over the claims of our earthly families. Jesus had always respected his family. He kept the fifth commandment by honoring his father and mother. He honored her all the way to the cross, when in his dying hour he arranged for her support and care (see John 19:26–27). But even as Jesus recognized the claims of family, he knew that they had their limits, and in this case he refused to be distracted from his calling to preach the word of God. Without disowning his mother and brothers, or showing them any disrespect, or saying anything derogatory about them, he put things into proper perspective. The supremely important thing for him to do was the will of his Father in heaven, and at that moment, the demands of his family on earth were not in line with God's will.

Christians sometimes face the same dilemma. Often the demands of our families coincide with God's will for our lives. We have a God-given duty to love our families and provide for their needs. But there are times when family members demand unreasonable attention, or even when they stand in the way of the ministry that God has called us to do. This kind of conflict is especially common when someone with non-Christian parents gets called to the mission field, or when family members selfishly believe that their needs are the only ones that matter. Thus there are times when the claims of family need to be set aside for the higher calling of our kinship with Christ. This needs to be done lovingly and respectfully, but also clearly and firmly.

The major lesson to draw from Luke 8:21 is that the true members of God's family are the men and women and boys and girls who do what Jesus says; they "hear the word of God *and* do it." This was the main thing that Jesus was saying. He took the request that his family made and used it as an opportunity to explain what it means to belong to the family of God. Thus his comment was not so much directed at his own family as it was to the people who were listening to his teaching. As Darrell Bock explains it, "The remark is not a repudiation of family, as much as it is an endorsement and exhortation to disciples to be receptive to the word."[6]

There is no higher privilege or greater blessing than to belong to the family of God through a relationship with Jesus Christ. This is one of the grand themes of the Bible and one of the great hopes of the soul: to be a son or a daughter of the Most High God. Going back to the Old Testament, this was the special status of Israel: the children of Israel were the children of God (see Rom. 9:4). But in the New Testament the apostle John taught that we become God's children through the regenerating work of the Holy Spirit (John 3:3–5), and he marveled that by the love of God (1 John 3:1), through faith in Jesus Christ, we have the right to become the children of God (John 1:12–13): "The Father himself loves you" (John 16:27).

The apostle Paul spoke not in terms of a new birth, but in terms of adoption. He said that we were "predestined for adoption through Jesus Christ" (Eph. 1:5; cf. Gal. 4:4–5). But like John, Paul said that we become children of God through faith in Jesus Christ (Gal. 3:26). He said that as the sons and daughters of God, we have the Spirit of his Son working in our hearts

6. Bock, *Luke 1:1–9:50*, 751.

(Rom. 8:14–16; Gal. 4:6). He also said that we have a full right to the inheritance of our Father, which is eternal life in Jesus Christ (Rom. 8:17, 29; Gal. 4:7). By the grace of God, we are the children of God, with all the rights and responsibilities that come with belonging to his household. Even if we have no living relatives, or if our earthly families reject us, God still says, "I will be a father to you, and you shall be sons and daughters to me" (2 Cor. 6:18).

We do not gain this high privilege by working our way into the family. Like every other aspect of salvation, adoption is by grace. But there is a way for us to show that we belong to the family of God. There is an unmistakable mark of the family resemblance. As Jesus said, speaking as our elder brother, "My mother and my brothers are those who hear the word of God and do it" (Luke 8:21). The distinguishing feature of the family of God is obedience to the word of Christ.

This fits everything Jesus has been saying about hearing and doing his will. It is not just *saying* that we belong to God's family that makes us the children of God; it is living as obedient sons and daughters. God's true children are the ones who do what Jesus says, who live with the light of his gospel.

Some of the most shining examples turned out to be the members of Jesus' own family. When Jesus spoke of people hearing the word of God and doing it, his mother Mary was included. After all, she was the one who said, "Behold, I am the servant of the Lord; let it be to me according to your word" (Luke 1:38). But Mary was not the only one. After the resurrection, the disciples met together in Jerusalem. As they did this, they were obeying the word of Christ, who told them to wait for God to send them the Holy Spirit. In the book of Acts, Luke tells us that they were "devoting themselves to prayer, together with the women and Mary the mother of Jesus, and his brothers" (Acts 1:14). The members of Jesus' earthly family also had a place in his heavenly family. We know this because they listened to Jesus and did what he said; the family resemblance is unmistakable.

Membership in the family of God is open and available to everyone who comes to Jesus Christ in faith. We can be as close to Jesus as his own mother and brothers. They say that blood is thicker than water, but we are tied to the family of God by the person and work of the Holy Spirit—a bond that is even thicker than blood.

If we are the children of God, then we must bear the family resemblance, which we learn to do by following Jesus Christ. Jesus has called us his siblings, which makes him our older brother in the family of God. In any family, younger brothers and sisters should always follow the good example of their older brother. I pray for this in my own household, where a little boy shares a bedroom with his older brother. That little boy loves his older brother. He admires him and looks up to him. He likes to say what his big brother says, play what his big brother plays, and even wear what his big brother wears. He lives in the hope that one day he will be able to do all the things that his big brother does.

My prayer for my household is also the prayer of my own heart. I, too, have an Older Brother whom I love and admire. I want to be like him. As a child of light through faith in Jesus Christ, I am called to listen to my older brother, and to do the word of God.

31

WHO *IS* THIS GUY?

Luke 8:22–25

*He said to them, "Where is your faith?" And they were afraid,
and they marveled, saying to one another, "Who then is this,
that he commands even winds and water, and they obey him?"*
(Luke 8:25)

There was something strange about the breeze: not only its extraordinary heat, like the breath out of an oven, nor its uneasy, unsettled gusting but something else that he could not define. The young sun blazed clear in the pure eastern sky, terribly strong already, but over there in the west there was a lowering murk, and all along the horizon, rising some ten degrees, an orange-tawny bar, too thick for cloud.

"I do not know what to make of it," he said to himself. . . . "Of course," he reflected, "they expect me to know what to make of it. A captain is omniscient."

. . . at this moment a squall struck the *Niobe*, laying her over almost on her beam ends. . . . As the ship righted Jack recovered his feet, making his way through the tumble of chairs, table, papers and instruments. The moment he passed the cabin door he was enveloped in . . . a fine scene of confusion. Sailcloth was threshing wildly, the wheel, spinning round, had broken the helmsman's arm and flung him against the rail, the booms and the boats were all abroad, and a ghostly maintopmast staysail, blown almost out of its bolt-rope, streamed away to leeward. The situation was critical. . . . Some were running about the forecastle and . . . still more were swarming up the main and fore hatchways. Many of those on deck clung to the running rigging . . . another squall must lay her down, perhaps for good, certainly with great loss of life.[1]

Thus Patrick O'Brian describes a storm at sea in one of his splendid novels about the British navy during the time of the Napoleonic wars. Even for an experienced old sea captain, a sudden squall can be a terrifying experience, bringing not only chaos and confusion, but also the fear of death.

The Perfect Storm

There was once a storm like that on the Sea of Galilee. Like many stormy adventures at sea, the voyage started calmly enough, with Jesus deciding to go out for a leisurely sail. Luke tells us, "One day he got into a boat with his disciples, and he said to them, 'Let us go across to the other side of the lake'" (Luke 8:22). At first the water was calm, as it usually is on the Sea of Galilee: "So they set out, and as they sailed he fell asleep" (Luke 8:22–23). But then the weather started getting rough, and the tiny ship was tossed. As Luke tells it, "a windstorm came down on the lake, and they were filling with water and were in danger" (Luke 8:23).

It was the kind of storm that sometimes blows in to churn the waters of the Galilee. Although the sea is usually calm, when storms do come, they are usually violent. As one commentator explains, "The lake of Galilee is subject to sudden storms, situated as it is some 700 feet below sea level and adjacent to mountainous regions. Cold air from the heights is apt to sweep down through the precipitous gorges to the east and it can whip up the seas in a short time."[2] Galilee was the perfect place for a perfect storm.

This particular storm was as powerful as any that the disciples had ever seen. And remember, Peter and Andrew and James and John were

---

1. Patrick O'Brian, *Treason's Harbour* (New York: W. W. Norton, 1983), 176–78.
2. Leon Morris, *The Gospel According to St. Luke: An Introduction and Commentary*, Tyndale New Testament Commentaries (Grand Rapids: Eerdmans, 1974), 154.

fishermen by trade and had spent most of their lives in these waters. Yet they had never experienced anything like this. The storm hit them with a sudden and violent fury. Luke calls it "a windstorm" that "came down on the lake" (Luke 8:23). Matthew implies that it struck without warning (Matt. 8:24). A seaman would call it a squall—a sudden and violent gust of wind, usually accompanied by heavy rain.

The disciples did everything they could to deal with the situation. Their sailing vessel was rising and falling through the swells, riding to the top of one crest and then suddenly crashing down through the waves—as it seemed, almost to the bottom of the sea. The boat was filling so rapidly with water that it was in danger of getting swamped. The disciples pulled down their sails and began to bail for dear life. But they were still in danger, and soon they lost almost all hope of ever making it to shore. "We are perishing!" they said (Luke 8:24).

What a thunderous storm this must have been, for salty old sailors like Peter and John to give themselves up for lost. And what a picture this is of the sudden and dangerous storms that threaten us as we sail through life. Going back to the Old Testament, the Bible compares the troubles of life to the perils of the sea: "Save me, O God! For the waters have come up to my neck. . . . Let not the flood sweep over me, or the deep swallow me up" (Ps. 69:1, 15). As Jonah testified, "you cast me into the deep, into the heart of the seas, and the flood surrounded me; all your waves and your billows passed over me" (Jonah 2:3).

What the disciples went through on the Sea of Galilee is something we all go though in life: seas of difficulty and storms of trouble. People lose their jobs or suffer some other financial hardship, and they get tossed by waves of worry. They receive an unfavorable diagnosis or struggle with some chronic illness, and they are flooded with fear. They have painful interpersonal conflicts at home, in the neighborhood, at work, or in the church, and they feel as if they are sinking. They lose someone they love, and they are drowned in sorrow. Or perhaps they are simply swamped with all of the little duties and difficulties of everyday existence. We all must pass through the heavy seas of life's troubles. As the apostle Peter said—the same Peter who had been in the boat with Jesus—"Dear friends, do not be surprised at the painful trial you are suffering, as though something strange were happening to you" (1 Peter 4:12 NIV).

Often danger comes the way it came at Galilee: suddenly and unexpectedly. There the disciples were, sailing across the lake, without any sign of difficulty. Lulled into a false sense of security, they never imagined that within a few short hours, they would be fighting for their very lives. The same thing can happen to us. Although the seas of daily experience are sometimes calm, they are swept by sudden storms. Like the disciples, we are in a situation that we think we can handle. But then, completely unexpectedly, we are afraid that we are in danger of drowning. And then, most of all, we endure the testing of our soul.

MASTER AND COMMANDER

What should we do when trouble comes? How should we react in times of difficulty and danger, whether physical or spiritual? When the disciples were in danger—as the Bible says they were—they reacted by crying out for Jesus to save them: "And they went and woke him, saying, 'Master, Master, we are perishing!'" (Luke 8:24).

There was a problem with this response, as we shall see, but at least the disciples knew where to get help. Whenever we are in danger of drowning—or at least think that we are—we should cry out to Jesus. If we are burdened with our sins, we cry to him for mercy, asking him to save us through his cross and the empty tomb. If we are struggling to make ends meet, we cry to him for our daily bread. If we are buffeted by physical pain, we cry to him for patience and endurance. If we are torn apart by conflict, we cry to him for the peace of his Spirit. If we are overwhelmed with sorrow, we cry to him for the comfort of his presence. In every rough and stormy squall, even to the point of death itself, we call upon Jesus.

When we call upon Jesus, he is able and willing to help, as the disciples discovered. In times of trouble, there is no one better to call on than Jesus, because no one is better equipped to save us. When the disciples cried out to him, Jesus "awoke and rebuked the wind and the raging waves, and they ceased, and there was a calm" (Luke 8:24). The disciples were all in confusion, but Jesus was fully composed. Very calmly, and simply by the word of his power, Jesus told the storm to be still. He was not only the Master, but also the Commander—the commander of the waves and the storm and all the deadly power of the sea.

This was a genuine and immediate miracle. One moment the disciples were almost drowning in the heavy seas; the next moment they were floating serenely on the smooth surface of the Galilee. The storm ceased. The sea was calm. And there was no merely natural explanation for this. One commentator calls it "a mysterious, supernatural calm that testified to the sovereign power of Jesus but also the deep peace and security that belong to those who follow him."[3] The storm was stopped by the command of Christ. Jesus delivered his disciples—as he delivers everyone who calls to him in faith—by the divine power of his mighty word.

WHERE IS YOUR FAITH?

In the stillness after the storm, two crucial questions were posed. The first was a question Jesus asked, a question that we all need to answer about ourselves: Where is your faith? The second was a question the disciples asked, a question that everyone needs to answer about Jesus: Who is this man?

The first question comes at the beginning of Luke 8:25, where Jesus says to his disciples, "Where is your faith?" This was a rebuke—a gentle rebuke, but a rebuke nonetheless. The obvious implication was that the disciples were not really trusting in Jesus. Kent Hughes points out the irony here: the storm did not wake Jesus, but the unbelief of his disciples sure did![4]

To be sure, the disciples had cried out to Jesus for help. But there was something rather desperate about the way they did it. The boat was not the only thing getting swamped that day; the fear of the disciples overwhelmed their faith. They looked only at the danger, forgetting that they were safe with Jesus. They asked for help only as a last resort, and when they did, they were frantic, almost hysterical. Rather than trusting God to take care of them, they immediately assumed the worst. "We are perishing!" they said (Luke 8:24). In other words, "We're dying out here!" Their assumption was that Jesus did not know and did not care about their situation.

We can sympathize with the disciples in their lack of faith. In fact, most of us can probably empathize with them. It is only natural to be afraid

3. Donald A. Hagner, *Matthew 1–13* (Dallas: Word, 1993), 222.
4. R. Kent Hughes, *Luke: That You May Know the Truth*, 2 vols., Preaching the Word (Wheaton, IL: Crossway, 1998), 1:299.

of death, and it is easy to panic in a crisis. It is easy to be overwhelmed by the wind and the waves of life's troubles. When the water is high, and the storm is rising, it is easy to think that we are going down for the last time. It is also easy to think that God does not know and does not care that we are drowning. If he did, then obviously he would wake up and do something about it, right?

Yet no matter how desperate our situation is, we should always trust God to bring us safely back to shore. The story of Jesus calming the storm gives us three strong reasons to trust God in every rough and stormy gale. Each of these three great truths is like a life preserver for the soul, lifting us up to a faith that will not go under at the first sign of danger.

We should trust Jesus, first, *because even the storms of life are under his sovereign control.* Here we need to go back to the beginning of this episode, where Jesus said to his disciples, "Let us go across to the other side of the lake" (Luke 8:22). The disciples were in the storm because Jesus himself told them to go out on the lake. As Michael Wilcock comments: "We cannot avoid the fact that Jesus was altogether in control of the whole chain of events in this passage. *He* took his disciples across the lake, where a storm was going to burst upon them."[5]

Having a personal, saving relationship with Jesus Christ does not mean that somehow we will escape all of life's troubles. On the contrary, Christians suffer the same natural disasters, the same sinful abuse, and the same daily misfortunes as everyone else. In fact, sometimes knowing Jesus takes us right into the storm, especially when in some way we suffer for our faith. We can be "in the center of God's will," as people say, and yet still find ourselves at the center of the storm, as the disciples did.

This does not mean that God is always the cause of our suffering (some of our sufferings are caused by the sins of others, or by our own sin), for he can never be the author of evil. But it does mean that our sufferings never catch God by surprise. He always knows when we are headed for stormy troubles. Sometimes, in order to accomplish his work in our lives, he even guides us into them. That was certainly true in this case, because Jesus was the one who told the disciples to cross the lake. This was for the testing of their faith and the training of their souls.

---

5. Michael Wilcock, *The Message of Luke*, The Bible Speaks Today (Downers Grove, IL: InterVarsity, 1979), 101.

Whenever we are tossed about by life's troubles, we need to remember that God is still sovereign. He is never taken by surprise. Whatever troubles we are facing, God has brought us to this point in our lives, and he is using our present experiences to make us more like Jesus, shaping us into the glorious image of his Son. "By affliction He teaches us many precious lessons, which, without it we should never learn. By affliction He shows us our emptiness and weakness, draws us to the throne of grace, purifies our affections, weans us from the world, and makes us long for heaven. In the resurrection morning we shall all say, 'it is good for me that I was afflicted.' We shall thank God for every storm."[6]

In the meantime, we can pray that God will use our troubles for spiritual gain. We can ask him to teach us through our afflictions, praying that our suffering will help us to grow in grace. It was with this thought in mind that Ruth Graham prayed, "Dear God, let me soar in the face of the wind: up . . . through cold or the storm with wings to endure. Let the silver rain wash all the dust from my wings. Let me soar as He soars . . . let it lift me. . . . Let it buffet and drive me, but, God, let it lift."[7]

ALL IN THE SAME BOAT

A second reason for us to trust God—even in stormy troubles—is that *Jesus has set the perfect example.*

One of the most surprising things about this episode is that somehow Jesus managed to sleep his way through most of it—on the cushion, as Mark tells us (Mark 4:38). This testifies to the true humanity of Jesus Christ. To stay asleep in such a storm he must have been completely exhausted. No doubt he was weary from the heavy demands of his teaching ministry, worn out by the constant demand to help people. Jesus needed a nap badly—so badly that he could sleep anywhere. He was as prone to fatigue as anyone else, and his physical weakness was a sign of his genuine humanity. To see Jesus asleep in the boat is to know that he had a real body, with all of its needs and limitations.

But it is also to know this: that Jesus had complete confidence in the loving care of his Father. How was Jesus able to rest easy during such a

6. J. C. Ryle, *Mark* (Carlisle, PA: Banner of Truth, 1985), 83.
7. Ruth Graham, quoted in Hughes, *Luke,* 1:297.

violent storm? Partly because he was so tired, but also because he had faith in his Father. If Jesus had to look after his own life, undoubtedly he would have awakened when the first wave crashed over the stern. There is a way to sleep, and yet remain alert. But Jesus slept as if he did not have a care in the world. In a way, he didn't, because he was resting in his Father's arms. Deep down he knew that no harm could come to him, that his Father would wake him when he needed to be awakened.

When Jesus said, "Where is your faith?" he was challenging his disciples to live with the same kind of trust, to rest in their Father's care. In the words of Keith Nickle, Jesus "modeled for them the tranquility that comes from perfect trust. He went to sleep in the shalom of God. It was not that he had overlooked the gale warnings in the weather reports, nor that he was such a landlubber that he did not grasp the perilous vulnerability of being out on the sea in an open boat. It was, rather, that he knew God was in control, and he was willing to rely on that knowledge absolutely."[8]

Jesus calls us to live by the same kind of faith, believing that God is in control, and absolutely relying on him. So often we feel that we need to stay alert for every danger. We worry about our finances. We are afraid of what might happen to our children. We agonize over situations at work. These and many other concerns keep us up at night. Somehow we always feel that we need to keep an eye on things, just to be safe. But this quickly becomes exhausting, and it is all because we are not trusting God to look after us. We do not rest in our Father's care the way that Jesus did.

A third reason for trusting God through wind and wave is the most comforting of all. We have this trust *because Jesus is with us in the boat.* The first thing Luke tells us is that Jesus "got into a boat with his disciples" (Luke 8:22). He was with them when they sailed across the lake. He was with them when the wind began to rise and the waves crashed over the bow. He was with them when they cried for help. So why were they so afraid? Norval Geldenhuys asks the question like this: "How could they have feared that they would perish as long as He was in the ship? Even although He was asleep, He is the Almighty Lord who

8. Keith F. Nickle, *Preaching the Gospel of Luke: Proclaiming God's Royal Rule* (Louisville: Westminster John Knox, 2000), 83.

watches over the safety of His followers. How could they have feared that God would allow His Son, the promised Redeemer, and His disciples to perish?"[9]

Jesus is on board with us as we ride out the storm. He has given us the promise of his everlasting presence, and we can depend on him in every desperate situation. If ever we find ourselves in any difficulty, we have this promise as an anchor for the soul: "Fear not, for I have redeemed you; I have called you by name, you are mine. When you pass through the waters, I will be with you; and through the rivers, they shall not overwhelm you. . . . For I am the LORD your God, the Holy One of Israel, your Savior" (Isa. 43:1–3). And if anyone asks us, "Where is your faith?" we can tell them: "Our faith is in the God who rules the universe, and in his Son, Jesus Christ, who has died on the cross for our sins."

What a difference it makes, especially in treacherous waters, to know that Jesus is in the same boat with us. This is true not only for the individual believer, but also for the church. Since the time of the New Testament, Christians have often used the boat as a symbol of the church of Jesus Christ. This idea goes all the way back to Noah and the ark, but it is also based on what happened to Jesus and his disciples out on the Sea of Galilee. Charles Spurgeon said, "I scarcely know of an apter picture of a church than a ship upon the treacherous Galilean Sea with Jesus and His disciples sailing in it. . . . Every sail of the good ship which bears the flag of the High Admiral of our fleet must be beaten with the wind, and every plank in her must be tried by the waves."[10]

This is a great encouragement, because it guarantees that even when the storm tide is rising, the ship of God's church will not sink. Jesus is on board, and no matter how fiercely the storm rages, we can trust that our Master and Captain will see us safely through. Therefore, whenever we feel that we are drowning, we need to ask ourselves, "Now what difference would it make in this situation if I were really to trust in Jesus, believing that he is in the same boat with me, and knowing that he is able to save me? Where *is* my faith?"

9. Norval Geldenhuys, *The Gospel of Luke*, New International Commentary on the New Testament (Grand Rapids: Eerdmans, 1951), 252.

10. Charles Haddon Spurgeon, *The Parables and Miracles of Our Lord*, 3 vols. (Grand Rapids: Baker, 1993), 1:121.

This was the question that Jesus asked his disciples, and he asked it because he knew that they had every reason to trust in him. We have even more reason to trust in Jesus. We have seen his love in the cross; we have experienced his power through the empty tomb; and we have been given his Spirit to stay with us wherever we go. Therefore, when the storms come, we trust Jesus to get us safely back to shore.

WHO IS THIS JESUS?

For their part, the disciples also had a good question to ask, a question about the true identity of Jesus Christ. When they saw that the sea was calm, the disciples "were afraid, and they marveled, saying to one another, 'Who then is this, that he commands even winds and water, and they obey him?'" (Luke 8:25).

The disciples had been afraid of the storm, but now they were even more afraid—not in the sense that they thought Jesus would harm them, of course, but in the sense that they were in awe of what he had done. Jesus had just proved that he was even more powerful than the mightiest storm at sea. This overwhelmed them with feelings of reverent fear and transcendent awe.

It also made them wonder who Jesus really was, after all. And this would seem to be the main point of this passage. The goal of Luke's Gospel is to help us become more certain about the person and work of Jesus Christ. Each episode expands our understanding of who Jesus is and what he has come to do for our salvation. Here in chapter 8, the disciples raise the question that is really the central concern of the whole Gospel: "Who *is* this Jesus?"

Ironically, the disciples also provided the answer, although they seem not to have fully recognized it themselves. They said, "he commands even winds and water, and they obey him" (Luke 8:25). "Command" was just the word for it, because Luke tells us that Jesus "*rebuked* the wind and the raging waves, and they ceased" (Luke 8:24). Jesus spoke to the storm as if it had to answer to his authority. Apparently, the storm *did* have to answer to Jesus, because it obeyed what he commanded.

Now who, do you suppose, has the right to speak that way to the sea? This question may have been a real stumper for the disciples, but the answer is

389

obvious to anyone who reads Luke's Gospel: Jesus is God. His miracle on the Sea of Galilee was proof positive of his divine nature and omnipotent deity.

This becomes especially clear when we read the story against the background of the Old Testament, where God alone had the power and authority to rule the chaos of the sea. We encounter this motif throughout the Psalms, where God is praised as the one "who stills the roaring of the seas" (Ps. 65:7). "You rule the raging of the sea," wrote the psalmist, "when its waves rise, you still them" (Ps. 89:9). Psalm 106 goes so far as to say that God "rebuked the Red Sea" when he saved Israel out of Egypt (see Ps. 106:7–9; cf. 104:7). But perhaps the most striking parallel comes in Psalm 107, which sounds very much like what happened to the disciples on the Sea of Galilee:

> Some went down to the sea in ships,
>   doing business on the great waters;
> they saw the deeds of the LORD,
>   his wondrous works in the deep.
> For he commanded and raised the stormy wind,
>   which lifted up the waves of the sea.
> They mounted up to heaven; they went down to the depths;
>   their courage melted away in their evil plight;
> they reeled and staggered like drunken men
>   and were at their wits' end.
> Then they cried to the LORD in their trouble,
>   and he delivered them from their distress.
> He made the storm be still,
>   and the waves of the sea were hushed. (Ps. 107:23–29)

The commanding power that Jesus had over the wind and the waves was a clear demonstration of his deity. Jesus Christ is Lord of the sea, which makes perfect sense, because he created it. Key passages throughout the New Testament testify that Jesus is the Creator God. At the beginning of his Gospel, John tells us, "All things were made through him, and without him was not any thing made that was made" (John 1:3). "For by him all things were created," Paul tells us—"all things were created through him and for him" (Col. 1:16; cf. 1 Cor. 8:6). Or again, the book of Hebrews tells us that it was through Jesus that God created the world (Heb. 1:2). And the book of Revelation praises Jesus as the God who made all things, and by whose will they were created (Rev. 4:11).

So when Jesus calmed the storm, he was claiming his right to rule the world that he made. Creation's Creator is also creation's Lord. The disciples witnessed this firsthand when their Master stood up in the boat and rebuked the sea. Who is this Jesus? He is the Lord of the storm, the Ruler of nature, and the God of all creation.

This same Jesus—who has the power to save—calls us to have faith in him through the winds and the waves of every storm. This does not mean that we will never suffer any harm. But it does mean that Jesus will see us through. David Gooding's comments are worth quoting at length. He writes:

> We live in a universe that is lethally hostile to human life. . . . Within our earth itself wind, wave, lightning, storm, flood, drought, avalanche, earthquake, fire, heat, cold, germ, virus, epidemic, all from time to time threaten and destroy life. Sooner or later one of them may destroy us. The story of the stilling of the storm is not, of course, meant to tell us that Christ will never allow any believer to perish by drowning, or by any other natural disaster. Many believers have so perished. It does demonstrate that he is Lord of the physical forces in the universe, that for him nothing happens by accident, and that no force in all creation can destroy his plan for our eternal salvation or separate us from the love of God which is in Christ Jesus our Lord.[11]

It was the love of God in Christ that led Charles Wesley to write his famous hymn "Jesus, Lover of My Soul." Charles had joined his brother John on a mission to Georgia in the colonies of America. The trip had been a disappointment in nearly every respect. As the Wesleys sailed home to England in the fall of 1736, both of them disillusioned by the sufferings of ministry, they were caught in a frightening storm out on the Atlantic Ocean. When it appeared that all would be lost, Charles did not pray for deliverance, but for the faith to trust in God and to encourage the other passengers on board. The sea grew calm, the ship was

11. David Gooding, *According to Luke: A New Exposition of the Third Gospel* (Grand Rapids: Eerdmans, 1987), 143.

saved, and many people gave their lives to Jesus Christ.[12] Afterwards, Wesley wrote:

> Jesus, Lover of my soul,
> Let me to thy bosom fly,
> While the nearer waters roll,
> While the tempest still is high;
> Hide me, O my Savior, hide
> Till the storm of life is past;
> Safe into the haven guide;
> O receive my soul at last!

Everyone who trusts in Jesus Christ has this comfort. Jesus has saved us through his death on the cross and his resurrection from the dead. He is sovereign over everything that threatens to harm us. Now by his Spirit he is on board with us through all of life's troubles, until at last he will receive us into the haven of his everlasting love.

12. Rosalie de Rosset, "Jesus, Lover of My Soul," in *Christianity and the Arts* (Spring 1999): 31.

32

What Has He Done For You?

Luke 8:26–39

The man from whom the demons had gone begged that he might be with him, but Jesus sent him away, saying, "Return to your home, and declare how much God has done for you." And he went away, proclaiming throughout the whole city how much Jesus had done for him. (Luke 8:38–39)

The famous twentieth-century British philosopher Sir Bertrand Russell wrote a provocative book called *Why I Am Not a Christian.* The first time I opened the book, I did so with some trepidation, fearing that perhaps it might contain powerful arguments that would shake the foundations of my Christian faith. But there was hardly any reason to be afraid. Russell's evangelism for atheism is far from persuasive, and in fact some of his arguments are nearly laughable.

Among other objections, Russell argues that Jesus Christ was neither the best nor the wisest of men. He makes his case by referring directly to things that Jesus said or did in the Gospels, including a memorable incident recorded in Luke 8. "There is the instance of the Gadarene swine," Russell writes, "where it certainly was not very kind to the pigs to put the devils into them and make them rush down the hill to the sea. You must remember that He was omnipotent, and He could have made the devils simply go away; but He chose to send them into the pigs. . . . I cannot myself feel that either in the matter of wisdom or in the matter of virtue Christ stands quite as high as some other people known to history."[1]

The philosopher was referring, of course, to the miracle in which Jesus saved a wretched man by casting a legion of demons into a herd of pigs, which proceeded to perish by running headlong into the Sea of Galilee. But what shall we make of Russell's criticism? Was it wise and good for Jesus to send the demons into the swine? The truth is that this miracle was a powerful demonstration of the deity of Jesus Christ and the total transformation that comes to anyone who receives his grace. Far from being embarrassed by what Jesus did, the incident draws us to trust in him for salvation and to tell people how much he has done for us.

THE MADMAN IN THE GRAVEYARD

The miracle took place on the far side of the Sea of Galilee. Luke tells us that after stilling the storm, Jesus sailed with his disciples "to the country of the Gerasenes, which is opposite Galilee. When Jesus had stepped out on land, there met him a man from the city who had demons. For a long time he had worn no clothes, and had not lived in a house but among the tombs" (Luke 8:26–27).

No sooner had Jesus stepped out of the boat than he met a man who was in a loathsome and pitiable condition. Cyril of Alexandria provided an apt description: "In great misery and nakedness, he wandered among the graves of the dead. He was in utter wretchedness, leading a disgraceful life . . . deprived of every blessing, destitute of all sobriety, and entirely deprived even of reason."[2]

The man was naked; he did not even have the decency to put on some clothes. He was alone, his antisocial behavior having alienated him from society and left him completely isolated. The man was also dangerous. Luke does not mention this explicitly, but Matthew tells us that he was "so fierce

1. Bertrand Russell, *Why I Am Not a Christian, and Other Essays on Religion and Related Subjects*, ed. Paul Edwards (New York: Simon & Schuster, 1957), 18–19.
2. Cyril of Alexandria, "Commentary on the Gospel of Luke" in *Luke*, ed. Arthur A. Just Jr., Ancient Christian Commentary on Scripture, NT 3 (Downers Grove, IL: InterVarsity, 2003), 139.

that no one could pass that way" (Matt. 8:28). Here is how one traveler described a similar encounter in the same part of the world: "On descending from the height of Lebanon, I found myself in a cemetery. . . . The silence of the night was now broken by fierce yells and howlings, which I discovered proceeded from a naked maniac, who was fighting with some wild dogs for a bone. The moment he perceived us, he left his canine companions, and bounding along with rapid strides, seized my horse's bridle and almost forced him backwards over the cliff."[3] The man that Jesus met was just as wretched—more like an animal than a human being.

Most strangely of all, the man made his home among the tombs outside the city. People in those days would have considered this complete degradation, and rightly so. To live in the God-forsaken place of the dead is a sign of sheer lunacy: "The healthy man has a horror of a decaying corpse and avoids defilement; it is only deranged people who have any desire for death and decay."[4]

The man that Jesus met was in nearly the worst condition that anyone could imagine. He was naked, lonely, violent, and insane; he was walking among the dead. Yet even for all his misery, we can see ourselves in his situation, because sin has similar effects on all of us. It exposes us naked in our guilt. It alienates us from one another, leaving us lonely and alone. It makes us violent, at least in our attitudes, if not in our actions. Spiritually speaking, we walk among the dead. Thus the madman in the graveyard shows the wretchedness of our condition outside of Christ.

A LEGION OF DEMONS

This man's degradation was more deadly than most because he was possessed by many demons. This was obvious from the way that he accosted Jesus: "When he saw Jesus, he cried out and fell down before him and said with a loud voice, 'What have you to do with me, Jesus, Son of the Most High God? I beg you, do not torment me.' For he had commanded the unclean

---

3. Eliot Warburton, *The Crescent and the Cross*, quoted in J. C. Ryle, *Expository Thoughts on the Gospels, Luke* (1858; reprint Cambridge: James Clarke, 1976), 1:271.

4. A. Schlatter, *Das Evangelium des Lukas* (Stuttgart, 1931), quoted in Norval Geldenhuys, *The Gospel of Luke*, New International Commentary on the New Testament (Grand Rapids: Eerdmans, 1951), 258.

spirit to come out of the man. (For many a time it had seized him. He was kept under guard and bound with chains and shackles, but he would break the bonds and be driven by the demon into the desert)" (Luke 8:28–29).

The madman was in such a desperate condition because he was demon-possessed—not just by one demon, but by many. "Jesus then asked him, 'What is your name?' And he said, 'Legion,' for many demons had entered him" (Luke 8:30). The Bible does not say exactly how many demons there were, but since there were up to six thousand soldiers in a Roman legion, there must have been thousands (at least two thousand, if the number of pigs is any indication; see Mark 5:13).

Demons are fallen angels. Although they were created for the glory of God, they follow Satan in his rebellion and torment the children of men. Demonic activity seems to have been especially prevalent during the time of Christ. Perhaps this was because Satan had turned all his evil energies against the land of the Savior's promise. Charles Spurgeon even wondered whether Satan—that old counterfeiter—had witnessed the incarnation and was trying to imitate it by sending demons into people's minds and souls.[5] But whatever the reason, Jesus encountered many people who were possessed by evil spirits.

There are two errors that people commonly make about demons. One is to minimize them, or even to deny their existence altogether, like the journalist Kenneth Woodward, who claims that they are merely a "trivial personification . . . hardly adequate to symbolize the mystery of evil."[6] Demons love to be downplayed like this because it makes it easier for them to gain control. The other error is nearly as dangerous: to so exaggerate their importance that every sin or spiritual difficulty is attributed to the direct agency of demons. When people think this way, they stop taking responsibility for their actions and forget the depravity of their own sinful hearts.

The Bible provides a balanced view of demonic activity. To begin with, it recognizes the reality of spiritual oppression. There are evil spirits in the world who prey upon human weakness. Despite what some Christians say,

5. Charles Haddon Spurgeon, *Miracles and Parables of Our Lord*, 3 vols. (Grand Rapids: Baker, 1993), 1:545.

6. Kenneth Woodward, quoted in R. Kent Hughes, *Luke: That You May Know the Truth*, 2 vols., Preaching the Word (Wheaton, IL: Crossway, 1998), 1:303.

not every sin or psychological disorder is the work of a demon. Often our own iniquity is explanation enough. But demons do exploit spiritual weakness to gain control over certain individuals, warping their personalities and twisting their actions to evil purpose. David Gooding rightly describes the madman in the Gospel as "an extreme example of what satanic forces can do with a human personality that has come under their complete domination. Unlike the Holy Spirit, who always sets a man free, develops his personality and increases his self-control and dignity, satanic forces seem to strive to overpower a man's personality, and ultimately to break down his self-control, and to rob him . . . of self-respect."[7] The man whom Jesus met was a sad example. Mark tells us that the man tried to injure himself (Mark 5:5); the demons inside were trying to dominate, distort, and destroy a precious person made in the image of God. Evil spirits are nothing to trifle with. Given the chance, they are controlling, abusive, and violent.

In his best-selling book *People of the Lie*, psychiatrist M. Scott Peck explains how he came to believe in the reality of supernatural evil. Peck had been inclined to dismiss the very idea of demonic oppression. Then he met Charlene, who despite his best efforts, never made any personal progress. Eventually he reached the conclusion that she was evil, in fact that she was trying to destroy him. Peck writes: "Charlene's desire to make a conquest of me, to toy with me, to utterly control our relationship, knew no bounds. It seemed to be a desire for power purely for its own sake." When Peck asked her about the meaning of life, Charlene replied that she had been raised in a Christian home, where she was taught to glorify God. But then she protested, "I cannot do it. There's no room for me in that. That would be my death. I don't want to live for God. I will not. I want to live for me. My own sake!"[8]

This is what demons always do. Whether they do it openly and overtly (by possessing a person, as we often see in the Gospels), or whether they do it more secretly and covertly (by corrupting the structures of society, as is more common today, at least in America), they always oppose the glory of God. "For we do not wrestle against flesh and blood," the Scripture says, "but against the rulers, against the authorities, against the cosmic powers

7. David Gooding, *According to Luke: A New Exposition of the Third Gospel* (Grand Rapids: Eerdmans, 1987), 144.

8. M. Scott Peck, *People of the Lie* (New York: Simon & Schuster, 1983), 168.

over this present darkness, against the spiritual forces of evil in the heavenly places" (Eph. 6:12).

There is a cosmic struggle for the heart and soul of every human being, and the man with the legion of demons gives us a shocking picture of what happens when Satan is winning. The man was alienated from society. He was harmful to himself and dangerous to others. He was out of his mind. He was living among the dead. Worst of all, although he was aware of the demons inside his head, he was powerless to resist them. His life had become a living hell.

This is what sin does to us all, even if our own situation seems less extreme. The Bible tells us that the sinful mind is "hostile to God" (Rom. 8:7). It describes us as "dead in trespasses and sins" (Eph. 2:1). It says that apart from a saving relationship with Jesus Christ, we are "alienated and hostile in mind" (Col. 1:21). Worst of all, we cannot save ourselves. On the contrary, we are "utterly indisposed, disabled, and made opposite to all that is spiritually good."[9] This is all because "the god of this world has blinded the minds of the unbelievers, to keep them from seeing the light of the gospel of the glory of Christ" (2 Cor. 4:4).

When Pigs Flew

If ever a man seemed beyond any hope of salvation, it was the crazy man who lived at the cemetery. Yet he was about to have a life-changing encounter with Jesus Christ. This is always what people truly need when troubled by evil spirits: they need the gospel. This is the other side of the biblical balance. The evil power of demons has to be recognized and respected, but it does not have to be feared. Fallen angels cannot triumph over the almighty power of Jesus Christ.

The demons themselves know this all too well. According to James, "the demons believe—and shudder" (James 2:19). In other words, they know that there is an omnipotent God, and for this reason, they live in mortal fear. This explains their reaction to Jesus. The legion of demons knew exactly who he was: the "Son of the Most High God" (Luke 8:28). As fallen angels, they had known the Second Person of the Trinity since the

9. Westminster Larger Catechism, A. 25.

foundation of the world. When they saw Jesus, therefore, they discerned his deity; they knew that he was God the Son incarnate, and they were terrified.

We can smell the fear of these demons in the way they pleaded with Jesus. First they begged him not to torment them (Luke 8:28). Then "they begged him not to command them to depart into the abyss" (Luke 8:31). "The abyss," as the demons called it, is the place of the dead (see Rom. 10:7)—what Revelation describes as "the bottomless pit" where Satan will be condemned (Rev. 20:1–3). The demons know that this is their final doom. They know that Jesus will defeat them. They know that they will be cast into a terrible place of everlasting torment (see Rev. 21:8), and so they tremble with fear. Some people may not believe in hell, but the demons certainly do! We should believe in hell, too, and repent before it is too late for us, as it already is for them.

Jesus did not send these demons into the abyss; it was not yet time. Instead, he did something that many people find rather strange: "Now a large herd of pigs was feeding there on the hillside, and they begged him to let them enter these. So he gave them permission. Then the demons came out of the man and entered the pigs, and the herd rushed down the steep bank into the lake and were drowned" (Luke 8:32–33). People like Bertrand Russell are offended by this miraculous stampede. They believe that it was a form of cruel and unusual punishment, at least for the pigs, if not for the demons. How can we defend Jesus from their accusations?

We might defend him by pointing out that he was not the one who destroyed the pigs; the demons did it. Of course Jesus gave them permission, as the Bible says, but it was still the demons who hatefully drove the swine over the cliff. Or we could argue that this was better than the alternative, which was to turn the demons loose to torment the general population. Or we could say that the pigs were ceremonially unclean, and that therefore they were an appropriate receptacle for demons. Or we could point out that hog farming was against the law of Moses (e.g., Lev. 11:7). It was not kosher for Jews to raise bacon, even if they were only selling it to Gentiles. So depending on who owned the pigs, this may have been an act of divine justice. We could even say that Jesus created these pigs in the first place, and that as their Creator, he had the right to do with them as he pleased.

There may be some truth in all of these arguments, but it is better to say that the pigs lived and died for the glory of God. These fine swine are the most famous pigs in history. What other herd of pigs can claim to have demonstrated the divine power of Jesus Christ over the dark powers of hell? Jesus cast out the demons as easily as he had commanded the sea. He is the ruler of both the natural and the supernatural realms. In order to prove this, he permitted the demons to enter the pigs. In this way, everyone could witness what had happened in the unseen world of the spirits: Jesus had delivered a man from his demons. The pigs were an essential part of demonstrating the full extent of the miracle that had taken place.

There are many mysteries in the invisible war between God and Satan, and many things that we struggle to understand. Like Jesus, we believe that demons exist; like the demons, we believe that Jesus exists, and that he has the authority to crush every power that opposes his will. Whenever we are confronted with supernatural evil—when we believe that someone may be tormented by demons, for example, or when it seems that Satan is having his way in a family or community—we cry out for deliverance. We can never defeat the powers of hell in our own strength, but only by trusting in Jesus Christ, who "must reign until he has put all his enemies under his feet" (1 Cor. 15:25).

Afraid of What?

The way people responded to this extraordinary exorcism was as important as the miracle itself. We see a clear contrast between the hog farmers and the madman that Jesus saved. Both of them went away and told other people what had happened, but only one man did this for the glory of God. Luke begins with the farmers:

> When the herdsmen saw what had happened, they fled and told it in the city and in the country. Then people went out to see what had happened, and they came to Jesus and found the man from whom the demons had gone, sitting at the feet of Jesus, clothed and in his right mind, and they were afraid. And those who had seen it told them how the demon-possessed man had been healed. Then all the people of the surrounding country of the Gerasenes asked him to depart from them, for they were seized with great fear. So he got into the boat and returned. (Luke 8:34–37)

It is not every day that lunatics find religion, or that pigs commit mass suicide, so the word spread quickly. People wanted to come and see what had happened, and soon Jesus was confronted by an angry mob. The pigs were gone, and people were amazed to find that crazy old man who used to scare people at the cemetery sitting down and listening to Jesus. This frightened them so much that they demanded Jesus to depart.

Why were they so afraid? Perhaps they were looking after their financial interests. Notice that they confronted Jesus after hearing "how the demon-possessed man had been healed" (Luke 8:36). In other words, they knew that Jesus had cast demons out of the man and into the pigs. Now that the pigs were gone, they may have been afraid that Jesus would take away all their business. After all, two thousand pigs is a lot of bacon! The English poet John Oxenham imagines them saying something like this:

Rabbi, begone! Thy powers
Bring loss to us and ours.
Our ways are not as Thine.
Thou lovest men, we—swine.
Oh, get you hence, Omnipotence,
And take this fool of Thine!
His soul? What care we for his soul?
What good to us that Thou hast made him whole,
Since we have lost our swine.[10]

If this is why people were worried, it shows how wrong their priorities were. They cared more about their precious pigs than they did about the priceless treasure of a life transformed by the grace of Jesus Christ. This challenges our own priorities. What do we really value? Are we more concerned about getting our work done, or about taking time for people who need to know Christ? Are we willing to give up what we own—to support gospel work with sacrificial giving—so that others can come into the possession of salvation?

The people of the Gerasenes had the wrong priorities: they were afraid of losing any more of what they had. But they had an even deeper fear—the fear of Jesus himself, and of his saving power. Luke tells us that they

10. John Oxenham, "Gadara, A.D. 31," quoted in Hughes, *Luke,* 1:310.

"came to Jesus and found the man from whom the demons had gone, sitting at the feet of Jesus, clothed and in his right mind, and they were afraid" (Luke 8:35). They could see what Jesus had done, and yet they still rejected him. They were full of fear—not fear in the sense of reverence and awe, but trembling and terror. They were afraid of Jesus. They were afraid of his power and authority. They were afraid of his ability to change someone's life in ways they could not begin to understand. Perhaps most of all, they were afraid of what Jesus would change in their own lives if they let him stay around any longer.

This may seem irrational, yet it often happens. People have a life-changing encounter with Jesus Christ. By the transforming work of the Holy Spirit, they turn away from their sins and receive the free gift of eternal life, placing their own personal trust in the death and resurrection of Jesus Christ. The change is so dramatic that everyone knows it has to be the work of God. Yet sometimes the friends and family members who ought to be rejoicing respond instead with ridicule and rejection. They almost seem frightened to see someone read the Bible, go to church, and start talking about spiritual things. Deep down, what they are really afraid to confront is their own need of a Savior. They are close enough to see who Jesus is and what he can do. But instead of being open to consider the changes that God wants to make in their own lives, they find it much easier to send Jesus away.

This is always a tragic mistake. How sad it was that the Gerasenes drove Jesus away! If only they had let him stay, he could have saved them forever. He would have put them into their right minds, whether or not they were demon-possessed. He would have taught them everything they ever needed to know.

GOING HOME WITH THE GOSPEL

We know this because Jesus did all this—and more—for the man he saved. It is one of the most radical transformations in the Gospels. Jesus took a man who was crazy, naked, and dangerous—a man walking with the dead—and changed his whole life forever. Here is how Darrell Bock summarizes the transformation:

In a complete reversal of the previously possessed man's demeanor, he is now clothed, whereas before he had been naked; he is now seated, whereas before he had been roaming; he is now associating with others as he sits at Jesus' feet, whereas before he sought solitude; he is now of sound mind, whereas before he had been crying out in a loud voice; he is now comfortable in the presence of Jesus, whereas before he wanted nothing to do with him.[11]

Notice all the things that Jesus did for this man. Luke describes him as "the man from whom the demons had gone" (Luke 8:35). So Jesus delivered him from demons. His evil spirits were gone. He was no longer oppressed and possessed by fallen angels. Jesus Christ was in control of his life, and wherever Jesus takes control, there is freedom from Satan.

The man was sitting at the feet of Jesus. Jesus had calmed the restless storm that raged inside his soul, and now he was able to sit quietly and listen to careful instruction. No longer alone and isolated, he had a saving relationship with Jesus Christ, and as a result, soon he would have many other healthy relationships as well. He was coming back into community. He was also fully clothed, and this too was spiritually significant. Previously he went around naked, without any sense of modesty or decency, but now he was wearing proper clothes. The orderly way he was behaving was a sign of the discipline Jesus was bringing to his soul.

Another way to say this is that the man was finally thinking sensibly. He was "in his right mind," as Luke puts it. What a wonderful expression of what it means to know Jesus Christ! Until we come to Christ we are out of our right minds, but once we turn to him in faith we begin to think about everything the way we ought to think about it, in a Bible-based, Christ-centered, God-glorifying way. In a word—the word the herdsmen used to describe what had happened—the man was *healed* (Luke 8:36).

This is a marvelous picture of what happens in salvation. We leave the sinful power of Satan and come under the control of Jesus Christ. We enter into a wonderful new personal relationship with him, and also with his people in the community of the church. Now we are clothed in the righteousness of Jesus Christ. We are able to sit still and listen to what he has to teach us. We have a whole new way of thinking about things, because the

11. Darrell L. Bock, *Luke 1:1–9:50*, Baker Exegetical Commentary on the New Testament 3A (Grand Rapids: Baker, 1994), 1:777–78.

Word of God is transforming our minds. This is the experience of every person who trusts in Jesus Christ for salvation. Now we know Jesus for sure. As J. C. Ryle said, "Never is a man in his right mind till he is converted, or in his right place till he sits by faith at the feet of Jesus, or rightly clothed till he has put on the Lord Jesus Christ." Real conversion, Ryle goes on to say, "is nothing else but the miraculous release of a captive, the miraculous restoration of a man to his right mind, the miraculous deliverance of a soul from the devil."[12] As we come to know Christ more and more, we experience his healing—healing from sin, from Satan, from loneliness, from indecency, from wrong ways of thinking, and even from the power of death.

Considering all the things that Jesus had done for this man, it is not surprising that he responded very differently from everyone else who was there that day. Instead of sending Jesus away, he was ready to follow him anywhere: "The man from whom the demons had gone begged that he might be with him" (Luke 8:38). When he saw that Jesus was leaving, the man pleaded for permission to climb in the boat and join his disciples. This is what we have come to expect in Luke's Gospel, that when people come to Christ, they leave everything else behind and begin to follow him. But God had a different plan for this man's life, as he often does: "Jesus sent him away, saying, 'Return to your home, and declare how much God has done for you'" (Luke 8:38–39).

There is more than one way to serve Jesus, and more than one pathway of discipleship. This man would still be following Jesus, but not in the way that he expected. The gospel begins at home, so rather than going somewhere across the sea, he would go back and witness for Christ among his own people. This is usually the first calling we have after coming to Christ: not going off on some exotic adventure, but going back home to share the good news about Jesus with our family and friends.

The man who had been delivered from demons did just that. He was not only saved *from* something, but also *to* something: a life of evangelistic discipleship. The story thus ends with him going back and "proclaiming throughout the whole city how much Jesus had done for him" (Luke 8:39). Here Luke uses an important turn of phrase. Jesus told the man to say how much *God* had done for him, but when he went to share the gospel, it was

12. J. C. Ryle, *Expository Thoughts on the Gospels, Luke* (1858; reprint Cambridge: James Clarke, 1976), 1:270.

404

all about what *Jesus* had done. No difference. Somehow he knew that Jesus had saved him with the very power of God.

The man must have had a dramatic testimony. Think of the stories he could tell, from his time among the tombs to the running of the pigs. And think how much Jesus had done for him. Here was a violent, demon-possessed man who had lived naked among the dead. But Jesus had cast out his demons. He had restored his dignity, brought him back to his senses, taught him the truth, and given him a reason to live by calling him to glorify God in sharing the gospel. Jesus had done so much for him that he told the whole city about it.

Anyone who has come to Jesus in faith has a wonderful story to tell. The details are always a little different, but the story is still the same. God has forgiven all our sins—even the dark and secret misdeeds that no one else knows about, and that we are almost afraid to admit to ourselves. He has done this through the cross, where Jesus died for our sins, and in the empty tomb, where Jesus was raised to give us eternal life. God has covered us with the righteousness of Jesus Christ, so that we are no longer naked in our guilt. He has put us into our right mind, so that we know who we really are, and who God really is. He has settled us down to listen to his word. He has given us a saving relationship with his Son. This is how much Jesus has done for us, even if we sometimes forget. If this is what Jesus has done for us, then we need to tell people about it, so that he can do the same thing for them.

33

Only Believe

Luke 8:40–56

*While he was still speaking, someone from the ruler's house came
and said, "Your daughter is dead; do not trouble the Teacher any
more." But Jesus on hearing this answered him, "Do not fear; only
believe, and she will be well." (Luke 8:49–50)*

The Gospels generally present the life of Jesus Christ as a series of
separate incidents: one story after another. Each self-contained
episode has its own cast of characters, its own plot, conflict, and
resolution. This makes the Gospels ideal for teaching and preaching. One story
equals one lesson or one sermon—all nice and tidy.

Yet from time to time we catch a glimpse of the commotion that constantly swirled around Jesus. There were no narrators to announce the next
miracle, or subtitles to identify each parable. No one was there to help the
disciples find their places or to hold up cue cards so they would remember
their lines. It was life on the move, with one incident flowing into the next.
The scene was constantly changing. People were always jostling around
Jesus, clamoring for his attention, waiting to speak with him.

We see Jesus getting pushed and pressed at the end of Luke 8. After a time
of teaching, Jesus had sailed across the Galilee to perform two miracles—

one out on the water, and one on the far shore. "Now when Jesus returned," Luke tells us, "the crowd welcomed him, for they were all waiting for him" (Luke 8:40). Jesus was a major attraction; people wanted to see more. But as soon as he arrived, he was called away to perform another healing miracle. Then, while he was on his way to perform that miracle, he was interrupted to perform yet another one.

This was a typical day in the life of our Savior: so much to do, for so many people. Here at the end of chapter 8 Luke brings two miracles together into one narrative. He gives us two for the price of one because this is the way it happened, of course, but also because he wanted to teach something significant about salvation. Here we meet two very different people, yet they are joined by their desperate need, by the first beginnings of saving faith, and by their experience with Jesus and his healing power.

TWO PEOPLE, ONE NEED

The first person we meet was one of the most prominent men in the community. As the crowds welcomed Jesus back on shore, "there came a man named Jairus, who was a ruler of the synagogue" (Luke 8:41). The synagogue was the social and spiritual center of life in the Jewish community, and this man was one of its elders. As ruler of the synagogue, Jairus had the responsibility to oversee its teaching ministry and lead in the public worship of God. He was well respected for his godliness.

But no one had ever seen him like this: "And falling at Jesus' feet, he implored him to come to his house, for he had an only daughter, about twelve years of age, and she was dying" (Luke 8:41–42). Jairus was desperate. His daughter—his only daughter, the little girl that he loved—was dying. As she lay dying, he did everything he could to save her, as any parent would, but nothing seemed to help. She was the priceless treasure of his heart, and he had all but given her up for lost.

Finally, Jairus went to see Jesus. Generally speaking, Jesus did not find favor with the religious establishment, but this man was desperate. He had heard about Jesus and the miracles he performed. Whether he was a believer or not, it was certainly worth a try, so Jairus came begging for help. Rather than sending one of his servants, he came in person, and as a sign of his humble submission, he fell at Jesus' feet. He was up against our last and deadliest enemy. Death had brought him to his knees.

Providentially, Jesus was able and willing to help. Immediately he set out for the man's home, but "as Jesus went, the people pressed around him. And there was a woman who had had a discharge of blood for twelve years, and though she had spent all her living on physicians, she could not be healed by anyone" (Luke 8:42–43).

All of a sudden, here was someone else in desperate need—different in many ways from the ruler of the synagogue, but nearly as needy. Although we do not know her name, we do know her medical history. She had been bleeding for more than a decade—as long as the little girl on her deathbed had been alive. Very likely she was suffering from some kind of uterine hemorrhage, but in any case, she simply could not stop bleeding.

The case was serious, possibly even life-threatening. At the very least, the hemorrhage had ruined the woman's life. According to the law of Moses, a woman with a discharge of blood was considered ceremonially unclean (see Lev. 15:19ff.). She was not allowed to enter the temple or participate in public worship. She was not even allowed to touch other people, because if she did, then they too would become defiled.

People suffering from chronic illness often struggle with isolation, as their physical limitations cut them off from social interaction. This woman's alienation was profound. She was an outcast. Out of necessity, she had pulled away from all physical contact, including with members of her own family. It had been twelve long years since anyone had embraced her. During that time she constantly had to be careful not to touch anyone, or to let anyone touch her. Maybe her condition was not a matter of life and death, but something had died inside her all the same.

Not surprisingly, the woman had tried everything to find a cure. Mark says she "had suffered much under many physicians, and was no better but rather grew worse" (Mark 5:26). From what we know of the ancient practice of medicine, this is hardly surprising. Here is what the Talmud advised for someone in this condition: "Take of the gum of Alexandria the weight of a small silver coin; of alum the same; of crocus the same. Let them be bruised together, and given in wine to the woman that has an issue of blood. If this does not benefit take of Persian onions three pints; boil them in wine, and give her to drink, and say 'Arise from thy flux.' If this does not cure her, set her in a place where two ways meet, and let her hold a cup of wine in her right hand, and let some one come behind and frighten her, and say, 'Arise from thy flux.'"[1] Needless to say, these remedies were far from effective. In fact, they sound more like cures for the hiccups than for chronic illness!

Luke is somewhat less critical of the woman's doctors, but he does mention her medical bills: "though she had spent all her living on physicians, she could not be healed by anyone" (Luke 8:43). Well, the more things change, the more they stay the same! The woman's illness had cost her everything she had: her money, her relationships, and her strength.

In some ways, she was very different from Jairus. They stood at opposite ends of the social spectrum. One was at the top of the scale, while the other wasn't even on it. But they were both desperate for a cure. They both had critical problems they were unable to solve for themselves, which reminds us of our own tragic situation in this fallen world. In spite of all the medical progress that we have made, we are still powerless to stop our suffering. Both Jairus and the woman with the discharge of blood were beyond human help, and so are we. Whether they are physical or spiritual, we all have needs we cannot meet and problems we cannot solve. We struggle with besetting sins, broken relationships, incurable disabilities, chronic diseases, and areas of personal weakness that leave us feeling discouraged and defeated. And in the end, no matter what else we do or do not have to suffer, death will bring us to our knees.

THE HEALING TOUCH

Where do you turn when you have tried everything else and nothing seems to help? Often it is out of the most desperate sense of need that people finally turn to Christ. When every other attempted remedy has failed, when we have spent everything we have and still have not found the cure, when everyone else has let us down and all our other supports have given way, Jesus is ready and waiting to save us. As the needy people in this story discovered, he is ready to heal anyone who falls down before him in faith, or who reaches out to touch the garment of his grace.

---

1. Quoted in M. R. Vincent, *Word Studies in the New Testament* (Wilmington, DE: Associated Publishers and Authors, 1972), 103.

The woman was saved first. At first she was afraid to have any direct contact with Jesus. That would be too embarrassing. But she thought that perhaps she could just get close enough to touch his robe. We can imagine her waiting on the fringes of the crowd, working her way a little closer and a little closer, and then spotting his robe just within her reach. Luke tells us, "She came up behind him and touched the fringe of his garment, and immediately her discharge of blood ceased" (Luke 8:44).

It was a marvelous and miraculous healing. The woman was saved by the mighty power of Jesus Christ. All she touched was the corner of his garment, but even that was enough to save her. She was healed completely; for the first time in more than a decade, she was no longer bleeding. She was healed freely; this was the first cure she did not have to pay for, not to mention the first one that actually worked! She was healed instantly. All it took was one little touch, and she could feel supernatural power coursing through her body, healing her damaged tissues.

Jesus could feel it too. He asked, "Who was it that touched me?" (Luke 8:45). It seemed like a dumb question, at least to Peter. Jesus was in a crowd, and all kinds of people were touching him. So when everyone denied it, Peter said, somewhat impatiently, "Master, the crowds surround you and are pressing in on you!" (Luke 8:45). But Jesus would not be denied. Whether or not he performed this miracle by deliberate intent, he knew what had happened. He could tell that his divine power had been released into someone's life. So he insisted, "Someone touched me, for I perceive that power has gone out from me" (Luke 8:46).

This comment is mysterious, because it seems to imply that Jesus could heal people unawares, that he could perform a miracle without intending to do so. Maybe the woman was healed by a direct act of God the Father, or by a supernatural work of the Holy Spirit. But if so, one wonders why something like this did not happen more often. People were always touching Jesus, but they were not always getting healed.

It is also possible that Jesus really *did* know who touched him, and that he knew it all along. People generally assume that when Jesus asked who touched him, he was asking for the sake of his own information. This is not impossible. By becoming a man in his incarnation, God the Son voluntarily assumed certain limitations, including limitations of intellect and cognition. His mind was as human as the rest of him, so with respect to his humanity (not his deity), he did not know all things. But in this case it is more than likely that Jesus knew exactly what had happened, that in fact he had willed it to happen. Therefore, he was not asking for his own benefit, but for the sake of the crowd, and for the woman herself.

Notice the effect that this question had on her. She was desperately hoping not to be noticed. When Jesus asked his question, she must have been mortified. Remember, she was not permitted to touch anyone. So if people found out that she had pushed her way through the crowd—or worse, that she had dared to lay a hand on Jesus—they would be indignant. They would humiliate her publicly. This is why she wanted to remain anonymous. In fact, we get the impression that she had already started to slip away. But now she was exposed. She knew that Jesus knew, and everyone else knew it too: "And when the woman saw that she was not hidden, she came trembling, and falling down before him declared in the presence of all the people why she had touched him, and how she had been immediately healed" (Luke 8:47).

Now we can see why Jesus asked who touched him. Rather than letting this woman remain anonymous, Jesus called her out to give a public testimony of God's saving work in her life. At first was this more than a little bit scary. The woman was afraid to be exposed. But Jesus was not trying to embarrass her; he was giving her an opportunity to glorify God. Now everyone knew how she had been healed: by reaching out and touching Jesus. By openly declaring this, she brought honor to her Savior's name.

Some people would prefer to keep salvation a secret. They are willing to reach out for Jesus in their own private way, as long as no one else knows about it. They want to be healed by a secret touch, but they don't want to make a stand for Jesus.

Whatever else we may say about such people, it is doubtful that they are Christians, because Christians make an open confession of Jesus Christ as Savior and Lord. Jesus said, "Everyone who acknowledges me before men, I also will acknowledge before my Father who is in heaven, but whoever denies me before men, I also will deny before my Father who is in heaven" (Matt. 10:32–33). The truest confession of our faith is not a private moment alone with Jesus, but a public witness to his grace, even if we give it—as this woman did—with fear and trembling.

411

"Never keep silence," wrote Abraham Kuyper, "or accustom yourself to reticence. You must speak out for the Christ. He who does not do so, or who is loathe to do so because of embarrassment, becomes guilty of denying his Savior."[2]

BELONGING TO CHRIST

Jesus had another reason for asking who touched him. Not only did it give the woman a chance to confess her faith, but it also brought her into a relationship with her Savior. Salvation means much more than touching Jesus once and getting healed. It means entering into a personal relationship with him. Thus the conversation ends with Jesus saying, "Daughter, your faith has made you well; go in peace" (Luke 8:48).

In these few short words, Jesus teaches us what it means to belong to him. First he speaks about the grace of adoption, calling this woman "Daughter." This is the first and only time in the Gospels that Jesus speaks to someone this way. For twelve agonizing years she had been alienated from human society. There must have been many times in her long suffering when she felt completely rejected, even by God. All she wanted was someone to hold her and take care of her. Now she was wrapped up in the embrace of her Savior. Jesus had not called her out to humiliate her after all, but to save her, to heal her, and to love her as God's own dear child.

Next Jesus speaks about the gift of saving faith, telling the woman it was her faith that made her well. We could even say that her faith "saved" her, because the word Jesus used for healing is a form of the basic New Testament word for salvation *(sozo)*. Of course, it was really the power of God in Christ that healed her, but the way she gained access to that healing power was by reaching out to Jesus with the hand of her faith. However timid she may have been, when she touched the corner of his robe, she believed that she could be healed. This was not some kind of magical superstition; it was simple faith in the person and work of Jesus Christ. This daughter of God trusted Jesus for her salvation, and by faith she gained access to his saving power.

2. Abraham Kuyper, *The Implications of Public Confession*, trans. Henry Zylstra, 6th ed. (Grand Rapids: Zondervan, 1934), 53–54.

Then Jesus sent the woman on her way with the blessing of his peace. She had come to him in all kinds of turmoil, desperate for a saving cure. But she departed in peace. She had physical peace; her body was restored. She had spiritual peace; she had entered into a personal saving relationship with Jesus Christ. And she had social peace; now that her cure was public knowledge, she would no longer suffer scorn and prejudice, but she would be reintegrated into the community of God's people.

These are blessings that Jesus has for everyone who reaches out to him in faith. He gives us his love, making us the sons and daughters of God. We do not have to hold back, alone and afraid, avoiding other people and hardly daring to approach God. No matter what we have done, or what we have suffered, Jesus will welcome us into the Father's love with open arms. And he will give us his peace, watching over us forever with the benediction of his grace. Within his own person, on the basis of his crucifixion and resurrection, Jesus has the power to heal us in all the ways we need to be healed—from sorrow, abandonment, abuse, depression, and the guilt of our sin. All we need to do is grab hold of him by faith and trust his power to save.

Faith, not Fear

This might seem like a good place to stop, but there is more to the story. The whole time that Jesus was speaking with the woman he had healed, Jairus was waiting with groaning impatience. His little girl was dying, and there was not a moment to lose. Why did Jesus keep stopping to help people? Every minute he delayed was another minute his daughter suffered, and another minute that brought her closer to death.

Then someone came running up with the news that Jairus had been dreading for days: "While he [Jesus] was still speaking, someone from the ruler's house came and said, 'Your daughter is dead; do not trouble the Teacher any more'" (Luke 8:49). This gives the impression that Jairus had been trying to hustle Jesus along, tugging at his sleeve and reminding him to hurry. But now it was too late. Jesus had waited too long. The girl was dead, and all that anyone could do was to mourn her passing. As the servant said, there was no reason to trouble Jesus any longer.

413

This statement echoed the words of the centurion back in chapter 7, when he said, "Lord, do not trouble yourself. . . . But say the word, and let my servant be healed" (Luke 7:6–7). On that occasion, telling Jesus not to trouble himself was a statement of faith. The centurion believed that Jesus did not have to go in person; all he had to do was say the word. But this time it was an admission of unbelief. The servant simply assumed that whatever power Jesus had could not possibly extend beyond the grave. Obviously there was nothing more that he or anyone else could do.

When Jesus overheard what the servant said, he immediately interrupted. "But Jesus on hearing this answered him, 'Do not fear; only believe, and she will be well'" (Luke 8:50). Now we can see why these two stories are paired together, and perhaps also why Jesus took so long to get to Jairus's house. It was all in the providence of God. If he had wanted to, Jesus could have healed the girl without even going to the house. Instead, he followed Jairus home, and along the way, performed a healing miracle that demonstrated the power of faith. Now Jesus would give a more complete demonstration of his saving power, and the first miracle that he performed would help Jairus trust in his power to perform the second. There were two miracles, both of which call us to faith in Jesus Christ.

All Jairus had to do was believe, but even that must have seemed impossible. The moment he heard that his daughter was dead, grief overwhelmed his soul and fear clutched at his heart. But Jesus told him not to be afraid. He told him to have faith, which is the very antithesis of fear.

Faith and fear always stand in opposition. This means that we have a choice to make: either we can be afraid of all the things that might go wrong, and have gone wrong, or we can trust Jesus to see us through. We face this choice all through life. Am I afraid of what might happen to my children, always fretting about their physical and spiritual safety, or do I entrust them to God's fatherly care? Am I afraid of what people will say if I take a stand for Christ, or do I trust God to vindicate me? Am I afraid of losing everything I own, or do I trust God to provide what I truly need? Am I afraid that I will never get what I want out of life, or do I trust God to give me the desires of his heart? In every anxious situation, Jesus calls us to trust in him.

A simple illustration of the way fear finds its answer in the Christian's faith comes from the Blitz, when the Nazis were bombing London:

> A father, holding his small son by the hand, ran from a building that had been struck by a bomb. In the front yard was a shell hole. Seeking shelter as soon as possible, the father jumped into the hole and held up his arms for his son to follow.
>
> Terrified, yet hearing his father's voice telling him to jump, the boy replied, "I can't see you!"
>
> The father, looking up against the sky tinted red by the burning buildings, called to the silhouette of his son, "But I can see you. Jump!"[3]

Jesus calls us to exercise the same kind of trust in him, not leaping blindly in the dark, but falling into his arms because we hear his voice. We trust him for the forgiveness of our sins through his death on the cross. We trust him for spiritual healing from the wounds we have suffered in a fallen world. We trust him for the grace to endure trials with patience and perseverance. We trust him for the reconciliation of relationships, and for the salvation of the people we love.

THE AWAKENING

What was remarkable in this situation is that such faith was extended beyond the grave. Jesus told Jairus not to be afraid, even in the face of death, but only to believe. What he told him to believe was that his daughter would be well—literally, that she would be saved (Luke 8:50). This sets the stage for one of the most dramatic scenes in the Gospel: "And when he came to the house, he allowed no one to enter with him, except Peter and John and James, and the father and mother of the child. And all were weeping and mourning for her, but he said, 'Do not weep, for she is not dead but sleeping.' And they laughed at him, knowing that she was dead" (Luke 8:51–53).

The mourners had already gathered, and the sound of their lamentation filled the house. Jairus and his wife were weeping, too, in the inconsolable

3. Donner Atwood, *Reformed Review*, quoted in Craig Brian Larson, *750 Engaging Illustrations for Preachers, Teachers, and Writers* (Grand Rapids: Baker, 2002), 196.

agony of parents grieving the loss of their little girl. Jesus was not unsympathetic. After all, as we saw in the previous episode, he knew what it meant to love someone like a daughter. Nevertheless, Jesus told them not to weep. But when he told them why, they scoffed at his obvious ignorance of basic medicine. The girl was dead, they said.

And the girl *was* dead. But Jesus said, "she is not dead but sleeping" (Luke 8:52). When he said this, Jesus was not offering a different diagnosis. Instead, he was introducing a whole different perspective on what it means to die, based on his divine power over life and death. Jesus knew that this girl would rise to live another day, so he said that she was only asleep. As one old commentator says, there is an entire sermon in the word "sleeping."[4] The girl's death was not permanent. The girl was dead to her family and friends, but as far as Jesus was concerned, she was only asleep.

So "taking her by the hand he called, saying, 'Child, arise'" (Luke 8:54). It was the simplest thing. Jesus touched the girl with his healing hand and said what her mother probably said to her every morning: "Get up, my child."[5] And she *did* get up, because by the power of Jesus, life came back into her body, reuniting her body and her soul: "And her spirit returned, and she got up at once. And he directed that something should be given her to eat. And her parents were amazed, but he charged them to tell no one what had happened" (Luke 8:54–56).

The girl came back to life as if waking from a dream. They gave her something to eat, so she could regain her strength. Then Jesus told the people who were in the room—her immediate family and his closest disciples—not to tell anyone what had happened. It would be their little secret, at least for the time being. The Gospel does not tell us why. They could not keep it a secret forever, of course; people would discover that the girl had come back to life. But whether he was trying to protect the little girl, or waiting for another time to reveal his resurrection power, Jesus was not looking for a lot of immediate publicity.

Bear in mind that the girl's resuscitation was only temporary because she had not yet received her resurrection body. So although Jairus and his

---

4. Jones of Nayland, as stated in J. C. Ryle, *Expository Thoughts on the Gospels, Luke* (1858; reprint Cambridge: James Clarke, 1976), 1:289.

5. See Leon Morris, *The Gospel According to St. Luke: An Introduction and Commentary*, Tyndale New Testament Commentaries (Grand Rapids: Eerdmans, 1974), 162.

daughter had their happy reunion, eventually they would be parted by death, and one of them would have to grieve all over again. The only real hope for them and for us is not resuscitation, but resurrection—the raising of our bodies to everlasting splendor in the kingdom of God.

The really important question is whether there is a resurrection for the dead, not just for a little while, but forever. Part of the purpose of this miracle was to prove that there is. What happened to Jairus's daughter is a picture of what will happen to every believer in Christ. Death is not the end for us. As soon as we die, our souls immediately enter the presence of Christ. As the Scripture says, to be "away from the body" is to be "at home with the Lord" (2 Cor. 5:8). Meanwhile, our bodies rest in the ground, waiting for the final resurrection. That resurrection is so absolutely certain that the Bible sometimes describes death as a kind of sleep: "For since we believe that Jesus died and rose again, even so, through Jesus, God will bring with him those who have fallen asleep" (1 Thess. 4:14).

Death is not the end for believers in Christ. In the same way that Jesus was raised on the third day, we too will be raised. Our bodies will sleep in death, but they will rise again. How do we know this? By faith—faith in Jesus Christ. And since faith is the antithesis of fear, we do not need to fear our own death, or the death of the people that we love in Christ. This story is a special comfort for parents who like Jairus suffer the loss of a child. One poet wrote:

When sickness, pain, and death
Come o'er a godly child,
How sweetly, then, departs the breath!
The dying pang, how mild!

It gently sinks to rest,
As once it used to do
Upon the tender mother's breast,
And as securely too.

The spirit is not dead,
Though low the body lies;
But, freed from sin and sorrow, fled
To dwell beyond the skies.

That death is but a sleep
Beneath a Savior's care;
And He will surely safely keep
The body resting there.[6]

Through faith in Christ, we have this hope for ourselves, and for all the children and friends we have loved and lost. Their souls live. Their bodies are only sleeping in the dust of death, and we will see them again at the resurrection. "Do not fear," Jesus says; "only believe, and all will be well."

---

6. Author and title unknown, quoted in James W. Bruce III, *From Grief to Glory: Spiritual Journeys of Mourning Parents* (Wheaton, IL: Crossway, 2002), 131.

34

AN INTERNSHIP FOR
THE APOSTLES

Luke 9:1–9

*And he called the twelve together and gave them power and
authority over all demons and to cure diseases, and he sent them
out to proclaim the kingdom of God and to heal.* (Luke 9:1–2)

*T*he best way of learning is by doing. A chef does not master the
art of fine cuisine from reading a cookbook, but rather from
stirring the sauce in the kitchen. A football player does not
learn how to block or tackle by staring at "X's" and "O's" on the chalkboard,
but by putting on some pads and hitting people. A seamstress does not
become a dressmaker by watching sewing demonstrations, but by working
with fabric and thread. Learning comes by doing.

So it was for the apostles. This band of brothers had been traveling
with Jesus ever since he called them to follow him (Luke 6:12–16).
They watched him perform miracles. They listened to him teach, puzzling over his parables and pondering the answers he gave to their endless questions. But the training of the twelve was not yet complete. The
disciples needed practical experience in the ministry of word and deed.

419

So Jesus "sent them out to proclaim the kingdom of God and to heal" (Luke 9:2).

Today people might call this an internship, like the ones that seminary students undertake to learn all the practical things they really cannot learn in the classroom. Or perhaps it was more like a short-term missions trip. In any case, it was an exciting moment. Jesus was coming to the end of his ministry in Galilee, but before he set his face towards Jerusalem and the cross (Luke 9:51), and before he gave his disciples their Great Commission to reach all nations with the gospel, he wanted to give them practical experience in ministry. So he sent them out on a mission into the surrounding communities.

A DOUBLE MISSION

In order for any internship to be effective, an intern needs to know his calling. This is something that the Presbyterian Church in America (PCA), to give just one example, takes very seriously. Pastoral interns work with church leaders to produce a detailed internship proposal, including a job description. Then, once their proposal is approved, interns are given a solemn charge: "In the name of the Lord Jesus Christ, and by that authority which He has given to the Church for its edification, we do declare you to be an intern of this Presbytery as a means of testing your gifts for the holy ministry wherever God in His providence may call you; and for this purpose may the blessing of God rest upon you, and the Spirit of Christ fill your heart."[1]

When Jesus sent out his apostles to test their gifts for ministry, he gave them a solemn charge as well, but in different and somewhat unusual terms. There were three main parts to the charge: first, their mission as apostles, which was a double mission to preach and to heal (Luke 9:2); second, the power and authority they needed to fulfill their mission (Luke 9:1); and third, the manner in which they were to execute their mission (Luke 9:3–5). Luke then shows us how the apostles fulfilled their mission (Luke 9:6), as well as how people responded (Luke 9:7–9).

---

1. The Book of Church Order of the Presbyterian Church in America, 5th ed. (Office of the Stated Clerk of the General Assembly of the Presbyterian Church in America, 2001), 19–10.

The apostolic mission was twofold. Jesus sent his disciples out "to proclaim the kingdom of God and to heal" (Luke 9:2). Thus their ministry involved both preaching and healing. They ministered to people's bodies as well as their souls.

Preaching came first. The primary calling of the apostles was to proclaim the good news of the kingdom of God. This also happened to be the primary calling of Jesus Christ. Back in chapter 4, when people were clamoring for him to keep healing, Jesus said, "I must preach the good news of the kingdom . . . ; for I was sent for this purpose" (Luke 4:43). This was the apostles' purpose as well: to preach the gospel of God's kingdom.

After spending time with Jesus, the apostles had many things to teach. They could instruct people in the proper understanding of the law, as they had received it from Christ. They could call people to repentance, pleading with them to turn away from sin. They could teach them to love their enemies, to build their lives on the rock, to receive God's word the way rich soil receives good seed, and to do all the other things that Jesus had taught them to do. But the best way to summarize their ministry of God's word is to say that they preached the kingdom.

The kingdom of God is not a territory protected by an army or an empire on a map, but a sovereign dominion over the hearts of God's people. God's kingdom is God's rule—his royal authority and sovereign reign. God is the King, so wherever he is, the kingdom is. The kingdom is present wherever God exercises his kingly power, and wherever people honor and serve him as their King.

Jesus had been preaching the kingdom ever since he began his public ministry (Luke 4:43). Now the apostles were to preach the same message, proclaiming that the kingdom had come in the person of Jesus Christ. "Proclaim" was just the word for it. This biblical word for preaching (kēryssō) has its origins in the royal court, where a herald would go out and announce the arrival of the king or some other news of public importance. In a similar way, the apostles went out as gospel heralds to announce the coming of Christ as King.

Then, in order to confirm the truth of their message, the apostles performed miracles of healing. Like Jesus himself, they cured the sick, cast out demons, cleansed lepers, and gave sight to the blind. Their miraculous healing ministry proved that what they said was true: the kingdom had come.

Christ had arrived as King to redeem people from the curse of the fall. He had come to save people body and soul, delivering them from death and disease. He cared for people's physical needs; he had the power to make them whole.

This was all confirmed by the miracles of the apostles, which in one way or another were signs of salvation. The apostles were not trying to call attention to themselves, but to Christ and his gospel. Their miracles showed that what they said about salvation was true. Obviously they could not heal everybody, and even the people they healed would get sick again, and eventually die. The most important thing, therefore, was not giving people some kind of temporary healing, but offering them eternal life through faith in Jesus Christ. The apostolic performance of miracles proved the proclamation of the apostolic gospel.

Our Mission

Preaching and healing had always been the main hallmarks of the public ministry of Jesus Christ. The apostolic mission to preach and to heal was therefore an extension of his saving work. This had been God's plan from the beginning. Rather than taking his gospel around the world himself, Jesus would in turn give it to his disciples, and they would carry it to the ends of the earth. By doing this, Jesus was multiplying his ministry. Together the apostles would preach the gospel to more people in more places than Jesus could ever do all by himself.

The gospel of his kingdom is still spreading. Today the ministry of Jesus and his apostles is extended through the church. As remarkable as it may seem, Jesus does his work in the world through the ordinary men, women, and children of the church. Together we are called to preach the good news of the kingdom of God. We proclaim the apostolic message of the cross and the empty tomb, announcing that through the death and resurrection of Jesus Christ, sinners can receive forgiveness from God, with the free gift of eternal life. This is our first and fundamental calling. In the words of J. C. Ryle, preaching is "God's chosen instrument for doing good to souls. By it sinners are converted, inquirers led on, and saints built up. A preaching ministry is absolutely essential to the health and prosperity of the visible church. The pulpit is the place where the chief victories of the Gospel have always been won, and no Church has ever done much for the advancement of true religion in which the pulpit has been neglected."[2]

We are also called to heal—in other words, to minister to people's material as well as spiritual needs. At certain times and in some places, this ministry may be miraculous, especially when the gospel first penetrates a culture. In order to confirm the truth of his word, God certainly can and sometimes may heal people in miraculous ways. But whenever and wherever the church gets established, the church itself becomes the confirmation of the gospel. How did people know that the apostles were telling the truth about God's kingdom? In part, because their miracles proved it. How do people know that *we* are telling the truth about salvation, especially when they cannot see Jesus in person? People do not know this by our miracles, ordinarily, but as a community of God's people we confirm the truth by our love, our suffering, and the sacrificial way we care for people's needs.

Like Jesus and the apostles, the church has a double mission. We are called to a ministry of *both* word and deed, and these two aspects of ministry should never be separated. As the church, we seek to meet people's physical as well as spiritual needs. This means caring for the sick, feeding the hungry, clothing the naked, visiting prisoners, welcoming strangers, and showing hospitality to the homeless. We do these things because Jesus did them. We do them because God cares for our bodies as much as he cares for our souls. And we do them because meeting people's needs helps confirm the truth of our message. Often people are not ready to receive Christ until they see his love demonstrated in a tangible way through the healing service of the church. Norval Geldenhuys summarizes by saying:

We must go into the world and (1) preach the kingdom of God—summon mankind to the realization that His divine and saving sovereignty has been fully manifested in the advent, passion, and triumph of Christ, and that they must repent so that they may, to His honour, share in the wealth of His mercy as He even now imparts it to every member of His kingdom and as He will impart it fully at the end of the age; (2) we must continue His works of mercy by working also for the deliverance of mankind from their physical need—through poor-relief work, care for orphans, hospital services (especially in

2. J. C. Ryle, *Expository Thoughts on the Gospels, Luke* (1858; reprint Cambridge: James Clarke, 1976), 1:292.

the mission field), institutions for the blind, prayers for the sick, work among prisoners and other undertakings in the service of suffering humanity.[3]

At some level, this is the calling of every church and every Christian. Proclaim the kingdom of Christ in word and deed. Care for people's physical and spiritual needs. Share the gospel, giving your life away in sacrificial service. Unless we do these things, we fail to fulfill our mission to the world. But if we do them, the kingdom of God is demonstrated in word and deed.

Mission Possible

It is one thing to have a clear mission, and another thing to complete it. The television show *Mission: Impossible* always began by describing a dangerous situation. The director would say, "Your mission, should you choose to accept it," and then he would explain the mission. But what he could not do was to guarantee its success. That was left up to the team on the mission, to their resources, and of course, to the ingenuity of the people who wrote the screenplay.

The apostles had much more than this to work with. When Jesus gave them their mission, he also gave them the divine authority and almighty power they needed to complete it: "And he called the twelve together and gave them power and authority over all demons and to cure diseases" (Luke 9:1). Power is the ability to do something; authority is the right to do it; the apostles needed both.

Obviously, the apostles needed the power to perform miracles. Otherwise, they would make complete fools of themselves. They were claiming that the kingdom had come, and they needed to be able to back up this claim by demonstrating the power of the kingdom. If they offered to heal people, and then failed to heal them, their gospel would have no credibility. So Jesus gave them his own divine power over demons and diseases. The apostles had seen him demonstrate this mighty power day after day, cleansing lepers, mending broken bones, raising the dead, and performing all kinds of healing miracles. Now, in the name of Jesus, they would have the

---

3. Norval Geldenhuys, *The Gospel of Luke*, New International Commentary on the New Testament (Grand Rapids: Eerdmans, 1951), 265–66.

same mighty power. They would cast out demons, give sight to the blind, and enable the lame to walk.

In addition to power, Jesus also gave his apostles the authority to perform these miracles. This is stated explicitly in verse 1, and also implied in verse 2, which says that Jesus "sent out" the twelve. The word "send" (*apesteilen*) is a form of the biblical word for "apostle" (*apostolos*). In the technical sense, an apostle is someone who is sent—specifically, someone sent to serve as an official representative, like an ambassador. The apostles in the biblical Gospels were the personal representatives of Jesus Christ. Those who were sent had "instructions to teach and act in the name of the Sender, on His authority."[4] This ensured that any power they were given would not be used for their own purposes, but only under the divine direction of Jesus Christ.

So the disciples were given power and authority; they had both the ability and the right to carry out their commission. Sometimes people have the power to do something, but not the authority. Then, if they proceed to use their power, they are abusing it. For example, a street gang may have the power to control an urban neighborhood, but it does not have the rightful authority. By contrast, a police officer may have the authority to stop gang violence, but if he does not have any backup, he may not have the power. The apostles had both power and authority—the power and authority of God the eternal Son.

This was especially important when it came to casting out demons. What right did these mere men have to command the demons? No right at all. Yet Luke tells us that Jesus gave the apostles authority over "all demons." Not even one fallen angel, except perhaps for Satan himself, could resist their will. If the apostles decided to cast out a demon, they could cast it out, freeing people from their bondage to demonic darkness.

The authority of these apostles was unique. They alone were fully authorized to serve as personal representatives of Jesus Christ, preaching the good news of his kingdom and performing its miraculous signs. To this day, we recognize their unique authority by reading their New Testament writings as the very Word of God. God has not given us the same power and authority that he gave to them as apostles. Nevertheless, God *has* given us power

4. Geldenhuys, *Luke*, 266.

and authority. Jesus Christ now does his saving work in the world through his people. Under his lordship, we have the authority to preach the gospel, saying, "Believe in the Lord Jesus, and you will be saved" (Acts 16:31). On the basis of God's Word, it is our responsibility and our right to tell people that if they trust in Jesus Christ, then on the basis of his sufferings and death on the cross, their sins will be forgiven.

We not only have the authority to do this, but also the power. We have the gospel of Jesus Christ—the good news that through his death and resurrection, Jesus has opened the way to eternal life—and this gospel "is the power of God for salvation to everyone who believes" (Rom. 1:16). We also have the Holy Spirit. When Jesus sent us out into the world to spread the gospel, he sent us with his Spirit. The Spirit has the power to save sinners, granting them the gift of faith and turning their hearts to God. The Spirit also gives us the power to continue serving God in the work of the gospel, even when we are weak and struggling. The Scripture says we are "strengthened with power through his Spirit" (Eph. 3:16). So whenever we are tempted to doubt that what we do for the Lord is accomplishing anything, we may ask God to empower us again by the inward work of his Holy Spirit.

Room and Board

The apostles had a twofold mission, with the power and authority to fulfill it. They were called to preach and to heal with the gospel. But to carry out this mission, they also needed to know how, so Jesus gave them a special set of instructions: "Take nothing for your journey, no staff, nor bag, nor bread, nor money; and do not have two tunics. And whatever house you enter, stay there, and from there depart" (Luke 9:3–4).

Jesus told the apostles to travel light. By way of comparison, former Philadelphia Eagles quarterback Koy Detmer once told reporters that he wore only one set of clothes on team road trips for the entire season. He never carried any luggage. But even Mr. Detmer, as light as he traveled, said that he stuck a toothbrush in his back pocket before he got on the airplane to leave town. The apostles traveled even lighter: no clothes, no food, no money—just their sandals and the robes on their backs. They were not even allowed to take a bag, perhaps because this might give the impression that they were beggars.

The apostles simply went as they were, and wherever they went, they did not stay long. Jesus told them to enter, stay, and leave from the same house. Maybe this meant that they should not look for luxury. Rather than moving from house to house, always searching for better lodgings, they were supposed to be content with what God provided. But something else seems to be going on here too. In those days, the conventions of hospitality did not allow long visits; people were careful not to overstay their welcome. So when Jesus told his disciples to leave from the same place they arrived, he was telling them that after a few days, they should move on to another town.

This schedule helps to convey the urgency of their mission. Jesus did not want his apostles to be distracted from their ministry, or to waste any time preparing for it. Thus they went "in haste, carrying not an ounce of superfluous equipment, relying entirely on hospitality, and wasting no time upon the inhospitable and unreceptive."[5] They were utterly dependent on God. This was an important part of their apostolic internship. Rather than relying on their own resources, the apostles had to entrust themselves entirely to God's providential care. In this way, they would learn to trust God for *everything*.

From time to time some Christians have concluded that every missionary should travel the same way: not taking any supplies or asking for any money. This is a good example of bad exegesis. To begin with, Jesus gave these instructions most specifically to the apostles, but never to the rest of the church. Furthermore, the apostles were still in Israel, serving the people of God, from whom they had a right to receive hospitality. In addition, Jesus later told the apostles to do almost exactly the opposite. At the end of the Last Supper he said, "But now let the one who has a moneybag take it, and likewise a knapsack" (Luke 22:36). So not even the apostles lived this way all the time. There is more than one way to trust God, and more than one godly way to gain the support we need for missionary work.

Having said that, however, we should remember how little we truly need, and how much God can be trusted to provide for the work of the gospel. One thinks of the missionary work of Hudson Taylor, who trusted God

5. G. B. Caird, *The Gospel of St. Luke* (London: Pelican, 1963), 126.

alone to provide for the China Inland Mission. Or one thinks of of the faith ministry of George Muller, who ran a famous orphanage in Bristol, England. Muller never did any fund raising for his ministry, but simply prayed and trusted God to provide. Christians in ministry often have more than they need, but never too little to do the work that God has called us to do. God always supplies what we truly need.

THE ULTIMATE QUESTION

God certainly provided the apostles with what they needed. He gave them power and authority for ministry, he met their daily needs, and he enabled them to carry out their mission. Carry it out they did, taking the good news of Jesus Christ into all the surrounding communities. As Luke tells us, "they departed and went through the villages, preaching the gospel and healing everywhere" (Luke 9:6). In other words, the apostles fulfilled all the requirements of their internship. This was an important step in their progress towards ministry, but it was also important for another reason: the gospel they preached was a matter of spiritual life and death.

When Jesus gave the apostles their instructions, he obviously attached special importance to the way people responded to their gospel. Some would receive the good news by faith. They would welcome the apostles into their own homes, and believe the gospel of the kingdom. But others would not even give them basic hospitality. This was more than bad manners; it was a rejection of God and his gospel. Remember, the apostles were representatives of Jesus Christ. To reject them, therefore, was to reject Christ himself.

Jesus told his disciples what to do when people rejected them: "And wherever they do not receive you, when you leave that town shake off the dust from your feet as a testimony against them" (Luke 9:5). This gesture amounted to a public rebuke. In effect, the apostles were to reject the town the same way that the town had rejected them. Shaking dust off their feet was a sign that people in that community were outside the kingdom of God. As Leon Morris explains, "There was a rabbinic idea that the dust of Gentile lands carried defilement, and strict Jews are said to have removed it from their shoes whenever they returned to Palestine from abroad. The disciples' shaking of the dust from their feet . . . declared in symbol that Israelites who rejected the kingdom were no better than Gentiles. They did not belong to the people of God."[6] This was a matter of spiritual life and death. Because these people rejected the apostles, they were cut off from Christ.

The same thing happens whenever we preach the gospel today. We proclaim the forgiveness of sins and the free gift of eternal life through the crucifixion and resurrection of Jesus Christ. People respond to this message in different ways. Some people believe it and are saved, while others reject it to their own condemnation. But either way, the gospel clarifies people's condition; it shows where they really stand spiritually. Until they hear the good news, it is our responsibility to give it to them; but once they hear it, it is their responsibility to believe it, or else to be lost forever.

There is a striking example of how one man responded to the gospel at the end of this passage. It is the example of Herod. This was Herod Antipas, the son of the infamous Herod the Great, who had sought to have Jesus killed when he was only a baby. Luke tells us that "Herod the tetrarch heard about all that was happening, and he was perplexed, because it was said by some that John had been raised from the dead, by some that Elijah had appeared, and by others that one of the prophets of old had risen" (Luke 9:7–8).

It is hard to know what all is included in the phrase "all that was happening." Perhaps this refers to everything that Jesus had done since the beginning of his public ministry—all the miracles that he had performed. Or perhaps it refers more specifically and immediately to the ministry of his apostles. Suddenly Jesus seemed to be everywhere. People all over Galilee were talking about his ministry. This is because the apostles had done their work well, not advancing themselves, but preaching Jesus Christ and performing miracles in his name. When they moved on to the next place, therefore, the people they left behind were all talking about Jesus. This is the perfect model for Christian ministry: touching people's lives in a way that leaves them deeply impressed—not with us, but with our Savior.

---

6. Leon Morris, *The Gospel According to St. Luke: An Introduction and Commentary,* Tyndale New Testament Commentaries (Grand Rapids: Eerdmans, 1974), 164.

Everyone in Israel was talking about the Savior. Who was this Jesus? People had different opinions. Some thought he was like John the Baptist, who was famous for preaching the kingdom of God. Others thought he was the second coming of Elijah, no doubt thinking of Malachi's great promise that Elijah would come again before the day of the Lord (see Mal. 4:5). Still others said that Jesus was one of the ancient prophets, back from the dead.

Understandably, Herod was confused. Some said this, while others said that, and it was hard to get the story straight. Frankly, all the talk about John the Baptist was starting to frighten him. Herod said, "John I beheaded, but who is this about whom I hear such things?" (Luke 9:9). From this question we learn, almost incidentally, that John the Baptist had been murdered. The last we heard, John was languishing in prison, wondering whether Jesus really was the Christ (see Luke 7:18–23). Now we know that John is dead—beheaded by the cruel hand of Herod.

To all of this Luke adds a haunting comment: "And he sought to see him" (Luke 9:9). Herod's curiosity was getting the best of him. He wanted to see Jesus. He wanted to know who he was. Maybe he just wanted to make sure that Jesus wasn't John the Baptist after all. Perhaps his guilty conscience made him afraid of John's ghost.

But whatever his reasons for wanting to see Jesus, Herod was asking the right question. It is the ultimate question that we each have to answer for ourselves and that ought to be at the center of our ministry. It is the question that Luke comes back to again and again in his Gospel: Who is Jesus? Each time someone asks, the question comes with greater and greater urgency, demanding an answer: Who is this Jesus? Each time the answer becomes clearer and clearer. Yet Herod never did get it right. He never came to faith in Jesus Christ. We know this because he did nothing to save Jesus from the cross, but instead allowed his soldiers to abuse him on the way to his execution (Luke 23:6–12; cf. 13:31).

Herod's example shows how absolutely crucial it is to make a firm decision for Christ. If we do not receive him by faith, we are really rejecting him, and eventually he will reject us. This is true even if we express some interest in Jesus. Herod was interested in Jesus, too. He found Jesus fascinating. He wanted to meet him and know more about him. But he never trusted him for salvation.

It takes more than idle curiosity for someone to come to Christ. It takes repentance for sin and faith that Jesus is the Son of God and the Savior of sinners. We need to do more than take a look at Jesus; we need to come to the right conclusion about him, knowing for sure that he is our Savior. Once we do, we will want other people to know Jesus too. We will go everywhere in the power of his Spirit and the authority of his name to preach the gospel and to heal people with the love of Christ.

35

FIVE LOAVES, TWO FISH, TWELVE BASKETS

Luke 9:10—17

> *And taking the five loaves and the two fish, he looked up to heaven and said a blessing over them. Then he broke the loaves and gave them to the disciples to set before the crowd. And they all ate and were satisfied. And what was left over was picked up, twelve baskets of broken pieces.* (Luke 9:16–17)

Sometimes I forget how to follow Christ and have to learn all over again. If it has happened to me once, it has happened a thousand times: I learn some basic lesson in Christian discipleship, but soon I forget, and then I find myself struggling spiritually. When I stop to ask why, I discover that I have been missing one of the basics—something I already know but somehow have managed to forget, again.

What are some of the basic lessons that Christians sometimes forget to remember? We forget to study the Bible, not remembering that God's Word gives us life. We forget the power of prayer, not remembering that God's blessing is ours for the asking. We forget that we cannot make it on our own, not remembering our deep dependency on the Holy Spirit. We forget that we do not have to work our way to heaven, not remembering that God has accepted us in Christ. We forget how much God loves us, not remembering that we are his sons and daughters. We forget that our Father knows best, not remembering to trust his sovereign plan for our lives. And we forget that God will provide, not remembering his promise to give us our daily bread.

Whenever we come down with this kind of spiritual amnesia, we go into spiritual decline. Our relationship with Christ ceases to be a joy and starts becoming a chore. Instead of being carried along by the wind of the Spirit, we trudge along under our own power, weighed down by the guilt of unconfessed sin. We experience unnecessary feelings of loneliness, doubt, discouragement, and anxiety. Very soon, unless we learn how to follow Christ all over again, we will be ineffective in our service to God. How quickly we forget, and how badly we need to remember.

A RETREAT INTERRUPTED

The apostles had the same problem. They seemed to forget almost as much as they learned from Jesus, especially in the early days of their discipleship. There is a notable example of this in Luke 9, where Jesus feeds the five thousand. This is one of Jesus' most famous miracles—one of only two miracles to appear in all four Gospels (the other is the resurrection). It comes near the end of Jesus' ministry in Galilee, at one of the climax points of the Gospel. Soon Peter will make his confession of the Christ. But first Jesus had one last great miracle to perform in Galilee, at the world's most famous picnic.

Everyone knows the story, but people do not always remember the context. The apostles had just completed their internship, so to speak. They had been preaching the kingdom and healing people all over Galilee—an amazing experience of God's power and provision in ministry. Now it was time for the disciples to go on a retreat and report on their short-term mission trip. According to Mark, they had not even had a chance to sit down and eat, so Jesus invited them to come away and rest (Mark 6:31). They must have been exhausted. What they needed most—and what we always need the most after a busy time in ministry—was time away with Jesus.

Jesus and his disciples were hoping to enjoy a little privacy, away from the public eye, but they could not escape for long: "On their return the apostles told him all that they had done. And he took them and withdrew apart to a town called Bethsaida. When the crowds learned it, they followed him, and he welcomed them and spoke to them of the kingdom of God and cured those who had need of healing" (Luke 9:10–11).

This is a powerful witness to the compassion of Christ and his servant-hearted ministry. The hordes of people that followed Jesus were invading his privacy and disturbing his rest. Most people would have been tempted to ask them to come back later, or to send them away altogether. But Jesus welcomed all comers. He was willing to be inconvenienced and interrupted, as long as he had an opportunity to preach the kingdom and perform its miracles. The way Jesus welcomed these people reminds us that we can go to him at any time; he will listen to our cry for help. It also sets the pattern for our own ministry. Even when we are tired and weary, wanting to take a break from other people and their problems, we need to be ready to give them the gospel and to help them in any practical way we can.

Jesus was always ready to receive people in need, and when he received them, he was always able to help them. Luke tells us that Jesus cured anyone and everyone who needed healing. There was not one single case that he could not resolve. This is a powerful testimony to his grace. There is hope for everyone in Jesus, because he is able to save anyone who comes to him for help. This is as true for us spiritually as it was for the crowds medically. By the power of his grace, Jesus is able to forgive our sins, renew our spirits, and comfort our sorrows. He is able to touch the wounded places in our hearts and make us whole.

All of this provides the background to a very practical difficulty: "Now the day began to wear away, and the twelve came and said to him, 'Send the crowd away to go into the surrounding villages and countryside to find lodging and get provisions, for we are here in a desolate place'" (Luke 9:12). The sun was going down in the desert. The hour was late, the shadows were lengthening, and before long it would be getting dark. As the day wore on, the disciples began to have some logistical concerns. They wondered where everyone would get something to eat, not to mention a place to stay. They were out in a remote area, far from anything resembling a roadside hotel, and it was hard to imagine where so many people could find room and board.

434

Apparently the disciples were thinking about others, but the way they approached Jesus seems a little suspect. They were hungry too, and one wonders how much this had to do with their request, especially since it was more like a demand. Basically, the disciples told Jesus to get rid of the crowds. That way, everyone else could look after their own needs, while the disciples had Jesus all to themselves. But there were some things that they were forgetting and needed to remember.

Jesus Tests His Disciples

Jesus responded with a demand of his own. It was a test of their fitness for ministry—the final exam for their internship. Jesus said to his disciples, "You give them something to eat" (Luke 9:13).

This was a command, not a question. But what are we to make of it? Was Jesus serious, or not? Maybe he was trying to get the disciples to recognize their own inadequacy. On this interpretation, he wanted them to see that they were *unable* to give people something to eat, in the hope that they would remember to depend on him to supply whatever was needed.

This may be the right interpretation, but there is another one that we should at least consider. The statement Jesus made was emphatic, and the emphasis fell on the word "you." Jesus was putting the onus on the apostles. He was saying, "*You* give them something to eat." They were the ones who noticed what the people needed, and who wanted to send them away to get it. They were also the ones who had a responsibility to provide. Jesus was insistent: "You feed them!" Here it helps to remember the context. The apostles had just completed a short-term missions trip on which they had performed many miracles. Could it be that in the name of Christ, they also had the power to feed the hungry?

We will never know, because the disciples never obeyed Christ's command. Instead, they said that they were powerless to help: "We have no more than five loaves and two fish—unless we are to go and buy food for all these people" (Luke 9:13). The very idea sounded absurd, especially when we learn that "there were about five thousand men" (Luke 9:14), not including the women or children. How could the disciples provide food for so many people? All they had was five loaves and two little fish—hardly enough to go around. Nor did they have the money to buy what was needed. Feeding everyone would have cost a fortune (eight months' wages, according to Philip; see John 6:7), especially for men traveling without any money. The only reason the disciples even mentioned the idea of buying groceries was to show how impossible it was, and perhaps to show how ridiculous it was for Jesus even to suggest such a thing.

The trouble with the disciples was that they were looking at things from a merely human perspective. They were acting like men without a God, thinking only in terms of what they had on hand and what they had the ability to provide from their own resources, not considering the power and the providence of their God. David Gooding remarks that Jesus' question ought to have "startled them into thinking that there might be more to the kingdom of God and the powers of Jesus than they had yet realized. Instead of that, the highest their thoughts could rise to was the possibility of going to the nearest merchants (wholesalers, of course) and of buying the necessary quantity of food."[1] The disciples were forgetting that they had a God, not remembering his power to provide.

At the very least, they should have asked Jesus to supply what they were unable to give. To be sure, the disciples had never seen this kind of miracle before. Jesus had been unveiling his powers gradually, healing one person at a time. He had not yet demonstrated his divine power to give people the bread of life. So we can understand why the disciples did not anticipate this miracle in advance. Yet by now they should have learned to expect the unexpected from Jesus, and to ask for his help whenever things were humanly impossible.

The feeding of the five thousand reminds us not to forget that God is not limited by our inadequacies. Rather, our very limitations can display the glory and the grace of Jesus Christ whenever he does what we are unable to do: His power is made perfect in our weakness (2 Cor. 12:9).

One man who understood this principle well was Robert Morrison, the famous missionary to China. In 1805 the London Missionary Society recruited Morrison to go to China. It was the time of the Napoleonic wars, however, and the only British ships traveling to China belonged to the East India Company, which refused to transport missionaries. So Morrison went to the United States, hoping to book passage to Canton. When the owner

---

1. David Gooding, *According to Luke: A New Exposition of the Third Gospel* (Grand Rapids: Eerdmans, 1987), 162.

of the ship heard about Morrison's plans, he was skeptical. "And so, Mr. Morrison," he said, "do you really expect that you will make an impression on the idolatry of the great Chinese Empire?" "No, sir," Morrison quickly replied, "I expect God will."[2] Through Morrison's ministry, in all its weakness, God *did* make an impression on China's idolatry, with spiritual results that last until the present day. It is when we know that we are at the end of our own resources that we are ready to see what God will do.

Dinner Impossible

In this particular case, what God did was to make a miraculous provision, through his Son and our Savior, Jesus Christ:

> And he said to his disciples, "Have them sit down in groups of about fifty each." And they did so, and had them all sit down. And taking the five loaves and the two fish, he looked up to heaven and said a blessing over them. Then he broke the loaves and gave them to the disciples to set before the crowd. And they all ate and were satisfied. And what was left over was picked up, twelve baskets of broken pieces. (Luke 9:14–17)

Everyone was astounded. Most Christians have heard this story so often that we forget how utterly amazed the people must have been. The tense of the Greek verb indicates that Jesus kept breaking and breaking the bread. The more he broke it, the more there was for everyone to eat, until finally everyone was satisfied. Five loaves were multiplied to feed five thousand. To put this miracle into perspective, imagine the logistics involved in planning a meal for five thousand people. Better yet, try to imagine having five thousand people show up unexpectedly for dinner. Then imagine trying to feed them all from the leftovers in the refrigerator!

The feeding of the five thousand was truly a miracle. This may seem obvious, but it needs to be said, because people sometimes deny the miracles of Christ, and this miracle has been treated with as much skepticism as any of the others. What some people doubt is that Jesus had the power to do anything that went beyond the ordinary laws of nature,

2. The story is recounted in David Aikman, *Jesus in Beijing* (Washington, DC: Regnery, 2003), 36.

as this miracle obviously did. By multiplying the loaves and fishes, Jesus was making new matter, which the skeptic says can neither be created nor destroyed.

So what really happened? Skeptics often say that everybody shared. They were so inspired by the person who contributed the five loaves and the two fish (a little boy, John tells us; John 6:9) that they all opened their bags and began to share whatever they had. The real miracle, some people say, was a miracle of generosity.

Such an interpretation robs Jesus of his glory. Curiously, it also requires nearly as much faith as it takes to believe in the miracle itself. Where would people who ran after Jesus on the spur of the moment get so much food? If they had brought their own food, then why were the disciples worried about them? And what would be the point of passing it all in and then having Jesus pass it all out again?

The real difficulty, however, is that a merely natural explanation contradicts what we read in Luke and the other Gospels. The Bible gives four different accounts of what happened that day—two that come directly from eyewitnesses (Matthew and John)—and they all agree on the basic events. Jesus did this miracle out in the open, where everyone could see it. To their complete astonishment, people saw Jesus give them more and more food from the same five loaves and the same two fish. It was so impossible that none of them could explain it, but none of them could deny it either: it was a real miracle.

THE MEANINGS OF THE MIRACLE

The most obvious meaning of this miracle is that God will provide. As he provided for his people in the wilderness, so he will provide for us—not in the same miraculous way, perhaps, but by the same powerful grace.

We need to remember this because sometimes we are tempted to forget. God has promised to provide for our needs, both as the church and as individual Christians. He will give us our daily bread, providing food, clothing, and shelter. He will meet our needs for friendship and fellowship. He will give us the guidance that we seek in faith. He will provide a way for us to serve him. And when God gives us the opportunity to serve, he will give us all the resources we need to fulfill our calling. We are not limited by what we have on hand, or by what we are able to provide for ourselves; we are enabled by the power and providence of God.

God's provision is abundant. The disciples kept going back to Jesus for more food, and every time they went back, there was always more. In the words of Alexander Maclaren, "The pieces grew under his touch, and the disciples always found his hands full when they came back with their own empty."[3] Even after everyone was fully and finally satisfied, there was still more left over: twelve full baskets of broken pieces (Luke 9:17). In other words, there was one basket of leftovers for each and every disciple. This was a powerful object lesson in the abundance of God's grace. The weight of those baskets would help the disciples remember that Jesus had provided far more than they ever expected.

Every time God meets our needs, we should savor the abundance of his provision, so that the next time we find ourselves in need, we do not forget to trust in him. Even if we have learned this lesson before, there are times when we need to learn it all over again. God has provided for us in the past, and he can be trusted to provide for us again in the future. How long will his provision continue? All through life, and then on through eternity. In the words of one little poem, "Yesterday, God helped me, / Today He'll do the same. / How long will this continue? / Forever—praise his name."[4]

When we think of the feeding of the five thousand, we probably think first of material provision. That is not the only meaning of this miracle, however. Jesus really did meet the material needs of the people who listened to him preach, and unless he did, there is nothing else for us to learn from this miracle. The only God who can help us is a God who is able to provide. Nevertheless, meeting people's physical needs was not the miracle's only purpose. Like all of his miracles, the feeding of the five thousand teaches us even deeper truths about the person and work of Jesus Christ.

To begin with, the miracle testifies to the deity of Jesus Christ. When Luke describes the location of this miracle as "a desolate place" (Luke 9:12), he

3. Alexander Maclaren, *The Epistles of St. Paul to the Colossians and Philemon*, The Exposition Bible (New York: A. C. Armstrong, 1903).

4. Anonymous, quoted in R. Kent Hughes, *Luke: That You May Know the Truth*, 2 vols., Preaching the Word (Wheaton, IL: Crossway, 1998), 1:331.

calls us to think back to Israel's wanderings through the wilderness between Egypt and the Promised Land (see Ex. 16). This connection is made even more explicit in the Gospel of John, who tells us that after Jesus performed this miracle, people asked him about the manna in the wilderness (John 6:31). They were making a connection between what Jesus provided for them and what God had provided for his people during the exodus from Egypt. This was the right connection to make. Just as God had provided daily manna in the days of Moses, so now once again God was providing bread in the wilderness, in the person of his Son.

Incidentally, this provides a clear answer to Herod's earlier question (Luke 9:9): Who is this Jesus? The answer is that he is God the Great Provider. This is something to remember, and not to forget: Jesus is one and the same as the God of the Old Testament, who cares and provides for his people.

What else does this miracle teach? The power of prayer. The feeding of the five thousand teaches us to trust God for what we need, not worrying about how we will get it, but asking God to provide. Here Jesus is our great example. The disciples were anxious about where people could get some food. But Jesus was not worried at all; he simply prayed. Thanking God, Jesus "looked up to heaven and said a blessing" (Luke 9:16). In contrast to his disciples, who were only looking at the difficulties of their situation, Jesus looked to his Father in heaven. Perhaps when he blessed God he used the ancient Jewish table benediction: "Blessed art Thou, O Lord our God, King of the universe, who bringest forth bread from the earth."[5] But whatever he said, Jesus said it with his eyes turned to his Father, in dependence upon his grace.

We can turn in the same direction. Through faith in Jesus Christ, we are sons and daughters of our Father in heaven. Now, whenever we find ourselves in any need, we remember to turn to our Father in prayer, trusting him to provide. Then we turn to him again in thanksgiving, as Jesus did, blessing him for our daily bread.

This miracle also shows that we have a part to play in the work that Jesus is doing on earth. Jesus was the one who broke the bread, but he gave it to his disciples to distribute. Of course Jesus could have handled the distribu-

---

5. Norval Geldenhuys, *The Gospel of Luke*, New International Commentary on the New Testament (Grand Rapids: Eerdmans, 1951), 271.

tion himself. If he had the power to produce the bread, then obviously he had the power to pass it out as well. Instead, "he broke the loaves and gave them to the disciples to set before the crowd" (Luke 9:16). Earlier Jesus told the disciples to give the people something to eat, and now they were doing it. They could not provide the food themselves; only Jesus could do that. But there were some things that they could do. They could recognize people's needs; they could give Jesus what they had—the loaves and the fish; and they could give away what Jesus provided. Thus the people would be fed through their ministry.

This miracle is virtually a parable for Christian ministry. From time to time we see what people need, spiritually and otherwise. Whatever we have to give is woefully inadequate, but we offer our time and our talents, the best that we are able to give. Then Jesus takes it, and by the supernatural power of his grace, he uses it to help people. He also uses *us* in the process, so that we join in the work of his kingdom. This is what the apostles experienced in the early church. God gave them gifts of preaching, prayer, and evangelism. In their own strength they would have accomplished nothing, even for all their gifts. But they offered themselves in ministry to the service of Jesus Christ, and by the provision of his grace, they were able to spread the gospel all over the world.

We need to remember that we have the same privilege today. God is using us to teach his Word, share the gospel, and demonstrate the love of Christ through deeds of mercy. Even if we do not feel that we have very much to offer, God can multiply our ministry. We must never forget to give what we have for the work of God's kingdom, and then ask God to use it for the glory of Jesus Christ. Norval Geldenhuys comments:

> It is vain for us to attempt by ourselves to give real food to needy mankind with our five little loaves and two fishes—the insignificant gifts and powers possessed by us. But when we place at His disposal, in faith and obedience, everything we have received from Him, He will, in spite of our own insignificance and poverty, use us nevertheless to feed souls with the bread of eternal life. He sanctifies, blesses and increases our talents and powers, everything consecrated by us to His service.[6]

6. Geldenhuys, *Luke*, 270–71.

441

THE SUFFICIENCY OF CHRIST

These are all valuable lessons to learn. One of the reasons this miracle has such a special place in the hearts of God's people is that it speaks to so many of our needs. But after everything else has been said about this passage, the main lesson is simply this: all we really need is Jesus.

The miraculous feeding of the five thousand met people's physical needs. In fact, once they had tasted the bread that Jesus provided, they wanted to eat it all the time. In the Gospel of John, Jesus accuses them of only coming to him for physical food. "You are seeking me," he said, "because you ate your fill of the loaves" (John 6:26). But if that is all that people wanted, they were missing the point. "Do not labor for the food that perishes," Jesus went on to say, "but for the food that endures to eternal life" (John 6:27). In other words, the meaning of the miracle is spiritual and eternal, not merely temporal and physical.

Going back to the Old Testament, physical bread was always a symbol of spiritual sustenance. This was true of the manna in the wilderness. Moses told the children of Israel that God gave them special bread so they would "know that man does not live by bread alone, but man lives by every word that comes from the mouth of the LORD" (Deut. 8:3). Similarly, Isaiah describes salvation in terms of eating bread that truly satisfies (Isa. 55:1–3). Bread means life, and the Bible uses this physical symbol to speak of the spiritual life that we have in God.

By feeding the five thousand, Jesus was teaching us to find our life in him. We could probably infer this from the Gospel of Luke, but in case there is any doubt, the Gospel of John makes it perfectly explicit. There Jesus says "the bread of God is he who comes down from heaven and gives life to the world" (John 6:33). "I am the bread of life" (John 6:35), he goes on to say; "I am the living bread that came down from heaven. If anyone eats of this bread, he will live forever" (John 6:51). Jesus is our nourishment and provision, our sustenance and satisfaction. "The heart of man," wrote J. C. Ryle, "can never be satisfied with the things of this world. It is always empty, and hungry, and thirsty, and dissatisfied, till it comes to Christ."[7] It is

---

7. J. C. Ryle, *Expository Thoughts on the Gospels, Luke* (1858; reprint Cambridge: James Clarke, 1976), 1:303.

in Christ that we have the forgiveness of sins, a new relationship with God, and all the other blessings of salvation.

Jesus gives us this life through his death on the cross and his resurrection from the grave. Later he said, "The bread that I will give for the life of the world is my flesh" (John 6:51). In other words, he would offer his very body for our salvation. Jesus was speaking of his crucifixion, of the life that he gave for our sins when he died on the cross. Of all the things that we need to remember and never forget, this is the most important: the provision of eternal life that comes by trusting in Christ crucified.

What we need is Jesus. Only Jesus. The Jesus who offers his body as the true and everlasting bread. Are you still remembering this, or have you been forgetting?

36

Confessing Christ Crucified

Luke 9:18–22

Then he said to them, "But who do you say that I am?" And
Peter answered, "The Christ of God." And he strictly charged
and commanded them to tell this to no one, saying, "The Son
of Man must suffer many things and be rejected by the elders
and chief priests and scribes, and be killed, and on the third
day be raised." (Luke 9:20–22)

Suddenly it all becomes so clear. For a long time we cannot seem
to gain perspective, but in a moment everything opens out and
we are able to see with perfect vision. The mind unexpectedly
seizes on the solution to a mathematical equation. As an airplane lost in the
fog drops below the cloud deck, the pilot can see the runway lights. Moun-
taineers climb above the timberline, and in an instant they see the whole
valley stretched out below them. Everything becomes clear.

So it is with faith in Jesus Christ. For a time—maybe a long time—we
cannot seem to gain the spiritual perspective that we seek. God seems to
remain just beyond our grasp. We see the shapes shifting in the mist of eternity, but we struggle to make out the meaning of life. We wander through

the dark forest of doubt, wondering if we will ever come out into the clearing. Then suddenly it happens: our souls are bathed in sunlight, and we see the salvation of God in the person of his Son.

C. S. Lewis writes about this kind of experience in his spiritual autobiography, *Surprised by Joy*. Lewis had been wrestling with the claims of Christ, and as God pursued him, gradually he came to believe in Christianity more and more. Still, he had not yet fully accepted the deity of Jesus Christ. Then one day it happened. Lewis writes: "I know very well when, but hardly how, the final step was taken. I was driven to Whipsnade one sunny morning. When we set out I did not believe that Jesus Christ is the Son of God, and when we reached the zoo I did. Yet I had not exactly spent the journey in thought. Nor in great emotion. . . . It was more like when a man, after long sleep, still lying motionless in bed, becomes aware that he is now awake."[1]

Who Is Jesus?

The first disciples had a similar experience. For months or even years they had been following Jesus, listening to his words and witnessing his miracles. During that time Jesus was inviting them to consider his identity, in the hope that they would trust in him for their salvation. He brought them along slowly, allowing them to reach their own conclusions on the basis of inductive reasoning. But finally the time came for Jesus to ask them directly: Who did they think he was?

Jesus asked this question when he was alone with his disciples, away from the crowds. He began by inquiring about the opinion of others: "Now it happened that as he was praying alone, the disciples were with him. And he asked them, 'Who do the crowds say that I am?'" (Luke 9:18). What was the word on the street? What verdict were people reaching in the court of public opinion? Jesus was not asking these questions for his own information, but testing his disciples so they would recognize his person and work.

The disciples gave several plausible answers, all based on what they had heard: "John the Baptist. But others say, Elijah, and others, that one of the prophets of old has risen" (Luke 9:19).

1. C. S. Lewis, *Surprised by Joy: The Shape of My Early Life* (New York: Harcourt Brace Jovanovich, 1955), 237.

445

At least on this occasion, John the Baptist was the number one answer. To us this may sound strange, because we know that Jesus and John were two entirely different people. They came from two different families, they were given two different names, and they had two different missions in life: John was the herald, while Jesus was the King. Nevertheless, we can understand why people made this mistaken identity. Many people in Galilee had never met John; they knew him only by reputation. Since what they knew about Jesus sounded so much like what they had heard about John, it was natural for them to associate the two men in their minds, especially since they were cousins. Both men had a large following, both men were present at the same baptism, and both men preached the same basic message about the kingdom of God. The association was so close that people who knew of John's beheading may even have thought that Jesus was the second coming of the Baptist (see Luke 9:7).

Another leading vote getter was the prophet Elijah. This was largely because of Malachi's prophecy: "Behold, I will send you Elijah the prophet before the great and awesome day of the Lord comes" (Mal. 4:5). On the basis of this promise, pious Jews were waiting for Elijah with eager expectation. In truth, Malachi's prophecy was about John the Baptist and his ministry in preparing the way for Christ. As one of the angels announced near the beginning of Luke's Gospel, John came "in the spirit and power of Elijah" (Luke 1:17). Yet we can understand why some people made the connection with Jesus. Jesus was a great prophet, and some of the miracles that he performed—like giving people bread, for example, or raising a widow's son from the dead—were similar to miracles that Elijah performed (see 1 Kings 17:8–24). Could it be that he was the second coming of Elijah?

Other people had other opinions. Some drew a comparison with the prophet Jeremiah. Many said he was like Moses, teaching the law and providing bread in the wilderness. Still others were not entirely sure which prophet he was, but they knew they were in the presence of someone great, like one of the mighty men they had read about in the Scriptures. People had many different opinions about Jesus.

The same is true today. People disagree about the true identity of Jesus of Nazareth. Some say he is only a legend, that his Gospels are merely a fiction. Others admit that Jesus existed—no serious historian can reasonably doubt that he did—but they deny his deity. Their only interest is in his teaching, not his miracles, and certainly not his atoning death or resurrection from the dead. They believe that Jesus was a noble prophet, a moral teacher, a successful politician, or a wise sage, but they do not believe that he was the Son of God. In the words of one theologian, the "Jesus of Nazareth who came forward publicly as the Messiah, who preached the ethic of the Kingdom of God, who founded the Kingdom of Heaven upon earth, and died to give His work its final consecration, never had any existence."[2]

Then there are many people who recognize that there is something special about Jesus, but are not quite sure what it is. They respect his teaching and admire his life, but they do not worship him as their Savior and their God. They are wandering in the mist of spirituality, still waiting to get a clear vision of Jesus. They are not yet awake to his true identity as the Son of God and the Savior of the world.

WHAT DO *YOU* BELIEVE?

It is always interesting to hear what people think about Jesus. Asking about this is a great way to start a conversation about spiritual things. But the question for us is what we ourselves believe about Jesus, and this is exactly where Jesus was heading with his disciples. What other people were saying was all very interesting, but it was not nearly as important as what was happening in their own minds and hearts. So Jesus asked the disciples for their own opinion about his true identity.

We know this question is important because Jesus prayed before he asked it. More than any other Gospel writer, Luke mentions the times that Jesus spent in prayer. He wanted to show that before each new phase of ministry, the Son of God went to his Father in prayer. Jesus prayed at his baptism (Luke 3:21). He prayed in the wilderness before he began to preach (Luke 4:1ff.). He prayed before he called his first disciples (Luke 4:42), and again when it was time to choose the twelve (Luke 6:12). Now it was time to pray again; this encounter took place "as he was praying alone" (Luke 9:18). Maybe Jesus was praying to see if this was the right time to ask his disciples who he was. Or maybe he was praying that they would come up with the right answer. But whatever the reason, it was a good time to pray. Jesus was

2. Albert Schweitzer, *The Quest for the Historical Jesus* (New York: Macmillan, 1959), 398.

about to ask the most important question in the world: "Who do you say that I am?" (Luke 9:20).

Luke has been asking and answering this question since the beginning of his Gospel. As he explained in the dedication, Luke wrote this Gospel to help people be more certain about Jesus Christ (see Luke 1:4). To that end, he carefully wrote down the events surrounding the Savior's birth, including messages from angels. He told about Jesus' childhood and gave his genealogy. He recorded his first sermon and documented his early miracles. Luke also reported how people responded to Jesus. His goal in all of this has been to help us be absolutely sure who Jesus is.

Now it was time for Jesus himself to put the question directly to his disciples: "Who do you say that I am?" The word "you" in this question is emphatic. "Some people say one thing, and others say something else, but *you*, what do *you* say?" Jesus was bringing his disciples to a point of personal commitment. What mattered was not what other people were saying, but what they believed for themselves.

Jesus was asking his disciples, but as we read the Gospel, he is also asking us. Who do *you* say that Jesus is? This is the most important question in the world, because Jesus is the most important person in the universe. The Bible says, "all things were created through him and for him" (Col. 1:16), and "in him all things hold together" (Col. 1:17). So if we truly want to understand anything about anything, we have to know who Jesus is. But the question is also important because the answer we give determines our destiny. Heaven and hell are hanging in the balance. The Bible says that the free gift of eternal life is only for those who know Jesus Christ (see Rom. 10:9–10), but how can we know him for sure if we do not even know who he is?

So Jesus asked the crucial question: "Who do you say that I am?" (Luke 9:20). When he asked, the whole universe could have stopped to wait for the answer. The very Son of God was asking for someone to declare his true identity. But before any suspense could build, Peter blurted out the answer: You are "the Christ of God" (Luke 9:20).

How typical it was for Peter to answer first. He was by far the most outspoken disciple, often serving as the spokesman for the others. Peter always had something to say, even if he did not always raise his hand first, and even if he had a knack for saying the wrong thing at the wrong time. But on this occasion, Peter got the answer absolutely right: Jesus is the Christ.

Peter had many good reasons to say this. Like the other disciples, he had thought through some of the alternatives. He had considered whether Jesus might be John the Baptist, or Elijah, or one of the other prophets. But none of those answers quite seemed to fit. There was a connection between Jesus and these prophets, all of whom pointed to his ministry. But calling Jesus another prophet did not go far enough in recognizing his unique supremacy. Peter knew this because he had been with Jesus from the beginning. He watched Jesus demonstrate his power over demons, disease, and death. He saw him rule the wind and the waves. He even tasted the bread that Jesus brought down from heaven. As Peter considered everything he had seen and heard, suddenly it all became perfectly clear: Jesus is the Christ of God.

This was more than a matter of inductive reasoning, however; it was also a matter of faith. As we learn from the Gospel of Matthew, Peter said this because God the Father revealed it to him (Matt. 16:17). This is how anyone comes to know Jesus as the Christ—by studying what he has said and done in the Gospels, and also by the supernatural work of God's Spirit, who alone can reveal his true identity. When people are struggling with the claims of Christ, it is not just more evidence they need, but a gracious work of God that changes their minds and hearts. This is the true biblical doctrine of salvation, that *God* enables us to confess our faith in Christ. It is rational to believe in Jesus for salvation, but no one ever comes to him by reason alone. Only the Spirit of God is able to persuade us to believe that Jesus is the Christ.

WHAT DOES *CHRIST* MEAN?

What does it mean to confess that Jesus is the Christ of God? *Christ* is not Jesus' last name, but a title of honor. It is the Greek equivalent to the Hebrew word *Messiah*. To say that Jesus is the Christ, therefore, is to say that he is the Messiah. But what does Messiah mean? Literally, the Messiah or the Christ is "the anointed one"—the one who has been chosen by God and consecrated for sacred office.

Here it helps to know some Old Testament background. When a prophet, priest, or king was set apart for the holy service of God, he was anointed with oil. For example, when Aaron was ordained as high priest over Israel, Moses was instructed to "take the anointing oil and pour it on his head and anoint him" (Ex. 29:7). The other priests of Israel were consecrated the same way, with the anointing of oil. On occasion, prophets were also anointed. Thus Isaiah was able to say, "the LORD has anointed me to bring good news" (Isa. 61:1; cf. Luke 4:18).

Anointing was for prophets and priests, but especially for kings. In fact, most of the Old Testament references to anointing relate to royalty. So it was that Samuel anointed David king over Israel (1 Sam. 16), Zadok anointed Solomon (1 Kings 1:39), and Elisha anointed Jehu (2 Kings 9). The anointing of the king with oil was a physical symbol of his spiritual calling. From that time forward, the king was called "the anointed one," the Messiah, the Christ (e.g., 1 Sam. 2:10; 2 Sam. 22:51; Ps. 89:20).

Many prophets, priests, and kings were anointed to lead Israel. But along the way there were hints that one day God would send the greatest Prophet, the highest Priest, and the mightiest King of all. The people of God knew these ancient promises. They knew that one day a deliverer would crush Satan's head (Gen. 3:15). They knew that God would raise up a prophet like Moses from among his brothers (Deut. 18:18). They knew that a mighty king would come from the royal city of David (Mic. 5:2). They knew that his kingdom would endure, that he would rule "on the throne of David and over his kingdom" forever (Isa. 9:7; cf. 2 Sam. 7:12–16; Ps. 89:4). So the people of God waited in hope for *the* Anointed One, *the* Messiah, *the* Christ.

Different people had different ideas about what the Messiah would do when he came. Many people expected some kind of political deliverance, the establishment of an earthly dominion, with the defeat of Israel's enemies and the exaltation of Jerusalem. The disciples themselves were prone to this kind of thinking. Even after Jesus was raised from the dead, they wondered when it would be time for Jesus to "restore the kingdom to Israel" (Acts 1:6). Others understood the more spiritual aspects of his kingdom. But whatever people were expecting, it took them a while to recognize Jesus as the Christ.

Luke has been dropping hints about the true identity of Jesus since the beginning of his Gospel. He has carefully shown that Jesus came from the royal house of David (Luke 1:27), that he was born in Bethlehem (Luke 2:4), that he had the right to reign on David's throne (Luke 1:32–33), that he came to fulfill the ancient promises of salvation (Luke 1:68ff.), that in the explicit words of the Christmas angels, he is "the Savior, Christ the Lord" (Luke 2:11). Luke even showed how Jesus was anointed with the Holy Spirit (Luke 3:21–22; cf. Acts 10:38).

Peter may not have known all of this, but he had seen Jesus in action. He had witnessed his authority over demons and his power over creation. He had watched Jesus raise the dead and offer the forgiveness of sins. He was an eyewitness to many miracles, culminating in the feeding of the five thousand. Peter had been taking it all in, thinking about what it all meant. Therefore, when he was asked who Jesus was, the answer came right out: Jesus is the Chosen One, the anointed King, the expected Messiah, the Christ of God.

By using this particular title, Peter was declaring that Jesus came from God. The phrase "of God" indicates origin, so the expression "Christ of God" declares that Jesus is the Messiah sent from God, the Savior that God had always promised to send. The title is virtually an intimation of Christ's deity. It means that Jesus is the divinely appointed Savior, who came from the very throne of God to bring salvation to everyone who believes in him.

Are you able to make the same confession that Peter made? Consider your response to Jesus as he is presented in the Gospel. Is it clear to you that he came from God? Do you see that he is the Savior whom God promised? It is not enough to admire Jesus as a great man. Even Muslims believe that he is a prophet, and many secular historians admit the wisdom of his teaching. The question about Jesus—the most important question in the universe—is whether he is in fact the Christ, the true God and unique Savior of the world. Anyone who confesses this will be saved.

CHRIST, CRUCIFIED

Peter's confession of the Christ is the climax (to this point) of Luke's Gospel. Thus it would seem like a moment to celebrate. After months of training, the disciples finally understood who Jesus was. Surely it was time for them to rejoice in Jesus as the Christ, and for Jesus to praise them for their profound understanding of his person.

Instead, Jesus immediately began preaching to them the gospel of his crucifixion and resurrection. Before there could be any misunderstanding

451

about what it meant for him to be the Messiah, Jesus "strictly charged and commanded them to tell this to no one, saying, 'The Son of Man must suffer many things and be rejected by the elders and chief priests and scribes, and be killed, and on the third day be raised'" (Luke 9:21–22). Knowing that Jesus was the Christ was not the end; it was only the beginning. As soon as the disciples knew who he was, Jesus began telling them what he had come to do. We do well to follow the same pattern in our own personal evangelism, introducing people to Jesus and his saving work. Knowing his person is a prerequisite for fully understanding his work. A good place for us to begin, therefore, is by telling people that Jesus of Nazareth is God the Son.

We can scarcely imagine the disciples' confusion and dismay as they heard Jesus' extraordinary words about suffering, death, and resurrection. What on earth was Jesus talking about? Why was he talking about suffering and dying, and why was he so adamant in refusing to let them tell anyone that he was the Christ? For months they had been struggling to figure out who he was, watching his miracles, listening to his words, searching the Scriptures, talking amongst themselves, and trying to determine their teacher's true identity. Who was this man? Now they finally had their answer. When they heard Peter confess Jesus as the Christ, they knew that this *had* to be right. But as soon as they got the right answer, Jesus started talking about things that raised all kinds of further questions.

Jesus also swore his disciples to silence, giving them strict orders not to share it with anyone else. Why wouldn't he let them tell people who he was? Scholars still debate the purpose of this so-called messianic secret, but the reason is fairly obvious: the disciples were just beginning to understand who Jesus was, and they had no clear idea what he had come to do. If they started to tell everyone who Jesus was, they were bound to give people the wrong idea. At most they would give a half-gospel that was really no gospel at all. It would be like when a parent starts giving instructions to a child, and the child runs off before the instructions are finished. The job will not get done right, if it gets done at all.

Waiting for instructions was especially important in this case because most people were looking for the wrong kind of Messiah. Their aspirations and expectations were largely military. They were looking for a Christ who could deliver them from the Romans, and thus enabled them to live in a nation that was ruled by the law of God. So if the disciples did not wait until they had a better understanding of what Jesus had come to do, the gospel would get all mixed up with politics. Later Jesus would send them out to tell the whole world who he was (see Luke 24:44–49). But that would only be after the training of the twelve was complete, when they were ready to go global. For now, they needed to keep listening to what Jesus had to teach. No one can share the gospel without first knowing what the gospel is.

Waiting was also important because when Jesus started teaching about his saving work, the disciples had no idea what he was talking about. Jesus said that he would suffer and die, which was just about the last thing the disciples ever imagined that he would say. As far as they were concerned, the Messiah was a mighty deliverer and a triumphant ruler. For him to suffer and to die was incomprehensible, which explains why the disciples abandoned Jesus at the cross. They did not understand what was happening, even though Jesus had tried to explain it to them in advance. For the disciples, a rejected Christ was virtually an oxymoron. Of all the things Jesus ever said to them, this was the most confusing, the most shocking, the most impossible to understand. But Jesus did not come to meet their expectations, or our expectations, or anyone else's expectations. He came to do his Father's will in the plan of salvation, which meant suffering and dying for sin. The only Christ there is to confess is Christ crucified.

All of the prophecies Jesus made to his disciples came true. He suffered many things: the accusations of enemies, the betrayal of friends, the abuse of soldiers, and the scorn of low criminals. He was rejected by the rulers of Israel—"the elders and chief priests and scribes." This refers most specifically to the trial where the Jewish council known as the Sanhedrin denied that Jesus was the Christ. Leon Morris comments: "The word *rejected* seems to be a technical term to denote rejection after a careful legal scrutiny held to see whether a candidate for office was qualified. It implies here that the hierarchy would consider Jesus' claims but decide against Him."[3] This too was part of his suffering: that his own people rejected him for not being the very Savior that he actually was. Then Jesus was killed. The apotheosis of his suffering and rejection was the crucifixion: his painful, shameful death on

3. Leon Morris, *The Gospel According to St. Luke: An Introduction and Commentary*, Tyndale New Testament Commentaries (Grand Rapids: Eerdmans, 1974), 169.

the cross. Jesus was nailed to the cursed tree and left to die a slow, bloody, excruciating, God-forsaken death.

It was not simply that these things *would* happen, but that they *had* to happen. It was a divine necessity. Jesus said, "The Son of Man *must* suffer many things and be rejected and killed" (Luke 9:21). He was under divine compulsion. Jesus was the Christ, and these were all things it was necessary for him to endure in order to do the work of the Christ. They were necessary because they were promised in the Scriptures and because they were part of God's plan, the covenant between the Father and the Son, the everlasting agreement for our salvation. They were also necessary because in the court of eternal justice there was no other way for sin to be forgiven except through the atoning death of the perfect Son of God.

CHRIST, RISEN

Jesus knew all this in advance and embraced it long before it happened. The things he suffered were not incidental or accidental, but fundamental to his person as the Christ. Thus as soon as Peter made his confession, Jesus said, "Yes, I am the Christ, but if you want to make that confession you must confess me as the *crucified* Christ."

Even this is not all. Jesus would also be raised from the dead on the third day. This too was part of the plan. There would be triumph in the end, a crown to follow the cross. After the Christ was crucified, he would rise from the dead in glorious splendor, promising eternal life and all the blessings of God in heaven to everyone who believes in him. Here was the first preaching of the full gospel: not just the kingdom and the cross, but also the empty tomb. This is what it meant for Jesus to be the Christ. It is what the gospel is all about: suffering, rejection, and crucifixion, before dying and rising again.

Can you even imagine what the disciples must have been thinking when Jesus told them this? If so, can you also understand why they were not yet ready to proclaim him as the Christ? Cyril of Alexandria wrote,

> There were things yet unfulfilled which must also be included in their preaching about him. They must also proclaim the cross, the passion, and the death in the flesh. They must preach the resurrection of the dead, that great and

truly glorious sign by which testimony is borne him that the Emmanuel is truly God and by nature the Son of God the Father. He utterly abolished death and wiped out destruction. He robbed hell, and overthrew the tyranny of the enemy. He took away the sin of the world, opened the gates above to the dwellers upon earth, and united earth to heaven. These things proved him to be, as I said, in truth God. He commanded them, therefore, to guard the mystery by a seasonable silence until the whole plan of the dispensation should arrive at a suitable conclusion.[4]

It will take the whole rest of the Gospel for these events to unfold. Luke has spent nine chapters introducing us to the *person* of Jesus. He has given us a clear answer to his first great question: Who is Jesus? The answer is that he is the Christ, the Messiah, the Son of God anointed to be our Savior. From here on out Luke will focus on the *work* of Jesus. What did he come to do? The answer the Gospel gives is that he came to suffer and to die for our sins, and then to rise again with the free gift of eternal life for everyone who confesses him as the crucified and risen Christ.

What is your confession? Who do *you* say that Jesus is, and what do you believe that he came to do? The Gospel of Luke testifies that Jesus is the Christ of God, who suffered and died on the cross for sinners, and who was raised from the dead to give eternal life. Even the disciples did not understand all this the first time Jesus explained it to them. They needed to hear the gospel many times before it began to make sense to them. But eventually they believed it and were saved.

Is the gospel clear to you? If it is, then you can say, on the basis of what you read in the Bible, and by the work of God's Spirit in your mind and heart, that "Jesus is the Christ." Your soul is alive to the full realization that Jesus died for your sins and rose again to give you eternal life. Maybe all of that is clear to you. Then again, maybe it is not yet clear at all, and you are still trying to understand it. The way to understand the gospel is by hearing the same message that Jesus first preached to his disciples, and by asking God for the faith to believe in the crucified and risen Christ.

---

4. Cyril of Alexandria, "Commentary on the Gospel of Luke" (Homily 44), in *Luke*, ed. Arthur A. Just Jr., Ancient Christian Commentary on Scripture, NT 3 (Downers Grove, IL: InterVarsity, 2003), 155.

37

THE CROSS OF DISCIPLESHIP

Luke 9:23–27

And he said to all, "If anyone would come after me, let him deny himself and take up his cross daily and follow me. For whoever would save his life will lose it, but whoever loses his life for my sake will save it." (Luke 9:23–24)

*T*he only way to follow Jesus is to follow him to the very death, every day. Frankly, most Christians wish there could be some other way to follow Jesus—an easier way. We had hoped that Jesus would refrain from making too many costly demands, that he would endorse the plans we already had for our lives, or at least that he would let us live for him with as little inconvenience as possible. We said we wanted to follow Jesus, but what we really meant was that we would follow him as long as he was going more or less the way we were planning to go. Instead of giving up the life that we had, we wanted to find a way to add Jesus to it.

If that is what we had hoped for, we were badly mistaken. There is no easier way, no more convenient Christianity. Jesus calls us to make a comprehensive and costly sacrifice. To every one of his disciples he says, "If anyone would come after me, let him deny himself and take up his cross daily and follow me" (Luke 9:23).

456

The Terms of Discipleship

Like everything else that Jesus said, these words need to be understood in their proper context. Peter had just made his dramatic confession of Jesus as the Christ (Luke 9:20). On the basis of what he had seen and heard, and by the inward witness of God the Holy Spirit, Peter correctly identified Jesus as the Messiah, the Anointed One. This was a major revelation: the disciples finally recognized Jesus as the Christ of God.

This was only the first step, however. In addition to knowing the person of Jesus, the disciples also needed to understand his work. So Jesus immediately began to teach them the things he needed to do for their salvation. He would endure suffering, rejection, and death before rising on the third day. Jesus *had* to do these things because he was the Christ, and these were the things that the Christ was sent to do. The only Christ that Peter or anyone else can confess is Christ crucified and risen.

All of this was very hard for the disciples to understand. When Jesus began speaking about his crucifixion and resurrection, they basically had no idea what he was talking about. But then Jesus said the hardest thing of all: just as he would suffer unto death, so also his disciples would suffer and die on the cross of daily self-denial. So here, in the space of just a few short verses, Jesus proclaimed the whole gospel message and applied it to daily life. He said, "Look, here is what is going to happen to me, and if you want to follow me, the same thing will happen to you. You will have to follow me all the way to the cross, because that is where I am going."

Truly this is what it means to confess Jesus as the Christ. It means much more than simply knowing who Jesus is, or what he came to do. It means that his life, in all its suffering, becomes the pattern for our lives. The only Christ that anyone can confess is Christ crucified, and the only way to confess him is to follow him all the way to the cross. Thus Jesus said, "If anyone would come after me, let him deny himself and take up his cross daily and follow me" (Luke 9:23). This is Christ's own definition of what it means to be a Christian—the terms of discipleship.

Jesus gave these terms "to all," but he was speaking especially to his would-be disciples. In the interest of full disclosure, he wanted them to know exactly what they were getting into. Furthermore, he was speaking to *all* of his disciples: there were and are no exceptions. When Jesus said, "If *anyone* would come after me," he meant that this was the only way to follow him at all. A life of sacrifice and self-denial is not just for super-Christians who share the gospel door to door or travel to a dangerous mission field; this life is for anyone and everyone who wants to be his disciple.

As Jesus issued the terms of discipleship, he used three different verbs to describe what every disciple must do: deny, take up, and follow. These are really three different ways of saying the same thing, but each has a slightly different emphasis.

The first verb is "deny," and what Jesus calls us to deny is our selves, meaning especially our sinful selves, with all the selfish desires of our fallen nature. The Greek verb "to deny" *(arneomai)* is a strong word of negation that in this case means to forget oneself entirely, to reject any thought of doing what will please ourselves rather than God. Instead of gratifying ourselves or indulging ourselves in all the ways our sinful nature desires, we are called to deny ourselves, rejecting anything and everything that will get in the way of offering ourselves for God's service. This is almost exactly the opposite of the selfish way our culture is always telling us to live. We are constantly invited to get what we want out of life, to pamper our every whim and satisfy our every craving. We get so used to having things our way that when we do not get what we want, when we want it, we get angry.

Yet Jesus calls us to deny ourselves. By doing this, we are following his example. In becoming a man, Jesus denied himself the glories of heaven. In fulfilling the law, he denied himself the pleasures of sin. In dying on the cross, he denied himself protection from pain—not just physical pain, but also the spiritual anguish of being forsaken by his Father. Now Jesus calls us to deny ourselves so that we too may do the work that God has called us to do. This means saying no to sin, no to ungodly attitudes, no to unhealthy relationships, no to self-indulgent acquisitions, no to things that waste our time, and no to physical pleasures that sap our spiritual strength. It also means saying no to many things that are good in themselves, but are not God's will for us, at least at the present time. What are you accepting for yourself that Jesus wants you to deny? What are you holding on to that he is calling you to give up or give away?

At the same time that we deny ourselves, there is something that Jesus wants us to "take up" *(airō)*, namely, our cross. This is the second term of discipleship, and in it we have a premonition of the awful agony that

458

Jesus would endure in his crucifixion. The disciples did not yet know this, of course. Later the cross would become a symbol of everything that Jesus did for them (and for us) in salvation. But for the present, the cross was simply a means of execution, like an electric chair or the syringe for a lethal injection.

In all likelihood, the disciples had seen what Jesus was describing: a rebel dragging his cross out to his own execution, according to the Roman custom. To take up one's cross was to go out and die. So this was a more radical way of talking about self-denial. As Leon Morris comments, "When a man from one of their villages took up a cross and went off with a little band of Roman soldiers, he was on a one-way journey. He'd not be back. Taking up the cross meant the utmost in self-denial."[1] It meant the very death of self.

Cross-bearing is something that goes well beyond the ordinary trials of daily life. When people complain about their problems, they sometimes say something like, "Well, I guess that's just my cross to bear." But Jesus was not talking primarily about the difficult people in our lives, or our work situation, or our physical limitations, or our financial hardships, unless we are suffering these things because of our faith. No, he was speaking specifically about the suffering that we endure for his sake, the hardships we face due to the very fact that we are trying to follow Christ. Norval Geldenhuys explains this well:

> He who desires to become His disciple and servant will every day have to be willing to put his own interests and wishes into the background and to accept voluntarily and wholeheartedly the sacrifice and suffering that will have to be endured in His service. The "cross" is not the ordinary, human troubles and sorrows such as disappointments, disease, death, poverty and the like, but the things which have to be suffered, endured and lost in the service of Christ—vituperation, persecution, self-sacrifice, suffering, even unto death, as a result of true faith in and obedience to Him.[2]

Joni Eareckson Tada takes this principle and applies it to daily life. As a quadriplegic, Joni has suffered more than most people, and in her suffering

1. Leon Morris, *The Gospel According to St. Luke: An Introduction and Commentary*, Tyndale New Testament Commentaries (Grand Rapids: Eerdmans, 1974), 170.

2. Norval Geldenhuys, *The Gospel of Luke*, New International Commentary on the New Testament (Grand Rapids: Eerdmans, 1951), 276.

she has also learned the difference between the ordinary struggles of life and true Christian cross-bearing. She writes:

> I have learned that it's a passion for God that will give you a passion for people. And this utter delight in Him will come from the toughest of trials that you are about to face. Our affliction becomes that which pushes and shoves us down the road to the cross. . . . And that's what it means to become like Him in His death. Don't think that the cross is simply the wheelchair, or an irritating job, or an irksome mother-in-law. The cross is the place where you die to sin and live to God.[3]

When Jesus speaks about the cross we bear for him, he says that it must be part of our everyday experience. "If you want to be my disciple," he says, "take up your cross *daily*." So Jesus is not speaking about something we do only at the beginning of the Christian life, or about the occasional sacrifice we make along the way, but about our everyday discipleship. Being a Christian does not mean going to church on Sunday, serving in a ministry or going to a small group Bible study once a week, and then living for ourselves the rest of the time. It means laying ourselves on the altar of daily obedience. How could a Savior who gave his life for us be content with anything less than seeing us live our lives for him? Jesus is calling us to daily crucifixion on our own personal cross.

The third verb that Jesus used was "to follow" *(akoloutheō)*. To be a disciple is to deny ourselves, take up our cross, and follow Jesus. By now it is perfectly clear that when Jesus called people to follow him, he meant following him all the way to the death. He has just said that he himself will endure suffering, rejection, and even death. Now anyone who follows this Savior must be prepared for the same kind of rejection. The Christian life is a life after Christ, marked by suffering and death. He bore the cross for us; now we bear the cross for him.

Is this the kind of life that you are leading? Are you following Jesus all the way? If so, then it should be easy to identify the things you are giving up for the gospel and the rejection you are suffering for the cause of Christ. If we keep the terms of Christian discipleship, then inevitably we

3. Joni Eareckson Tada, "Sent to Serve," *Wheaton* (Autumn 2005): 59.

suffer. We are bound to hear cynical remarks from our neighbors and to face ethical dilemmas at work. We are bound to have people criticize our uncompromising commitment to sexual purity or walk away from us because they do not want to hear us give them the gospel. We are bound to have occasional pangs of regret over things that we are giving up for the gospel, as we put more of our time and money at God's disposal.

If we are not experiencing these kinds of hardships it is doubtful whether we are following Christ in the biblical way. Confessing Christ means much more than simply believing in his cross; it also means taking up a cross of our own.

THE TRADEOFF OF DISCIPLESHIP

If we are going to accept the terms of discipleship and follow Jesus to the very death, then we must have some supremely compelling reason for doing so. Jesus gives us a good reason in the following verse. Why should we deny ourselves and take up our cross to follow him? Jesus says, "For whoever would save his life will lose it, but whoever loses his life for my sake will save it" (Luke 9:24). This is one of the great paradoxes of the Christian faith—the tradeoff of discipleship: to save your life is to lose it, but to lose your life for Jesus is to save it.

What does it mean to "save" your life, and what does it mean to "lose" it? The manner of Jesus' expression is important. He speaks first of those who "*would* save" their lives. As it turns out, they will not save them after all, but they would like to. In other words, their aspiration is self-preservation. Their ambition in life—what they will to do—is to protect themselves.

People who want to save their lives in this sense believe that their satisfaction and security are up to them. Thus they pursue their careers with blind ambition, working so hard that there is little time for anything else, even the people they claim to care about. Or they organize their lives around their entertainments, the pleasures they like to pursue. They want to get what they want to get out of life, so they keep their lives pretty much to themselves. They are not willing to make any costly, interpersonal investments in the kingdom of God. They call themselves

461

Christians, but they are not willing to suffer for the cause of Christ. They never go anywhere difficult or dangerous with the gospel. They rarely, if ever, have conversations with people that might expose their own spiritual commitments. Then, at the first sign of any hardship or persecution, their instinct for self-preservation takes over, and they pull back inside their comfort zone.

There is a tradeoff for all of this. Ironically, and very tragically, people who want to save their lives end up losing them. The word "loss" here suggests a total forfeit, like a ship that is lost at sea with all hands. What we lose in seeking our own salvation is absolutely everything, even our very lives. What Jesus means by this is not so much our physical lives, but our spiritual lives—not just now, but forever.

By contrast, whoever loses his life in Christ will save it. Notice that Jesus does not say, "whoever *would* lose his life," but "whoever *loses* his life" (Luke 9:24). The case is not theoretical, but factual. Jesus is speaking about something more than being willing to lose our lives; he is speaking about actually giving our lives for him. This is in keeping with his terms for discipleship, which demand that we carry the instrument of our own crucifixion with us wherever we go. God has not given us our lives to keep for ourselves, but to give away for him.

One young man who gave his life away for Jesus was James Franklin Pyles, a Wheaton College student who went to live in poverty among the Palestinians. Sadly, while Pyles was losing his life for Jesus in the summer of 2004, he was killed in a tragic accident. In both his life and his death, Pyles confirmed the truth of something he had once written about the cross of discipleship: "To give is merely to part with something that we possess. To sacrifice is to part with something that we possess, and will miss. There is a certain pain present in sacrifice that is not found in mere giving. . . . God did not merely give us forgiveness, but sacrificed Himself in order to give us redemption. It is this very cross of sacrifice that we are called to take up in order to follow Jesus."[4]

People who follow Jesus and take up the cross of discipleship end up saving their lives. This is true in the present because they save their lives from being wasted. Rather than squandering themselves for earthly

4. James Franklin Pyles, quoted in *Wheaton* (Autumn 2004): 49.

gain, they spend themselves for the glory of God, which is the only way to avoid leading a meaningless existence. Then in the life to come they will gain an even greater prize: everlasting joy in the presence of God. To give your life to Jesus is to save it, now and forever.

It was this tradeoff that led Jim Elliot to say, "He is no fool who gives what he cannot keep to gain what he cannot lose." Elliot was one of five famous missionaries to Ecuador who were killed by the Auca Indians in 1956. The Aucas were headhunters, and Elliot knew the danger of going to them. But he was willing to give up what he could not keep—life itself—in order to give them the gospel. He prayed, "Father, take my life, yea, my blood if Thou wilt, and consume it with Thine enveloping fire. I would not save it, for it is not mine to save. Have it, Lord, have it all. Pour out my life as an oblation for the world."[5] Elliot's prayer was answered. His life-blood was poured out as an oblation, but he was no fool, because in losing his life for Jesus, he gained something he could never lose: the everlasting pleasure of God.

Thankfully, we do not have to become martyrs to gain this prize, for there is more than one way to lose our lives. We lose them by giving ourselves completely over to Jesus in faith. We lose them by living for others, and not for ourselves. We lose them by showing kindness to strangers and compassion to children in distress. We lose them by giving people the gospel, even if they end up rejecting it, and rejecting us. We lose our lives by giving sacrificial support to the ministry of God's Word, locally and internationally.

As we give our lives away, by the grace of God, we end up saving them. This is the tradeoff that compels us to take up the cross of discipleship:

Everyone who tries selfishly to secure for himself pleasure and happiness in life will in fact doom his life to failure—he will never find real joy or full life. He commits spiritual suicide. But he who lays his life upon the altar in the service of Christ, who strives for His honor and for the extension of His kingdom, while keeping self in the background, will spontaneously find true joy and life—here and hereafter.[6]

5. R. Kent Hughes, *Luke: That You May Know the Truth*, 2 vols., Preaching the Word (Wheaton, IL: Crossway, 1998), 1:341.
6. Geldenhuys, *Luke*, 276.

THE TRAGEDY OF MAKING THE WRONG DECISION

The tradeoff of discipleship forces us to make some serious choices. Will we follow Jesus, or go our own way? Will we take up our cross, or leave it behind? Will we keep our lives for ourselves, or give them away for Jesus? The decisions we make determine our destiny.

With so much at stake, Jesus wanted to make sure that people knew how to calculate their alternatives. So he took the person who wanted to save his life and placed him in the best of all possible circumstances. He imagined someone living for himself and gaining everything the world had to offer— all its power, prosperity, and prestige. Then Jesus asked whether all of this would be worth the price of the person's soul. "For what does it profit a man," he said, "if he gains the whole world and loses or forfeits himself?" (Luke 9:25).

The question was a rhetorical one, of course, but the answer is that it profits a man absolutely nothing. A person's soul is more precious than anything else in the universe because it is made in the image of God and bound for eternity. To lose one's soul, therefore, is to lose one's most valuable possession and suffer eternal loss.

If not even the entire world can offset the cost of losing your soul, how much less the things that are in the world! Consider everything the world has to offer: its proud ambitions, its monumental achievements, its exciting entertainments, its luxurious pleasures. Then consider the smaller treasures you strive for every day—the purchases you are planning to make, the pleasures you feel you cannot live without, the position you are trying to gain. Is it really worth it to let these things stand in the way of obedience to Christ? Are they worth the price of your soul?

There is a poignant scene near the end of *A Man for All Seasons*, Robert Bolt's play about England's famous Lord Chancellor Thomas More. More fell out of favor with Henry VIII because he refused to support the king's marital infidelity. At length Henry arranged for More to be convicted on false charges and put to death. The king's accomplice in this nefarious plot was Richard Rich. In exchange for the kingdom of Wales, Rich had agreed to testify against Thomas More. At the end of the trial, as More passed by his accuser, he grabbed the medallion around Rich's neck, signifying his lordship over Wales, and said, "Why, Richard, it profits a man nothing to give his soul for the whole world . . . but for Wales?" If a man's soul is not worth the world, then it is not worth the kingdom of Wales, still less the things that we settle for.

Jesus was arguing from the greater to the lesser. If a man's soul is not worth the world, then it is not worth anything in the world either. Jesus was also speaking in the light of eternity. The reason worldly things do not profit is that our souls are bound for either heaven or hell. To make this perfectly clear, Jesus went on to say: "For whoever is ashamed of me and of my words, of him will the Son of Man be ashamed when he comes in his glory and the glory of the Father and of the holy angels" (Luke 9:26). This emphatic statement places the losing and saving of our souls in the context of the final judgment. Jesus knew that one day he would judge the world. He was looking beyond his cross to the crown that he will receive on the last day. He will come again in all his glory— his own glory and the glory of his Father, with all the heavenly angels. On that day he will judge every person who ever lived. He will render the final verdict that will determine our eternal destiny. Some he will welcome into the joy of his Father's heaven; others he will condemn to the fires of hell.

Consider what great joy there will be for people Jesus acknowledges as his own disciples. But consider as well what dreadful terror awaits those who will be abandoned by God. To lose or forfeit one's self, wrote J. C. Ryle, "is to lose God, and Christ, and heaven, and glory, and happiness, to all eternity. It is to be cast away for ever, helpless and hopeless in hell!"[7]

The Crown after the Cross

Who will suffer this great loss? Those who are ashamed of Jesus Christ, and of his words, and who therefore refuse to deny themselves and take up the cross of discipleship. This is a sobering warning, because there are times when we too are tempted to be ashamed of Christ. We hesitate to let people know that we are Christians. We are too timid to speak a word in his defense, or take a stand on a moral issue. We are afraid to

---

7. J. C. Ryle, *Expository Thoughts on the Gospels, Luke* (1858; reprint Cambridge: James Clarke, 1976), 1:311.

read our Bibles or pray in public. If we are so ashamed of Jesus, will he be ashamed of us?

The words of Jesus haunt us because there are times—too many times—when we *are* ashamed of him. But as haunting as these words are for us, they must have been all the more haunting for the disciples. They were even more ashamed of Jesus than we are, and at the time when it mattered the most. As Jesus went to his own cross—unashamed to take our guilt upon himself, and unashamed to die naked for our sins—his disciples were ashamed of him. Rather than denying themselves, they denied Jesus, as Peter did during his trial. Rather than taking up their crosses, they left Jesus to take up his cross alone, and afterwards, rather than proclaiming Jesus and his word, they gathered in secret shame.

Yet Jesus had grace for his disciples. He went to the cross to die for their shame, and when he was raised from the dead, he went back to give them the courage to meet the terms of his discipleship. By the power of the Holy Spirit, he enabled them to give their lives away for him and for his gospel. One day they will receive the blessed reward that Jesus has promised to all his disciples.

There is a reminder of this reward at the end of the passage, when Jesus says, "But I tell you truly, there are some standing here who will not taste death until they see the kingdom of God" (Luke 9:27). Whom was Jesus talking about, and what did he mean when he said that they would see the kingdom of God?

To "taste death" means to die, so Jesus was saying that some of his disciples would not die until they had seen the kingdom of God. Simply put, the kingdom of God is the rule of God. But when did the disciples see this? Obviously, Jesus was talking about something that happened long before his second coming, when his kingdom will come in all its glory. Different scholars offer different explanations. Some say this promise relates to the resurrection, or to the ascension, when Jesus left his disciples and returned to heaven in a cloud of glory. Still others say that Jesus was talking about sending his Spirit at Pentecost, when the apostles received the power of his kingdom to establish his church, or that this promise relates in some way to the destruction of the Jewish temple in A.D. 70. All of these events are connected to the kingdom in one way or another, and reveal its heavenly glory.

Or perhaps Jesus was talking about the transfiguration, which is the next incident in Luke's Gospel, and in which three of his disciples first saw him in all the glory of his everlasting kingdom. The experience of these disciples was exceptional, but Jesus has the same grace for us. He died for our shame as much as anyone else's. Now the Savior who suffered rejection for us is with us as we endure rejection for him. Soon he will welcome us into his Father's glory, if only we will answer his call to take up the cross of discipleship.

The renowned English novelist W. Somerset Maugham wrestled with the terms of discipleship at the end of his illustrious life. When he died in 1965, at the age of ninety-one, Maugham was still enormously popular, receiving more than three hundred fan letters a week. He was also fabulously wealthy. His nephew Robin describes what it was like to visit his uncle Willie in those days:

> I looked round the drawing room at the immensely valuable furniture and pictures and objects that Willie's success had enabled him to acquire. I remembered that the villa itself, and the wonderful garden I could see through the windows—a fabulous setting on the edge of the Mediterranean—were worth 600,000 pounds.
>
> Willie had 11 servants, including his cook, Annette, who was the envy of all the other millionaires on the Riviera. He dined off silver plates, waited on by Marius, his butler, and Henri, his footman. But it no longer meant anything to him.
>
> The following afternoon I found Willie reclining on a sofa, peering through his spectacles at a Bible which had very large print. He looked horribly wizened and his face was grim.
>
> "I've been reading the Bible you gave me. . . . And I've come across the quotation, 'What shall it profit a man if he gain the whole world and lose his own soul?' I must tell you, my dear Robin, that the text used to hang opposite my bed when I was a child."

Then, in that intimate moment, as he weighed the tradeoff of discipleship, with his soul hanging in the balance, the great writer said this: "Of course, it's all a lot of bunk." His nephew sadly went on to describe the bitterness of his uncle's last days, when he would cry out in terror: "Go away! I'm not ready. . . . I'm not dead yet. . . . I'm not dead yet, I tell you."[8] Somerset Maugham had gained the whole world, but when he tried to save his life, he lost it, to the forfeit of his own soul.

Do not waste your life. Do not be ashamed of Jesus. Do not lose your soul. But deny yourself, take up the cross of discipleship every day, and follow Jesus. He will save your life.

8. This story, which first appeared in the *London Times*, is recounted in Hughes, *Luke*, 1:342–43.

38

THE GLORY OF GOD THE SON

Luke 9:28–36

And as he was praying, the appearance of his face was altered,
and his clothing became dazzling white. . . . And a voice came
out of the cloud, saying, "This is my Son, my Chosen One;
listen to him!" (Luke 9:29, 35)

re you ever tempted to envy the apostles? Rather than simply reading the Gospels, as we do, the apostles lived them. When Jesus healed the sick and calmed the storm, they were there to see it. They were the first to learn the Lord's Prayer, to puzzle over his parables, and to learn everything else that Jesus had to teach. They were present when Jesus suffered his passion, returned from the grave, and ascended to heaven. The apostles witnessed Jesus when he made redemptive history.

On the basis of such experiences the apostle John was able to testify, "That which was from the beginning, which we have heard, which we have seen with our eyes, which we looked upon and have touched with our hands, concerning the word of life—the life was made manifest, and we have seen it, and testify to it and proclaim to you the eternal life, which was with the Father and was made manifest to us" (1 John 1:1–2; cf. John 1:14, 18). John was speaking about his relationship with the Son of God. He had heard the

Savior with his own ears, seen him with his own eyes, and touched him with his own hands. John had been with Jesus.

Sometimes it is tempting to think that the apostles had a relationship with Jesus that we could never experience, and that therefore it was easier for them to carry the cross of discipleship. Oh, to be among the apostles! We may not covet their sufferings for the gospel, but we wish we could have walked in their sandals with Jesus.

JESUS TRANSFIGURED

Of all the things the apostles witnessed, none was more spectacular than their vision of the glorified Christ. When Jesus called his disciples to take up the cross, he also said, "I tell you truly, there are some standing here who will not taste death until they see the kingdom of God" (Luke 9:27). It is not entirely certain what Jesus had in mind when he spoke about *seeing* God's kingdom, but he may well have meant the glorious revelation three of his disciples were given on the mount of transfiguration. It was their unique privilege to see something before they died that most believers see only after they die: the glory of God the Son.

This glorious encounter began with a private retreat for prayer: "Now about eight days after these sayings he took with him Peter and John and James and went up on the mountain to pray" (Luke 9:28). We get the impression that these three men were especially close to Jesus, forming an inner circle of disciples. One of the ways Jesus nurtured his friendship with these men and prepared them for spiritual leadership was to spend time with them in prayer. Really, this is how anyone develops a closer relationship with Jesus Christ: by spending time with him in prayer.

The prayers of these men were a sign that something important was about to happen, because in the Gospel of Luke, Jesus prays before each new phase of ministry (e.g., Luke 3:21; 6:12; 11:1). The Bible teaches us to pray at all times (see 1 Thess. 5:17), maintaining constant communion with Christ, but this is most necessary when we are about to take up a new calling, such as school, work, ministry, marriage, parenthood, or retirement. By his own example, Jesus teaches us to take time away with God in prayer.

This was no ordinary prayer meeting, because "as he [Jesus] was praying, the appearance of his face was altered, and his clothing became dazzling white" (Luke 9:29). The disciples had only ever seen Jesus in the limitations of his flesh, which was part of the humiliation of his incarnation. As they walked up the mountain, they saw him, as they always had, under the veil of his ordinary humanity. But then in a single instant, a flash of time, Jesus was revealed to them in all his divine splendor.

What, exactly, did the apostles see? In what can only be described as a major understatement, Luke says that "the appearance of his face was altered" (Luke 9:29). Matthew says more, telling us that Jesus "was transfigured before them, and his face shone like the sun" (Matt. 17:2). His appearance was not simply altered, but transfigured. In other words, it was illuminated with visible glory. Peter, James, and John saw a blinding display of light, as if they were caught in the high beams of heaven. Jesus radiated with divine incandescence, his deity shining through the veil of his humanity. As the disciples gazed into his face, they saw a radiant luminescence that revealed the glory of God's Son. Even his clothes were dazzling; as Mark says, they "became radiant, intensely white, as no one on earth could bleach them" (Mark 9:3).

As the disciples gazed upon this glorious revelation, they were catching a glimpse of something from the past. They were seeing the glory that the Son had with the Father before the world began (John 17:5)—the eternal splendor of his divine being. They were seeing a visible manifestation of God's invisible glory. Here, for the first time in the Gospels, they were witnessing the majesty of God the Son. As Luke puts it, "they saw his glory" (Luke 9:32).

The disciples were also seeing something from the present—not something from this world, but something from the hidden world of God's heavenly kingdom. They were seeing what the poet Edwin Muir described as "the unseeable one glory of the everlasting world."[1] There is more to reality than meets the eye. Beyond this world there is a supernatural realm of spiritual reality. The effect of the transfiguration, writes David Gooding, was to convince the disciples

> beyond any shadow of doubt of the real existence of the other world, the eternal kingdom. Our world is not the only one: there is another. Next they

1. Edwin Muir, "The Transfiguration," in *Chapters into Verse: Poetry in English Inspired by the Bible*, vol. 2: *Gospels to Revelation*, ed. Robert Atwan and Laurance Wieder (Oxford: Oxford University Press, 1993), 114–16.

were given to see that that other world is not just future to our world, but concurrent with it, though also before it and beyond it. They further saw that though that world is normally invisible to ours, Christ had contact with both worlds simultaneously; and what is more, though he was still on earth, his person and clothes could and did take on a radiance suited to the glory of the other world. [2]

Then too the apostles were seeing something from the future. They were catching a glimpse of the glory that God would reveal in Jesus Christ. They had heard Jesus speak about his sufferings and death, but here was a tangible sign that after his humiliation there would be exaltation, that after his crucifixion there would be glorification. Jesus would rise in a shining resurrection body, he would ascend to heaven to sit on God's majestic throne, and he would return with clouds of glory at his second coming. When Jesus was transfigured, the disciples glimpsed his everlasting glory. "He was bright as the lightning on the mountain," wrote Gregory of Nazianzus, "and became more luminous than the sun, initiating us into the mystery of the future." [3]

Two Men from the Past

Jesus was not alone on the mountain, but he was joined by two famous men from the Bible: "And behold, two men were talking with him, Moses and Elijah, who appeared in glory and spoke of his departure, which he was about to accomplish at Jerusalem" (Luke 9:30–31).

These two short verses are fascinating for all the things they tell us about the life to come. They raise all kinds of questions that we cannot answer—questions about what Moses and Elijah looked like, and what they had been doing for the last thousand years—but they also give us hope for the future. These verses teach us that there is an afterlife. Moses and Elijah had been gone for centuries, yet they were still very much alive, kept safe in the hands of God. They also teach us that in the life to come, believers have a relationship with God and with one

2. David Gooding, *According to Luke: A New Exposition of the Third Gospel* (Grand Rapids: Eerdmans, 1987), 167.

3. Gregory of Nazianzus, "On the Son" (Oration 3.19) in *Luke*, ed. Arthur A. Just Jr., Ancient Christian Commentary on Scripture, NT 3 (Downers Grove, IL: InterVarsity, 2003), 161.

another. They teach us as well that people who know Christ will share in his glory, for both Moses and Elijah are said to have "appeared in glory" with Jesus (Luke 9:31).

For everything these two men teach us about the future, what they teach us about Jesus Christ and the salvation we have in him is much more important. It is no accident that Moses and Elijah were the men who appeared with Jesus, because together they represent the entire Old Testament. Moses was the hero of the exodus, the man who led Israel out of Egypt. He was famous for giving God's people the Ten Commandments, which he wrote on stone tablets and brought down from the mountain. Moses stood for the Law.

Elijah stood for the Prophets. After Moses, he was one of the greatest prophets in the Old Testament. Elijah raised the dead. He shut the rain up in heaven as judgment for Israel's sin. He prayed down fire to defeat the prophets of Baal. He did not die, but was carried up to heaven in a chariot of fire. God promised further that one day Elijah would return. Therefore, people looked to him as their once and future prophet.

In those days people referred to the Old Testament as "the Law and the Prophets," and together Moses and Elijah stood for the whole thing. Therefore, their presence testified that Jesus had come to fulfill the Law and the Prophets (see Matt. 5:17), that he was the culmination of everything promised in the ancient Scriptures. When Moses and Elijah appeared with Jesus on the mountain, it was as if the whole Old Testament was standing up to say that everything was coming together in Christ.

Moses and Elijah were not simply standing there, looking glorious; they were also having a serious conversation. The tense of the verb for talking in verse 30 suggests that this was an ongoing discussion. But notice especially their theme. These men enjoyed talking together, especially about theology. But of all the things that Moses and Elijah might have discussed, there was one thing that demanded their attention above all others, one thing they wanted to ask Jesus about more than anything else: his departure.

What "departure" did they have in mind? This uncommon word was sometimes used to refer to someone's death. Later Peter would use it this way in one of his epistles (2 Peter 1:15). So Moses and Elijah were talking about the death of Jesus. But here the word seems to carry even weightier significance, for it is actually the Greek word *exodus*. Moses and Elijah were talking about the exodus of Jesus Christ.

Immediately this word calls to mind the great Old Testament story of salvation: Israel's exodus from Egypt. Moses knew all about that great deliverance, of course, because he had helped to bring it about. But somehow Moses knew that Jesus was about to bring a new and greater deliverance. He would finally deliver his people from their slavery to sin, and he would lead them to the Promised Land—the heaven of his Father's glory. Jesus would do this through his exodus, his departure, his death.

When Moses and Elijah spoke of this exodus as something Jesus "was about to accomplish at Jerusalem" (Luke 9:31), they were making clear and obvious reference to his death on the cross, and perhaps also to his resurrection from the grave. Jesus had work to do. He had something to accomplish, something both Moses and Elijah knew about because it was prefigured in their prophetic ministries. Furthermore, their own salvation depended on the work that Jesus needed to do. Like all the other saints of the Old Testament, Moses and Elijah were saved by grace through faith in the Savior whom God promised to send. Now their Savior was about to do his saving work. Is it any wonder that this was the topic of their conversation?

If only we had a digital recording: Moses and Elijah talking to Jesus about the gospel! These great men knew that Jesus was getting close to fulfilling their promises, yet probably they still had all kinds of questions. Moses perhaps would have considered the connection between the Passover lamb and the blood that Jesus would shed on the cross. Or he would have asked Jesus to explain how his death related to the sacrifice of atonement made in the Holy of Holies. Meanwhile, Elijah might have wondered whether God would again send fire from heaven to accept this sacrifice. And how did it all relate to the coming day of the Lord, which was prophesied in Elijah's ministry? There was so much to talk about!

There still is. God has accomplished a great new exodus through the death and resurrection of Jesus Christ. This new exodus is the most important thing that ever happened in the universe. It brings deliverance from bondage—the forgiveness of our sins, with the promise of eternal life. Therefore, it is and ought to be a source of endless fascination for us. What Jesus accomplished in his exodus is worth a lifetime of careful study, and after that, an eternity of joyful praise.

What Peter Said

For his part, Peter wished that the conversation would never end. Luke tells us: "Now Peter and those who were with him were heavy with sleep, but when they became fully awake they saw his glory and the two men who stood with him. And as the men were parting from him, Peter said to Jesus, 'Master, it is good that we are here. Let us make three tents, one for you and one for Moses and one for Elijah'—not knowing what he said" (Luke 9:32–33).

The disciples were at it again. First they fell asleep. If there was one thing the disciples excelled at—and this may have been the only thing—it was their extraordinary ability to slumber, especially when it was time to pray. Then once they were fully awake to the glory on the mountain, they made what one commentator calls "a most unfortunate suggestion."[4] Peter made it, of course. He wanted the moment to last, so when he saw that Moses and Elijah were leaving, he blurted out the first thing that came to his mind.

The stories in Luke's Gospel always push us to respond to Jesus in faith. They do this by showing both the right responses and the wrong responses that people made to Jesus during his earthly ministry. Here we see one of the wrong responses. We know this because Luke tells us that Peter had no idea what he was talking about—not because of his sin, but because of his weakness. Apparently, Peter was trying to make the glory last. He wanted to hold on to this mountaintop experience. He wanted the glory of Jesus to keep shining. He wanted to find a way to keep Moses and Elijah up on the mountain. So he offered to build three tents or tabernacles.

There were two basic problems with this suggestion. To begin with, it put Moses and Elijah on the same level with Jesus. Each prophet would be given his own tabernacle, as if he deserved the same honor and recognition as Jesus himself. Peter should have known better, of course. Only a week before, he had confessed that Jesus was *not* Elijah or "one of the prophets" (Luke 9:19–20), but that he was, in fact, the Christ. Yet apparently Peter did not fully understand the supreme greatness of Jesus Christ. The other great prophets are not on level terms with Jesus. He is their Savior and their God, and thus they bow before him. Moses and Elijah were not there to show that Jesus was one of the prophets, but to testify that he is the one and only Christ.

4. Gooding, *Luke*, 169.

This reminds us not to give Jesus any less honor than he truly deserves. Jesus Christ does not have any peers. When he spoke with Moses and Elijah—as great as those men were—he was not consulting with his colleagues. On the contrary, his greatness is unique, and whatever glory the disciples saw in him was the inherent, intrinsic splendor of his own supreme majesty. Jesus Christ deserves all worship and honor and glory and praise. To give him anything less than everything we have is to rob the Son of his glory.

Peter's suggestion also interfered with God's plan of salvation. In a way, Peter was right: it *was* good for the disciples to be with Jesus on the mountain. Every believer has a deep desire to see the glory of God in the face of Christ, and to gaze on him forever. But the time for that everlasting glory had not yet come. Peter was getting ahead of himself, and ahead of God. As he should have known from what Jesus had said, the Son of Man still needed to suffer many things, to be rejected and killed before rising on the third day.

Not willing to wait, Peter wanted the glory right away. To make it last, he proposed setting up some little tents, like the ones people erected for the feast of tabernacles. Presumably, he was thinking as well of the tabernacle that Moses made in the wilderness as the place for God's glory. Once the tents were made, people could come and see Jesus, Moses, and Elijah in all their glory. Soon, the area would become a religious shrine, perhaps with little souvenir stands popping up all over the mountainside.

Jesus Christ does not need a shrine. He rejects any attempt to localize him or institutionalize him, to lock him into a particular religious experience or devotional routine. He refuses to be worshiped according to human superstition. Most importantly, he refused to be dissuaded from the sufferings of the cross. Praise God that he did, because if Jesus had stayed on the mountain, it would have delayed his departure, and possibly even bypassed his exodus altogether. Jesus needed to come down from the mountain and finish his saving work. It was only after he died for sin that he would be revealed in his full and final glory.

What God Said

It is hardly surprising that Peter had the wrong response to Jesus and his transfiguration. Left to ourselves, we are bound to come up with all kinds of wrong ideas about Jesus and how to worship him. This is why we need something more than a merely human perspective on his person and work. We have heard from the disciples, but what does God the Father say about Jesus? "As he [Peter] was saying these things, a cloud came and overshadowed them, and they were afraid as they entered the cloud. And a voice came out of the cloud, saying, 'This is my Son, my Chosen One; listen to him!'" (Luke 9:34–35).

Here was a greater manifestation of divine glory. The disciples had seen the person of Jesus shining in splendor, but now a glorious cloud came down out of heaven from God to envelop Jesus and the prophets, and possibly also the disciples themselves. This glory-cloud made the disciples tremble with fear, and well it should, because it was nothing less than the glory of God. The disciples were seeing what Moses saw when God descended on the tabernacle (Ex. 40:34–35), what Solomon saw when God's presence filled Israel's house of worship (2 Chron. 7:1–3), and what Ezekiel saw rising from the temple on the wings of the cherubim (Ezek. 10). They were seeing the glory of almighty God—his Shekinah glory—the radiant cloud that gave people a visible manifestation of his invisible majesty.

The cloud alone would have been enough to confirm God's presence and blessing. But God also spoke. It was *his* voice, of course, that came from the cloud, and unlike Peter, God knew exactly what he was talking about. He identified Jesus as his Son and Chosen One—the One to whom the disciples must listen. God may have said this partly to encourage Jesus in his preparation for the cross. Just as the Father spoke at the Son's baptism (see Luke 3:22), so now again at the transfiguration he speaks to confirm the Son's calling as his chosen servant.

What God said was mainly for the benefit of the disciples, however, and also for us. People had long been speculating about the true identity of Jesus. The disciples themselves were beginning to confess him as the Christ, without fully understanding what that meant. But here now was an authoritative revelation from God. Who is Jesus? He is the Chosen Son of God.

What God the Father said to Peter, James, and John needs to be understood against the background of the Old Testament. When the Father called Jesus his Son, this of course reflected their eternal relationships within the triune being of God. There is only one God, and this one God exists in three persons: the Father, the Son, and the Holy Spirit. Jesus Christ is God the

477

eternal Son. Surely this is part of what the Father meant when he declared Jesus to be his Son.

Yet the sonship of Jesus Christ also refers to his kingship. In the Old Testament Psalms of David, God sometimes spoke to the king of Israel as his son: "You are my Son; today I have begotten you. Ask of me, and I will make the nations your heritage, and the ends of the earth your possession" (Ps. 2:7–8). Therefore, when God the Father calls Jesus his Son, he is granting him a royal title—a title that testifies to his kingly authority. God glorified Jesus as his royal and eternal Son.

Jesus is also the Chosen One (see also Luke 23:35). This title comes from the Old Testament. It appears in the Psalms with reference to David (e.g., Ps. 89:3), and also in the book of Isaiah, where God says, "Behold my servant, whom I uphold, my chosen, in whom my soul delights" (Isa. 42:1). As we read on in Isaiah, we discover that God's chosen servant will offer his life as a sacrifice for God's people. He will be wounded for their transgressions; he will be crushed for their iniquities; his soul will make an offering for their sin, so that they can be counted righteous by God (see Isa. 52:13—53:12). By calling the Son his servant, therefore, God the Father was confirming everything Jesus had said to his disciples about his sufferings and death. To put this another way, God wanted to talk about the same thing that Moses and Elijah wanted to talk about: the salvation that Jesus would bring through his death on the cross as the Suffering Servant. God glorified Jesus for his suffering in our salvation.

Then God told the disciples to listen to Jesus. This too is an echo from the Old Testament, from Deuteronomy 18, where God said to Moses: "I will raise up for them a prophet like you from among their brothers. And I will put my words in his mouth, and he shall speak to them all that I command him. And whoever will not listen to my words that he shall speak in my name, I myself will require it of him" (Deut. 18:18–19). Jesus Christ is the great prophet of the ancient promise. To listen to him is to hear the voice of God.

When God speaks, people should listen. Here, in the space of just a few short words, God speaks volumes of sacred truth about the person and work of Jesus Christ. Jesus is God's royal and eternal Son, the chosen servant of our salvation, the prophet who speaks the truth of God. It is no wonder, then, that he was transfigured in glory. The Father was glorifying

Jesus as the Son of everlasting glory, as the King who rules us, as the Savior who died for us, and as the Prophet who teaches us everything we need to know for salvation.

OUR RESPONSE

How should we respond to the glory of Jesus Christ and to God's revelation of his saving work?

The disciples who were there that day were not quite sure how to respond. Luke tells us: "And when the voice had spoken, Jesus was found alone. And they kept silent and told no one in those days anything of what they had seen" (Luke 9:36). When the glory passed, and Moses and Elijah disappeared, Jesus was still there, ready to do the work that he alone could do for our salvation. But the disciples were speechless. Possibly they had learned from Peter's example not to talk about things they did not yet understand. They needed some more time to think things through. It was only later—after the sufferings of the cross and the glories of the resurrection—that they bore witness to what they had seen on the mountain.

But we *do* know how to respond, or at least we ought to. We respond by following God's command to listen to Jesus. This command is for us as much as it was for the first disciples. We are called to listen to what Jesus says about trusting in him for eternal life. As Calvin said, "We are placed under His tuition alone, and commanded from Him alone to seek the doctrine of salvation."[5] We are called to listen to what Jesus says here in Luke 9 about his death and resurrection, about our own self-denial and cross-bearing, and about following him to the very death.

Beyond that, we are called to listen to everything Jesus says. What is Jesus saying to you right now that demands your attention? Listen to his promise that he will forgive your sins. Listen to his assurance that he will receive you into the family of God. Listen to the comfort that he will never abandon you, that he will be with you through all of life's troubles. Listen to the invitation of rest for your soul. Listen to the imperative to love God more than anything else, and to love your neighbor as yourself. Listen to the reminder

5. John Calvin, quoted in J. C. Ryle, *Expository Thoughts on the Gospels, Luke* (1858; reprint Cambridge: James Clarke, 1976), 1:320.

that his power is made perfect in your weakness. Listen to the exhortation to leave bitterness behind and find your joy in him. Listen to his call to costly discipleship. Listen as well to the rebuke that you need to turn away from some particular sin. Whatever Jesus is saying, God commands that we listen.

Some people say they would be willing to listen to Jesus if only he would speak to them in an audible voice. They want God to speak to them directly. If only they could hear what Peter and the other disciples heard on the mountain! And if only they could see what those men saw!

The apostle Peter himself wrote about this in his second epistle. He said, "We were eyewitnesses of his majesty. For when he received honor and glory from God the Father, and the voice was borne to him by the Majestic Glory, 'This is my beloved Son, with whom I am well pleased,' we ourselves heard this very voice borne from heaven, for we were with him on the holy mountain" (2 Peter 1:16–18). That is all very well for Peter, but what about us? Of course we take his word for it that these things really happened, but how does that help us if we never have the same mountaintop experience?

Peter goes on to make this remarkable comment: "And we have something more sure, the prophetic word, to which you will do well to pay attention as to a lamp shining in a dark place, until the day dawns and the morning star rises in your hearts" (2 Peter 1:19). According to Peter, what the Scripture says about Jesus is even *more* certain than what he heard and saw on the mountain! The gospel is more complete; it contains everything we need to know about Jesus, and not just the glorious glimpse that the disciples were given. It is also more permanent. What Peter experienced on the mountain lasted for only a little while, but God's Word is eternal. Whenever we have any questions about Jesus, or about the true way of salvation, or about what God wants us to do, we can go back to the Bible again and again. The way to know Jesus and his glory for sure is to believe the Bible.

When we pay attention to what the Bible says about Jesus, we see his glory for ourselves. Peter says that faith in Christ is like the rising of the morning star. The morning star is the planet Venus, rising in all its beauty on a clear morning, piercing the dusky horizon with its steady gleam. This is what it is like when we listen to Jesus and look to him for our salvation. In a darkened world, the glorious Son of God gives us eternal light and beauty and joy.

Has the morning star of salvation risen in your heart? Do you believe what God says about Jesus Christ in the gospel? Live by his light until the day when he comes again with the glorious clouds of heaven, when we will join the fellowship of Moses and Elijah and all the saints, and when we will see the everlasting glory of God the Son.

39

FOUR MISTAKES THAT MOST CHRISTIANS MAKE

Luke 9:37–50

> *An argument arose among them as to which of them was the*
> *greatest. But Jesus, knowing the reasoning of their hearts,*
> *took a child and put him by his side and said to them, "Who-*
> *ever receives this child in my name receives me, and whoever*
> *receives me receives him who sent me. For he who is least*
> *among you all is the one who is great." (Luke 9:46–48)*

*I*t is sad to say, but sometimes Christians keep people from making a commitment to Christ. It happens something like this: a woman feels as if she is missing the meaning of life, or a man decides that he wants to know more about God. They start exploring the various religious options, and sooner or later they consider Christianity. After all, it seems to be such a popular religion. They begin to read the Bible. They are attracted to the person of Christ. Eventually they decide to go to church, where they meet some real live Christians, and that is when the trouble starts.

One would hope that Christians, of all people, would provide a good recommendation for Christianity. Sometimes we do, and people are won to Christ through the love of his people. But not always. Outsiders are quick to sense our hypocrisy—the reality gap between what we say and the way we live. They are turned off by the way we sometimes blur the line between our theology and our politics. They are offended by the inflammatory or reactionary comments they hear us make on cultural issues.

The real issue, of course, is not what people think about us, but what they think about Jesus. Criticizing Christians can easily become just another excuse for not coming to Christ. Some of these criticisms may also be unfair. But sometimes people's perceptions of the church are far more accurate than we are willing to admit. Rather than helping people come to Christ, we get in the way. If only our lives were as attractive as the Christ we claim to follow.

NOT TRUSTING GOD TO DO WHAT ONLY HE CAN DO

If we want to help lead people to Christ, there are some things we need to avoid—four mistakes that most Christians make, and that the disciples made in Luke 9.

The first mistake is not trusting God to do what only he can do. The disciples made this mistake after the transfiguration of the Son of God. Peter, James, and John came back down the mountain from that glorious vision into the daily routine of ministry, where they faced the powers of hell's darkness: "On the next day, when they had come down from the mountain, a great crowd met him. And behold, a man from the crowd cried out, 'Teacher, I beg you to look at my son, for he is my only child. And behold, a spirit seizes him, and he suddenly cries out. It convulses him so that he foams at the mouth; and shatters him, and will hardly leave him'" (Luke 9:37–39).

Some scholars have thought that this boy suffered from epileptic seizures; many of the symptoms are similar. Yet the Bible clearly states that whatever physical problems he may have had, the boy was under the influence of supernatural evil—what his father called "a spirit," and what Luke called "the demon" and "the unclean spirit" (Luke 9:42). Here is an example, then, of the way that Satan desires to destroy us and our children. Mark

483

tells us that the demon often threw the boy into fire and water, trying to kill him (Mark 9:22). This is what the devil always wants to do: kill our souls, if not our bodies.

Needless to say, the boy's father was desperate for help. Maybe Jesus was busy at the time, or maybe he was still up on the mountain, but whatever the reason, the man first went to the disciples. "I begged your disciples to cast it out," the man said, "but they could not" (Luke 9:40).

What was the reason for this failed exorcism? Remember that Jesus had given the disciples "power and authority over all demons and to cure diseases" (Luke 9:1). They had done this kind of thing before, and if anything, they had even more reason for confidence now that they confessed Jesus as the Christ, and now that some of them had seen his glory. Nevertheless, they failed. The painter Raphael captured the irony of this in his final masterpiece, which shows the dramatic contrast between the divine light the disciples saw transfigured on the mountain and the demonic darkness they were unable to dispel when they came back down to earth.[1]

The disciples did not fail for lack of effort, but due to their lack of faith. It was not because they had lost their powers, or because they used the wrong technique for exorcising demons, but because of their unbelief. This is clear from the way that Jesus answered the boy's father: "O faithless and twisted generation, how long am I to be with you and bear with you?" (Luke 9:41). So Jesus took matters into his own hands and said, "Bring your son here." Then, as the boy was coming forward, the demon made one last desperate attempt to keep him away from Jesus. Satan never gives up any of his victims without a fight, and often it is right before someone comes to Christ (whether literally or spiritually) that he makes his most violent assault. In this particular case, "the demon threw him to the ground and convulsed him" (Luke 9:42). This must have been terribly frightening. "But Jesus rebuked the unclean spirit and healed the boy, and gave him back to his father. And all were astonished at the majesty of God" (Luke 9:42–43). So it was that Jesus performed a miracle that his disciples apparently could have performed themselves, if only they had believed. Both scenes are depicted in the same painting, which seems to

---

1. Raphael, *The Transfiguration*, 1520.

show that although the disciples had seen the light of the glory of God, they were not yet able to turn back the darkness.

This deliverance includes many of the same elements that we have seen in other miracles. Once again, Jesus showed compassion for children. Once again, he gained an easy victory over demonic powers. Once again, Jesus restored someone to his right mind and reconciled a family. As David Gooding explains it, we see in this miracle "the tragic effect of the physical distortions and personality changes induced by demon-possession which had in a very real sense taken the boy away from his father and ruined the enjoyment of the relationship; and the delightful outcome of the healing, that the boy was 'given back' to his father and the enjoyment of the relationship restored."[2] In all of this, people saw yet another display of the majesty of God in the work of Jesus Christ.

What is different in this case is that Jesus rebuked his disciples for not trusting in his saving power. When he spoke about a "faithless and twisted generation" (Luke 9:41), he was referring to Israel's experience after the exodus, when Moses told God's people that they were "a twisted generation" (Deut. 32:5). When Jesus said this, he was speaking about the disciples as much as anyone else. Obviously, he was not speaking about the boy's father, who had done what any godly parent ought to do with a child in trouble: he brought his boy to Jesus and said, "Look at my son." That good man was faithful, not faithless. In fact, this was the very man who in the Gospel of Mark said to Jesus, "I believe; help my unbelief!" (Mark 9:24). So Jesus was not speaking about the boy's father. Possibly he was speaking about others who were there that day, and who doubted his power to save. The word "generation" would seem to refer to a wider group. But the faithless people in this instance were primarily the disciples, who did not have the faith to cast out the boy's demon.

This grieved Jesus deeply. We can sense his sorrow in the question he asks: "How long am I to be with you and bear with you?" (Luke 9:41). This was not sinful impatience, but holy frustration with the unbelief of his own people, including his closest friends. Like a mother who wonders when her son will start taking responsibility for his actions, or a

2. David Gooding, *According to Luke: A New Exposition of the Third Gospel* (Grand Rapids: Eerdmans, 1987), 171.

schoolteacher who wonders when his student will ever learn to follow instructions, Jesus longed for his disciples to trust him with a simple faith. One of the great sufferings of his earthly pilgrimage was the unbelief of his own disciples.

Sometimes we grieve Jesus the same way. This is one of the mistakes that most Christians make. We say we believe in God, but do we trust him to do what only he can do? All too often we try to serve him in our own strength, as the disciples did, and then nothing happens, or at least nothing that demonstrates the majesty of God.

The main point of this episode is not that we need to trust God to help us cast out demons—which is something that rarely happens—but that we need to trust God to do *all* the spiritual work that only he can do. We have all the more reason to trust God than the disciples did, because we have received the full benefits of Christ's finished work, and the Holy Spirit is now at work in us to help us trust in God. We need this faith in our struggle against temptation. We come up with all kinds of methods to manage our sin, but the real transformation comes by trusting in the gospel to change our hearts and minds. We need this faith in our relationships, which can be restored only by the healing work of God's Spirit. We need this faith in our ministry, both as individual Christians and as a church, both locally and around the world. We may be very busy serving the Lord in practical ways, but this makes a spiritual difference only when we depend on God to use what we do to advance his gospel. We need this faith in our evangelism; leading someone to Christ does not depend on the skill of our witness, but on the grace of God. We need this faith in our discipleship. No matter how much good advice we give, we cannot be the Holy Spirit for anyone else; only God can change someone's life. Then we need this faith in our ongoing war with Satan, who is seeking to destroy everything we do for God. The only way to be safe from the Evil One is through faith in Jesus Christ and in his mighty power.

Make no mistake: God is the only one who can do any of these things. Therefore, we are called to trust in him through Jesus Christ. When we do this, we see his majesty in our own spiritual growth, in the healing of wounded relationships, in the salvation of sinners, and in the triumph of the church over spiritual darkness.

Taking Our Eyes Off the Cross

A second mistake that most Christians make is to take our eyes off the cross. We are easily distracted, and even when we think about spiritual things, we may be more interested in the power and the glory than in suffering and the cross. Jesus knew that his disciples faced the same temptation, so immediately after he healed the boy with the unclean spirit, "while they were all marveling at everything he was doing, Jesus said to his disciples, 'Let these words sink into your ears: The Son of Man is about to be delivered into the hands of men'" (Luke 9:43–44).

By saying this, Jesus was calling his disciples to look again at the cross, and perhaps also to connect his power over demons to the main event in his battle with the devil. He did not want them to get so caught up in marveling over his miracles that they missed the main point of his ministry. It had only been a week since he first told them that he would have to suffer many things and be killed before rising again. Now he wanted them to hear it again: the main message of the gospel is not that Jesus can perform exorcisms and work other wonders, although of course he can, but that he came to suffer and die for our sins.

The disciples did not know it then, but when Jesus spoke about being "delivered into the hands of men," he was talking about his crucifixion. Soon, through the treachery of a close friend, a conspiracy of religious leaders, the cowardice of the governor, the violence of an angry mob, and the cruelty of wicked soldiers, Jesus would be nailed to a rough piece of wood and left to die.

The disciples did not understand any of this. This was now the second time that Jesus had predicted his death, but it did not make any more sense to them this time than it did the first time. They knew that Jesus was the Messiah, but they did not yet understand that he had come to suffer for sinners. The idea that someone as powerful as Jesus would die in weakness was unthinkable. Luke tells us, "But they did not understand this saying, and it was concealed from them, so that they might not perceive it. And they were afraid to ask him about this saying" (Luke 9:45). This quadruple negative could hardly be more emphatic. The disciples had turned their eyes completely away from the cross, not seeing what Jesus was showing them about his sacrifice, and not willing to ask the questions that would lead them into a sure and certain knowledge of salvation.

We know better because, unlike the disciples, we know the end of the gospel story. Through the eyes of faith we have seen Jesus dying on the cross and rising again. We know the meaning of his crucifixion and resurrection: through the saving work of Jesus Christ, God has forgiven our sins and promised to receive us into his everlasting glory. We know all this better than the disciples did, or at least we ought to. If we do not know this, all we need to do is open our Bibles and, unlike the disciples, ask Jesus to help us understand the gospel.

Yet we still make the same mistake the disciples made, albeit in a different way. We keep the cross near the center of our worship, but we do not always keep it at the center of our daily discipleship. Jesus has called us to follow him all the way to crucifixion. He has called us to deny ourselves, take up our crosses daily, and follow him. But are we giving people the kind of sacrificial love that shows we serve a crucified Savior?

Too often we take our eyes off the cross. We are not satisfied with Jesus; instead, we want all of the other things that life has to offer. We are not willing to suffer the embarrassment of talking about Jesus with friends, or to risk harming our careers by taking our stand on a biblical principle, or to give up the comforts of life as we know it to take the gospel to the far places of the world. We do not want to suffer, even for Jesus, and so we take our eyes off the cross.

Make no mistake: Jesus calls us to keep the cross at the center, the way the apostle Paul did when he resolved to know nothing "except Jesus Christ and him crucified" (1 Cor. 2:2), or when he refused to boast about anything "except in the cross of our Lord Jesus Christ" (Gal. 6:14). The cross must remain at the center of our personal evangelism, of what we tell people about the Christian faith. It must remain at the center of our stewardship, of the costly decisions we make about investing our time and our money in gospel work. It must remain at the center of our family life, as we serve one another in love. The cross must also remain at the center of our commitment to see the world won for Christ, starting in our own community.

SEEKING GREATNESS FOR OURSELVES

The mistake of taking our eyes off the cross is closely related to a third mistake, which is to seek greatness for ourselves rather than for God. This brings us to what may be the most pointless debate in the history of human argumentation: "An argument arose among them as to which of them was the greatest" (Luke 9:46).

The Bible does not tell us how this argument started. Maybe Peter or John or James had been bragging about going up the mountain with Jesus. "You know, he likes us the best," one of them might have said. "Oh, yeah? I heard he took you up there because he didn't think he could let you out of his sight!" And so it went, with all of the petty jealousies, vain conceits, and unrighteous reasonings of their sinful hearts.

This dispute was foolish because, like us, none of the disciples were all that great in the first place. Remember, these were men who could hardly stay awake to the end of a prayer meeting. Trying to determine the greatest disciple was a little bit like trying to find the world's tallest pygmy: even if it were possible to figure out the answer, it would hardly matter. It was also foolish because the disciples were striving to reach the wrong end of the scale. Jesus had been telling them to deny themselves, but rather than carrying their crosses, they were still trying to climb to the top of the spiritual ladder.

It was a silly argument—the kind that little children have on the playground. To show how childish it was, "Jesus, knowing the reasoning of their hearts, took a child and put him by his side and said to them, 'Whoever receives this child in my name receives me, and whoever receives me receives him who sent me. For he who is least among you all is the one who is great'" (Luke 9:47–48).

What Jesus did and what Jesus said were both important. What he did was to take a child by the hand. This in itself was a meaningful gesture. It gives us a glimpse of the kind of relationship that Jesus loves to have with children. There is no better place for any child to be than close beside the Savior. The rabbis generally ignored children altogether. According to one of their ancient commentaries, chattering with children would bring a man to ruin.[3] But Jesus notices children and brings them close, as he did in this instance.

Then Jesus said that the way his disciples treated little children would indicate what kind of relationship they had with him and with his Father

---

3. See Albrecht Oepke, "*pais*," in *Theological Dictionary of the New Testament*, ed. Gerhard Kittel and Gerhard Friedrich, trans. Geoffrey W. Bromiley, 10 vols. (Grand Rapids: Eerdmans, n.d.), 5:646.

in heaven. Part of his point was that it takes humility to make friends with a child. To have a meaningful relationship, an adult has to get down on the child's level and talk in a way the child can understand. According to Jesus, when people have the humility to welcome children in this way, they are really welcoming the triune God.

This is one of the upside-down values of the kingdom of God, in which the least are the greatest. Notice, though, that Jesus does not say anything about anyone being the greatest. He simply says that whoever is least is great, without making any comparisons. True greatness in the eyes of God comes when we take the lowest place, seeking no recognition for ourselves, but showing concern for the weak and the helpless. As followers of Christ, we are called to care for people who usually get overlooked because to some people they do not seem all that important, like children. True spiritual greatness is determined by the company we keep.

Jesus himself is the perfect example. Rather than holding on to the privileges of his own exalted position as the Son of God, he humbled himself to live among us and offer his life for our sins. This aspect of Christ's ministry was deeply impressive to Charles Colson. In contrast with the corrupt ambition that he witnessed in the Nixon administration and in his own personal life, Dr. Colson said that Jesus

> served others first; He spoke to those to whom no one spoke; He dined with the lowest members of society; He touched the untouchables. He had no throne, no crown, no bevy of servants or armored guards. A borrowed manger and a borrowed tomb framed his earthly life. Kings and presidents and prime ministers surround themselves with minions who rush ahead, swing the doors wide, and stand at attention as they wait for the great to pass. Jesus said that He Himself stands at the door and knocks, patiently waiting to enter our lives.[4]

Part of our Savior's true greatness is that he did not seek greatness for himself. What a mistake it is, therefore, for us to play the kind of spiritual one-upsmanship that the disciples played. "My church is better than your church." "My worship is more pleasing to God than your worship." "My ministry is more important than your ministry." "My way of living

4. Charles Colson, *Kingdoms in Conflict* (Grand Rapids: Zondervan, 1987), 85.

the Christian life, or of educating my children, or of witnessing for Jesus is better than yours." These are the kinds of things that Christians think, and sometimes say, even if we do not always say it in such an obvious way. Sometimes we even try to gain an advantage by being more broken for our sin or more sacrificial in our giving than someone else—anything to prove our own true spiritual greatness.

Make no mistake: there is nothing great about us. "Of all creatures," wrote J. C. Ryle, "none has so little right to be proud as man, and of all men none ought to be so humble as the Christian."[5] Everything we have is a gift of God's grace. One of the best ways for us to show our gratitude is by loving the people who usually get overlooked. This means caring for our children in a Christ-like way, seeking what is best for them. It means getting involved in the spiritual education of children inside and outside the church. It means paying attention to children in our neighborhoods and showing compassion to orphans and street children around the world. It also means visiting prisoners, helping people with disabilities, embracing people who are overwhelmed by difficult problems, showing hospitality to immigrants, and giving ourselves to people who have nothing to give us in return. To do such things is to receive the Son and the Father, honoring their greatness rather than our own.

FIGHTING THE WRONG ENEMY

As he heard what Jesus was saying about true spiritual greatness, John thought back to a recent encounter with someone else in ministry. Then he said to Jesus, "Master, we saw someone casting out demons in your name, and we tried to stop him, because he does not follow with us" (Luke 9:49).

It is not entirely clear why John said this. Possibly he was confessing his sins, acknowledging that he had failed to treat someone else's ministry with proper humility. Maybe he was simply looking for clarification: had he done the right thing in rebuking the man, or not? But it seems more likely that John was raising an objection. It was all very well for Jesus to talk about being least in the kingdom of God, but surely some

5. J. C. Ryle, *Expository Thoughts on the Gospels, Luke* (1858; reprint Cambridge: James Clarke, 1976), 1:327.

distinctions still had to be made. Were not the disciples at least better than people who went around doing things in Jesus' name, but were not even part of their fellowship?

John's argument had a certain logic to it. Apparently, this "freelance exorcist" was not following Jesus in the way of discipleship.[6] Surely there was something wrong with someone working in the name of Christ but not following him in the biblical way. Shouldn't he be stopped, and wasn't it up to the disciples to stop him?

In response, Jesus might have pointed out that when the disciples rebuked the man, they had spoken out of sinful self-importance. They did not have a monopoly on doing God's work. He might also have pointed out that the disciples had recently failed to cast out a demon, so they were hardly in a position to stop someone else from doing what they were unable to do themselves! Instead, Jesus simply said: "Do not stop him, for the one who is not against you is for you" (Luke 9:50).

This statement is hard to understand, especially since Jesus later said something that sounds nearly the opposite: "Whoever is not with me is against me" (Luke 11:23). But as we shall see, on that occasion Jesus was talking about the work of Satan, with whom there can be no compromise. In both instances, Jesus was making it clear that there is no middle ground: people are either for Jesus or against him. Here John was talking about someone who was trying to serve Christ, however imperfectly, and who (unlike the disciples) trusted him enough to cast out demons! So in this case Jesus warned his disciples not to make the mistake of fighting the wrong enemy. The man casting out demons was not against their ministry, and therefore they had no business trying to stop him. In fact, this was a greater sin than anything that might have been wrong with the other man's ministry.

This principle is important to remember any time we look at the way other people are serving Christ and are tempted to think that they should do things differently. (I am not speaking here about fundamental matters of doctrine, but of the various ways that people who are fighting against the powers of Satan do their gospel work.) Unless we are in a position of spiritual oversight, then even if we are right about

6. R. Kent Hughes, *Luke: That You May Know the Truth*, 2 vols., Preaching the Word (Wheaton, IL: Crossway, 1998), 1:366.

some of the ways that other Christians are wrong, it is not our responsibility to correct them. Whenever we perceive a problem in the Christian church, we always need to ask if it is our God-given responsibility to address it. If, in our misguided zeal to defend the cause of Christ, we try to be the Holy Spirit for people, we may actually get in the way of what God is doing. J. C. Ryle laments the way that thousands of Christians,

> in every period of Church history, have spent their lives in copying John's mistake. They have laboured to stop every man who will not work for Christ in their way, from working for Christ at all. They have imagined, in their petty self-conceit, that no man can be a soldier of Christ, unless he wears their uniform, and fights in their regiment. . . . We forget that no Church on earth has an absolute monopoly of all wisdom, and that people may be right in the main, without agreeing with us. We must learn to be thankful if sin is opposed, and the Gospel preached, and the devil's kingdom pulled down, though the work may not be done exactly in the way we like. . . . Above all, we must praise God if souls are converted, and Christ is magnified—no matter who the preacher may be, and to what Church he may belong.[7]

Make no mistake: other Christians are not the enemy. Satan is the enemy, and we should do everything we can to encourage other Christians in their battle against him. We are in a holy alliance against the powers of darkness, and rather than having us attack one another, our Supreme Commander orders us to keep fighting the right enemy.

How Long?

Luke 9 presents a series of four little episodes that show four mistakes that most Christians make: not trusting God to do what only God can do; taking our eyes off the cross; seeking glory for ourselves; and fighting the wrong enemy. The first mistake comes from a lack of faith; the second from a lack of focus; the third from a lack of humility; and the fourth from a lack of wisdom.

7. Ryle, *Luke*, 1:328.

All four of these mistakes compromise our witness for Christ. When we serve the Lord in our own strength, people are unable to see the power of the Holy Spirit. When we take our eyes off the cross, we stop giving the sacrificial service that leads people to Christ. When we seek our own greatness, no one can see how great and how glorious God is. And when we fight amongst ourselves, we drive people away from our fellowship rather than drawing them in. Kent Hughes says that these common mistakes give us "a telltale aroma, and others can smell it, especially those outside the church. Sometimes it is an acrid air of condescension or subtle, smiling hostility, or aloofness, or clubbish exclusivity, or doubt about God's blessing on all who are not in the approved circle. This stench has kept multitudes away from the church and, more important, a knowledge of Christ."[8]

Which mistakes are you making? Sooner or later, most Christians make them all. We do things in our own strength, not trusting in the power of God's grace. We take our eyes off the cross, seeking satisfaction in earthly things rather than giving our lives away for Jesus. We elevate ourselves rather than putting others first. We wound our own brothers and sisters with the "friendly fire" of a critical spirit.

The first disciples made all these mistakes, too, which might make us wonder whether Jesus made a mistake in choosing them. But here is a great comfort: Jesus has mercy and grace for people who make spiritual mistakes. The Gospel of Luke proves it. Here in Luke 9 Jesus is already prepared to give up his life, but it will take him fourteen more chapters to get to the cross. Why the delay? In part because he still had so many things that he needed to teach his disciples. Looking back on all of their early mistakes, Michael Wilcock asks: "What then can Jesus do with a group of disciples still so unbelieving, slow-witted, swollen-headed, and narrow-minded, except take them with him on another year's course of teaching?"[9]

This takes us back to the question that Jesus asked in verse 41: How long would he have to bear with the unbelief of his disciples? The answer was as long as it took to finish the work of their salvation

8. Hughes, *Luke*, 1:364.
9. Michael Wilcock, *The Message of Luke*, The Bible Speaks Today (Downers Grove, IL: Inter-Varsity, 1979), 113.

and teach them the right way to serve. Jesus has the same patience with us. Even after all the mistakes we have made—including ones that dishonor God and hinder people from coming to Christ—God is still working with us, forgiving our sins and calling us again and again to follow Jesus. How long will he keep doing this? According to the gospel, he will keep doing this as long as it takes to save us.

40

Don't Look Back

Luke 9:51—62

*Yet another said, "I will follow you, Lord, but let me first say fare-
well to those at my home." Jesus said to him, "No one who puts
his hand to the plow and looks back is fit for the kingdom of God."*
(Luke 9:61–62)

HERE comes a time in every great man's life when he has to
make his stand. If he is going to fulfill his destiny, he must
carry out his calling. With single-minded devotion and whole-
hearted courage, he must pursue what lies ahead, never turning aside, and
never looking back. He must do that one great thing he was chosen to do.
So it was that "when the days drew near for him to be taken up," the greatest
man who ever lived "set his face to go to Jerusalem" (Luke 9:51).

THE JOURNEY TO JERUSALEM

This verse marks a major turning point in the Gospel of Luke. To this
point Jesus has been preaching the gospel of the kingdom and performing
miracles of power in Galilee. He still has many more things to do and to
teach; he has not yet completed his training of the twelve. But the end is

near. As we know from Luke 9, Jesus must suffer many things, including the rejection of his people unto death. Soon he will have to carry the very cross that he has been preaching to his disciples. This was his destiny, and knowing this, Jesus made Jerusalem his destination.

Jerusalem was the city of God's king, and thus it was the place the Messiah went to receive his royal welcome. Jesus made his journey there over many months, leisurely making his way through the towns and villages where he still needed to preach the gospel. This journey—which was as much spiritual as it was geographic—runs all the way to chapter 19, where Jesus finally goes up to the great city on a donkey, weeping because he knows that Jerusalem has rejected God and will be destroyed.

What did Jesus do when he arrived there? In Jerusalem he corrected the religious leaders for corrupting the temple and rejecting his authority. In Jerusalem he taught his last parables. In Jerusalem he prophesied the destruction of the temple, the overthrow of the city, and the end of the world. And in Jerusalem he celebrated his last Passover supper with his disciples before going up the Mount of Olives to pray.

There was danger for Jesus in that great city. Jerusalem was the city where many prophets had gone to die (see Luke 13:33). Thus for Jesus to go there was to face mortal danger. In Jerusalem people plotted against him. In Jerusalem he was betrayed with a kiss, arrested by the temple police, and abused by soldiers. In Jerusalem Jesus was brought before the Jews on false charges, taken to Pilate the governor, and then on to Herod the king, before being sent back to Pilate. In Jerusalem an angry mob called for his crucifixion, until finally the governor gave in to their violent demands. In Jerusalem his disciples left him. And in Jerusalem Jesus was stripped naked and nailed to a cursed tree—in Jerusalem he was dead and buried.

Jesus knew all of this when he was still in Galilee, at least in general terms, if not in precise detail, and it was with all of this in mind that he "set his face to go to Jerusalem" (Luke 9:51). This expression indicates firm resolution and complete fixity of purpose. Like the Suffering Servant in Isaiah, who set his "face like a flint" (Isa. 50:7), Jesus was absolutely determined to go up to Jerusalem and do everything he was called to do for our salvation. What Jesus suffered was not some unfortunate accident, but the direct result of his deliberate obedience to his divine calling as the Savior of the world.

It was not merely to die that Jesus went to Jerusalem, however. Luke reveals his deeper purpose and higher destiny by telling us when Jesus set his face towards the city. He did this "when the days drew near for him to be taken up" (Luke 9:51). This is the only place where the unusual expression "to be taken up" *(analēmpseōs)* occurs in the New Testament. What does it mean? Possibly it refers to the way that Jesus was carried off by his enemies. Yet elsewhere the verbal form of this expression refers to his ascension (e.g., Acts 1:2; 1 Tim. 3:16), to that momentous occasion when the risen Christ went up into heaven, trailing clouds of glory. Luke tells us where Jesus was heading so we can see the whole of his saving work. Jesus was nearing "the consummation of his saving work in the crucifixion, resurrection, and ascension."[1] He was moving towards the cross and beyond: to his resurrection from the dead and the glory that would follow forever.

Jesus would reach this everlasting glory by way of Jerusalem. Jerusalem had to come first. There he would forgive his enemies, promise paradise to a dying thief, and make atonement for our sin. But after he completed his saving work, he would be raised from the dead and taken up to the glorious throne of God. When Jesus set his face toward Jerusalem, therefore, he was looking ahead to the cross *and* to the crown that he would gain by dying for sinners. Once he fixed his gaze in that direction, he would never look back. Nothing would deter him or distract him from doing what he was called to do, the work that was his everlasting destiny and that he desired to do for our salvation.

Jesus Rejected

What kind of response did Jesus meet along the way? As he made his journey to Jerusalem and beyond, how did people react to Jesus and his call to discipleship? We get an early indication from an incident that took place in Samaria, where Jesus sent his advance men to make reservations: "And he sent messengers ahead of him, who went and entered a village of the Samaritans, to make preparations for him. But the people did not receive him, because his face was set toward Jerusalem" (Luke 9:52–53).

---

1. Leon Morris, *The Gospel According to St. Luke: An Introduction and Commentary*, Tyndale New Testament Commentaries (Grand Rapids: Eerdmans, 1974), 178.

People had rejected Jesus from the very first time he preached the gospel. They would not even accept him in his own hometown. But from this point forward, the opposition seemed to intensify. Generally speaking, the closer Jesus got to Jerusalem and the cross, the more sharply he came into conflict with people who rejected him as the Messiah.

In this case, the people who rejected him were Samaritans, and the reason they refused to receive him was precisely that he was on his way to Jerusalem. There is a cultural background to this. The Samaritans, who were cousins of the Jews, believed that the place to worship God was not Jerusalem, but their own Mount Gerizim. There was a long history of conflict over this issue, including incidents of armed violence. When Jewish pilgrims traveled through Samaria on their way up to Jerusalem, they sometimes met with an angry response. The last thing a Samaritan wanted to do was help a Jew get to Jerusalem.

The way the Samaritans rejected Jesus foreshadows all the rejection that would follow. The people in this village may have rejected him for reasons of ethnic pride, but Luke presents this as part of a wider pattern. Jesus was on a saving mission from God, but whether through ignorance or malice, some people refused to welcome him as their Savior or follow him as their Lord. Apparently, there was no more room for Jesus in Samaria than there had been in Bethlehem, or than there would be in Jerusalem. This pattern of rejection leads us to ask how much room we are making for Jesus in our own hearts. What kind of welcome do we give to his saving work?

When James and John heard that the Samaritans refused to give Jesus a room, they wanted to do something about it. They said, "Lord, do you want us to tell fire to come down from heaven and consume them?" (Luke 9:54). This request can hardly be faulted for a lack of faith, to say nothing of zeal. Not for nothing did Jesus call these brothers "Sons of Thunder" (Mark 3:17)! Once again (see Luke 9:49), James and John were ready and willing to set people straight. They believed that if they prayed like Elijah of old (see 2 Kings 1:9–12), God would send fire down from heaven to destroy their enemies. These disciples had a bold faith in God, with a passionate zeal for the honor of Jesus.

These disciples can be faulted, however, for their lack of charity, not to mention their bad sense of timing. So Jesus "turned and rebuked them [James and John]. And they went on to another village" (Luke 9:55–56).

This was not yet a day for judgment; it was still a time for mercy. Admittedly, the Samaritans had done wrong. They were guilty of ignorant prejudice against the Jews and against Jesus. God would hold them accountable for their sins. But they still had time to repent, and thus it was wrong for James and John to seek their destruction before their time.

The error of these disciples reminds us how wrong Christians can be, even when we know we are right. James and John had faith in the power of God. They spoke out of concern for the honor of Christ, and with a clear biblical precedent. Yet they were still in the wrong. Their zeal was not according to knowledge. J. C. Ryle wisely comments:

> It is possible to have much zeal for Christ, and yet to exhibit it in most unholy and unchristian ways. It is possible to mean well and have good intentions, and yet to make most grievous mistakes in our actions. It is possible to fancy that we have Scripture on our side, and to support our conduct by Scriptural quotations, and yet to commit serious errors. It is clear as daylight, from this and other cases related in the Bible, that it is not enough to be zealous and *well-meaning*. Very grave faults are frequently committed with good intentions. From no quarter perhaps has the Church received so much injury as from ignorant but well-meaning men.[2]

We need more than good intentions; we need righteous actions. We need more than zeal for God's glory; we need hearts that are filled with the compassion of Christ. We need more than the knowledge of Scripture; we need spiritual insight to know how to apply it to our own situation. Never is this more important than when we think we have a responsibility to defend God's cause. We may be right about the sin in someone's life, or a problem in the church, or some ungodliness in government, or the prevailing errors of our culture. But are we responding in a way that demonstrates the kindness of God, the mercy of Christ, and the truth of the Spirit speaking in Scripture?

Jesus rejects any form of violent response from the church acting as the church. There will be a day of judgment, but that fiery verdict is for God to render. In the meantime, this is the day of salvation, when there is still

2. J. C. Ryle, *Expository Thoughts on the Gospels, Luke* (1858; reprint Cambridge: James Clarke, 1976), 1:333–34.

time for people to repent—even people who have rejected Jesus Christ. Our present calling is not to seek revenge against God's enemies, but to serve them in love, asking God to temper the harsh edge of our zeal with the compassion of Christ.

God did this transforming work in John's life. Given what we read in Luke, we would hardly guess that John became the apostle of God's love. Yet we know from his epistles that the love of God in Christ became the grand theme of his life and ministry. Later John even proved his love to the Samaritans. The book of Acts tells us that he and Peter took the gospel "to many villages of the Samaritans" (Acts 8:25). We can only wonder whether John may have visited the same village that he had once sought to destroy by fire. What we know for certain is that God transformed him from a fighter into a lover, and that by his grace God can work the same kind of change into our own hearts. Whenever people arouse our anger, we can ask the Holy Spirit to help us show them the love of God.

ON THE ROAD TO THE CROSS

The Samaritans refused to help Jesus on his journey, but there were others who had a different response. When they saw where Jesus was going, they wanted to go with him. So Luke 9 ends with three brief encounters that Jesus had with three would-be disciples on the road to Jerusalem. Each of these encounters teaches us something about what it means to follow Jesus. In fact, "follow" is the key word in this section, occurring in verses 57, 59, and 61. All three of these people had every intention of following Jesus. Yet when we learn more about them, we have to wonder whether they really had what it took to follow Jesus all the way to Jerusalem, which leads us to ask whether we ourselves are ready to follow Jesus all the way.

The first encounter teaches us that if we want to follow Jesus, we have to be willing to give up everything, even the comforts of home. The person who learned this lesson was more than willing to follow Jesus. Luke tells us, "As they were going along the road, someone said to him, 'I will follow you wherever you go'" (Luke 9:57). Here was someone who knew something about the demands of discipleship. He understood that following

Jesus meant going wherever he went. Without raising any questions or making any conditions, this man volunteered to go anywhere and everywhere with Jesus.

Yet for all his confidence, the man really had not counted the cost of discipleship. "He spoke with so much self-confidence," writes Norval Geldenhuys, "because he had no inkling of the way of sorrows and death which the Lord would yet follow and also because he did not realize his own weakness and instability."[3] Before we say that we are ready and able to follow Jesus, we need to know where he is going, and what hardships we are likely to face along the way.

Jesus never denied the more difficult aspects of discipleship, but always announced them in advance. He never presented the Christian life as a life of ease, but always of sacrifice. His message was, "I love you and have a difficult plan for your life." So Jesus said to the first would-be disciple: "Foxes have holes, and birds of the air have nests, but the Son of Man has nowhere to lay his head" (Luke 9:58).

These famous words remind us of the many things that Jesus himself gave up in becoming a man. He was the Son of Man, the glorious Lord who came down from heaven to bring salvation. From eternity past, he had lived in palaces of light, basking in the incandescent glow of his mutual love with the Father and the Spirit. Then he came down to this dark world, where he had scarcely a place to lay his head. This was true in Bethlehem, where there was no room for him at the inn. It was true in Samaria, where people refused to put him up for the night. And it was true throughout his earthly ministry, when he traveled as a homeless evangelist. Even the animals have their homes, but Jesus had nowhere to live and nothing to call his own. When he said this, he was not complaining, but simply stating the facts: Jesus gave up everything to come and be our Savior.

Now Jesus calls us to give up everything for him. This does not mean that we are not allowed to own property. By his generous grace, God often blesses us with material possessions that we may use for his glory. But it *does* mean that we must never allow earthly things to get in the way of true discipleship. Jesus has not called us to a life of luxury, but to

---

3. Norval Geldenhuys, *The Gospel of Luke*, New International Commentary on the New Testament (Grand Rapids: Eerdmans, 1951), 295.

a life of suffering service. He is calling us to follow him where he went: to Jerusalem and the cross. This means laying aside our earthly ambitions. It means letting go of creature comforts to make costly gifts to Christian ministry. For some it will mean giving up the security of our homes to follow God's calling. James Boice writes: "It is true that Jesus may never ask us to break with our families for his sake or sell all we have and give to the poor in order to follow him. Indeed, in the great majority of cases, this is not required at all. But *we must be willing* to obey in these or any other areas if Jesus asks it, and we must actually do it, if he does."[4]

This can be very costly for us, as it was for Jesus. One missionary described the dense fog that descended to darken her soul when she left her home in America to serve God in Eastern Europe. "I have been trying to maintain contentment," she wrote in a newsletter to friends back home, but "I don't quite *fit*. Life lacks the homey familiarity of the States and this new culture persists in its multi-faceted strangeness. *'Where is my home?'* With my heart in a quandary, I have continued seeking to be a stable mom and wife, yet feeling anything but steady in the ongoing wrestling match with the unfamiliar."

As she wrestled with these issues, the missionary came to a radical redefinition of what it meant for her to be at home. Here is how she explained it:

> Then today the Lord brought transcending comfort through a special, wise friend who had experienced this same sense 16 years ago when the Lord moved her family to Europe. With resonant empathy, she breathed words of encouragement straight from the Word of God into my heart: "Lord, Thou hast been our dwelling place in all generations" (Ps. 90:1). She reminded me that the Lord Himself is my dwelling place, the Place that never changes, *my Home;* a sense of stability began to infuse me and the fog began to burn away.[5]

When God is our dwelling place, we can leave everything to follow Jesus, and still be at home.

---

4. James Montgomery Boice, *The Gospel of Matthew,* vol. 1: *The King and His Kingdom* (Grand Rapids: Baker, 2001), 134.

5. Minda Garner, "The Chronicles of Sofia," Sept. 2004.

No Time to Lose

The next encounter dealt not with the comforts of home, but with the claims of family. Jesus said to another would-be disciple, "Follow me." But the man answered, "Lord, let me first go and bury my father" (Luke 9:59). Rather than being too quick to promise, like the first would-be disciple, this man was too slow to perform.[6] Here was someone else who wanted to follow Jesus, but first he wanted to negotiate the terms of his discipleship. The word "first" is important because it shows where the man's priorities were. He wanted to honor a commitment to his family *before* he began to follow Jesus.

Here it helps to know the cultural background. On a first reading, most people assume that this conversation took place sometime between the death of the man's father and his proper burial. But in all likelihood, his father was not yet dead. In those days Jewish people buried their dead within twenty-four hours, and family members sat with the body of the deceased until it was laid to rest. If the father had died already, his son would not have been talking with Jesus at all, but sitting at home with his family in mourning.

What, then, was the nature of this request? When the man asked for permission to bury his father, he was asking Jesus to let him care for his father during his declining years, until finally he died. Here the man had a strong claim. Honoring our parents is one of the Ten Commandments, and caring for them in old age is one of the best ways we can ever honor them. But Jesus discerned that this man was using his family situation as an excuse for delaying his discipleship. What hinders us from following Christ is not always something sinful; sometimes it is something good in itself that nevertheless gets in the way of what God really wants us to do. That must have been how it was for this man, because "Jesus said to him, 'Leave the dead to bury their own dead. But as for you, go and proclaim the kingdom of God'" (Luke 9:60).

If this statement sounds harsh, it may be because we still do not understand the demands of discipleship. There are many duties we can safely leave in the hands of unbelievers—people who are spiritually dead. Caring for an elderly parent is one example, or at least it was in that culture.

6. See Boice, *King*, 130.

Even people without deep spiritual insight have some idea how to take care of their own families. But who will go out and preach the kingdom of God? Only a true follower of Jesus Christ. So Jesus told this man to leave his family obligations in the hands of other relatives—letting the spiritually dead bury the naturally dead—while he himself went out to proclaim the good news. Maybe some of the first people who needed to hear his gospel were members of his own family, but even to do that effectively the man needed to see that his highest and most urgent duty was to follow Jesus. Unless he understood this, how could he minister effectively to his family's deepest need?

Do not put Jesus off even one more day; follow him without delay. If this man waited until his father died, it might take him most of the rest of his life. Indeed, he might never get around to becoming a disciple. This is why Jesus never lets us put him off. He always wants us to start following him right away, and then for the rest of our lives, and for all eternity. David Gooding comments: "If Jesus is God's Son, our first duty is towards him. A man who considers that he has a prior duty to fulfill before he is free to become a follower of Christ, has no concept of who Christ is."[7] Nothing is more important than following Jesus, not even the claims of our own families, which are the strongest of all earthly claims. If it comes down to a choice—as it sometimes does—we must do what Jesus wants us to do, not what our family wants us to do. In the words of Cyril of Alexandria, "the fear of God is to be set even above the reverence and love due to parents."[8]

We need to be careful how we apply this principle, especially since elsewhere Jesus warned against making service to God an excuse for *not* caring for our parents (see Mark 7:9–13). Of course there are times when caring for our families is the very way that Jesus wants us to follow him. The claims of family have their God-given place in life, and honoring these claims is part of our service to God. Even missionaries may be called to set aside their work for a season so they can minister to a dying parent. But we must never let a false sense of duty get in the way of our real duty to Christ, whatever that is in our own particular situation.

7. David Gooding, *According to Luke: A New Exposition of the Third Gospel* (Grand Rapids: Eerdmans, 1987), 194.

8. Cyril of Alexandria, "Commentary on Luke," in *Luke*, ed. Arthur A. Just Jr., Ancient Christian Commentary on Scripture, NT 3 (Downers Grove, IL: InterVarsity, 2003), 169.

It was in this context that a third person spoke to Jesus on the Jerusalem road: "Yet another said, 'I will follow you, Lord, but let me first say farewell to those at my home'" (Luke 9:61). In all likelihood, this man had heard what Jesus said about the dead burying the dead. He did not want to do that. He did not feel the need to wait around for the rest of his father's life before he started to follow Jesus. He was willing to go much sooner. But first—there's that word again—he wanted at least enough time to go and say good-bye.

Once again, this may seem like a reasonable request. As a matter of common courtesy, surely it was appropriate for this man to go back home and say farewell to his family. There was even a good biblical precedent for this. When Elisha answered God's call to leave the family farm and follow the prophet Elijah, he was granted permission to kiss his father and mother good-bye (1 Kings 19:20). Elisha went home, burned his plow, slaughtered his oxen, and held a farewell feast for his family and friends.

Jesus may well have had that incident from Elisha's life in mind, because he said, "No one who puts his hand to the plow and looks back is fit for the kingdom of God" (Luke 9:62). To see the connection with Elisha, we need to consider both situations carefully. When he talked about putting one's hand to the plow, Jesus was saying that the "normal courtesies of family affection must give way to the overriding demands of the kingdom of God."[9] The proverb he used to make this point came from the fields, where the best way to plow a straight furrow is to keep looking ahead at some fixed point in the distance. Farmers who keep looking backwards, trying to figure out if they are still lined up properly, end up zigzagging all over the countryside. That is not what Elisha did at all. When he went back home to say good-bye, he made a definitive break with his old way of life. Once Elisha burned his plow and slaughtered his oxen, he was done with farming forever. But apparently if the man that Jesus met went back home, he would be tempted to stay. Something else was first in his heart, and knowing this, Jesus told him not to go back, even for a moment, but to follow him right away. Like a soldier going off to battle, or even like a daddy leaving home for work in the morning, this man needed to do his duty without delay.

9. Michael Wilcock, *The Message of Luke*, The Bible Speaks Today (Downers Grove, IL: InterVarsity, 1979), 118.

Sometimes we wrestle with the same temptation. We want to wait a little longer before embarking on our journey with Jesus, or before setting off on a new pathway in our pilgrimage. Once we start, we are tempted to look back at everything we used to love. But as J. C. Ryle wisely said, "Those who look back want to go back," and "If we are looking back to any thing in this world we are not fit to be disciples."[10] If we keep second-guessing our decision for Christ, or looking back fondly on our old affections, or even worse, going back to the places where we used to sin, then we will never get anywhere with Jesus. If we want to be his disciples, we need to follow him without any further delay.

John Wesley once gave some helpful advice to people who wanted to know how to follow Jesus. He said: "Do all the good you can, by all the means you can, in all the ways you can, in all the places you can, at all the times you can, to all the people you can, as long as you ever can."[11] To this helpful summary we should add the phrase "as soon as you can." Disciples of Jesus do all the good they can, by all the means they can, in all the ways they can, starting as soon as they can.

I Will Follow

As we consider these three would-be disciples, it is hard not to wonder what became of them. Did they ever decide to follow Jesus? Was the first man willing to be homeless for the sake of the gospel? Did the second man let the dead bury their dead so that he could preach the gospel? Did the third man go home and say good-bye, or did he start following Jesus right away? It would be interesting to know what they all did, but Luke does not tell us. Maybe this is because his main concern was to help us write the ending to our own story—the story of our journey with Jesus.

The one thing we do know is what Jesus did after this: he kept on going to Jerusalem. Having set his face toward that great city, nothing could deter him from reaching his appointed destination. He had already given up all the things he was calling his disciples to give up as they followed him. He had given up the comforts of home and the claims of family. More than

10. Ryle, *Luke,* 1:341.
11. John Wesley, quoted in Rick Warren, *The Purpose-Driven Life* (Grand Rapids: Zondervan, 2002), 259.

that, he had given up the glories of heaven to suffer the indignities of earth. With single-minded, wholehearted devotion to the glory of God, Jesus made it to Jerusalem and the cross, before being taken up into glory.

Now Jesus calls us to go where he has gone, to make whatever sacrifices he calls us to make, and to suffer the kinds of losses that he suffered. Are you ready to follow Jesus to the cross before going on to glory? Then you must be willing to leave the comforts of home and accept a lower standard of living, claiming nothing for yourself, but giving what you have for the gospel. Will you go anywhere and do anything for Jesus?

In the same way that Jesus once set his face toward Jerusalem, God is calling us to set our hearts on Jesus and follow him. Look to Jesus, the Scripture says, "who for the joy that was set before him endured the cross, despising the shame, and is seated at the right hand of the throne of God" (Heb. 12:2). Look to Jesus, and never look back.

41

THE KING'S MESSENGERS

Luke 10:1—16

After this the Lord appointed seventy-two others and sent them on
ahead of him, two by two, into every town and place where he him-
self was about to go. And he said to them . . . "The one who hears
you hears me, and the one who rejects you rejects me, and the one
who rejects me rejects him who sent me." (Luke 10:1–2, 16)

T he China Gospel Fellowship—also known as Tanghe—is a
large network of Chinese house churches. Early in 1994 the
fellowship began collecting donations for a special missionary trip. Since most of the group's members live in poverty, their giving
was sacrificial. People sold their chickens or gave up money they had
been saving for marriage. No matter what the cost, they wanted God to
be glorified in China.

When sufficient funds had been raised, the fellowship held a worship
service at which they commissioned seventy young evangelists to go out
two-by-two and preach the gospel in the far provinces of China. The missionaries were young and single, some of them still in their teens. Given
only enough money for a one-way journey, they were told to trust God to
provide for their needs. This trust was well placed, for God was faithful to

provide. Six months later all of the missionaries returned home safely, having established new churches in twenty-two of China's thirty provinces.[1]

In sponsoring this mission, the Tanghe were carrying out the Great Commission to go into all the world and preach the gospel. They were also following the example of Jesus Christ, who "appointed seventy-two others and sent them on ahead of him, two by two, into every town and place where he himself was about to go" (Luke 10:1).

THE SENDING OF THE SEVENTY-TWO

Previously Jesus had sent out his twelve apostles to cast out demons, heal diseases, and preach the kingdom of God (Luke 9:1–2). Now he was sending out a larger group to multiply his ministry. He was on his way to Jerusalem, and he still had many places where he wanted to preach the gospel. To that end, he sent messengers ahead to prepare for his coming.

For the sake of their own encouragement and accountability, this small army of evangelists went out two by two. There were seventy-two of them in all, or perhaps only seventy, depending on which ancient manuscript one consults. Scholars have debated the significance of this number. Some say it corresponds to the seventy nations listed in Genesis 10 and relates to the calling these messengers had to take the gospel to Gentiles living on the far side of the river Jordan. Others say the number comes from the end of Genesis, when seventy members of Jacob's family went down to Egypt. In the same way that the twelve apostles correspond to the twelve patriarchs, the seventy evangelists correspond to the seventy original Israelites: Jesus was establishing a new Israel. Still others say the number refers to the seventy (or seventy-two) elders of Moses (Num. 11:16–30), or to the seventy members of the Sanhedrin who provided religious leadership for the Jews.

Whatever the precise connection, the point would seem to be the same: the gospel work of Christian evangelism is not for the apostles only, but for other people who claim to follow Christ. As far as we know, these seventy-two evangelists never held any positions of spiritual leadership. They were ordinary Christians, so to speak. But like the twelve apostles, they were called to go and preach the gospel. Their short-term missionary trip—recorded

---

1. David Aikman, *Jesus in Beijing: How Christianity Is Transforming China and Changing the Global Balance of Power* (Washington, DC: Regnery, 2003), 84.

only in the Gospel of Luke—is one of the earliest indications of the missionary calling of the church. The same Lord Jesus who calls us to follow him also calls us to go out and preach the gospel. Every cross-carrying disciple has a cross-proclaiming witness for Christ.

The work of these witnesses is most clearly described in verse 9: "Heal the sick and say to them, 'The kingdom of God has come near to you.'" Like the twelve apostles, the seventy-two evangelists were called to a ministry of both word and deed. Their basic message was the coming of the kingdom of God—the advent of God's righteous rule through the person and work of Christ, the King. This message was the mainstay of their ministry.

Jesus also gave these evangelists the power to perform miracles, so that they could minister to the body as well as to the soul. This was an immediate blessing to everyone touched by their ministry, but it also had a further purpose: it confirmed the truth of their message. When people saw these evangelists healing the sick, they knew that what they said was true. As Norval Geldenhuys explains it, "The wonder-working healings will serve as an indication and proof of the fact that the royal sovereignty of God is exercised in and through Christ and His disciples. Thus the inhabitants of the towns and villages that are to be visited will have the opportunity of recognizing and accepting the kingly sovereignty of God and will thus be able to experience its beneficial working in their own hearts and lives."[2]

The confirmation of the ministry of the word by the deed is still vitally important today. At certain times and in certain places—especially when the gospel first penetrates a pagan culture—God may still work miracles. But whether he works miracles or not, the church is called to demonstrate the love of God in practical deeds of mercy, and this is essential to effective gospel communication. How do people experience the reality of the kingdom of God? In those days they experienced it through the message of the gospel, which was confirmed by miracles of healing. Today people experience the kingdom of God through the preaching of the gospel, which is confirmed by the loving care of the people who preach it.

One worker in Vietnam explained how God used the ministry of word and deed to bring a former student to faith in Christ:

2. Norval Geldenhuys, *The Gospel of Luke*, New International Commentary on the New Testament (Grand Rapids: Eerdmans, 1951), 301.

His first encounter with Jesus was when he was in 9th grade. He had a motor-bike accident with a Christian brother. When neither was seriously injured, although their bikes were totaled, the brother offered praise to God above. This deeply impressed the student, but he didn't think about it again until after he'd graduated and come to Hanoi seeking work. God arranged various circumstances so that brothers and sisters were instrumental in meeting his physical needs (he'd come without a job and knowing no one!). Their care spoke eloquently to his heart, and he read the New Testament over and over to learn more about their worldview. They invited him to a sharing service at the local church, and that night he truly met and accepted Jesus Christ. Now he works in an orphanage, sharing love with the children there.[3]

It was the gospel message that saved this young student, of course, but God used the loving care of Christian people to give the gospel entrance into his heart. This is how God brings people to Christ: by the good news we give them about the death and resurrection of Jesus Christ, and also by the love we show the homeless, the prisoner, the orphan, the stranger, and anyone else who is battered and broken by sin.

LABORERS FOR THE HARVEST

As Jesus sent out these seventy-two evangelists to do gospel work in word and deed, he gave them some very specific instructions. These instructions show the priority of prayer, the presence of danger, the promise of provision, the peace of welcoming the kingdom, and the peril of rejecting it.

First, Jesus said to his disciples, "The harvest is plentiful, but the laborers are few. Therefore pray earnestly to the Lord of the harvest to send out laborers into his harvest" (Luke 10:2). Jesus said something similar on other occasions (see Matt. 9:37–38; John 4:35). This was his consistent perspective on the missionary calling of the church. When Jesus spoke of the harvest, as he often did, he was speaking about people's souls. The world is like a field, and every person is like a plant—either a fruitful blade of wheat that God will gather to himself, or a pernicious weed that he will destroy with fire. God is planning to gather a great harvest of souls from every time in history and every tribe among the nations.

3. Personal correspondence from Bradley Baurain, Nov. 2004.

This is a great encouragement in gospel work. We are sometimes discouraged by what seems to be slow progress in missions, but the harvest is plentiful. God is still bringing people to salvation every day. As Jesus said to Paul when he was doing dangerous missionary work in Corinth: "Do not be afraid . . . for I have many in this city who are my people" (Acts 18:9–10). These people had not yet come to Christ, but they were coming soon, and thus in a sense they were already his.

The same is true today. According to God's sovereign plan, people all over the world and in our own community are predestined to come to Christ. Therefore, we always have great opportunities for giving people the gospel, both in our own personal ministry and through the missionary work of the church. The harvest is as plentiful today as it has ever been. There are open opportunities for the gospel to spread through urban outreach, church planting in immigrant communities, overseas theological education, Bible translation, and other forms of Christian work. Jesus calls us to take his perspective and believe that the fields are white for the harvest, even in dark places dominated by Hinduism and Islam.

There is a problem, however. The plenty of the harvest is inversely proportional to the number of harvesters. "The laborers are few," Jesus said. Not many people are willing to do the hard labor of the gospel: sowing seeds of salvation by sharing the good news, or gathering people in by leading them to Christ. We are not nearly as fruitful in our evangelism as we ought to be. Nor do we have nearly as many missionaries as we need. Wycliffe estimates that an additional two thousand workers are needed to translate the gospel for the more than three thousand people groups that still do not have the Bible in their own language.[4] Or, to give another example, although there are more than a billion Muslims in the world today, it is generally believed that less than 2 percent of all American missionaries are working in Muslim communities.[5]

Where will we get the missionaries we need? The answer is not better recruitment, although of course this has its practical place in the church. The answer is not better conferences, although God can use missionary gatherings to carry forward the good work of the Great Commission. The

---

4. For up-to-date information on the global status of Bible translation, see www.wycliffe.org.

5. This information comes from Todd Johnson, Director of the Center for the Study of Global Christianity.

answer is not better seminaries, although of course theological education can help prepare people for service. The answer is persistent prayer—prayer for God himself to raise up new workers for the great harvest. "Pray earnestly to the Lord of the harvest," Jesus said, "to send out laborers into his harvest" (Luke 10:2). Prayer has the priority. Even as the seventy-two evangelists went out to preach, they were still to pray, because prayer was the chief part of their labor.

We pray to God because he is the Lord of the harvest. Three times in the opening verses of Luke 10 Jesus either identifies himself or is identified as the Lord who sends workers out into the field. He alone is able to supply the need. Just as he once sent out the seventy-two, so now he invites us to pray that he will send out others. Is this missionary need a regular part of your prayer life?

Every believer is called to labor for the harvest, but God also sets apart certain men and women for the work of gospel witness. For this we must pray, asking the sending Lord to provide preachers, evangelists, Bible translators, church planters, and other Christian workers to reach the unreached around the world. As we pray, we also tell God that we are willing to be part of the answer to our own prayers: we too will go and labor in his gospel field, right where we are and wherever he sends us.

GOD'S PROTECTION AND PROVISION

This work is difficult, as the word "labor" would suggest. It was more than difficult, however; it was also dangerous, for Jesus said to the seventy-two: "Go your way; behold, I am sending you out as lambs in the midst of wolves" (Luke 10:3). This was his second instruction: a warning about the presence of danger in gospel work.

When Jesus sends his servants out to preach the gospel—especially where it has never been preached—they are vulnerable to attack, like sheep going out to face hungry wolves. Spiritual enemies are waiting to tear them to pieces with angry words and violent assaults. This was often true in the early church, when the enemies of Christ made murderous threats against his people, and when most of the apostles became martyrs. It was true in the pioneer days of African missions, when missionaries packed their possessions in a coffin. Not expecting to return home, they were planning ahead for an easy burial. The peril is still present today wherever cutting-edge evangelists confront the dark powers of communism, paganism, and Islam. To go out and preach the gospel is to be exposed to difficulty, danger, and perhaps even death.

Jesus warns us about this so that we will know what to expect. Although sending agencies take reasonable precautions to protect their missionaries, anyone who goes out to preach the gospel needs to be ready for hardship and willing to die for Jesus. But Jesus also tells us this so that we will rely on his protection. We may go out as sheep among the wolves, but we still have a shepherd who has promised to walk with us all the way, even through the valley of the shadow of death. The presence of spiritual danger does not drive us to fear, but to a deeper trust in the help of our God.

Along with his protection, God also promises his provision, which brings us to the third instruction that Jesus gave the seventy-two: "Carry no moneybag, no knapsack, no sandals, and greet no one on the road" (Luke 10:4). These evangelists were told to go as they were, without even taking so much as an extra pair of shoes.

These instructions were unique to that time and place, when Jesus was on his way to Jerusalem, and when his disciples had left their homes to follow a Savior who had nothing to call his own (Luke 9:58). In fact, for reasons that will become clear when we get to chapter 22, later Jesus would tell his disciples to make sure that they *did* have a moneybag and a knapsack (Luke 22:36). Every call is different, and the demands of short-term pioneer missionary work are different from the demands of a full campaign, where ongoing support is needed for long-term faithfulness. But in this particular case, Jesus sent his servants out with nothing but the gospel and the hope of a plentiful harvest.

The seventy-two evangelists had to trust God for all their needs. This trust was well placed, because God had promised to provide, as he always provides for people who do his work. As the evangelists went about their ministry, traveling from place to place, some people would welcome them with warm hospitality. Jesus said that in such cases they were to "remain in the same house, eating and drinking what they provide, for the laborer deserves his wages. Do not go from house to house. Whenever you enter a town and they receive you, eat what is set before you" (Luke 10:7–8).

515

It was appropriate for the seventy-two evangelists to accept the kindness of strangers. People doing gospel work are entitled to the basic necessities of life. But for their part, the evangelists were to be content with whatever God provided. Jesus told them not to move from one house to the next, looking for better lodgings or hoping for better hospitality. He also told them to eat whatever people gave them, not insisting on a gourmet menu or worrying about whether their hosts kept kosher food laws the same way they did.

Again, these special instructions have a wider application. Missionaries and other Christian workers (including pastors) should strive to maintain a deep and steady contentment with what God provides. Do not use your calling for financial gain; resist the temptation always to want more. This perspective is essential for missionaries, but it is godly counsel for any believer. Be thankful for everything you have, not longing for luxury. Be easy to please and grateful for what other people offer.

Our attitude about material possessions needs to be guided by the urgency of our mission. These seventy-two evangelists had a crucial calling. They were messengers of the King, sent ahead to herald the approach of his kingdom. They did not have time to prepare for their journey; they just had to get up and go. They did not even have time to greet people on the road, especially in the ancient Near East, where formal greetings could take hours on end. These men were not out to make a social visit, but to preach the gospel without distraction and without delay. In the words of the English poet Robert Herrick:

> Christ, I have read, did to His chaplains say,
> Sending them forth, *Salute no man by th' way:*
> Not, that He taught His ministers to be
> Unsmooth, or sour, to all civility;
> But to instruct them, to avoid all snares
> Of tardidation in the Lord's affairs.
> Manners are good: but till his errand ends,
> Salute we must, nor strangers, kin, or friends.[6]

6. Robert Herrick, "Salutation," in *Chapters into Verse: Poetry in English Inspired by the Bible,* vol. 2: *Gospels to Revelation,* ed. Robert Atwan and Laurance Wieder (Oxford: Oxford University Press, 1993), 122.

We need to apply this principle in our own service to God. What Robert Herrick called "snares of tardidation" are things that slow us down in our discipleship. They may be things that are good in themselves (like extra clothes and nice things to eat, for example), yet they delay us from doing the work that God has for us to do. The time is too short, and the work of the gospel is too important for us to dilly-dally. Too many Christians lead divided, distracted lives. We rush from one thing to the next without ever taking the time to make sure that what we are doing is the best way to fulfill our commitment to Christ. Is it any wonder, then, that sometimes we doubt whether we are really making a difference in the world?

The people who make the biggest difference for Christ and his kingdom are people who keep their focus on the work that God has called them to do, whether at home, at church, in the workplace, or overseas. According to J. C. Ryle, the austere instructions that Jesus gave to his evangelists

> ought to remind us of the necessity of simplicity and unworldliness in our daily life. We must beware of thinking too much about our meals, and our furniture, and our houses, and all those many things which concern the life of the body. We must strive to live like men whose first thoughts are about the immortal soul. We must endeavour to pass through the world like men who are not yet at home, and are not overmuch troubled about the fare they meet with on the road and at the inn. Blessed are they who feel like pilgrims and strangers in this life, and whose best things are all to come![7]

Peace or Peril

Jesus sent his evangelists out empty-handed so that they would learn to trust the promise of his provision. But there was also another reason: their poverty would force people to make a decision. Either people would welcome the evangelists into their homes, or they would leave them out in the cold. But either way, they had to make a spiritual choice. Here is how David Gooding explains it: "If the missionaries had enough money to support themselves, then letting them hire a room in a hotel would be a simple commercial transaction carrying no spiritual implication.

---

7. J. C. Ryle, *Expository Thoughts on the Gospels, Luke* (1858; reprint Cambridge: James Clarke, 1976), 1:349.

But if the people were faced with penniless, destitute men claiming to be Messiah's own ambassadors, they would be forced to decide whether they would receive and entertain them as such, or reject them."[8]

Understand what was at stake when these evangelists preached the gospel, and indeed, what is at stake whenever anyone preaches the gospel. The seventy-two were royal messengers. Their message was the King's message, and therefore the way that people responded would indicate what kind of relationship they wanted to have with the King. There would be peace for those who welcomed the kingdom, but peril for those who rejected it. Jesus made this perfectly clear at the end of his instructions: "The one who hears you hears me, and the one who rejects you rejects me, and the one who rejects me rejects him who sent me" (Luke 10:16). The seventy-two evangelists may not have seemed very impressive. All they had was the gospel. Yet that gospel came from the King himself, offering the true way of salvation in Christ. These messengers were there in the name of the King. Therefore, the way people responded to them would determine their eternal destiny.

Some people would respond in faith. Jesus said to his messengers, "Whatever house you enter, first say, 'Peace be to this house!' And if a son of peace is there, your peace will rest upon him. But if not, it will return to you" (Luke 10:5–6). What Jesus calls a "son of peace" is someone who welcomes the gospel message. In verse 8 he describes such people as "receiving" his messengers. They welcome both the good news of God's kingdom and the people who preach it; it is virtually one and the same.

People who gave the gospel this kind of welcome would enjoy the blessing of God's peace. The evangelist would say, "Peace be to this house!" and the members of the household would have God's peace. These were not idle words; they were a benediction from God. But they did not work like magic, as if the words themselves had the power to bring peace. Like any other gift from God, these words had to be received by faith to convey any real blessing. Anyone who believed the gospel message had peace with God through Jesus Christ—a peace that would last forever.

The same thing still happens today whenever people receive the good news by faith. Someone comes preaching the gospel message that Jesus was born to bring salvation, that he died on the cross to pay the price for our

8. David Gooding, *According to Luke: A New Exposition of the Third Gospel* (Grand Rapids: Eerdmans, 1987), 197.

sin, and that he rose again to give the free gift of eternal life. That message may not seem very impressive. Nevertheless, anyone who preaches the true gospel is a royal messenger from God, and therefore anyone who receives the message by faith receives God himself. The King of all kings is summoning us to salvation, and if we welcome his royal summons by trusting in Jesus Christ, we will have the blessing of his everlasting peace.

People who reject this gospel message do so at their own peril. Nowhere did Jesus make this any clearer than in these very instructions. First, he told his evangelists what to do when people rejected them: "But whenever you enter a town and they do not receive you, go into its streets and say, 'Even the dust of your town that clings to our feet we wipe off against you. Nevertheless know this, that the kingdom of God has come near'" (Luke 10:10–11). If in a particular town no one showed the evangelists any hospitality, they were to take their message to the streets and give a spiritual object lesson. Shaking the dust off their feet was a sign of rejection and exclusion, even condemnation. It meant that the people of that community were outside the people of God, that as far as God was concerned, their town was foreign soil.[9]

To reject a royal messenger is to reject the royal person of the king who sent the messenger. This is almost always a serious mistake, but never more so than when the King is the Sovereign Lord of the entire universe. Jesus proceeded to pronounce this woe against communities that rejected his messengers: "I tell you, it will be more bearable on that day for Sodom than for that town. Woe to you, Chorazin! Woe to you, Bethsaida! For if the mighty works done in you had been done in Tyre and Sidon, they would have repented long ago, sitting in sackcloth and ashes. But it will be more bearable in the judgment for Tyre and Sidon than for you. And you, Capernaum, will you be exalted to heaven? You shall be brought down to Hades" (Luke 10:12–15).

The word "woe" expresses deep regret and sad dismay. Jesus uses it here to show the anguish he felt over his rejection in places where he had once preached the gospel: Chorazin, Bethsaida, and Capernaum, which was his home-away-from-home. These were towns in Galilee where Jesus performed mighty miracles. The people of those communities had every

---

9. R. Kent Hughes, *Luke: That You May Know the Truth*, 2 vols., Preaching the Word (Wheaton, IL: Crossway, 1998), 1:377.

opportunity to trust him for their salvation. They saw Jesus in the flesh; they witnessed his divine power and heard his words of salvation. Nevertheless, they remained unrepentant; sadly, they did not receive Jesus by faith. As a result, they were in grave peril.

When Jesus spoke of "that day" (Luke 10:12), he was plainly referring to the day of judgment, when God will render his verdict on every person who has ever lived (see, for example, Obad. 15; 1 Peter 2:12). Some people will be received into his everlasting peace, but others will be condemned to everlasting destruction. As it says in verse 15, they will be "brought down to Hades," which is not simply a place for the dead, but "a place of punishment and condemnation, which was ordained exclusively for the ungodly."[10]

Here Jesus makes a sobering and surprising comparison. The day of judgment will be unbearable for any sinner who dies outside of Christ. Nevertheless, it will be even more unbearable for unbelievers from places like Chorazin and Capernaum than for unbelievers from wicked cities like Sodom, Sidon, and Tyre (see Isa. 23; Ezek. 26–28). Sodom was so infamous for its immorality that God destroyed it by fire (see Gen. 19). What city could ever be worse off than Sodom? According to the Bible, the answer is any city that ever heard the gospel but still rejected Jesus.

This is a sober warning for anyone who hears the good news about Jesus Christ but refuses to receive him as Savior and King. God holds us responsible for whatever we know about Jesus Christ: the greater the opportunity, the greater our responsibility. Whenever the gospel is preached, the kingdom of God is near. To reject the gospel is to reject Jesus; to reject Jesus is to reject the kingdom of his Father in heaven; and the more clearly the gospel has been preached, the greater responsibility we bear for rejecting it. We would hardly expect a bunch of pagans in a place like Sodom to trust in God. But what about people who worship in an evangelical church or read Bible commentaries? What can we expect from them, and more importantly, what does God expect? Once we have heard that salvation comes only through Jesus Christ, we can never claim ignorance again. We will have to face the eternal consequences of our response to Jesus and his gospel. There will be no excuses.

10. H. L. Strack and P. Billerbeck, *Kommentar zum Neuen Testament aus Talmud und Midrasch*, 6 vols. (Munich: Beck, 1922–1961), 4:1022.

What is your response to the gospel message? By the logic of what Jesus said about Sodom and Chorazin, the day of judgment will be most unbearable of all for people who worshiped in Bible-teaching, gospel-preaching churches but never entered the kingdom of God. If we have heard the royal message of salvation, then we need to respond to Jesus in faith, trusting the gospel of his kingdom. Jesus could hardly make it any clearer than he does in this passage. There are two and only two destinations: a heaven of peace for those who receive him by faith, and a hell of peril for those who reject him in unbelief.

Once we have made our decision for Christ, we need to do whatever we can to get the gospel to others. This means praying for missionaries to labor in the harvest fields of the gospel. It means serving God with practical compassion, so that the truth of his Word is confirmed by the deeds of our mercy. For some, getting the gospel out will mean answering God's call to go somewhere far away and preach the gospel. For others it will mean living for Christ close to home and supporting the global work of the gospel through prayer and giving. But there is something desperately urgent for everyone to do. People are dying and going to heaven or hell every day. What will you do with the message you have received from the King? How will you labor to share it with others?

42

JOY, JOY, JOY!

Luke 10:17—24

> *The seventy-two returned with joy, saying, "Lord, even the
> demons are subject to us in your name!" . . . In that same hour he
> rejoiced in the Holy Spirit and said, "I thank you, Father, Lord
> of heaven and earth, that you have hidden these things from the
> wise and understanding and revealed them to little children; yes,
> Father, for such was your gracious will." (Luke 10:17, 21)*

Whether they have been away for many years or gone for only a short trip, missionaries love to go home and report on their gospel work. If the work has been difficult and discouraging, as it often is, they are likely to need special care. But if by the grace of God they have seen the gospel working with power, they will be full of infectious joy for what God has done.

China's Tanghe fellowship experienced this joy late in 1994 when seventy evangelists (see ch. 41) returned from a six-month missionary trip. Following Christ's example, these evangelists had gone out two by two, carrying the gospel to China's far provinces. Six months later all seventy missionaries returned to report on their work. Here is how one leader described their joyous reunion:

> It was a testimony meeting. We had given the missionaries one-way tickets. We told them, "You can't fail. If you are not successful in planting churches, nobody will give you money to come back." When we heard their testimonies, everybody was crying. They wore out their shoes, they were rejected by people. They lived in ditches and in forests. Some of them lived with pigs. In the meeting, God showed his love to us. We were joyful because they all came back alive.[1]

They were also joyful because God had blessed their ministry. Seventy missionaries went out with almost nothing except the gospel, and by the grace of God, they established new house churches all over China, including some congregations that now number in the hundreds of thousands. The missionaries saw the gospel working with power, and they returned rejoicing.

THE GREAT JOY OF GOD'S VICTORY OVER SATAN

The seventy-two evangelists Jesus sent out to announce the coming of God's kingdom experienced the same emotion. Jesus sent them out to heal the sick and to say, "The kingdom of God has come near to you" (Luke 10:9). When they had fulfilled their mission, "The seventy-two returned with joy, saying, 'Lord, even the demons are subject to us in your name!'" (Luke 10:17). This is the first of three great joys in the middle of Luke 10: the great joy of God's victory over Satan.

When Jesus first sent these missionaries out to preach the gospel, he gave them sober warnings. He said he was sending them out "as lambs in the midst of wolves" (Luke 10:3). He told them that people would reject them, that in some communities they would not even get a bite to eat or a place to stay. But whatever hardships they may have faced, when the evangelists returned to Jesus they were absolutely elated. Their mission had been a resounding success. They had healed the sick, they had preached the good news, and to their happy amazement, they had cast out demons.

---

1. Xing Liaoyuan, quoted in David Aikman, *Jesus in Beijing: How Christianity Is Transforming China and Changing the Global Balance of Power* (Washington, DC: Regnery, 2003), 84.

Even the fallen angels who served the kingdom of darkness by tormenting the souls of men were subject to their ministry. The missionaries could hardly believe it, and they could not wait to tell Jesus about it.

We can well imagine the missionaries running up to Jesus, bubbling with enthusiasm, their faces glowing with excitement. They had the kind of spontaneous joy that comes with unexpected success. "Joy" is just the word for it, because these evangelists were celebrating what God had done, and not simply what they had done. This is one of the differences between happiness and joy: we can be happy with ourselves, but true joy comes only when we get outside of ourselves to glorify God. Happiness may be self-centered, but joy is always God-centered. The evangelists had this God-centered joy because they knew that they did not cast out demons by their own strength, but only in Jesus' name: "Satan-crushing power resided neither in their persons nor in their office, but in Jesus."[2] The Lord Jesus Christ is the only exorcist. He alone has power over the devil and his demons. But like the evangelists, we may share in his triumph, and in the joy that his triumph brings.

This joy is one that Jesus shares. When the evangelists told Jesus about their victory over the demons, he said, "I saw Satan fall like lightning from heaven. Behold, I have given you authority to tread on serpents and scorpions, and over all the power of the enemy, and nothing shall hurt you" (Luke 10:18–19). With these words, Jesus confirmed that he had given his evangelists power over the devil and his demons. But two questions about these verses are still hard to answer: Exactly when did Jesus see Satan fall from heaven, and how can we apply what Jesus said about having authority over the enemy?

Satan is the archenemy of God and the accuser of God's people. His very name means "adversary." Created as one of God's most beautiful angels, he rebelled against his creator, and as punishment for his pride, he was banished from glory. Perhaps this is when Jesus saw Satan fall from heaven: at the time of his rebellion, when he arced toward earth and his glory was extinguished. If so, then in verses 18 and 19 Jesus was explaining why the demons were subject to his seventy-two evangelists. It was because "the might of Satan, the prince of all diabolical powers, [was] already broken."[3] In the words of Cyril of Alexandria, God threw

---

2. Dennis E. Johnson, "The Joys of the Coming Kingdom," *Evangelium* 5.2 (Apr. 2007), 10.

3. Norval Geldenhuys, *The Gospel of Luke*, New International Commentary on the New Testament (Grand Rapids: Eerdmans, 1951), 302.

Satan down "from on high to earth, from overweening pride to humiliation, from glory to contempt, from great power to utter weakness."[4]

God did all of this even before the coming of Christ. But when Jesus spoke of Satan falling from heaven, he may have been referring to something more immediate and more directly related to the ministry of his messengers. When they cast out demons in his name, Jesus caught a glimpse of his own impending victory over Satan through his crucifixion and resurrection (see 1 Cor. 15:54–57; Col. 2:15; 1 John 3:8). The apostle John wrote about this in his apocalypse:

> And the great dragon was thrown down, that ancient serpent, who is called the devil and Satan, the deceiver of the whole world—he was thrown down to earth, and his angels were thrown down with him. And I heard a loud voice in heaven, saying, "Now the salvation and the power and the kingdom of our God and the authority of his Christ have come, for the accuser of our brothers has been thrown down, who accuses them day and night before our God. And they have conquered him by the blood of the Lamb." (Rev. 12:9–11)

The great victory that Jesus won over Satan through the cross will be made complete at the final judgment, when God will throw Satan down into the lake of fire, and he will be "tormented day and night forever and ever" (Rev. 20:10). But there were signs of that ultimate victory already in the ministry of the evangelists: "in the grand offensive by the seventy against the might of Satan it could plainly be seen how Satan had already lost his exalted position of power."[5] Jesus perceived that when his servants cast out demons, Satan was falling from the high seat of his rebellion—as quick as a flash, like a bolt from the blue sky. As John Keble wrote in one of his religious poems:

> See Lucifer like lightning fall,
> > Dashed from his throne of pride;
> While, answering Thy victorious call,
> > The Saints his spoils divide.[6]

---

4. Cyril of Alexandria, "Commentary on Luke," in *Luke*, ed. Arthur A. Just Jr., Ancient Christian Commentary on Scripture, NT 3 (Downers Grove, IL: InterVarsity, 2003), 175.

5. Geldenhuys, *Luke*, 302.

6. John Keble, "See Lucifer like Lightning Fall," in *Chapters into Verse: Poetry in English Inspired by the Bible*, vol. 2: *Gospels to Revelation*, ed. Robert Atwan and Laurance Wieder (Oxford: Oxford University Press, 1993), 122.

Then Jesus went on to give his evangelists "authority to tread on serpents and scorpions, and over all the power of the enemy," and he said "nothing shall hurt you" (Luke 10:19). Jesus gave both power and authority—the ability to gain victory over Satan, and also the right to do so. Jesus could give his servants power and authority because, as the Son of God, he himself has power and authority over Satan. The Scripture says that Jesus "has gone into heaven and is at the right hand of God, with angels, authorities, and powers being subjected to him" (1 Peter 3:22). But what does it mean for Jesus to give *us* this authority?

Some Christians have interpreted Luke 10:19 so literally that they have made snake-handling a test of fellowship. The only true Christian evangelist, they say, is someone who can handle poisonous snakes and remain unharmed. They find confirmation for their view in the story of Paul at Malta, when the apostle shook a viper into the fire (see Acts 28:1–6). But it seems more likely that Jesus was speaking figuratively.[7] The real issue here is not physical danger from poisonous vipers, but spiritual danger from that old snake, the devil. Going all the way back to the Garden of Eden, the serpent is a familiar biblical image for Satan (see Ps. 91:13), and most likely the scorpions here refer to his demons.

The point of these symbols of spiritual evil is that in the name of Jesus Christ, we have the authority to resist the devil. The power of God constrains the power of Satan in the life of the believer. Through faith in Christ, God gives us a way to escape the devil's temptations, and through the ministry of his Spirit, he will keep us safe from the devil until we reach glory. Satan can never do us any ultimate harm. We may suffer hardships and even death, as the apostles did, but nothing can ever separate us from the love that God has for us in Christ (see Rom. 8:38–39). Therefore, we should never believe—even for a moment—the devil's own lie that we are powerless against him.

What a great triumph it is—and what a great joy—whenever we claim God's victory over Satan through Jesus Christ. This happens whenever God's Word is preached in the power of the Holy Spirit. It happens whenever a sinner comes to faith in Christ. It happens whenever secret sin is brought into the light of the cross. It happens whenever a Christian stands

7. Here Jesus may also refer to Israel's experience in the exodus; see Deut. 8:15.

firm against the temptation to lust after life's pleasures, or to be embittered by life's disappointments, or to rage against a hard providence, or to do anything else contrary to God's will for our lives.

How is Satan tormenting you, and what victory are you gaining over him? One little boy was visiting a friend when he accidentally broke a little toy frog. His first impulse was to hide the toy so that no one would know. But by the witness of the Holy Spirit in his conscience, it occurred to him that this was exactly what Satan wanted him to do. So instead of hiding the frog, he went right away and showed his friend's mother what had happened. By doing this, the boy gained a real triumph over Satan. The high archangel of darkness is utterly defeated when even the littlest Christian claims victory in Jesus' name.

THE GREATER JOY OF ETERNAL LIFE

As much joy as the seventy-two evangelists had in their triumph over Satan, Jesus told them that something else should give them even greater joy: the promise of eternal life. "Nevertheless," he said, "do not rejoice in this, that the spirits are subject to you, but rejoice that your names are written in heaven" (Luke 10:20).

When Jesus told his disciples not to rejoice over Satan, he was not being a killjoy. As we have seen, the seventy-two evangelists had good reason to rejoice, and Jesus rejoiced with them. Rather than forbidding this joy, Jesus was really making a comparison, phrased in terms of an apparent contradiction or negation. He was telling them that they had another reason for rejoicing that ought to take precedence. "Yes," he was saying, "it is good to rejoice in your authority over the demons, but this cannot compare with the deeper joy of everlasting life."

Jesus referred to this everlasting life by using a familiar metaphor. He called his messengers to rejoice that their names were "written in heaven" (Luke 10:20). Here we encounter the common biblical image of the book of life. When Moses interceded for the children of Israel, offering his life for their sins, he prayed, "Please blot me out of your book that you have written" (Ex. 32:32). Later, when the Israelites were living as exiles in Babylon, the prophet Daniel promised: "Your people shall be delivered, everyone whose name shall be found written in the book" (Dan. 12:1).

Moses and Daniel both believed that God kept a written record of all the people who belonged to him. The apostle Paul believed this too, and thus he spoke of coworkers "whose names are in the book of life" (Phil. 4:3). Similarly, the writer to the Hebrews described people who come to God through faith in Christ as being "enrolled in heaven" (Heb. 12:23). The apostle John went so far as to say that the names of God's people were "written before the foundation of the world in the book of life of the Lamb that was slain" (Rev. 13:8).

This idea of the book of life was deeply rooted in the culture of the ancient Near East. Kings who ruled great empires loved to keep long lists of the names of their subjects. A good example comes from the Christmas story, when Caesar Augustus issued a decree that a census should be taken across the entire Roman world (Luke 2:1). In those days people were familiar with the bureaucracy of government record-keeping. Typically, having one's name "in the book" served as proof of citizenship. In New Testament times, Roman officials would keep detailed registers of the people who belonged to their city-state, and who therefore had the full rights of membership in their community. A person whose name was in the book was entitled to property and protection.

What, then, does it mean to have our names written in heaven? It means that the High King of heaven knows and remembers that we belong to him. It means further that he is keeping an accurate record of our citizenship in his everlasting city (see Phil. 3:20). It means that we have a right to all the privileges of heaven, even before we arrive. And it means that we have God's own guarantee of eternal life. Jesus says of anyone who trusts in his righteousness, "I will never blot his name out of the book of life. I will confess his name before my Father and before his angels" (Rev. 3:5). So when Jesus tells us to rejoice that our names are written in heaven, it is to reassure us that he is keeping track of our salvation. David Gooding makes the perceptive comment that unless we were certain of this, we would not be able to rejoice at all.[8] Instead, we would always be anxious about our eternal destiny, wondering whether God will remember that we belong to him. But the book of life gives us eternal security. To quote an old gospel song, we know that when the roll is called up yonder, we'll be there.

8. See David Gooding, *According to Luke: A New Exposition of the Third Gospel* (Grand Rapids: Eerdmans, 1987), 200.

Nevertheless, the book of life still makes some people feel anxious, especially because Revelation tells us that this book will be opened at the final judgment (Rev. 20:12), and "if anyone's name was not found written in the book of life, he was thrown into the lake of fire" (Rev. 20:15). I can remember how, as a small boy, I wanted to make sure that my name was written in the book of life. So even after I prayed to receive Jesus Christ, I went back to God again and reminded him to make sure that he wrote down my name. How can we end the uncertainty and know for sure that our names are written in the book of life?

We do not come to this assurance by climbing up into heaven, searching God's archives, and paging though his royal registry. Instead, we know that our names are written in heaven the same way we know everything else about our salvation: by believing in Jesus Christ as he is offered to us in the gospel. We know that we have eternal life, not because we have read the book of life, but because we have faith in the manger, the cross, and the empty tomb. The people whose names are written in heaven are the people who trust in Jesus.

Once we know that we have a title in heaven, this becomes our great joy in life—even greater than the joy we have in claiming God's victory over Satan. Eternal life is a greater joy because it is more all-inclusive. When the seventy-two evangelists cast out demons, they experienced only one small part of their salvation. Eternal life includes victory over Satan in spiritual warfare, but it encompasses all of the other blessings that God also has for us in Jesus Christ: the forgiveness of our sins, the resurrection of our bodies, and the fellowship of knowing God as our loving Father. The joy of eternal life is also more permanent. Whatever other joys we experience could never last for long if we could not be certain that God will always love us. But having our names written down in the book of life is a joy that will last forever.

Our joy in eternal life keeps us from being downcast during difficult times of ministry, when Satan does not seem to be cast under our feet, or when God chooses to use others more prominently in gospel success. Sometime late in 1980, Iain Murray visited the aging Dr. Martyn Lloyd-Jones. The famous London preacher was drawing near to death and could only sit up for an hour or two each day. Murray asked an obvious question: "How are you coping now that your ministry is so confined?" After all,

Lloyd-Jones had preached to countless thousands, bringing many to faith in Christ. He had also had a leading role in establishing important evangelical institutions like Tyndale House, The Westminster Conference, and The Banner of Truth. Lloyd-Jones replied, "Do not rejoice that the demons are subject to you in my name, but rejoice that your name is written in heaven." Then he said, "I am perfectly content." This is the deepest source of the believer's joy through life and on into eternity: our salvation is not based on what we have done, but on God's saving grace, for our names are written in the book of life.[9]

THE GREATEST JOY OF ALL

Is any joy greater than the joy we have in knowing eternal life? Yes, there is a greater joy—the greatest joy of all: the joy that God the Son has in God the Spirit and God the Father. Luke tells us: "In that same hour he rejoiced in the Holy Spirit and said, 'I thank you, Father, Lord of heaven and earth'" (Luke 10:21).

The word that Luke uses here for rejoicing is more intense than any other word for joy, including the other terms that he has used in this very passage. The Greek word *agalliaō* is a word for exuberant ecstasy, for complete exultation in the fullness of joy. When we see why Jesus was rejoicing, we can understand why Luke used it here. Jesus rejoiced to see Satan defeated and to give the free gift of eternal life. But here was an even greater joy because it took place within the triune being of God, who exists eternally as one God in three persons.

Of its very nature, the joy of Jesus is greater than any joy that we could ever experience. Because Jesus is God the Son, his joy is a divine rejoicing. It is a perfect joy, unspoiled and undiminished by sin. Here his joy is especially intense because he is rejoicing in the revelation of the Holy Spirit and in the secret, saving work of his Father. Luke is showing us the joy at the heart of the universe, the rejoicing that takes place within the Godhead, where God is both the subject and the object of his own joy. The Father, the Son, and the Spirit glory in one another. When Jesus was baptized (Luke 3:22), and again when he was transfigured (Luke 9:35), we saw the pleasure that the

9. The story was related to me in personal correspondence from D. A. Carson.

Father takes in his own beloved Son. Now Jesus rejoices in the Spirit and the Father, and as he rejoices, we catch a glimpse of God glorifying and enjoying himself. There can be no greater joy than this: the eternal joy that God himself enjoys in the being of God.

On this occasion, Jesus was so overwhelmed with triune joy that in a spontaneous outburst he rejoiced out loud. He rejoiced in the Holy Spirit, finding his enjoyment in the Third Person of the Trinity. He also rejoiced in the Father, praising him for his supreme greatness over heaven and earth. But many people would be surprised at the occasion for this joy. Why was Jesus rejoicing? Because, he said to his Father, "you have hidden these things from the wise and understanding and revealed them to little children; yes, Father, for such was your gracious will" (Luke 10:21–22). Jesus was rejoicing over the sovereignty of God in salvation, over the doctrine of election, over the fact that God reveals the truths of salvation only to his own beloved children.

People often consider the sovereignty of God's grace to be a dark and difficult doctrine. Why does God bring some people to a saving knowledge of Jesus Christ, while others are left to perish in their sins? The Bible never gives us the full answer, except to say that God does it for his own glory. But far from treating this mystery as an occasion for anxiety, the Bible presents it as a comfort for the soul. The doctrine of election, which proves God's sovereignty in salvation, is a doctrine of joy. We find this on Christmas night, when the angels sing "Glory to God in the highest!" and bless the people who are in God's pleasure (Luke 2:14). We find it in Romans 9 to 11, where Paul's exposition of election ends with a grand doxology of praise. We find it in Ephesians 1, where the fact that God has chosen us in Christ is celebrated with high praise to God. We also find it here in Luke 10, where God's sovereignty in salvation brings joy to the very Godhead.

Jesus rejoices in the Father's gracious will to reveal salvation to some but not to others. To be specific, God has hidden the secrets of his gospel from people who think that they are wise, and revealed them instead to little children (literally, to babies)—in other words, to people who know that they do not know everything, and who therefore come to him in simple, childlike faith.

When Jesus spoke about "the wise and understanding," he may well have been referring ironically to members of the religious establishment

531

like the Pharisees and the Sadducees—theological know-it-alls who refused to believe that he was the Christ. When he spoke about "little children," he was referring to his ordinary disciples, who for all their weakness were learning to follow him in faith and obedience. It is not ignorance that Jesus is praising here, but humility. Norval Geldenhuys has rightly observed that the contrast here is "not that between 'educated' and 'uneducated' but between those who imagine themselves to be wise and sensible and want to test the Gospel truths by their own intellects and to pronounce judgment according to their self-formed ideas and those who live under the profound impression that by their own insight and their own reasoning they are utterly powerless to understand the truths of God and to accept them."[10]

Which of these two categories describes your own attitude towards Jesus Christ? Are you still trying to evaluate Christianity according to your own belief system, or are you ready to learn what God wants to teach you? If in our arrogance we insist that God has to meet our own intellectual standards, we will never be saved. As David Gooding has said, "The mysteries of his person, his mind, his heart, his salvation are infinitely too exalted and wonderful to be penetrated and understood simply by submitting them to a sufficiently powerful intellectual analysis. By God's own choice and decree they remain hidden to the wise."[11] But by the grace of God, the Holy Spirit plainly reveals these same profound mysteries to humble sinners who come to God with nothing except their need for him. God is not an intellectual elitist. There is no minimum IQ for membership in the family of God. The gospel is not restricted to people who are smart enough to understand it. All we need is a teachable spirit and a childlike trust in Jesus Christ.

A powerful example of this kind of humility may be seen in the life of Eta Linnemann, the learned German theology professor who abandoned her attacks on the Bible to become a believer in Jesus Christ. Dr. Linnemann had been a protégé of the infamous Bible critic Rudolf Bultmann. The spiritual emptiness of liberal scholarship eventually led her into addictions to alcohol and television. But when she reached her lowest point of her personal despair, Linnemann found the grace of God. She writes:

10. Geldenhuys, *Luke*, 306–7.
11. Gooding, *Luke*, 201.

At that point God led me to vibrant Christians who knew Jesus personally as their Lord and Savior. I heard their testimonies as they reported what God had done in their lives. Finally God himself spoke to my heart by means of a Christian brother's words. By God's grace and love I entrusted my life to Jesus. He immediately took my life into his saving grasp and began to transform it radically. My destructive addictions were replaced by a hunger and thirst for his Word and for fellowship with Christians. I was able to recognize sin clearly as sin rather than merely make excuses for it as was my previous habit. I can still remember the delicious joy I felt when for the first time black was once more black and white was once more white. . . . By God's grace I experienced Jesus as the one whose name is above all names. I was permitted to realize that Jesus *is* God's son, born of a virgin. He *is* the Messiah and the Son of Man.[12]

When she spoke at Philadelphia's Westminster Theological Seminary in the early 1990s, Dr. Linnemann was asked what had brought about this radical change in her life and theology. To her the answer was so obvious that she was almost astonished by the question. She said, "Why, I became a child of God!" It was as simple as that. It is always that simple: anyone who comes to God in childlike trust will gain a clear knowledge of salvation in Christ. All we need to do is come to Jesus in simple faith, asking him to be our Savior and our God.

Giving grace to the humble is one of God's greatest joys. As Jesus rejoiced in the Spirit, he went on to say: "All things have been handed over to me by my Father, and no one knows who the Son is except the Father, or who the Father is except the Son and anyone to whom the Son chooses to reveal him" (Luke 10:22). In verse 21 Jesus had rejoiced in the revelation of the Father; here in verse 22 he rejoices in his own revelation as the Son. It is all interconnected. Jesus Christ is God the Son. Therefore, everything that belongs to the Father—such as his sovereign power and divine authority—also belongs to the Son.

When Jesus said that the Father had given him all things, he was making the strongest possible claim to his own deity. All things belong to Jesus Christ, the Son of God. Not a single atomic particle in the entire universe is outside his supreme lordship. Due to his divine identity, the Son has

12. Eta Linnemann, *Historical Criticism of the Bible: Methodology or Ideology?* trans. Robert W. Yarbrough (Grand Rapids: Baker, 1990), 18–19.

perfect knowledge of the Father, in the same way that the Father has perfect knowledge of the Son. The Father and the Son share mutual intimacy with the Spirit in the fellowship of their triune being. Only God can know God perfectly, and therefore no one knows the Son as does the Father, or the Father as does the Son.

And yet (and this is the reason Jesus rejoices) we ourselves are able to have fellowship with the triune God. By the grace of the Father, according to the will of the Son, through the revelation of the Holy Spirit, we know the living God. It is the work of the Son to bring us into fellowship with the Father, and Jesus rejoices that this is so. God the Son came into the world so that we could enter his joy—the joy of knowing and loving God. David Gooding writes: "As Son of the Father he enjoyed unique knowledge of the intimate relationship that lies at the heart of the Godhead, and with that unique knowledge the unique privilege of communicating it to whomever he pleased."[13]

A JOYOUS BENEDICTION

Jesus ended this conversation with a blessing that came from a heart full of joy—a blessing that must have made his disciples' joy complete: "Then turning to the disciples he said privately, 'Blessed are the eyes that see what you see! For I tell you that many prophets and kings desired to see what you see, and did not see it, and to hear what you hear, and did not hear it'" (Luke 10:23–24).

This joyous benediction is in keeping with what Jesus already said about the secrets of salvation belonging only to God. The Father and the Son have exclusive, mutual, intimate fellowship within their triune being. But according to the Father's gracious will, by his own sovereign choice and through the revealing work of the Holy Spirit, the Son invited his disciples— and his disciples alone—to share in their fellowship. Theirs was the high privilege of knowing the Father and the Son, with the Spirit.

To make sure they understood what a great privilege this was, Jesus referred to all the men who desperately wanted to have this knowledge, but never lived to see the day. He was referring explicitly to the prophets

13. Gooding, *Luke,* 202.

and kings of the Old Testament who prayed for the coming of the Christ. How these men longed to see the promise of the ages fulfilled in the long-awaited Messiah! Imagine what Jeremiah would have given to see the righteous Branch raised up from David (Jer. 23:5), or Isaiah to see the son conceived to the virgin (Isa. 7:14), or Micah to see the baby born in Bethlehem (Mic. 5:2). Imagine what David would have given to see his God-forsaken Savior poured out like water or laid in the dust of death (Ps. 22:1, 14–15), or Isaiah to see the Suffering Servant wounded for his transgressions and buried in a rich man's tomb (Isa. 53:5, 9). Imagine what Job would have given to see his risen Redeemer standing on the earth (Job 19:25). With a holy jealousy, these mighty kings and faithful prophets longed to know the Christ as the disciples knew him. What a blessing it was for the twelve to see the ancient promises fulfilled in the birth, life, death, resurrection, and ascension of Jesus Christ. What a blessing—and what a joy!

Only one thing could add to the disciples' joy, namely, our own believing response to their gospel. The apostle John—who had been with Jesus the day he rejoiced in the Spirit—wrote about this saving response in his first epistle. John began by testifying to the things that he had heard with his own ears and seen with his own eyes—the gospel realities that were the envy of prophets and kings. Then he celebrated the joy he had in knowing God. "Our fellowship," he rejoiced to say, "is with the Father and with his Son Jesus Christ" (1 John 1:3).

John's joy was not yet complete, however. There was one thing he still desired, which was for us to join him by trusting in Jesus for our salvation. John wrote, "That which we have seen and heard we proclaim also to you, so that you too may have fellowship with us" (1 John 1:3). "We are writing these things," he went on to say, "so that our joy may be complete" (1 John 1:4). The joy of the apostles is complete whenever we join their fellowship with the Father and the Son through Jesus Christ.

Their joy becomes our own when we come to Christ. The ancient kings would have laid down their crowns, and the old-time prophets would have left behind their ministries to know Jesus the way we know him in the gospel: as our Savior from sin and our God forever. What joy is ours! We have the great joy of having our names written in heaven, and the still greater joy of knowing the Father, the Son, and the Spirit in their rejoicing. No one is more greatly blessed than we are, and therefore no one should live with greater joy.

43

WHOSE NEIGHBOR AM I?

Luke 10:25–37

"Which of these three, do you think, proved to be a neighbor to the man who fell among the robbers?" He said, "The one who showed him mercy." And Jesus said to him, "You go, and do likewise."
(Luke 10:36–37)

*I*f you were on your way to do something important—to give a presentation, for example—and you saw someone in trouble, would you stop and help? Would it be worth the inconvenience? And what if you were running late? Would you still take the time to help someone in need?

Two psychologists from Princeton University tried to answer these questions in an experiment about good and bad neighbors. Seminary students were unexpectedly asked on short notice to give a talk to a group of their professors. Some were asked to speak on the parable of the good Samaritan, while others were asked to address the relevance of Christian ministry to daily life. Some students were given adequate time to prepare, while others were told that they were running late. On their way to give their talks, they all encountered a man who was moaning for help. But who would stop to help him?

One would hope that all of them would stop. They were seminary students, after all, and some of them had just read the story that Jesus told about helping people along life's way. Unfortunately, they did not all stop. Some of them did, but some of them didn't, mainly because they were in too much of a hurry to be good neighbors.[1] If we want to avoid making the same mistake ourselves, we need to be willing to stop and help the people God is giving us to help, even when it may be terribly inconvenient. To be ready to do this, it helps to know what Jesus really said about the good Samaritan.

What Must I Do to Be Saved?

Most people know this parable, but they do not always remember the context. Jesus had been rejoicing over the way his Father had hidden the secrets of salvation from people who thought they were wise and revealed them instead to people with childlike faith. "And behold"—as if to prove the point that Jesus was making—"a lawyer stood up to put him to the test, saying, 'Teacher, what shall I do to inherit eternal life?'" (Luke 10:25).

In Israel, to be a lawyer was to be an expert in God's law—a Bible scholar and a theologian. This man knew the laws of God from the Scriptures of the Old Testament, and he sought to apply them to daily life. In this case, his question dealt with a matter of supreme importance: eternal life. What could be more important to know than the way of everlasting life? Since God has "put eternity" into our hearts (Eccl. 3:11), we all want to know if there is a way for us to live forever.

Yet as important as this question is, there were some problems with the way the lawyer asked it. One was his motivation. Luke tells us that he was putting Jesus to the test. How foolish it is to test God on his theology, and yet people do the same thing today. Rather than accepting Jesus on his own terms, believing that he is the Son of God and Savior of sinners, they evaluate him according to the principles of their own theology. Yet the Bible explicitly warns us *not* to put God to the test (Deut. 6:16). The real question is not what we think about Jesus, but what he thinks about us.

1. Malcolm Gladwell, in an interview with *Christianity Today*, (August 7, 2000); 65.

There was also a problem with the way the lawyer phrased his question: "What shall I *do* to inherit eternal life?" To put the question more literally, "Having done what will I inherit eternal life?" as if to say that one single good deed was all it took to gain salvation. Phrased this way, the question is self-contradictory. On the one hand, the man referred to eternal life as an inheritance—something granted as a gift. On the other hand, he assumed there was something that he could do to gain eternal life, that his salvation would come by some good work. This was typical of Judaism in those days. Of course there was still a remnant that depended on God for grace, but it was more common for people to make their salvation contingent on their religious performance. "Great is Torah," went one rabbinical saying, "for it gives to them that practice it, life in this world and in the world to come."[2] Many people make the same mistake today. They assume that if there is a heaven at all, they will gain entrance only if the good that they do outweighs the bad.

This is not an assumption that God happens to share. To help the lawyer see this, Jesus responded with a question of his own: "What is written in the Law? How do you read it?" (Luke 10:26). By referring the Bible scholar back to his Bible, Jesus was reclaiming the agenda. The way to eternal life is written in God's Word, and what does that Word say? As the lawyer well knew from his own careful study and daily worship, it said, "You shall love the Lord your God with all your heart and with all your soul and with all your strength and with all your mind, and your neighbor as yourself" (Luke 10:27).

This was a good answer because it came straight out of God's law. It came from Deuteronomy 6, which pious Jews recited every day: "Hear, O Israel: The LORD our God, the LORD is one. You shall love the LORD your God with all your heart and with all your soul and with all your might" (Deut. 6:4–5). The man's answer also came from the book of Leviticus: "You shall not take vengeance or bear a grudge against the sons of your own people, but you shall love your neighbor as yourself: I am the LORD" (Lev. 19:18). These verses summarized all Ten Commandments, the whole law of God (see Matt. 22:37, 39). So Jesus told the lawyer that he had given a good answer: "You have answered correctly; do this, and you will live" (Luke 10:28; cf. Rom. 10:5).

2. Mishnah *Pirke Aboth* 6.7, quoted in Kenneth E. Bailey, *Through Peasant Eyes* (Grand Rapids: Eerdmans, 1980), 36.

All that the lawyer had to do—all that anyone has to do—was to keep the two great commandments by loving God and loving his neighbor. If he did this (and kept on doing it; in contrast to the lawyer, Jesus used the present tense) he would gain eternal life. But keeping these commandments is easier said than done, and therein lies the problem. The love that God requires is perfect love—not just once, as the lawyer seemed to think, but all the time. To love God truly with heart, soul, mind, and strength is to love him with everything we are and have. To love our neighbors properly is to love them with the same intense interest and constant concern that we have for ourselves. But who has ever loved in such a wholehearted and supremely selfless way?

Jesus was answering the lawyer on his own terms, giving a legal answer to a legal question. Is there anything we can do to gain eternal life? Yes, the law of God offers salvation to anyone who fully satisfies its demands. "Do this," Jesus said, "and you will live." But who is able to do it? No one, except the sinless Son of God. As the Scripture says, "by works of the law no human being will be justified in his sight, since through the law comes knowledge of sin" (Rom. 3:20; cf. Gal. 3:10). In other words, we can never be saved by keeping the law—not because there is anything wrong with the law, but because there is something wrong with us. This was the obvious implication of what Jesus said to the lawyer. He was laying down an impossible challenge designed to drive sinners to seek a Savior.

Whom Do I Have to Love?

At this point, the lawyer should have prayed for grace. He should have fallen to his knees and said something like this: "Help me, Lord, for I am a sinful man. I cannot love God the way he demands to be loved, and I have never loved anyone nearly as much as I love myself. Tell me how a sinner like me can be saved."

If the lawyer had done that, Jesus undoubtedly would have explained the true way of salvation, which is not by anything that we can do, but only by what Jesus has done—his perfect fulfillment of the law in love for his Father and for us as his neighbors. But instead of asking God for justifying grace, the lawyer, "desiring to justify himself, said to Jesus, 'And who is my neighbor?'" (Luke 10:29).

The lawyer was trying to save face. He had asked a question to show his intellectual and spiritual superiority. But Jesus responded with an answer so basic that it made him look stupid for even asking. Love God and love your neighbor—these were simple answers that even the youngest scholar at the synagogue knew from learning his catechism. Jesus was getting the better of him; probably his colleagues were starting to snicker. So he tried to show that things were really much more complicated than Jesus was making them. "Yes, yes, of course, we all need to love our neighbors," the man was saying, "but exactly how do you define the word 'neighbor'?" This question assumed that some people fell into the category of "nonneighbor." C. H. Talbert thus paraphrased the lawyer's question: "How can I spot others who belong to God's people so that I can love them?"[3]

In all likelihood, the lawyer also raised this question because he knew that he did not love his neighbor after all, at least not the way that Jesus demanded. He was looking for some sort of loophole (as sinners often do). His desire to "justify himself" related not merely to his initial question, but to his whole life before God. Obviously, he could not love everyone. That would be impossible. But if he could find a way to limit the size of his neighborhood, then maybe, just maybe, he really could love his neighbor, and then he would be able to justify himself before God.

This is what always happens when we try to be saved by our own works. Rather than upholding the law in all its perfection, we undermine the law by reducing it to something we think we might be able to keep. Thus the lawyer tried to make God's second great commandment more manageable. David Gooding imagines him reasoning as follows:

> Are we expected to treat every man jack in the whole of the world as our neighbor and love him as ourselves? And if that is impossible, where are we to draw the line? And are we to treat outrageous sinners and vicious tyrants and blaspheming heretics as our neighbors and love them, along with all others, as ourselves? Or may we with good common sense take the commandment as meaning by "neighbor" the people in our family, or street, or synagogue, or at a stretch our fellow-nationals, but no more? Can we take it

---

3. C. H. Talbert, *Reading Luke: A Literary and Theological Commentary on the Third Gospel* (New York: Crossroad, 1982), 122.

also that our political or national enemies, by being enemies, have ceased to be our neighbors?[4]

This ethnocentric attitude was common in those days. When the Israelites spoke about their neighbors, they were referring almost exclusively to their fellow Israelites, to members of their own covenant community, and not to people from neighboring nations. According to scholars, "An Israelite's neighbor is any member of his nation, but not one who is not an Israelite."[5] So as far as loving one's neighbors was concerned, some people counted, and some people didn't. Some people were inside the circle of neighborly love, but everyone else was left outside. The Israelites took care of their own, but they did not think that they had an obligation to care for anyone else. "After all," they said, "we can't help everybody; we have to draw the line somewhere."

This attitude is equally common today. Sometimes we draw the boundary along ethnic lines, excluding people from a different background. Sometimes we draw it along religious lines. We do a decent job of caring for other Christians, but we have much less concern for people outside the church. Sometimes we draw the boundary along social lines, making a distinction between the deserving and the undeserving poor. Sometimes we simply exclude people whose problems seem too large for us to handle. But wherever we draw the line, we find the lawyer's logic compelling. We have to make choices in life. Our love has to have limits. Since we cannot help everybody, only certain people qualify as our neighbors. Everyone else will have to go somewhere else to get whatever help they need.

NOT GOOD NEIGHBORS

Rather than offering a theoretical definition of the concept of neighbor, Jesus answered the lawyer's question by telling a story. This parable answered the lawyer's question, at least indirectly, by redrawing the boundaries of his neighborhood. Jesus got the man to think outside of his usual categories

4. David Gooding, *According to Luke: A New Exposition of the Third Gospel* (Grand Rapids: Eerdmans, 1987), 203.

5. Hermann L. Strack and Paul Billerbeck, quoted in Norval Geldenhuys, *The Gospel of Luke*, New International Commentary on the New Testament (Grand Rapids: Eerdmans, 1951), 313.

by putting a Samaritan at the center of the story. More importantly, the parable showed that he was asking the wrong question altogether. The real question is not "Who is my neighbor?" but "Whose neighbor am I?"

The story began with a dying man in desperate need. As Jesus told it, "A man was going down from Jerusalem to Jericho, and he fell among robbers, who stripped him and beat him and departed, leaving him half dead" (Luke 10:30). This situation was not uncommon. As it made its long and winding descent from Jerusalem, the Jericho road passed through treacherous country. With its narrow passages and dangerous precipices, it was an ideal place for thieves and bandits to ambush lonely travelers. In ancient times people called it "the bloody way."[6] So it proved to be for the victim in Jesus' story. Stripped and beaten, his battered body was soaking the trail with its blood. The man was almost dead.

As he lay dying, several people had a chance to save the man's life. The first two people who passed by the crime scene were both religious leaders. They were fine, upstanding citizens—exactly the kind of people one would expect to stop and help. Sadly, they did nothing at all: "Now by chance a priest was going down that road, and when he saw him he passed by on the other side. So likewise a Levite, when he came to the place and saw him, passed by on the other side" (Luke 10:31–32).

Both men were guilty of a sin of omission: they failed to save a man's life. They passed the victim by, pretending not to notice. The cruelty of their neglect was all the more wicked because they were coming from Jerusalem, where they had almost certainly been to worship. The people who heard this story would assume that these religious leaders had been in Jerusalem to serve at the temple, where they had recited the law and offered sacrifices on God's altar. But however fervently they worshiped at God's house, when these men went out on the road they failed to keep the law of God's love or to offer themselves as living sacrifices for a neighbor in need.

Scholars wonder why these men failed to stop and help. Was it because they were in a hurry to get home? Was it because they were afraid of being ambushed? Was it because they did not want to get blamed for beating the man up? Was it perhaps because they thought that he was already dead? According to God's law, priests were forbidden to touch a dead body

6. J. C. Ryle, *Expository Thoughts on the Gospels, Luke* (1858; reprint Cambridge: James Clarke, 1976), 1:380.

(Lev. 21:1–3), and according to custom, Levites who became ceremonially unclean had to go through a costly and time-consuming week-long ritual of purification.[7] Thus the lawyer who was listening to the parable may well have thought that such men had a duty *not* to stop and help. Or did these men fail to stop simply because they were too busy to be bothered by the inconvenience of helping someone in desperate need?

Jesus does not tell us why the priest and the Levite refused to help, yet it hardly matters. What excuse could possibly justify their refusal to save a man's life? If they were in a hurry, their families could wait. If there was a chance they might get ambushed, they should have died trying to save someone's life. Even if there was a chance that the man might be dead, their higher duty to try to save a life superseded any claim of the ceremonial law. These men had a righteous responsibility to stop and help, and when they failed to do so, they became accomplices to the man's murder.

The poor example of these religious leaders shows us some of the characteristics of bad neighbors. When am I a bad neighbor? When I avoid people in obvious need. When I come up with flimsy excuses for refusing to get involved with someone who has a legitimate claim on my love. When I have little concern for those who are wounded and dying, whether their injuries are spiritual or physical. When I see someone who might be in trouble, but refuse to stop and find out what kind of help I might be able to offer. When I walk away from worship with a heart as hard as the one I came in with. When I am too selfish to interrupt what I am doing or to be inconvenienced by someone else's problems. Whenever I make lame excuses for not doing what I know, deep down, that Jesus wants me to do for someone else. I am a bad neighbor whenever I refuse to be a good neighbor to someone in need.

When Charles Spurgeon preached from this passage, he imagined some of the excuses these men might have made for their shocking sin of omission. As he considered the possibilities, he noticed members of his congregation smiling at their absurdity. Then he challenged them to see the absurdity of their own failure to love their neighbors:

> I shall leave you to make all the excuses you like about not helping the poor
> and aiding the hospitals, and when you have made them they will be as good

7. Bailey, *Through Peasant Eyes*, 45.

as those which I have set before you. You have smiled over what the priest might have said, but if you make any excuses for yourselves whenever real need comes before you, and you are able to relieve it, you need not smile over your excuses, the devil will do that; you had better cry over them, for there is the gravest reason for lamenting that your heart is hard toward your fellow-creatures when they are sick, and perhaps sick unto death.[8]

What kind of neighbor are you? Are you stopping to help needy people, or are you making all kinds of excuses for passing them by?

THE GOOD SAMARITAN

At this point we might expect a good, honest Israelite to come along and help—not another proud clergyman, but a pious layman. Instead, Jesus adds a surprising twist to the story. The hero is not a Jew at all: "But a Samaritan, as he journeyed, came to where he was, and when he saw him, he had compassion. He went to him and bound up his wounds, pouring on oil and wine. Then he set him on his own animal and brought him to an inn and took care of him. And the next day he took out two denarii and gave them to the innkeeper, saying, 'Take care of him, and whatever more you spend, I will repay you when I come back'" (Luke 11:33–35).

A Samaritan was just about the last person that anyone in Israel would expect to stop and help. In centuries past the Samaritans had defied God's law by intermarrying with the Assyrians. Over time they had developed their own version of the Torah and set up their own center for worship. Thus, as far as the Jews were concerned, the Samaritans were half-breed heretics. By the time of Christ, there was a settled animosity between the two people groups. As John tells us in his Gospel, "Jews have no dealings with Samaritans" (John 4:9). In fact, some rabbis had a serious debate as to whether a Jew had any responsibility to save a Samaritan.[9] Others said that such heretics "should be pushed (into the ditch) and not pulled

8. Charles H. Spurgeon, "The Good Samaritan," *The Metropolitan Tabernacle Pulpit* (Pasadena, TX: Pilgrim, 1972), 23:357.

9. Greg W. Forbes, *The God of Old: The Role of the Lukan Parables in the Purpose of Luke's Gospel*, Journal for the Study of the New Testament Supplement Series 198 (Sheffield: Sheffield Academic Press, 2000), 64.

out."[10] For their part, the Samaritans had been known to give Jews trouble on the highway. Jesus knew all about this because the Samaritans had rejected him only a short time before, when they refused to receive him on his way to Jerusalem (see Luke 9:52–53).

People often call this parable "The Story of the Good Samaritan," but as far as the Jews were concerned, there were no good Samaritans. The term was an oxymoron—a contradiction in terms. It is difficult to come up with a contemporary comparison that conveys the same sense of social surprise, but we do not really understand this story until we make a racial and religious comparison that seems to go too far. Maybe it would be something like an Islamic fundamentalist helping an evangelical Christian who was injured in a terrorist attack. It was the last thing anyone would expect, and in fact if the injured man had not been so desperate, he may have refused the Samaritan's help altogether. These men were not neighbors at all; they were enemies. Nevertheless, the Samaritan stopped to help, giving us the superlative example of what it means to be a good neighbor.

What are the characteristics of a good neighbor, as exemplified by the good Samaritan? A good neighbor notices people in need, as the Samaritan did when he saw the victim lying in the road. The priest went down the road, and the Levite went to the place where the man lay, but the Samaritan went to the man himself. A good neighbor has compassion for people who suffer. The Greek word for compassion (*splanchna*) expresses strong feelings of pity and tenderness. The word is often used to indicate God's compassion for us in Christ (e.g., Luke 7:13), but here it is used to express the Samaritan's heart-response to someone in desperate need. Even without knowing who he was, the Samaritan had pity on the man's condition.

Yet being a good neighbor involves more than an emotional response: it also requires practical deeds of mercy. A good neighbor is willing to stop and help, even when it is inconvenient. So the Samaritan stopped in the middle of his journey, got down from his donkey, and began to administer first aid—binding, soothing, and disinfecting his neighbor's wounds. As he poured out his oil and wine, he was pouring out his love. A good neighbor refuses to draw artificial boundaries in order to avoid getting involved. A good neighbor helps strangers. Without prejudice, he loves people who do

---

10. This rabbinical saying is quoted by J. Jeremias in *The Parables of Jesus* (London: SCM, 1963), 202.

not belong to his own ethnic or religious group. The Samaritan was willing to help this man simply because he needed the help.

A good neighbor also makes costly sacrifices of time and money to serve people in trouble. As J. C. Ryle said in his comments on this passage, "The kindness of a Christian towards others . . . should be a practical love, a love which entails on him self-sacrifice and self-denial, both in money, and time, and trouble. His charity should be seen not merely in his talking, but his acting—not merely in his profession, but in his practice."[11] The good Samaritan let his neighbor ride his own animal. He led him to an inn where he proceeded to give him further medical attention. Then he arranged for the long-term care he needed to recover from his injuries. Two denarii would last a couple of weeks, and if the man needed more help after that, the Samaritan would put it on his own tab. There were things he needed to do; he could not stay with the man indefinitely. But rather than abandoning him, the Samaritan commended him to the care of others. This is what a good neighbor does: he follows through by doing whatever it takes to ensure that full help is provided.

In short, a good neighbor is someone who loves others as he loves himself. A notable example of the application of this principle comes from the life of Ernest Gordon. As mentioned back in chapter 22 of this commentary, Gordon was a British Army officer interned in the infamous Japanese prison camp on the River Kwai. Late in the war, as Gordon and other prisoners of war traveled through the jungles of Asia, they happened upon a train full of wounded Japanese soldiers nearly dying of neglect. Out of love for Christ, Gordon and many of his fellow officers began to administer aid to these soldiers, their enemies.

One of their fellow officers was deeply offended. "What bloody fools you all are!" he said. "Don't you realize that those are the enemy?" Of course they did realize this. It was exactly the point, as Gordon tried to explain:

> "Have you never heard the story of the man who was going from Jerusalem to Jericho?" I asked him. He gave me a blank look, so I continued, "He was attacked by thugs, stripped of everything and left to die. Along came a priest; he passed him by. Then came a lawyer, a man of high principles; he passed by as well. Next came a Samaritan, a half-caste, a heretic, an enemy. But he didn't

11. Ryle, *Luke,* 1:378.

pass by; he stopped. His heart was filled with compassion. Kneeling down, he poured some wine through the unconscious lips, cleaned and dressed the helpless man's wounds, then took him to an inn where he had him cared for at his own expense."

"But that's different!" the officer protested angrily. "That's in the Bible. These are the swine who've starved us and beaten us. They've murdered our comrades. These are our enemies."

Gordon responded by saying, "Who is mine enemy? Isn't he my neighbour? . . . Mine enemy *is* my neighbour!"[12]

WHO IS THE GOOD NEIGHBOR?

Jesus ended his story by making a point of practical application. To help his lawyer friend understand this point for himself, Jesus asked him the all-important question: "Which of these three, do you think, proved to be a neighbor to the man who fell among the robbers?" (Luke 10:36). Carefully avoiding any use of the hated word "Samaritan," the man nevertheless answered correctly: "The one who showed him mercy." To which Jesus replied, "You go, and do likewise" (Luke 10:37).

This parable is partly about what it means to be a good neighbor. It is not simply about stopping to help people on the road, of course, although sometimes that's part of it. Nor is the point that all good Samaritans will be saved. Apparently, this was one of those times when an unbeliever (like the Samaritan) puts a believer (as the priest and the Levite were supposed to be) to shame. Nor is it primarily about racial reconciliation, although this parable has important implications for cross-cultural relationships. The main point is that a neighbor is something we are, not something we have, and that for believers in Christ, neighborly love is a whole way of life.

The lawyer wanted to know who was (and perhaps more importantly who wasn't) his neighbor. If you ask the question that way, the answer is, "My neighbor is anyone in need—anyone at all—whom in the providence of God I may be able to help." Jesus took the lawyer's theoretical question and gave him a practical answer: "Whenever we come across somebody in

12. Ernest Gordon, *To End All Wars* (Grand Rapids: Zondervan, 1963), 197–98.

our pathway in great need, we are to have compassion on them and help them as we would like them to help us if we were in need."[13]

But Jesus also wanted the lawyer to consider a deeper question—not "Who is my neighbor?" but "Whose neighbor am I?" Hence the wording of his question: "Which of these three, do you think, proved to *be* a neighbor?" (Luke 10:36). Rather than letting him get away with keeping the issue at arm's length, Jesus brought it straight to his heart. The real question is not what someone else has to do to qualify for my assistance, but what kind of neighbor am I anyway? As one commentator observes, "One cannot define one's neighbor; one can only be a neighbor."[14] Or again, "Neighbor is not a concept to be debated or defined, but a flesh-and-blood person in the ditch waiting to be served. You can't define your neighbor in advance; you can only be a neighbor when the moment of mercy arrives."[15]

To say this another way, a person becomes my neighbor when I treat him in a neighborly way. So instead of wasting our time trying to come up with a more precise definition of "neighbor," we need to get busy and help the people right in front of us. Whom are you able to help, but have been trying to ignore? How will you respond the next time you encounter someone in need?

Jesus told the lawyer—and he tells us—to do what the good Samaritan did and show mercy. At one level, this is simply a call to emulate the good Samaritan. As it says in the text of Johann Sebastian Bach's Cantata 77, "And give me too, my God, a Samaritan's heart, / That I may love my neighbour as well / And be troubled for him / In his anguish, / That I do not pass him by / And abandon him in his extremity."[16] As believers in Christ, we are called to love our neighbors, and when we do this, our lives demonstrate the love of Christ. If all we ever do is talk about love, our talk is only talk, and people easily ignore us. But when we show them love by being good neighbors, our actions and affections confirm the story we tell about Jesus, the cross, and the resurrection.

13. Gooding, *Luke*, 203.

14. Heinrich Greeven, quoted in Arland J. Hultgren, *The Parables of Jesus: A Commentary* (Grand Rapids: Eerdmans, 2000), 99.

15. William M. Cwirla, "What Must I Do? A Question of the Law," *Modern Reformation* (Nov./ Dec. 2002): 6.

16. From Johann Sebastian Bach, "Du sollt Gott, deinen Herren, lieben" (1723), in *The Complete Church and Secular Cantatas*, trans. Richard Stokes (Lanham, MD: Scarecrow, 1999), 128.

At another level, however, this parable shows us our own deep need for the gospel. Remember the context: the lawyer wanted to know what he had to *do* to be saved. Jesus gave him the answer that is written in the law: if you love God and love your neighbor, you will live. But knowing how difficult it is to love one's neighbor, the lawyer asked Jesus to place some kind of limit on the law, so that it would be possible to keep. Jesus refused. Instead, he made it clear that loving our neighbor means making costly sacrifices for anyone in need, including our enemies.

By doing this, surely Jesus wanted us to see that this is a law we cannot keep. Who is able to offer such mercy to all his neighbors? If everyone is my neighbor, then how can I possibly love my neighbor the way God wants me to love? If we tried to do this out of our own selfish hearts, we would quickly get exhausted by people's problems and grow to resent all the claims they place on our love. To quote again from Bach's cantata on this biblical text: "Ah, there abides in my love / Naught but imperfection! / Though I often have the will / To accomplish God's commandments, / It is not yet possible."[17]

Whatever else the law may be able to do for us, it cannot make us love our neighbors, especially if God demands that we count our enemies among them. Here is how Kenneth Bailey summarizes the meaning of the parable: "I must become a neighbor to anyone in need. To fulfill the law means that I must reach out in costly compassion to all people, even to my enemies. The standard remains even though I can never fully achieve it. I cannot justify myself and earn eternal life."[18]

The story of the good Samaritan is a law parable, therefore, that shows us how much we need the love God has for us in the gospel. The good news of the gospel is that through the death and resurrection of Jesus Christ, God has loving grace for law-breaking sinners who are not good neighbors. As we read about the good Samaritan, we cannot help but be reminded of the saving work of Jesus Christ, who always practiced what he preached. The church has a long history of reading (and in some cases misreading) this parable as an allegory for the gospel. Augustine wrote, "The Lord Jesus Christ meant that he was the one who gave help to the man lying half-dead on the road, beaten and left

17. Bach, "Du sollt Gott," 129.
18. Bailey, *Through Peasant Eyes*, 55.

by the robbers." This interpretation goes too far, especially when it tries to make the details of the parable correspond with specific aspects of the gospel. For example, it is not clear that Augustine was right to say that Jesus meant the Samaritan's oil and wine to stand for the sacraments of baptism and the Lord's Supper, or that the two denarii represent the Father and the Son, as Origen claimed. Nevertheless, this parable does bear witness to Jesus Christ. Is it surprising that the man who had such a profound understanding of what it means to be a good neighbor later became the ultimate neighbor when he died on the cross for our sins?

Yet to say that Jesus is the good Samaritan, as many scholars and preachers have said, is to give him too little praise. For the mercy he has shown to us is far greater. When Jesus came to our aid to give us life, we were not merely dying but dead, dead in our trespasses and sins. Jesus came out of his way to help us, not just crossing the road, but traversing the infinite distance from heaven to earth. Furthermore, it took him more than a day or two of his time and a couple coins from his pocket to gain our salvation. It cost him the sufferings of earth, the blood of his body, and the agonies of his soul on the cross. Jesus traveled a much greater distance, to help people in much greater need, at much greater cost. He is equally committed to seeing our salvation through to the end, for he has promised to come back and carry us all the way to glory. As David Gooding has said: "We were not his neighbors nor he ours. But he chose by incarnation to come where we were; and in spite of the fact that human beings hounded him to a cross, he rescued us at his own expense, and has paid in advance the cost of completing our redemption and of perfecting us for unimaginable glory."[19]

Now this Good Neighbor says, "You go, and do likewise" (Luke 10:37)—be a good Samaritan to the people you meet along life's way. Who is the person that needs your help? Is it a child in your class, perhaps, or a colleague at work? Maybe it is a person in your neighborhood, or someone in the church who can never seem to get it together. Or perhaps it is someone in trouble halfway around the world. Do not make excuses, but accept the responsibility to be a good neighbor for Christ. Do not look

19. Gooding, *Luke*, 205.

away, but see what needs to be done. Do not cross over to the other side, but take the time to stop and help. Do not quit before the job is done, but by the grace of God, carry things all the way through. Do not do these things to gain eternal life, but because when you were beaten, bloodied, and left for dead, Jesus came and showed mercy to you.

44

HAVING A MARY HEART
IN A MARTHA WORLD

Luke 10:38–42

*But the Lord answered her, "Martha, Martha, you are anxious
and troubled about many things, but one thing is necessary.
Mary has chosen the good portion, which will not be taken
away from her." (Luke 10:41–42)*

How will it all end? Will the late, great United States be destroyed by some unforeseen cataclysm? Will we collapse under the weight of our own decadence? Or will we simply fade away, going not with a bang, but with a whimper?

Consider another possibility: maybe it will all end in a blur. Living at hyper-speed, the images flicker ever more rapidly across the screens of our lives. Hyped up and supercharged, we live from one surge of adrenaline to the next. We are busier now than we were a year ago, and we will be even busier next year.[1] According to James Gleick, we are witnessing "the acceleration of just about everything."[2] So maybe we will just keep moving faster

1. Richard A. Swenson explains why in *Margin* (Colorado Springs: NavPress, 1992, 1995).
2. James Gleick, *Faster: The Acceleration of Just About Everything* (New York: Pantheon, 1999).

and faster until, as we approach the speed of light, we suddenly disappear in a blur that smudges the cosmos.

Where is the time in all of this to nurture the life of one's soul? Because if there is one thing we cannot accelerate, it is our growth in godliness.[3] How can our love for Jesus deepen without time away to read our Bibles, or to pray, or even to stop and think?

SISTER, SISTER

This struggle is not a new one. Even before the fastest culture ever, people were distracted from spiritual things. We see this in the story of two sisters who were close friends with Jesus Christ: "Now as they went on their way, Jesus entered a village. And a woman named Martha welcomed him into her house. And she had a sister called Mary, who sat at the Lord's feet and listened to his teaching" (Luke 10:38–39).

These two sisters had two very different personalities. Their character-types are not hard to recognize in women we know today. "Mary's bent," writes Joanna Weaver, "was to meander through life, pausing to smell the roses. Martha was more likely to pick the roses, quickly cut the stems at an angle, and arrange them in a vase with baby's breath and ferns."[4] Not surprisingly, these two women had two distinct ways of serving God: Martha served him with her hands, while Mary served him with her mind and her heart. But both sisters wanted to honor God with true devotion to Jesus Christ. There were some problems with Martha's attitude, as we shall see, but we do her an injustice if we fail to recognize the sincerity of her love for Jesus. Like Mary, this godly woman deserves our admiration.

Martha was the responsible one, the type who is always volunteering and always making sure that everything is done to her standards. She was one of the 20 percent who end up doing 80 percent of the work. And if there was one area where Martha excelled, it was in the gift of hospitality. Today people would call her "the hostess with the mostest." Think Martha Stewart, with her panache for stylish homemaking.

3. Donald Whitney makes this point in an unpublished paper entitled "The Almost Inevitable Ruin of Every Minister . . . and How to Avoid It."

4. Joanna Weaver, *Having a Mary Heart in a Martha World* (Colorado Springs: Waterbrook, 2002), 5.

As soon as Martha heard that Jesus was coming, perhaps with little warning, all her domestic instincts took over. She welcomed him into her home as an honored guest. Even as she offered him the best seat in the house, her mind was probably racing down her mental list of all the things that needed to be done for Jesus and his disciples. Any woman who has ever welcomed a special guest into her home knows all the things that needed to be done: cleaning, buying, chopping, cooking and baking, to say nothing of washing up. Everything had to be just right. Martha was the type to put place cards on the table, goat cheese in the salad, and wine with every place setting.

Martha was right to give this kind of welcome because hospitality is one of the noble virtues of godliness. "Seek to show hospitality" (Rom. 12:13), the Scripture says. "Show hospitality to one another without grumbling. As each has received a gift, use it to serve one another, as good stewards of God's varied grace" (1 Peter 4:9–10). Martha used her gift of hospitality to serve others, and when she had the opportunity to do this work for Jesus, she wanted to shine. As the Son of God, he deserved the best welcome that she could give him. We know from other places in the Gospels that Jesus visited this home more than once. Could it be that Martha's gracious hospitality was one of the things that drew him there?

While Martha was busy getting everything ready for dinner, Mary was also attending to Jesus—not in the kitchen, but in the living room. From the moment she heard that Jesus was coming, one thought had consumed her. Unlike Martha, this thought did not concern what she could do for Jesus, but what Jesus could do for her. He could teach her his word, drawing her deeper into a relationship with him.

Mary wanted to know Jesus, and as he taught, she was the very model of attention. Mary sat in the front row, right at Jesus' feet. She did not want to miss a word; she wanted to hear everything her Teacher said. To sit at someone's feet implies not only attention, but also submission. Mary was not standing up to confront Jesus, like the lawyer who asked what he had to do to inherit eternal life (Luke 10:25). Instead, she was sitting at his feet, ready to listen, ready to learn, and ready to believe. Mary shows us how attractive it is when a woman devotes herself to learning what Jesus says. She is a perfect example of the kind of listening Paul had in mind when he said, "Let a woman learn quietly with all submissiveness" (1 Tim. 2:11). The apostle is teaching submission, but like Jesus, he is also opening the door for women to learn theology.

Mary's posture seems all the more remarkable when we remember that in those days women were not exactly encouraged to become theologians. Somehow people had the idea that theology was mainly for men, but not for women, as if it were some kind of gender-specific specialty rather than what it actually is: the knowledge of God that everyone needs. Some rabbis permitted women to study the Torah, but forbade them to sit at their feet for formal instruction. Jesus not only permitted it; he positively encouraged it. To him it was as important to teach women the doctrines of disciple-ship as it was to teach the men. Sound theology helps us to know God, and of course women have as much need for this as men do.[5] Every believer is called to grow in his or her understanding of the gospel of Jesus Christ, the teaching of the Bible, the doctrines of the Christian faith, and the way these truths apply to daily life. Mary reveled in her opportunity to do just that. While Martha was busy preparing a banquet, Mary was already having one—she was feasting on the word of Christ.

WHAT MARTHA THOUGHT

Unfortunately, this heartwarming scene of gracious hospitality and theological instruction was soon disturbed by the storm that was build-ing in Martha's heart. As Jesus went on teaching, Martha became increas-ingly agitated, until finally the storm cloud burst and the angry words came pouring out: "But Martha was distracted with much serving. And she went up to him and said, 'Lord, do you not care that my sister has left me to serve alone? Tell her then to help me'" (Luke 10:40).

There was nothing wrong with what Martha was doing, but there were some problems with her attitude. We should give them careful notice because these problems are all too common in people who work hard for the Lord. It is possible to serve the Lord, as Martha did, and yet do it in a very unattractive way.

Martha was guilty of at least three sins. One was distraction. As Luke tells us, she was "distracted with much serving." Martha was guilty of

---

5. The importance of theology for women is emphasized by Carolyn Custis James in *When Life and Beliefs Collide: How Knowing God Makes a Difference* (Grand Rapids: Zondervan, 2001).

inattention to the word of Christ. The primary meaning of the Greek verb for distraction *(perispaō)* is to be dragged away. This implies that Martha was doing or wanting to do one thing, but ended up getting pulled away from it. This is what it means to be distracted. First we are attracted to something, but then we get distracted, and our attention turns away.

Martha had lost her focus, and it was her service, of all things, that distracted her attention away from Jesus. With her strong sense of duty, Martha had a long list of all the things she had to do. They were all things she wanted to do for Jesus, but she got so caught up in doing them that she lost sight of Jesus himself. Charles Spurgeon comments: "Her fault was not that she served. The condition of a servant well becomes every Christian. Her fault was that she grew 'cumbered with much serving,' so that she forgot him and only remembered the service."[6] Martha's ministry was keeping her from Jesus.

How easy it is for us to get distracted, even when we are serving the Lord. We begin serving because we are attracted to Jesus and want to show him our love. So we get involved in helping children, or reaching out to the poor, or teaching the Bible, or some other form of Christian service. Our motivation is to honor God by loving our neighbors. But soon we get distracted by the problems we have in ministry, or even by the work of ministry itself. We have discipline problems in the classroom, and we forget why we ever wanted to work with children in the first place. Or we get so caught up in getting ready to teach others that we fail to listen to what God is saying to us in his Word. Sometimes we even forget to pray for God's blessing, without which our service can accomplish nothing at all.

Distraction soon gives way to self-pity. The more Martha thought about all the things that had to be done—at least according to her own high standards for hospitality—the more overwhelmed she began to feel. As she continued slaving away in the kitchen, she began to feel sorry for herself. We know the feeling, because like Martha, we start sulking whenever we feel that we are the ones doing all of the work. We think more and more about how hard we are working; little by little, our feelings of self-pity take over.

---

6. Charles H. Spurgeon, quoted in Weaver, *Having a Mary Heart*, 62.

Soon we have stopped serving Jesus at all. We are serving ourselves, and thinking only about what our ministry is or is not doing for us.

Self-pity inevitably gives rise to resentment. Martha did not stay feeling sorry for herself for long, however. Quickly she realized that there was someone else to blame—someone who wasn't lifting a finger. It just wasn't fair! Martha did not have to be doing all this work by herself; if only that lazy Mary would get back in the kitchen where she belonged! For if there was one thing that Martha hated, it was a slacker:

> It was not of course that she did not enjoy his conversation: she would have enjoyed it as much as Mary; but she had very clear and very strong ideas on what things just had to be done when you were entertaining so important a guest as the Lord. If asked, she doubtless would have explained that true love is practical, and that work must be put before pleasure; and it was this that filled her with resentment when Mary left off working and went and sat at the Lord's feet and listened to his word. It meant that Mary was getting all the pleasure, and Martha was getting all the work, her own share and Mary's as well. To Martha's way of thinking, Mary was being selfish, unprincipled and unfair.[7]

In her resentment, Martha self-righteously assumed that her sister ought to be serving Jesus the same way that she was. This attitude is common in the church, especially among people who think they are working hard in Christian ministry. We assume that others should have the same priority that we have, and we look disapprovingly on their lack of commitment. Why isn't anyone volunteering to help? Why aren't more people supporting this ministry? Why don't people notice what I am doing? Whether we are involved in children's ministry, or adult discipleship, or mercy ministry, or missionary work, or some other form of Christian service, we resent it when people do not make our ministry their priority.

All of these sinful attitudes go together. First we get distracted. However much we say that we want to worship like Mary, our inner Martha keeps bossing us around, and we grow inattentive to Christ and his word.[8] This makes us vulnerable to self-pity. Since we are no longer focusing on

7. David Gooding, *According to Luke: A New Exposition of the Third Gospel* (Grand Rapids: Eerdmans, 1987), 213.

8. Weaver, *Having a Mary Heart*, 2.

Jesus, we can only focus on ourselves. Our difficulties loom large, our work seems overwhelming, and we start to feel sorry for ourselves. Then in our frustration we look for other people to help us, and when they fail to meet our expectations, our resentment begins to burn. As Kent Hughes explains, "There is a tendency for people who are wound tight like Martha to give everything to their particular area of calling or interest and to allow that interest to so dominate their lives that they have little time to let God's Word speak to them. Without the benefit of the Word, they adopt a mind-set of narrowness, judgmentalism, or fault-finding. And eventually the creativity and vitality they once gave to their area of ministry sours."[9]

This can happen very quickly. For Martha it happened during the time it took her to start preparing a meal. One minute she was welcoming Jesus into her home with joy; the next minute she was busy in the kitchen; the minute after that she was making a scene out in the living room.

Perhaps Martha tried banging on a few kitchen utensils and casting some dirty looks before she said anything, but if she did, of course it was useless because Mary only had ears and eyes for Jesus. By the time Martha spoke, her blood was on the boil. Out spilled all of her irritation, maybe even outrage. Indeed, she was almost as angry with Jesus as she was with Mary, because he was part of the problem! By letting her sit at his feet, Jesus was actually encouraging Mary to neglect her domestic duties. We can hear the tone of reproach in Martha's words: "Lord, do you not care that my sister has left me to serve alone?" Then she presumed to tell Jesus what he should be doing: "Tell her then to help me" (Luke 10:40).

By this point Martha's attitude was more than unattractive; it was ugly. She had stopped serving and started scolding. She interrupted Jesus and interfered with her sister's relationship with her Savior. If she could, Martha would even usurp the place of God in Christ by telling Jesus what to do.

This is where the unattractive attitudes in our own service to Christ will lead. It may not seem all that serious to neglect the Word of God. At first we can hardly tell the difference it makes not to read our Bibles or to pray. But soon a subtle self-pity creeps in. Rather than rejoicing in the promises of God, we feel sorry for ourselves because of the difficulties we are facing. We are increasingly critical, finding fault with others for what they are doing or

9. R. Kent Hughes, *Luke: That You May Know the Truth*, 2 vols., Preaching the Word (Wheaton, IL: Crossway, 1998), 1:398.

not doing for us. Before long we will be trying to tell God his business. This will all happen when in our service *for* Jesus we get distracted *from* Jesus.

WHAT MARY CHOSE

How did Jesus respond to Martha's complaint? Given everything she was doing to get dinner on the table, her request for a little help would seem more than reasonable. Jesus did not see it that way, however: "But the Lord answered her, 'Martha, Martha, you are anxious and troubled about many things'" (Luke 10:41). Or as the New English Bible expresses it, "you are fretting and fussing about so many things."

Notice what Jesus did not do. He did not take sides. He did not send Mary back to the kitchen. Nor did he tell Martha that she ought to be more like her sister. He did not even tell her to stop doing what she was doing. This is because Jesus did not "disapprove of Martha's activities as such, for they were also the outcome of love for Him and were meant to serve Him. It is her wrong attitude as revealed in her condemnation of Mary and her dissatisfaction with Himself that had to be set right and rebuked."[10] The issue was not who was doing what, but what kind of relationship Martha had with Jesus, and what kind of relationship she needed to have.

It is important in all this to see that Jesus loved Martha as much as he loved Mary. He loved Mary by protecting her time with him and praising her choice to sit at his feet. But he also loved Martha. We know this because the apostle John says so in as many words (John 11:5), and also because of the way that Jesus spoke to her. "Martha, Martha," he said, calling her back to attention. It was out of love for Martha that Jesus gently rebuked her. He did this by identifying the sin in Martha's heart; he exposed her underlying idolatry. The Bible tells us not to be anxious about anything (Phil. 4:6), but Martha was anxious about almost everything. She had a to-do list as long as her arm. She did not know how to let some things go, and she did not know how to stop worrying about all the things she could not get done, or that she could not get done according to the unreasonable standards of her own perfection. Kent Hughes comments: "Martha's self-appointed responsibilities distracted her from what mattered most. So it is with us.

10. Norval Geldenhuys, *The Gospel of Luke*, New International Commentary on the New Testament (Grand Rapids: Eerdmans, 1951), 316.

The self-imposed necessities of ministry smother us, and serving becomes drudgery."[11]

Martha's rebuke shows that behind all our self-pity and resentment are the worries of an anxious heart. Knowing this helps us know how to preach ourselves the gospel. When we find that we are feeling sorry for ourselves because we have suffered a setback, or that we are snapping at people over little things, we need to ask ourselves what we are really worried about. Then we need to recall the promises of God that speak to our anxieties. If we are worried that we will not get what we need, we need to remember God's promise to provide. If we are worried what people will think, we need to remember God's promise to accept us in Jesus Christ. If we are worried about will happen or will not happen in the future, we need to remember God's promise to love us to the very end. Behind every unattractive attitude in the distracted heart there is an ungodly anxiety, and for every anxiety God has a promise in the gospel.

After showing Martha what was really in her heart, Jesus crumpled up her to-do list, so to speak, and said, "One thing is necessary. Mary has chosen the good portion, which will not be taken away from her" (Luke 10:42). Martha had a whole list of things she thought were necessary; Jesus said there was only one. But what, exactly, was the one and only necessary thing?

This question has caused a fair amount of consternation, because Jesus never says. He does not define the one thing that is necessary for the life of discipleship. Instead, he points to Mary's example. Rather than giving us a proposition, he shows us a picture. What is necessary is to sit at Jesus' feet, the way that Mary did, and listen to what he says, and in this way come to know Jesus for sure. This picture shows us Mary's devotion to Christ, specifically her commitment to his teaching. Mary loved Jesus and his Word.

Some scholars emphasize the context for these words. Jesus was on his way to Jerusalem and the cross. Time was short. So Martha did not need to make a fuss over his meals. Dinner could wait. What Martha really needed to do was to sit down and listen to some of the last important things that Jesus had to say.

11. Hughes, *Luke*, 1:398.

What Jesus said about the one needful thing also has a wider application. There is only one thing that is necessary for any of us. It is not anything that we can ever do for God. This was Martha's mistake. She thought that what was really important was her service for God. Yet our service for God can never be necessary in the absolute sense, because he does not need us at all. As the apostle Paul said, God is not "served by human hands, as though he needed anything" (Acts 17:25). God can do perfectly well without our service. But we, on the other hand, are in desperate need of him. Therefore, what is necessary for every Mary or Martha is not to serve Jesus, but to be served by him.

To be more specific, the one thing necessary is to receive the Word of God through the ministry of Jesus Christ. It is by this Word that God gives us the saving knowledge of his Son. The one thing that is truly necessary for us, therefore, is to hear what Jesus has to say about the way of salvation:

> Amid all life's duties and necessities there is one supreme necessity which must always be given priority, and which, if circumstances compel us to choose, must be chosen to the exclusion of all others. That supreme necessity is to sit at the Lord's feet and listen to his word. It must be so. If there is a Creator at all, and that Creator is prepared to visit us and speak to us as in his incarnation he visited and spoke to Martha and Mary, then obviously it is our first duty as his creatures, as it ought to be our highest pleasure, to sit at his feet and listen to what he says.[12]

With this in mind, Jesus told Martha that her sister had made the right decision: "Mary has chosen the good portion, which will not be taken away from her" (Luke 10:42). This expression fits the context perfectly, because the Greek word for portion *(merida)* often refers to a meal. While Martha was preparing one meal, Mary was having another, better one. She was feeding on the Living Word.

Strictly speaking, Jesus did not say that Mary chose something better, but simply that she chose "the good portion." Nevertheless, he still seems to be making a comparison. It is good to serve the Lord, as Martha did, but better still to love him and learn from him. To be sure, practical service has its place in the Christian life. Jesus values our service; more than that, he

---

12. Gooding, *Luke*, 212.

demands it. In fact, as Mary sat listening to Jesus she may well have heard him say something about serving God by serving others. But what we do for Jesus is not the heart of our relationship with him. He prizes our friendship and our fellowship more highly than all our service. He wants us to be with him and to know him. He wants us to give ourselves to him, just as he gives himself to us. The good portion is Jesus himself.

Doing Martha's Work with Mary's Heart

What portion are you choosing? The story of Mary and Martha confronts us with a choice. It may not be the choice that we usually have in mind, however. Some people see it as a choice between two different ways of living: the active life and the contemplative life. Thus there are two kinds of Christians in the world: the Mary Christians and the Martha Christians, the listeners and the doers. The Marthas are the ones who do most of the work. They volunteer a lot, and usually end up running a ministry. The Marys lead a more thoughtful existence. They are the ones who start the prayer groups and set up the monasteries.

There is some truth in all of this because Mary and Martha represent such familiar personality types. We have all known our Marys and Marthas in the church (especially the Marthas). But we do not have to choose one of these personalities as a Christian lifestyle. After all, every Martha needs a prayer life, and every Mary is called to serve. Nor do we need to think that a contemplative life is superior to an active one. Jesus loved both Mary and Martha, and he loves the Mary and Martha in all of us.

Others see the story of Mary and Martha as a choice between two different duties. One duty is to serve God in practical ways like Martha, and the other duty is to spend time alone with God in prayer and Bible study. Martha's problem, then, was that she chose the wrong duty. Here is how one commentator explains the choice:

> We cannot do everything; there is not enough time. Like Mary, therefore, we shall have to choose and choose very deliberately. Life's affairs will not automatically sort themselves into a true order of priorities. If we do not consciously insist on making "sitting at the Lord's feet and listening to his word"

our number one necessity, a thousand and one other things and duties, all claiming to be prior necessities, will tyrannize our time and energies and rob us of the "good part" in life.[13]

This is closer to the truth, but still needs some correction. We do need to make the time and take the time to be with Jesus, not only by worshiping with other believers, but also by spending our own private time in God's Word. One of the main lessons of this story is: "Don't be so distracted and concerned about doing good that you neglect what is most important, namely, to sit at the feet of Jesus and hear the Word of God."[14] However, we need to think about this the right way. Our quiet time with Christ is *not* another item on our to-do list—yet one more thing that we have to do for Jesus; rather, it is an opportunity for him to do something for us. Remember what is necessary: not something we do for Jesus, but something he wants to do for us as we listen to him. Do you see the difference? When the Marthas read this story, we usually think we need to add another duty to the list: time with Jesus. We do need time with Jesus, of course, but not if we think of that time as fulfilling our religious obligation. Jesus is not asking for something more from us; he is asking for less, so that he can give us more of himself.

When we make this kind of time for Jesus—quality time to meet him in his Word and through prayer—we are choosing the good portion. Jesus is the perfect antidote for all the unattractive attitudes that poison our service when we turn our attention away from him. His gospel is the cure for our distraction, as we are drawn to the beauty of his grace. His peace is the cure for our anxiety, as we trust him through the worries of life. His love is the cure for our self-pity, as we forget ourselves in serving others for his sake. His mercy is the cure for our resentment, as we offer others the same forgiveness that Jesus has given to us. This is the good portion that God offers to Marys and Marthas everywhere: Jesus himself, in all his grace. What we gain in knowing Jesus cannot be taken away from us, any more than Martha could take away Mary's golden opportunity to sit at her Master's feet.

Happily, we do not have to choose being with Jesus to the exclusion of serving him. God has given us the time to do everything he has truly called

13. Gooding, *Luke*, 216.
14. Arthur A. Just Jr., *Luke 9:51–24:53*, Concordia Commentary (St. Louis: Concordia, 1996), 458.

us to do, including spending some of our time in private communion with Christ. But he has also given us his Holy Spirit, and this means that we can commune with Christ in our daily activities. Part of Martha's problem was that she could not serve in the kitchen and be with Jesus in the living room at the same time. But we can. Through the inward work of the Holy Spirit, who makes Christ to live in us by faith, we can pray and listen to Jesus right in the middle of all our activities—even in the kitchen. As much as we need time away with Jesus, we also need to know his presence when we are with others, and when we are busy with our work. The Holy Spirit makes this a reality in the Christian life. By his ministry we can have a Mary heart in a Martha world, offering Martha's kind of service with Mary's attention to Jesus.[15]

One Christian who learned to do this well was the French monk Nicholas Herman, better known as Brother Lawrence. Brother Lawrence made it his ambition to "do everything for the love of God, and with prayer." He found this hard to accomplish in the busy life of his daily routine. There were so many distractions, especially when he served in the kitchen. But eventually Brother Lawrence learned to meet with Christ in the kitchen as much as anywhere else. He said: "The time of business does not with me differ from the time of prayer, and in the noise and clatter of my kitchen, while several persons are at the same time calling for different things, I possess God in as great tranquility as if I were upon my knees."[16] Brother Lawrence learned this not so much by doing something different, but by doing what he always did in a different way—doing it for Jesus instead of for himself.

The best examples of this kind of spiritual repose are Mary *and* her sister Martha. We must include Martha because she was listening when Jesus gave her his kind rebuke. We know this because of what happened later when the two sisters were grief-stricken at the death of their brother Lazarus. Their house was full of guests. Doubtless Martha was concerned to be a gracious hostess, even through her tears. But when she heard that Jesus was coming, she knew that only one thing was necessary. So she abandoned all her guests and ran outside the village to meet her Lord.

15. This theme is helpfully developed in Weaver, *Having a Mary Heart.*
16. Brother Lawrence, *The Practice of the Presence of God* (Virginia Beach: CBN University Press, 1978), 10.

Martha was still Martha, however, and we can hear the reproach in her first words to Jesus: "Lord, if you had been here, my brother would not have died" (John 11:21). Yet even these words were spoken in faith, because Martha went on to affirm her trust in Jesus and his resurrection power. She had learned to know Jesus, and even in her disappointment with him she could not bring herself to deny what she knew to be true about his grace. When he asked if she believed that he is the resurrection and the life, she made one of the first great confessions of the Christian faith: "Yes, Lord; I believe that you are the Christ, the Son of God, who is coming into the world" (John 11:27). Martha got it. When the crisis came and she had to look death in the eye, her theology did not let her down. When she was in the living room with Jesus, she learned what was most necessary of all: not anything that she could ever do for God, but what God was doing for her through Jesus Christ.

And what of Mary? She also listened to what Jesus was saying, and while sitting at his feet, she learned something that nearly all of the other disciples missed: Jesus was going to suffer and die. Then, out of the extravagance of her love, she responded to this awful news by anointing Jesus with sweet perfume, preparing him for burial (John 12:1–8).

We may even say that these two sisters were the first disciples to believe the gospel. Mary believed in the cross, even before the crucifixion, whereas Martha believed in the power of the resurrection. They believed these things because they both did the one thing that is needed, which is to listen to Jesus with the full attention of a loving heart.

45

When You Pray

Luke 11:1–4

*Now Jesus was praying in a certain place, and when he finished,
one of his disciples said to him, "Lord, teach us to pray, as John
taught his disciples." (Luke 11:1)*

e believe in the power of prayer. We believe that the living God hears us when we cry out to him in the name of Jesus Christ. We believe that the "effectual fervent prayer of a righteous man availeth much" (James 5:16 KJV). We believe that whatever we ask in prayer we will receive, if we have faith (Matt. 21:22). We believe that, as Martyn Lloyd-Jones once said, prayer is "the highest activity of the human soul."[1] We believe that secret, fervent, believing prayer is at the heart of all personal godliness. We believe that the neglect of prayer can only lead to ruin. But have we learned to pray the way that Jesus prayed?

JESUS PRAYS

Usually we think of the life of Christ as a series of miracles, parables, and personal conversations, culminating in the events of his passion, and occa-

1. Martyn Lloyd-Jones, *Studies in the Sermon on the Mount*, 2 vols. (London: Inter-Varsity, 1960), 2:45.

sionally interrupted by seasons of prayer. But we could just as well see his life the other way around: as a series of private prayer times, interspersed with the ordinary events of his daily ministry. Jesus Christ was a great man of prayer.

Nowhere is this made clearer than in the Gospel of Luke, which records nearly a dozen prayer times, including many that are mentioned nowhere else in the Gospels. As he tells the gospel story, Luke portrays Jesus as praying his way from Galilee up to Jerusalem and the cross. He usually mentions these prayer times in passing, so it would be easy to miss this theme in his Gospel. But when we take careful notice of all the times when Jesus (and others) went to pray, the cumulative effect is impressive. Luke wanted to show that faithful intercession is essential to the life of godliness.

The first example comes in connection with Jesus' baptism, which marked his formal entrance into public ministry. Luke tells us that when Jesus "had been baptized and was praying," the Holy Spirit descended like a dove and God the Son received the blessing of his Father (Luke 3:21–22). Luke also tells us that as his popularity began to grow, and great crowds gathered to hear him and be healed, Jesus "would withdraw to desolate places and pray" (Luke 5:16). Luke tells us further that when Jesus was about to choose his twelve disciples, "he went out to the mountain to pray, and all night he continued in prayer to God" (Luke 6:12). Jesus prayed early and often; on occasion, he prayed for a good long time.

After Jesus fed the five thousand, he was alone with God in prayer once again (Luke 9:18). Maybe he was praying for his disciples, because on this occasion Peter confessed him as the Christ. Eight days later, Jesus went out to pray again, and this time he took three of his disciples with him. While they were saying their prayers, the Spirit came down to glorify Jesus, and the disciples saw him transfigured in radiant splendor (Luke 9:28–29). Jesus prayed again—rejoicing in the Spirit and giving thanks to the Father—when the seventy-two came back from their first gospel mission (Luke 10:21–22). It seems that whenever anything of major importance happened in the life and ministry of Jesus Christ, it was surrounded by prayer.

As we come to the beginning of chapter 11, we find Jesus at prayer once again: "Now Jesus was praying in a certain place" (Luke 11:1). With these words, we are reminded of all the times that Jesus went to pray, and of everything we learn from this example. We learn the necessity of regular prayer. If Jesus took the time to talk things over with his Father, how much more are we in need of time away with God in prayer? If we want to follow God in the way of obedience and fulfill our true mission in life, as Jesus did, we need to lead the same life of prayer.

Jesus also teaches us the power of prayer. Through prayer Jesus received the Holy Spirit, with wisdom for teaching and the power to do miracles. Through prayer Jesus made disciples, choosing the twelve. Through prayer Jesus did the work of evangelism, calling people to trust him as the Christ. Through prayer Jesus glorified God, and was glorified by him. Through prayer he carried forward the missionary work of the gospel. Therefore, if we want to see God work powerfully to change people's lives through our own teaching, discipleship, and missionary evangelism, we need to spend time with him in prayer. We will accomplish as much or more by praying than by all our doing.

The disciples were beginning to learn this lesson by watching Jesus pray, and they wanted to experience it for themselves. So when Jesus finished praying, "one of his disciples said to him, 'Lord, teach us to pray, as John taught his disciples'" (Luke 11:1). It was common practice in those days for rabbis to teach their followers a specific form of prayer. Apparently, John the Baptist had done this for his disciples, although his prayer is not recorded in Scripture. Now the disciples wanted Jesus to do the same thing for them. They were in awe of his prayer life, and they wanted to know the secret of closer communion with God. Thus they asked Jesus how to pray.

This request fits the movement of Luke's Gospel. The story of Mary and Martha showed the supreme necessity of knowing God through the teaching of his Son. But there is another side to this. We need to speak to God as well as listen to him, and here Jesus shows us how. The disciples' request also fits their own spiritual need. They were still learning to follow Jesus, and they were only just beginning to learn how to pray. Although they came from a praying people, they had never seen anyone pray like this. In Jesus they saw a unique passion for prayer, with unusual zeal and unprecedented intimacy. When they saw this, they wanted it for themselves.

We should eagerly desire the same kind of prayer life for ourselves. J. I. Packer wrote, "Prayer is the spiritual measure of men and women in a way that nothing else is, so that how we pray is as important a question as we can ever face."[2] Like the disciples, we have only just begun to learn how to pray. We need to go deeper. But to do this, we need someone to show us how. Therefore, we come to Jesus with the same request his disciples made: "Lord, teach us to pray."

DIFFERENT VERSIONS, SAME PRAYER

How did Jesus answer this all-important question? With surprising simplicity. Jesus said, "When you pray, say: 'Father, hallowed be your name. Your kingdom come. Give us each day our daily bread, and forgive us our sins, for we ourselves forgive everyone who is indebted to us. And lead us not into temptation'" (Luke 11:2–4).

Anyone who knows the Lord's Prayer will notice immediately that there seems to be something wrong with this prayer. It does not sound quite right. The prayer is similar to what we have heard before, but its cadence is different. This is because there are two different versions of the Lord's Prayer—one in Matthew and one in Luke. Since the one from Matthew is much more familiar (see Matt. 6:9–13), the differences in Luke are all the more conspicuous. What are some of these differences?

Matthew's version begins with "Our Father in heaven," whereas in Luke Jesus simply says, "Father." Both prayers continue with "hallowed be your name" and "your kingdom come," but then Matthew includes a petition that Luke omits: "your will be done, on earth as it is in heaven" (Matt. 6:10). What the prayer says about daily bread is the same in both Gospels, but the wording of the confession is slightly different. In Matthew Jesus says, "forgive us our debts, as we also have forgiven our debtors" (Matt. 6:12), but in Luke he says, "forgive us our sins, for we ourselves forgive everyone who is indebted to us" (Luke 11:4). The sense is similar, but the wording is different. Then, after the petition about temptation, Matthew adds a line we do not find in Luke: "but deliver us from the evil one" (Matt. 6:13). There is one final point of agreement between the two prayers, but this too may come as a surprise. Neither prayer ends with the famous doxology of the early church, which was largely taken from one of David's ancient prayers:

2. J. I. Packer, *Knowing Christianity* (Guildford, Surrey: Eagle, 1995), 95.

"For thine is the kingdom, and the power, and the glory, forever. Amen" (Matt. 6:13b KJV; cf. 1 Chron. 29:11).[3]

Although some of these variations are significant, we do not need to be troubled by them, for the prayer is substantially the same in both Gospels. Even Matthew's two "extra" petitions are virtually entailed by other petitions that Luke does include. To pray for God's will to be done on earth as it is in heaven is another way of praying for his kingdom to come. And it is in temptation most of all that we need God to deliver us from evil. The Bible may give us two different versions, but they are different versions of the same prayer.

Nevertheless, some people *are* troubled by the differences. They want to know which prayer is the "real" Lord's Prayer. In fact, some people go so far as to see the differences as errors or contradictions. Either Luke included the wrong prayer in his Gospel, they say, or Matthew tried to improve on Luke by expanding his prayer.

The answer, of course, is that Jesus taught his disciples to pray on at least two occasions. The prayers that he gave were substantially the same, but not identical. This is hardly surprising. Good teachers often repeat what they say, but they rarely say it exactly the same way twice. Sometimes they give the same message to a new audience, like a preacher who delivers the same sermon in two different worship services. But sometimes teachers give the same message to the same audience, especially if what they have to say is important, or if they are not sure their students understood them the first time. The disciples, of all people, needed this kind of repetition. They understood almost nothing the first time they heard it, and Jesus needed to tell them many things again and again. It is hardly surprising that he should speak to them more than once on such an important subject as prayer, or that his disciples would ask him to teach them again something he had taught them before.

Clearly Matthew and Luke wrote about two different episodes. In Matthew Jesus teaches the Lord's Prayer in Galilee, as part of his Sermon on the Mount. As Jesus taught his disciples a new way to live, he showed them the difference between making a big show of praying in public, as some

3. For more information about the history and proper use of this traditional doxology, see Philip Graham Ryken, *When You Pray: Making the Lord's Prayer Your Own* (Phillipsburg, NJ: P&R, 2006), 173–84.

religious leaders did, or babbling on and on like pagans, and the simplicity of true Christian prayer. The prayer that Luke records comes later in Jesus' ministry, and in a different context. Jesus was on his way to Jerusalem, and after he stopped to pray, one of his disciples asked for further instruction in the fine art of intercession. By way of reminder, Jesus taught him a briefer form of the same prayer that he had once taught on the mountain.

Far from causing any difficulty, the differences between these two prayers teach us something important about the Lord's Prayer. Christians often recite the Lord's Prayer verbatim. It is good for Christians to use the very words of Jesus when they pray, especially in public or family worship. Cyprian was right when he asked, "What prayer can have greater power with the Father than that which came from the lips of the Son?"[4] Calvin agreed with this logic and included the Lord's Prayer in his Genevan liturgy, as many other churches have done all over the world. This is not the only way to pray the Lord's Prayer, however. The variations between Matthew and Luke show that Jesus was giving us a normative pattern for prayer, but not a rigid form. The Lord's Prayer is a model, not a mantra. The important thing is not using the exact words that Jesus uttered, but following the same structure and incorporating the same themes into our own life of prayer.

GOD OUR FATHER

The prayer in Matthew is the one that people generally use for worship, probably because it is a little longer, but the prayer in Luke is also worthy of our study. It teaches us how to pray in the fewest possible words. As Matthew Henry once said, this prayer is at the same time "remarkably concise and yet vastly comprehensive."[5]

The Lord's Prayer has two movements. The first goes in the direction of God: "Father, hallowed be your name. Your kingdom come" (Luke 11:2). We address God as our Father, praying for the honor of his name and the coming of his kingdom. This is where we should always begin in prayer: with the power and the glory of God. The Lord's Prayer teaches us to offer

4. Cyprian, quoted in Derek Thomas, *Praying the Saviour's Way* (Fearn, Ross-shire: Christian Focus, 2002), 11.

5. Matthew Henry, quoted in Terry L. Johnson, *When Grace Comes Alive: Living through the Lord's Prayer* (Fearn, Ross-shire: Christian Focus, 2003), 19.

God-centered prayer. First things first: we need to begin by praising God for who he is and what he is doing. Only then do we tell God about the things that we need: daily bread, the forgiveness of sins, and deliverance from evil. Thus in the second movement of the Lord's Prayer we turn from the majesty of God to the needs of his people—from the vertical to the horizontal.

Each part of the Lord's Prayer is important, starting with the form of address: "Father." We are so used to talking to God this way that we forget that this was a radical new way to pray. The people of the Old Testament had many names and titles for God, but rarely addressed him directly as "Father" when they prayed (Isa. 63:16 is the notable exception.) Even though he was the Father of his people Israel, the Israelites did not address God in personal terms, or speak to him the way that children speak to their father. This was a revolutionary new development in the history of prayer.

Jesus taught his disciples to pray this way because it was the way that he prayed. Every time Jesus spoke to God in heaven, he called him "Father." The only exception proves the rule. As Jesus endured the agonies of the cross, there was a time when he suffered the full weight of God's wrath against our sin. At the time when he knew that he was separated from the Father by the curse of our sin, he cried out, "My God, my God, why have you forsaken me?" (Matt. 27:46). But at every other moment of his life on earth, Jesus knew the joy of God's presence and called him "Father." This was even true of his final moments on the cross, when by faith he said, "Father, into your hands I commit my spirit!" (Luke 23:46).

No one had ever spoken to God this way before. When Jesus used this form of address, he was lifting the veil on the mystery of the Trinity. There is only one God, and this one God exists in three persons: the Father, the Son, and the Holy Spirit. The relationships among the three persons of the Godhead are eternal relationships. So even when the Second Person of the Trinity became a man, he continued to know the First Person of the Trinity the way that he had always known him, as the Father of the Son. Therefore, it was perfectly natural for him to call God his "Father."

What is surprising is that Jesus invites *us* to pray the same way. When we pray, we repeat the form of address that our Savior used and call God "Father." We speak to him "in just such a familiar, trusting way as a child would with his father."[6] The Bible says that when we believe in Jesus Christ, God gives us "the right to become children of God" (John 1:12). Then, to help us know that we really are his children, God sends us the Holy Spirit, and part of the Spirit's work is to help us pray as children to a Father. The Scripture says, "you have received the Spirit of adoption as sons, by whom we cry, 'Abba! Father!' The Spirit himself bears witness with our spirit that we are children of God" (Rom. 8:15–16). With the help of the Spirit, and through faith in the Son, we pray to God as our Father, coming to him as loving sons and daughters.

Have you learned to call God your Father through faith in Jesus Christ? This is hard for some people to do, especially people whose fathers have done them harm. One young woman with an abusive father had tremendous difficulty understanding what it meant to know God as her loving Father. One of her girlfriends pointed to the example of a father they both knew. "Have you ever seen the way his daughter runs into his arms?" she asked. "Yes," the woman said, "I have seen it; but I can't even bear to look."

How can someone with such a background ever learn to call God Father? Or what about orphans, who never had a father at all? Fortunately, we do not know God as Father by looking at earthly fathers in all their sin, although in the best of fathers we may catch an occasional glimpse of the fatherhood of God. Nor do we know God as Father by viewing him through the lens of our own family experience, although that always has an influence on our spiritual life. No, we come to know God as Father by seeing him in the Scriptures. There we learn that he is the ideal Father, who cares for his children, who listens to us, who understands what we need, who loves us with an everlasting love, and who always knows what is truly best for us.

It is on the basis of God's love for us as our Father that we come to him in prayer. The opening word of the Lord's Prayer governs everything that follows. When we pray for God's name to be hallowed, we are seeking our Father's honor. When we pray for his kingdom to come, we are praying for the establishment of our Father's authority. When we pray for our daily bread, we are asking our Father to meet our needs. When we pray for forgiveness, we are asking our Father to show us mercy. When we pray against temptation, we are asking our Father to keep us safe. As we bring each of

6. J. Jeremias, quoted in R. Kent Hughes, *Luke: That You May Know the Truth*, 2 vols., Preaching the Word (Wheaton, IL: Crossway, 1998), 1:406.

these petitions before the throne of grace, we are praying to God as our loving Father, who loves to do what we ask in his name.

Two Petitions for God

The first petition of the Lord's Prayer in Luke is for God's name to be hallowed. God's name is much more than a title. In biblical usage, the name of God refers to all that God is. For example, when King David says, "we trust in the name of the Lord our God" (Ps. 20:7), he is not putting his confidence in a particular combination of Hebrew letters. On the contrary, he is trusting God himself, in all his glory and grace. God's name represents who God is.

When we pray for God's name to be hallowed, therefore, or "made holy," we are acknowledging the purity of his eternal being. We are declaring that God's character is set apart from sin, that his attributes are absolute in their perfection. We are also praying for God to display his holiness. We are not praying for him to become holy, as if he could ever be any holier than he already is, but that he would be known to be holy. "Hallowed be your name" is a petition that pertains to God's reputation. It is a prayer that God would be known to be God, in all his holiness.

We offer this prayer first of all for ourselves, asking that our lives would demonstrate God's holiness. This means being careful not to dishonor God's name by using it in a profane or casual way. More than that, it means treating everything that pertains to God with complete seriousness. It means listening to what he says in his Word. It means showing reverence for him in worship. It means living with the kind of personal purity that is in keeping with his character. When we ask God to hallow his name, we are praying that he would enable us to obey the words of Peter, when he said: "in your hearts regard Christ the Lord as holy" (1 Peter 3:15).

We make the same petition for others, asking that our family and friends, our church and our community, our nation and indeed the entire world would know the holiness of our God. This petition, writes Norval Geldenhuys, "is that God should so work inwardly upon the one who prays, and upon all others, that they shall recognize Him in His Self-revelation and serve Him as the Holy One—that they should render to Him, the divine

Father, all honor and adoration and should love and obey Him with their whole heart."[7] When you pray, begin by honoring God's holy name.

After praying for God's reputation, we then pray for his rule: "Your kingdom come" (Luke 11:2). Jesus had been preaching about the kingdom of God since the beginning of his public ministry. Here in the second petition he teaches his disciples to pray for its coming.

The kingdom of God is not a nation-state, a system of government, or a geographic region on a political map. Very simply, God's kingdom is God's rule. It is the sovereign administration of his authority over creation, over his enemies, and over the people who honor him as their King. Thus the second petition is a prayer for the glory of God. To pray for the kingdom is to pray for God's glorious rule to bring all things under its control. We pray this first of all for ourselves, asking God to reign in our hearts by faith. We ask God to help us do things his way, not our way. We want to obey his royal commands and serve his royal will.

We pray the same thing for our families, asking that our homes would be outposts of the kingdom—places where God's divine dominion is acknowledged in our household prayers, our mutual service, and the ordinary routines of daily life. We pray this for our churches, asking God to conform our lives and relationships to the gospel. We pray this for our city, asking that it would become a community where strangers become neighbors, the poor receive protection, the weak are defended, business prospers, and the arts flourish to the glory of God. We pray this for our nation, asking that truth and sacrifice would prevail over selfishness and greed. Then we pray this for our world, asking that one day very soon Jesus would return to set everything right.

THREE PETITIONS FOR US

Once we have prayed for the holiness and the kingdom of our Father God, we are ready to pray for our own needs. The order is important: God comes first, giving the vertical priority over the horizontal. Yet there is still a place for our own concerns—a secondary place, but a place nonetheless. As Tertullian observed, "Divine Wisdom arranged the order of this prayer with

---

7. Norval Geldenhuys, *The Gospel of Luke*, New International Commentary on the New Testament (Grand Rapids: Eerdmans, 1951), 319–20.

exquisite choice. After the matters that pertain to heaven—that is, after the name of God, the will of God and the kingdom of God—it should make a place for a petition for our earthly needs too!"[8] Thus in the last three petitions we ask God for daily provision, daily pardon, and daily protection.

Ordinarily we would think of these as personal needs. In this context, however, they are also presented as communal needs. The last three petitions are prayed in the first person plural. We are not praying for ourselves as individuals, but for ourselves as a church. The Lord's Prayer is a family prayer for the people of God, a corporate prayer for the covenant community. Although we may certainly use it in our own personal prayer times, Jesus gave us this prayer to offer with and for one another.

First we pray for our daily bread. Scholars have long debated the precise meaning of the term "daily" *(epiousion)* in the original Greek. Does it refer to the bread I need today, or the bread I will need for tomorrow—the coming day? Either way, the petition teaches us to live day by day, asking God for what we need from one day to the next.

By teaching us to pray this way, Jesus is calling us to daily, ongoing dependence on our Father in heaven. We are inclined to trust our own ability to provide for our daily needs, and thus to take what God gives us for granted. But even the food we buy with money we earn is a gift from God. The only reason we have our daily bread is that God is good and faithful in providing it. To make sure we know where this bread comes from, Jesus teaches us to ask God for it. Ordinarily God answers this prayer through earthly means, including our own diligent labors. But even when we buy the bread, God is the one who puts it on the table. Our Father cares for our earthly needs.

In this petition Jesus is also teaching us that our true needs are few. All we really need is bread, a basic necessity. Jesus did not tell us to pray for a chocolate éclair. What he has taught us to pray for every day (and what he has promised to provide) is bread. This implies that we should be content with what God provides—even if he provides only the bare necessities of life—and not crave what God has not promised to give. This does not mean that we can never pray for anything that goes beyond our daily bread. Out of the abundance of his grace, God often gives us even greater gifts, and we may pray for many good things in life. But the Lord's Prayer teaches us to

8. Tertullian, "On Prayer," in *Luke*, ed. Arthur A. Just Jr., Ancient Christian Commentary on Scripture, NT 3 (Downers Grove, IL: InterVarsity, 2003), 187–88.

know the difference between our needs and our "greeds." In the daily life of prayer, our main petition is for things we truly need.

As much as our Father cares for our physical needs, he cares even more for our spiritual needs. Jesus put these two kinds of needs in their proper proportions, giving us only one petition for the body, but two for the soul.

After we ask God for our daily bread, we beg his forgiveness for our sins. This is how we must always come to God: not confident of our own righteousness, but pleading for his mercy and grace. The Lord's Prayer is a sinner's prayer, in which we acknowledge that we are unworthy sinners before a holy God. This is something we need to acknowledge every day. Just as we ask for daily provision, so also we need to ask for daily pardon. The confession of sin is an ongoing part of our relationship with God. Our sins are forgiven through Christ's death on the cross. Now, whenever we sin, as we continue to do, we can claim God's forgiveness in Jesus' name. As Martin Luther frequently and famously said, the whole Christian life is one of repentance.

Like the prayer in Matthew, the Lord's Prayer in Luke makes a connection between the forgiveness we receive and the forgiveness we offer: "Forgive us our sins, for we ourselves forgive everyone who is indebted to us" (Luke 11:4; cf. Matt. 6:12). The connection almost seems to be a condition, but it is really presented as an assertion: as the children of God, we forgive people who owe us something because of their sin.

This petition plainly acknowledges the sinfulness of sin—not just our own sin, but also the sins of others. When people do us wrong, they put themselves in our debt. The same is true of our own sin against God: it deserves to be punished. We owe God the penalty for our rebellion, which is eternal death. But God has mercy for sinners. He is willing to cancel our debt if only we will come to him in faith and repentance. One of the strongest proofs that we have received such forgiveness from our Father is our own commitment to forgiving others, no matter what they have done. It is simply a fact: the children of God forgive their debtors. By forgiving our debtors, therefore, we show our family resemblance to our Father in heaven.

Who is your debtor? What person has done you wrong? If we refuse to forgive, our hearts must not be right with God. The forgiven forgive, and thus our refusal to forgive shows that we do not understand the grace of

God. Anyone who is sincere in praying the Lord's Prayer must be willing to offer forgiveness to others. This does not mean that God's forgiveness is based on our forgiveness. As Leon Morris has explained, the Lord's Prayer "does not make a human action, the forgiveness of others, the ground of forgiveness. The New Testament is clear that forgiveness springs from the grace of God and not from any human merit. Rather the thought moves from the lesser to the greater: since even sinful men like us forgive, we can confidently approach a merciful God."[9]

We confess our sins because we keep on sinning, but it would be better if we did not sin at all. Therefore the Lord's Prayer ends with the prayer that God would "lead us not into temptation" (Luke 11:4). This petition does not imply that God is ever the one who tempts us. The Bible warns us never to say that God is tempting us, "for God cannot be tempted with evil, and he himself tempts no one" (James 1:13). Whenever we are tempted, therefore, it is by the wicked allure of our own sinful desire. But God is able to protect us in the time of temptation, and even to keep us away from a particular temptation entirely, which is what we are asking when we pray the Lord's Prayer.

Frankly, sometimes we enjoy being tempted—almost as much as we enjoy giving in. One advertisement for Jaguar automobiles preyed upon this weakness in our fallen nature. After listing the traditional "Seven Deadly Sins" of lust, greed, pride, sloth, envy, wrath, and gluttony, the brochure read, "Prepare to shift effortlessly from temptation to exhilaration. The all-new XJ8L—where will it lead you? Can you resist?" When it comes to our temptations, all too often the answer is "No, I feel powerless to resist." Therefore, we need to pray this last petition every day.

The Bible teaches that when we are tempted, God always provides a way of escape (1 Cor. 10:13). It also teaches that God can use the trial of our temptation for spiritual good (James 1:2–3). But when we pray the Lord's Prayer, we make a frank acknowledgment of our spiritual weakness. Even if we always have a way of escape, it is safer for sinners like us not to be tempted at all. So in the Lord's Prayer we ask God to lead us away from temptation.

9. Leon Morris, *The Gospel According to St. Luke: An Introduction and Commentary*, Tyndale New Testament Commentaries (Grand Rapids: Eerdmans, 1974), 194.

The Lord's Prayer

This, then, is the way that Jesus taught us to pray. We begin with our Father God, asking him to enhance his reputation and extend his rule. Then we turn to our own needs, asking God for daily provision, daily pardon, and daily protection.

When we pray this way, we are standing against the prevailing values of our fallen world. In a culture that is increasingly secular and profane, we pray for holiness. In a culture where people want to promote their own agendas, we pray for the kingdom of God. In a culture that fosters its independence and lives for its luxuries, we trust God for daily bread. In a culture that is convinced of its own righteousness, we beg forgiveness. In a culture that revels in its temptations, we ask God to lead us away.

Most Christians call this countercultural form of intercession the Lord's Prayer because it was given by Jesus Christ, our Lord. But there is another reason to call it his prayer, which is that Jesus himself is the answer to every one of its petitions. We pray to God as our Father, but we can do this only through the saving work of His Son. As Jesus said, "No one comes to the Father except through me" (John 14:6), and this principle applies to prayer as much as it applies to any part of the Christian life.

When we pray to our Father, first we pray for his name to be made holy. This prayer is answered in Jesus Christ, "the Holy One of God" (Mark 1:24). It is also answered in us by the powerful sanctifying work of God's Spirit, who makes us holy like Christ. As Christians, we now bear the name of Christ. God is thus known to be holy through us—of all people—as we are conformed to the holiness of Christ.

When we pray for God's kingdom to come, we are praying for the kingdom of our Lord Jesus Christ. Jesus told his disciples, "the kingdom of God is in the midst of you" (Luke 17:21). He said this because he is the King, and where the King is, the kingdom is. Christ's kingdom has been established through his death and resurrection, and soon it will come into its full dominion at his second coming. Jesus is the answer to all our prayers for the kingdom of God.

Next we pray for our daily bread, and this prayer is answered in Jesus as well, because he said, "I am the living bread that came down from heaven. If anyone eats of this bread, he will live forever. And the bread that I will give for the life of the world is my flesh" (John 6:51). Our daily physical bread points to the eternal spiritual bread that we have in Christ. Then, rather obviously, Jesus is the answer to our prayer for forgiveness, because it is only through his atoning work on the cross that we can ever be forgiven. What about temptation? Jesus himself resisted all the temptations of the devil, and now he is able to help us in our time of trial. We are delivered from temptation by trusting in Christ.

The Lord's Prayer is a gospel prayer that finds its answer in Jesus Christ. Jesus taught us to pray this way so that we would know how to talk with our Father and also so that we would know how to walk with him as the Son. When we pray the Lord's Prayer, we are not simply learning a prayer that Jesus taught his disciples a long time ago, but a prayer that God is ready to answer for us through the saving work of his Son.

46

BOLDLY PERSEVERING IN PRAYER

Luke 11:5–13

"And I tell you, ask, and it will be given to you; seek, and you
will find; knock, and it will be opened to you. For everyone
who asks receives, and the one who seeks finds, and to the one
who knocks it will be opened." (Luke 11:9–10)

I have just two words for anyone who needs help from me in the middle of the night: *Good luck!* For it is only with the greatest difficulty that anyone can rouse me from what Shakespeare famously described as the sleep that "knits the raveled sleeve of care."[1]

Whenever we have had a newborn baby in the house, people from church have thoughtfully inquired as to whether or not I am getting enough sleep. No need to worry: I can sleep through almost anything. Blissfully I sleep away, waking only rarely to confront all of the things that happen in the night. The children have long since learned to go to Mommy's side of the bed!

So if you ever need something after bedtime, don't count on me. But if perchance you did manage to wake me in the middle of the night, I would

---

1. This line comes from Shakespeare's *Macbeth*.

try to help—really, I would. I would make at least some effort to hear what you were saying and then get out of bed. If you were patient and persistent enough, eventually you could get what you needed, even from me. This is the real-life context for what Jesus taught his disciples about boldly persevering in prayer.

THE FRIEND AT MIDNIGHT

Seeing the consistency of his prayer life, and sensing his intimacy with the Father, the disciples asked Jesus how to pray. In response, he gave them the flexible form of intercession that has been the basis for Christian prayer ever since. Jesus taught his disciples to pray to God as their Father, seeking the honor of his name and the glory of his kingdom, and asking him to meet their daily needs for food, forgiveness, and freedom from temptation. We call it the Lord's Prayer: the prayer that Jesus taught us to pray, and that is answered by his grace.

Then, having given his disciples the basic content for their prayers, Jesus proceeded to show them how boldly they should ask for what they needed, and how generously their Father would answer. Jesus did this by telling them a story:

> Which of you who has a friend will go to him at midnight and say to him, "Friend, lend me three loaves, for a friend of mine has arrived on a journey, and I have nothing to set before him"; and he will answer from within, "Do not bother me; the door is now shut, and my children are with me in bed. I cannot get up and give you anything"? I tell you, though he will not get up and give him anything because he is his friend, yet because of his impudence he will rise and give him whatever he needs. (Luke 11:5–8)

This story is meant to be absurd. Whenever Jesus introduces a parable with a statement or a phrase like "Which of you . . . ?" (e.g., Luke 12:25; 14:5, 28), we know that he is about to describe something that would never happen. The question is a signal that the answer is "No one": no self-respecting member of the covenant community would refuse to help a neighbor in need.

To see the absurdity of it all, it helps to know the cultural context. In biblical times hospitality was a sacred duty. When a guest arrived—

582

especially a friend—the host had a holy obligation to provide a bountiful meal. There are several notable examples in Scripture, from the feast that Abraham scrambled to provide for three visitors (Gen. 18:1–5) to the fatted calf that the welcoming father killed for his long-lost son (Luke 15:22–24).

Travel was difficult in those days, there were few reliable inns, and travelers usually arrived hungry. Thus the first order of business was putting a good meal on the table. Bread was essential, not just to eat, but to use for dipping and sopping everything else. It was "the knife, fork, and spoon with which the meal [was] eaten."[2] Thus the man in the story was in a real bind. His bread was gone, and needless to say, there were no twenty-four-hour minimarts or all-night bakeries. So when the man's friend arrived at midnight, he found himself unable to meet the high demands of biblical hospitality.

There was only one thing to do, which was to see if the people next door had anything left to eat. Under ordinary circumstances, he would not think of putting their friendship to the test by bothering them at midnight. But the demands of hospitality required him to take action. He had to find some bread, so he went to the neighbors and pounded on their door, making a reasonable request at an unreasonable hour: Could he please borrow a little bread—not for himself, but for a friend from a far place?

The neighbor's response is reminiscent of the time that Winnie-the-Pooh went visiting and Rabbit, not wanting to be bothered, pretended not to be at home. When Pooh saw Rabbit's hole he wondered about stopping by for a little snack, so he bent down and called out:

"Is anybody at home?"
There was a sudden scuffling noise from inside the hole, and then silence.
"What I said was, 'Is anybody at home?'" called out Pooh very loudly.
"No!" said a voice; and then added, "You needn't shout so loud. I heard you quite well the first time."
"Bother!" said Pooh. "Isn't there anybody here at all?"
"Nobody."

2. Kenneth E. Bailey, *Poet and Peasant: A Literary-Cultural Approach to the Parables in Luke* (Grand Rapids: Eerdmans, 1976), 123.

Rabbit was trying to avoid the obligations of playing host to a hungry bear. But eventually Pooh's persistence paid off, and Rabbit had to invite him to come inside (where Pooh proceeded to eat more than he should have, but that is another story).[3]

Much the same thing happened in the parable of the friend at midnight. His neighbor was already in bed, his whole family sleeping together in a one-room cottage. Just about the last thing the man wanted to do at that hour of the night was to get out of bed. So he told his neighbor "No" four different ways. It was a quadruple refusal: "Do not bother me; the door is now shut, and my children are with me in bed. I cannot get up and give you anything" (Luke 11:7). None of these excuses is very persuasive. If the door was shut, it could be opened; if the children woke up, they could be tucked back in. The real issue was not that the man *could* not help, but that he *would* not. He heard the request and he had the bread, but he did not bother to get up and help.

Nevertheless, his neighbor insisted. His hospitality was at stake, so he would not take "No" for an answer. Jesus does not give us the rest of the dialogue, but if anyone has ever tried to persuade you to do something that you did not want to do, you know basically how the conversation goes. Eventually the man in bed realized, to his annoyance, that it would be easier just to give the man what he wanted. So with a sigh of exasperation, he rolled out of bed and gave his neighbor what he needed, being careful not to step on the children. He did not do it for love or friendship, but simply because he wanted to be left alone. He did it because his neighbor had the audacity to come at midnight and keep asking until he got what he wanted.

AUDACIOUS, PERSISTENT PRAYER

We should come to God with the same kind of bold perseverance when we pray. The key phrase in the parable—a phrase that is notoriously difficult to interpret—comes in verse 8: "because of his impudence he will rise and give him whatever he needs." There are two difficulties here: one is to determine which pronoun goes with which character in the story, and the other is to determine the precise meaning of the Greek word *anaideian*,

3. A. A. Milne, *Winnie-the-Pooh* (1926; reprint London: Methuen, 1993), 21–22.

which the English Standard Version translates as "impudence." Grammatically, the phrase "his impudence" might refer to the man in bed. However, it is difficult to see how this attitude can serve as an adequate rationale for his decision to get up and help his neighbor. Nor can we accept interpretations that try to explain this by saying that the word *anaideian* refers in some way to having a sense of honor.[4]

No, the man who has the *anaideian* is the man who needs the bread. But what does this word mean? The King James Version translates the term as "importunity," which means "making persistent or pressing requests" (*Oxford Encyclopedic English Dictionary*). The New International Version uses the word "persistence." The English Standard Version has more of an edge to it: "because of his impudence." To be impudent is to be impertinent; it is to be shamelessly presumptuous. This is probably the most accurate translation. The Greek word *anaideian* refers to someone who "acts without any sensibility to shame or disgrace."[5] We all know the type: someone who does not particularly care what the neighbors think, and who has the sheer audacity to come right out and ask for something that no one else would dare to mention.

This, then, is how we should pray: not timidly dropping God hints about what we need, but boldly, even shamelessly presenting our petitions before God and then continuing to pray about them until we get an answer.

We need to be careful here, because if we press the details of the parable too far we will end up making some serious errors. Jesus is not saying that God gets annoyed when we bother him at midnight, or that he has to be cajoled into giving us what we need, or that we should never take "no" for an answer. In fact, God is not like the man in bed at all. Jesus is making a contrast to show that God is ready and willing to help us. If even the surliest of neighbors can be persuaded to help us in the middle of the night, then how much more will our Father in heaven hear us when we pray! We know that God neither slumbers nor sleeps (Ps. 121:4), and that he loves to help his people in need (Ps. 34:15). We also know that when we pray, we should always submit our requests to his perfect will (Matt. 6:10).

---

4. Arland J. Hultgren's arguments against connecting *anaideian* to the man in bed are decisive. See his book *The Parables of Jesus: A Commentary* (Grand Rapids: Eerdmans, 2000), 230–32. Some have argued that the man in bed is "shameless" in the sense that he gets up to avoid the public shame of failing to help his neighbor in showing hospitality. But as Hultgren shows, if the man acts on the basis of what other people will think, he is not shameless at all, but keeping up his appearances.

5. Hultgren, *Parables*, 231.

Prayer is not a way of getting God to do what we want, or of persuading him to do something that he does not want to do. But prayer *is* an audaciously bold request for God to do what he has promised to do. So when we ask God to hallow his name, to establish his kingdom, to give us bread, to forgive our sins, and to save us from temptation, we may do it with shameless persistence. As Michael Wilcock says, Jesus teaches us to pray this way "not *because* God *will not* answer otherwise, but *as if* he *would not*."[6] Of course God always has the prerogative to say "no" to our petitions, but when we pray the way that Jesus taught us to pray, we may come to God with the holy boldness of a confident faith.

By way of example, this is the way to pray for a friend who needs to know Christ. Humanly speaking, we may not be sure how our friends will ever receive the gospel, but we believe that God can save them. So we pray, and as we pray, we may appeal to God on the basis of his own character. Sometimes we can see how God has begun to work in someone's life, and then we can pray that because of his faithfulness he is now obligated to finish what he had started. Or we can tell God that if he has given us a love for our friends, then out of the perfection of his divine love, he should love them all the way to salvation. We can also tell God that saving our friends would serve his greater glory. Can God still refuse such requests? Of course he can—he is God, after all. But like the friend who came at midnight, we should pray as *if* he *could not* refuse.

Then we should keep praying. According to Leon Morris, the lesson of this parable is: "We must not play at prayer, but must show persistence if we do not receive the answer immediately. It is not that God is unwilling and must be pressed into answering. The whole context makes it clear that He is eager to give. But if we do not want what we are asking for enough to be persistent, we do not want it very much."[7]

How much do you want the things for which you pray? Do you boldly persevere, or do you get discouraged and give up, not daring to beg God for an answer? Terry Johnson writes:

6. Michael Wilcock, *The Message of Luke*, The Bible Speaks Today (Downers Grove, IL: InterVarsity, 1979), 126 (emphasis in original).
7. Leon Morris, *The Gospel According to St. Luke: An Introduction and Commentary*, Tyndale New Testament Commentaries (Grand Rapids: Eerdmans, 1974), 195.

One of the reasons we lack spiritual depth in our day is because of our failure to persist in prayer. Where do we lack it? We lack it in our family life. Our families are not as strong and as spiritually stable as they ought to be. We lack it in our personal lives. We are not progressing in sanctification as we ought. We lack it as a church. We are not seeking revival to any significant degree in our day. We are failing to reach our neighbors and our neighborhoods. Why are these things so? Because we don't pray, and, when we do pray, we trifle at it.[8]

So let me ask again: Are you boldly persevering in prayer? This means praying and praying for people to be saved. George Muller prayed for one of his friends for more than sixty years. "Never give up until the answer comes," Muller wrote. "He is not converted yet, but he will be."[9] And the man *was* saved, even though his conversion came after Muller's death. Persevering in prayer means praying and praying for the global work of the gospel. If the lost Muslim, Hindu, and Buddhist nations of the world are to be saved, it will be in answer to the persistent prayers of God's people. Persevering in prayer means praying and praying for the church, asking God to send the Holy Spirit in all his renewing, reviving, and reforming power. To persevere is to pray and pray for God's transforming work in our families, healing our wounds and making us strong to serve one another. It is also to pray and pray for our own growth in godliness, asking God to win the victory over our selfishness and sin.

Why do we pray this way? *Not* because God is counting our prayers and waiting until we reach a certain number before he will answer, but because when Jesus taught us to pray, he told us to have the audacity to keep telling our Father what we need.

ASKING, SEEKING, KNOCKING

It is hard to pray this way and keep on praying. J. C. Ryle once wrote, "It is far more easy to begin a habit of prayer than to keep it up.... Thousands take up a habit of praying for a little season, after some special mercy or

---

8. Terry L. Johnson, *When Grace Comes Alive: Living Through the Lord's Prayer* (Fearn, Ross-shire: Christian Focus, 2003), 208.

9. George Muller, *The Kneeling Christian*, 95, quoted in Johnson, *Grace*, 216.

special affliction, and then little by little become cold about it, and at last lay it aside. . . . Let us resist this feeling, whenever we feel it rising within us. Let us resolve by God's grace, that however poor and feeble our prayers may seem to be, we will pray on."[10]

To help us pray on, Jesus applied his parable with some of the most encouraging words in the Bible: "And I tell you, ask, and it will be given to you; seek, and you will find; knock, and it will be opened to you. For everyone who asks receives, and the one who seeks finds, and to the one who knocks it will be opened" (Luke 11:9–10).

As we have seen, this parable is more about how we should pray than about how God answers. But in the application of the parable, *both* our part and God's part are clearly in view. Our duty is to ask, seek, and knock. There seems to be a progression here. It is one thing to ask, but to seek requires a higher level of commitment. To seek is to pursue what is asked. Then to knock is to pound at the very door for an answer. These three verbs move in the direction of a more serious intention to get what God has to offer.

What is even more important, however, is the form of these verbs. All three of them describe a continuous action. Luke 11:9 does not say, "ask, seek, knock," but "asking, seeking, knocking." Jesus is not just telling us how to come to God in the first place, but how to go to him again and again: "keep asking, keep seeking, keep knocking."

We do this for the very first time when we ask God to save us through the death and resurrection of Jesus Christ. We *ask* God to give us eternal life; we *seek* to know for sure what the Bible says about the cross and the empty tomb; and we *knock* on the door of salvation until Jesus opens the way to God. But even after we come to Christ, we are to keep on pursuing God in prayer, asking for what we need, seeking what God has for us to find, and knocking on the door of spiritual knowledge. "The sense of the verse," writes Terry Johnson, is "keep on asking and it will be given to you, keep on seeking and you will find, keep on knocking and it will be opened to you. Jesus ties together persistence and efficacy. Prayer works as you work at prayer."[11]

10. J. C. Ryle, *Expository Thoughts on the Gospels, Luke* (1858; reprint Cambridge: James Clarke, 1976), 2:11.
11. Johnson, *Grace*, 205.

Prayer has this kind of efficacy not because of the way we pray, but because of the way God answers. He is a generous Father who loves to give us what we truly need. When we have the audacity to pray the way that Jesus taught us to pray, God has promised to hear us and answer us. In the dialogue of prayer, we are pressing God for something that he is longing to give.

In these verses Jesus assures us that God will answer our prayers. He offers this assurance, not just once or twice, but six times—three in verse 9 and three in verse 10. In verse 9 Jesus says, "Ask, and it will be given to you; seek, and you will find; knock, and it will be opened to you." Our asking, seeking, and knocking will not be in vain. God will give, God will reveal, God will open. In case we have any doubt about this, Jesus goes on to say, "For everyone who asks receives, and the one who seeks finds, and to the one who knocks it will be opened." Jesus repeats himself to give us extra assurance that our prayers will be answered.

Of course Jesus is not saying that God will give us anything and every-thing we want. In this context, he is talking about the way God answers the petitions we make in the Lord's Prayer. As we will discover when we get to the end of verse 13, he is talking most specifically about the spiritual blessings that God gives to every believer in Jesus Christ. If we ask for these things, we will receive.

Notice that this promise is for *everyone* who asks, seeks, and knocks. This gives special encouragement to anyone who has never come to God the Father in the name of Jesus Christ, or who is afraid that God will not give a gracious welcome. Everyone who asks in faith will receive. Everyone who seeks with a sincere heart will find. Everyone who knocks on the door of Jesus Christ will go in and be saved. Jesus is telling us not to hold back, but to go to God and ask for what we need.

Good Gifts from Bad Fathers

The promises that Jesus makes in verses 9 and 10 are so immense that they may seem impossible to keep. So to prove that God really is this gener-ous, Jesus added two little parables that come from family life: "What father among you, if his son asks for a fish, will instead of a fish give him a serpent; or if he asks for an egg, will give him a scorpion?" (Luke 11:11–12).

Once again, Jesus asks a question that is meant to sound absurd. What kind of father would give his son a snake instead of a fish, or a scorpion instead of an egg? A man who did such a thing would be a fiend, not a father. Sadly, there are such men in the world, but the point still stands: no ordinary father would be so cruel as to give his son something dangerous when he asks for something good.

Having made this point, Jesus proceeded to argue from the lesser thing to the greater: "If you then, who are evil, know how to give good gifts to your children, how much more will the heavenly Father give" (Luke 11:13).

At this point, some of us might be tempted to say that Jesus is being too hard on fathers. Is it really right for him to say that we are "evil"? After all, he was speaking to his disciples, who may not have been the best of fathers, but probably were not the worst either. But of course it is right for Jesus to say this. Here he is speaking from his intimate knowledge of our total depravity. He knows that fathers are capable of doing something good. In fact, his two little parables assume this. But he also knows that the hearts of fathers are as wicked as anyone else's, and that in our sinful nature we are as likely to harm our children as to help them.

Nevertheless, for all our shortcomings, most of us fathers know what our children need. When they ask for something, we listen to what they are saying. We provide what they truly need, and if we are able, we do much more than that. The point is that if even bad fathers know to give good gifts, we can trust our perfect heavenly Father to give us the best gifts of all.

Knowing that we can count on God's fatherly care gives us confidence when we pray. I witness this kind of confidence in my study at Tenth Presbyterian Church in Philadelphia. When the door is closed, most people knock rather cautiously and wait for an answer, so as not to disturb me. Not my eldest son, however. If he remembers to knock (which he doesn't, always), he knocks loudly and immediately enters. His knock is more like an announcement, and then he has the audacity and the impertinence to walk right in. Rightly so, for he is my son! What would be impudent for anyone else is for him a proper recognition of his privileged status as his father's son.

This is the way that Jesus has taught us to pray: with a boldness based on the benevolence of our Father's love. God wants to answer even more than we want to ask. Do you believe this when you pray? Richard Phillips tells the story of a man who approached Alexander the Great with a financial need. The famous conqueror referred the man to his royal treasurer, with the promise that he would have whatever he needed. Soon the treasurer came running up in a state of alarm because the man had asked for a vast sum of money. Surely there must have been some mistake! But Alexander calmly gave the man what he wanted, saying, "He has treated me as a king in asking, and so I shall be as a king to him in giving."[12]

Our Father God loves to be a King to us in giving: "He who did not spare his own Son but gave him up for us all, how will he not also with him graciously give us all things?" (Rom. 8:32). God has given us his generous invitation, offering us everything we need in Jesus Christ. The question is whether we will go to him and ask for what we need, seeking and knocking until he answers.

THE FATHER'S GREATEST GIFT

The last thing to notice is the surprising twist that comes at the very end of this passage. Jesus had been teaching his disciples how to pray to their Father. First he gave them a model for their daily prayers, which we usually call "the Lord's Prayer." Then he told them how to approach God in prayer with sanctified audacity. Next he encouraged them that when they came to God asking, seeking, and knocking, he would hear them as a loving Father. But what, exactly, would God do for them? This is where the surprise comes. Jesus said, "How much more will the heavenly Father give the Holy Spirit to those who ask him!" (Luke 11:13).

This is surprising because the Holy Spirit is not specifically mentioned anywhere in the Lord's Prayer, or in the instructions that Jesus gives about asking, seeking, and knocking. It is also surprising because Jesus seemed to be talking about earthly blessings. The parables of the friend at midnight and the father's gifts all deal with material needs. Nevertheless, when Jesus comes to the end of his instructions on prayer, he promises that when we ask, God will give us the Holy Spirit.

To some this may seem a slight disappointment, but in fact it is the climax of the whole passage: the Son promising that the Father will give us

12. Richard D. Phillips, *Turning Your World Upside Down: Kingdom Priorities in the Parables of Jesus* (Phillipsburg, NJ: P&R, 2003), 45.

591

the Spirit. Of all the gifts that God could possibly give us, none is greater than the gift of God himself in the person of the Holy Spirit. If we do not believe this, it is only because we do not know the greatness of the Spirit's person or the scope of the Spirit's work. To demonstrate the unique blessing of having the Spirit, one need only consider the extraordinary ministry of the apostles once they received the gift of the Holy Spirit at Pentecost: they had the power to perform miraculous wonders and to preach a gospel that changed the world.

The Spirit is a great gift because he is divine. There is one God in three persons—Father, Son, and Holy Spirit. The Spirit fully shares the divine majesty; he is to be worshiped with the Father and the Son. Therefore, when the Son promises that the Father will send us the Spirit, he is promising that God himself will live within us.

What will the Spirit do in us? He will reveal the truth of God through the teaching of Scripture, which he himself first revealed. He will give us the conviction of sin, granting us the gift of repentance. He will persuade us of the truth of the gospel, working in us the gift of faith. By faith he will unite us to Jesus Christ, so it is only through the Spirit we receive the blessings of salvation: justification, sanctification, and adoption. That is not all; it is only the beginning. The Spirit will win us the victory over sin. The Spirit will equip us with gifts for ministry. The Spirit will grow in us the fruit of godliness. The Spirit will assure us that we are the children of God. One day the Spirit will raise us from the dead, just as he raised Jesus from the dead, and by his transforming grace he will change us into glory.

Do you see what a great blessing it is when Jesus promises us the Holy Spirit? J. C. Ryle summarized by saying, "The Holy Spirit is beyond doubt the greatest gift which God can bestow upon man. Having this gift, we have all things, life, light, hope, and heaven. Having this gift, we have God the Father's boundless love, God the Son's atoning blood, and full communion with all three Persons of the blessed Trinity. Having this gift, we have grace and peace in the world that now is, glory and honor in the world to come."[13] In short, to have the Holy Spirit is to have everything that God has to give us. Jesus has promised that this Spirit is ours for the asking.

13. Ryle, *Luke*, 2:12.

Have you asked the Father for the gift of the Spirit in the name of the Son? One man who made this request was John Newton, the infamous slave trader who by the grace of God became a famous preacher and hymn writer. Newton was captain of the *Greyhound* when the ship was caught in a violent storm at sea. In the middle of the night the upper timbers of the ship were shattered and water gushed into Newton's cabin. As he clambered onto the deck, the man next to him on the ladder was swept overboard and perished. The captain took the helm of the ship, and in the desperate hours that followed, he reflected on the life that he had wasted by living without God. He thought to himself, "there never was, nor could be, such a sinner as myself. Then, comparing the advantages I had broken through, I concluded at first that my sins were too great to be forgiven." How could a wretched sinner like John Newton ever find grace?

As he held on for dear life, Newton began to reason that the best way forward was to ask for the power of the Spirit and then to live by the truth of the gospel. His thinking was influenced, he later said, by his reading of Luke 11:13, where God promised to "give the Holy Spirit to them that ask him."[14] When Newton asked for the Spirit, God made good on his promise and gave him the greatest of all gifts, saving that wretched sinner by his amazing grace in the power of the Spirit. God is ready and willing to do the same thing for you, because this is a request Jesus has guaranteed that the Father will answer. All you have to do is ask.

---

14. Steve Turner, *Amazing Grace: The Story of America's Most Beloved Song* (New York: HarperCollins, 2002), 41–44.

47

JESUS OR THE DEVIL

Luke 11:14–26

"Every kingdom divided against itself is laid waste, and a divided household falls. And if Satan also is divided against himself, how will his kingdom stand?" (Luke 11:17–18)

*I*n June of 1858 more than a thousand delegates met at the Illinois statehouse to elect Abraham Lincoln as the Republican candidate for the United States Senate. That night the great man gave one of his most famous speeches. Referring to the civil strife then threatening to tear the nation in two, he said, "A house divided against itself cannot stand. I believe this government cannot endure, permanently half slave and half free."

Abraham Lincoln borrowed his image of the divided house from something Jesus said in the Gospel of Luke: "Every kingdom divided against itself is laid waste, and a divided household falls" (Luke 11:17). Jesus made this statement in the form of a proverb, and like any proverb, it applies to many situations in life. So when Lincoln used it to describe the peril of a country torn between slavery and freedom, he was making a national application of a biblical principle.

As is the case with many things that Jesus said, however, we often forget the original context. When we take the time to study the Gospel carefully, we find that as important as Lincoln's speech was for the cause of freedom, what Jesus said was even more important. For when Jesus spoke about the divided house, he was referring to a deadlier war over a crueler slavery that required a stronger deliverance. He was speaking about the triumph of his kingdom over the fallen house of Satan.

A MIRACLE OF SPEECH

This episode begins with one of the shortest miracle stories: "Now he was casting out a demon that was mute. When the demon had gone out, the mute man spoke, and the people marveled" (Luke 11:14).

This was only the latest in a long series of conflicts between Jesus and the devil, starting with the temptation in the wilderness, when Satan tried to turn Jesus away from the cross (Luke 4:1–13). In the months that followed, Jesus often defeated the works of the devil by casting out demons (Luke 4:41). On one occasion he cast out an entire legion of demons (Luke 8:26–39). On another occasion he rescued a boy who was afflicted with dangerous and diabolical seizures (Luke 9:37–43). This time Satan had silenced a man's tongue.

Luke tells us that a demon was making the man mute. He was unable to express himself fully, either to his neighbors or to God. This poor man could not even say the words of the Lord's Prayer, or call out to his heavenly Father verbally the way that Jesus had been teaching his disciples to pray. Because of his demonic disability, he was virtually a prisoner inside his own body. It was all because of Satan:

> This is self-evidently the work of the enemy. . . . If it is God's desire and design, and man's chief glory, that he should be the priest of creation and articulate creation's response to the Creator, that he should talk with God as a son with a father, then it is obvious why it should be of prime strategic importance to the enemy to cripple man's ability to speak with God, to lock up man's spirit within himself, and as far as God is concerned to turn this earth into a silent planet.[1]

1. David Gooding, *According to Luke: A New Exposition of the Third Gospel* (Grand Rapids: Eerdmans, 1987), 222.

This is what Satan wants to do to every one of us: he wants to break off communication, isolating us from one another and separating us from God. Even if we are not literally mute, there are times when we might as well be. Whenever we fail to speak words of spiritual blessing or forget to pray, we forfeit the use of our tongues for their highest and best purpose, which is to glorify God. By not speaking for God or to God we become the devil's tool, like the demon-oppressed man in Luke's Gospel.

What a great deliverance it was when Jesus cast out his demon and enabled him to speak! What joyous words of thanksgiving the man must have uttered, and what high words of praise! In an instant he was saved from the devil that had his tongue. Now, to the amazement of all the people, he was able to glorify God.

This exorcism teaches us many precious truths about salvation. It teaches us that Jesus is stronger than any demon, and that he has the power to restore people in body, soul, and speech. It also teaches us what happens when we come to know Christ: our mouths are restored to their right and proper use. Instead of cursing God and warring against others with our words, we are able to pray to God and speak truth to our neighbor. This can only happen by the grace of God, because without Christ we can only speak words that come from a godless, graceless heart.

Anyone who has not yet learned to speak gracious words for God should pray the way that King David prayed: "O Lord, open my lips, and my mouth will declare your praise" (Ps. 51:15). And anyone who has received this grace should do what the people did when they saw Jesus perform this miracle: they marveled at what Jesus had done, giving glory to God. By the grace of our Lord Jesus Christ, we too can say, "He put a new song in my mouth, a song of praise to our God" (Ps. 40:3).

THE ANTAGONISTS AND THE SKEPTICS

Sadly, some of the people who witnessed this miracle had a very different reaction, and their response is the main reason that this episode appears in the Gospel. Luke spends far more time telling us what happened *after* this miracle than telling us about the miracle itself.

These proportions are in keeping with the overall movement of Luke's Gospel. Most of the miracle stories come in the first half of Luke, before

Jesus set his face toward Jerusalem (Luke 9:51). But from that point on he faced increasing opposition, until finally he was crucified. In this episode, the important thing is not so much the miracle itself, but the obvious skepticism and antagonism of the people who witnessed it. People were amazed when Jesus made this man talk. They knew that he had done something supernatural, but not all of them acknowledged that it was the work of God: "some of them said, 'He casts out demons by Beelzebub, the prince of demons, while others, to test him, kept seeking from him a sign from heaven'" (Luke 11:15).

All of these people agreed that Jesus had cast out a demon, no doubt about it. The question was how he had done it, and why. Some responded with antagonism, claiming that this was really the work of the devil, while others responded with skepticism, demanding some clearer sign from God.

To identify Jesus with Beelzebul was a wicked and pernicious blasphemy. "Beelzebul" was an ancient term for a pagan deity. We find the term in secular literature, used with reference to one of the gods of Canaan. We also find it in the Old Testament, where it refers specifically to the god of Ekron (see 2 Kings 1:2). In time the Jews came to identify Beelzebul as one of the arch demons of hell, or even as Satan himself. To say that Jesus was casting out demons by Beelzebul, therefore, was to say that he was the devil's tool. Since these people denied that Jesus was the Son of God, they had to give some other explanation for his power to cast out demons. The only thing they could come up with was that he was doing it by the devil's own power.

Many people slander Jesus the same way today. Rather than acknowledging that his church is God's agent for doing good in the world, people think or say that what the church does is evil. Of course it is true that many wrong things have been done in the name of Christ, and that in its weakness and sin the church sometimes acts in ways contrary to the will of God. But when the church is standing up for what is righteous—defending the unborn, for example, or proclaiming that Jesus is the only way to God, or promoting biblical standards for sexual purity—it is a wicked lie to say that the church is unloving or ungodly. When such opposition comes, as it often does in a post-Christian society, it is an attack on Christ himself.

Others are less antagonistic to Jesus, but still remain skeptical. This was true of the people who wanted God to give them a sign. They were not sure whether Jesus was doing the work of the devil or not. Maybe his power really did come from God. They were open to that possibility, but they demanded proof. What Jesus was doing was not enough, as far as they were concerned; they wanted something more. Here is how Norval Geldenhuys describes their attitude:

> Others, who did not go so far as to suggest that He acted through the power of Satan, would nevertheless not see and acknowledge in His power over the evil spirits and in all His other words and deeds evidence that He was the Messiah. Without showing any signs of true desire for salvation, they demand that, if He were to be acknowledged as Messiah, He should cause an indisputable, divine miracle to take place which might prove openly the fact of His Messiahship. Otherwise, they reasoned in their unbelief and pride, they could not be sure whether the accusation of His acting through the power of Satan was not perhaps true.[2]

If anything, this attitude is even more common today. Whatever they may think of Christianity and the church, most people do not think they are hostile to Jesus Christ. They are spiritually open, and thus they are willing to consider what Jesus has to offer. But before they make a commitment, they think they need a sign that Jesus really is the Savior and God that he claims to be.

This kind of skepticism may seem less evil than outright antagonism, but it is no less dangerous. Whether we deny Jesus altogether or simply dismiss him until we get more evidence, we do not trust him by faith. In fact, the skeptic may not actually be any closer to God than the antagonist! Many people who say that they are skeptics have no sincere desire to know God at all. They are only using their skepticism as an excuse for avoiding the hard realities of sin, death, and judgment. As J. C. Ryle once said, "It is always one mark of a thoroughly unbelieving heart, to pretend to want more evidence of the truth of religion."[3] The truth is that God has given more than enough evidence. What holds people back is the pride of their own skepticism.

---

2. Norval Geldenhuys, *The Gospel of Luke,* New International Commentary on the New Testament (Grand Rapids: Eerdmans, 1951), 329.

3. J. C. Ryle, *Expository Thoughts on the Gospels, Luke* (1858; reprint Cambridge: James Clarke, 1976), 2:21.

How Jesus Answered

Jesus began to meet the challenge of these two objections—the antagonistic accusation that he was working by the devil's power and the skeptical demand for a sign—by pointing out that the claim of demonic influence was illogical: "But he, knowing their thoughts, said to them, 'Every kingdom divided against itself is laid waste, and a divided household falls. And if Satan also is divided against himself, how will his kingdom stand?'" (Luke 11:17–18).

In other words, why would Satan try to undo the very work that he had been doing? One of his cruel demons had muted a man made in the image of God, accomplishing the devil's purpose of silencing the man's praise. Why then would Satan deliver the man from the very bondage he had worked so hard to bring about? This did not make any sense! A self-divided kingdom cannot stand. Therefore, it was unreasonable for people to say that this miracle was the work of the devil. In their denial that Jesus was doing the work of God, they were in defiance of common sense.

Not only was their accusation illogical, but as Jesus pointed out, it was also inconsistent: "For you say that I cast out demons by Beelzebul. And if I cast out demons by Beelzebul, by whom do your sons cast them out? Therefore they will be your judges" (Luke 11:18–19).

Apparently there were other people in the Jewish community who also had the power to cast out demons. It was generally acknowledged that whenever a religious leader performed such an exorcism, it was a sign that God was working through him. That is not what the critics were saying about Jesus, however. When *he* cast out demons, they said it was the work of the devil. This was inconsistent. If they said that Jesus was working for the devil, then obviously they should be saying the same thing about their own exorcists. Yet they had always believed that exorcism was the work of God. So Jesus caught them in a contradiction. In denying that his power came from God, they were denying one of their own basic principles for judging the truth.

These attacks on Jesus were illogical and inconsistent. But in the final analysis, every attempt to deny God's work is illogical and inconsistent. Since God is our Creator, we cannot even try to reason him out of existence without using the minds that he gave us. Nor can we shake an angry fist at him without clenching the hand that he so marvelously made. Any attack on our Creator is self-refuting, because in making the attack we can only use (or rather, misuse) the gifts that he gave us.

Another example of this inconsistency is the way that people curse. Often the very people who deny that God has anything to do with their daily lives will shout his name when they get angry. Do they believe that God has the power to damn, or not? If not, then why do they keep talking to him like that? Taking God's name in vain unwittingly shows the illogical inconsistency of rejecting Jesus Christ.

THE FINGER OF A STRONGER SAVIOR

So how did Jesus do it? If he was not working for the devil, then where did he get his power over demons? Jesus said, "But if it is by the finger of God that I cast out demons, then the kingdom of God has come upon you" (Luke 11:20). In other words, the situation was exactly the opposite of what people were saying. They were claiming that Jesus was working by the power of Satan, when in fact he was doing the will of God.

To be more specific, Jesus was doing this work "by the finger of God." This expression has its origins in Exodus, where Pharaoh's magicians used it to describe one of the deadly plagues they suffered in Egypt (see Exod. 8:19). The Egyptians were touched by the finger of God. But in Matthew Jesus uses a slightly different expression. There he says, "But if it is by the *Spirit* of God that I cast out demons" (Matt. 12:28; emphasis added). The "finger of God" thus refers to "Spirit of God." Jesus performed this miracle of speech by the power of the Holy Spirit. As Cyril of Alexandria explained: "The Son is called the hand and arm of God the Father because he does all things by the Son, and the Son in a similar way works by the Spirit. Just as the finger is attached to the hand as something . . . belonging to it by nature, so also the Holy Spirit . . . is joined in oneness to the Son. . . . The Son **does** everything by the Spirit."[4]

People were asking for a sign, but really this should have been sign enough. They had just witnessed a direct demonstration of the power of God's Spirit. They had seen a man touched by the very finger of God, with

---

4. Cyril of Alexandria, "Commentary on Luke," in *Luke*, ed. Arthur A. Just Jr., Ancient Christian Commentary on Scripture, NT 3 (Downers Grove, IL: InterVarsity, 2003), 193.

the result that he was delivered from the devil. Jesus was beginning to exercise his royal authority over Satan. This was a clear sign that God's kingdom was coming in Christ.

To further explain what he was doing, Jesus gave an illustration—almost like a parable: "When a strong man, fully armed, guards his own palace, his goods are safe; but when one stronger than he attacks him and overcomes him, he takes away his armor in which he trusted and divides his spoil" (Luke 11:21–22).

The strong man, of course, is Satan. Jesus portrays him as a wealthy prince taking his ease in a fortified palace, surrounded by treasure. He is so strong that his fortress seems unassailable. This is a frightening picture of the devil's dominion over lost sinners. The goods in his palace are the souls of people who are still in bondage to sin, whom Satan has claimed to be his own property, and who have yet to be rescued from his dominion. Anyone who doubts Satan's strength to do this only needs to look at what is happening in the world. The devil is always going about his evil work, and like a greedy miser standing guard over his treasure, he wants to hold on to everything he has worked so hard to gain. This means that the "sinner's heart must be carried away by storm if it be ever taken, for there is no hope of taking the Evil Spirit by surprise."[5]

Perhaps you can even see Satan's strength in your own spiritual condition. If you have not been touched by the finger of God's Spirit, then you are still under the devil's control, whether you are aware of this or not. Try as you might, in your own strength you will never be able to break free from his palace, because he is always standing guard over your soul.

Praise God, there is someone who is stronger than Satan. Here Jesus describes a stronger one who attacks the devil's palace, overthrows his guard, strips him of his armor, and claims the goods that Satan once claimed for his own. As we read the rest of the gospel story, we discover that Jesus himself is the Stronger One who overthrows the devil through his crucifixion. As Jesus was paying the suffering price for our sins, he was disarming the devil and putting him to public shame (see Col. 2:13–15). The Scripture says Jesus died so that "through death he might destroy the one who has the power of death, that is, the devil, and deliver all those who through fear of death were subject

---

5. Charles H. Spurgeon, "The Strong One Driven Out by a Stronger One," *The Metropolitan Tabernacle Pulpit* (1865; reprint Pasadena, TX: Pilgrim, 1970), 76.

to lifelong slavery" (Heb. 2:14–15; cf. 1 John 3:8). The Scripture says further that Jesus defeated the devil through his resurrection, by which he turns people "from the power of Satan to God" (Acts 26:18). It is through the cross and the empty tomb that Jesus drives Satan out and rescues his own.

Jesus is so much stronger that Satan's resistance is futile. As strong as the devil seems, he is utterly overwhelmed by the superior strength of God in Christ. One man who witnessed this power firsthand was a secretary in China's Communist Party—a man named Fang Tiancai. Fang sought to decapitate the leadership of the large Christian community in Henan Province. In particular, he wanted to kill the well-known pastor and evangelist Li Tianen. Suddenly Fang fell out of favor with his superiors, and found himself in prison. In the providence of God, he ended up in the same death row prison cell as Li Tianen—the very man he had targeted for execution:

> "Are you Li Tianen?" Fang asked, kneeling down and trembling on arrival in the cell. Li said he was.
>
> "God in Heaven, you are an awesome power!" Fang exclaimed. Then he went on, "I was ready to execute you three times, but the Jesus you believe in protected you. Marx was not able to save me. Now I believe the Gospel you believe in is real."[6]

With Jesus, or Against Him?

Do you believe in the reality of the gospel? Have you seen the power of Jesus Christ? Do you trust in his death and resurrection for your deliverance? When we come into contact with Jesus Christ, we have a choice to make: either we believe in his divine power and receive him as our Savior and Lord, or else we decide to keep running with the devil. There is no middle ground; we have to take sides. This is the application that Jesus makes from the story of the strong man and the Stronger One: "Whoever is not with me is against me, and whoever does not gather with me scatters" (Luke 11:23).

This may sound like the contradiction of something from earlier in the Gospel, when Jesus said to his disciples, "the one who is not against you is for you" (Luke 9:50). That was in a very different context, however. Here

---

6. David Aikman, *Jesus in Beijing: How Christianity Is Transforming China and Changing the Global Balance of Power* (Washington, DC: Regnery, 2003), 70.

is how J. C. Ryle explains the difference: "In the former case, our Lord was speaking of one who was really working for Christ, and against the devil, and was doing good, though perhaps not in the wisest way. . . . He works against the same enemy that we work against, and therefore he is on our side. In the case before us, our Lord is speaking of men who refused to join Him and become His disciples."[7]

This is a choice that every individual has to make: Will I be for Jesus Christ, or against him? Many people would rather not have to choose. We see this in Luke 11. Some of the people who saw Jesus cast out demons thought he was doing the work of the devil. These people were openly and obviously against him; others did not know what to think. They were against demons and disabilities, so they certainly did not want to accuse Jesus of being on the devil's payroll. They were even open to the possibility that he could be the Christ. Yet they did not want to make a firm commitment or take a strong position.

We see the same thing today. Most people do not think of themselves as being *against* Jesus Christ, but they are not entirely *for* him either. They are willing to admire Jesus from a distance as long as he does not make too many demands on their obedience. This is even true in the church, where people worship on Sunday and then go back to their worldly ways the rest of the week. But Jesus warns us that we cannot have it both ways. With him there is no middle ground. He says, "Look, if you are not completely for me, then you are really against me."

There is no neutrality. Either we are for Christ and his kingdom, or we are against him. If we are for him, then we will join him in his great work of gathering souls to God. But if we are against him, then we will only drive people away, scattering them to Satan. Are you standing with Jesus or against him? "Let it be the settled determination of our minds," wrote J. C. Ryle, "that we will serve Christ with all our hearts, if we serve Him at all. Let there be no reserve, no compromise, no half-heartedness."[8]

UNCLEAN SWEEP

If we do not follow Christ without reserve, we are in serious spiritual danger. This is the point of the closing illustration that Jesus gives

7. Ryle, *Luke*, 2:28.
8. Ibid., 2:25.

about the demon who leaves and later returns: When the unclean spirit has gone out of a person, it passes through waterless places seeking rest, and finding none it says, "'I will return to my house from which I came.' And when it comes, it finds the house swept and put in order. Then it goes and brings seven other spirits more evil than itself, and they enter and dwell there. And the last state of that person is worse than the first" (Luke 11:24–26). This mysterious passage lifts the veil on the spiritual realities of the unseen world. It tells us that demons can enter people, leave people, and later return. It says that demons are restless creatures who sometimes wander in the wilderness, but are always seeking to find a home. It says further that they are seeking to find this home in the soul of a human person, and that in some cases a person may be possessed by many demons.

Why does Jesus speak about these things here? Obviously the theme of demon possession is connected in some way to the miracle that he had just performed. But what practical lesson is he trying to teach us? Simply this: that we are safe from Satan only when we have the Spirit of Christ living within us. Indeed, if all we ever have is a self-made attempt at personal reformation, without a saving work of God's Spirit, we will end up worse off then ever.

Jesus describes a person who had experienced the departure of a demon without full deliverance. The wandering spirit left for his own reasons, on his own initiative. He was not expelled by the power of Jesus Christ. Once the evil departed, the person was able to tidy things up inside. Since he was no longer dominated directly by a demon, he was able to make some kind of moral recovery. But he never invited someone stronger to take possession of his soul. Satan left, but the Spirit never entered. The man swept his soul, but never asked God to cleanse it. He was partially reformed, but not totally renewed. So when the unclean spirit decided to return, the house—be it ever so tidy—remained unoccupied. Upon finding that he could still have possession, the demon went out to get seven even more diabolical friends to come and devour the man's soul. Here is a man, said Charles Spurgeon, who was "for a time reformed, but eventually subjected to the worst forms of evil."[9]

9. Spurgeon, "Strong One," 74.

How frightful it would be for us if Satan were to find himself at home in our souls! Yet this is what happens when we try to make moral improvement by our own religious effort. According to Michael Wilcock, Jesus is showing "how useless (indeed dangerous) is the expulsion of an evil power, by whatever means, if no corresponding good power comes in to bar the door against its return. And this is always true, whether it is by exorcism or by sheer determination that men try to rid themselves of the evil within them."[10] At first when we try to reform ourselves, it may seem as if we are making progress. We think we are in spiritual recovery. But unless we put our faith in Jesus Christ, we do not have his Spirit living within us. Where the Holy Spirit dwells, no evil spirit will enter, but without the Spirit there is no one to bar the door against the devil. Sooner or later all the old demons will return, and as Jesus says, we will be even worse off than before (Luke 11:26; cf. 2 Peter 2:20–22).

We are either for Jesus or against him. If we are for him, then his Spirit lives inside us, and our soul is secure. But if we are not for Jesus, then some day Satan will come and take possession. "There is no safety," wrote J. C. Ryle, "except in thorough Christianity.... The house must not only be swept ...; a new tenant must be introduced.... The outward life must not only be decorated with the formal trappings of religion; the power of vital religion must be experienced in the inner man. The Devil must not only be cast out; the Holy Spirit must take his place. Christ must dwell in our hearts by faith."[11]

See how dangerous it is to be satisfied with any religious change that falls short of complete conversion by the Spirit of God. Moral reformation without spiritual regeneration even leads to demonic domination. People who try a little harder to live a little better need to know this: it will never work. In order to experience real and lasting spiritual change, we need something more than personal advice, or a self-help program, or a recovery group. Not even casting out a demon is enough. What we need is the indwelling of the Holy Spirit, whom Jesus has promised that the Father will give to anyone who asks (see Luke 11:13). We need to pray for the Stronger One to give us the supernatural, transforming grace of the Holy Spirit, who

10. Michael Wilcock, *The Message of Luke,* The Bible Speaks Today (Downers Grove, IL: Inter-Varsity, 1979), 128.
11. Ryle, *Luke,* 2:26.

alone can replace our lust with purity, our worry with trust, our greed with contentment, our anger with patience, our profanity with peace, and our addictions with selfless zeal for the glory of God.

There can be no vacancy in the heart, and no joint tenancy. It is either Jesus *or* the devil. When Abraham Lincoln gave his famous "house divided" speech, he said, "I do not expect the Union to be *dissolved*—I do not expect the house to *fall*—but I *do* expect it will cease to be divided. It will become *all* one thing or *all* the other." The same may be said of every human soul. However conflicted we may sometimes feel, we must and we will become all one thing or all the other. If that is the case, then, will you be all for Jesus?

48

A SIGN FOR ALL TIMES

Luke 11:27–36

> *"This generation is an evil generation. It seeks for a sign, but no sign will be given to it except the sign of Jonah. For as Jonah became a sign to the people of Nineveh, so will the Son of Man be to this generation."* (Luke 11:29–30)

The academic world was amazed to learn that Antony Flew had decided to believe in God. For more than fifty years the erudite British philosopher had been an outspoken critic of Christianity. Flew was one of the most famous atheists in the world, and as an atheist, he believed that "the onus of proof is on the theists since atheism is *prima facie* the more reasonable position."[1] Thus he would believe in God only if God provided more evidence.

Then Antony Flew changed his mind. To the amazement of his fellow philosophers, he announced just before Christmas that, come to think of it, there *was* enough evidence for the existence of God. Speaking in *Philosophia Christi*, the journal of the Evangelical Philosophical Society, Flew said,

---

1. Antony Flew, *A Dictionary of Philosophy* (New York: St. Martin's, 1979), 28.

"It seems to me that the case for a God who has the characteristics of power and also intelligence is now much stronger than it ever was before."[2]

Flew's abandonment of atheism was welcome news. He only became a theist, however, not a Christian. Although Flew said that he was open to the possibility of divine revelation, he also said that he did not believe in the God of the Bible, or the gospel of Jesus Christ. Presumably he was still looking for a little more evidence.

There were people like that in the Gospel of Luke—people who believed in God but were still making up their minds about Jesus. Some people had chosen to follow him, becoming his disciples. Others had decided to reject him, claiming that he was of the devil. But still others were looking for more evidence. Even when they saw Jesus perform miracles, they "kept seeking from him a sign from heaven" (Luke 11:16). Their faith was postponed by their doubts. Before they believed in Jesus, they wanted indisputable evidence that he was the Son of God. What sign would he show them?

Who Is Truly Blessed?

Before we see the answer, we need to hear how Jesus responded to a woman who wanted to praise him. Jesus had just cast out a demon, and some people were claiming that he had performed this miracle by the power of Satan, while others were demanding a clearer sign from heaven. Jesus responded that he was serving God, not the devil, and he warned people that if they were not with him, they were against him.

One woman was there taking it all in. As she listened to Jesus, she was overcome with admiration. She said to herself, "I wish I had a son like that; his mother must be very proud!" Suddenly she spoke out loud, raising her voice and saying, "Blessed is the womb that bore you, and the breasts at which you nursed!" (Luke 11:27). Spoken like a true mother! This woman was praising Jesus by blessing the mother who raised him, perhaps reflecting the ancient idea that a woman may find her own greatness by bearing a famous son. But Jesus quickly answered, "Blessed rather are those who hear the word of God and keep it!" (Luke 11:28).

2. Antony Flew, *Philosophia Christi*, as quoted by David Roach in "Famed atheist sees evidence for God, cites recent discoveries," *BPNews*, Dec. 13, 2004.

By saying this, Jesus was not so much contradicting the woman as he was correcting her with a comparison. What she said was true, as far as it went. The mother of Jesus *was* blessed. Mary said so herself back in chapter 1, when she first heard that she would give birth to a son: "from now on all generations will call me blessed" (Luke 1:48). The woman in Luke 11 was one of the first people to make that call, yet she was in danger of missing the message. As blessed as it was for Mary to nurse Jesus at her breast, it is even more blessed to hear and to do the word of God. This blessing is available to all men and women, whether they are related to someone famous or not.

Mary herself is a good example. Some people have tried to honor Mary in their worship. This is the practice of the Roman Catholic Church, which teaches that Mary has an eternal motherhood, that she does saving work in bringing people to God, and that adoring her is intrinsic to Christian worship.[3] Adoring Mary in this way is a mistake, because only God deserves our worship. But like any other godly woman, Mary may be imitated. Jesus said, "Blessed are those who hear the word of God and keep it" (Luke 11:28), which is exactly what Mary did. When God called her to be the mother of the Messiah, she believed what God promised, and then acted on her faith.

It is not Mary's person that calls for blessing, therefore, but her trust in Christ and her obedience to the word of God. Rather than becoming an object of our praise, Mary serves as an example to our faith. In the end, her most important relationship to Jesus was not as a mother to her son, but as a sinner to her Savior, and a disciple to her Lord. As Augustine said in his treatise on *Holy Virginity*, "Mary was more blessed in accepting the faith of Christ than in conceiving the flesh of Christ."[4] This blessing is available to everyone who trusts in Jesus Christ. We do not have to be members of his biological family to have his blessing. We only need to listen to what he says. The people God blesses are the people who hear his word, and then do it.

3. See *Catechism of the Catholic Church*, 2d ed. (Washington, D.C.: United States Catholic Conference, 1997), 252–53.

4. Augustine, "Holy Virginity," in *Luke*, ed. Arthur A. Just Jr., Ancient Christian Commentary on Scripture, NT 3 (Downers Grove, IL: InterVarsity, 2003), 195. Similarly, J. C. Ryle wrote: "It was a greater honor to the Virgin Mary herself to have Christ dwelling in her heart by faith, than to have been the mother of Christ, and to have nursed Him on her bosom" (*Expository Thoughts on the Gospels, Luke* [1858; reprint Cambridge: James Clarke, 1976], 2:31).

THE SIGN OF JONAH

The trouble is that some people want something more from God. Not content with a word to hear and believe, they demand another sign to see and prove. This attitude was common in the time of Christ, but Jesus did not give in to its demand: "When the crowds were increasing, he began to say, 'This generation is an evil generation. It seeks for a sign, but no sign will be given to it except the sign of Jonah'" (Luke 11:29).

In one sense, Jesus had given many signs of his true identity as the Son of God and the Savior of the world (e.g., Luke 5:17–26; 9:37–43). Every miracle he performed, including the demon he had just cast out, was a sign of the kingdom of God. People did not need any more signs; they needed to believe the signs they had already been given. If they did not believe those signs, then what sign *would* they believe? "The fact is," writes David Gooding, "that the people who demanded another sign would not have been convinced by it or by any number of signs. Their seeking of a sign was not an indication of their willingness to believe if only adequate evidence were provided, but a rationalizing of their unwillingness to believe the perfectly adequate evidence they already had."[5] This is a warning to anyone who says, "I will believe in Jesus as soon as God gives me a sign." God has not promised to give us a sign. Rather than looking for one, therefore, we ought to believe the word that he has spoken.

There is one exception, however. Jesus told the crowds that he would give them one last sign of his salvation, what he called "the sign of Jonah" (Luke 11:29):

> For as Jonah became a sign to the people of Nineveh, so will the Son of Man be to this generation. The queen of the South will rise up at the judgment with the men of this generation and condemn them, for she came from the ends of the earth to hear the wisdom of Solomon, and behold, something greater than Solomon is here. The men of Nineveh will rise up at the judgment with this generation and condemn it, for they repented at the preaching of Jonah, and behold, something greater than Jonah is here. (Luke 11:30–32)

5. David Gooding, *According to Luke: A New Exposition of the Third Gospel* (Grand Rapids: Eerdmans, 1987), 227.

To understand what Jesus was saying about Jonah and Nineveh—not to mention Solomon and the queen of the South—we need to know the Old Testament. Jonah was the prophet whom God called to go and preach to the pagans in Nineveh. In sinful rebellion Jonah bought himself a one-way ticket to sail in the opposite direction, but God sent a great fish to swallow him alive. After three days under water, the prophet repented and the fish vomited him back up. This time Jonah did go to Nineveh, where he warned people that judgment was imminent, and then watched them repent of their sins.

As Jesus looked at Jonah's ministry, he saw a connection with his own saving work. Just as Jonah was a sign to the Ninevites, so Jesus would be a sign to his generation. But what, exactly, was the connection? Was it his ministry as a prophet? His preaching of judgment? His call to repentance? These things may be part of it, but there is something more. A sign is something miraculous, and strictly speaking, there was nothing miraculous about Jesus' preaching. Furthermore, when Jesus spoke about this sign, he clearly referred to something that would happen in the future, and not just to his present ministry as a preacher. So what was the sign?

Luke does not mention it explicitly, but there *was* a miracle in Jonah's ministry: a miracle that signified the resurrection. We know this because in the Gospel of Matthew, after Jesus speaks about "the sign of the prophet Jonah," he goes on to say this: "For just as Jonah was three days and three nights in the belly of the great fish, so will the Son of Man be three days and three nights in the heart of the earth" (Matt. 12:40). Jesus was referring to his own death, burial, and resurrection from the dead. In the same way that Jonah was entombed in the belly of the sea, so Jesus would be buried for three days before rising again. The sign of Jonah is the death and resurrection of Jesus Christ.

God has given us the same sign. What has God done to point us to the truth of his gospel? How do we know that Jesus lived a perfect life on our behalf? How do we know for sure that God has accepted Christ's sacrifice for our sins? How do we know that Jesus has the power of eternal life? How do we know that we will live forever? The answer, in each case, is that God has raised Jesus Christ from the dead. Even Antony Flew seems to admit that the resurrection is a sign for all times. "The evidence for the resurrection is better than for claimed miracles in any other religion," he says. "It's

611

outstandingly different in quality and quantity, I think, from the evidence offered for the occurrence of most other supposedly miraculous events."[6]

To put all of this in another way, the sign that God has given us is the gospel. The gospel is simply the good news of salvation through the crucifixion and the resurrection of Jesus Christ. And this is the sign that God has given to all generations: the death of Jesus on the cross *and* his return from the empty tomb. The sign is Jesus himself, dying and rising again. Is this the kind of sign that gives incontrovertible proof to the demanding skeptic? No, but it is a sign nonetheless, a true sign that points to God's salvation in Jesus Christ. If we believe this sign, we will be saved.

The African Queen

Everyone who believes that Jesus died and rose again will inherit eternal life. But we must believe! Jesus used two examples from the Old Testament to prove this. One is the example of Jonah, to which we shall return momentarily; the other is the story of Solomon and the queen of Sheba.

King Solomon was and still is world-renowned for his extravagant wealth and extraordinary wisdom. An African queen had heard about this famous king, and she wanted to see for herself. So she traveled from Africa to Israel with a caravan of treasure. There she tested the king's wisdom, toured the treasuries in the king's palace, and worshiped in the temple that he built for God. What she saw and heard took her breath away. She said to King Solomon: "I did not believe the reports until I came and my own eyes had seen it. And behold, the half was not told me. Your wisdom and prosperity surpass the report that I heard. . . . Blessed be the Lord your God, who has delighted in you and set you on the throne of Israel!" (1 Kings 10:7, 9).

Here was a woman who desperately wanted to know the truth. She went to great trouble and expense to find out if what she had heard was really true. Luke tells us, "she came from the ends of the earth to hear the wisdom of Solomon" (Luke 11:31). And because she was seeking the truth sincerely, she found what she was looking for.

What a contrast to people in the time of Christ! They were in the presence of someone even greater than golden King Solomon: Jesus Christ, who

---

6. Flew, quoted in Roach, "Famed atheist."

is wisdom incarnate and who reigns as the King of all kings. As great as Solomon was in wealth and wisdom, Jesus is infinitely greater—and in all humility, he did not hesitate to say this. His kingdom spans the globe, his riches are the splendors of the universe, and "in [him] are hidden all the treasures of wisdom and knowledge" (Col. 2:3). As Alexander Maclaren once said, Jesus Christ is the "the perfect encyclopaedia of all moral and spiritual truth."[7] Yet the men of his day would not even take the trouble to know him as their Savior and Lord. Jesus was present with them in Israel; they did not have to travel anywhere else to find him. They had every opportunity to know Jesus as the Christ—all they had to do was to believe. Yet instead of believing, they demanded another sign.

At the last tribunal, the queen of Sheba will stand up and judge these men for their unbelief. As Jesus said, she "will rise up at the judgment with the men of this generation and condemn them" (Luke 11:31). And rightly so, because that woman—that Gentile!—went much farther than they did to meet a lesser king.

What will the queen of Sheba say about us? We too have been given every opportunity to know the wisdom of God incarnate. We have read his Word and heard his gospel. But have we taken the trouble to study these things and know them for sure? Are we willing to seek after Jesus until we find our salvation in him?

If we do not believe in Jesus, then the queen of Sheba will not be the only witness against us. The other example Jesus took from the Old Testament was the prophet Jonah. It was not simply Jonah's three days in the belly of the sea that interested Jesus, but also the way that the people of Nineveh responded to his ministry. They believed in the gospel of the risen prophet. When he warned them about the coming judgment, they believed his message, repented of their sins, and were saved.

Jesus longed to say the same thing about the people of his own generation. When they witnessed his death and resurrection—the gospel sign of Jonah—he wanted them to trust in him for their salvation. After all, those pagans back in Nineveh listened to a man who came back from the sea. What would God's own people Israel do when they saw a man come back from the very dead? One might expect them to listen to his word, but

7. Alexander Maclaren, *The Epistles of St. Paul to the Colossians and Philemon*, The Exposition Bible (New York: A. C. Armstrong, 1903), 166.

Jesus was far from hopeful. He said, "The men of Nineveh will rise up at the judgment with this generation and condemn it, for they repented at the preaching of Jonah, and behold, something greater than Jonah is here" (Luke 11:32).

The people who heard Jesus say this were given every opportunity to believe. They were in the presence of a greater prophet than Jonah, a greater king than Solomon. They heard him preach and they saw him die and rise again, but many of them still did not believe. Thus at the final judgment the men of Nineveh will condemn them for their unbelief.

What will the Ninevites say about us? God has spoken to us more clearly than he ever did to them. All they heard was a message of judgment, spoken by an almost complete failure of a prophet. We have heard a message of grace, spoken by the very Son of God. The only sign they were given was a man swallowed by a big fish and then brought back up. We have been given the sign of a man swallowed by death itself, and then rising again in triumph. Do you believe this gospel sign?

At the final judgment we will be held responsible for what we have done—or failed to do—with Jesus. If we have heard the good news of the crucified and risen Christ, then God will hold us accountable to repent like the Ninevites and believe like the queen of Sheba. If we receive Jesus, then we will still be standing on the day of judgment. But if we reject Jesus, God will reject us forever.

THE LAMP OF THE BODY

In our unbelief, we generally assume that the problem lies somewhere outside of us. "Yes, I am willing to believe in God," people say, "if only he will show me a sign." But the examples that Jesus gave prove that this is not the real problem. The sign is there; the problem is that we do not believe it. This is also the point of the rather intricate illustration that Jesus gave at the end of this conversation. He said:

> No one after lighting a lamp puts it in a cellar or under a basket, but on a stand, so that those who enter may see the light. Your eye is the lamp of your body. When your eye is healthy, your whole body is full of light, but when it is bad, your body is full of darkness. Therefore be careful lest the light in

you be darkness. If then your whole body is full of light, having no part dark, it will be wholly bright, as when a lamp with its rays gives you light. (Luke 11:33–36)

Elsewhere Jesus uses light as an illustration of the believer's witness to the world; we are called to shine for Jesus. But that is not how he uses the image here. In this context the light refers to Jesus himself. He is not hiding somewhere in the shadows; the candle of his gospel is not hidden underground. On the contrary, Jesus has done his saving work on the open stage of human history, where everyone can see it. All his words and all his works are radiant with the revelation of God's glory. To this day his gospel is publicly proclaimed all over the world. Like the lamp blazing from a lighthouse, it shines for all to see. Cyril of Alexandria said, "The Father gave us the Son to be a lamp to the world, to illumine us with divine light and to rescue us from satanic darkness."[8] Or as Jesus himself said, he came "so that those who enter may see the light" (Luke 11:33).

If we fail to see Jesus, therefore, it is not because he does not wish to be seen. There are enough lumens in his lantern. The problem rather is that our eyes are too dim to see his glorious grace. Here Jesus describes the eye as the lamp of the body. In other words, the eye is the organ that gathers light and brings illumination to the rest of the body, much the way a lamp illuminates a room. A clear eye sees the light, but a bad eye keeps the body in darkness:

When the eye is sound and right and light is shining, the eye enables you to make full use of the light—you can see where you are, how to walk and how to do your work. But when there is something wrong with your eye you cannot make use of the light even when you are irradiated by the brightest light. Your whole body is then, as it were, wrapped in darkness, for you cannot see where to put your feet in order to walk, where to take hold with your hands to perform your work, and so forth. So, for all practical purposes, when your eyes are "wrong" you are in utter darkness.[9]

8. Cyril of Alexandria, "Commentary on Luke," in *Luke*, ed. Arthur A. Just Jr., Ancient Christian Commentary on Scripture, NT 3 (Downers Grove, IL: InterVarsity, 2003), 196.

9. Norval Geldenhuys, *The Gospel of Luke*, New International Commentary on the New Testament (Grand Rapids: Eerdmans, 1951), 337–38.

The same thing is true spiritually. This optical illustration is about spiritual perception. When the eyes of the soul are clear, we are able to see the light of Jesus Christ shining in the gospel. We perceive that he really is the Son of God and the Savior of the world. We see the cross and the empty tomb—the signs for all times. We believe that Jesus died for our sins on the cross and rose again to give us eternal life. The love of Christ shines brightly in our hearts, and we start walking in the light of his love. But when our spiritual eyes are bad—when they are covered with the cataract of unrepentant sin or blinded by the skeptical demand for more and more evidence—then we cannot see Jesus as our Savior. The problem is *not* that we do not have enough light, as if God needed to give us a more brilliant sign. No, God has given us enough light in his gospel. The problem is that we cannot see it because our hearts are still in darkness.

This is what was wrong with the people who demanded that Jesus give them a sign. Jesus was shining on them with a bright, clear light, but they could not see it. To shift the blame, they said that *he* was the problem, when in fact the problem all along was their own inward darkness. By using this analogy, Jesus was trying to get them to see that their spiritual vision was obscured by dark clouds of unbelief. The reason they "still live in darkness and do not see and accept Him as the Messiah is not to be attributed to a concealment of the light of His revelation of salvation, but is to be imputed to the wickedness of their own hearts."[10]

So Jesus gave them this warning: "be careful lest the light in you be darkness" (Luke 11:35). This warning is for religious people who know something about Jesus but have not yet received him as their Savior and their God. Often they are worshiping somewhere in a church. They think that they have seen the light. But is it the light of the gospel? Do they believe the Word of God? Are they trusting the crucified and risen Savior? If not, then even the eye that they were given to see spiritual truth is keeping out the light of salvation. What a tragic condition!

> If there is darkness in our spiritual life, this is never the fault of the light of the Gospel—for this light shines in full glory and power. It is man's wrong inner nature—unbelief, worldly-mindedness and other sins—that prevents the light of Christ from irradiating and renewing his life. What a tragedy that

10. Geldenhuys, *Luke,* 337.

so many are struggling in darkness while the Gospel light is there all the time to make everything in their life bright and beautiful! As soon as man opens his life to Christ in faith His glorious light streams in.[11]

When I think of what it must be like to struggle with this kind of spiritual darkness, I cannot help but think of my own brother-in-law, an airplane pilot who lost his sight to bacterial meningitis. His eyes are sound, yet the damage to his optic nerve has left him blind. He cannot see. Though sad, this situation is not hopeless, because my brother-in-law will see again at the resurrection. But what about people who are still walking in spiritual darkness, who have not yet escaped the blindness of their sin? What hope is there for them?

What we need is not some other sign, but the spiritual ability to see the sign that God has already given: Jesus Christ, crucified for sinners and raised again with the power of life. We can see Jesus by asking for the Holy Spirit to come and open our eyes. Jesus has promised that God will give the gift of his Spirit to anyone who asks. The Spirit's work is to reveal the light of Jesus Christ to the eyes of our faith, so that we may see the glory of God. "If then your whole body is full of light," Jesus said, referring to this ministry of the Spirit, "having no part dark, it will be wholly bright, as when a lamp with its rays gives you light" (Luke 11:36).

This is God's glorious promise: when the Spirit opens our eyes to see the full brightness of his salvation, the light of Jesus will illuminate all the dark corners of our lives, until the dawn breaks on the eternal day, the dark shadows are chased away, and all is light.

11. Geldenhuys, *Luke*, 339.

49

WHEN YOUR SOUL IS AN
UNMARKED GRAVE

Hypocrisy

Luke 11:37–44

> *"Woe to you Pharisees! For you love the best seat in the synagogues
> and greetings in the marketplaces. Woe to you! For you are like
> unmarked graves, and people walk over them without knowing it."*
> (Luke 11:43–44)

hat is the biggest danger the church faces in the twenty-first century? Is it secular hostility to biblical truth? The spread of Islam and other false religions? The doctrinal errors of postevangelical theology? These are all serious dangers, but judging from what Jesus said in the Gospels, the gravest danger may come from theologically informed, religiously active, morally conservative people whose hearts are far from God. Nothing is deadlier to the life of true godliness than spiritual hypocrisy.

TABLE TALK

Hypocrisy is the theme of important remarks that Jesus once made over dinner. People had been demanding a sign from him, but in response, Jesus said that *he* was the only sign they would get, as he died on the cross and rose again. What people really needed was not some other sign, but faith to believe what God said in his Word and in the person of his Son. Jesus was giving people plenty of light in the gospel, but the blindness of their sin was keeping them in the dark.

During this conversation Jesus received a dinner invitation: "While Jesus was speaking, a Pharisee asked him to dine with him, so he went in and reclined at table" (Luke 11:37). This was a familiar position for Jesus. We often find him sitting down to break bread with people and confront them with the claims of his gospel. This is a good example for us to follow. We should be sociable with all kinds of people, taking advantage of every opportunity to build relationships, including with people who do not know Christ. But we must always be sure to point them to God. All too often Christians accept this kind of dinner invitation without using it to full spiritual advantage.

On this particular occasion, Jesus was eating at the table of a Pharisee who wanted to hear more of what he had to say. The Pharisees enjoyed an excellent reputation in those days. If anyone tried to lead a life that was pleasing to God, it was the Pharisees. They were morally straight, keeping God's law. They were theologically conservative, defending the faith. In fact, they were generally considered to be the holiest people in Israel, with the most obvious concern for personal godliness.

One would have thought, therefore, that the Pharisees were just the kind of people Jesus would enjoy. Yet even before anyone took the first bite, Jesus offended his host, maybe intentionally. As Luke tells it, "The Pharisee was astonished to see that he did not first wash before dinner" (Luke 11:38). The man was shocked—shocked!—that Jesus would eat without washing his hands.

To understand why this was considered socially unacceptable, it helps to know that the Pharisees really did believe that cleanliness was next to godliness. The issue for them was not personal hygiene, but ceremonial purity. So before they had anything to eat, they "had water poured over their hands to remove the defilement contracted by their contact with a sinful world."[1]

1. Leon Morris, *The Gospel According to St. Luke: An Introduction and Commentary*, Tyndale New Testament Commentaries (Grand Rapids: Eerdmans, 1974), 203.

Some Pharisees carried this concern to an obsessive extreme, going through an elaborate cleansing ritual before meals and on other occasions. The following passage from the Mishnah gives a good idea what people like the Pharisees meant when they said, "Go wash your hands before dinner":

> The hands are susceptible to uncleanness, and they are rendered clean up to the wrist. Thus if a man had poured the first water up to the wrist and the second water beyond the wrist, and the water flowed back to the hand, the hand becomes clean; but if he poured both the first water and the second beyond the wrist, and the water flowed back to the hand, the hand remains unclean. If he poured the first water over the one hand alone and then bethought himself and poured the second water over the one hand, his one hand is clean. If he had poured the water over the one hand and rubbed it on the other, it becomes unclean; but if he rubbed it on his head or on the wall it remains clean.[2]

Shock

Given such specific regulations, we can well imagine what the Pharisee thought when Jesus did not wash his hands at all. He had the same reaction the mother of the bride would have if her daughter walked down the aisle wearing shorts and flip-flops, or the queen of England would have if a grubby mechanic laid a hand on her royal person. It simply wasn't done— not at the house of a Pharisee.

It is important to understand that there was nothing morally wrong with what Jesus did. The only thing Jesus violated was a man-made rule for religiously acceptable conduct. The Pharisees had a thousand and one of these extrabiblical rules, which they believed God had given to Moses on Mount Sinai, and were subsequently handed down by oral tradition. They further believed that breaking any one of them was a serious breach of holiness. This is why Jesus caused offense. But the law of God said nothing about washing up before dinner. It was a matter of spiritual indifference, and knowing this is crucial for everything that follows. The Pharisee had his own ideas about right and wrong, but they went well beyond the Word of God.

As Christians we need to learn to tell the difference between the law of God and our own personal preferences. We may have all kinds of opin-

---

2. *Yadayim* 2.3, as quoted in R. Kent Hughes, *Luke: That You May Know the Truth*, 2 vols., Preaching the Word (Wheaton, IL: Crossway, 1998), 2:22.

ions about things like what people ought to wear, what they should eat, how they should run their household, how they should spend their money, what priorities they should have in ministry, or what political position they ought to take. Some of these opinions may be strongly held. We may even believe that there are good spiritual reasons for our opinions. The Pharisee certainly had spiritual reasons for thinking that Jesus should wash his hands. But are we properly distinguishing between the commands of God and our own code of conduct? When we get offended, we need to make sure it is only for things that God himself truly finds offensive, instead of just pontificating on the basis of our own opinions.

The Heart of Hypocrisy

Taking offense is not necessarily a sign of holiness. Often it is a sign of immaturity, even hypocrisy. That was clearly the case here. We know this because as Jesus proceeded to reveal what was in the Pharisee's heart, he exposed the sin of self-righteousness. Perhaps the Holy Spirit will use what Jesus said to expose the same sinful spirit in us, bringing us to repentance. Self-examination promotes spiritual health by extracting the poison of a hypocritical heart. J. C. Ryle said:

> Let me counsel every true servant of Christ to examine his own heart frequently and carefully before God. This is a practice, which is useful at all times; it is especially desirable at this present day. When the great plague of London was at its height, people took note of the smallest symptoms that appeared on their bodies in a way that they never noticed them before. A spot here, a spot there, which in time of health, men thought nothing of, received close attention when the plague was decimating families and striking down one after another! We ought to watch our hearts with double watchfulness. We ought to give more time to meditation, self-examination and reflection. It is a hurrying, bustling age; if we would keep from falling, we must take time for being frequently alone with God.[3]

Jesus made four specific criticisms that can help us spot the first symptoms of our own self-righteousness. When am I a hypocrite? *I am a hypocrite*

3. J. C. Ryle, *Churches Beware!* (Darlington, UK: Evangelical Press, 1998), 76–77.

when I am more concerned with outward appearances than inward godliness.
Jesus said to his host, "Now you Pharisees cleanse the outside of the cup and
of the dish, but inside you are full of greed and wickedness" (Luke 11:39).

Here Jesus drew a comparison between the Pharisee's mealtime ritual
and his true spiritual condition. When a Pharisee sat down to eat, he carefully observed the formality of wiping his cup and dish. But imagine how
disgusting it would be if somebody cleaned only the outside without ever
cleaning the inside. Usually I keep a drinking cup near the desk where
I write. Sometimes I forget to empty it out when I travel, and upon my
return, things are growing in it. Needless to say, whenever this happens I
wash the inside of my cup as well as the outside!

This analogy applies to the spiritual life. Some people think it is enough
to act good on the outside, no matter what they are like on the inside. The
Pharisees were like that. For them the really important thing was their
observable conduct—the part of their spiritual lives that other people
could see. So they maintained strict outward conformity to their rules for
godly conduct. They went to public worship. They made a big show of saying their prayers. They let other people know about their charitable giving.
By performing these external rituals, they were cleaning the outside of their
cup and dish.

What were they really like on the inside? Jesus said they were filthy! Like
the scum inside a cup of foul liquid, they were full of greed and wickedness. They thought they were holy, and other people thought so too. But
they were really like the people Isaiah prophesied about: "This people draw
near with their mouth and honor me with their lips, while their hearts are
far from me" (Isa. 29:13). The Pharisees were only keeping up religious
appearances: "Their scrupulous ritual cleansing of cups and plates from
ceremonial defilement allowed them to feel they had attained to a high
degree of holiness, when all the while they were doing little or nothing
about the vastly more serious greed and wickedness which was filling their
inner selves with real moral uncleanliness."[4] These men may have had clean
hands, but they had unclean hearts.

This was foolish, and Jesus said so: "You fools! Did not he who made the
outside make the inside also?" (Luke 11:40). In other words, the inside is

4. David Gooding, *According to Luke: A New Exposition of the Third Gospel* (Grand Rapids: Eerdmans, 1987), 231–32.

as important to God as the outside. The soul is as important as the body, because God made them both. So God is at least as concerned about what is inside as he is with the outside. Who we are matters more than what we do. As God said to the prophet Samuel, "Man looks on the outward appearance, but the LORD looks on the heart" (1 Sam. 16:7).

What is inside of you? Are you as good on the inside as you want people to think you are on the outside? If not, how big is the gap between your outside Christianity and your inside hypocrisy? Maybe you speak courteously to people, while inside you are thinking unkind thoughts. Maybe you never use bad language (or almost never), but your inner dialogue is laced with profanity. Maybe you resist having sex outside of marriage, but secretly feed on a forbidden lust. Maybe you spend more time talking about prayer requests than actually praying. Maybe you say you trust what God is doing, while inside you are full of angry resentment. Or maybe you are hiding some other sin that you know could be your downfall. But whatever secret sin lurks inside, understand that outward obedience without inward godliness is the heart of hypocrisy.

WOE TO HYPOCRISY

When else am I a hypocrite? *I am a hypocrite when I am more concerned about my own little rules than about the big things that matter more to God.* Jesus said, "But woe to you Pharisees! For you tithe mint and rue and every herb, and neglect justice and the love of God" (Luke 11:42). When Jesus pronounced this woe on the Pharisees—the first of three woes—he was not making a threat, but expressing his regret. "Woe" means "Alas!" Here it is a word of sadness for the sorry condition of the Pharisees, who were majoring on the minors, while completely omitting the really important things.

If anything interested the Pharisees more than hand-washing it was tithing. Tithing was something God commanded. According to the Old Testament law (e.g., Num. 18:21–24), members of the covenant community were to give one tenth of their gross income to support the worship and work of God's house. But the Pharisees took this commandment to an excessive extreme by carefully cutting an exact tenth from their smallest herbs. This was a distinguishing characteristic of their community. Instead of making a rough overestimate in their giving to God, they calculated their offerings down to the last decimal point.

Somewhere in all of their obsessive arithmetic, the Pharisees had lost the joy of giving generously to God. There was an even deeper problem, however. Not only were they unnecessarily precise in one small area of the law, but at the same time they were completely missing more fundamental areas of obedience. They did not love God, and they did not love their neighbors by doing justice. As J. C. Ryle explains it, "They were scrupulous to an extreme about small matters in the ceremonial law;—and yet they were utterly regardless of the simplest first principles of justice to man and love toward God."[5] The Pharisees were not defending the weak, protecting the poor, welcoming strangers, helping widows, adopting orphans, or doing any of the other things that the Bible calls justice (e.g., Isa. 1:17). While they were busy keeping one little rule, they were breaking the basic commandments of God.

This is the heart of hypocrisy: keeping the letter of the law in one or two minor areas of obedience, while at the same time neglecting the big things that matter more to God. Do not make the same mistake the Pharisees made by getting things out of proportion. Are you giving God at least 10 percent of what you own? I hope so, because by grace we should give at least as much as God's people gave under the law. But doing justice is more important. What we do with our money is one test of our godliness, but an even better test is how we treat people in need. Who is the weak person that you are protecting, the poor person that you are helping, the stranger that you are welcoming, and the child that you are receiving into the family of God? To open your wallet without opening your heart is hypocrisy.

Confusing the little things with the big things was not the only reason that Jesus pronounced woe on the Pharisees. He also said, "Woe to you Pharisees! For you love the best seat in the synagogues and greetings in the marketplaces" (Luke 11:43).

The Pharisees were always jockeying for a better position. The men with the best reputation—the men who kept their hands pristine and their tithes precise—were given priority seating at the local synagogue. The better a man's reputation, the closer he sat to the front, and a few privileged men

5. J. C. Ryle, *Expository Thoughts on the Gospels, Luke* (1858; reprint Cambridge: James Clarke, 1976), 2:45.

even sat facing the congregation. Christians followed a similar practice in many colonial churches, like Boston's famous Old North Church, where the box pews near the front were reserved for the most prominent men in the city. The Pharisees would have loved this kind of seating arrangement. They also loved to be greeted with special respect in the city streets. The more elaborate the greeting, the better. For them it was not enough to be greeted as a friend, but as a gentleman and a scholar, an elder and philanthropist, a doctor of sacred theology, a protector of piety, a defender of righteousness, and so on.

This was all part of their hypocrisy. As we have seen, the Pharisees were more concerned about outward appearances than about inward godliness. So to them it was desperately important to get the recognition they thought they deserved. This was their motivation, and it helps us to see another sign of our own hypocrisy: *I am a hypocrite when I crave for people to recognize my spiritual accomplishments.*

We live in a competitive culture, in which people are always comparing themselves to others. Who has the latest style? Who got the highest grade? Who made the biggest financial contribution? Who won the best promotion? Sadly, we bring the same attitude into the church. We want people to notice what we are doing for the Lord. Even if we say we do not care for recognition, secretly we glory in people's praise. If we are making progress in some spiritual discipline, we want people to know about it. We gain a sense of self-importance from our ministry, especially in comparison to others. Sometimes even the difficulties we acknowledge when we ask for prayer are a way to gain sympathy for all the hard work we are doing for God.

Then when people fail to give us the attention we think we deserve, we grow resentful. We say, "Nobody even notices what I am doing!" "I am just as gifted as so-and-so, so I should have the same place of ministry." "I'm not sure it is worth doing this any more; here I am doing all this work, and I never get any credit."

Jesus shows us a different way to live. He teaches us to be faithful in service, to take the lowest place, to give other people credit, to make our sacrifices in secret, to wait patiently for him to put us in the position where we belong, and to care nothing for other people's opinions. Jesus teaches us to live this way because it is the way that he lived, all the way to the cross. But sometimes we are more like the Pharisees, wanting people to recognize our accomplishments. This is the heart of hypocrisy. We cannot seek God's glory and our own glory at the same time.

Deadly Hypocrisy

The last woe is the most distressing: "Woe to you! For you are like unmarked graves, and people walk over them without knowing it" (Luke 11:44). This too is hypocrisy: *I am a hypocrite when I am spiritually dead inside, and no one knows, maybe not even myself.*

When I was in junior high school I traveled to England with a group of students from Wheaton College. We spent a day and a night near Salisbury Cathedral. That evening some of us wandered onto the cathedral grounds and started to play Frisbee. Soon a couple of local residents walked over and told us off in proper English fashion. We were playing in a graveyard, they said, and we needed to cease and desist. As we looked around we saw that there were indeed some old flat gravestones, although they were so covered with grass that we had hardly noticed.

If we had been Israelites, touching an unmarked grave like this would have rendered us ceremonially impure for one full week. According to the regulations in the book of Numbers, anyone who touched a grave was unclean for seven days (see Num. 19:16).

Because of these regulations, the Israelites were usually very careful to whitewash their graves so that people would notice them and avoid them. But Jesus said the Pharisees were like *un*marked graves. This was a condemning comparison. They were not just unclean inside, like a dirty cup, but also dead inside, like a box of rotten remains. The Scottish theologian Thomas Boston had personal experience with this when he was a young boy. His schoolhouse was in a churchyard, where he inadvertently stumbled across an open grave: "I was providentially made to see there, within an open coffin, in an unripe grave opened, the consuming body just brought to the consistence of thin mortar, and blackish; the which made an impression on me, remaining to this day . . . not to be beheld with the eye but with horror."[6]

What Boston saw in that horrible grave is a stark image of spiritual death. This is what our hearts are like when we are living for God only on

---

6. Thomas Boston, *Memoirs*, in *The Complete Works of the Late Rev. Thomas Boston of Ettrick*, ed. Samuel M'Millan, 12 vols. (London, 1853; reprint Wheaton, IL: Richard Owen Roberts, 1980), 12:14.

the outside. We may not even know it, but we are dead inside. Other people may not know it either. The week I am writing this, a prominent evangelical leader found out that one of his most trusted colleagues was involved in an adulterous relationship that had been going on for many years. The man's wife had to redefine her husband, his children had to redefine their father, and his church had to redefine their pastor. For years his heart was dead in its hypocrisy, like an unmarked grave, and nobody even knew it.

That is not the worst of it, however. By using this image of the unmarked grave, Jesus was also saying that the Pharisees had a corrupting influence on anyone who came into contact with them. Because they had a reputation for strict holiness, people followed their spiritual example. Yet rather than leading to holiness, this would bring them into contact with something deadly. Soon they would be guilty of the same sins the Pharisees were committing. How ironic! The very men who were trying to keep things spiritually clean were in fact sources of spiritual defilement. The hypocrisy of the Pharisees was deadly to other people's souls.

Can you see how deadly your own hypocrisy is? Trying to be one thing on the outside when you are another thing on the inside; focusing on the little things but missing the big things; craving more recognition—these things are spiritually deadly, not just to you, but also to others. Even if nobody knows it, the corpse inside is corrupting your family, your friends, and your church. "All of us inevitably communicate what we are," writes Kent Hughes. "We can externally do all the right religious things, . . . but we will ultimately impart what is within. The people around us will see the artificiality, the affectedness, the elitism, the anger, the hostility, the hatred, the suspicion, the sourness, the inner blasphemies. We leave our fingerprints on each other's souls, for Christ or for unbelief."[7]

INSIDE OUT

How sad Jesus was to see the contagious corruption of the Pharisees, as he must be sad to see our own hypocrisy. Their woeful pride in their spiritual accomplishments and their woeful lack of concern for what really mattered to God had a woeful effect on the people around them. What makes

7. Hughes, *Luke*, 2:27.

627

this so sad is that the Pharisees wanted to do the right thing. Yet despite all of their good intentions, they were the most spiritually dangerous people in Israel. Woe to them, and woe to us, who are like them in so many ways.

What these men needed in order to heal their hypocritical hearts—and what every hypocrite needs—is the gospel of Jesus Christ to change us from the inside out. This is the essential difference between any merely human religion and the supernatural work of God's Spirit. Even without God we can perform at least some acts of outward obedience. We can work a little harder to live a little better, and when we do, we may well be able to fool other people into thinking that we are righteous. But only God can give us a heart for godliness. This new heart comes from the saving work of Jesus Christ, on the basis of his death on the cross and resurrection from the dead. It is given by the Holy Spirit, who makes Christ to dwell in our hearts by faith, and who is even now working to change us from the inside out.

The powerful gospel of Jesus Christ working in the heart is the remedy for all our hypocrisy. The hypocrite is more concerned with outward appearances than inward godliness, but the gospel gives a new heart that expresses itself in a new life. Of course there always have to be some outward changes, but these come from the inside, where God is working in our hearts. What makes our lives clean is not an outward washing with water, as the Pharisees thought, but the inward cleansing of the Holy Spirit.

Jesus said to the Pharisees, "But give as alms those things that are within, and behold, everything is clean for you" (Luke 11:41). Since he had been talking about a cup and a dish, some have taken "those things that are within" as a reference to food and drink. Instead of washing the outside of our cups and dishes, we need to give what is inside them to the poor—namely, something to eat and drink.

That is true enough. However, here Jesus is speaking spiritually. The first thing we need to give to God is what is inside of us—our heart, soul, mind, and strength. Then everything else we offer to God will be acceptable in his sight. J. C. Ryle said, "Give first the offering of the inward man. Give your heart, your affections, and your will to God, as the first great alms which you bestow, and then all your other actions, proceeding from a right heart, are an acceptable sacrifice, and a clean offering in the sight of God. . . . Give yourselves first to the Lord, and then He will be pleased with your gifts."[8]

The hypocrite is always hoping that people will not find out what his heart is really like. But the believer knows that what is happening on the inside is far more important than what seems to be happening on the outside. So the believer prays, as John Calvin famously prayed, "I offer you my heart, Lord, promptly and sincerely."

The gospel also helps us know the difference between the big things and the little things, so we can give full attention to what matters most to God. When Jesus spoke to the Pharisees about tithing, he said, "These you ought to have done, without neglecting the others" (Luke 11:42). In other words, it is fine to keep giving an exact tithe, as long as you make sure to love God and to do justice. It is not either/or; it is both/and. You certainly should give God at least a tithe, even if you take it to a trivial extreme, as the Pharisees did. But you should love God most of all, and your neighbor as yourself. This love will never come from your own sinful heart. It can only come from the Savior who loved you enough to die for your sins. By his grace we have true love for God and for others.

The gospel also helps us see ourselves the way God sees us, so that it no longer matters very much what other people think. The hypocrite is always desperate for more recognition, but the gospel convinces us that nothing we do for God has any merit of its own. We want to see ourselves the way God sees us: as forgiven sinners, accepted in Christ. Whatever good there may be in us is only by the grace of God. We do not want people to praise us; we want them to praise him! One missionary learned this lesson in a powerful way when he went to China. He writes:

> I was with an elderly woman who had been running from the police for many years. She had distributed thousands of Bibles without state permission. As we sat together with our translator, I learned that for her family's security she could only arrange to see her husband once a year. What honor, what hope, had the world given to this grandmother? I told her I would carry her heroic story to America. She giggled politely behind

8. Ryle, *Luke*, 2:48–49.

her hand at this idea. "Oh, don't tell them about me," she declared hopefully. "Tell them about Jesus."[9]

This is what the gospel does. It gives you true spiritual life, so that you are no longer dead inside, but wonderfully, vitally alive. It delivers you from the hypocrisy of external religiosity and pretentious piety, so that you can live with a clean, pure heart for Jesus. Only this kind of heart can offer the life of Christ to anyone else.

Are you ready to receive the new heart that God offers? You can have it right now; it is yours for the asking. If you have already asked for that new heart, are you fully ready for God to make it as holy, as pure, as clean, as genuine and sincere as he wants it to be? Let us leave this passage, as J. C. Ryle wrote,

> with a settled determination to watch and pray against hypocrisy in religion. Whatever we are as Christians, let us be real, thorough, genuine, and sincere. Let us abhor all . . . affectation, and part-acting in the things of God, as that which is utterly loathsome in Christ's eyes. We may be weak, and erring, and frail, and come far short of our aims and desires. But at any rate, if we profess to believe in Christ, let us be true.[10]

Yes, let us be true. Let us truly be the people we are called to be in Christ, from the inside all the way out.

---

9. Tom White, "Jesus—Our Gift of Hope," *The Voice of the Martyrs* (Dec. 2004): 2.
10. Ryle, *Luke*, 2:47.

50

THE BLOOD OF THE PROPHETS

Luke 11:45—54

"Therefore also the Wisdom of God said, 'I will send them prophets and apostles, some of whom they will kill and perse-cute, so that the blood of all the prophets, shed from the foundation of the world, may be charged against this generation.'"
(Luke 11:49–50)

*J*esus never hesitated to offend people—especially people in spiritual leadership—provided that it might do them some spiritual good. At the end of Luke 11, we see that he did not even mind offending people in their own homes.

A Pharisee invited Jesus to dinner at his home. Jesus promptly offended the man by neglecting to wash his hands, forgoing the ritual cleansing that the Pharisees considered essential to personal godliness. Then, as if that were not bad enough, Jesus proceeded to denounce the Pharisees for being more concerned with outward appearances than inward godliness. He pronounced three woes against their deadly hypocrisy. The Pharisees had a lethal influence on the people who looked to their example, and they needed to start getting honest with God about their inner sinner.

Nevertheless, what Jesus said also happened to be personally offensive and culturally inappropriate. People must have choked on their pita bread when they heard him say it. In fact, one of the men at the table tried to give Jesus the hint that he was insulting people, himself included: "One of the lawyers answered him, 'Teacher, in saying these things you insult us also'" (Luke 11:45). The man thought that perhaps a word of caution would hinder Jesus from saying anything further. Surely he did not intend to offend a fine, upstanding, God-fearing man like himself!

If that is what the lawyer thought, he was badly mistaken. In a way, he was asking for it, because Jesus went right ahead and proceeded to offend every last lawyer in the room. Maybe what he said will offend us too, but if so, it is not because Jesus has bad etiquette, but only because he knows how badly we need to be confronted with the sinfulness of our sin.

WOE TO THE LEGALISTS

In his rebuttal to the lawyer, Jesus pronounced three more woes: woe to legalism, woe to murderous rebellion against the Word of God, and woe to false teaching that keeps people from hearing the gospel. By adding these woes to the ones he had already given the Pharisees, Jesus was showing the woeful condition of the men who were supposed to be Israel's spiritual leaders.

The first woe was against legalism: "Woe to you lawyers also! For you load people with burdens hard to bear, and you yourselves do not touch the burdens with one of your fingers" (Luke 11:46).

To understand what Jesus was saying, we first need to know who the lawyers were. They were not personal injury prosecutors who sued on behalf of their clients or defense attorneys who made closing arguments in a court of law. Rather, they were Bible scholars and theologians. For the Israelites of that day, the Old Testament was God's law for daily life. In order to help people follow that law, certain men devoted their lives to interpreting and applying the Holy Scriptures. The men who did this analysis and exegesis were the lawyers; they were teachers of the law.

What, then, was the difference between these lawyers and the Pharisees? Whereas the term "Pharisee" referred to a religious party—almost like today's Christian denominations—the term "lawyer" referred to a professional occupation. Some lawyers were Pharisees, but not all of them, because not all lawyers followed the customs of the Pharisees. There were also some Pharisees who were lawyers; they were Bible scholars by profession. Yet many Pharisees were involved in some other line of work. In fact, many of them were lay people.

To give a contemporary analogy, we might compare the Pharisees to fundamentalists and the lawyers to seminary professors. Obviously, not all fundamentalists are seminary professors (most of them do something else for a living), and not all seminary professors are fundamentalists (some are liberals, for example). But some people are both. That was the situation here. Some of the guests around the dinner table were lawyers; some were Pharisees; and some were lawyers who belonged to the party of the Pharisees.

Each group had its own characteristic sins. The lawyers were guilty of legalism. Jesus said they loaded people with heavy burdens. In other words, in their interpretation and application of God's law, they came up with all kinds of picky rules that people had to follow—"the traditions of the elders." For example, the law commanded God's people "to remember the Sabbath day, to keep it holy" (Ex. 20:8). But how, exactly, was this command to be obeyed? To give just one example, here is what the lawyers said about carrying something on the Sabbath: A man may not carry an object "in his right hand or in his left hand, in his bosom or on his shoulder." However, he may carry it "on the back of his hand, or with his foot or with his mouth or with his elbow, or in his ear or in his hair or in his wallet (carried) mouth downwards, or between his wallet and his shirt, or in the hem of his shirt, or in his shoe or in his sandal."[1]

Supposedly such rules were intended to help people follow God's law, but in fact they had a harmful effect on the spiritual life of the covenant community. Although they believed that they were teaching people God's will, in fact the lawyers were adding fallible human regulations to the infallible Word of God. By doing this, they were distracting people from what God truly wanted them to hear and to do. In fact, some Bible scholars believed— there is a saying about this in the Mishnah—that what the scribes said was more important than the Scripture itself because what they required

---

1. *Shabbath* 10.3, quoted in Leon Morris, *The Gospel According to St. Luke: An Introduction and Commentary*, Tyndale New Testament Commentaries (Grand Rapids: Eerdmans, 1974), 205–6.

was clearer![2] Rather than upholding the law, therefore, the lawyers were actually undermining it by putting something else in its place.

As a result of this kind of thinking, people began to obey the rules of men rather than the laws of God. They were led to believe that such legalistic obedience was necessary for their salvation. In the words of one old commentator, the lawyers laid down "many vexatious and trifling rules" that people had to keep "if they would be saved."[3] This weighed people down with a heavy burden of man-made religion. "So complicated were these rules and regulations," writes David Gooding, "that one would have needed to be a highly qualified lawyer oneself to know whether one was breaking the law or not; and a serious attempt to keep the rules turned moral and religious duty into an intolerable burden."[4] Imagine being held accountable to a study Bible produced by the Internal Revenue Service, and you will get some idea what this was like. It was virtually impossible for any ordinary person to know everything the lawyers required, let alone actually to do it.

To make matters worse, the lawyers did nothing to help people who were struggling under the weight of this burden. They did not lift even one little finger to help. Instead of giving more grace, they kept laying down more law, and then they looked down on people who failed to keep it. Meanwhile, they themselves knew all the loopholes, so that they could usually figure out a way to avoid keeping any law they did not want to keep. Again, it was like the IRS: the better you knew the regulations, the less you had to pay. So, for example, a man who knew all the Pharisaic rules for keeping the Sabbath could find a way to carry what he needed wherever he wanted it to go.

The poor example of these spiritual leaders is a warning to pastors and elders and anyone else in spiritual authority. We must not hold people to a standard that goes beyond the plain teaching of Scripture. This is one of the problems with the Roman Catholic Church: it raises human tradition to the level of divine truth. It is also the problem with many step-by-step methods for spiritual improvement in the evangelical church. Rather than living by faith and obedience to biblical principles, people slavishly adhere

2. *Sanhedrin* 11.3, quoted in Morris, *Luke*, 205.
3. Morris, *Luke*, 55.
4. David Gooding, *According to Luke: A New Exposition of the Third Gospel* (Grand Rapids: Eerdmans, 1987), 234.

634

to some human method for spiritual growth or family management. This is the problem too with all the unwritten rules we have for our own style of living the Christian life, with all of its personal preferences. We pay more attention to our human traditions than to the will of God. Ironically, rather than upholding the law, our legalism always destroys it.

Furthermore, we must not hold people to a standard that we are not striving to reach ourselves. This is part of what Jesus meant when he accused the lawyers of not shouldering the burden. If we tell people to be holy, we must be holy; if we tell them to be pure, we must be pure; if we tell them to make sacrifices, we must make sacrifices. Not that we must attain perfection before we can even begin teaching the will of God. If that were the case, then no one could ever teach at all. But our works must agree with our words; what we practice must be consistent with what we preach. Our calling is to help people glorify God, and we will never do that by weighing them down with all kinds of legalistic expectations that we do not even try to meet ourselves.

Above all, we must not present the Christian faith as a law to keep rather than a gospel to believe. The obedience we offer is not some desperate attempt to gain God's favor, but a grateful response to the salvation he has provided through the crucifixion and resurrection of Jesus Christ. When we turn to Jesus in faith—trusting him to forgive our sins and give us eternal life—he releases us from the oppressive burden of legalistic righteousness so that we are free to live for the glory of God. Jesus says, "Come to me, all who labor and are heavy laden, and I will give you rest. Take my yoke upon you, and learn from me, for I am gentle and lowly in heart, and you will find rest for your souls. For my yoke is easy, and my burden is light" (Matt. 11:28–30).

WOE TO THE REBELS

Jesus pronounced a second woe against the teachers of the law for their murderous rebellion against the Word of God. He began by pointing to the splendid tombs they were then building for the ancient prophets. "Woe to you!" Jesus said. "For you build the tombs of the prophets whom your fathers killed. So you are witnesses and you consent to the deeds of your fathers, for they killed them, and you build their tombs" (Luke 11:47–48).

Today visitors to Jerusalem can see similar tombs in the Kidron Valley, built in the memory of various prophets from the Old Testament. Making these memorials was considered a pious act, a way to honor the ministry of Israel's former prophets. It was also a way to atone for the sins of their fathers, who had put so many of those noble prophets to death. So people said. Yet Jesus saw things rather differently. As far as he was concerned, when people built these tombs they were finishing the work their forefathers had only started. This was a case of "like father, like son." In effect, the people of Jesus' generation were becoming unwitting accomplices to the murder of the very men they sought to honor. Rather than honoring the prophets by building these tombs, they were joining their ancestors in killing them. Here is how one scholar paraphrased what Jesus was saying: "They killed the prophets: you make sure they are dead."[5]

The tombs themselves were not the issue. The issue was the rebellion in the hearts of the spiritual leaders as they refused to listen to God's Word. It was much easier for them to live in the past by admiring some dead prophet than it was to live for God in the present by doing what the prophet said. The lawyers of that day made a grand show of outward piety, but their hearts were far from God. They had the same sinful attitudes as their fathers before them, and thus they shared in their guilt. They had the same ungodly lifestyle as the people whom the prophets had criticized throughout the Old Testament. They were guilty of pride, hypocrisy, and injustice. Therefore, even while they tried to honor the prophets with their tombs, they dishonored them with their lives.

The proof would come in what these men did with the greatest prophet of all. Jesus showed this by taking the history of the prophets and connecting it to the world-changing events of his own time:

> Therefore also the Wisdom of God said, "I will send them prophets and apostles, some of whom they will kill and persecute," so that the blood of all the prophets, shed from the foundation of the world, may be charged against this generation, from the blood of Abel to the blood of Zechariah, who perished between the altar and the sanctuary. Yes, I tell you, it will be required of this generation. (Luke 11:49–51)

5. T. W. Manson, quoted in R. Kent Hughes, *Luke: That You May Know the Truth*, 2 vols., Preaching the Word (Wheaton, IL: Crossway, 1998), 2:32.

When Jesus spoke about the "Wisdom of God," he was not referring to some extrabiblical book, as some have speculated, but to the wise counsel of God's sovereign will. Here the Son is lifting the veil on the Father's purpose in sending the prophets. Why did God send his people the prophets? He sent them to teach the will of God, of course, but he did it with full knowledge that they would be persecuted and killed. This was God's plan, in all its wisdom: he would send prophets to his people, and his people would put them to death.

The history of the ancient prophets is a litany of suffering. It began with the murder of Abel, who was killed by his brother because he believed in the need for blood atonement (Gen. 4:1–8). It ended with Zechariah, who was stoned in the courtyard of the temple when he rebuked people for breaking God's law (see 2 Chron. 24:20–22). According to the Hebrew Scriptures, which traditionally ended with 2 Chronicles, Zechariah was the last of the martyrs. In between Abel and Zechariah were all the other suffering prophets: Joseph, who was abandoned by his brothers; Elijah, who was persecuted by his king and queen; Jeremiah, who was thrown into a pit and left to die; and all the rest of them. Again and again the Israelites rejected the messengers of their salvation.

The sufferings of all the prophets would culminate in the death of Jesus Christ. His crucifixion would be the nadir of their persecution. Jesus of Nazareth was the greatest of all the prophets and the clearest revelation of the gospel. As the Son of God, he was the Word of God. In his public ministry he proclaimed the true gospel message of repentance and faith. So what would they do with him? Here Luke gives us another hint that he would be despised and rejected, a man of sorrows and acquainted with grief. Here Jesus himself bears witness that the guilt of his blood would be charged against the people of his generation.

Like all the words of Christ, this prophecy came true. The leaders of Israel—the lawyers and the Bible scholars—were the very ones who arrested Jesus in the middle of the night, brought him up on a false accusation, dragged him before Pilate, incited the crowds against him, and demanded his death. When they did this, they took full responsibility for it, uttering some of the most chilling words ever spoken: "His blood be on us and on our children!" (Matt. 27:25). By putting Jesus to death, they became guilty for the blood of the Son of God.

It was not just the blood of Jesus that was charged against them, however; it was also the blood of all the prophets. All of the prophets testified about Jesus. So when the lawyers killed Jesus, they were in murderous rebellion against all the prophets of God. In consenting to murder God's Son, they were "more guilty than their ancestors because of their rejection of the greater prophets and apostles. Rightly and justly then the vengeance would fall on this generation for the murders of all the prophets from the beginning of the world."[6]

We should take encouragement from the woe that Jesus pronounced on these men because it shows that God is holy and just. Everyone who persecutes Christ and his church will be held accountable. God will not forget the sufferings of his people. Justice will be required. The guilt of righteous blood will be charged against them.

But we too should be warned. This woe is mainly for people who think that they are righteous, as the lawyers did, and as we probably do. Do we honor the prophets, or are we in rebellion against the words that they spoke for God? We most truly honor the prophets, not by venerating them, but by obeying them. The way to honor Hosea is to worship God with our love rather than with burnt offerings (see Hos. 6:6–7). The way to honor Amos is to give the needy a pair of sandals and to raise the poor from the dust (see Amos 2:6). The way to honor Micah is to do justice, love kindness, and walk humbly with our God (see Micah 6:8). The way to honor Habakkuk is to live by faith (see Hab. 2:4). The best way to honor God's messengers is not by erecting their tombs, but by living the way they taught us to live. Otherwise, we too are in rebellion against the Word of God.

What is the best way for us to honor Jesus Christ as the greatest Prophet of all? We honor him by confessing the guilt of our sin—the sin that sent him to the bloody cross—and by claiming his blood as our atonement. We honor him by knowing him for sure as the Son of God and Savior of sinners. We honor him by living on the basis of his grace rather than our own extrabiblical law.

WOE TO THE FALSE TEACHERS

Jesus had one last woe to pronounce against the teachers of the law. He said woe to their legalism, woe to their murderous rebellion against the

---

6. Gooding, *Luke*, 236.

Word of God, and finally woe to their distortion of the gospel: "Woe to you lawyers! For you have taken away the key of knowledge. You did not enter yourselves, and you hindered those who were entering" (Luke 11:52).

This was highly ironic. The lawyers were called to lead people to salvation. Because they taught the Scriptures, they were supposed to hold the key to saving knowledge. But Jesus said they had taken the key away. Now, because they had lost the key, they themselves could not enter eternal life. Even worse, they were keeping other people from entering as well. The very men who were supposed to usher people to God were blocking the way! They spent all their time reading, studying, debating, and teaching the Bible; yet rather than making its message clear, they were only confusing people about the truth.

So what *is* the key of knowledge, the secret that unlocks the mysteries of salvation? Jesus Christ is the key, just as he is the way, and the truth, and the life. The key to saving knowledge is the grace that God offers to guilty sinners through Jesus Christ. The way to be saved—the way to have eternal life—is not by works of our own obedience. Rather, it is to confess our sins and put our trust in Christ alone for our salvation. As Cyril of Alexandria said in one of the first commentaries on the Gospel of Luke, the key of knowledge is "justification in Christ."[7]

According to Jesus, the lawyers should have known this. After all, they were the ones who knew the Scriptures which taught that God would raise up a Prophet to save his people from their sins. Therefore, they should repent of their sins and trust in the saving mercy of their God. This was the whole message of the Bible, and now it was fulfilled in Jesus. Really, the lawyers should have been proving from the Scriptures that Jesus was the Christ. Instead, they were busy putting all kinds of extra religious demands on people, as if they could be saved by their own obedience. Because the lawyers did not trust Jesus by faith, they discouraged other people from trusting him too.

This woe teaches us to trust in Christ alone for our salvation. He is the key to everything, and without the key we cannot enter eternal life. The only true and saving knowledge of God comes through Jesus Christ. Only through him can we ever be saved. Once we understand this, we need to do

7. Cyril of Alexandria, "Commentary on Luke," in *Luke*, ed. Arthur A. Just Jr., Ancient Christian Commentary on Scripture, NT 3 (Downers Grove, IL: InterVarsity, 2003), 202.

everything we can to help other people understand it too, especially if we have any kind of teaching responsibility in the church. Woe to us if we take away the key of knowledge.

How are we tempted to do this? What are some of the ways that we might hinder people from coming to Christ? Here are a few suggestions. We take away the key of knowledge when:

- We fail to be clear and simple in telling people about Jesus.
- We speak about the business of the church but not about the saving work of Jesus Christ.
- We add works to faith as the basis for our standing before God.
- We focus on outward religious rituals rather than the inward transforming work of the Holy Spirit.
- We treat the Bible as a text to analyze rather than as a Word from God to believe and obey.
- We get caught up in complex theological arguments that are not vitally connected to the person of Jesus Christ.
- We so overemphasize one particular doctrine that we distort the message of salvation.
- We confuse our Christianity with our politics.

We also take away the key of knowledge when in our fear and indifference we fail to give people the gospel at all.

WOE IS ME!

Given everything that Jesus said at the Pharisee's house, can you even imagine the tension around the table as the dinner party ended? By the time Jesus was through, he had offended everyone at the table, exposing each person's hypocrisy, pride, hatred, and legalism. He had accused them all of keeping people away from God and contaminating others with the deadly corruption of their ungodly hearts. No wonder they wanted to kill him! "As he went away from there, the scribes and the Pharisees began to press him hard and to provoke him to speak about many things, lying in wait for him, to catch him in something he might say" (Luke 11:53–54).

In saying this, Luke is giving us another premonition of the crucifixion; he is preparing us for Good Friday and the cross. At the end of chapter 9 Jesus had set his face toward Jerusalem (Luke 9:51), and from that point on, he came into increasing conflict with the leaders of Israel. With murderous hostility, they tried to get him to say something to incriminate himself. They were after him like a wild beast, for the vocabulary that Luke uses comes from the world of hunting and trapping. Like stalkers in the underbrush, they were waiting to pounce on Jesus, catching him unawares.

This proved the truth of what Jesus had been saying about the hostility of these men. They hated Jesus, and even though they never caught him doing anything wrong, they went right ahead and put him to death, so that his blood was charged to their account. When Jesus offended them, it only made them angry, and many of them took their outrage with them all the way to hell!

What should they have done instead? When Jesus offended them, they could have responded a different way altogether, the way that we should respond when the words of Jesus offend our own self-righteous pride. We do well to respond the way Isaiah did when God pronounced woe against the people of his day. At the end of Luke 11 Jesus pronounces six woes on the leaders of Israel, three against the Pharisees and three against the lawyers. This is reminiscent of Isaiah 5, where God pronounces six woes against the wickedness of his people. In both cases, we might wonder where the seventh woe is. In the Bible things often come in sevens, so is there a missing woe?

In Isaiah the seventh and final woe comes in chapter 6, when the prophet says, "Woe is me! For I am lost; for I am a man of unclean lips, and I dwell in the midst of a people of unclean lips; for my eyes have seen the King, the LORD of hosts!" (Isa. 6:5). Isaiah knew that in God's eyes he was just as guilty as anyone else. Therefore, rather than being offended by what God said about his sin, he repented of it, and was saved.

If the lawyers and Pharisees had made the same confession, they would have given true honor to the example of the prophet Isaiah, and they too would have been saved. But rather than pronouncing woe upon themselves, they plotted to put Jesus to death.

What choice will you make?

Do not put Jesus away as the lawyers wanted to do. Instead, fill in the missing woe and say, "Woe is me, Lord, for I am the heartless legalist, I am the hateful rebel who hinders people from coming to Christ. God, save me by the cross where my sins sent Jesus to die." On that blood-stained cross the greatest of all prophets took the woe of our sin upon himself, and by the mercy of that cross we may be saved from all our self-righteous sins.

51

UNAFRAID AND UNASHAMED

Luke 12:1–12

"And I tell you, everyone who acknowledges me before men,
the Son of Man also will acknowledge before the angels of God,
but the one who denies me before men will be denied before
the angels of God." (Luke 12:8–9)

Elizabeth's story is a profile in Christian courage. She was raised in a small village in Southeast Asia, where her parents taught her to trust God for her daily needs and where she dreamed of getting a good education. When she was sixteen, a relative offered to help her find a high-paying job in another country, so that she could help her family and earn the money she needed for college.

What Elizabeth did not know, however, was that her relative would betray her into the sex trade. When she reached the border, she was sold into slavery and taken to a house of prostitution, where she was raped by customer after customer.

Seven months later, by the mercy of God, investigators from the International Justice Mission found Elizabeth and persuaded the local police to raid the brothel where she was being held against her will. When her rescuers arrived, they found the following words written on the wall of her room:

"The Lord is my light and my salvation. Whom shall I fear? The Lord is the strength of my life. Of whom shall I be afraid?"[1]

From where does this kind of courage come? How can a suffering young girl, living in Satan-infested squalor, hold on to her fearless hope that God will save her? To apply this more personally, how can we, who are so easily intimidated by even the slightest hostility to our Christian faith, learn to live with the same courageous confidence?

THE LEAVEN OF HYPOCRISY

At the beginning of Luke 12 Jesus teaches his disciples at least five valuable lessons about how to live unafraid and unashamed. The first lesson is that I am ready to take a strong stand for Christ *when my heart is free from hypocrisy*.

Jesus had been having dinner with some religious leaders, and over the course of the meal he denounced their deadly hypocrisy. By the time they were finished having dinner—if they even made it to dessert—they wanted to catch Jesus and kill him. This is the context for what Jesus said: "In the meantime, when so many thousands of the people had gathered together that they were trampling one another, he began to say to his disciples first, 'Beware of the leaven of the Pharisees, which is hypocrisy'" (Luke 12:1).

So many people were coming to hear Jesus that it was becoming a mob scene. But before speaking to the masses, Jesus gave some personal instructions to his disciples. From this point on, he was in mortal danger from his enemies. Eventually his disciples would be in danger, too. But rather than being afraid of what the Pharisees might do to their bodies, Jesus told them to watch out for their souls. The real threat was spiritual, so Jesus warned his disciples to beware of the leaven of the Pharisees.

Leaven is yeast that works its way through the dough and makes bread rise. In the Bible it is a common image for something small that spreads silently, almost secretly, but ultimately pervasively—like the kingdom of God, for example (Luke 13:20–21). The image is usually negative, however, and often relates to sin. Here Jesus uses it for hypocrisy, which is the reality gap between our outward appearance of godliness and the sinner that lives

1. Andy Crouch, "The Cruel Edges of the World," *Christianity Today* (June 2004): 60.

inside. The Pharisees had a reputation for righteousness, but their hearts were far from God. Jesus knew that like the yeast in a batch of dough, their deadly hypocrisy would gradually work its way into other people's hearts. If the disciples were not careful, soon they would be Pharisees too—making an outward show of their religious rituals without loving God from the heart.

We need to beware of the same danger. How easy it is to say things and do things that make us seem more spiritual than we really are. We try to leave people with the impression that we are active in ministry and faithful in our commitment to Christ, when in fact our hearts may well be growing colder to the things of God. How easy it is to be a hypocrite . . . and how deadly! J. C. Ryle described Pharisaism as a "subtle leaven," which "once received into the heart infects the whole character of a man's Christianity."[2] If we claim to follow Christ, then we need to be who we seem to be and strive earnestly to become the people God wants us to become in Christ.

One reason to pursue this kind of integrity is that the day will come when the real condition of our hearts is truly known. Jesus said, "Nothing is covered up that will not be revealed, or hidden that will not be known. Therefore whatever you have said in the dark shall be heard in the light, and what you have whispered in private rooms shall be proclaimed on the housetops" (Luke 12:2–3). In other words, it will all come out in the end; all our secret sins will be revealed. We may be able to cover our tracks for a little while, but we cannot hide our hypocrisy forever.

Sin often gets exposed in this life. The student gets caught handing in somebody else's work; the executive gets caught fixing the books; the church leader gets caught using pornography; the mother gets caught abusing her child. When they get caught, everyone knows the truth. What was concealed gets revealed. What was kept in the dark is brought to light. What was whispered in secret is reported on the evening news. It happens every day.

But even the sins that do not get exposed in this life will be revealed at the last judgment. We cannot hide them forever. God is omniscient; he knows all things. The Bible says he "will bring every deed into judgment, with every secret thing, whether good or evil" (Eccl. 12:14; cf. Rom. 2:16). There will be full disclosure. It will all come to light: every proud conceit,

2. J. C. Ryle, *Expository Thoughts on the Gospels, Luke* (1858; reprint Cambridge: James Clarke, 1976), 2:58.

petty theft, angry word, abusive blow, lustful fantasy, thought of self-pity, spin of the truth, and whisper of gossip.

What is your secret, and when will it be exposed? If we do not confess our sins, including the ones that nobody else knows about, then we will live in fear of being discovered. The only way to be unafraid and unashamed is to make a full confession, trusting God to forgive our sins through Jesus Christ. The Scriptures say, "Whoever conceals his transgressions will not prosper, but he who confesses and forsakes them will obtain mercy" (Prov. 28:13). Then, once we have confessed our sins, we will be ready to take a strong stand for Christ.

FEAR ITSELF

We need to be free from the hypocrisy of secret sin. We also need to fear God more than we fear other people. This too will enable us to be courageous for Christ. I am ready to take a strong spiritual stand *when I fear God more than I fear other people.* Here is how Jesus made the comparison: "I tell you, my friends, do not fear those who kill the body, and after that have nothing more that they can do. But I will warn you whom to fear: fear him who, after he has killed, has authority to cast into hell. Yes, I tell you, fear him!" (Luke 12:4–5).

We cannot eliminate fear altogether. It is part of our frailty as fallen creatures living in a vast universe ruled by a sovereign God. Our souls were made for eternity. How can we help but fear our own mortality?

There is more than one kind of fear, however—a wrong fear and a right fear. Jesus tells us *not* to fear people who can harm only our bodies. This is a hard teaching because we love our bodies and instinctively protect them any way we can. We are afraid of physical pain and shudder at the prospect of death. Nevertheless, Jesus tells us not to be afraid of people who can only kill our bodies. Clearly he is drawing a distinction between this life and the life to come. For the believer, death is only temporary. Therefore, our real concern ought to be what will happen to us in eternity. If we belong to God through faith in Jesus Christ, we know that death will be our entrance into glory. "What terror of death can assail us," wrote Cyril of Alexandria, "now that life has abolished death? Christ is the resurrection and the life."[3]

3. Cyril of Alexandria, "Commentary on Luke," in *Luke,* ed. Arthur A. Just Jr., Ancient Christian Commentary on Scripture, NT 3 (Downers Grove, IL: InterVarsity, 2003), 60.

If we should not be afraid of people who can kill us, then far less should we fear people who can only scorn us. Many Christians are far too easily frightened. They are afraid to take a moral stand at work that might cost them their careers. They are afraid to defend a consistent Christian position in the college classroom, or the faculty lounge. They are afraid to challenge their friends when they are going in the wrong spiritual direction. They are afraid to talk to strangers about the gospel. But Jesus said we should not even fear people who could put us to death; we should not be afraid of them.

There is only one right and proper fear, and that is the fear of God. When Jesus speaks here about someone who "has authority to cast into hell" (Luke 12:5), he is not talking about Satan; he is talking about almighty God! Hell is not Satan's dominion, but only his prison. *God* is the one who has authority over heaven and hell.

This is one of several places where Jesus speaks frankly about hell. The word he uses relates to the physical geography of Israel. *Gehenna*, as the place was called, was a valley outside Jerusalem. It was a ravine of smoking refuse, an accursed place of perpetual burning. The Bible uses this God-forsaken valley to describe the torments of hell as an everlasting fire. Some people may not believe in hell, including some people who call themselves Christians, but Jesus certainly did! Jesus plainly taught that God will banish unrepentant sinners to hell; therefore, he is to be feared.

Fearing God is far from popular these days. If people are looking for God at all, they are hoping to find a more user-friendly deity. They no longer worship God with reverent trembling, not even in church. Instead, they worship with casual triviality. But Jesus said that God is to be feared. He is to be treated with respect and awe, because he holds the power of eternal judgment.

When we tremble at God's authority over heaven and hell, we are ready to defend his cause in the world, little fearing what other people will think. We will be like John Knox, the man who brought the Reformation to Scotland. Knox never backed down from a challenge, spiritual or otherwise. He wielded his sword in battle; he rebuked reigning monarchs; he turned the heart of his nation back to God. At the end, as his body was lowered into the ground, someone at the graveside pronounced Knox's epitaph: "Here lies one who feared God so much that he never feared the face of man."[4]

The first disciples were men of such courage. According to the New Testament, they boldly preached the gospel all over the ancient world. According to tradition, all of them also died violent deaths, except for John. They faced suffering with great courage—defying their enemies—because Jesus taught them to fear God more than anything or anyone else.

When John Hooper was sentenced to die for preaching the gospel during the English Reformation, some of his friends encouraged him to recant. If only he would deny the gospel of justification by faith, the Roman Catholic Church would be satisfied, and his life would be spared. But Hooper was viewing things from an eternal perspective, and thus he did not fear those who could only kill his body. "Life is sweet," he said, "and death is bitter. But eternal life is more sweet, and eternal death is more bitter."[5] When we learn to make this taste comparison ourselves, we will have the courage of our Christian convictions.

His Eye Is on the Sparrow

Whenever we talk about the fear of God, there is always the danger of a serious misunderstanding. We should fear God with reverence and awe, but if we belong to him through faith in Jesus Christ, we should *never* be afraid that God is out to harm us. On the contrary, he has promised to love us to the very end. So after warning about hell, Jesus went on to tell his disciples *not* to be afraid of God, but to trust in his gracious care: "Are not five sparrows sold for two pennies? And not one of them is forgotten before God. Why, even the hairs of your head are all numbered. Fear not; you are of more value than many sparrows" (Luke 12:6–7).

By clearly distinguishing between two different kinds of fear, Jesus gave his disciples another basis for Christian courage. The same God who holds the power of judgment is also the God who knows me and loves me. Far from getting ready to throw me into hell, he is watching over me to keep me safe forever. Knowing this helps me to be a more courageous Christian.

4. William Barclay, *The Gospel of Luke* (Philadelphia: Westminster, 1956), 164.
5. Bishop Hooper, quoted in Ryle, *Luke*, 2:61.

I am able to take a strong stand for Christ *when I fully trust that God knows me and cares about me.*

Jesus proves this point by making a famous comparison between a sparrow and one of his disciples. Sparrows are a dime a dozen. We can see how little they are worth by comparing Luke to Matthew, where Jesus says that two sparrows are "sold for a penny" (Matt. 10:29). This almost seems like a contradiction: in Matthew Jesus says two for a penny, while in Luke he says five for two pennies. But anyone who knows anything about marketing can explain the discrepancy. Sparrows cost a penny a pair, but if you bought two pair at the market, the seller would give you a volume discount and throw in an extra sparrow. A sparrow is such a little bird that it is worth next to nothing. Yet God never forgets even a single sparrow. He sees them safely hatch from their shells. He scatters the seed that provides their daily food. When they fall to the ground, he knows where they lie. One prison inmate was inspired by watching the sparrows flit around the barbed wire outside his prison cell. Most of the sad and broken men around him despaired of ever finding freedom. But the sparrows gave the prisoner gospel hope:

> Yet I am happy and I'm free
> Though tombed within this Hell,
> For mighty acts of God I see
> Through cold bars of my cell.

> For sparrows play outside my wall
> And flit from fence to tree;
> I know He grieves their every fall
> And He is here with me.[6]

Martin Luther observed that when Jesus compared us to sparrows, he was "making the birds our schoolmasters and teachers." In the gospel, Luther said, the sparrow becomes "a theologian and a preacher to the wisest of men."[7]

6. Robert Raines, *To Kiss the Joy* (Waco: Word Books, 1973), 88–89.
7. Martin Luther, *The Sermon on the Mount*, trans. Jaroslav Pelikan, in *Luther's Works* (St. Louis: Concordia, 1956), 21:197–98.

For if God takes such good care of sparrows, what will he do for us? God knows everything about us, down to the very last hair on our heads. Scientists say that the average person has at least one hundred thousand hairs. Every last one of those hundred thousand hairs is known by God—a remarkable testimony to his divine omniscience! God knows *everything* about us. Nothing in our lives is too small for him to notice, or so insignificant that it is unworthy of his attention.

God uses this vast knowledge for our benefit, because we are far more precious to him than "many sparrows" (Luke 12:7). This expression preserves the dignity of the birds as his creatures. But people are worth far more to him because we are made in his very image and likeness. Now God has placed his ultimate valuation on us through the cross where Christ died for our sins. If God loves the little sparrows, how much more does he love us! "He who did not spare his own Son but gave him up for us all, how will he not also with him graciously give us all things?" (Rom. 8:32).

Knowing God's love and care for us is a comfort to all our fears. Every time we see a sparrow—which is every day, if we will take the trouble to notice—we see a creature that is known by God, individually. If his eye is on the sparrow, then we know for sure that he watches us. The God we revere is a God who knows us and loves us. He will be with us in times of trouble. He will provide for our daily needs. He will give us guidance for the future. He will rescue our broken relationships. He will heal the deep wounds in our heart. Rather than holding back, therefore—refusing to take some bold step of faith because secretly we fear that God will let us down—we should have courageous confidence that God is always watching over us.

CONFESSING CHRIST

As reassuring as it is to know that God will remember us in this lifetime, it is infinitely more important for him to acknowledge us in the life to come. So Jesus gives us this promise: "And I tell you, everyone who acknowledges me before men, the Son of Man also will acknowledge before the angels of God, but the one who denies me before men will be denied before the angels of God" (Luke 12:8–9).

With these words, Jesus again puts our relationship with him into eternal perspective. He summons us to the tribunal of heaven, where the greatest of all judges holds court with all his angels. Then Jesus connects what he will say about us at the final judgment to what we say about him here on earth, teaching a fourth lesson in courageous Christianity: I am unafraid and unashamed *when I know that if I stand up for Jesus now, Jesus will stand up for me later.*

To acknowledge Jesus before men is to be open and honest about our total life-commitment to him as our Savior and our Lord. It is to show that we are Christians by the things that we do and we say. It is to work for Christ, play for Christ, and witness for Christ in our daily lives. It is to make a verbal confession of our faith, both inside and outside the church. The Scripture says, "If you confess with your mouth that Jesus is Lord and believe in your heart that God raised him from the dead, you will be saved" (Rom. 10:9). To confess Christ is to do all these things regardless what persecution or opposition we may suffer.

Jesus has promised that if we do this, then he will acknowledge us at the last day. What comfort this brings to the soul! When we stand before God for judgment, all of our secrets will be revealed. We will be condemned by the law, condemned by our sin, and condemned by Satan himself. But if we confess Christ, then the very Son of God will rise to our defense. He will testify that we belong to him by faith. He will claim that through his death on the cross he has taken our shame upon himself and fearlessly paid the full penalty for our sin. He will plead for his Father to declare us righteous in his sight. And he will win our case, because his appeal will be based on God's own justice and mercy. The very justice of God will demand our justification.

If Jesus has promised to do all this for us, then we should have the courage to do all that we can for him. J. C. Ryle said:

> The difficulty of confessing Christ is undoubtedly very great. It never was easy at any period. It never will be easy as long as the world stands. It is sure to entail on us laughter, ridicule, contempt, mockery, enmity, and persecution. . . . The world which hated Christ will always hate true Christians. But whether we like it or not, whether it be hard or easy, our course is perfectly clear. In one way or another Christ must be confessed.[8]

But what if we do *not* confess Christ? What if we are not willing to acknowledge him in a church service, or in a class at school, or in the break

8. Ryle, *Luke*, 2:65.

room at work, or over the counter at the pharmacy, or anywhere else? What if we are ashamed to be known as Christians? What if we are afraid to take a public stand for Christ on the crucial issues of our day, such as homosexual marriage, for example, or the claim that Jesus is the only way to God? What will become of us then?

If we do not confess Christ, we deny him, and if we deny him, he will deny us. This is only fair, but it is also frightening, because Jesus will deny us when it matters most of all: at the final judgment. "The one who denies me before men," he says, "will be denied before the angels of God" (Luke 12:9). On the day when all secrets are revealed before the throne of God, Jesus will not testify that we belong to him or claim the merits of his death on our behalf. Instead, he will send us to hell—and all because we were too afraid to make our stand for Christ.

This ought to lead to some serious self examination. Am I confessing Jesus Christ, or denying him? If I have been denying him, I need to offer full repentance for my sin and make a true confession of my faith. If I do this, God will forgive me, for Jesus said, "everyone who speaks a word against the Son of Man will be forgiven" (Luke 12:10). However, Jesus also went on to give this sober warning: "but the one who blasphemes against the Holy Spirit will not be forgiven" (Luke 12:10). This is a hard verse to understand. What does it mean?

To speak against the Son of Man is to speak against Jesus Christ without fully understanding who he is or what he has done. Obviously it must not be the kind of full and final denial that Jesus was talking about in verse 9. Nevertheless, it is still a sin—a sin of weakness that God can and will forgive. A good example of such forgiveness is the forgiveness Jesus offered the men who taunted him on the cross, saying, "Father, forgive them, for they know not what they do" (Luke 23:34).

Somehow blasphemy against the Holy Spirit must be a different and more serious sin. From similar passages in Matthew and Mark, it appears to be the sin of someone who knows that Jesus is the Christ, but attributes his power to Satan instead (see Matt. 12:31–32; Mark 3:28–30). According to one old commentator, the sin here "must consist in a conscious, willful, intentional blasphemy of the clearly recognized revelation of God's grace in Christ through the Holy Ghost, a revelation which nevertheless out of hate and hostility is ascribed to the devil."[9] It is of the very nature of the case that such a person—hardened by sin—will not be forgiven, not because of any deficiency in God's grace, but because such a person denies the only gospel that can ever save anyone. The great Dutch theologian Herman Bavinck thus described blasphemy against the Holy Spirit as

> a sin against the Gospel in its clearest revelation, . . . not in doubting or simply denying the truth, but in a denial which goes against the conviction of the intellect, against the enlightenment of conscience, against the dictates of the heart; in a conscious, willful, and intentional imputation to the influence and working of Satan of that which is clearly recognized as God's work, ... in a willful declaration that the Holy Ghost is the Spirit of the abyss, that truth is a lie, and that Christ is Satan himself.[10]

The blood of Christ is sufficient for any sinner who truly repents—even a sinner who on occasion has denied the name of Christ. But if instead of believing the gospel a sinner stubbornly persists in repudiating Jesus and even calling him the devil, how can he be forgiven?

THE HELP OF THE SPIRIT

Rather than committing unforgivable blasphemy against the Holy Spirit, Jesus calls us to believe the witness of the Spirit and to rely on his assistance whenever we speak for Christ. This is a final basis for Christian courage: I am ready to take a strong stand for Christ *when I trust the Holy Spirit to help me in my witness.*

When Jesus told his disciples to be unafraid and unashamed, he did not expect them to do this in their own strength. On the contrary, he promised that his Spirit would be with them to help them: "And when they bring you before the synagogues and the rulers and the authorities, do not be anxious about how you should defend yourself or what you should say, for the Holy Spirit will teach you in that very hour what you ought to say" (Luke 12:11–12).

---

9. Impeta, quoted in Norval Geldenhuys, *The Gospel of Luke*, New International Commentary on the New Testament (Grand Rapids: Eerdmans, 1951), 352.

10. Herman Bavinck, *Gereformeerde Dogmatiek*, quoted in Geldenhuys, *Luke*, 352.

Jesus was preparing his disciples for persecution. In coming days they would be dragged before various religious and political authorities—both Jewish and Gentile—and they would be forced to defend their faith. In fact, this began to happen only days after Jesus ascended into heaven, when Peter and John were arrested by the temple police and hauled before the Sanhedrin (Acts 4:1ff.). Under the threat of such opposition, it would be tempting for them to be afraid—if not of the persecution itself, then of failing to be a good witness for Christ. Jesus told them not to worry, however, because the Holy Spirit would teach them what to say.

God fulfilled this promise. Every time the apostles appeared in court, they had another opportunity to proclaim the gospel. We see this again and again in the book of Acts. The apostles fearlessly preached in the power of the Spirit, and many people were saved through their ministry.

Although this promise was especially for the apostles, it also applies to other believers. We too can trust the Holy Spirit to help us whenever we witness for Christ. Yet many Christians are reluctant to share their faith because they are afraid that they will not know what to say. How can we overcome this sinful fear and become bolder in our evangelism?

Part of the answer is to be better prepared to give a simple presentation of the gospel. As the Scripture says—and this comes from Peter, who also knew what it meant to trust the Spirit—we always need to be ready to give a reason for the hope that is in us (1 Peter 3:15). But there are some situations for which it is impossible to prepare. When that happens, we can trust the Spirit to help us. We do not need to know all the Bible verses, have all the answers, or even persuade people to repent and believe the gospel. All we need to do is speak a word for Christ and pray that the Holy Spirit will use what we say—however inadequate—to do his saving work in people's lives.

This is where true spiritual courage comes from. It comes from freely confessing our sins, fearing God more than we fear other people, trusting the watchful care of the Father, knowing that Jesus will defend us at the final judgment, and depending on the help of the Holy Spirit.

One man who struggled to have the courage of his Christian convictions was Thomas Cranmer, the famous archbishop of Canterbury and author of the Book of Common Prayer. Cranmer was at the forefront of the English Reformation, and served Christ faithfully for many years. But when Bloody

Mary took the throne, the Roman Catholic Church condemned Cranmer to die. He was forced to watch in anguish as his friends Hugh Latimer and Nicholas Ridley were burned at the stake in the center of Oxford. For a time Cranmer faltered. Fearing the pains of his body more than the authority of his God, he recanted his faith in the gospel. He did this, writes one of his biographers, because he saw "the poignant contrast between the pleasant prospect of life and the vivid horror of an agonizing death."[11]

Happily, on the eve of his execution, Cranmer's courage returned. He repented of his sin and retracted all his recantations. As he looked to eternity, he realized that he feared God more than he feared the queen of England or the fiery pains of death. And by the help of the Holy Spirit, Cranmer went to his death making one last courageous confession of his faith in Jesus Christ. In his farewell remarks he exhorted people "to care less for this world and more for God and the world to come," and not to fear the queen, but only the power of God.[12]

God is not asking you to burn at the stake (not yet, at any rate). He is asking you to do some things that are far less painful, like taking a stand for righteousness at work, or telling a friend about Jesus, or giving your life to Christian service. Do not hold back, but have the courage to take your stand for Christ, unafraid and unashamed.

11. Albert Frederick Pollard, *Thomas Cranmer and the English Reformation, 1489–1556* (New York and London: G. P. Putnam's Sons, 1905), 369.
12. Ibid., 379.

52

A FOOL AND HIS MONEY

Luke 12:13–21

"But God said to him, 'Fool! This night your soul is required of you, and the things you have prepared, whose will they be?' So is the one who lays up treasure for himself and is not rich toward God." (Luke 12:20–21)

ohn Grisham's novel *The Testament* opens with the dying words of a man who will soon be parted from all his money. Here are his last thoughts on earth:

Day, even the last hour now. I'm an old man, lonely and unloved, sick and hurting and tired of living. I am ready for the hereafter; it has to be better than this. . . . My assets exceed eleven billion dollars. I own silver in Nevada and copper in Montana and coffee in Kenya and coal in Angola and rubber in Malaysia and natural gas in Texas and crude oil in Indonesia and steel in China. My companies own companies. . . . My money is the root of my misery. I had three families—three ex-wives who bore seven children, six of whom are still alive and doing all they can to torment me. . . . I am estranged from all the wives and all the children. They're gathering here today because I'm dying and it's time to divide the money.[1]

Whether rich or poor, this is how life always ends: with the dead leaving it all behind, and the living dividing whatever is left. Yet the living are not always satisfied with the way things get divided. This was certainly true of the man in the crowd who said to Jesus, "Teacher, tell my brother to divide the inheritance with me" (Luke 12:13).

A SELFISH REQUEST

The situation is all too familiar. A man had died, and two sons were squabbling over the money he had left behind. Both men wanted to get what they had coming to them. One of them was sure he was getting shortchanged, so he asked Jesus to adjudicate. That is not quite what the man was asking, however. He was not looking for an objective opinion about a fair distribution; he wanted Jesus to settle the estate in his favor.

Remember the context. Jesus had been teaching people how to take a spiritual stand, fearlessly living for Christ against all opposition. But rather than listening to what Jesus was saying, the man was preoccupied with his own situation. He wanted his rights! So he did what people sometimes do when they are having a disagreement: he asked a spiritual leader to get involved, in the hope that he would settle the matter by telling other people what they needed to hear. Most ministers are familiar with this kind of request. Michael Wilcock wryly comments that here Jesus has "the sympathy of every clergyman who finds himself asked to make pronouncements, sign forms, join committees, and generally 'lend his weight' to matters which have little to do with his real work!"[2]

Yet Jesus refused to get involved. In fact, he gave the man the apparent brush-off, saying, with obvious disapproval, "Man, who made me a judge or arbitrator over you?" (Luke 12:14). Jesus was clear about his calling. One day he would stand in judgment over everyone for everything. But the day for judgment had not yet come, and in his earthly ministry, it was not his

1. John Grisham, *The Testament* (New York: Doubleday, 1999), 1–2.
2. Michael Wilcock, *The Message of Luke*, The Bible Speaks Today (Downers Grove, IL: InterVarsity, 1979), 133.

calling to resolve this dispute. Israel had a legal system for settling small claims; Jesus had come to seek and to save the lost.

How important it is to know the difference between what we are and are not called to do. We are not called to do everything, including some things that we are asked and able to do. To know what things God truly wants us to do, we need to be clear about our calling, as Jesus was. In this case, it was not his place to decide who got what, but to challenge people about their ultimate priorities. He was "not showing indifference to the claims of legal justice, but was insisting that there is a greater gain than getting an inheritance and a greater loss than losing it."[3]

A Sober Warning

Jesus did not give the man what he wanted, but what he needed. Instead of settling the estate, Jesus responded to the man's selfish request by giving a sober warning: "Take care, and be on your guard against all covetousness, for one's life does not consist in the abundance of his possessions" (Luke 12:15).

Jesus loved to make this kind of editorial comment. He would take a conversation and turn it into a teaching opportunity. Here his warning was partly for the man who wanted to get more of his father's inheritance. Jesus knew the man's heart, and he could see that he was guilty of the great sin of coveting, of what the Puritan Thomas Watson described as "an insatiable desire of getting the world."[4] The man wanted to take what belonged to his brother and grab it for himself. Jesus may also have been speaking to the man's brother, because he seems to have been greedy too: he was keeping the whole inheritance for himself. It is possible that both men were coveting, one by refusing to divide the inheritance and the other by demanding to have it divided.

This helps us see that the warning Jesus gave is really for all of us. Whether we are among the haves or the have-nots, we are all tempted by the consuming desire to have things that God has given to others rather than to us. The poor are tempted to want all the things they do not have, while the rich

3. D. G. Miller, *Saint Luke* (London: SCM Press, 1959), 110.
4. Thomas Watson, *The Ten Commandments* (1692; reprint Edinburgh: Banner of Truth, 1965), 174.

are tempted to want even more of what they have. So Jesus warns us all to be on our guard against *all kinds* of covetousness.

The Greek word used here for coveting *(pleonexia)* has to do with excess. It refers to the acquisitive attitude of always wanting more, beyond what we even need. The covetous heart is never satisfied. Janwillem van de Wetering offers this memorable description: "Greed is a fat demon with a small mouth, and whatever you feed it is never enough."[5] Even when you get what you want—the job, the home, the automobile, the furniture, the clothing, the merchandise—you soon find yourself craving something more.

The Scripture says, "He who loves money will not be satisfied with money, nor he who loves wealth with his income" (Eccl. 5:10). That is why Jesus did not give this man his inheritance. It would not have satisfied his real need. That is also why Jesus tells us to be content with what we have, not coveting what God has not given. Rather than always wanting a higher standard of living, Jesus calls us to be satisfied with what we already have.

This requires constant vigilance. Jesus is giving an emphatic imperative here. When he tells us to "take care," he is telling us to watch out. Far from saying that greed is good, as some economists might say, Jesus is warning us that there is real danger here, and that we need to be wary. Take heed against greed! Even something we have never coveted in the past may become a temptation for us yet. Our wants may seem small: a nicer vacation, a more reliable car, a slightly larger house, a somewhat bigger paycheck. But little by little we get drawn into discontent. Possessions are always trying to possess us, until finally we give in to the cravings of a covetous heart.

Jesus warns us that this is not what life is all about. Life does not consist in the abundance of our possessions. Here again the word he uses has to do with excess. Abundance *(perisseuein)* in this sense means surplus, a superfluity of stuff.

Having more than we need does not add anything to our lives. Even if we had all the things we could possibly want out of life, we would not have any more of life itself. How can we find life in things that we consume? T. W. Manson commented, "It is true that a certain minimum of material goods is necessary for life; but it is not true that greater abundance of goods

---

5. Janwillem van de Wetering, *Just a Corpse at Twilight*, quoted in Richard A. Kauffman, "Reflections," *Christianity Today* (March 2003): 70.

means greater abundance of life."[6] Possessions do not add life to us. In fact, with all the demands they make on our time and effort they usually end up taking life away, as we work harder and harder to keep living in the manner to which we have become accustomed. J. C. Ryle said, "The more acres a man has, the more cares. The more his money increases, the more of his time is generally consumed and eaten up in thinking about it."[7]

Some people live for money, and for all the things that money can buy. It is how they keep score, how they find their sense of satisfaction. Their daily thoughts are driven by the debts they have to pay off. Or they are consumed with the financial goals they have set. "By the time I'm forty, I want to have this," they say, "or I want to be able to do this when I'm sixty." But that is not what life is all about:

> Not what we possess, but what we are, is the important matter. . . . The real life of a man has little relation to what he possesses. Neither nobleness nor peace nor satisfaction . . . has much dependence on property of any sort. . . . Covetousness is folly because it grasps at worldly good, under the false belief that thereby it will secure the true good of life, but when it has made its pile, it finds that it is no nearer peace of heart, rest, nobleness, or joy than before, and has probably lost much of both in the process of making it. The mad race after wealth, which is the sin of this luxurious, greedy, commercial age, is the consequence of a lie—that life does consist in the abundance of possessions.[8]

If that is the lie, what is the truth? The truth is that all life is found in God, not in us or anything in this world. The Bible says that Jesus is the life (John 14:6). It says that true life is to know the only true God and his Son Jesus Christ (John 17:3). It says that we do not live to ourselves, but to the Lord (Rom. 14:7–8). It says that to live is Christ (Phil. 1:21; cf. Gal. 2:20). So this is life: to know Jesus and to live for him.

The things of this world cannot make us live. In fact, to the extent that they pull us away from finding satisfaction in Christ, they only keep us from really living. They may give us a temporary lift—the surge of

6. T. W. Manson, *The Sayings of Jesus* (London: SCM Press, 1937), 271.
7. J. C. Ryle, *Expository Thoughts on the Gospels, Luke* (1858; reprint Cambridge: James Clarke, 1976), 2:76.
8. Alexander Maclaren, *Expositions of Holy Scripture* (Grand Rapids: Eerdmans, 1952), 6:339–40.

pleasure that comes when we get what we want. But watch out! Nothing in this world can give you life.

THE MISER'S DILEMMA

To strengthen his warning about wanting more than we have, Jesus told his disciples a parable about a man who had too much:

> The land of a rich man produced plentifully, and he thought to himself, "What shall I do, for I have nowhere to store my crops?" And he said, "I will do this: I will tear down my barns and build larger ones, and there I will store all my grain and my goods. And I will say to my soul, Soul, you have ample goods laid up for many years; relax, eat, drink, be merry." (Luke 12:16–19)

The man had it made. He had everything this world has to offer. He had a lot of money. He had good food and fine wine, with plenty of time to enjoy them—or so he thought. His riches were getting richer. He had just harvested a bumper crop. In fact his biggest problem now was storage. Listen again to his pitiful lament: "What shall I do, for I have nowhere to store my crops?" (Luke 12:17). How ironic! The man kept accumulating more and more until finally he did not have enough space to keep it all. What an indictment this is of our own excess! Many Americans have so much more than we need that we do not even know where to keep it all. Yet we keep thinking of more things that we would like to have. How ironic! How pathetic!

As we look over this man's portfolio, and overhear his plans for retirement, the words we can use to describe his attitude toward life may also describe our own spiritual condition. The man was thankless. Verse 16 makes it clear that his prosperity did not come from his own hard work or his superior skill at business, but from the natural bounty of his land. It should have been obvious, therefore, that everything he had was a gift from God, who sends rain from heaven to water the crops that grow. Yet the man was so ungrateful that he did not praise God, or bring him an offering.

The man was also selfish. He did not give his neighbor any more thought than he gave to God. Rather than giving his extra grain to the poor, he was going to keep it all for himself. Think how many ways he could have resolved his supposed dilemma of not having enough room to store his grain. He could have given the excess to poor people in his neighborhood. Augustine commented that "the bellies of the poor were much safer storerooms than his barns. . . . If he stowed it away in the bellies of the poor, it would of course be digested on earth, but in heaven it would be kept all the more safely."[9] Alternatively, the man could have given it to his local priest for the worship of God. The man's real dilemma was how to give it all away, not how to hoard it all for himself! But instead of seizing the opportunity to share, he decided to build himself some bigger barns.

The man did this because he was selfish. Indeed, we could go farther and say that he was self-absorbed. The man was so in love with himself that he was seemingly incapable of thinking about anything or anyone else. Of the fifty-four words in the parable in the original Greek, fully eighteen of them are first-person words like "I," "me," and "my."[10] The man was obsessed with himself. One clear sign of his self-absorption was his inner monologue. Jesus depicts him as constantly talking to himself about himself. He not only asked himself the questions, but he also gave himself the answers!

Another word we can use to describe the man in this parable is anxious—anxious about how to look after all his possessions. When he says, "What shall I do?" we can almost see him wringing his worried hands. He was also acquisitive and possessive. His repeated use of the word "my"—my crops, my barns, my grain, my goods—conveys a strong sense of ownership, not stewardship. Rather than thinking of what he owned as belonging to God, and therefore to be used for his glory, he thought of it all as belonging to himself, to be used for his own pleasure.

The mention of pleasure suggests another term to describe this miserly man: self-indulgent. He wanted to live what some people call "the good life." As he looked ahead to the golden years of his retirement, he anticipated spending them in the pursuit of idle pleasure. Now that he was financially secure, he could give his life to wine, women, and song. Or he could do nothing at all—whatever he pleased. The man was self-indulgent.

9. Augustine, Sermon 36.9, in *Luke*, ed. Arthur A. Just Jr., Ancient Christian Commentary on Scripture, NT 3 (Downers Grove, IL: InterVarsity, 2003), 208.

10. Dan Doriani, "What Shall We Do with Our Possessions?" *Covenant Magazine* (Oct./Nov. 1998): 5.

We could also call him presumptuous because he assumed that he would live indefinitely. This explains why he decided to make a capital investment in additional storage for his nondurable assets. It also explains why he said to himself, "Soul, you have ample goods laid up for many years" (Luke 12:19). He thought his money was his security for the future. Maybe he would not live forever, but he was sure to live long enough to enjoy himself. In short, the man was doing exactly what Jesus warned his disciples not to do: he was making his money his life.

The Miser's Folly

All of these words are accurate descriptors, but Jesus had a much simpler way of saying it. He called the rich man a fool. The first part of the parable shows the man's own worldview. In verse 17 he identifies his dilemma; in verse 18 he comes up with his solution; in verse 19 he charts his course for the future. Only then does Jesus give us God's perspective: "But God said to him, 'Fool! This night your soul is required of you, and the things you have prepared, whose will they be?'" (Luke 12:20).

These words are chilling in their irony. When God tells the man that his soul will be "required," he uses the same terminology a banker would use to call in a loan.[11] God is telling the man that his loan is now due—the loan of his mortal existence. His life has always belonged to God, and now God is coming to claim it. But that is not the only irony. How ironic that a man who has been having his own private monologue has been overheard by God. How ironic that a man who thinks he will live for many years is down to his last few hours on earth! How ironic that a man who wants to keep it all for himself will have to leave it all behind. And how ironic that a man who gives not one thought to God must still answer to God for his very soul. How ironic, how tragic, and according to Jesus, how foolish!

Why did Jesus call this man a fool? Maybe it was because his life was so short. He was running out of time, and he did not even know it. He assumed he had years and years left to enjoy himself—decades to take things easy and spend all his money. In all his financial planning, in all his efforts to take control of his future, he never counted on his own untimely

11. Kenneth Bailey, *Through Peasant Eyes* (Grand Rapids: Eerdmans, 1980), 67.

demise. Yet death was already outside the door. A fool and his money are soon parted, and this man was going to die before he had the chance to enjoy even one single day of his retirement. How foolish to make all those plans for a day that would never come!

How foolish also to worry so much about so many things that he could not keep! Jesus asks the man a rhetorical question: "The things you have prepared, whose will they be?" (Luke 12:20). The answer is that whomever they will belong to, they will not belong to him, which is all he really cared about. Fool that he was, he was taking all sorts of trouble about stuff that soon would belong to someone else. He could not take it with him. No one ever can. However rich we may be, we will die poor, leaving everything behind for someone else. In the words of the psalmist, "The fool and the stupid alike must perish and leave their wealth to others" (Ps. 49:10).

The farmer was a fool for this reason as well: he thought that life consisted in the abundance of things—the very attitude that Jesus warned against. He thought that life was all about getting more and more for himself. What a fool he was, to think that money and pleasure are the most important things in the world! It was not just death that made him look like a fool. He would have been a fool even if he did not die for decades. He was a fool already, because he was living for all the wrong things: "Man whose life hangs by a thread and who may be called upon at any time to give account of himself is a fool if he relies on material things."[12]

But the man was mainly a fool for this reason: he did not know God. This is what the Bible usually means when it describes someone as a fool. The fool is the man who "says in his heart, 'There is no God'" (Ps. 14:1). He does not believe in the existence of God at all, or if he does, he does not acknowledge his presence in daily life. The rich man in the parable was like that. He did not thank God for the plentiful produce of his land, he did not ask God what he should do with all his extra grain, and he did not offer his time and talents for God's service. He did not acknowledge God's sovereignty over his lifespan or prepare to meet God when he died. He did not give one thought to God at all. The man thought he had a storage problem, but what he really had was a spiritual problem: he was an atheist.

12. Leon Morris, *The Gospel According to St. Luke: An Introduction and Commentary*, Tyndale New Testament Commentaries (Grand Rapids: Eerdmans, 1974), 213.

Rich toward God

The practical point of this parable is very simple: Don't be a fool! Don't be the kind of fool who lives for this world and gives no thought to God. Instead, be wise to thank God for every blessing, knowing that everything comes from him. Be wise to pray about practical problems, asking God what to do. Be wise to offer the best of your abilities for whatever God needs to be done, even in retirement. Be wise to know that life is short, that any day may be your last, and therefore that your future belongs to God. Be ready to meet God for judgment, trusting him to save you from your sins through Jesus Christ.

Jesus was a good preacher, and a good preacher almost never ends his sermon without bringing things to a point of practical application. Here is how Jesus applied the parable of the rich fool: "So is the one who lays up treasure for himself and is not rich toward God" (Luke 12:21). This command is for everyone, for rich and poor alike. Nothing is said here about what we have or how much we make. Having or not having treasure is not the issue. The issue is our attitude about what we have—our heart motivation for what we do with it.

Some people lay up treasure for themselves. Like the fool in the parable, they live for money and all the things that money can buy. Their goal is getting things for themselves. If that is what they want, it is all they will ever get. They will never gain the pleasures that come from knowing God, or the treasures of eternal life.

Jesus calls us away from such poverty of soul to be rich toward the God who has been so rich toward us. God has lavished us with the gifts of his good creation: food, clothing, shelter, and millions of other material blessings. More than that, he has lavished us with the gifts of his saving grace: the forgiveness of our sins, freedom from guilt, and the hope of eternal life. He has done this through the extravagant grace of our Lord Jesus Christ, who gave his lifeblood for our sins when he died on the cross. Though he was rich, yet for our sakes he became poor, so that we through his poverty might be made rich (see 2 Cor. 8:9).

Now we have a choice to make: will we lay up more treasure for ourselves, or will we be rich toward God? Sadly, when it comes to giving to God, most of us are middle-class Christians at best. We know all too well what it means to lay up treasure for ourselves. Evangelicals in America are the wealthiest Christians in the history of the world, yet we give less than 4 percent of our gross income to gospel work—a clear indication of where our real treasure lies.

But what would our lives be like if we were not so stingy? What does it mean to be rich toward God? I am rich toward God when his glory is my highest goal, when his worship is my deepest joy, and when his fellowship is my greatest satisfaction. I am rich toward God when I offer all my abilities for his work, without reserve. I am rich toward God when I take the time to serve people in need and give the first portion of everything I get to Christian ministry. I am rich toward God when I make the needs of the poor a priority in my financial giving and embrace a simple lifestyle that gives me more freedom for ministry. I am rich toward God when I decide there are some things I can live without so that I will have more to give to people who do not even have the gospel. I am rich toward God when I give and give until all I am and all I have is dedicated to his glory.

Will we lay up treasure for ourselves, or will we be rich toward the God who has been so generous to us? This was the question Jesus wanted the crowds to consider. Here is how Kent Hughes describes the choice we all must make:

> We can enlarge our savings and build huge accounts to hold it all. We can plan our retirement so we will have nothing to do but change positions in the sun. We can plan our menus for the twilight years so that nothing but the finest cuisine crosses our lips. We can live as if this is all of life. We can laugh our way to the grave—only to discover at the end that we have nothing and are in God's eyes fools. Or we can be rich toward God because we gave and gave and gave.[13]

This chapter began with a scene from John Grisham's best-selling novel *The Testament*, in which a dying billionaire dies unloved, but not alone. Greedy relatives gather around his bedside, hoping for their share of his massive inheritance. But the book has a surprise ending. After the old man dies, the family gathers to read his last will and testament, signed shortly

13. R. Kent Hughes, *Luke: That You May Know the Truth*, 2 vols., Preaching the Word (Wheaton, IL: Crossway, 1998), 2:50.

before his death. To their complete shock, the entire fortune is granted to an illegitimate daughter none of them has ever known. It turns out that this unexpected heiress is serving as a Christian missionary to people in Brazil.

A lawyer is sent to find her so that she can sign the necessary paperwork. When he finally tracks the woman down, she refuses to accept any part of the inheritance. The lawyer is dumbfounded, of course, because from his perspective life consists in the abundance of one's possessions. Yet because of her faith in Christ, the missionary has a completely different set of priorities. "You worship money," she tells the lawyer. "You're part of a culture where everything is measured by money. It's a religion."[14] But the missionary belongs to a different religion and serves a different God, so in the end she decides to put every last penny into a trust fund for the worldwide work of the gospel, including practical care for poor people in Brazil.

What has God given you to give away? The issue is not how much you have, or do not have, but your attitude about what you do not have, and your generosity with what you do have. Jesus is calling you to give more to God, to the point of costly personal sacrifice. You would be a fool not to give everything you are, and everything you have.

14. Grisham, *Testament*, 285.

53

ANXIOUS FOR NOTHING

Luke 12:22—34

And he said to his disciples, "Therefore I tell you, do not be anxious about your life, what you will eat, nor about your body, what you will put on. . . . Instead, seek his kingdom, and these things will be added to you." (Luke 12:22, 31)

According to *Panic-Anxiety.com*, there are three major components to anxiety. First, there is the physiological component, which features physical symptoms such as muscle tension, sweating, and palpitations of the heart. Second, there is the psychological component, which is characterized by emotional symptoms such as restlessness, sleeplessness, irritability, failure to concentrate, and feelings of fear. Finally, there is the social component, as people suffering anxiety cling to other people for reassurance, hoping that someone can help him or her feel safe.

The causes of anxiety are many. They include fears about the future, feelings of inadequacy, financial pressures, work-related stress, loneliness, family conflict, grief, and the fear of death. The proposed remedies are even more numerous. The Internet is replete with stress-relieving pharmaceuticals, herbal elixirs, aromatherapies, breathing techniques, self-help programs, and a thousand other treatment options.

No doubt some of these remedies are useful in certain ways. Nevertheless, Jesus offers his disciples a more complete cure from the worries of life. "Do not be anxious," he says, "because you have a good Father who knows what you need."

NOT TO WORRY

Jesus said this while he was challenging his disciples to be more generous. Rather than laying up treasure for themselves—like that fool of a farmer who kept building bigger barns—Jesus told his disciples to be rich toward God (Luke 12:21). Yet as soon as we think about giving away what we have, the worry always arises: How can I be sure that I will still have everything I need? So Jesus "said to his disciples, 'Therefore I tell you, do not be anxious about your life, what you will eat, nor about your body, what you will put on'" (Luke 12:22).

This is one of the clear commands of Christ: Don't worry. Jesus is speaking here in the imperative. In fact, it is a double imperative: Do not worry about either food or clothing—the basic necessities of life. Then Jesus explains why: "For life is more than food, and the body more than clothing" (Luke 12:23; cf. 1 Tim. 6:8). In other words, there are more important things in life than waiting around for the next meal. Furthermore, your body is more than a mannequin to dress up with this outfit or that fashion. Your life and your body are for God and the glory of his kingdom. So do not make food and clothing your reason for living. Do not treat them as ends in themselves, but only as means to the higher end of living for God.

To prove his point, Jesus gave two examples from the natural world—one for food and one for clothing. In verses 24 to 26 Jesus uses the raven as an illustration of the way God provides good things to eat, and then in verses 27 to 28 he uses the lily as an illustration of the way God provides good things to wear. In both cases, his point is to show how much more graciously God the Father will care for us as his children.

First, "Consider the ravens: they neither sow nor reap, they have neither storehouse nor barn, and yet God feeds them. Of how much more value

are you than the birds!" (Luke 12:24). Ravens are not terribly attractive birds. They are like crows, only bigger—great, squawking creatures
with wild, fierce eyes. Under Old Testament law ravens were ceremonially
unclean. Leviticus goes so far as to call ravens detestable (see Lev. 11:15).
Nevertheless, God graciously provides everything they need: "He gives . . .
to the young ravens that cry" (Ps. 147:9). So God put the question to Job:
"Who provides for the raven its prey, when its young ones cry to God for
help, and wander about for lack of food?" (Job 38:41). The answer is that
God provides for the ravens, as he does for all his creatures.

Jesus pointed out that these birds get what they need without sowing,
reaping, or storing. Ravens are not farmers; they are scavengers. They take
whatever they can get from the produce of the land. Nevertheless, they get
what they need, because this is the way God feeds them.

Jesus used this illustration to make a "how much more" argument. He
reasoned from something lesser to something greater. If God takes care of
ravens—of all creatures—then he will certainly take care of us. The point
is not that we should live like ravens. The way God provides for us is different from the way he provides for them. In point of fact, human beings *do*
sow and reap and store. God cares for each creature according to its own
nature, but if God provides for birds that are living claw to beak, he will certainly provide for us. Of course we need to work hard, plan for the future,
and give reasonable attention to the things God has placed in our care.
Yet there is no sense worrying about our daily needs. Hudson Taylor, the
great missionary to China, became famous for trusting God to meet all his
needs, even when there seemed to be little hope of any provision. Yet even
Hudson Taylor recognized the importance of faithful obedience and hard
work as the ordinary means of God's provision: "the use of means ought
not to lessen our faith in God: and our faith in God ought not to hinder
our using whatever means he has given us for the accomplishment of his
own purposes."[1]

How unnecessary it is—indeed, how absurd it is—for us to be anxious
about things that God has promised to provide. Worry gains us nothing,
and therefore we really are anxious for nothing, as Jesus went on to say:
"And which of you by being anxious can add a single hour to his span of

---

1. Hudson Taylor, quoted in Marshall Broomhall, *The Man Who Believed God* (London: China
Inland Mission, 1929), 53.

life? If then you are not able to do as small a thing as that, why are you anxious about the rest?" (Luke 12:25–26).

There are two ways to understand what Jesus is saying here. According to the King James Version, Jesus said, "Which of you can add to his stature one cubit?" whereas in the English Standard Version he asks, "Which of you can add a single hour to his span of life?" Both translations are possible, but the latter meaning is more common and seems to make more sense. However nice it is to be tall, what most people really want is more time—more time to get things done and more time to live. If only we had one more hour in the day, one more day in the week, one more week in the year! Yet we will not get anything more by worrying about it. All our worrying will not add even a single day to our lifespan. It will not help us one little bit.

In fact, far from adding anything, anxiety always subtracts. Worry is a thief: it steals our time. Our thoughts turn to our troubles, and then rather than praying about them or doing the things God is calling us to do, we waste time worrying about them. Worry steals our rest. We lie awake at night, anxious about tomorrow, and then we get up too tired to work hard, and this only adds to our anxiety. Worry steals our health, as we suffer the physical effects of our anxiety. Worry steals our obedience, as it tempts us to other sins like irritability, addiction, and laziness, or on the other hand, overwork. Worry steals our hope, as we fear the worst about the future. All kinds of difficulties arise in our minds—most of which will never come to pass. Kierkegaard said it like this: "Worriers feel every blow / That never falls / And they cry over things / They will never lose."[2]

What a sad waste it all is! Worry shrivels the soul, robbing our joy, leaving us ill-equipped to face the spiritual and emotional challenges of each new day. Few things are as discouraging to our spirit, or as destructive of our contentment, or as detrimental to our witness as the anxious worries of a troubled heart. So Jesus asks, "Why are you anxious?" (Luke 12:26).

Well, why *are* you so anxious? If there is nothing at all to gain by worrying, and so much to lose, why worry about your daily needs? Consider the ravens, and see every bird on the wing as a witness that God will provide.

---

2. Søren Kierkegaard, quoted in R. Kent Hughes, *Luke: That You May Know the Truth*, 2 vols., Preaching the Word (Wheaton, IL: Crossway, 1998), 2:53.

CONSIDER THE LILIES

Jesus' second illustration related to clothing and came from the world of botany: "Consider the lilies, how they grow: they neither toil nor spin, yet I tell you, even Solomon in all his glory was not arrayed like one of these" (Luke 12:27). It is easy to imagine Jesus standing in a field of wildflowers when he said this, just as it is easy to imagine that there were ravens in the vicinity. The "lilies" to which he referred were not Easter lilies, but various flowers of the field, which Jesus used to make some striking comparisons.

Flowers do less work than we do. In fact, they do not do any work at all. They do not toil; they just grow. They do not spin fabric to use for clothing; they just wear what God gave them. Yet how marvelously they are adorned! Not even Solomon could compete with their beauty. As the wealthiest of kings, Solomon wore the gold and purple of his royal office; yet even the littlest flower surpasses his splendor. Here Jesus was taking pleasure in the beauty of his own creation. As the Son of God he had personally designed every blossom. The bright flowers of the field were a reflection of his divine beauty. With evident satisfaction, Jesus pointed to the lilies and rightly declared their superlative splendor. Although they do less work than we do, by the grace of God, they far surpass us in the finery of their raiment.

Furthermore, flowers live much shorter lives than we do. This was another aspect of the comparison: "But if God so clothes the grass, which is alive in the field today, and tomorrow is thrown into the oven, how much more will he clothe you, O you of little faith!" (Luke 12:28). Once again Jesus used a "how much more" argument, reasoning from something lesser to something greater. Wildflowers are not known for their longevity. Jesus knew the words of Isaiah: "The grass withers, the flower fades" (Isa. 40:7). Flowers have a transitory existence. So why take the trouble to make them so beautiful? Why waste so much effort on their adornment? Nevertheless, the Creator God has lavished the flowers of the field with ravishing beauty, from the morning dew on the first tulip, to the high meadow carpeted with mountain blossoms in springtime.

If God squanders such beauty on little flowers, what will he do for the people he made in his image and saved through the gift of his Son? What will he do for the children he loves as a Father and has destined to live forever? Jesus answers by saying, "how much more will he clothe you" (Luke 12:28).

We should reason from the lesser to the greater and make the application to our own daily needs: God will take care of us! Every flower we see is a testimony to his loving providence. Martin Luther said it like this: "The flowers stand there and make us blush and become our teachers. Thank you, flowers, you who are to be devoured by the cows! God has exalted you very highly, that you become our masters and teachers."[3] We should learn, therefore, what the flowers are there to teach us.

If we have not yet learned not to worry about our basic needs, it must be because of our unbelief. Jesus plainly identifies the heart issue at the root of all our anxiety when he says, "O you of little faith!" (Luke 12:28). Worry comes from not believing in the God who feeds the ravens and dresses the lilies. Worry is inversely proportional to our faith. To the extent that we worry, just to that extent we are not trusting in God, and therefore we are sinning against him. Most people think of worry as one of the smaller sins, if it is a sin at all. We tell ourselves that worrying about things is not nearly as wrong as lusting after them or getting angry about them. Yet Jesus says that anxiety is unbelief, and there is no greater sin than not believing in God.

When we worry, we deny God's promise that he will give us whatever we truly need. We deny his wisdom, not trusting that he fully appreciates the difficulties of our situation. We deny his goodness, not believing that he has our best interests at heart. We deny his sovereignty, not waiting for him to provide what we need in his own good time. Our anxiety is a direct attack on the God-ness of God as it relates to the needs of our own daily lives.

This means that the remedy for all our fearful worries is more faith in our faithful God. As soon as we start to feel anxious, we need to stop thinking about our troubles and start thinking about the character of our God—his wisdom, his goodness, his sovereignty, and all the promises he has made to us in Christ.

Seek the Kingdom

When we start trusting God to provide, we are liberated from the grasping pursuit of temporary things and can start living for God's eternal kingdom.

3. Martin Luther, *Sermons of Martin Luther*, ed. John Nicholas Lenker, vol. 5 (Grand Rapids: Baker, 1983), 115.

Having given a clear command not to worry, with two vivid illustrations, Jesus told his disciples that there are two and only two ways to live. One is to live for ourselves and the things of this world, and the other is to live for God and his kingdom. Jesus said: "And do not seek what you are to eat and what you are to drink, nor be worried. For all the nations of the world seek after these things, and your Father knows that you need them. Instead, seek his kingdom, and these things will be added to you" (Luke 12:29–31).

The key verb in these verses is "seek." To seek is to set your heart on something, to make it your main objective. What you seek is what you think about; it is what you pursue; it is what you live for.

Some people live for this world. They are like the rich fool who was worried about having enough storage space for all his stuff. Such people are preoccupied with food, clothing, and material possessions. Their attention is dominated by the things they do not have and want to get, or the things they are about to purchase, or the things they already own but still have to pay off. They are strongly attracted to the merchandise in the mail order catalog and the lifestyle portrayed in the glamour magazines: fine dining, fabulous clothes, and a better-looking body. Or maybe they are just struggling to get by, but all they can think about is getting ahead in life. This is what most people live for. It is what people have always lived for, all over the world.

Jesus tells us to live a different way. He tells us to seek the kingdom of God. In other words, he tells us to pursue the establishment of God's royal rule in every area of life. The kingdom of God comes through the proclamation of salvation through the death and resurrection of Jesus Christ. By faith in Christ, the grace of God begins to rule in our hearts, and then as we live in loyal subjection to our king, that grace is extended into the lives of others. This should always come first for us in our worship, our work, our play, our families and our neighborhoods: the kingdom of grace that God is establishing through his Son. We do not pursue earthly possessions, therefore, but live for the work that God is doing to establish his eternal kingdom. We need to reason the way the famous missionary C. T. Studd reasoned in his life motto: "If Jesus Christ is God and died for me, then no sacrifice can be too great for me to make for him."[4]

Of course we still need our daily bread. Of course we need to work so that we can eat. Of course we need to provide for our families and plan for

---

4. C. T. Studd, quoted in Norman P. Grubb, *C. T. Studd—Cricketer and Pioneer* (London: Lutterworth Press, 1972), 141.

the future. The Bible speaks to all of these issues. But Jesus tells us not to seek these things, or at least not to seek them *first*.

Jesus also tells us not to worry about them. The word he uses for worry at the end of verse 29 (*meteōrizesthe*) originally referred to ships tossed about by the waves of a stormy sea. While this is not what the word still meant at the time of Christ, its etymology provides an apt analogy for the turmoil that comes when we abandon God's kingdom for the anxious pursuit of worldly possessions. Worry tosses the soul like a ship in stormy seas. The issue is not what we have or do not have. The issue is what we are striving after, what we are living for, and therefore what we are anxious about. When Jesus tells his disciples not to seek food and drink, he

> does not in any way mean that they must be lazy and neglect their ordinary work and duties, but that they must not allow their hearts to become so attached to material things that their inner lives are controlled by those, and they are not to be vexed and anxious about these things. Everyone must perform his daily task, which God gives him, whole-heartedly and to the best of his ability, but the inner life of the believer must not be caught in the clutches of materialism and of anxiety with regard to worldly things.[5]

What delivers us from all such worldly anxiety is faith in our loving Father. According to Jesus, the reason we do not need to seek after material things is that our Father already knows what we need. The truth of this promise is expressed in the gentle humor of a little nursery rhyme:

Said the Raven to the Sparrow,
"I should really like to know
Why these anxious human beings
Rush about and worry so."

Said the Sparrow to the Raven,
"Friend, I think that it must be
They have no Heavenly Father,
Such as cares for you and me."[6]

5. Norval Geldenhuys, *The Gospel of Luke*, New International Commentary on the New Testament (Grand Rapids: Eerdmans, 1951), 358.
6. Adapted from an anonymous rhyme quoted in Hughes, *Luke*, 2:52.

The truth is that we *do* have a heavenly Father, who has given his own Son for our salvation, and who knows exactly what we need. What delivers us from the senseless pursuit of worldly things is knowing for sure that we have a good Father, who knows what we need and has the wisdom to provide it at just the right time, in exactly the right way. When we seek the kingdom, all the other things we need—meaning the basic necessities of life, not the luxuries that we do not truly need—will be added to us. We can let God "worry" about all those things. As a Father who loves his children, it is his pleasure to provide. He will keep on providing for us every day until we finish the work he has called us to do for his kingdom.

Edith Schaeffer testifies to God's provision in her wonderful book about L'Abri, the Christian shelter that she and her husband, Francis, established in Switzerland. God had called the Schaeffers to make a home in Europe for young people who needed to find Christ. Yet their visas were about to expire, and unless they found a permanent residence, they would be expelled from Switzerland. In desperation, Edith prayed out loud, "Oh, Heavenly Father . . . if You want us to stay in Switzerland, if Your word to me concerning *L'Abri* means our being in these mountains, then I know You are able to find a house, and lead me to it in the *next half hour. Nothing* is impossible to You. But You will have to do it."[7]

Suddenly Edith Schaeffer heard someone in the street calling her name. It was a real estate dealer who wanted to know if she had found anything yet. Soon he was driving her to a mountain chalet that was unexpectedly available. Her prayers were answered; God had found the house. Yet there was a further difficulty. The chalet was for sale, but the Schaeffers did not have any money to buy it, and they were nearly out of time. As Edith prayed that night, she had faith that God would still provide. But she also asked for a sign: "Oh, please show us Thy will about this house tomorrow, and if we are to *buy* it . . . send us one thousand dollars before ten o'clock tomorrow morning."[8]

The next morning a letter came with the post by train. It was from a couple who had been praying for the Schaeffers, but had never supported them financially because they had so little to give. However, the couple had come into some money unexpectedly, and this time they were sending a

---

7. Edith Schaeffer, *L'Abri* (Wheaton, IL: Tyndale, 1969), 92.
8. Ibid., 97.

check in the amount of . . . one thousand dollars! Within a matter of days the rest of the money came in—none of it asked for, but all of it prayed for. As the Schaeffers sought the kingdom, their Father added what was needed.

But of course the best example of trusting in God's fatherly care is Jesus himself, who traveled through the wilderness and had no place to call his own, but never went begging for bread. Because he fully trusted his Father to provide for all his needs, Jesus was able to seek the kingdom with all his heart, mind, soul, and strength. His Father cared for him right to the very end of his kingdom work, when he died on the cross for our sins, and when he prayed that the Father would raise him from the dead. When Jesus tells us to trust the Father for everything we need, he is telling us to do what he did in his own life and saving death. Now Jesus will help us to do the same thing by the gracious work of the Holy Spirit, who whispers to our hearts that the Father loves us.

PUT YOUR MONEY WHERE YOUR HEART IS

Most Christians would be happy for Jesus to stop there. We find it hard enough to trust God for the things we need. But as we have seen over and over again in the Gospel of Luke, Jesus always wants to take us deeper in our discipleship. He wants us to make more and more costly sacrifices for the kingdom of God, until we know the joy of living only for his glory. So here Jesus goes beyond telling us not to worry about what we need and tells us to give away what we have: "Fear not, little flock, for it is your Father's good pleasure to give you the kingdom. Sell your possessions, and give to the needy. Provide yourselves with moneybags that do not grow old, with a treasure in heaven that does not fail, where no thief approaches and no moth destroys. For where your treasure is, there will your heart be also" (Luke 12:32–34).

To put this in financial terms, Jesus was calling his disciples both to divest and to invest. There are things we have that Jesus wants us to give away, and when we give them away we need to put them in the right place. The Christian life is a continuous transfer of funds in which we divest from the world in order to invest in the kingdom of God.

We start by giving more of what we have to people who are going without. Up to this point Jesus has been talking about food and clothing. But

677

what should we do about all our other possessions? We should start by tithing them—giving away at least 10 percent of our gross income for Christian work. Next, we should seek to raise the percentage of our giving, asking God to increase our faith, so that we can increase our giving. Then, as we learn about various needs in our community and in the wider world, we should give above and beyond what we were planning to give, and even above and beyond what we once thought we were able to give. We should strategize about making do with less, so that we have more to give for the work of God's kingdom. The deeper we grow in our commitment to Christ, the more we are able to give.

Of course Jesus is not saying that no Christian can ever own anything, or that we all have to live in poverty. We know from what Luke wrote in the book of Acts that many of the first Christians had money and property to call their own (see Acts 4:34–37; 5:4). We also know from other places in Scripture that it is permissible for Christians to have possessions and use them for the glory of God (e.g., Ex. 20:15, 17; Eph. 4:28; 1 Tim. 6:17–19). But let those passages preach themselves! Here we need to preach the radical investment strategy that Jesus preached to his disciples: "Sell your possessions, and give to the needy" (Luke 12:33).

This is the safest investment we can ever make. Earthly riches are so uncertain. Many wealthy people suffer sudden reversals and end up destitute. Moneybags grow old; treasure fails; robbers steal; moths destroy. Or to put this in more contemporary terms, our earthly investments are subject to depreciation, loss, theft, and liquidation. But whatever we invest in the kingdom of God is safe forever. When we give to gospel work—especially to the poor—our funds are transferred directly to heaven, where they are exchanged for the currency of glory. "Give away these earthly things," said Cyril of Alexandria, "and win that which is in heaven. Give that which you must leave, even against your will, that you may not lose things later. Lend your wealth to God, that you may be really rich."[9]

People say, "You can't take it with you," but the truth is that you *can* send it on ahead, as long as you invest in the eternal kingdom of God. Do not settle for short-term investments that will only help you when you retire. Extend your planning horizon into eternity, where nothing ever depreci-

9. Cyril of Alexandria, "Commentary on Luke," in *Luke*, ed. Arthur A. Just Jr., Ancient Christian Commentary on Scripture, NT 3 (Downers Grove, IL: InterVarsity, 2003), 211.

ates, and everything accrues to the glory of God. "Store up your treasure on earth," writes David Gooding, "and it will inevitably pull your heart in the direction of earth. Store it in heaven, and it will pull your heart, and with it your goals, ambitions and longings, toward heaven."[10]

We know that this is the best investment advice we could ever receive, yet we still hold on to our earthly treasure. Why is this? It is partly because we do not really trust our Father to provide. Our anxiety gets in the way of our generosity. Here we need to see how the teaching Jesus gives in this passage all fits together. We are not to worry because our Father knows what we need, and because our Father knows what we need, we do not need to be afraid of giving away what we have.

Another reason we make so many poor investments is that our hearts are in the wrong place. Jesus said, "Where your treasure is, there will your heart be also" (Luke 12:34). We cannot help but spend our wealth on the things that we love the most. When we love ourselves more than we love God, we forfeit the opportunity to give to mercy ministry, local evangelism, church planting, world missions, and all the other Christian work that advances the kingdom of God. But how much more is gained when we learn to love the things that God loves and then put our money where our heart is.

There is another side to Edith Schaeffer's story of trusting her heavenly Father to provide what she needed to purchase a chalet for the work of L'Abri. The thousand-dollar check she received from her friends came with the following letter:

> Three months ago Art came home from work with an unexpected amount of money. . . . We decided at first to buy a new car, then came to the conclusion that we didn't need a new car. Our next thought was to invest in buying a little house, which we would rent. We went to look at houses, and as we looked over a very likely small house I suddenly saw signs of termites in the beams. "Look, Art," I said, "Doesn't that remind you of the verse which says, Lay not up for yourselves treasures upon earth, where moth and rust doth corrupt, and where thieves break through and steal: but lay up for yourselves treasures in heaven, where neither moth nor rust doth corrupt, and where thieves do not break through nor steal." I then asked, "Art, would you be willing to take this money and invest it literally in heaven? . . . rather than investing it in

10. David Gooding, *According to Luke: A New Exposition of the Third Gospel* (Grand Rapids: Eerdmans, 1987), 241.

another house on earth for added income? Would you be willing to give it to the Lord's work somewhere?" He replied, "Yes, Helen, I would."

Well . . . that was three months ago, and all during these three months we have been asking God to show us what He would have us do with this money . . . now tonight we have come to a definite decision, and both of us feel certain that we are meant to send you this money . . . to buy a house somewhere that will always be open to young people.[11]

What investments are you making? Jesus says we will put our treasure where our heart is. So where is your heart? For some it is with the clothing on the rack, the product on the Internet, the improvement to the house, and all the dreams for financial security. For others it is with the homeless in the city, the orphans in Africa, the suffering church in the persecuted world, and the gospel ministry of the local church.

It is always easy to tell where someone's heart is: it is wherever you are putting your treasure. Therefore the real question is, "Is your heart in the right place?" Because when your heart is in the right place, your treasure will end up in the right place too.

11. Schaeffer, *L'Abri*, 97–98.

54

READY, OR NOT?

Luke 12:35—48

"But know this, that if the master of the house had known at
what hour the thief was coming, he would not have left his house
to be broken into. You also must be ready, for the Son of Man is
coming at an hour you do not expect." (Luke 12:39–40)

eady or not, Jesus is coming. Once he came to die for sinners, and once again he will come to judge the world. We
know this for sure because it was promised by angels. On
the great day when Jesus ascended to heaven, two angels told his disciples,
"This Jesus, who was taken up from you into heaven, will come in the same
way as you saw him go into heaven" (Acts 1:11). We also know that he is
coming again because the apostles repeated this promise to the church. So
Paul testified that "the Lord himself will descend from heaven with a cry
of command, with the voice of an archangel, and with the sound of the
trumpet of God" (1 Thess. 4:16). Jesus said it himself: "Behold, I am coming
soon, bringing my recompense with me, to repay everyone for what he has
done" (Rev. 22:12).

Yet even apart from these promises, we know that Jesus *must* come again
to consummate his saving work. How else can every wrong be righted and

every evil brought to justice? How else can Satan be defeated and con-demned to hell? How else can Jesus gather his people to himself? How else can he receive the honor that he alone deserves, unless he comes again in power and glory?

Jesus is coming—just as he promised—to judge the world. Are you ready, or not?

READY FOR THE MASTER

Jesus had been teaching his disciples not to live for earthly treasure, but to seek first the kingdom of God. To prepare them always to be ready for his second coming, he taught them the parable of the waiting servants, fol-lowed by a second, closely-related parable about a faithful steward. The first parable went like this:

> Stay dressed for action and keep your lamps burning, and be like men who are waiting for their master to come home from the wedding feast, so that they may open the door to him at once when he comes and knocks. Blessed are those servants whom the master finds awake when he comes. Truly, I say to you, he will dress himself for service and have them recline at table, and he will come and serve them. If he comes in the second watch, or in the third, and finds them awake, blessed are those servants! (Luke 12:35–38)

Ready servants who watch for their master will be blessed at his coming. Jesus begins by imagining a master who has gone to celebrate a wedding. In those days the feasting and the dancing would last late into the night. Who could tell when the master would return? Maybe he would come back home around midnight, or maybe later—sometime in the last watches of the night.

Whenever the master returned, his servants would be ready. All night long they would "stay dressed for action." Today this would mean they rolled up their sleeves; in those days it meant taking their long, flowing robes and tucking them into their belts, so as not to trip over them when they sprang up to open the door. They also kept the home fires burning. A good servant would tend the flame in his oil lamp, so that when his master returned, he could light the way.

Watchful and wakeful, these men waited for their master, ready at any moment to serve as his door opener and light switch. Here is how Kent Hughes imagines the welcome their master received: "Warm light streamed from the windows, breathless, smiling, eager servants bearing shining lamps gathered at the door, and no doubt there was a choice nocturnal snack on the table."[1]

This picture of ready service reminds me of the remarkable service that diners receive at Philadelphia's *Le Bec Fin*, reputed to be one of America's finest restaurants. As you walk up to the restaurant, the doors open and the wait staff is ready to receive you, to help with your coat, and to seat you at a table. Then they cater to your every culinary desire. The servers are so alert and attentive that it feels as if you have your own personal servant. Almost before you know that you need something, it is already provided.

This is the kind of service that the master in the parable always enjoyed. His servants were eager to please; they kept a sharp edge to their preparedness. Not knowing when their master would return, they were in a state of perpetual readiness. The quality of their service was a joy to their master's heart. As he walked home from the wedding that night, it may have occurred to him to wonder whether his servants would still be waiting, or whether perhaps they might have fallen asleep. It was so late that it would be perfectly understandable if they had gone to bed. But no sooner had the man knocked than the door was opened, and he found his servants at the ready.

Here the parable takes a surprising turn, because Jesus imagines the master becoming a servant to his servants. He is so overjoyed with their faithfulness in waiting for his return that he tucks his robe into his own belt, invites his servants to sit around his table, and begins to serve them an impromptu feast. This was the master's blessing on the ready servants who watched and waited for his coming.

For us this is a heartwarming scene of late-night fellowship, but for the people listening to Jesus this role reversal was almost unthinkable. What master would ever wear a servant's clothing, or invite his slaves to sit down to his own feast? What master would ever make himself nothing by taking the form of a servant?

1. R. Kent Hughes, *Luke: That You May Know the Truth*, 2 vols., Preaching the Word (Wheaton, IL: Crossway, 1998), 2:61.

A master like Jesus, of course! What would be unthinkable for anyone else was at the very heart of our Savior's mission to the world. He was the Master of the universe, the Lord of all creation. Yet he had come to serve his people, and by serving them, to set them free. This parable of the waiting servants could only be told by the kind of God who would wear the weakness of his people by taking on the flesh of their humanity, who would strip his robes to wash the feet of his disciples, and who would serve as their substitute by dying on the cross for their sins.

When we know the rest of the gospel story, we can see that Jesus put himself into this parable. We can also see what a blessing it is to serve him as our master. Jesus has worn the garments of our servitude. He has served us to the very death. He has invited us to sit down at his table, where he feeds our needy souls. Now we wait for him to come again, ready and waiting for the day when we will enter the fullness of our Master's joy.

NOT READY

Not everyone is as watchful as the servants in the parable. So Jesus used a slightly different image to give a word of caution: "But know this, that if the master of the house had known at what hour the thief was coming, he would not have left his house to be broken into" (Luke 12:39).

Once again Jesus describes an unexpected arrival at someone's house. Only this time the master is the one who should have been ready, and the person who arrives does not come to bless, but to burgle. After the crime has been committed, the master of the house laments his lack of preparedness. If only he had known when the thief was coming, he could easily have protected his property. This is what people always say when they suffer an unexpected and preventable loss: If only we had known in advance!

Some people are ready, some are not. The point of this mini-parable is that people who are not prepared will suffer great loss at the coming of Christ. Here is how Jesus made the application: "You also must be ready, for the Son of Man is coming at an hour you do not expect" (Luke 12:40).

There are two important questions to answer about this verse. First, which coming did Jesus have in mind: his first or his second? Jesus came once to die for sinners, and he is coming again to judge the world. Right now we are living "between the times"—that is, between the first and second comings of Christ. But when Jesus told his disciples to be ready, was he referring to his first advent or his final triumph?

Some scholars say this command refers to his earthly ministry, culminating in his death and resurrection. Jesus was helping his original disciples be more prepared for the impending crisis of his crucifixion. What sense would it make to tell them to get ready for his second coming? Such a command would not even come into effect until after he ascended to heaven. At this point they did not even understand that Jesus was going to die for their sins, let alone rise from the dead and return to heaven.

Nevertheless, it seems likely that Jesus was indeed looking ahead and helping his disciples know how they should live in the time between his ascension to heaven and his coming on the clouds with glory. Jesus often prepared his disciples for things in advance, and he taught them many things they did not fully understand until after he rose from the dead. In this case, he taught them something that also has a great deal of relevance for us, namely, that we need to be ready for his second coming.

The title that Jesus uses for himself here—"the Son of Man"—is associated with the end of history. This Old Testament title referred to the glory of Christ's deity, and especially to his final triumph. In his vision of the last days, the prophet Daniel saw "one like a son of man" coming on the clouds to receive an everlasting dominion (Dan. 7:13–14). This is not something that happened the first time that Jesus came, but something that will happen only when he returns.

Jesus is coming again. His second coming is the next big event in salvation history, and one of the main promises of the New Testament. The promise is made in nearly every New Testament book—more than three hundred times in all. Jesus is coming again. His coming will be personal: Jesus himself will return, in his own glorious resurrection body (see Phil. 3:20–21). His coming will be visible: "Behold, he is coming with the clouds, and every eye will see him" (Rev. 1:7). His coming will be glorious. The Scripture describes it as "the appearing of the glory of our great God and Savior Jesus Christ" (Titus 2:13). This personal, visible, glorious return is also imminent. Jesus said, "Surely, I am coming soon" (Rev. 22:20). This is the advent that Jesus had in mind when he told his disciples to be ready for the coming of the Son of Man.

Another good question to ask about these verses is, why does Jesus compare his coming to a thief in the night? Although this may not seem like a flattering comparison, it is common in Scripture: "the day of the Lord will come like a thief in the night" (1 Thess. 5:2; cf. 2 Peter 3:10). As Jesus said to the church in Sardis, "If you will not wake up, I will come like a thief, and you will not know at what hour I will come against you" (Rev. 3:3; cf. 16:15).

Jesus uses this comparison because his coming will be so unexpected. Thieves are stealthy; no one ever knows when they are coming. So it is with the second coming of Christ: no one knows when he will return. But there is also a second point of comparison, which is the loss that some people will suffer when that day comes. When Jesus returns, people who are not ready for his coming will suffer eternal loss: "Just as the master of the house who is not constantly on the watch is surprised and robbed by the thief, so also those who *are not ready* for His second coming (who neither believe in Him nor obey Him) will suffer irrevocable loss—His coming will bring with it their everlasting destruction."[2]

Are you ready, or not? Jesus says we always need to be ready, because we never know when he will come again. Being ready means getting right with God by trusting in Jesus Christ. Unless we have prayed to receive Jesus as Savior and Lord, we are not ready. How can we possibly be prepared to meet Jesus if we have not asked him to forgive our sins? Being ready also means having a sense of urgency about sharing the gospel. Other people need to be ready to meet Jesus, too. He is coming very soon. But how will people be ready to meet him unless someone loves them enough to give them the gospel?

Being ready means praying for the kingdom to come, asking God to expand his rule in our own lives, in the church, in our community, and around the world. It also means devoting our lives to Christian service. Given what the parable says about servants and masters, probably this should be our primary application. If we are God's servants, then we need to be busy teaching God's Word, healing the sick, feeding the hungry, visiting prisoners, caring for children, helping the elderly, or doing whatever humble service we have the ability and the opportunity to do. Time is short, and we need to make

2. Norval Geldenhuys, *The Gospel of Luke*, New International Commentary on the New Testament (Grand Rapids: Eerdmans, 1951), 363.

the most of it. The Son of Man may come today, tonight, or tomorrow. But whenever he comes, Jesus says we must be ready. Are you ready, or not?

Faithful in God's House

Peter had another question for Jesus. It was not a question about when Jesus was coming, or why he compared his coming to a thief in the night. Instead, Peter wanted to know whether Jesus was speaking only to his disciples, or to everyone, so he asked, "Lord, are you telling this parable for us or for all?" (Luke 12:41).

Peter had noticed that sometimes Jesus spoke to the multitudes (especially when he spoke in parables), but that on other occasions he spoke more specifically to his own followers (such as when he explained his parables). Peter wanted to know which kind of conversation this was, especially since Jesus had just been talking about some people suffering loss at his coming.

Jesus did not give Peter a direct answer, but responded with a question of his own. This question really amounted to another mini-parable about servants and their rewards: "Who then is the faithful and wise manager, whom his master will set over his household, to give them their portion of food at the proper time?" (Luke 12:42). Jesus was still talking about servants and masters, but with a slightly different emphasis. In the parable about the late night wedding, the servants were praised for their watchfulness; here the servant is praised for his faithfulness.

Once again, the master is away from his house and appoints one of his slaves to serve as his steward. The steward was still a servant, but he was responsible to provide whatever rations the other servants needed, and to that end, he was entrusted with his master's goods. If the steward did his work wisely and faithfully, the household would flourish and he would receive his master's praise. In fact, he would probably get what people today would call a promotion. Jesus said, "Blessed is that servant whom his master will find so doing when he comes. Truly, I say to you, he will set him over all his possessions" (Luke 12:43–44). A famous example from the Bible is Joseph's promotion to the head of Potiphar's house in Egypt. The general principle is that faithful servants gain their master's reward.

In one sense, this principle applies to everyone. Throughout this discourse Jesus had been challenging people to make wise use of their material goods. The parable of the rich fool, the examples of the raven and the lily, the statement about putting your heart where your treasure is—in all of these illustrations Jesus had been teaching people what to do with what they had. Here again, in the example of the wise steward, Jesus is talking about portions of food and household possessions, calling us all to be faithful stewards.[3]

We are not the masters of the house—God is. Whatever things we "own" are really on loan from God. Therefore, we must exercise good stewardship, using what God has given to us for the benefit of others. The master entrusts his goods to the steward with the expectation that the steward will use them to feed others and not simply to stuff himself. In the same way, God has given us goods to use for others, and not only for ourselves. Here Jesus is teaching about being rich toward God, seeking the kingdom, and giving to the needy. If you are a faithful steward of your possessions, you will gain your Master's reward.

There is another way to take these verses, however. A steward is put in charge of a household, and this is exactly the responsibility Jesus gave to Peter and the other apostles. The New Testament describes the church as God's household (e.g., 1 Tim. 3:15), with the apostles serving as its stewards (e.g., 1 Cor. 4:1). As the stewards of God's house, the apostles were entrusted with the responsibility of feeding people the Word of God. In time, this sacred trust was passed on to other men: the pastors and elders of the church. So while the example of the faithful steward applies to all of us in the use of our material possessions, it also has a more specific application to people who have teaching authority in the church. One old commentator offered the following paraphrase: "The precepts that I have given apply to every individual, but with greater force to you who are in the situation of stewards, to whom much has been entrusted, and from whom consequently much will be required."[4]

---

3. On the connections between Luke 12:41–48 and the rest of the chapter, see David Gooding, *According to Luke: A New Exposition of the Third Gospel* (Grand Rapids: Eerdmans, 1987), 245.

4. John Richardson Major, quoted in J. C. Ryle, *Expository Thoughts on the Gospels, Luke* (1858; reprint Cambridge: James Clarke, 1976), 2:93.

God has given pastors and elders spiritual responsibility. They must be faithful in their calling to feed the family of God, giving each person "their portion of food at the proper time" (Luke 12:42). This means preaching the Word of God in public worship, teaching the Word of God in classes and small group Bible studies, and sharing the Word of God in private counseling and personal discipleship. Every member of God's household needs his or her portion of Scripture, and if we are called to any kind of teaching ministry in the church, we must be faithful to give the people of God good spiritual nourishment.

Here Jesus promises that faithful servants will gain their Master's reward. What a blessing it is for workers when the boss walks in and finds them doing their jobs. Jesus applies this principle to Christian service. In verse 43 he says God will bless us when he finds us doing his will. Then in verse 44 he says God will promote us to positions of greater responsibility, especially on the day when we begin to rule with Christ in the kingdom of God. Charles Spurgeon said: "May the Lord keep you waiting, working, watching, that when he comes, you may have the blessedness of entering upon some larger, higher, nobler service than you could accomplish now, for which you are preparing by the lowlier and more arduous service of this world!"[5]

Will you be ready for that kind of responsibility, or not? It all depends on whether you are faithful or not—faithful to your calling in the household of God.

WITH THE UNFAITHFUL

Sadly, not every servant is faithful in doing his master's will. This is especially true when the master is absent. How tempting it is to slack off when no one is there to check up on your work. It is only human nature: When the boss is away, the workers will play! But sooner or later the day of reckoning comes. In most situations, this only means that people have to get back to work, but the situation that Jesus described was rather more serious: "If that servant says to himself, 'My master is delayed in coming,' and begins to beat the male and female servants, and to eat and drink and get drunk, the master of that servant will come on a day when he does not expect him, and

5. Charles H. Spurgeon, "Watching for Christ's Coming," *The Metropolitan Tabernacle Pulpit* (Pasadena, TX: Pilgrim, 1975), 39:165.

at an hour he does not know, and will cut him in pieces and put him with the unfaithful" (Luke 12:45–46).

What terrible judgment will fall on every unfaithful servant! Here Jesus describes a situation of gross negligence. The steward deceives himself into thinking that his master will not come home any time soon. So rather than nourishing the other servants, he abuses them. Rather than keeping his sacred trust, he squanders his master's provisions by gorging himself on the best food in the pantry and the finest wine in the cellar. The man is an abusive, drunken, gluttonous disgrace.

Many people treat God the same way today. They scoff at the idea that Jesus is coming again (see 2 Peter 3:4). They take advantage of the time God is giving them to repent by constantly putting God off. They abuse the good things God has given by squandering their resources on themselves. They are not faithful in serving Jesus Christ, and **they are not** ready for his return. This is even true in the church. How many pastors and elders are guilty of the very sins that Jesus describes in verses 45 and 46—abusive in their treatment of the men and women under their care, negligent in their ministry of God's Word, and careless in their indulgence of earthly pleasures?

These are matters for serious self-examination. Do I believe that Jesus is coming soon, or do I live as if he has been delayed? Am I using my possessions for the good of others and the glory of God, or am I careless in my stewardship, using things mainly for myself? Am I teaching others the grace of God, or am I silent about my faith? These are good tests of our readiness for Christ's return. Here is another good test, to use throughout the day: Am I a faithful servant, or would I be embarrassed if Jesus returned right now and found me doing what I am doing? Always act, said Charles Spurgeon, "just as you would wish to be acting if he were to come."[6]

There will be a day of judgment. Here Jesus describes the terrible fate of an unfaithful steward who is unprepared for his master's coming. His master will come when he is least expected and "cut his servant in pieces" (Luke 12:46). Such a grisly punishment was not unheard of in the ancient world, yet some scholars wonder whether Jesus was speaking literally. This may perhaps have been a manner of speech, like today when people

---

6. Spurgeon, "Christ's Coming," 39:162.

say, "My boss is going to *kill* me when he finds out about this!" But in any case, the punishment for an unfaithful steward will be severe.

It will be somewhat less severe for any other servants who, like the steward, are unfaithful. Jesus said, "And that servant who knew his master's will but did not get ready or act according to his will, will receive a severe beating. But the one who did not know, and did what deserved a beating, will receive a light beating" (Luke 12:47–48). Here we learn that judgment is according to knowledge. The more a servant knows about what his master requires, the more serious his sin in failing to obey, and the more strictly he will be punished for any unfaithfulness.

This same principle holds true for the final judgment, which is what this parable is really about. People sometimes ask if it is really fair for God to condemn people who have never heard the gospel. From what Jesus says here, their punishment will be less severe. The more knowledge we have, the greater our responsibility, the greater our guilt if we fail to live up to what we know, and therefore the more severe our condemnation. The worst punishment of all will be for church leaders who should have known better but were still unfaithful to God.

Notice that no matter how much we know, or do not know, every unfaithful servant is still condemned. Basil the Great rightly observed: "When I consult the New Testament, I find that our Lord Jesus Christ does not absolve from punishment even sins committed in ignorance, although he attaches a harsher threat to deliberate sins."[7] No matter how much we know about the gospel, we all know something about God, and God will hold us accountable for it (see Rom. 1:18). In this parable some receive a heavier beating, and some receive a lighter beating, but they are all counted among the unfaithful.

So it will be at the final judgment, when the faithful in Christ will enter his glory, but all the unfaithful will be banished from the presence of God forever: "For those servants of Christ who labor faithfully and devotedly in His service every moment expecting the coming of their Lord and joyfully looking forward to it, the second coming of Jesus will be a matter of the greatest joy and of the most glorious gain. But for those who doubt His promises and who live in selfishness, imperiousness and

---

7. Basil the Great, "Preface on the Judgment of God," in *Luke*, ed. Arthur A. Just Jr., Ancient Christian Commentary on Scripture, NT 3 (Downers Grove, IL: InterVarsity, 2003), 216.

worldly-mindedness, the second coming will be fraught with terror and irrevocable loss."[8] The most severe penalty in this passage is not to be cut into pieces, or to receive a beating, but to be counted unfaithful by God, and therefore condemned to everlasting destruction in hell. In the words of one commentary, "Neglectful Stewardship Leads to Utter Wretchedness with Unbelievers."[9]

How Much Is Required?

These parables about servants and masters are some of the weightiest parables in the Gospels. They bring us face to face with our destiny, and show us that we all need a Savior. For whether we are more or less ignorant, and whether we have been more or less unfaithful, we have all been neglectful in our stewardship. Who can say that we have always been at the ready, or that we have made the best use of all the good things that God has given us, or that today we are living in full expectation of the coming of Christ? This is why we need a Savior—a Savior to suffer the punishment that we deserve for our sins. Jesus Christ is the true and faithful servant who took all our unfaithfulness upon himself when he died on the cross, and then buried it in the grave before coming back to life. Christianity is not a religion for faithful servants, but a gospel for unfaithful servants.

Now, having done everything that needed to be done for our salvation, Jesus calls us back into God's service. He tells us to be watchful and faithful as we wait for his coming. Then he gives us this concluding exhortation: "Everyone to whom much was given, of him much will be required, and from him to whom they entrusted much, they will demand the more" (Luke 12:48).

This statement is in keeping with the principle Jesus had just been explaining. The more you have been given, the greater your responsibility to use it for the glory of God. If I may be permitted a word of personal testimony, God has used this verse—as much as any other verse in the Bible— to shape my life as a Christian and my calling as a minister of the gospel. My grandmother would give this verse to me when I was a little boy. She would remind me how much I had been given: my family, church, abilities,

8. Geldenhuys, *Luke*, 364.
9. Section heading in Just, *Luke*, Ancient Christian Commentary on Scripture, 215.

education, and so forth. Then she would say, "To whom much is given, of him shall much be required." From time to time, as I thought about what God wanted me to do with my life, I would remember this verse. I would consider how much God had given to me, and how much he would require. In the end, this is one of the main reasons I became a minister.

Perhaps you are able to give a similar testimony. Whether or not you came to know Christ at an early age, and whether or not you serve in the church full-time, God has called you into his service and prepared you for that calling. He has provided for your daily needs. He has given you sound spiritual instruction through the preaching of the gospel, through good Christian literature, and through the personal discipleship of godly men and women. How much God has given you! And how much he will require on the day when Jesus comes again! Are you ready to give him that much, or not?

55

BEFORE THE FIRE FALLS

Luke 12:49–59

*"I came to cast fire on the earth, and would that it were already
kindled! I have a baptism to be baptized with, and how great is my
distress until it is accomplished! Do you think that I have come to give
peace on earth? No, I tell you, but rather division." (Luke 12:49–51)*

I was standing where the fire jumped the trail. At first it was no bigger than a small
Indian campfire, looking more like something you could move up close to and
warm your hands against than something that in a few minutes could leave your
remains lying in prayer with nothing on but a belt.... The fire ... stopped for only
a moment when it reached the trail we were hoping to use as a fire-line.... Then it
jumped.... I broke and started up the hillside.... [The fire] was in front of me, as
well as behind me, with nowhere to go but up. Above, it was little spot fires started
by a sky of burning branches. The spot fires turned me in my course by leaping
into each other and forming an avalanche of flame that went both down and up
the mountain. I kept looking for escape openings marked by holes in smoke that
at times burned upside down. Behind, where I did not dare to look, the main
fire was sound and heat, a ground noise like a freight train.... It came so close it
sounded as if it were cracking bones, and mine were the only bones around.[1]

1. Norman Maclean, *Young Men and Fire* (Chicago: University of Chicago Press, 1972), 5–6.

So Norman Maclean describes his life or death experience as a smoke-jumper in the mountains of Montana. Maclean made it to the top of that hillside, where the fire reached its limit, and thus he lived to tell his story. By the grace of God, when fire fell with lightning from the sky, Maclean escaped the conflagration. He was terrified, and in a way, he was also purified, but the important thing is that he was saved.

BAPTISM BY FIRE

Luke 12 ends with a fiery blaze of judgment and an urgent warning to find safety in Christ before it is too late. Jesus had been teaching his disciples about his second coming and about their calling to be faithful as they watched and waited for his return. He then proceeded to connect his future coming in judgment with his more immediate work of suffering and dying for sinners: "I came to cast fire on the earth, and would that it were already kindled! I have a baptism to be baptized with, and how great is my distress until it is accomplished!" (Luke 12:49–50).

To understand what Jesus was saying, we need to know what kind of fire he was talking about, and what kind of baptism. Some see this fire as a reference to the Holy Spirit. Others see it as a symbol of God's Word, or of the gospel. But in the Bible, the image of fire most frequently refers to divine judgment. So Jesus was talking about coming in judgment and fulfilling John the Baptist's promise that he would baptize "with the Holy Spirit and with fire" (Luke 3:16).

The Scripture says, "Our God is a consuming fire" (Heb. 12:29). When he is present in his holiness, God burns with a pure and powerful flame. This fire has a twofold effect: it consumes whatever is destined for destruction, while at the same time purifying whatever God ordains to refine. Fire always consumes or purifies, depending on the nature of what it burns. It is an instrument of judgment, revealing things for what they are. This is what Christ came to cast on the earth: the consuming, purifying fire of God's judgment. Fire is "the spiritual power exercised by the Lord through His Word and Spirit—to the undoing of those who reject Him and to the refining of those who believe in Him."[2]

2. Norval Geldenhuys, *The Gospel of Luke*, New International Commentary on the New Testament (Grand Rapids: Eerdmans, 1951), 367.

695

There is a second image in these verses—the image of baptism. In coming to cast his fire, Jesus also had a baptism to undergo. Obviously this does not refer to his baptism in the Jordan River, because he had already received that baptism, and here he is looking ahead to something not yet accomplished. Yet it will be accomplished soon, for Jesus is not talking about something far in the future, like his second coming, but about something more immediate. In verses 49 and 51 he clearly refers to his first coming, not his second. Then in verse 56 he challenges the crowd to "interpret the present time." So whatever baptism Jesus had in mind, it was a baptism he would receive in the course of his earthly ministry.

Jesus was speaking, of course, about his baptism into death by crucifixion, the fiery trial he would go through when he suffered the wrath of God against our sin on the cross. He was speaking about the waves of hellish curse that he would endure for our salvation. Before casting his consuming fire on the earth to destroy and to purify, Jesus must suffer the scorching heat of divine judgment; he "must first be plunged into the flood of pain and suffering."[3]

This baptism by fire was something Jesus had a burning desire to fulfill. In verse 49 he expresses his longing to cast fire on the earth, and then in verse 50 he says that he will be under duress until he goes through his baptism. The word "distress" *(synechomai)* shows the anguish of our Savior's soul as he anticipated what he would suffer for our salvation. The cross was costing him something even before he was crucified. He knew what terrible anguish awaited him, but the distress of this anticipation was only temporary, and Jesus was looking beyond it to accomplishing our salvation.

At the end of chapter 9 Jesus set his face towards Jerusalem (see Luke 9:51). That was a major turning point in Luke's Gospel, as Jesus resolutely turned his steps in the direction of the cross. By the time we get to the end of chapter 12, Jesus wants to push the pace. With every passing day he has a growing sense of urgency about the great work that he must do. Already he is suffering for it, but he is not shrinking back. Here, with holy impatience, he tells his disciples that his soul will not be satisfied until he does what he has come to do.

I. Howard Marshall offers the following paraphrase of Luke 12:50: "How I am totally governed by this until it be finally accomplished."[4] What a joy

<hr/>

3. Ibid., 366.
4. I. Howard Marshall, *The Gospel of Luke*, New International Greek Testament Commentary (Grand Rapids: Eerdmans, 1978), 547.

it is for us to see our Savior say this on his way to the cross! Jesus was going there to suffer for our sins, to die in our place, and he would not rest until the job was done. This was the governing ambition of his life and ministry. With his heart set on accomplishing the great work of our salvation, he pressed relentlessly towards his baptism of the cross. Apart from this willing sacrifice, we could never be saved.

A House Divided

We have already seen how the coming of Christ divides and discriminates. Some are destroyed by the fire he casts, while others are refined by it. This is a hard teaching. Many people would prefer to think that God will save everyone in the end, and that no matter what we believe, we are still spiritually unified. In an interview on *60 Minutes*, comedian Jim Carrey said, "I'm a Buddhist, I'm a Muslim, I'm a Christian. I'm whatever you want me to be . . . it all comes down to the same thing."[5]

Even some Christians are starting to think this way. Here is how the *Wall Street Journal* described their view of salvation: "Personally, I am trusting Jesus Christ as my means of gaining God's permanent favor and a place in heaven—but someone else could get to heaven based upon living an exemplary life."[6] There is nothing that divides us, the thinking goes—not even Jesus or his gospel.

Jesus himself took a rather different view. "Do you think that I have come to give peace on earth?" he asked. "No, I tell you, but rather division. For from now on in one house there will be five divided, three against two and two against three. They will be divided, father against son and son against father, mother against daughter and daughter against mother, mother-in-law against her daughter-in-law and daughter-in-law against mother-in-law" (Luke 12:51–53).

If Jesus had waited for his disciples to answer the question he asked, they would have said "Yes." Did Jesus come to give peace on earth? Of course he did! This is what the Messiah was for. The Jews of that time generally believed that when their Savior came, he would establish peace on earth

5. Jim Carrey, quoted in Derek W. H. Thomas, "The Gospel According to Jim Carrey," *The First Epistle* 37.47 (Dec. 2, 2004): 2.

6. David Shiflett, "Uncertain Crusaders," *Wall Street Journal*, Nov. 14, 2003.

by defeating Israel's enemies and building a golden kingdom. This expectation was based on all the ancient prophecies about the Prince of Peace (e.g., Isa. 9:6). To some extent, this popular expectation gets reinforced in the Gospels. Before Jesus was born, Zechariah prophesied that God would "guide our feet into the way of peace" (Luke 1:79). Then at the time of his nativity the angels announced, "On earth peace among those with whom he is pleased" (Luke 2:14). "Go in peace," Jesus would sometimes say (e.g., Luke 7:50; 8:48). Later, the apostles picked up this theme in their preaching, declaring that there is peace between Jews and Gentiles in Christ (Eph. 2:17). Did Jesus come to give peace on earth? Absolutely.

However, the peace of Christ will not be perpetual until the end of the age, when Jesus comes again to consummate his kingdom. Only then will we experience full and lasting peace. Only then will the lion lie down with the lamb and the swords be beaten into plowshares. In the meantime, "we have peace with God through our Lord Jesus Christ" (Rom. 5:1). We have the peace of the Holy Spirit. We have the inner peace that comes from knowing our heavenly Father loves us and cares for us. But we do not always have peace with other people.

This is especially true when it comes to our religion. Jesus is divisive. At the time he spoke these words, people were still making up their minds about him, but soon they would have to make a decision. Soon he would die and rise again, and then people would be forced to make a choice: Is Jesus the Son of God and the Savior of sinners, or not? There is no way to take both sides of the question. If we believe that Jesus is who he says he is, then we must receive him as our only Savior and follow him as our only Lord. If we do not believe him, then we are free to dismiss him as a legend from the past, or as a mere human being. But everyone has to make a choice. All roads do not lead to God. We are either for Jesus or against him, and this division draws a line right down the middle of the human race. This is what Jesus came to bring: not peace, but division.

Knowing this helps us have the right expectations. Some people expect that knowing Christ will make life happier and easier, and in some ways it does. But as followers of Christ we are called to share in his sufferings, and often this includes facing hostility from people who do not know Christ. We see this all through the history of the church, from the Roman persecutions right up to the attacks many Christians suffer today from Muslim extremists and totalitarian governments. Even if what we face is less severe, we see the same hostility in our own culture, where people ridicule biblical convictions and sometimes treat evangelical Christianity as a form of fascism. This is not surprising. Jesus did not come to give peace on earth, but to bring division.

Nowhere is this division more painful than in our own families. When someone from a non-Christian family comes to faith in Christ, it often disrupts family relationships, and sometimes threatens to destroy them. By the grace of God, many of these relationships will get restored, but what heartache any conflict brings!

Sometimes the division comes when we start sharing the gospel with our families. This is partly our own fault if we try to tell them the truth without showing them God's love. But the division is also there because some of our family members do not want to know Christ. In fact, depending on where we live in the world, they may try to put us to death.

Other times the division comes when a Christian repents, turning away from sin. Friends and family members may find this threatening. They say that the new believer is being judgmental, but often the real issue is their own guilty conscience. They resent having someone around who challenges their lifestyle, or who reminds them that they are not right with God.

Then there are times the division comes when a Christian makes a commitment to full-time ministry. Unless they are Christians themselves (and sometimes even if they are), parents may feel that Christian service is a second-class calling—the waste of a perfectly good education. Or they may resent the fact that their children are moving into a needy urban neighborhood, giving their grandchildren a Christian education, or going overseas with the gospel. They do not mind having their children get religious, as long as they do not take it to any extremes.

Most of the time there is less hostility. Relationships remain close, even with family members who do not have a commitment to Christ, but there is always some underlying tension, as well as the distress of knowing that there are spiritual things you can never share. Then there is the anguish we suffer when we see the people we love—members of our own families—living and dying without making a personal faith commitment to Jesus Christ.

Whatever the precise reason for the division, sooner or later Jesus always causes a conflict. Some family members have their own plans for our lives, and when they do, inevitably the claims they make on us will come into conflict with the lordship of Jesus Christ. This will also happen at school, at work, in the neighborhood. It will even happen in the church, because there are unbelievers there, too—people who call themselves Christians but really do not know Christ. Our first allegiance is to Jesus Christ, and there are times when his claim on our lives brings us into conflict with other people.

However much we are grieved by this, we should not be surprised by it. Jesus told us this would happen. He said that he did not come only to unite, but also to divide. What causes the division is that some people refuse to come to him in faith. J. C. Ryle thus offered this wise counsel: "Let us never be moved by those who charge the Gospel with being the cause of strife and divisions upon earth. . . . It is not the Gospel which is to blame, but the corrupt heart of man. . . . So long as some men and women will not repent and believe, and some will, there must needs be division. To be surprised at it is the height of folly. The very existence of division is one proof of Christ's foresight, and of the truth of Christianity."[7]

A Sign of the Times

Jesus was not content to leave things there, but pressed his listeners to make a decision. He had come to cast fire on the earth—the fire of judgment. He had a baptism to endure—the baptism of the cross. His work as Savior and Judge would cause a division that would cut right down the center of the human race. But which side will you be on? This was the question that confronted the crowd, that confronts everyone. We are either with Jesus or against him. When the fire falls, we will either be refined, or else destroyed. Either we trust in Christ and his cross, or else we ignore him and reject him. We are either with the people of God, or against them.

Jesus said to the crowds: "When you see a cloud rising in the west, you say at once, 'A shower is coming.' And so it happens. And when you see the south wind blowing, you say, 'There will be scorching heat,' and so it happens. You hypocrites! You know how to interpret the appearance of earth and sky, but why do you not know how to interpret the present time?" (Luke 12:54–56).

7. J. C. Ryle, *Expository Thoughts on the Gospels, Luke* (1858; reprint Cambridge: James Clarke, 1976), 2:98.

Weather forecasting was not terribly sophisticated in those days, but in that predictable climate it was reasonably accurate. For example, a cloud rising in the west, coming off the Mediterranean Sea, was likely to bring rain (e.g. 1 Kings 18:44–45), whereas a wind blowing up from the south, coming off the desert, would typically bring a heat wave. Everybody knew about the weather simply by observing nature.

What did people know about spiritual things? As they watched Jesus go about his teaching and healing ministry, they should have seen what was happening. They should have recognized the spiritual signs, like those noble sons of Issachar we read about in the Old Testament—"men who had understanding of the times" (1 Chron. 12:32). But they could not see it, or if they did, they would not admit it (which would explain why Jesus called them "hypocrites"). They knew how to read the sky, with its clouds of blessing and its scorching winds, but they could not interpret current events as they pertained to Jesus, the coming judgment, and the way of everlasting life.

What, specifically, should they have seen? Luke is the Gospel of knowing for sure, and it has shown us what Jesus was saying and doing. People should have learned from his teaching that he spoke with divine authority. This was the man who took the old promises about salvation and said, "They are fulfilled in my ministry" (see Luke 4:21). They also should have seen from his miracles that he had true divine power. This was the man who ruled the waves and who cast out demons "by the finger of God" (see Luke 11:20). If people had been able to interpret the times, they would have recognized that Jesus was the Messiah who had come to bring salvation.

They also should have seen that judgment was coming. Jesus was just the kind of prophet who always got persecuted, and probably killed. Already the religious leaders were plotting against him (see Luke 11:53–54), and this served as a storm warning. If people had been able to interpret the times, they would have seen the gathering clouds and taken cover. Yet they never saw it coming. Because of their spiritual blindness, "they do not see the cloud of grace and blessings which appears with Him to all who believe in Him, nor do they observe the glowing heat of the judgment which He brings for those who are disobedient."[8]

8. Geldenhuys, *Luke,* 368.

Many of the people in the crowds never did understand who Jesus was, or what he had come to do. It would be tempting to come up with excuses for them. After all, how could they know that Jesus was the Savior until he had finished his saving work? Not even the disciples understood what Jesus was saying about dying and rising again. How could anyone be expected to interpret his ministry before the cross and the empty tomb? Nevertheless, Jesus said they should have been able to read the signs. They should have seen what was starting to happen and trusted him as their Savior.

If *they* should have seen it, then *we* certainly should. We have the testimony of the Gospels, which not only tell us what Jesus did, but also explain what it means. Then we have the rest of the New Testament to give us the true interpretation of Jesus and his salvation. Furthermore, we are living on the other side of the resurrection. God has raised Jesus from the dead. This is the sign that his sacrifice for sin has been accepted, and that now, through faith in him, our sins are forgiven and we have the hope of eternal life. See the signs of the cross and the empty tomb. Understand what they mean. Trust Jesus for your salvation.

SETTLING OUR CASE

Judgment is coming, and before the fire falls, we need to make sure that we have a right relationship with God. Jesus said we need to do this now, before it is too late: "And why do you not judge for yourselves what is right? As you go with your accuser before the magistrate, make an effort to settle with him on the way, lest he drag you to the judge, and the judge hand you over to the officer, and the officer put you in prison. I tell you, you will never get out until you have paid the very last penny" (Luke 12:57–59).

Here Jesus shrewdly advocates the speedy resolution of a familiar legal situation. There are times when it is better for a defendant to go through all the trouble of a legal proceeding. This is especially true when he is innocent and has a good chance of winning his case. But when the defendant is guilty and there is no way to mount a defense, it is always more advantageous to settle out of court. Otherwise the guilty party will end up suffering the full penalty for his crime.

The legal situation is easy enough to understand, but what is the spiritual application? We need to be careful not to take this mini-parable too far, or